CORRECTIONS

The Fundamentals

BURK FOSTER

PEARSON

Prentice
Hall

Upper Saddle River, New Jersey 07458

Library of Congress Cataloging-in-Publication Data

Foster, Burk.
   Corrections : the fundamentals / Burk Foster.
      p. cm.
   Includes bibliographical references.
   ISBN 0-13-114328-X
   1. Corrections. 2. Corrections—History. I. Title.
HV8665.F67 2006
364.6—dc22   2004026752

Executive Editor: *Frank Mortimer, Jr.*
Assistant Editor: *Mayda Bosco*
Production Editor: *Judy Ludowitz, Carlisle Publishers Services*
Production Liaison: *Barbara Marttine Cappuccio*
Director of Manufacturing and Production: *Bruce Johnson*
Managing Editor: *Mary Carnis*
Manufacturing Buyer: *Cathleen Petersen*
Executive Marketing Manager: *Tim Peyton*
Editorial Assistant: *Kelly Krug*
Creative Director: *Cheryl Asherman*
Cover Design Coordinator: *Miguel Ortiz*
Cover Designer: *Marianne Frasco*
Cover Photo Credit: *Keith Stutes*
Composition: *Carlisle Communications, Ltd.*
Printing and Binding: *Hamilton Printing*

Pearson Education LTD.
Pearson Education Singapore, Pte. Ltd
Pearson Education, Canada, Ltd.
Pearson Education-Japan

Pearson Education Australia PTY, Limited
Pearson Education North Asia Ltd.
Pearson Educación de Mexico, S.A. de C.V.
Pearson Education Malaysia, Pte. Ltd.

10 9
ISBN 0-13-114328-X

In time all we are is what others remember.

This book is dedicated to the memory of my parents, Dean and Neta Foster, of Idabel, Oklahoma, and to my professional parent, Professor Samuel G. Chapman of the University of Oklahoma.

CONTENTS

PART II   SYSTEMS

5   Jails   93

6   State and Federal Prisons   120

7   Management and Custody   148

8   Corrections Policies and Issues   176

PART III   PRISONERS

9   Male and Female Prisoners   207

10   Prison Life   236

11   Special Needs Prisoners   282

14   Parole and Release from Prison   409

15   Probation and Community Corrections   455

16   Contrasting Philosophies: American and International Corrections Today   501

PREFACE

Corrections: The Fundamentals reflects my views on what ought to be included in an introductory college course for students who know very little about corrections. In teaching an introductory corrections course at the University of Louisiana–Lafayette for more than thirty years, I had long been saying that I wished someone would prepare a new text that was briefer in content, easily accessible to students, devoid of the pictures and graphics that have come to dominate college texts, and focused on the reality of corrections as it is practiced today. What I was proposing, I suppose, was a kind of "old-fashioned," narrative-dense text that could interest students in the evolution of corrections in America as a study in public policy—which is to say a government's course of action toward its own people over time.

Finally challenged by Frank Mortimer, criminal justice executive editor of Pearson/Prentice Hall, to prepare such a text myself, I took up the gauntlet and gave it a run. As I sat down to think about what I wanted to say, the guide I followed in writing the text is the basic outline I have followed in my introductory corrections course for more than twenty years. My definition of corrections is "that part of criminal justice that applies public policies to manage convicted criminals." In my own course, I concentrate on these aspects of corrections:

1. Its historical antecedents—that is, what we used to do and how we got from then to now
2. The institutions, staff, and functions necessary to manage secure custody of prisoners
3. The prisoners themselves and their lives in custody and out, emphasizing those features that most set them apart from other people not in prison
4. Options to secure custody—managing criminals outside of institutions

This text incorporates my concerns. Part I is history—early punishments, the creation of the penitentiary in the 1800s, the development of the modern corrections bureaucracy in the 1900s, and the impact of ideology and recent sentencing changes. Part II is the institutions that make up secure custody— jails, state prisons, and federal prisons, emphasizing management and custodial functions and critical policy issues. Part III is the prisoners—the background of men and women in prison, prison life, special needs prisoners, and prisoners' legal rights. Part IV is alternatives—rehabilitation, release from prison, probation and community corrections, and American corrections compared to the rest of world, featuring brief close-ups of seven other nations.

Most authors of introductory texts use some means of exposing students to ideas other than their own. What I have done in this text is select twenty-five commentaries by writers whose views I think students ought to hear. The essays chosen for the commentaries are intended to provide close-up attention to topics of particular interest—and also to provide material for outside writing assignments and classroom discussion. The commentaries come at the end of each chapter.

If you notice that many of the examples I use in my own writing make use of Louisiana, my adopted state, it is plainly because I have conducted research and worked inside jails and prisons—with both prisoners and staff—around the state for more than twenty-five years. Louisiana has the highest rate of incarceration in the world—officials from other states often come here now to see how to run a safe, orderly, inexpensive prison system—and its correctional policies and facilities provide abundant illustrations of points with which I strongly agree and other points with which I equally strongly disagree. It is also a state with a strong sense of corrections history centering on its state prison at Angola, the institution that has been at the center of my academic and professional career. I could not have done this book without the perspective I gained from working with prisoners and staff at Angola.

American corrections have undergone great changes from the days when I was working as a military police officer and first began teaching courses that touched on corrections. It is a "better" system objectively in regard to its components of care, custody, and control, but it is also a "bigger" system, much larger than it needs to be, in my view. When I consider existing policy and practice, I always contemplate how they came to be. The two questions I usually ask are these:

1. How did we confront this problem in the past?
2. How do others deal with the same issue or problem?

Dwight D. Eisenhower, who served two terms as president in the 1950s, once remarked, "The older I get, the more wisdom I find in the ancient rule of taking first things first—a process which often reduces the most complex human problems to manageable proportions." Take first things first—sound advice—but what are the first things that should be taken first?

The "first things" are the occasion of great debate in the United States today. My underlying concern, in viewing the totality of American corrections in its present context, is that we have become far more ideologically based rather than reality based in our management of criminals. My goal would be to give college students and other general readers a foundation—the fundamentals, the title my editors selected—in understanding not only the *what* of American corrections in the early twenty-first century but some portions of the *how* and *why* as well. How good a job did I do? If there is a second edition, I will get back to you.

ACKNOWLEDGMENTS

I have several groups of people to thank for their assistance and support during the two years that I worked on this book.

At the University of Louisiana–Lafayette:
Joni T. LeBlanc
Dr. Doris Meriwether
Leslie D. Schilling
Mary Matthews Clavelle
Dr. Craig Forsyth

In and around the prison system:
Douglas Dennis, *The Angolite*
C. M. Lensing Jr., Hunt Correctional Center
Dr. Stephen C. Richards, University of Wisconsin–Oshkosh
Marc Mauer, The Sentencing Project
Edmond Dantes

The reviewers who commented on the draft manuscript:
Susan Brinkley
University of Tampa
Tampa, FL

Linda Clark
Wharton County Junior College
Wharton, TX

Harold Frossard
Moraine Valley Community College
Palos Hills, IL

Sudipto Roy
Indiana State University
Terre Haute, IN

Kelli Stevens
Texas Christian University
Fort Worth, TX

At Pearson/Prentice Hall:
Frank Mortimer
Barbara Cappuccio
Mayda Bosco
Judy Ludowitz, Carlisle Publishers Services

From the free world:
Dr. Clifford Dorne, Saginaw Valley State University
Amanda Ripley, *Time* magazine
Michele D. Buisch, formerly of the American Correctional Association

Susan Clayton, American Correctional Association
Keith Stutes, assistant district attorney and photographer

Special thanks to Frank Mortimer, who initiated the project and persisted in assuring me that I could find the time to complete it.

My deepest personal thanks to P.L.F., in SALA.

COMMENTARIES & CONTRIBUTORS

1. Used with permission.

2. Used with permission.

3. Used with permission.

4. By Clifford Dorne, Assistant Dean, College of Arts and Behavioral Sciences, Saginaw Valley State University, and Donald J. Bachand, Dean, College of Arts and Behavioral Sciences, Saginaw Valley State University, Michigan. Original essay; used with permission.

5. By Sister Helen Prejean, Sisters of St. Joseph of Medaille, New Orleans, Louisiana. Appeared in *Salt of the Earth*, 1997, the online (salt.claretianpubs.org) publication of the Claretian Missionaries. Used with permission.

6. By Matthew Brady. Appeared in *Corrections Today* 58, no. 5 (August 1996):156–59. Reprinted with permission of the American Correctional Association, Lanham, Maryland.

7. By the Federal Bureau of Prisons. Appeared on the Bureau of Prisons Website at *www.bop.gov/ipag/ipafirst.html*. Used with permission of the Federal Bureau of Prisons.

8. By C. M. Lensing Jr., Warden, Hunt Correctional Center, St. Gabriel, Louisiana. Original essay; used with permission.

9. By Michele D. Buisch, formerly senior editor, American Correctional Association. Appeared in *Corrections Today* 63, no. 7 (December 2001): 16. Reprinted with permission of the American Correctional Association, Lanham, Maryland.

10. By Steve Rybolt, formerly of the Missouri Department of Corrections. Appeared in *Addiction Letter* 11, no. 3 (March 1995): 3. Reprinted with permission.

11. Used with permission.

12. By James A. Gondles Jr., Executive Director, American Correctional Association. Appeared in *Corrections Today* 64, no. 5 (August 2002): 6. Reprinted with permission of the American Correctional Association, Lanham, Maryland.

13. By Stephen C. Richards, Associate Professor of Criminal Justice, University of Wisconsin–Oshkosh, and Jeffrey Ian Ross, Associate Professor, Division of Criminology, Criminal Justice, and Social Policy at the University of Baltimore (Maryland). Original essay used with permission.

14. By Robert Johnson, Professor of Justice, Law, and Society, School of Public Affairs, American University, Washington, D.C. Appeared in *Corrections Today* 58, no. 4 (July 1996): 130–32. Reprinted with permission of the American Correctional Association, Lanham, Maryland.

15. By David W. Roush, Director, National Juvenile Detention Association Center for Research and Professional Development, Michigan State University, and Earl L. Dunlap, Executive Director, National Juvenile Detention Association, Eastern Kentucky University. Appeared in *Corrections Today* 59, no. 3 (June 1997): 21. Reprinted with permission of the American Correctional Association, Lanham, Maryland.

16. By Craig Turk, attorney, political consultant, and former managing editor of *The Public Interest*. Appeared in *The New Republic* 217, no. 8 (August 25, 1997):12–13. Reprinted with permission.

17. By Marc Mauer, Assistant Director, The Sentencing Project, Washington, D.C. Appeared in the May/June 2004 issue of *Focus* magazine, pp. 5–6, published by the

Joint Center for Political and Economic Studies, Washington, D.C. Reprinted with permission.

18. By Bob Herbert, columnist, *New York Times*. Appeared in *the New York Times*, May 31, 2004. Copyright © (2004) by The New York Times Co. Reprinted with permission.

19. By Christopher J. Alexander, formerly of the New Mexico State Penitentiary. Appeared in *Corrections Today* 60, no. 2 (April 1998): 18–20. Reprinted with permission of the American Correctional Association, Lanham, Maryland.

20. By Wilbert Rideau, former editor, *The Angolite,* Louisiana State Penitentiary. Appeared in *Time* 143, no. 12 (March 21, 1994): 80. Copyright © 1994 Time Inc. Reprinted with permission.

21. By Amanda Ripley, staff writer, *Time* magazine. Appeared in *Time* 161, no. 6 (February 10, 2003): 8. Copyright @ 2003 Time Inc. reprinted with permission.

22. By James Q. Wilson, Professor Emeritus, UCLA. Appeared in *Forbes* 167, no. 1 (January 8, 2001): 138. Reprinted by permission of *Forbes* Magazine © 2004 Forbes Inc.

23. By Clifford Dorne, Assistant Dean, College of Arts and Behavioral Sciences, Saginaw Valley State University, Michigan. Original essay; used with permission.

24. By John Pratt, reader in criminology at Victoria University, Wellington, New Zealand. Appeared in *Corrections Today* 64, no. 1 (February 2002): 64–66. Reprinted with permission of the American Correctional Association, Lanham, Maryland.

25. By the American Bar Association. Published online at *www.abanet.org;leadership/recommendations02/107.pdf.* Copyright © 2002 by the American Bar Association. Reprinted with permission.

ABOUT THE AUTHOR

Burk Foster is associate professor of criminal justice at the University of Louisiana–Lafayette, where he has been a faculty member since 1974. A former civilian police officer in Oklahoma, where he completed undergraduate and graduate degrees at the University of Oklahoma, he served as a lieutenant in the U.S. Air Force Security Police. After his move to Louisiana, his academic interests turned toward sentencing and corrections. He has testified as an expert witness in state and federal courts on issues related to corrections and the death penalty. Although he is not a convict and has never aspired to be one, he was a writer and contributing editor of *The Angolite,* the magazine of the Louisiana State Penitentiary, for sixteen years. Professor Foster and Angola inmate Lane Nelson are coauthors of *Death Watch: A Death Penalty Anthology* (2001). His primary research interests at present focus on the history of prisons and the death penalty. He is a longtime member of the Academy of Criminal Justice Sciences and the American Correctional Association. In addition to the criminal justice courses he teaches at UL–Lafayette, he also teaches and directs seminars in the university's Honors Program.

1 — EARLY PUNISHMENTS

It is evident that the intent of punishments is not to torment a sensible being, nor to undo a crime already committed. Is it possible that torments and useless cruelty, the instrument of furious fanaticism or the impotency of tyrants, can be authorized by a political body, which, so far from being influenced by passion, should be the cool moderator of the passions of individuals? Can the groans of a tortured wretch recall the time past, or reverse the crime he has committed?

The end of punishment, therefore, is no other than to prevent the criminal from doing further injury to society, and to prevent others from committing the like offense. Such punishments, therefore, and such a mode of inflicting them, ought to be chosen, as will make the strongest and most lasting impressions on the minds of others, with the least torment to the body of the criminal.

— Cesare Beccaria, *On Crimes and Punishments*, 1764

INTRODUCTION

This chapter considers the punishments early societies imposed on criminals before the development of modern prisons. The social and legal contexts of society before the 1700s were very different from what they are in most of the world today, and the types of punishments used on criminals were also very different from what we would expect today. After reading this chapter, you should be familiar with:

1. The forms of punishment most often used in societies through the 1700s.
2. The social and legal contexts within which punishments were applied.
3. Early and modern legal codes.
4. The impact of the Age of Enlightenment on eighteenth-century Europe.
5. The views of several important correctional scholars and reformers of this period.
6. The institutions early societies used to hold criminals and social misfits.

PUNISHING CRIMINALS: CORPORAL PUNISHMENTS

What penalties do we think of when we imagine the appropriate punishment for someone convicted of a serious crime today? In modern societies, we typically imagine a crime as being worth so much time in custody—three months, two years, ten years, or, in rare cases, the rest of the criminal's natural life. The amount of time we take out of the criminal's life ought to be proportionate to the harm done to the victim of the crime or to the greater society in which the criminal lives.

But this notion of punishment as time in custody is of recent vintage in humankind's history. If the recorded history of Western civilization stretches for about 2,000 years on either side of the birth of Christ—4,000 years total—the use of the modern prison to lock up convicted criminals is only about 200 years old. For the remaining 3,800 years, or 95 percent of the history we know much about punishments other than imprisonment predominated. What did early societies do with criminals before they started locking them up?

When we think of the punishments that pre-date the prison, we tend to imagine the abundant use of physical punishments, particularly corporal punishments and capital punishment. **Corporal punishment** is defined as any punishment that involves infliction of pain on the human body. A variety of such punishments come to mind—whipping, beating, branding, mutilation, and burning among the most common forms.

Over time, **whipping** emerged as the most prevalent method of physically punishing criminals in early Western societies. Whipping offered several advantages. It required no special equipment other than the whip. It could be done anywhere. Most corporal punishments were done at a central location where the entire community could turn out to watch. Whippings were also measured punishment in the sense that they could be counted—ten, twenty, or fifty lashes. This became more important when the idea that the punishment ought to be graduated in response to the seriousness of the crime became commonly accepted. Finally, whipping, while causing considerable pain and leaving the criminal's back scarred for life, was usually neither fatal nor incapacitating for life. The victim of a whipping might pass out, but he usually did not die, nor was he likely to be prevented from returning to a useful working life. After his injuries healed, he would bear the scars, but he would also be capable of resuming life as a productive citizen.

In 1530, during the reign of King Henry VIII of England, Parliament passed the Whipping Act, directed at keeping wandering vagrants in check. The act provided that vagrants were to be carried to some market town or other place and "there tied to the end of a cart naked, and beaten with whips throughout such market town, or other place, till the body shall be bloody by reason of such whipping."[1] Later, in the reign of Queen Elizabeth, the law was amended to strip offenders only half naked, and the whipping post was substituted for the cart. The poet John Taylor wrote these lines to open "The Praise and Virtue of a Jail and Jailers" in 1623:

> In London, and within a mile, I ween,
>
> There are jails or prisons full eighteen,
>
> And sixty whipping-posts and stocks and cages.[2]

Other corporal punishments had their place. **Branding** of criminals with a hot iron became a more common practice by the sixteenth and seventeenth centuries. Not only did it cause pain, but it was also a useful method of marking criminals—an early form of criminal identification. The "T" on the man's thumb meant he was a thief. The fleur-de-lis mark on the Parisian woman's shoulder meant she was a prostitute. Convicted criminals literally wore their criminal history as marks on their bodies; even if they changed identities, as it was easy to do in the early days, the marks of their crimes remained for the authorities to uncover beneath long sleeves.

Alice Morse Earle's 1896 text *Curious Punishments of Bygone Days* provides this account of the combination of punishments imposed on a Quaker in seventeenth-century New Haven, Connecticut (a criminal whose crime was being a Quaker in a place where Quakers were not welcome):

> "The Drum was Beat, the People gather'd, Norton was fetch'd and stripp'd to the Waste, and set with his Back to the Magistrates, and given in their View Thirty-six cruel Stripes with a knotted cord, and his hand made fast in the Stocks where they had set his Body before, and burn'd very deep with a Red-hot Iron with H. for Heresie."[3]

PUNISHING CRIMINALS: DEATH

Capital punishment in many forms was also common in early societies. The killing of a human being is the supreme penalty for a crime. Though the definition of a "capital offense" has changed considerably over time, the death penalty remains on the books in most countries today, including thirty-eight states of the United States and the federal government. Before the 1800s, the death penalty was generally available not only as a punishment for the most serious degree of homicide (as it is in the United States today) but also for any serious crime if the judge believed the offender deserved it. Torture before death was also commonplace.

The Code of King Hammurabi of Babylon, from about 1750 B.C., provided the death penalty for twenty-five different crimes. Sister Helen Prejean, the noted death penalty abolitionist, has often pointed out to death penalty proponents justifying their position as a biblical punishment that the Hebrew Law of Moses made dozens of crimes punishable by death, including cursing one's mother or father, sorcery, adultery, having sex with animals, homosexuality, and allowing one's own animals to cause the death of another person.[4]

As English common law developed, most felony offenses became capital crimes. The Death Penalty Information Center reports that by the early 1800s, 222 separate criminal offenses were punishable by death in England, including many forms of theft and property crimes (such as poaching game) that we would expect to be punished with a fine and suspended sentence today. The Colony of Virginia's "Divine, Moral and Martial Laws" of 1612 provided the death penalty for such offenses as stealing grapes, killing chickens, and trading with Indians.[5]

The forms capital punishment took in particular locales were up to local practice and the inventive minds of the persons imposing the sentence. Geoffrey Abbott's encyclopedic work *The Book of Execution* describes sixty-nine different methods of execution used around the world, everything from the ancient stoning and beating up to the most modern lethal injection, with dozens of curious sidetracks, including boiling alive, broiling on a gridiron, sawing in half, pressing to death, and tearing apart by horses.[6]

The prevalent methods of executing criminals changed over time. Early societies settled on simple methods, such as stoning, which was commonly used in biblical times. The Romans used crucifixion to make an example of political rebels and religious heretics; Spartacus was one, and Jesus of Nazareth was thought to be a bit of both. Later Roman executions were accomplished by beheading and relied on the person of the executioner to do the deed. Hanging of ordinary criminals and beheading of the nobility prevailed in England from the tenth century on. The mass executions of heretics under the Spanish Inquisition of the late 1400s were done by burning at the stake. Hanging and beheading were most common in the early modern era in Europe. In the first decade of the twenty-first century, shooting, beheading, hanging, and, in the United States, lethal injection are the principal methods employed by those nations still carrying out death sentences. Stoning is being used again in Iran and other countries practicing fundamentalist Islamic law.

PUNISHING CRIMINALS: EXILE

Many early societies (and a few more recent ones) avoided executing some deserving criminals by casting them out of society—sending them to some distant place and forbidding them to return home. This practice was called **exile** or **banishment** in its origins. In his historical writings, Robert Johnson has called the wilderness "the first penal colony," meaning a place to which criminals were sent. The British used the term **outlawry** to indicate a status outside the law. An outlaw was originally said to be *caput lupinum,* or to have a wolf's head. To declare a person an outlaw was to declare him a nonperson; his property was forfeited, he lost all civil rights, and anyone who killed him would not be charged with a crime since he no longer existed as a person. These extreme restrictions began to fade after the Norman Conquest.

From the 1600s through the mid–1800s, England practiced **transportation** of convicted felons to its colonies—first to America and later (after the independent United States was no longer available as the dumping ground for the wretched refuse of England's teeming shore) to Australia. The labor of these felons was sold to businessmen who were responsible for transporting them to their new colonial homes; the felons, men and women, generally owed seven years of labor to their masters or fourteen years if they had been pardoned from death sentences. Robert Hughes's book *The Fatal Shore* vividly describes the founding of Australia as a British penal colony at the end of the 1700s and the beginning of the 1800s. It was called Botany Bay, and to the convicts it meant a hellish place at the end of the earth from which there was no return.[7]

The status of these convicts was closely akin to the British practice of **indentured servitude** existing at the same time. Private persons (usually poor people in extreme financial difficulty) sold their labor to an entrepreneur; they were bound by contract for the duration. At the end of the term, the servants went free. Many thousands of poor Britishers came to the American colonies in this status.

Convicts were also bound, but they were not volunteers and signed no contracts. Their status was more like that of persons held under **slavery** except that slavery was for a lifetime (and into subsequent generations), while indentured servitude was for a specific period of years. The practice of using captured foreigners as slaves had existed from ancient times, and some societies provided that their own citizens could be sold into slavery in certain situations, particularly for debt. The Hebrew Law of Moses provided that criminals unable to make restitution to victims of property crimes should be sold into slavery and the money from their sale used to compensate the victims. This concept of penal servitude as being essentially equivalent to slave status would be very important to the evolution of the American prison after the founding of the penitentiary.

In modern times, the Soviet Union and China have frequently used internal exile of political dissidents. The basic idea is to isolate from major intellectual centers those persons whose ideas are dangerous to the regime. China places such persons under house arrest. The Soviet Union, before its abrupt decline, banished physicist and Nobel Peace Prize winner Andrei Sakharov to Gorky, 250 miles from Moscow, and kept the writer Alexander Solzhenitsyn (who would later win the Nobel Prize for Literature for his books critical of Soviet prisons) in exile in Kazhakstan after he had served eight years in prison and labor camps.

PUNISHING CRIMINALS: OTHER SANCTIONS

Early societies were not completely reliant on penalties imposing death, physical pain, banishment, or forced labor. From what we know of early legal systems, **economic sanctions** were commonly available for imposition on both property and violent criminals at the court's discretion. Today we think of economic sanctions as being of two types—fines and restitution. A fine is paid to the government, while restitution is paid to the victim. In earlier societies, the compensation went directly to the victim or the victim's family and not to the government. The problem that often arose was that, then as now, criminals were often lacking in economic means. When they (or their families) did not have the resources to repay their victims, they were sold as slaves. Later, when imprisonment for debt became a common practice and prisoners held in jail were required to pay their jailers fees for room and board, prisoners were under severe pressure to satisfy their obligations to both their private creditors and their public jailers. If they were too deeply in debt to get out, it was only one easy step to indentured servitude—and the opportunity to start life debt free in the New World after several years of uncompensated labor.

The tendency in the European nation-states in the early modern era, roughly the 1500s through the 1700s, was for criminal punishments to become more painful, large-scale public events—in a sense like big sporting events today, staged for mass entertainment (and perhaps education, as Robert Johnson has suggested), except that they ended with torture or killing. While Europe during this era was marked by the breakdown of traditional agrarian society and the growth of modern cities, with their diverse populations and the attendant problems associated with city life, the American colonies of the 1600s and 1700s were still small, rural communities of people who were very much like one another. They could be hard on the natives, on foreigners, or on people whose beliefs were very different from their own (as in the punishment of Quakers in Connecticut described previously), but they were often less inclined to do violence to members of their own communities, made up of family, neighbors, and friends.

In the American colonies, **public humiliation** of criminals was used more often than it was in Europe, and the European physical punishments were used less. Public humiliation took many forms. Minor offenders, such as drunks, lazy workers, or people who had violated religious laws, might be placed in a **pillory,** standing up with head and hands locked in a wooden frame, or the **stocks,** where a seated criminal would have both feet and hands locked in a frame. Displayed in a public place, offenders would be subject to the ridicule of people who knew them well; passersby felt free to insult the embarrassed offenders or pelt them with rotten vegetables. Women who nagged their spouses or gossiped might find themselves in a **ducking stool,** which was a chair on the end of a rope or the end of a seesaw in which they would be dunked in a creek a few times and given salutary warnings, such as "Don't nag" and "Don't gossip."

In Puritan communities, it was common practice to "brand" criminals with a cloth letter indicating their crime: "T" for thief, "D" for drunk, "F" for fighter. Nathaniel Hawthorne employed this device in *The Scarlet Letter,* telling the story of Hester Prynne, punished by having to wear a red "A" on her clothing for the crime of adultery. In the smaller, more homogeneous communities of the time, these forms of humiliation probably had as much impact on the offenders as other physical or economic penalties would have. The Quaker reformers of eighteenth-century Philadelphia would later object to public humiliation, in fact, as being harmful to the spirit of the lawbreakers; they would argue that incarceration was a better penalty. Today we wonder about the effects of such measures as "Drunk Driver" bumper stickers and "Sex Offender" signs placed in front yards.

THE SOCIAL AND LEGAL CONTEXT OF PUNISHMENT

When we look at the history of early punishments, it is apparent that practices varied greatly from one place to another. Some cultures were more violent than others. Most used torture, which was thought to be good for the soul, in dealing with criminals. In addition, practically all early cultures thought that any people not of their own were completely deserving of death and degradation—the more gruesome the better.

What determined the punishment practices of these societies? In the first place, we should think of the societies within which punishments were imposed. Early societies were generally smaller, relatively fixed or immobile, and made up of members who were more or less homogeneous—more like members of a small tribe who were always together. Everyone knew everyone else, and most people spent their entire lives surrounded by the same people. Aside from the rare adventurers who set off to the ends of the universe (most of whom reportedly fell off the edge of the earth or were devoured by dragons and never returned), people spent their entire lives never traveling very far from home. The epic journey of Mary and Joseph, from Nazareth to Bethlehem of Judea (if this is the right Bethlehem) preceding the birth of Jesus, covered all of seventy-five miles.

It is always easier to punish transients or strangers whom we do not know; it is not so easy to punish our family members, close friends, and neighbors. Indeed, one of the major determinants influencing public attitudes toward punishing criminals today is the homogeneity of the national population within which the crime occurs. The more homogeneous the people—the more alike they are in ethnicity, religion, and class and cultural values—the more lenient the punishment practices are likely to be. This is evident in the Scandinavian countries, where the concept of *folkhemmet,* meaning the nation as a family home, is said to apply, and in Japan. Conversely, the more heterogeneous a country's citizens and the more diverse their ethnic, religious, socioeconomic, and cultural backgrounds, the more punitive people are toward criminals (because they perceive that criminals are "different" from them, and indeed they often are). Russia and the United States come to mind here.

In many early societies, then, we can see that it would be much easier to expel a member who had committed some terrible crime (such as conspiring with the spirits of the other world) than to kill that person yourself. The expulsion into the wilderness, as Robert Johnson has noted, was really just as good as an execution and perhaps less painful for those doing the expelling. The person alone in the wilderness was virtually certain to die. Unless you happened to be a beautiful, long-haired woman in a skin suit (like the Raquel Welch character in *One Million Years* B.C. or Darryl Hannah as author Jean Auel's heroine Ayla in *The Clan of the Cave Bear*), no other society that you might encounter would take you in. If they found you wandering in the wilderness, they would know that it was because you had been cast out by your own people. They would kill you quickly to avoid the same kind of catastrophe your own people had been hoping to avoid when they got rid of you. Life in the wilderness was more than a bad camping trip waiting to be rescued by friendly rangers—it was a death sentence.

The other thought to keep in mind about the earliest historic societies was that their punishment practices were informal. Behavior was directed by social customs, called **folkways** and **mores,** more than by laws or formal rules. When someone violated these customs, by an act of illicit sex, violence, or sorcery, it was up to a community leader, typically a tribal or later a village elder, to decide the appropriate penalty, perhaps in consultation with other advisers. There was no reference book of sanctions. None of this was written down, and there was no appeal process. Execution of sentence was immediate. Even after some of the larger and more complex cultures began to write down their laws and apply some kind of uniformity to the process by which members were judged and punished, most other people on earth continued to live in cultures where justice was much more informal, personal, and spontaneous. This preference is expressed in the recent growth of interest in restorative justice.

EARLY LEGAL CODES

Over time, the more literate societies did develop written codes of laws. As the societies were typically small, in comparison to a modern country, their codes were much briefer and more direct than modern codes of laws. Modern codes, consisting of both substantive and procedural laws, are complex volumes containing thousands of statutes. Early codes, such as the Ten Commandments at the center of the Torah, the Hebrew Law of Moses, were simple, straightforward directives.

The Babylonian **Code of Hammurabi** is the oldest extant legal code. Preserved in the Louvre Museum in Paris today, the code consists of 282 civil and criminal laws engraved on a seven-and-a-half-foot tall rounded black stone. The stone was evidently put on display in a public place for all who could read to see. The statutes are very explicit and simply stated:

> 3. If any one bring an accusation of any crime before the elders, and does not prove what he has charged, he shall, if it be a capital offense charged, be put to death.
>
> 22. If any one is committing a robbery and is caught, then he shall be put to death.
>
> 117. If any one fail to meet a claim for debt, and sell himself, his wife, his son, and daughter for money or give them away to forced labor: they shall work for three years in the house of the man who bought them, or the proprietor, and in the fourth year they shall be set free.
>
> 132. If the "finger is pointed" at a man's wife, but she is not caught sleeping with the other man, she shall jump into the river for her husband.
>
> 154. If a man be guilty of incest with his daughter, he shall be driven from the place (exiled).[8]

Other well-known ancient codes include the Hebrew Law of Moses and various codes of the Greeks, particularly those of Draco and Solon. None of these ancient codes served as the direct basis of modern legal codes.

The thousand-year history of Roman law, from the Twelve Tables of about 450 B.C. to the *Corpus Juris Civilis* of the Byzantine emperor Justinian in the sixth century, was much more influential. The **Justinian Code,** published in two successive editions in 529 and 533 A.D. after work by two separate commissions of legal scholars, was a compilation of earlier Roman codes going back several hundred years. It would survive into the High Middle Ages; when scholars began teaching the law in early law schools, they taught from this code and from the **canon law** of the Roman Catholic Church. The Justinian Code was the principal secular, or worldly, law of the medieval period; canon law was ecclesiastical, or church, law. Canon law eventually diminished in importance as the influence of the medieval Church declined, but many of its principles were combined with Roman law to make up early continental or civil law. The two codes in combination provided the legal foundation of Western Europe as modern nation-states began to develop by the 1400s.

MODERN LEGAL CODES

Legal scholars of today define four major families of law—civil law, common law, Islamic law, and socialist law. Two of these, civil law and socialist law, are directly descended from Roman law. Common law developed in Britain between the time of the Norman Conquest (1066) and the seventeenth century. Islamic law is based on the Qur'an, written down in the seventh century by the disciples of the Prophet Muhammad, who had recited its verses to his listeners as he said they had been told to him by the angel Gabriel.

Civil law became the predominant legal family on the continent of Europe. Based on the Roman law tradition, its two most important codifications in the modern era were the Napoleonic Code of early nineteenth-century France and the Germanic Law of the People of the late nineteenth century. During the colonial era, civil law was spread to the countries that speak the continental European languages, so it is the most universal law on earth today. In its criminal context, civil law has several distinguishing characteristics:

1. It is concerned less with the rights of criminal defendants and more with getting at the truth.
2. It emphasizes the role of the judge, and private citizens are less often placed in decision-making positions.
3. Precedent is less important, and the trial is more open to useful evidence at the discretion of the judge.
4. The prosecutor and the defense attorney are less important figures, yielding to the authority of the judge.

Socialist law prevails in those countries that have adopted communism as an economic system. The two most important examples of socialist law are the Soviet Union and China, though the Soviet Union is now Russia again and has reverted to its earlier family of civil law, with some common law experimentations, such as trial by jury in some cases. Socialist law tended to be civil law but recast into a classless society in which the means of production were owned and managed by the state. As it was practiced in the Soviet Union and continues to exist in China, Cuba, and several other countries today, socialist law has these main features:

1. The law is used to serve the interests of the communist party, so it is perceived as being more directly under the control of political authorities.
2. The legal profession is less important, and direct public participation at all levels is emphasized.
3. As private property is less important, the protection of public property and community interests are more important.
4. Economic and political crimes, especially those affecting production, are more important than traditional property and violent crimes.
5. Judges are not expected to be independent but are acknowledged to be under the political control of the party, serving the interests of "socialist legality."

Common law is English law. It is found today in various forms among English-speaking countries. It developed over a period of several hundred years preceding its export to English colonies around the world. As it developed in England after the Norman lord William the Conqueror defeated the Saxons at the Battle of Hastings in 1066, common law was originally based more on tribal customs than on any existing legal code. Under the centralized legal system set up by William and his successors (particularly his grandson King Henry II, known as "the Lawgiver"), common law developed through the work of English judges over a long period of time. The law was based on precedent, or previous decisions, and it was applied in practice for many centuries before it was written down in code form. The common law came to have several defining features:

1. Concern with the due process rights of criminal defendants
2. The adversarial system emphasizing the opposing roles of prosecutor and defense counsel battling before a (supposedly) impartial judge
3. Greater concern with following procedural restrictions and the binding nature of precedent
4. The use of the jury of one's peers to render verdicts

Islamic law is important in Muslim countries. It is different from the other legal systems because in its pure form it is religious law, God's law as revealed to Muhammad and recorded in the Qur'an, the Muslim holy book. While most Muslim nations place Islamic law within a secular society and government, some elevate it to a higher place defining all aspects of government and social life. Fundamentalist Muslims view the other legal traditions as man-made, secular institutions designed to serve the ends of government. In their view, Islamic law, known as **Shari'a** ("the way"), is different in several respects:

1. Because its origins are in divine revelation, it is valid whether it is codified or not (so devout Muslims would be bound by Islamic law even in countries following codes based on other legal traditions).
2. It is not the product of human customs but a set of directives coming from God.
3. Legal expertise is also religious expertise, and the interpretation of the law is left more to religious scholars than to legal functionaries.
4. Crimes against God—including apostasy, rebellion, theft, adultery, and drug offenses—are the most serious criminal offenses.

Islamic law has increased in importance in recent decades as the fundamentalist movement has taken hold in several Muslim countries. In Saudi Arabia, Iran, Pakistan, and Sudan, Islamic law is the national law. In half a dozen other countries, the influence of Islamic law on the existing legal system, which is generally one based on European civil law, is increasing. This is not an easy balance, as Islamic law represents a step back in time for modern nations. In its criminal punishments, for instance, Islamic law provides for the death penalty by stoning, by sword, and by beheading (and, according to some texts, by live burial, specifically for the sex crime of sodomy); corporal punishments include whipping and amputation. In personal crimes, the victim's family may choose to accept *diyat*, or blood money, in compensation for injury or death. Under Islamic law, as was the case in many early societies hundreds of years ago, imprisonment is the punishment of last resort. The countries influenced by Islamic law, to a greater or lesser degree, generally have very low rates of imprisonment in contrast to the countries following other legal traditions.

THE AGE OF ENLIGHTENMENT

The punishment practices of the fundamentalist Muslim nations would compare with the practices followed in European countries through the 1700s, though European punishments would commonly have lacked the gravity and religious overtones of punishments under Islamic law. The eighteenth century was a time of important change in the West, a time of intellectual inquiry articulating new perspectives on government, law, and society. During this century-long **Age of Enlightenment,** the traditional methods of punishing criminals would be among many social institutions undergoing dramatic transformation.

In Europe, the Enlightenment was the bridge between the medieval age and the modern world. At the end of the 1600s, the European societies were predominantly rural, agricultural, politically conservative, and religiously orthodox. But doors to new worlds—geographical, scientific, and intellectual—were opening that would lead Europeans into the modern age by the end of the eighteenth century.

Colonization, begun on a smaller scale in the 1600s, would flourish in the 1700s. As Scott Christianson emphasizes in his historical work *With Liberty for Some: 500 Years of Imprisonment in America,* many of these early colonists were prisoners, debtors, slaves, indentured servants, soldiers, and sailors whose role as settlers was far from voluntary. Even so, they paved the way for future waves of immigrants.

The scientific discoveries of Copernicus, Galileo, and Newton shaped a new worldview—a vision of an orderly cosmos with natural laws that could be discerned and understood by ordinary humans. The scientific view weakened the traditional religious and mystical view of the world that had prevailed for over a thousand years. Society became more tolerant of new religious sects expressing contrary points of view (as in England's Tolerance Act of 1689).

As religion loosened its grip on society, intellectual curiosity flourished. Scholars questioned traditional ideas, especially those that had once supported absolutism. John Locke's *Two Treatises on Government* (1689) was particularly influential. Locke supported the concept of constitutional monarchy, as was then taking hold in Britain, based on the social contract between the government and its citizens. His argument contains many of the principles of modern democracy.

On the continent, other philosophers came to prominence in succeeding generations. Baron Charles Montesquieu's *The Spirit of the Laws* (1748) was a highly influential study of comparative government. Jean Jacques Rousseau's novel *Emile* and his work of political philosophy *The Social Contract,* both published in 1762, advocated an independent approach to religion and a democratic, communal civilization. He was labeled a "free-thinking heretic," his books were banned, and he fled to England from France to avoid arrest. Francois Arouet Voltaire, who was imprisoned twice as a young man for his controversial ideas, wrote plays, poetry, novels, history, and philosophy; he was critical of the Catholic Church and political absolutism but also skeptical of common people and democracy. The most prolific writer of his time, Voltaire argued for reason and tolerance within a nonideological worldview. In France also appeared what the British historian J. M. Roberts has called "the greatest literary embodiment of Enlightenment," *The Encyclopedie,* a series of twenty-eight volumes published between 1751 and 1772. Its principal editors were the writer Denis Diderot and the scientist Jean D'Alembert; they collected thousands of articles by writers and scientists, on topics from A to Z, an achievement of great cultural influence in the West at that time. *The Encyclopedie* was also banned by the Church, as its materialistic and rational ideas were considered too controversial for the time.

More and more, rational scholars rejected the absolute authority of church and state and advocated improving the lot of humanity by promoting tolerance and overcoming ignorance. Nowhere were the changes brought about by the Enlightenment more evident or profound than in France. France began the eighteenth century in the reign of King Louis XIV, the "Sun King," an absolute monarch to whom was attributed the remark "L'etat, c'est moi." ("I am the state.") But a century of inefficiency, extravagance, corruption, and disregard for the common good sent the divine right of kings into serious decline. France closed the 1700s with the French Revolution, which in 1793 saw the beheading of Louis XVI and Marie Antoinette, who had begun the revolution as king and queen but ended their lives on the scaffold as common citizens.

Change was not all about science and politics and abstract ideas. The lives of ordinary people changed greatly during this time. Cities grew in size and importance; more than a million people lived in London by the end of the 1700s. Literacy rates had climbed dramatically, and books and newspapers were in widespread circulation. Agriculture was more productive (which was important as the population, long held in check by disease and war, grew sharply), and the industrial revolution was under way in earnest.

The social problems that we associate with modern culture became evident in the new European cities. Crime was on the increase. Gambling, drunkenness, prostitution, and juvenile delinquency flourished in the poorer parts of cities. Punishments had grown more severe, and many criminals and social nuisances were shipped away to colonies across the sea, but the problems of crime and immorality grew more worrisome. Enlightenment philosophers had envisioned a progressive, healthy, civilized modern world, not a culture rotten to its core with crime, vice, and corruption. New ideas and approaches were needed to eliminate the thriving criminal habits that were accompanying the growth of modern urban society.

SCHOLARS AND REFORMERS

Many philosophers and practitioners influenced the changing views of law and crime that prevailed by the end of the 1700s. The most influential thinker of this era, in terms of his impact on the legal system, was the Italian nobleman **Cesare Beccaria** (1738–1794). In 1764, this twenty-six-year-old Milanese aristocrat published *On Crimes and Punishments,* a small volume of essays, some of them no more than one or two paragraphs, on the legal process and criminal punishments. Addressing such topics as "Of the Origins of Punishments," "Of Evidence and the Proofs of a Crime, and of the Form of Judgment," "Of the Advantage of Immediate Punishment," "Of the Punishment of Death," "Of Imprisonment," and "Of the Means of Preventing Crime," Beccaria set forth views that were in direct opposition to the secretive, arbitrary, physically punitive legal system of his time.

Reading Beccaria's work today is a bit like reading Shakespeare. The college sophomore, on first reading the plays of Shakespeare, exclaimed, "I can't believe we have to read this guy. He's so full of cliches." Well, Shakespeare invented more cliches than anyone else in the English language, and Beccaria originated many of the legal cliches that Western law incorporates today.

As one of the founders of the classical school of criminology, Beccaria emphasized the need for law to be in conformity with the rationality and free will of humanity. In his "Introduction," Beccaria argues that the law ought to provide "the greatest happiness of the greatest number," which became the central concept of Utilitarian philosophy. On severe punishments, he writes, "Crimes are more effectually prevented by the certainty than the severity of punishment." On the death penalty, which he strongly opposed, Beccaria writes, "The death of a citizen cannot be necessary but in one case; when, though deprived of his liberty, he has such power and connections as may endanger the security of the nation; when his existence may produce a dangerous revolution in the established form of government." Beccaria argued that penal slavery was a far better punishment than death; this idea of work during imprisonment would be at the core of the philosophy of the nineteenth-century penitentiary.

Beccaria was a shy, retiring man who thought and wrote well but apparently did not make much of a public speaker. He lived for another thirty years after *On Crimes and Punishments* was published, and he held several political positions in Italy, but he produced no more works that would rival this first short book in importance. It remains one of the classics defining the modern legal process.

Following a few years behind Beccaria was the British political activist, legal scholar, and social philosopher **Jeremy Bentham** (1748–1832), who is known as the founder of British **utilitarianism,** or philosophical radicalism. "Bentham claimed that all laws, ancient or modern, should be evaluated according to the single ethical principle of 'utility.' A law is good or bad depending upon whether or not it increased general happiness of the population."[9]

Bentham was known as the originator of the **hedonic calculus** (or hedonistic calculus), which is a measure of what he called our "two sovereign masters, pain and pleasure." The notion is that human action is based on our desire to maximize pleasure while minimizing pain.

Bentham had many interests and wrote prolifically for a long time. He was an activist as well as an abstract thinker. One practical reform of his, to which he devoted a good deal of energy in the 1790s, was a model prison called the **Panopticon.** First proposed in letters that he wrote from Russia in 1787, the Panopticon, or "Inspection-House," was a circular prison in which large square cells with glass front and rear walls would face a central guard tower. The person confined in the cell would be under the constant supervision of the persons in the central watch tower. Bentham thought this design would prove useful to any establishment in which persons were to be kept under inspection— schools, factories, asylums, hospitals, poor houses, and prisons.[10] Although the Panopticon is usually cited as an example of prison architecture, it should more correctly be seen as a model of prison discipline in which the intent was to create the perception of perpetual observation—to make the criminal think he was constantly under surveillance and to make the watchers think that someone was always watching them as well. The Panopticon was well suited to the maintenance of the superior–subordinate relationship on which the internal order of the nineteenth-century prison was based. No prison was ever built to his exact model, though the Stateville Prison in Illinois and several other American and British prisons used his basic circular design.

One of Bentham's contemporaries was the English sheriff and reformer **John Howard** (1726–1790). Although Howard, a prosperous landowner who had been briefly held prisoner by the French as a younger man, had a reputation as a Christian activist, it was his appointment as high sheriff of Bedforshire in 1773 that gave his life focus and earned him historical recognition as the "father of prison reform."

Howard devoted the rest of his life to inspecting jails and prisons throughout Great Britain and on the European continent. He kept meticulous notes of his observations, and in 1777 he published *The State of Prisons in England and Wales, with Preliminary Observations and an Account of Some Foreign Prisons*, a 489-page book printed at his own expense. Howard is said to be the first empiricist, meaning that he addressed the social problem of jails not by philosophy but by detailed observation and analysis. Providing specific, impartial information about conditions he had observed in person, Howard enjoyed great credibility among both public officials and prisoners.

Howard was a tireless advocate of correctional reform, yet he realized that the public was not much interested in the plight of prisoners and that change, if it came, would come slowly. The conditions of confinement in the 1700s were far different from what they are today, and Howard gave "his personal fortune, his health, and his safety" to the cause of changing these conditions, as his biographer Gordon Hay writes:

> What were the reforms John Howard advocated? Clean, healthy accommodation with the provision of adequate clothing and lines; segregation of prisoners according to sex, age, and nature of offense; proper health care: these were his priorities. There should be a chaplain service because he was of his age in believing that spiritual starvation was a major obstacle to reformation of character. Finally, he was a firm believer in the work ethic and the need for prisoners to be provided with work in order that the sin of idleness could be combatted.[11]

Howard introduced the word "penitentiary" to describe the ideal place to accomplish his reforms and induce penitence in the prisoner. The English Parliament, strongly influenced by his writing and advocacy, passed the Penitentiary Act of 1779, which provided for four major reforms—secure and sanitary structures, systematic inspections, abolition of fees for basic services, and a reformatory regime.[12] But these principles did not result in any great changes over the next few years.

In 1790, while visiting Russian military hospitals, Howard contracted the infectious disease **typhus,** also known as **gaol fever,** which was spread by fleas and body lice. He died and was buried at Kherson in the Crimea. His legacy lives on more than two centuries later through the work of the **John Howard Society,** the leading international correctional reform organization.

In America, the earliest correctional reformer of a stature comparable to Howard was the Quaker **William Penn** (1644–1718). Penn had been locked up several times as a young man in England when the government was trying to stifle the **Quakers** as a dissident religious sect. When he founded the colony of Pennsylvania in 1682, as a land grant from Charles II, Penn adopted a legal code, referred to as the **Great Law,** that was very different from other legal codes of its time.

Penn's code substituted imprisonment at hard labor for physical punishments. It first abolished the death penalty entirely, then reinstated it only for premeditated murder (similar to the capital offense of first-degree murder today). Caring for prisoners became a public responsibility, and prisons were required to provide free food and lodging rather than charging inmates fees, as was then common in England.

Penn's code was a very liberal and forward-looking set of laws, but it was considered too progressive for its time. After Penn died in 1718, Parliament reenacted a different, more conventional code, referred to as the "Sanguinary Laws" for its emphasis on bloody punishments, for the colony of Pennsylvania. These laws remained in effect until the American Revolution. The Quaker perspective would return to prominence after the Revolution in establishing the Pennsylvania model of the penitentiary.

EARLY CORRECTIONAL INSTITUTIONS: GAOLS

The true prison, in the modern sense, did not exist before the nineteenth century. The reformist ideas of the eighteenth century would eventually lead to the creation of a new social institution, the penitentiary, that would be used as the principal means of punishing serious criminals. In building this new institution, its planners and designers would have the examples of several earlier types of custodial facilities—asylums, gaols, hulks, bridewells, houses of correction, monasteries, and European prisons—to draw from and, in most instances, to avoid because of the inhumane conditions associated with their confinement practices.

From medieval times to the modern era, the basic English correctional institution (though critics might point out that it had no correctional purpose whatsoever) was the **gaol,** Americanized as **jail** but pronounced the same way. The jail was a small-town facility (or in a large city, such as London, a neighborhood facility) whose purpose was **detention,** or holding people for court. Gaols could range in size from one room to something the size of an old castle. Most colonial American jails were simply one-room wooden or stone structures that could be locked up.

Early gaols were different from those of today in several important respects. They were generally very small; indeed, Howard's inventory of gaols in England and Wales in the 1770s found fewer than 1,000 locked up in a nation approaching ten million in population. Their populations were diverse—debtors, pretrial inmates, sentenced inmates awaiting imposition of sentence, the poor and vagrants, the mentally ill, political dissidents and religious heretics (who were often confined in significant numbers in times of more rigid orthodoxy), and runaway servants.

A lot of the useful distinctions that we make among prisoners today meant very little in earlier times. Everyone was mixed up together—men and women, boys and girls, the insane and the sane, and civil and criminal commitments—typically in conditions of vice, idleness, filth, malnourishment, disease, and despair. Most institutions practiced no such thing as classification. Most of them were under the control of local authorities, which meant that they had limited or no economic resources and no standards to maintain.

Conditions of confinement varied according to the ability of the inmates to pay. Gaols operated on the **fee system,** which charged prisoners daily fees to make money for the sheriffs and businessmen who operated the institutions. Prisoners with money were typically able to get much nicer accommodations than would the poor. It is not only white-collar offenders today who seem to get preferential treatment within the legal system; rewarding wealthy and influential prisoners is a very old and established tradition.

Gustave de Beaumont and Alexis de Tocqueville visited the New Orleans jail on their American tour in 1831. This jail, which was the old Spanish colonial jail now owned by the city, consisted of thirteen cells housing up to 135 prisoners. The French visitors commented, "We found men together with hogs, in the midst of all odors and nuisances. In locking up the criminals, nobody thinks of rendering them better, but only of taming their malice; they are put in chains like ferocious beasts; and instead of being corrected, they are rendered brutal."[13]

EARLY CORRECTIONAL INSTITUTIONS: WORKHOUSES

From the 1500s through the 1800s, England developed a system of local workhouses to keep transient laborers (and the women and children who followed after them) from disrupting city life. In sixteenth-century London, the **Bridewell** came to be known as a particular type of this institution for the poor. Bridewell was a palace on the Fleet River built for King Henry VIII from 1515 to 1520. After 1550, King Edward VI supported a petition to turn the palace into a refuge and workhouse for the displaced rural poor flooding into London from the countryside. Richard Byrne reports, in *Prisons and Punishments of London*, that "simple charity became joined and confused with an attempt to remove the threat of idleness and lawlessness. . . . By 1556 the first prisoners had been received, and put to a wide variety of trades."[14]

The Bridewell was perceived to be a disciplined, charitable institution, in comparison to the vile squalor of the city jails, and it was held out as a model of reform, though whipping of both men and women inmates was a regular occurrence. Crowds used to go to Bridewell to watch the half-naked poor be whipped, which was intended to promote improved habits of industry in the poor. Many other English towns set up similar institutions, though theirs were not often housed in former palaces of the king.

Houses of Correction were created by statute in England in 1574 to house "rogues, vagabonds, and sturdy beggars," according to Richard Byrne. Bridewell was one of these, but many others were built (or existing buildings redesignated) to serve this purpose. All were intended initially to provide relief and job training to the poor, but as time went on they came to house prisoners of all sorts, including political and religious dissenters. As Byrne indicates, the later the houses of correction were built, "the further they departed from ideas of redemption through work."[15]

Across Europe, the **monastery** long played an important dual social role quite apart from its role as the center of religious teaching and learning. When church officials were guilty of criminal or grossly inappropriate conduct, they were rarely punished in the secular courts; if they needed to be removed from their positions, many were sent to monasteries where they could be isolated and punished—doing the same kind of penance later associated with the penitentiary. Indeed, the architectural model of the monastery was influential in the design of the nineteenth-century prison. We may say that old prisons resemble castles, but their architects and planners often looked back to the medieval monastery as the model of regimen and reform they had in mind for the penitentiary, particularly in the design of the individual cell to confine inmates and the simplified daily routine.

The other purpose of the monastery was to help the poor. Poor wanderers in need of a handout or a place to stay could always seek refuge in a monastery. As these institutions declined in number and resources, the poor were increasingly thrown into begging in public, which made them the kind of public nuisances that houses of correction were created to address.

The mentally ill were another problem for society in transition from medieval to modern times. From Roman times, persons suffering from mental disorders had been viewed as possessed by evil spirits. They were generally subjected to torture and confinement, right along with criminals, and later were placed in an institution, the **asylum,** which grew very large in size long before the modern prison.

EARLY CORRECTIONAL INSTITUTIONS: PRISONS

Prisons in their early days were often no more than caves or holes that could be secured in some fashion. The **Mamertine Prison,** which was a dungeon under the sewers of Rome, is often identified as the first known ancient prison. The early Christians were kept there along with other political and religious criminals until they were killed in the arena, sold into slavery, or otherwise eliminated.

Many other early prisons, as distinguished from jails, were often parts of older castles or other structures. Some dungeons or keeps held prisoners of different sorts for hundreds of years. Prisons were less likely to hold ordinary criminals and more likely to confine people held in safekeeping—untrustworthy royalty and nobility, political rebels, and religious heretics. It was common practice for these prisoners to be held in long-term isolation in a form of house arrest until it was safe to release them again. Jails held those whose punishment or disposition would come *after* they were removed from detention. Prisons often held those who might not ever be formally charged with a crime.

By the 1700s in England, institutions called by many names, their original specialized purposes often ignored, held prisoners in custody. Most confinements were of short-term duration, which was surely life affirming given the conditions of the time. Still, John Howard pointed out in his research, more criminals died in detention in English jails in the 1770s—usually of malnutrition and diseases such as smallpox, dysentery, typhus, and yellow fever—than were executed. Early American jails and prisons were no better.

Two continental European prisons were much admired as institutional models in the late eighteenth century. The **Hospice of San Michele** was built in Rome in 1704. It held delinquent youths and young men, like a modern reformatory. Inmates slept in separate cells and worked together in silence; rule violations were punished with flogging. As a church-supported institution, the hospice also subjected its teenage prisoners to moral training through Bible reading, not unlike the practices of several British and American prisons a century later. The inscription over the entrance to the hospice read: "It is insufficient to restrain the wicked by punishment unless you render them virtuous by corrective discipline."[16]

The other model institution was the **Maison de Force** in Ghent, Belgium. Opening as a workhouse in 1773, this institution for beggars and vagrants was widely admired for its humane, reformative approach. The Maison de Force's administrator, Jean-Jacques Vilain, maintained a system of strict discipline but avoided the excessive cruelty of that era. Inmates were classified by gender and crime severity. They slept in separate cells and worked in silence. Foreign visitors, including Sheriff John Howard, held Vilain's system in high regard.

At the other end of the scale, probably the very worst institutions of this time were not proper prisons at all; they were ships, old ships at anchor in the harbor. They were called prison ships, or **hulks,** as in rotting hulks, unseaworthy and sometimes sinking. It was not uncommon for prisoners held on the lower decks to drown in their chains—and they may have been the lucky ones, with the survivors facing conditions of filth, bad food, disease, and brutality that sometimes wiped out virtually the entire complement of prisoners on a given ship. This, of course, made space for another batch.

Conditions on the prisons ships were comparable to conditions on the slave ships transporting African slaves to the New World, with the obvious difference that the prison ships were at anchor and never went anywhere. The mortality rates on the hulks were the highest of any prisons of their era. The *HMS Jersey* and her dozen or so sister ships anchored in New York Harbor were responsible for more American deaths in the Revolutionary War—an estimated 11,500 sailors and soldiers dying in captivity—than all the deaths resulting from battle.

Although prison ships were considered a temporary solution to jail and prison overcrowding on dry land, they were in use in Britain (and during the Revolutionary War in America) for over a hundred years, until about 1875, when the construction of new prisons finally caught up with the population in confinement. By the time the hulks went out of service, a new institution, the penitentiary, moved front and center in corrections—a modern, civilized prison holding convicted criminals whose punishment was time, not blood. The physical punishments and institutions of the past were reduced to supporting roles as this modern invention found its place in society.

KEY TERMS

corporal punishment	economic sanctions	civil law	Panopticon
whipping	public humiliation	socialist law	John Howard
branding	pillory	common law	typhus
capital punishment	stocks	Islamic law	gaol fever
exile	ducking stool	Shari'a	John Howard Society
banishment	folkways	Age of Enlightenment	William Penn
outlawry	mores	Cesare Beccaria	Quakers
transportation	Code of Hammurabi	Jeremy Bentham	Great Law
indentured servitude	Justinian Code	utilitarianism	gaol
slavery	canon law	hedonic calculus	jail

detention	Houses of Correction	Mamertine Prison	hulks
fee system	monastery	Hospice of San Michele	
Bridewell	asylum	Maison de Force	

NOTES

1. William Andrews, *Old-Time Punishments* (New York: Dorset Press, 1991), p. 147.

2. Richard Byrne, *Prisons and Punishments of London* (London: Grafton, 1992), p. 2.

3. "Branding and Maiming," in Alice Morse Earle, *Curious Punishments of Bygone Days*, 1896, *www.rmr.net/~getch/punishments/curious/index.html*.

4. An introduction to Hebrew law is *Exodus*, chapters 20 (The Ten Commandments), 21, and 22.

5. "History of the Death Penalty, Part I," *www.deathpenaltyinfo.org/history2.html*.

6. Geoffrey Abbott, *The Book of Execution: An Encyclopedia of Methods of Judicial Execution* (London: Headline Book Publishing, 1994).

7. Robert Hughes, *The Fatal Shore: The Epic of Australia's Founding* (New York: Vintage Books, 1988).

8. "The Code of Hammurabi," *www.yale.edu/lawweb/avalon/medieval/hamcode.htm*.

9. "Jeremy Bentham, 1748–1832," *http://cepa.newschool.edu/het/profiles/bentham.htm*.

10. "The Panopticon," *www.cartome.org/panopticon1.htm*; "Irregular Times: Forward the Panopticon"; *www.irregulartimes.com/panopt.html*.

11. Gordon Hay, "Biography of John Howard," *www.johnhoward.ca/bio.htm*.

12. American Correctional Association, *The American Prison: from the Beginning . . . A Pictorial History* (Lanham, Md.: American Correctional Association, 1983), p. 16.

13. Gustave de Beaumont and Alexis de Tocqueville, *On the Penitentiary System in the United States and Its Application in France* (Carbondale: Southern Illinois University Press, 1964), p. 49.

14. *Byrne, Prisons and Punishments of London*, pp. 67–72.

15. Ibid., p. 71.

16. American Correctional Association, *The American Prison*, p. 1.

FURTHER READING

Abbott, Geoffrey. *The Book of Execution: An Encyclopedia of Methods of Judicial Execution.* London: Headline Book Publishing, 1994.

Beccaria, Cesare. *On Crimes and Punishments.* Indianapolis: Bobbs-Merrill, 1963.

Hughes, Robert. *The Fatal Shore: The Epic of Australia's Founding.* New York: Random House, 1986.

Morris, Norval, and David J. Rothman. *The Oxford History of the Prison: The Practice of Punishment in Western Society.* New York: Oxford University Press, 1995.

Van den Haag, Ernest. *Punishing Criminals: Concerning a Very Old and Painful Question.* New York: Basic Books, 1975.

WEB AND VIDEO RESOURCES

The Death Penalty Information Center is at *www.deathpenaltyinfo.org*.

The Website *http://crime.about.com* contains several historical articles and references among its current events and issues content.

1 Enlightenment Scholars and Modern Prisons

by Edmond Dantes

What would Enlightenment scholars think of prisons in the United States today? Since the *philosophes* advocated a way of thinking that left a lasting heritage of secularism, science, and humanitarian reform, it would be fair to say they'd think they had entered penal heaven. Initially, at least.

Of the eighteenth century's prevalent punishments for lawbreakers, only capital punishment remains. Floggings, mutilation, exile are gone. So are overcrowded, filthy, disease-infested gaols. In their place are spic-and-span "correctional facilities," whose ambiance and appointments would remind Enlightenment scholars more of their institutions of higher learning than of places where criminals are sent as punishment.

Cesare Beccaria, for instance, believed punishment should serve the dual purpose of incapacitation and deterrence, "with the least torment to the body of the criminal." Were he to walk through a modern prison, the sight of its neatly made bunks, gleaming floors, and freshly painted walls, its equally well-groomed prisoners and palatable (though bland) cuisine would make his humanitarian heart sing.

If John Howard, the old sheriff, pragmatist, and reformer, were to accompany Beccaria, he would behold his dream come true. Clean, healthy accommodations, adequate clothing and health care, and segregation of prisoners by sex, age, and, often, nature of crime are now the rule in U.S. prisons rather than the exception. The prevalence of Christian services and programs, divorced from a controlling role in prison operations, would not give him pause, though the popularity of Muslim religious teachings among black prisoners might.

Jeremy Bentham, the only one of these philosophers who lived long enough to see the advent and initial development of the penitentiary (he died in 1832), would be pleased to note, thanks to video cameras and increased funding to hire more guards, modern prisoners are under constant observation. Continuous surveillance of prisoners and staff, he believed, was integral to control of a prison.

If our stalwarts delved deeper into the mechanics of the American penal system, they would be dismayed. Learning that prison has become the preferred punishment for criminals would not disturb them, but finding so many prisoners serving extraordinary lengths of time for relatively minor offenses would. As humanitarians devoted to reason, they would be aghast at seeing hundreds of thousands of low-level street dealers and addicts locked up for years, sometimes decades, and at natural-life sentences imposed for stealing a piece of pizza or a few videotapes.

The very size of the system would stagger them. Beccaria, who advocated the principles of liberal democracy in a era when absolute monarchy prevailed, would be concerned about the prevalence of prisons. One of every hundred adult Americans is behind bars. George Orwell's *1984* described a totalitarian futuristic state in which "Big Brother is watching you." Beccaria and Howard would have misgivings about the tyrannical views expressed by some in power today, including U.S. Attorney General John Ashcroft.

The philosophers would be disheartened with the continued existence of the death penalty in 38 American states and the federal government. Beccaria advocated the death penalty only for flagrant revolutionaries and, as an alternative to its wider use, proposed perpetual slavery—a life term as a "beast of burden." They would be even more offended by the idleness, lack of productive work, and unpurposed atmosphere that prevail in most prisons—the sense of people doing nothing. They advocated regimented hard labor as punishment for prisoners, viewing it as necessary to their reformation.

Above all, after Beccaria, Howard, and Bentham had read the studies showing punishment has no effect on crime (imprisonment rates have no correlation with crime rates), proven during the past twenty-five years as incarceration has increased unceasingly while crime has leveled off or declined, they would be distressed to realize their treasured notion of deterrence—punishing the few for their criminal conduct to dissuade the many—is false doctrine. If our astonished philosophes then interviewed a scientific sample of our imprisoned felons, to ask them why they were not deterred, they would hear two answers: "I didn't think I'd get caught" or, "I was so angry (or so high) I didn't think about the consequences."

At this point, our Enlightenment scholars might do as their philosophical heirs are doing now—wring their hands and say, "If imprisonment doesn't control crime, what then?"

2 THE PENITENTIARY AND THE 1800S

It must be acknowledged that the penitentiary system in America is severe. While society in the United States gives the example of the most extended liberty, the prisons of the same country offer the spectacle of the most complete despotism. The citizens subject to the law are protected by it; they only cease to be free when they become wicked.

— Gustave de Beaumont and Alexis de Tocqueville, 1833

INTRODUCTION

This chapter considers the growth of the American penitentiary in the 1800s and the development of other alternatives as reformers and public officials saw what was happening to the "ideal" social institution they had created. The corrections system of today is the direct descendant of the institutions and alternatives devised in the nineteenth century. After reading the material in this chapter, you should be familiar with:

1. The penitentiary ideal.
2. The two contrasting models of American prisons.
3. Disciplinary practices in early penitentiaries.
4. Origins of probation and parole.
5. Separate prisons for women and juveniles.
6. Southern prisons and convict leasing.
7. Post–Civil War reforms and the reformatory movement.
8. The industrial prison model.

THE PENITENTIARY IDEAL

In telling the story of Creation, *Genesis* 1:2 says, "And the earth was without form." At the end of the 1700s, so was the penitentiary. It remained for humans—many of them with God in mind as they went about it—to give it form. Although the word **penitentiary** had been in use for more than twenty years among scholarly intellectuals and reformers, no modern penitentiaries as we think of them today had been built. The penitentiary was more of an idea or a set of principles than a physical institution with shape and form. It was a concept rather than a building. When people looked at buildings that held criminals, they saw jails, old prisons, and workhouses, none of them fitting the ideals of the penitentiary.

What was the penitentiary supposed to be? Its purposes were both secular and spiritual. It was supposed to be a place of humane punishment as opposed to the physical punishments still prevalent in Western societies. It was supposed to be a certain punishment, the common punishment of all serious criminals, to replace the diverse penalties applied (or often not applied) by judges. It was supposed to be clean and healthy in contrast to the jail and to avoid the kind of contamination both of body and of spirit that took place in the existing lockups. This meant that criminals in custody ought to be separated from each other as much as possible, preferably in isolation. Finally, and perhaps foremost as a social purpose, it was supposed to practice corrective discipline—to create habits of industry through the application of strictly enforced rules. Prisoners ought to work steadily at productive labor, not sit around idle as they often did in old jails and prisons.

In the spiritual province, the penitentiary was to be a place of penitence, or **penance,** meaning to express regret for the wrongdoing one has done. As a secular institution, the penitentiary was meeting the religious need for expressing contrition for sin. It allowed the criminal to say that he was sorry and to promise to do better; or, if this was too much to hope for, it provided the time and place in which the criminal, entering the institution in a criminal state of mind, would have the opportunity to ponder the error of his ways and see the need to reform. The principal goal of the penitentiary was to achieve the kind of spiritual transformation in a criminal being that was associated with the religious beings of the medieval monastery.

Many early advocates of the penitentiary were highly religious men (and a few were equally religious women). John Howard, the jail reformer, was a devout Congregationalist. **Thomas Eddy,** who secured passage of a humane penal code in New York in 1796, was a Philadelphia Quaker by way of Virginia and the New York insurance business. Eddy made a fortune quickly and turned to social and legal reforms. He lobbied for, built, and opened New York's first state prison, Newgate, in New York City in 1797. He served as warden of Newgate for several years and advocated humane imprisonment and the emancipation of slaves for the rest of his life.

The most influential prison reformers of the new United States of America were Pennsylvania Quakers. Following the lead of William Penn, the acknowledged father of prison reform in the colonies, the Quakers combined social reforms within religious principles. When the civic-minded Quakers of Philadelphia met at Benjamin Franklin's house in 1787, they organized the Philadelphia Society for Alleviating the Miseries of Public Prisons, known today as the **Pennsylvania Prison Society.** Under the leadership of Dr. **Benjamin Rush,** who is also cited for his contribution to early psychiatry, the society's immediate objective was to improve conditions in the decade-old **Walnut Street Jail** at Sixth and Walnut in downtown Philadelphia. The society objected to the public degradation of prisoners on work details (like modern-day chain gangs), to prisoners fed so meagerly that they were reduced to begging for food, to the jail's lack of sanitation and security, and to the absence of inmate classification. In the spiritual realm, Quakers believed that the jail ignored "the inner light" within each person, which they believed would be brought out by solitary confinement.

In 1789 and 1790, the Pennsylvania legislature passed laws to accomplish several reforms. John Roberts's *Reform and Retribution: An Illustrated History of American Prisons* calls the redesigned Walnut Street Jail "arguably the world's first penitentiary, because it carried out incarceration as punishment, implemented a rudimentary classification system, featured individual cells, and was intended to provide a place for offenders to do penance—hence the term 'penitentiary.'"[1]

The British might dispute this. Their own **Wymondham Gaol** at Norfolk, England, had opened in 1785, applying John Howard's penitentiary principles. But Walnut Street, with the construction of a new, three-story wing that opened in 1790, jumped a step ahead. John Roberts writes,

> It was that wing that became the prototype of the modern penitentiary. Convicted felons were housed in that wing—some in individual cells—separated from the rest of the inmate population. A work program was developed within the prison, with inmates engaged in handicrafts such as shoemaking, weaving, cutting and polishing marble, and grinding plaster of paris. Finally, through the work programs and the remorse and penitential reflection that was supposed to occur during incarceration, it was hoped that the inmates would undergo a period of correction; therefore, the Walnut Street Jail indeed had come to fit the definition of a "correctional" institution.[2]

A much larger, 500-cell prison opened at Gloucester, England, the following year, practicing solitary confinement, classification, and labor. It was considered a model of its time, especially for its hygienic and nutritional practices. Philadelphia's reformers found their own penitentiary regimen promising enough to argue for its adoption on a grander, more permanent scale, but improving the lot of convicts did not take high priority among Pennsylvania's public officials. Almost forty years would pass before the Walnut Street Jail felons would be moved into their new home at Eastern State.

CONTRASTING MODELS: EASTERN STATE

Several American states built new prisons from the 1790s to the 1820s, but the reformers of Philadelphia wanted a new and different design, an architecture incorporating the spirit of reformation into physical space. The legislature sponsored a contest, with a $100 prize for the winning design. **John Haviland,** a young British-born architect just starting his career, won the prize with a startling radial design unlike anything ever before seen in an American prison. An associate of John Howard, William Blackburn, had designed several small English prisons using the radial design between 1784 and 1805, most notably the Suffolk House of Correction at Bury St. Edmunds, completed in 1805. The radial design was prominent in England by the time John Haviland devised his grand scheme for the new Pennsylvania prison.

Haviland's **Eastern State Penitentiary,** built on the outskirts of Philadelphia in a farming area known as Cherry Hill, featured seven long cell blocks radiating like spokes from a central rotunda. The facade of the prison would resemble a Scottish castle from the late Middle Ages. A thirty-foot-high wall would enclose the site, sealing the convicts in and sealing the world out.

Haviland ended up being placed in charge of constructing the prison from his design. His original budget, which often means little as massive public works projects progress, was $100,000. Construction began in May 1822 and continued, one cell block at a time, until the last of the original seven blocks was completed in 1836. When construction of the original prison was completed in 1836, the total cost was $780,000. It was the most expensive public building in America at the time and one of the most admired. Tourists came from all over America and Europe to view this modern marvel—this building that claimed to change criminals into God-fearing, law-abiding citizens.

Haviland's original design incorporated the principles of Quaker reformative imprisonment—complete isolation of inmates, fair treatment, and opportunity for work, reflection, and reformation. In contrast to the oppressive, claustrophobic environment of many prisons built more recently, Eastern State's atmosphere was open and expansive. Corridors were wide, high, and arching. Cells were about ten feet long and eight feet wide (officially seven and a half by twelve), but the ceilings were very high, fifteen feet or more. Considering that prisoners in modern cells are provided only thirty-five square feet of floor space according to American Correctional Association standards, these cells were positively spacious.

Each cell contained a toilet that emptied into a drainage trench below, a worktable, and a bed. Overhead was a skylight, necessary for daytime illumination but also serving a symbolic purpose. It represented "the eye of God," the idea that God was watching each convict alone in his cell. In the back wall of the cell was a door to a walled exterior exercise yard—like an enclosed prison patio—about the same size as the cell.

The point of these arrangements was that the prisoner was held in total solitary confinement. The **Pennsylvania system** thus came to be known as the **separate system** or **isolate system.** When the prisoner was admitted to the prison, a woolen hood was placed over his head and a guard led him to his cell. He spent his entire time in confinement in the cell and the exercise yard—twice a day for thirty minutes at a time. He would never see any other part of the prison or have direct contact with other convicts. This separation was part of the Quaker plan—to maintain the isolation necessary for penitent reflection and to prevent the contamination that would occur if the convicts were allowed to mingle.

Prisoners were required to work in their cells at manual trades—weaving, leather working, carpentry, and shoe making. Keepers brought inmates three meals a day, putting the dishes through the narrow slots in the iron front door of the cell. Inmates could have a Bible and one other book at a time; no letters, magazines, or newspapers were allowed. The walls were too thick to allow conversation, social contact between guards and prisoners was forbidden, and no outside visitors were permitted. It was not even necessary to have guards on the perimeter walls, as prisoners were never in a position to get close to the walls. Guards in the central rotunda could keep the entire prison under observation from this one vantage point. This was the model of self-containment in which reformation was intended to take place.

How did this regimen work? When Beaumont and Tocqueville visited Eastern State on their 1831 prison tour, they interviewed forty-six inmates and came away favorably impressed. They spoke with Charles Williams, a light-skinned black farmer who had come to the prison in 1829 at age eighteen to serve two years for theft. He was Eastern State's Inmate Number 1. They wrote about Williams,

> This man works with ardor; he makes ten pairs of shoes a week. His mind seems very tranquil; his disposition excellent. He considers his being brought to the Penitentiary as a signal benefit of Providence. His thoughts are in general religious. He read to us in the Gospel the parable of the good shepherd, the meaning of which touched him deeply; one who was born of a degraded and depressed race, and had never experienced any thing but indifference and harshness.[3]

When Charles Dickens visited in 1842, he described Eastern State as a place of "solitary horrors." Although he was impressed by the prison keepers' "excellent motives" and the institution's "perfect order," he wrote in *American Notes, for General Circulation,*

> The system here, is rigid, strict, and hopeless solitary confinement. I believe it, in its effects, to be cruel and wrong. In its intention, I am well convinced that it is kind, humane, and meant for reformation; but I am persuaded that those who devised this system of Prison Discipline, and those benevolent gentlemen who carry it into execution, do not know what it is they are doing. . . . I hold this slow and daily tampering with the mysteries of the brain, to be immeasurably worse than any torture of the body, and because its ghastly signs and tokens are not so palpable to the eye and sense of touch as scars upon the flesh; because its wounds are not upon the surface, and it exhorts few cries that human ears can hear; therefore I the more denounce it, as a secret punishment which slumbering humanity is not roused up to stay.[4]

Dickens's doubts were insufficient to stem the worldwide tide of enthusiasm for Eastern State's model of reform. Of all nineteenth-century prisons built in America, Eastern State came closest to the penitentiary ideal. At least 300 prisons around the world were designed to incorporate its architectural and reformation model—both built on the idea of inmate labor under complete solitary confinement.

CONTRASTING MODELS: AUBURN

Even before Eastern State was open for business, a contrasting prison model was being developed in New York. At Auburn in western New York and at Sing Sing thirty miles north of New York City, two new prisons, **Auburn** and **Sing Sing,** were built to replace New York City's Newgate Prison. Auburn and Sing Sing were called prisons, not penitentiaries, when they opened; "penitentiary" was a term that originally meant a particular style of imprisonment that neither of these institutions used.

The first convicts were moved into Auburn in 1817. They were housed in small cells—seven feet long by three and a half feet wide by seven feet tall. The cells were stacked atop each other in tiers, and they had no outside exercise yards. Convicts were divided into three levels of control—from complete solitary to group work in the daytime and sleeping in single-person cells at night.

Auburn conducted an early experiment with solitary confinement, locking eighty hardened convicts in their cells for a year. At the end of the year, several had died, and most of the rest were sick. One jumped to his death as soon as he was released. Others were clearly deranged. The governor ordered several of them released immediately.

You can try this experiment at home if you wish. Have a trustworthy friend lock you in a closet for a year. Your friend has to bring you food and water two or three times a day and empty your waste bucket every day or two. At the end of a year, when the door opens, write down your thoughts about yourself, the other people in your life, and how your outlook has changed.

If you do not have a full year to devote to this experiment, try just one weekend. You may understand better why Auburn and the other prisons rejected solitary confinement except as a punishment or for control. The **Auburn system** of inmate management became known as the **congregate system.** It featured inmates living alone in their cells (at least until overcrowding became a persistent problem) while they spent most of their out-of-cell time in the company of other inmates—working, eating, and chapel, maintenance, and cleaning chores. The system was also called the **silent system.** When the prisoners were in contact with other prisoners, a rule of silence prevailed: no inmate was allowed to speak to another.

Auburn's early successes (or perhaps the lack of viable alternatives) led New York to build an even larger prison, originally called Mount Pleasant but known to the ages as Sing Sing, in the late 1820s. Sing Sing was built by convict labor. The prison was located on top of a quarry that produced fine marble, some of which was used in building the prison. The original cell block was five tiers high, a long, narrow building that held 1,000 one-man cells. Its cells were slightly smaller than Auburn's, barely allowing enough room for a bed and a bucket.

CONTRASTING MODELS: AND THE WINNER IS?

As the American states and many foreign nations turned away from punishments of the past and turned toward imprisonment as the principal means of punishing serious crimes, reformers and government officials trekked to Pennsylvania and New York to take a look at the two contrasting prison models. Which system was better: Eastern State or Auburn?

The purists agreed that the Pennsylvania model was closer to ideal. The environment was more penance inducing. The prison was orderly, quiet, and controlled. The prisoners were managed individually rather than in the congregate. Dr. Samuel Gridley Howe, the Boston social reformer and abolitionist, published *An Essay on Separate and Congregate Systems of Prison Discipline* in 1846. He pointed out that the congregate system treated prisoners as masses, whereas the solitary system treated each convict as an individual, which he favored.[5] But it was considerably more trouble to do it this way—to deal with one person at a time, in feeding them in their cells rather than in a group mess hall, or in ministering to other needs.

The Auburn model was cheaper to build and operate, requiring fewer guards to service and control the prisoners, and used the space within the walls more intensively. Most important, group labor made it economically more productive. A hundred men working with machinery in a prison shop were vastly more productive than a hundred men working alone in individual cells.

Eastern State's museum guidebook, "Behind the Walls," discusses the demise of its model in favor of the congregate model, citing three important reasons why Auburn won out. First, the aftermath of the Civil War brought a big increase in the prison population both as a result of the effects of the war and as a result of immigration and economic depression. Second, isolation caused some prisoners to suffer psychologically, leading critics to condemn solitary confinement as cruel and inhumane punishment. Finally, keeping a growing inmate population in solitary confinement was expensive. Inmates could do only individual handwork in their cells, so the prison could not profit from captive labor to produce more goods as congregate prisons did.[6]

In the end, it was like choosing between two homes: the fine mansion that you really like and the more ordinary house that you can afford. You may still have your dreams, but you settle for what is within your means. In its origins, the penitentiary was recommended for its humane, reformative purposes; over time, as its purpose came to be defined as housing convicts—the dregs of society—the emphasis shifted from goals to means—to cheapness, productivity, and efficient management (or "industry, obedience, and silence," as Scott Christianson described the Auburn environment).

In time, the few prisons built on the Pennsylvania model were converted to congregate prisons. Eastern State officially abandoned solitary confinement in 1913, though convicts had unofficially been in contact with each other since the end of the Civil War. Guard towers went up on the walls and over the central rotunda, and solitary confinement began to be used only as a punishment. Eastern State continued to have influence in other countries. Many nations used solitary confinement in some smaller prisons or as a new prisoner's first housing on entering the prison—as in the French progressive system requiring inmates to pass through several levels of confinement over time. In the 1990s, perpetual solitary was reborn in America in the form of the "supermax" prison, used with selected prisoners, but it no longer had any connection with penance or reform.

PRISON RULES AND DISCIPLINE

The architecture of the nineteenth-century prison—its imposing size, the medieval affect, and the stone and iron—were intended not only to control but also to intimidate, to break the spirit of the hapless criminals brought through the prison gate. More than one early prison carved in stone the line from Dante's *Inferno:* "All hope abandon, ye who enter here."

If prison officials expected convicts to become compliant participants in the new prison order, however, they were immediately disappointed. Criminals were not only humans, who can adapt to almost any situation, but they were also criminals who had established a pattern of antisocial behavior in society (the "free world," as convict slang says it). Locking them up in maximum-security, castle-like fortresses did not bring about any obvious positive transformation in most of the prisoners. More stringent measures were necessary.

Nineteenth-century prisons employed strict controls and severe disciplinary practices, commonly based on physical punishment. The most important restriction was the **rule of silence** that was applied in Auburn-style prisons.

Because most convicts spent much of their waking time in contact with others, silence was believed necessary to prevent the moral contamination that authorities feared would spread in prison. Prisons worked out elaborate systems of signaling, using whistles, bells, horns, and other sounds to structure the daily routine and hand signals to indicate requests and acknowledgments. Foreign visitors to these prisons were amazed to see large numbers of men working together in complete silence under the watchful eyes of a handful of guards.

Prisons then as now had lots of rules—rules regarding conduct, contraband, labor, sanitation, and sexual behavior. (Masturbation in particular was very strongly disapproved of, as it was believed to lead to blindness, insanity, tuberculosis, and other common prison ailments.) Guards were expected to be alert to any rule violation. At Eastern State, guards wore socks over their shoes when they went down the cell blocks to spy on prisoners, the better to catch unsuspecting prisoners engaged in nefarious conduct.

Prisoners were allowed fewer personal possessions than they are today, and they were far more isolated from the outside world. Some prisons had very specific lists of what possessions prisoners were allowed to have, but the whole matter was completely arbitrary. Prisoners in custody had no legal rights and no access to courts. What prisoners were allowed and how they were treated depended entirely on the administrators of their prison—in particular, the personality and beliefs of the warden, who created the custodial atmosphere.

The prototypical early American prison warden was Captain **Elam Lynds,** who was warden of Auburn prison and then built the new, improved Sing Sing in the 1820s. Lynds's view was that convicts were cowards and dogs and ought to be treated accordingly. Lynds invented two of the control devices associated with early prisons—**prison stripes** and the **lockstep.** He put inmates in striped uniforms to make them more visible and also to humiliate them, as it would be humiliating to you to have to wear pink pajamas with little bunny feet outside all day. The lockstep was a method of moving convicts around inside the prison; prisoners marched—shuffled their feet, actually—with a hand on the shoulder of the man in front of them. A long line of men going off to work or chow looked like a giant striped caterpillar, shuffling along in silence.

Lynds carried a bullwhip with him when he walked about the prison. He gave each of his guards a **cat-o'-nine-tails,** a whip with several knotted lines or cords attached to its handle. Guards were instructed to flog prisoners for any misconduct. That they carried out this order enthusiastically was documented in an early prison expose, *A Voice from Sing-Sing*, written in 1833 by the former army colonel Levi Burr. Burr called Sing Sing a "catocracy" for its extensive use of the cat-o'-nine-tails.

Elam Lynds was interviewed by Beaumont and Tocqueville on their prison tour, though by the time they interviewed him, Lynds was out of political favor and no longer a warden. In their "Interview with Mr. Lynds," the French visitors noted these observations from America's most prominent nineteenth-century prison warden:

> The director of a prison, particularly if he establish a new discipline, should be invested with an absolute and certain power.

I consider the chastisement by the whip, the most efficient, and, at the same time, the most humane which exists; it never injures health, and obliges the prisoner to lead a life essentially healthy. Solitary confinement, on the contrary, is often insufficient, and always dangerous. . . . I consider it impossible to govern a large prison without a whip.

A dishonest man is ever a coward.[7]

Elam Lynds, in a decade at Auburn and Sing Sing, practiced what came to be called the Auburn system of prison management. Based on its view of the prisoner as a weak, very inferior being, it established a prison regimen of several key elements:

1. Absolute silence
2. Hard labor
3. Unwavering routine
4. Total regimentation of the prisoners' lives
5. Breaking the convicts' spirit
6. Insisting that prisoners demonstrate a completely subservient attitude
7. Immediate physical punishments for all rule violations

This model of prison management became pervasive throughout American prisons in the nineteenth century. At its heart, it relied on physical punishment to maintain discipline by instilling fear in convicts. Sing Sing used flogging with the cat-o'-nine-tails, later replaced by the shower bath, in which a barrel of cold water would be dumped on the prisoner, and the iron cage, which would be locked around his head. San Quentin would use its own form of the shower bath, in which the prisoner would be sprayed with a high-pressure water hose. Most prisons used whippings, usually in view of other inmates, sometimes with the prisoner to be whipped tied to a whipping post or standing in a pillory. Delaware's "Red Hannah" whipping post, used into the 1950s, was one of the most enduring.

In contrast to the Pennsylvania system, which isolated convicts physically while treating them more humanely, Lynds's Auburn system allowed human contact but within an environment of repressive, often brutal, physical discipline. The penitentiary, which at least in the British and Pennsylvania models was intended to replace corporal punishments, instead reverted to these punishments to supplement imprisonment so that the nineteenth-century convict ended up with the worst of both worlds. The old convicts had been whipped and let go; the new convicts were whipped and returned to their cells to do more time.

PROBATION

When Beccaria and the other legal reformers of the 1700s were arguing against the use of physical punishments, one of their concerns was that physical punishments promoted judicial leniency—that judges often avoided punishing lesser or "tender" criminals, such as women and juveniles, not wanting to see them brutalized. Reformers argued that imprisonment, because it would be employed universally, without exception, would be a much greater deterrent than physical punishments that might or might not be applied, depending on the sympathetic mood of the judge.

Although probation, as an alternative to prison, is considered a modern sentence, it has roots in earlier practices under English and continental law. In these early systems, it was common to withhold punishment—what today we would call a **suspended sentence. Right of sanctuary,** under church doctrine, set aside holy places for criminals to seek protection from secular laws. In the Middle Ages, **benefit of clergy** allowed religious officials to avoid punishment in the criminal courts; their cases were referred to high church officials (which is how many of them came to be sent to monasteries for penance). Under English common law, persons who could recite Psalm 51, which begins, "Have mercy upon me, O God, according to thy loving kindness: according unto the multitude of thy tender mercies blot out my transgressions," were presumed to be church officials who would not be punished criminally. So many criminals memorized this chapter of the Bible that it became known as the **neck verse;** it was used like a "Get Out of Jail Free" card when facing punishment, especially the death penalty.

Other predecessors of probation in use in English and early American courts, such as **filing of cases** and **recognizance,** allowed judges to release deserving offenders without punishment. The suspended sentences these offenders received were less restrictive than contemporary probation; they did not require supervision or impose conditions of compliance on the criminal as probation does. The European model of **surcease** (or *sursis*) withheld punishment if the offender committed no new crime during the period of suspension. The suspended sentence is still used for many traffic and petty offenses in American courts.

The origins of modern **probation** in America are often traced to the work of **John Augustus,** a Boston shoe manufacturer and civic leader of the 1840s and 1850s. Augustus is often referred to as a "shoemaker," giving rise to an image of a kindly old cobbler abandoning his bench to rescue lost boys. In fact, Augustus was a wealthy, well-connected factory owner who spent most of his time and money helping the less fortunate.

Although probation was not then a legal sentence (all felons and many serious misdemeanants were supposed to go straight to prison, like today's mandatory sentences), Augustus used his influence to persuade judges in Boston courts to assign criminals to his care, beginning with a drunk in 1841 and continuing until his own death in 1858. Augustus would clean up the criminal, get him a job using his business connections, and help him find a place to live. A few months later, Augustus would accompany the criminal back to court, where the judge would terminate the sentence.

By his own published account, in seventeen years Augustus helped almost 2,000 people to straighten out their lives. What started as a one-time intervention became a full-time mission. Augustus reported a success rate of nearly 100 percent among these criminals, which would be unheard of today. Very likely, he did not keep good records about the lives of his probationers, or many of them disappeared and returned to their criminal ways in other places under other names.

Civic reformers in Massachusetts were greatly encouraged by Augustus's example. They got the state to pass the first probation statute in 1878, legally allowing the judge to suspend imprisonment. This was to be done only for the selected few who truly deserved it. By this time, court officials in many states were seeing what penitentiary life did to inmates, and several other states adopted probation laws over the next few years. Probation was initially an informal practice found mostly in urban courts and relying heavily on volunteers rather than paid probation officers. Over time, it became more formalized, under the control of state or county governments. The rise of the juvenile court in the early twentieth century promoted the continued expansion of formal probation services.

PAROLE

Today we say that probation is what you get instead of imprisonment; **parole** is what you get at the end of imprisonment. If the options that preceded probation had a long tradition, parole had none. We had to start keeping large numbers of people in prison for long periods of time before we could see that not everyone deserved to remain for the full sentence. The predecessor of parole could be called the king's **pardon** power or **clemency** power; criminals in the past had been set free from imprisonment or had death sentences canceled through the intervention of the king (or later the governor or president in the American legal system). When they were released through a pardon, however, they were completely free, not supervised postrelease as parole requires today.

Although the use of the term "parole" in its correctional sense is often attributed to Dr. Samuel Gridley Howe in 1840s Boston, parole comes from the Old French *parole d'honneur*, meaning "word of honor." The practice of parole is said to have originated in two British prison systems half a world apart—in Australia and Ireland in the 1840s and 1850s.

Alexander Maconochie was a British naval officer and prison critic who in 1840 was made superintendent of Australia's "Devil's Island"—the penal colony of **Norfolk Island** located about 800 miles due east of Brisbane. When convicts committed new crimes on the Australian mainland, they were banished to Norfolk Island. Its reputation was so severe that some men begged for death, preferring immediate execution to a lingering death in exile under brutal conditions.

Maconochie instituted reforms that turned Norfolk Island upside down. His basic premise was that convicts should be able to earn their way back to the main island through good behavior and hard labor. He set up the **marks system,** using a system of levels through which convicts would pass over time as they earned credits—"marks," as he called them—toward their discharge. When they had earned enough marks, they were allowed to leave Norfolk Island on a **ticket-of-leave.** This is called the first example of the modern **indeterminate sentence,** which in effect allowed the prison system to determine when the convict would be released. Maconochie left Norfolk Island in 1844 and returned to England. He was later placed in charge of the Birmingham Prison briefly but was fired because he was perceived as being too lenient—an early example of prisoner "coddling."

At about the same time, the Irish prison system was grappling with the problem of overcrowding, brought on by the Great Potato Famine and the deterioration of traditional society. John Roberts describes the Irish prison system of the mid-1800s as "the most enlightened of its day."[8] Under the direction of Joshua Jebb and **Walter Crofton,** this system

> combined religious, educational, and work programs with a graduated classification system, through which an inmate had to progress before being released. Inmates began their sentences in solitary confinement, with reduced rations and no work assignments. Good conduct won advancement to the next stage of incarceration, which included congregate labor and improved rations. In the final stage, the inmate was moved into a less restrictive prison environment, had a job assignment in the community, and could earn credits toward early release—again, if conduct seemed to indicate that the inmate had achieved rehabilitation.[9]

The sentence was indeterminate, and the release decision was that of the prison superintendent. When the prisoner was discharged, he was granted a ticket-of-leave to return home. His status was that of **conditional liberty** in that he was still serving his original sentence and could be returned to prison for violating the law. A police officer was assigned to maintain general surveillance of the former prisoner in the community and to recommend that he be put back in prison if he failed to follow the conditions of his release. The modern-day practice of parole, while considerably more bureaucratized, works essentially the same way.

Parole began to be used in the United States toward the end of the 1800s. Many prisoners were already leaving prison early through the use of **good-time** provisions that reduced time served for good behavior, and many prisoners benefited from the generous use of executive clemency by governors; pardons and commutations were frequent. Parole itself was identified specifically with the reformatory (discussed later in this chapter), which housed only a small percentage of prisoners in custody. Over time, its usage spread to all prisons. By the mid-1900s, virtually all inmates in American prisons were subject to parole review and conditional release.

WOMEN'S PRISONS

One of the perplexing problems of early jails and prisons was what to do with women prisoners. Rates of incarceration were much lower in those days than they are today, and the numbers of women in custody were very small—often just a handful among a much larger number of male prisoners. Jails before the 1800s had often treated women exactly as they treated men. Women were punished as men were, with the exception that pregnant women were often spared punishment until after they had given birth. Women were generally mixed with male prisoners and supervised by male jailers, which made the women doubly subject to abuse and exploitation. Since most women in custody were prostitutes or habitual thieves (and in America typically immigrants or minorities as well), no one worried much about their predicament.

This began to change in the early 1800s. **Elizabeth Gurney Fry** was an English Quaker and mother of eleven children. After a visit to Newgate prison in 1813, Fry began a ministry for the women of Newgate and eventually other London jails and prisons. She often visited prisons to read the Bible to inmates despite warnings that it was not safe for her to do so. Fry organized the Association for the Improvement of the Female Prisoners in Newgate in 1817. She took up many social causes over the next thirty years but is best known for her prison advocacy—arguing for separate prison facilities for women, run by women, and shaped toward the needs of women prisoners as a group different from men. She was a highly influential reformer. Like her predecessor John Howard, Fry's heritage is preserved in an international prison reform organization that bears her name.

In the United States, other reformers took up the separatist cause. **Eliza W. B. Farnham** was the head matron of the women's wing at Sing Sing Prison in New York from 1844 to 1848. She was noted for her efforts to make the women's prison environment more like a middle-class home and less like a prison; this included reform programs intended to transform low-life women criminals into middle-class homemakers—like turning Gangsta Girl into Martha Stewart (though since Martha Stewart's felony conviction, this analogy no longer seems so remote). Like many early reformers, Farnham was often in trouble with her superiors for being too nice to convicts. After she started an education program for the women inmates (and included works of fiction in the prison library), she was fired.

The **Indiana State Reformatory** was established in 1873 as the first separate prison for women in America. Several of the more progressive states, including Massachusetts and New York, opened separate women's prisons over the next few years. The Bedford Hills Reformatory for Women opened in New York in 1901. Its superintendent, **Katherine B. Davis,** brought in physicians and behavioral scientists to classify and study women prisoners and develop treatment programs. The women were housed not in cells but in separate cottage rooms, giving the prison a campus look. Jean Harris, a school headmistress who came to Bedford Hills much later as a convicted murderer, pointed out that women inmates were always referred to as "ladies," which expressed an ideal state for most of them.

As assistant attorney general of the United States in the 1920s, **Mabel Walker Willebrandt** was instrumental in the creation of the Federal Bureau of Prisons in 1930. Willebrandt was a Quaker who strongly advocated improving federal prison operations, particularly as they affected young people and women. It was under her direction that the **Federal Women's Reformatory** (initially named the Federal Industrial Institution for Women) at Alderson, West Virginia, opened in 1927. Dr. **Mary Belle Harris,** a Ph.D. in Sanskrit and a concert pianist, was the first warden of this prison, commonly known as **Alderson.** Located in the rolling hills of northern West Virginia, Alderson's cottage plan and absence of fences gave the prison the look of a weekend resort. Its female inmates denied the "country club" label often applied to low-security federal prisons. The popular saying among prisoners at Alderson in the early days was, "They work us like a horse, feed us like a bird, treat us like a child, dress us like a man—and then expect us to act like a lady."

While women prisoners in reformatories may have been expected to "act like ladies," the female inmates remaining in state prisons and local jails were more often treated like household servants and prostitutes. They worked as hard as the men, doing "women's work"—laundry, sewing, cleaning, and cooking. They were under the domination of men, both staff and the male trusties who were prominent in the day-to-day operation of the twentieth-century prison. Men on both sides of the bars were quick to take sexual advantage of women prisoners. Many states, notably in the South, did little to address the needs of women prisoners until after World War II. Louisiana, for instance, kept its women prisoners at the Angola prison farm until 1961, when they were moved into a separate prison south of Baton Rouge.

JUVENILE PRISONS

As some nineteenth-century reformers worked to improve the plight of women in prison, others focused on children. English and American legal systems had traditionally made no distinction in punishment based on age. Juveniles were locked up in jails right along with adults. Criminals as young as seven were given adult punishments if they were found to know the difference between right and wrong, and all youngsters became legal adults at fourteen. Several children under this age were executed in colonial times.

By the time of the Enlightenment, it was more common for judges to deal leniently with young offenders—particularly because so many of them had sad stories to tell, such as tales of abandonment and falling under the influence of adult criminals. One of the reasons legal scholars of this era advocated the use of imprisonment as a more general punishment was that they believed judges would be more likely to punish juveniles with confinement than with physical punishments, banishment, and other options of the time.

As the penitentiary became firmly established in the first half of the 1800s, reformers argued that young people should not be locked up in these institutions. They had three basic arguments:

1. The penitentiary regimen was too hard on tender youth.
2. Juveniles would learn bad habits from older criminals and be embittered by the experience of confinement.
3. Adolescents could be reformed if they were diverted early enough into institutions designed specifically for people their age.

Early efforts to reform juvenile justice were centered in America's large cities, where problems of criminal and antisocial behavior among youth were most concentrated and most noticeable. In the 1820s and 1830s, New York, Boston, and Philadelphia set up **houses of refuge** to keep juveniles out of jail. The first of these, opened in New York City on January 1, 1825, was like a combination shelter and detention center, accepting juveniles convicted of crimes or sentenced as vagrants, a catchall term for street youths.

By the 1850s, Massachusetts had opened separate **training schools** for boys and girls. Although juveniles were at this time still passing through the same legal system as adults, judges could send boys and girls deserving leniency to these training schools, where they would get the discipline, vocational training, and basic education to prepare them for a law-abiding, productive adult life. Training schools, which could be likened to involuntary vo-techs, pre-dated the reformatories for young adult criminals that would develop after the Civil War.

Urban courts of the Northeast and Midwest moved toward de facto age-based processing of criminals in the later 1800s. Juveniles often received more lenient treatment than adults, with a greater diversity of dispositional options. **Charles Loring Brace,** educated as a minister, instead became an early social worker, focusing his attention on the poor children of New York City. In 1853, he led a group that founded the Children's Aid Society, which emphasized noninstitutional assistance to poor and homeless children and their families. Brace theorized that institutional care "stunted and destroyed children,"[10] so his mission was to help their families or, failing this, to place them with new families. Brace became nationally known for organizing the **orphan trains** that sent many thousands (over 150,000 in seventy-five years, according to Children's Aid Society statistics) of abandoned, abused, and orphaned children out of New York City to small-town and farm families across America. This theme of removing children from the pernicious city environment to the good life of the country became known as the **child-saving movement.**

A century of efforts by reformers to not only separate juveniles from adults but also adopt a less punitive legal approach resulted in the establishment of the first **juvenile court** in Chicago in 1899. Operating on principles of informality, confidentiality, leniency, and paternalism (in the form of the judge taking parental control over the child), this court assumed jurisdiction over its clientele based on age. Its goal, variously expressed in the statutes of the time, was to save, help, or reform (later rehabilitate) youngsters from wasted and sometimes criminal lives. Over the next two decades, other states set up similar courts based on age and emphasizing probation and noncustodial alternatives. These juvenile courts did not immediately embrace all youthful offenders. In fact, most serious young criminals continued to be sent to adult prisons until after World War II. But the influence of the juvenile court grew steadily over time and eventually led to the bifurcated legal system of today, in which we follow completely separate routes and use different institutions for juveniles and adults.

SOUTHERN PRISONS AND CONVICT LEASING

As northern states developed the punitive institutions and alternatives that would bring them into the twentieth century, southern states followed a different track. In its approach to corrections, the South was different from the North in several key aspects:

1. Aside from its coastal cities, the South was much more rural than urban; local governments were much more influential than state governments.
2. Although individual reformers, often relocated from the North, made names for themselves in the South, reform movements never had the same effect on public policies in the South as they did in the North. Reforms tended to be discussed rather than acted on or, if put into effect, quickly abandoned.
3. Between one-third and one-half the population of southern states were blacks held in slavery, for the most part outside the civil and criminal legal system. It was difficult to be "progressive" when so much time and attention was devoted to maintaining an inherently regressive institution.

Many correctional reforms that resulted in important changes in the northeastern and midwestern states simply bypassed the South or were considerably watered down in their effects. Several southern states never concentrated their populations of convicted felons in penitentiaries in the 1800s. Instead, they left criminals in the custody of local sheriffs (often to be charged fees and worked as had been the practice in England) or leased convicts out to private entrepreneurs who assumed complete responsibility for the prisoners in return for their labor. Economy has always been an important issue in American corrections, but in southern prisons it was often elevated to paramount importance. Louisiana opened a modern penitentiary in Baton Rouge in 1835, a progressive prison based on the Auburn model, only to abandon its convicts to leasing in 1844, primarily because the new prison cost too much. Louisiana's convicts were leased to private businessmen until 1901.

Other states started leasing earlier, from the 1820s, and some continued it longer, into the 1920s, but the emphasis on economy was pervasive. The Civil War was an even more important influence. Louisiana historian Mark T. Carleton called the Civil War "the most decisive event in the history of the Southern penology."[11] By this he meant not that the war resulted in new theories or practices but that it freed the slaves and made them subject to equal punishment under law. Southern prisons, which before the war had been almost entirely white, quickly became majority black, in most states in even greater percentages than today. In the South, even during Reconstruction, prisons were seen as a necessary step in helping blacks make the transition from slavery to freedom (and the profit from their labor was helpful to the state budget).

After the Civil War, the **convict lease system** flourished in the South. Several southern states developed the predecessors of twentieth-century prison farms, following an obvious line of reasoning. Most new black convicts were accustomed to agricultural labor, so it made good business sense to keep them at it, whether on a public farm or one operated by a private owner. The last third of the nineteenth century was slavery rewritten as prison policy. Convicts were worked hard, with little thought for their health, safety, or improvement. Mortality rates were very high compared to northern prisons. Convicts privately leased had it the worst, laboring under deplorable conditions in the most primitive settings.

Convicts were viewed as a "species of slave labor" in postwar southern prisons. A speaker at the 1883 National Conference of Charities remarked, "Before the war we owned the negroes. If a man had a good negro, he could afford to take care of him: if he was sick, get a doctor. He might even get gold plugs in his teeth. But these convicts: we don't own 'em. One dies, get another."[12]

Reforms would eventually come to southern prisons in the 1900s. But the legacy of local control over prisoners, the emphasis on economy, the lack of attention to rehabilitation, and a racist culture in which white keepers controlled majority black prison populations would continue to make southern prisons much worse than prisons elsewhere. These historical problems would flare up again as litigation over substandard prison conditions flourished later in the twentieth century. As was the case with school integration and civil rights, lasting change occurred in southern prisons only when federal courts ordered that it take place.

THE REFORM MOVEMENT

The penitentiary was created as a reform; by the time of the Civil War, many penologists and social activists saw it as an evil—an institution badly in need of reform itself. The penitentiary was founded on the notion that criminal behavior could be eliminated or reduced by confining criminals. Where previous societies had emphasized the infliction of pain (through physical punishments) or banishment, fines, or indentured servitude, the penitentiary emphasized a combination of time and a very restricted environment as criminal penalties. It was a punishment much more suited to the rationality of the Enlightenment, to ideas about the progress of civilization, but, in fact, early results suggested it was working no better at controlling crime than the more primitive methods just abandoned.

In scarcely half a century, the penitentiary had gone from an institution representing optimism and hope of change to an institution representing suffering and mistreatment, as observed by the people running it. Norman Johnston's book on the history of Eastern State Penitentiary is subtitled *A Crucible of Good Intentions*. By the latter part of the 1800s, many of America's progressive penologists were giving up on the "good intentions" of the penitentiary.

In 1870, a well-known New York prison reformer, Dr. **Enoch Cobb Wines,** worked with other corrections critics to found the **National Prison Association.** This organization met in Cincinnati, Ohio, in October 1870. This first congress, as it was called, was attended by delegates from twenty-four states and several foreign countries. Its most recognized speaker was the Irish prison official Sir Walter Crofton, who spoke on his Irish system, while its most prominent American member was the Civil War general **Rutherford B. Hayes,** then governor of Ohio, soon to be president of the United States, and later to serve ten years as president of the association. Delegates met for several days, discussing prison reform ideals and penitentiary shortcomings, and in the end they adopted a "Declaration of Principles." First on their list was "Reformation, not vindictive suffering, as the purpose of penal treatment":

> The Declaration of Principles strongly endorsed the reformatory concept, indeterminate sentencing, separate facilities for women and for juveniles, classification, centralized prison management in each state, and the Irish system (of management and parole). It called for abolition of convict leasing, improvement of prison architecture, establishment of prison schools and hospitals, job training for staff, and rewards for good conduct by inmates.[13]

The Declaration of Principles, very ambitious for its time, reads like the road map of twentieth-century American corrections. Its creator, the National Prison Association, later changed its name to the American Prison Association and in the 1950s to the **American Correctional Association.** Today it is the largest professional organization of its type in the world. The ACA, as it is known, still holds its annual congress each year in August, and though it has been criticized for becoming too much like a sales meeting for private businesses hawking technology and equipment to corrections agencies, it remains the most important national forum for professional development and for addressing present and future policies in corrections.

THE REFORMATORY

One of the speakers at the Cincinnati National Prison Congress was an up-and-coming young prison warden, **Zebulon Brockway.** His paper was titled "Ideal for a True Prison System for a State." Six years later, Brockway got the chance to translate his ideals into reality—with the opening of the **Elmira**

Reformatory in New York. Receiving its first inmates on July 24, 1876, Elmira was intended as a radical departure from the other prisons of its time. It was supposed to work with young men, ages eighteen to thirty, who were first offenders and "redeemable."

The young men who came to Elmira were classified into three grades (low, intermediate, and high), earning more privileges and marks toward release as they advanced. The prison offered them a strong academic program and vocational training in several trades. Prisoners worked at contract labor for outside businesses, and in their free time they could take part in athletics, the prison band, the newspaper, and calisthenics.[14] When state law abolished contract labor, Brockway appointed an inmate colonel of the inmate corps and substituted military drill for work. Prisoners in uniform were soon marching in the quadrangle carrying wooden guns. The entire environment was much like the boot camps that became popular for younger criminals in the 1980s.

Influenced by the practices of Maconochie and Crofton, Brockway's **Elmira system** stood in sharp contrast to the penitentiary in several respects. It treated prisoners better (at least officially). The prison did not employ the silent system or the most degrading aspects of the Auburn system then still apparent in American penitentiaries. Prisoners were motivated with rewards, not fear. They earned marks according to their work and behavior. Typically, those starting with a five-year indeterminate sentence could earn release in a year if all went well. When approved for discharge (as being "reformed") by the board of managers, they were released on parole and required to remain in contact with the superintendent.

Brockway's model was extremely influential in late 1800s prison circles. The penitentiary stood for regimentation and uniformity, while the reformatory promoted individualized treatment based on classification. The penitentiary, following the ideas of Beccaria and the classical school, sought to make the punishment fit the crime; the reformatory used the indeterminate sentence to make the punishment fit the criminal. Reform in the early penitentiary clearly embodied religious concepts. While the reformatory incorporated religious and moral training, it viewed reform in social terms—seeking to return to society a responsible adult citizen capable of filling a productive place in the workforce.

The Elmira system was accepted as an alternative model for those criminals—men and women who were believed to be susceptible to rehabilitation through prison programming. This was an important change of principle. The penitentiary provided a place for self-motivated reform through reflection and penance; it worked in isolation. The reformatory carried its programs to the inmates; it viewed prison as a learning environment where behavior was changed through reformative experiences provided by the prison.

Between 1876 and 1913, most larger states of the Northeast and Midwest established reformatories as alternatives to their penitentiaries. Elmira actually looked like a penitentiary, with its maximum-security cell blocks and high walls, as did several later reformatories. Over time, however, reformatories adopted other architectural models. They incorporated dormitory and cottage housing and replaced walls with perimeter fences, a feature of most prisons built after World War II. Still, only a small percentage of convicts were referred to reformatories. Those who were repeat offenders or viewed as unsuitable candidates for rehabilitation (which apparently included most blacks, Indians, and other minorities) went to ordinary prisons to do hard labor.

Brockway was superintendent of Elmira until 1900, his last decade marked by controversy. He had always been viewed as highly religious and a strict disciplinarian, and along the way he became a devotee of the new science of criminal anthropology. He wrote in an 1884 article that "physical degeneracy . . . is a common subjective cause of criminal conduct; that the mental powers enfeebled, untrained, uninformed, characterize the mass of criminals on admission."[15] He argued that most criminals were degenerates of low intelligence who could not benefit from his reformative regime.

Brockway, who relied on corporal punishment so much that his nickname within the prison was "Paddler," was accused of severely whipping the most mentally and physically defective of his youths. The prison also suffered from overcrowding, poor medical treatment, and a social system that gave stronger "inmate monitors" control over younger, weaker boys. The Elmira system strongly influenced twentieth-century American corrections, but Brockway's misadministration of the Elmira Reformatory pushed him into retirement (after which he became a very successful local politician).

THE PRISON AS FACTORY

To most convicted felons of the late 1800s, these fancy-sounding terms—probation, parole, reformatory—meant nothing. You were a felon, you went to prison, you worked, and you went home. **Hard labor** really meant hard labor, and the reformative possibilities of imprisonment were generally forgotten about—a naively outmoded notion. From convicts laboring and meditating in their solitary confinement cells, the penitentiary had changed to convicts working together under severe discipline to produce goods that would be sold to pay for their own upkeep. The reform model changed to the labor model, and the penitentiary changed from a monastery to a factory.

A visitor to a northern prison of the late 1800s would have found a factory behind prison walls. Virtually all able-bodied inmates, men and women, did hard work six days a week. Either they worked in prison factories, producing goods for private businesses that bought their labor or items that the prison itself sold directly to the public, or they performed the cooking, cleaning, sewing, maintenance, and housekeeping functions necessary to keeping a big, enclosed society operating day to day.

Southern prisons were more difficult to categorize. In some states, sheriffs maintained custody of most state prisoners. Convict leasing meant, in several states, that there were no state prisons. Criminals were in the custody of private contractors who might disperse the leased convicts to farms, road camps, and railroad camps across the state. Other southern prisons adopted the northern industrial model.

In any case, two important features were missing from American penitentiaries at the end of the 1800s: prisoners sitting around idle and prisoners engaged in what we would today call rehabilitation activities. Rehabilitation was Sunday, a day off from work, the only day of rest. The only people who were idle the rest of the time were those who were too sick to work and those who were locked in solitary confinement—**the hole**—on a bread and water diet as punishment. Prison punishments were often physical, usually whippings. Solitary, which was supposed to have been good for reformation in the original Eastern State model, by the end of the century was used only to isolate disciplinary problems. Everyone else was supposed to be hard at work in the Big House.

KEY TERMS

penitentiary

penance

Thomas Eddy

Pennsylvania Prison Society

Benjamin Rush

Walnut Street Jail

Wymondham Gaol

John Haviland

Eastern State Penitentiary

Pennsylvania system

separate system

isolate system

Auburn

Sing Sing

Auburn system

congregate system

silent system

rule of silence

Elam Lynds

prison stripes

lockstep

cat-o'-nine-tails

suspended sentence

right of sanctuary

benefit of clergy

neck verse

filing of cases

recognizance

surcease

probation

John Augustus

parole

pardon

clemency

Alexander Maconochie

Norfolk Island

marks system

ticket-of-leave

indeterminate sentence

Walter Crofton

conditional liberty

good-time

Elizabeth Gurney Fry

Eliza W. B. Farnham

Indiana State Reformatory

Katherine B. Davis

Mabel Walker Willebrandt

Federal Women's Reformatory

Mary Belle Harris

Alderson

houses of refuge

training schools

Charles Loring Brace

orphan trains

child-saving movement

juvenile court

convict lease system

Enoch Cobb Wines

National Prison Association

Rutherford B. Hayes

American Correctional Association

Zebulon Brockway

Elmira Reformatory

Elmira system

hard labor

the hole

NOTES

1. John W. Roberts, *Reform and Retribution: An Illustrated History of American Prisons* (Lanham, Md.: American Correctional Association, 1997), p. 26.

2. Ibid., p. 27.

3. Negley K. Teeters and John Shearer, *The Prison at Philadelphia, Cherry Hill: The Separate System of Prison Discipline* (New York: Columbia University Press, 1957), p. 84.

4. Charles Dickens, *American Notes, for General Circulation* (London, 1842), pp. 146–47.

5. Scott Christianson, *With Liberty for Some: 500 Years of Imprisonment in America* (Boston: Northeastern University Press, 1998), p. 145.

6. "Behind the Walls: A Guide to Eastern State Penitentiary," no date, p. 7.

7. Gustave de Beaumont and Alexis de Tocqueville, *On the Penitentiary System in the United States and Its Application in France* (Carbondale: Southern Illinois University Press, 1964), pp. 161–65.

8. Roberts, *Reform and Retribution*, p. 59.

9. Ibid., pp. 59–60.

10. "The Children's Aid Society," *www.childrensaidsociety.org/about/history.*

11. Mark T. Carleton, *Politics and Punishment: A History of the Louisiana State Penal System* (Baton Rouge: Louisiana State University Press, 1971), p. 13.

12. Ibid., p. 45.

13. Roberts, *Reform and Retribution*, p. 62.

14. Ibid., p. 64.

15. Christianson, *With Liberty for Some*, pp. 179–81.

FURTHER READING

Beaumont, Gustave de, and Alexis de Tocqueville. *On the Penitentiary System in the United States and Its Application in France.* Carbondale: Southern Illinois University Press, 1964.

Christianson, Scott. *With Liberty for Some: 500 Years of Imprisonment in America.* Boston: Northeastern University Press, 1998.

Roberts, John W. *Reform and Retribution: An Illustrated History of American Prisons.* Lanham, Md.: American Correctional Association, 1997.

Rothman, David J. *The Discovery of the Asylum: Social Order and Disorder in the New Republic.* Boston: Little, Brown, 1971.

WEB AND VIDEO RESOURCES

For a good look at Eastern State Penitentiary, now open as a museum in Philadelphia, see *www.easternstate. org*. This site also has links to nearly 100 prison museums around the world.

A good overview of early American prisons can be found in the "Big House" series of documentary videos produced for the History Channel; see it at *www.history.org*.

An interesting Website is *www.notfrisco.com/prisonhistory/index.html*.

A collections of prison history links can be found at *www.asphistory.com/Links/links.htm*.

COMMENTARY

2 Penitence and Rehabilitation

by Edmond Dantes

In the context of criminals and prisons, are the terms "penitence" and "rehabilitation" the same, different, complementary, or all three?

"Penitence" was the concept guiding the highly religious men who, during the late 1700s and early 1800s, proposed and achieved construction of the first penitentiaries in the United States. They believed if criminals were isolated in tiny cells with nothing to read but the Bible, they would reflect upon their misdeeds, grow remorseful, and repent. This change would be deep and lasting, a transformation of godless wrongdoer into righteous believer, as the Christian-persecuting Saul was transformed on the road to Tarsus into Paul, the man of God.

"Rehabilitation" guided prison reformers of the late-1800s, the mid-1900s and, though fallen out of fashion, still lingers today. Probation, parole, and "good time" (time off for good behavior) were introduced in the nineteenth century as incentives for convicted criminals to behave themselves and either avoid imprisonment or get out of prison early. More incentives were added a century later, programs in-

tended to help prisoners become productive—citizens—education and vo-tech training—and others to ease them back into society—work—release and halfway houses. Also fed into the mix were psychological "treatment" programs of all sorts, from Alcoholics Anonymous to anger management, both during confinement and post-release. The aim was—and is—to take criminals entering the system and turn them into law-abiding citizens.

Penitence and rehabilitation, as used in the penal world, can be viewed as exactly the same. Each is considered a means by which keepers can transform the kept-for the better. To induce a metamorphosis, say, of criminal caterpillars into solid-citizen butterflies. Second, each carries the same fundamental flaw that caused them in practice to fall far short of the mark.

Penal practitioners of penitence and rehabilitation, the fervent Christians of the eighteenth and nineteenth centuries and the criminologists, psychologists, psychiatrists, and sociologists of the twentieth century, in their unbounded arrogance, believed they could impose lasting positive change in other people. In the first case, criminality was ungodly and criminals could be made to embrace God. In the other, criminality was a disease and criminals could be "treated" and "cured," i.e., rehabilitated.

Penitence and rehabilitation can also be seen as completely different. One is spiritual, the other secular. Setting aside the fact the penitentiary method of total isolation often induced psychosis rather than revelation, practitioners of penitence discovered (undoubtedly to their sorrow) that belief in Christianity did not necessarily preclude criminal activity. To use a current example, the disgusting discovery of a battalion of baby-raping Catholic priests more than proves the point. Setting aside sham, fakery and game-playing by prisoners, practitioners of rehabilitation discovered (to their chagrin) that educating prisoners, teaching them a trade, or "treating" them psychologically produced unpredictable results. Prisoners who had embraced rehabilitative programs, as well as those who had shunned "programming," got out and never returned. Many others committed new crimes and came back, often before the ink was dry on their release papers.

Still, penitence and rehabilitation were not total failures. The method was flawed, not the concepts. Remorse can lead to redemption and a forsaking of criminal ways. A number of ex-criminals use their Christian or Muslim faith as a barricade against unlawful temptations. Even more have benefitted from education, job training and psychological programs to become law-abiding, productive citizens. What ex-criminals have in common is, first, the desire to turn their lives around and, second, the will to achieve that goal despite every obstacle arrayed against them. Not the least of which is being considered toxic waste by society.

Penitence and rehabilitation can be complementary. A prisoner can have a religious epiphany, a "change of heart" (and many do), and still lack the education or job skills to compete in the labor marketplace. S/he is almost certain to return to prison. But rehabilitative programs are available, the odds change dramatically. Penitence and rehabilitation work when prisoners are helped to help themselves. Change has to come from within; it cannot be imposed.

3 TWENTIETH-CENTURY CORRECTIONS SYSTEMS

Penal and correctional institutions in the United States are difficult to describe because there are so many different types. In the first place there are the prisons, state and federal, for persons who have committed the more serious offenses or who have been sentenced for the longer terms. Most of these are for men, though there are a few women's prisons. Next there are the reformatories for younger offenders. There are reformatories for men and women. They are supposed to use reformatory methods but are in reality little different from junior prisons. In addition there are many city and county penitentiaries, workhouses, and houses of correction. For offenders younger than those committed to the reformatories, there are industrial and training schools for boys and girls. Finally there are the great number of institutions for short-term offenders and misdemeanants—county jails, municipal jails, county farms and chain gangs, and state farms for misdemeanants.

— FRED HAYNES, *THE AMERICAN PRISON SYSTEM*, 1939

INTRODUCTION

This chapter considers the growth of the prison system in the twentieth century. What began in the 1800s as a small, single-purpose institution to which all criminals were sent became, by the end of the 1900s, a diverse bureaucratic system using dual methods of control—specialized secure-custody institutions and various nonsecure alternatives to imprisonment. What started as "imprisonment" in the early 1800s was bureaucratically euphemized into "corrections" by the mid-1950s, as punishing and treating criminals became an industry involving local, state, and federal governments, with a subsidiary network of private organizations. After reading this chapter, you should be familiar with:

1. The "Big House" model of imprisonment of the early 1900s.
2. The rise and fall of labor in prison.
3. Prisons during and after World War II.
4. Contrasting models of rehabilitation and reintegration.
5. The prison population boom of the late 1900s.
6. Specialized prisons that developed in the 1900s.
7. The growth of state corrections departments.
8. An overview of the American penal system at the beginning of the twenty-first century.

THE BIG HOUSE

At the end of the 1800s, the small penitentiaries that had originated in the mid-Atlantic and New England states earlier in the century had spread across America, growing into much larger industrial prisons—factories behind walls. Prison had changed from a quiet, orderly place that isolated inmates much or all of the time to a mass institution in which hundreds or thousands of men (and a few women) labored in prison shops to produce merchandise for sale to the public. Old strict controls were vanishing—lockstep, shaved head, big stripes, rule of silence. Solitary was now for disciplinary punishment instead of penitence, and double bunking (or triple or quadruple bunking) of prisoners had become commonplace.

By 1900, huge prisons were the order of the day. Many state prisons held more than 1,000 inmates. San Quentin, suffering the effects of California's explosive growth and rampant crime problems, had more than 1,300 prisoners as early as 1880. New York's three prisons and one reformatory each held over 1,000 prisoners, as did Pennsylvania's Eastern State Penitentiary, which maintained its facade of solitary confinement even though more than half of its 732 "solitary" cells held more than one prisoner. The Ohio State Penitentiary at Columbus, built in the 1830s, had 1,800 cells by the end of the century. It was by far the largest prison in the world at the time, confining more than 2,000 inmates. But the most populous prison in America—and by many accounts the most wretched—was the Missouri Penitentiary at Jefferson City. Built in 1836 to confine forty-six convicts in forty cells, by the end of the century it held more than 2,300 convicts in 500 old cells. Missouri's governor called it "the largest school of crime in America."[1]

The beginning of the twentieth century saw continued prison population growth. Existing prisons were expanded, and new prisons were designed according to the architectural model that came to be known as the **Big House.** Borrowing from the plans of Haviland and other penitentiary builders of the early 1800s but on a much larger scale and incorporating industrial buildings, dining halls, chapels, and other functional buildings not considered in designs of the previous century, the Big House was like a self-contained medieval town. It was intended to be a model of **scientific management,** with a proficient guard force under centralized administration, maintaining custody of an ever-increasing number of prisoners within an efficient, secure environment.

The Big House had a certain look, captured on film in prison movies of the 1930s and 1940s, many filmed on site at Sing Sing, San Quentin, and other old penitentiaries. They looked like fortresses, with high, thick stone walls that rose twenty-five or thirty feet in the air (and usually extended ten to twenty feet below ground as well to prevent tunneling out). Towers for armed guards dotted the walls. Vehicular traffic entered and exited through heavy gates. The first building inside was usually the administration building, an imposing structure that resembled a city hall or state capitol. Behind this building lay cell blocks in different configurations—radial, telephone pole, square, and long lines. Everything was concrete or stone and iron and later steel. Gray was the dominant color—gray buildings; gray uniforms (after big stripes were abandoned); a dusty, gray yard; gray men working in factories or idling on the yard, their cigarettes trailing plumes of gray smoke. Prison gray, a drained, faded hue like the tint of an old photograph, became the hallmark of confinement.

The Big House grew even bigger by the 1920s. San Quentin could house 3,500 convicts; only insane inmates got a cell to themselves. The new State-ville Prison in Illinois had circular cell houses modeled after Jeremy Bentham's Panopticon design and had a capacity of 3,250 inmates. The old Jefferson City (Missouri) prison, still overcrowded, held more than 4,000 prisoners in its central unit and three prison farms. The Southern Michigan State Penitentiary at Jackson, the largest walled prison ever built in America, had a capacity of 5,510 inmates and held more than 3,000 inmates by the end of the 1920s.[2] These fortress prisons, though small in area, often held as many people as the towns that gave them their names and supplied their guard forces.

PRISON LABOR: FOR AND AGAINST

The essence of the Big House was **hard labor.** Some early proponents of the penitentiary argued that confinement without labor was more reformative, but by the 1830s, every American prison required labor from its convicts. In some, it was craft work that men and women could do alone in their cells. With the rise of the Auburn model, congregate labor in prison workshops prevailed.

Eastern State Penitentiary records reflect that over half the male convicts who arrived between 1855 and 1860 were assigned to either weaving and spinning or shoe making. The remainder were detailed to cane-seating chairs, varnishing, "segar-making," boot crimping, broom making, burnishing, blacksmithing, or domestic work (which meant institutional cleaning and maintenance).[3] Among the more than 1,000 inmates at Sing Sing and Auburn in the 1830s, the leading prisoner occupation was cooper (barrelmaker), with about 25 percent of the inmates assigned to this work. About 15 percent each were assigned as stoneworkers, weavers and tailors, and shoemakers. The others were assigned as blacksmiths, locksmiths, comb makers, furniture makers, saddle and harness makers, clock makers, cooks and bakers, machinists, or silk hatters.[4]

Whether the prison practiced the isolate or congregate model, labor was part of the regimen for two good reasons. First, it focused prisoners' time and energy productively, keeping them busy in unpleasant, sometimes traumatic, surroundings. Second, they turned out goods that were sold to recoup the prison's operating cost. The ideal was to turn a profit—to operate "in the black."

In early prisons, convicts commonly produced goods the penitentiary sold directly to the public on the open market. This was called the **public account** or **state account** system, meaning the prison was the merchant with no middleman. Over time, except for the sale of agricultural commodities, such as truck vegetables and, occasionally, inmate-made crafts, this practice declined as other forms of prison labor developed.

Fred Haynes, surveying prison labor systems in *The American Prison System* (1939), identified four separate systems of importance in the penitentiary's first century:

1. Public account
2. Convict lease
3. Contract or piece price
4. State use or public works and ways[5]

Public account was the original model. Under the **convict lease,** a private contractor rented prisoners from the state, assuming responsibility for their care and control in return. This model prevailed in the post–Civil War South. The **contract** model and its variant, the **piece price,** allowed private businesses to contract with the prison, either for a certain number of workers or for the number of items the workers could produce. Businesses typically set up workshops on prison grounds and paid prisoners a wage much lower than free-world workers would have been paid. The **state use** model and its variant, the **public works and ways** system, had prisoners producing goods bought by government agencies or working on public projects, such as constructing roads and buildings.

Private businesses were eager to employ convict labor, especially when the employer could select the "best" or most trustworthy laborers from the larger inmate pool. Moses Pilsbury, a post–Civil War penologist, calculated that a convict was worth about three-quarters of a free laborer. But if the convict was paid (or cost to lease) no more than a third of the free laborer's cost, it meant greatly enhanced profit. Historical evidence indicates that many businessmen made huge, quick profits from convict labor. The prison benefited economically as well, many state institutions operating profitably in good years in the era between the Civil War and World War I.

But, all was never entirely at ease on the prison-labor front. While the public and politicians might be pleased that prisoners were kept busy and productive, opposition came from three sources. Many private businesses were in direct competition with the contract and public account systems and strongly opposed prison-made goods being sold on the open market; it was bad for their business. In addition, laborers and, after the Civil War, labor unions argued that prisoners took jobs away from free people who were more deserving of employment. Finally, prison reformers deplored the way prisoners were worked, particularly under leasing in the South, where prisoners were underclothed, underfed, and overworked, often to death. Reformers wanted prisoners treated more like human beings (though acknowledging this would cut deeply into profits).

Battles were fought in state legislatures across the country over the prison-labor problem for the better part of a century. As Fred Haynes pointed out in 1939,

> Prison labor under the lease, contract, piece-price, and public account systems comes into direct competition with free industry, with the possibility of affecting prices, wages, and employment. Under the state-use and allied system, competition is less direct. It should be noted, however, that in the long run any articles produced by prison labor reduce the quantity of such articles to be purchased in the open market. Only the abolition of all prison labor can entirely prevent such competition with free labor. Even maintenance work may logically be regarded as reducing the amount of possible employment of free labor. Such a consideration would, of course, reduce the whole matter of an absurdity.[6]

THE DEMISE OF THE INDUSTRIAL PRISON

Political debate over prison labor intensified in the 1920s and 1930s. The prison population had almost doubled during the 1920s to about 150,000 in 1930, while the number of inmates productively employed declined steadily—from 75 percent in 1885 to 61 percent in 1923 to 52 percent in 1932. The increase in inmate idleness, placing a greater strain on vastly outnumbered security forces, and the increased burden on taxpayers as revenues from prison labor declined were important issues in prison management. **Sanford Bates,** director of the new Federal Bureau of Prisons, warned of the increased dangers of prison riots if inmate idleness persisted. He pointed out in 1933 that

> broadly speaking, the prisons of the country seem no nearer a solution of the employment problem than they were in 1923. I think I cannot be successfully contradicted when I say that today there is more idleness in most of the prisons of the country than ever. Those private manufacturers affected are more vociferous and uncompromising than heretofore; labor is still unsatisfied, and the public remains uninformed and indifferent.[7]

By the 1930s, opponents of prison labor had an important new ally: the Great Depression. Beginning in October 1929, this prolonged period of low business activity and high unemployment had profound long-term impact on society. President Franklin Roosevelt's New Deal policies in the 1930s led to the creation of the American version of a social welfare state. When national unemployment reached 25 percent at the peak of the Depression in 1933, getting people back to work became a national priority. The old argument about prison labor depriving free people of jobs took on new force.

State legislatures and the U.S. Congress took a harder look at the effects of prison labor on the larger society. Morgan Reynolds's 1996 study for the National Center for Policy Analysis reported the following:

> From 1929 onward a series of federal laws limiting shipment of prison-made goods made it increasingly difficult to provide productive employment for prisoners.
>
> The **Hawes-Cooper Act** (1929) mandated that prison-made goods transported from one state to another be subject to the laws of the destination state. The effect was to permit a state to ban the sale of all prisoner-made goods, whether made outside or within the state. Hawes-Cooper went into effect in 1934 and affected only states that banned the sale of prisoner-made goods.
>
> The **Ashurst-Sumners Act** (1935) made shipping prisoner-made goods to a state where state law prohibited the receipt, possession, sale or use of such goods a federal offense. Although the act strengthened Hawes-Cooper restrictions on interstate shipment of convict-made goods, protectionist businesses and unions were unsatisfied because the act relied on the states to ban such commerce.
>
> The **Sumners-Ashurst Act** (1940) made it a federal crime to knowingly transport convict-made goods in interstate commerce for private use, regardless of laws in the states.[8]

Other federal legislation from this era banned the use of convict labor on major federal contracts. Agricultural products were left out of this series of federal laws, leaving states with prison farms (particularly the belt of big plantation prisons from Texas across the South to the Atlantic coast) still able to sell their crops at home and abroad. The Big House, on the other hand, was devastated. These massive institutions, each on average holding 1,500 to 2,000 men behind their high walls, had been designed and built (or redesigned and rebuilt) as maximum-security factories. Suddenly cut off from the market, they had no use for prisoner labor, the center of their existence for a century. Many state prisons converted as much of their industrial output to the state-use model as quickly as they could, but there was simply no work available for most prisoners in what had been industrial prisons.

What were prisoners to do with their time? Some could be assigned to maintenance and internal chores—food service, laundry, cleaning, groundskeeping, records, and janitorial work. But how many prisoners can be assigned to mop a hall or mow a square of grass? When we think of prisons as places of idleness, where prisoners sit around doing nothing or hang out in the yard socializing, working out, and playing games, it is important to note that this was not the intention of penitentiary founders. They viewed labor as positive, even necessary to the prison's mission. Persistent opposition from outside undercut this philosophy and killed productive prison labor in the 1930s.

PRISONS IN WORLD WAR II

The abrupt demise of the industrial prison went virtually unnoticed for a time. In the 1930s, recovery from the Depression was the great national concern. Then came growing international conflict that resulted in World War II and that engulfed the United States in December 1941. The war had several major effects on prisons. Prison populations declined as many young men in trouble (including convicts who were paroled to work in war industries) were allowed to choose between military duty and prison. Active military service provided strong social control over young men, the demographic most likely to commit crimes, and the new rules against prison labor were relaxed to put prisoners to work in the war effort.

The **Prison Industries Branch** of the War Production Board was established in December 1941 to manage the industrial and agricultural output of state and federal prisons. The chairman of the War Production Board said in late 1942 that only about 10 percent of convicts were working in prison industries, which were producing at about a third of their estimated potential. As state political officials got more involved and federal restrictions were modified, prison production increased. By 1943, industrial and agricultural production in state prisons was estimated at about $25 million each. Prisons in Alabama, Michigan, and Oklahoma led in industrial production, while Louisiana, Ohio, and Texas led in agricultural production.[9] Prisoners manufactured assault boats, shell cases, bomb crates, bomb noses, truck bodies, submarine nets, cargo nets, Navy shirts, bush shirts, boiler suits, stretchers, flags, and leather insignia.

Federal prisons led the penal war effort. Inmates at McNeil Island Federal Penitentiary built Army patrol boats. Women at Alderson Reformatory sewed flags and bandoliers by day (working forty-eight hours per week) and volunteered to prepare Red Cross surgical dressings at night. Lewisburg Federal Penitentiary in Pennsylvania turned out thousands of bomb fins and steel mess trays. Atlanta Federal Penitentiary produced $4 million worth of defense materials annually by the middle of the war period.

State prisons in the West, South, and Midwest were also recognized for their productivity. California prisons, led by San Quentin under the direction of Warden Clinton Duffy, sewed mattress covers, manufactured submarine netting, assembled ration books, salvaged tin cans, repaired shoes, and recycled copper cable. San Quentin, the first state prison to win a war contract, also turned out bagging, trays, and reconditioned valves. Six hundred San Quentin prisoners worked in the jute mill making burlap bags. Alabama's prisons produced 12 million yards of cotton textiles annually, most of it shipped to other prisons to make fatigues and military clothing.

Prisoners were often cited for their patriotism and "can do" spirit. About half the state prisons won citations for excellence in production from the War Production Board. Many prisoners volunteered for extra duties on their own time. In Montana, North Carolina, and Virginia, prisoners helped farmers harvest potatoes and other crops. In California, the traditional animosity between labor unions and prisons was ignored for the duration of the war. Parolees were given union cards to work in prison industries and serve as merchant seamen. Buster Haley, a lifer who was chief of the salvage section at San Quentin, was featured in *Life* magazine. His three sons were on active duty in the Army.

World War II was good for prison labor. The industrial and agricultural output of prisons increased steadily. Prisoners got the opportunity to show the public that they, too, wanted to help in the war effort, and prison morale was high. Many barriers that had separated prisoners from free people were relaxed during wartime, only to be put back in place once the war ended in 1945. For American prisons, World War II would prove to be only a rest stop on the road they had been traveling for a hundred years.

PRISONS IN CRISIS

After the war, prisons faded from public view. Their populations went up again, industrial and agricultural production declined, and restrictions on interstate shipment of prison-made goods were restored. Prisons became institutions of idleness where growing numbers of prisoners were confined by penal officials who had nothing for them to do. Politicians who had advocated greater involvement of prisoners in the war effort turned a blind eye to prisons after the war. Prisoners, many of whom had exchanged military uniforms for prison gray, discovered that they were invisible once again.

Inside prisons, tensions built up that prison officials had no way of relieving. Violence had been a problem in American prisons going back to the Colonial era. In the twentieth century, as prisoners were gradually allowed more freedom of movement, inmate attacks on guards and other prisoners increased, as did escape attempts. Prisons had much smaller guard forces than they have now, and escape attempts, often on a large scale, were commonplace and frequently successful. Guards and wardens were taken hostage, injured, or killed by prisoners armed with guns, knives, or homemade weapons.

Prison riots were infrequent until after World War II, when several circumstances—relaxed controls over prisoners, idleness, inattention to grievances, and deteriorating buildings—combined to create an atmosphere ripe for explosion. Prison historian John Roberts reported,

> Scores of riots flared up in the 1950s. March through June of 1952 were especially violent months, with destructive riots at state prisons in Trenton, New Jersey;

Bordentown, New Jersey; Rahway, New Jersey; Jackson, Michigan; Concord, Massachusetts; Soledad, California; and elsewhere. Later in 1952, riots broke out at the Ohio State Penitentiary in Columbus; Menard State Prison in Illinois; the state penitentiaries in Utah and New Mexico; and at federal youth reformatories in El Reno, Oklahoma, and Chillicothe, Ohio.[10]

The New Jersey State Prison at Trenton was one of the most troubled, suffering three riots in 1952. Early in the year, the *Newark Star-Ledger* ran an exposé of prison life under this headline "Inside Trenton Prison: Dope, Sex, Booze, Dice—and Rule by Convicts." As prison officials tried to maintain order (which essentially meant retaking control over daily operations from the prisoners), convicts rebelled. On March 29, in Wing 5, where the hardest of New Jersey's prisoners were said to be housed, fifty-two convicts "chased their guards out of the wing, barricaded the entrance, and wrecked everything they could lay their hands on. They smashed cell toilets, shredded beds, broke windows, and set fires."[11] Forty-six hours later, after being tear gassed and sprayed with fire hoses, the prisoners gave up.

Two weeks later, sixty-nine convicts seized the print shop, took four staff members hostage, and threatened to slit their throats. When Commissioner Sanford Bates met with the prisoners, their spokesman, William Dickens, told reporters, "We are outlaws from the word go. We're the scum of society. You can send the National Guard on us but we won't give up. We know we're going to get the worst of it."[12] The prisoners presented a list of demands that prison officials rejected. A compromise was finally reached: the governor would appoint a state commission to study prison problems. Inmates surrendered after three days. While this riot was still under way, convicts at Rahway seized a cell block and held nine guards hostage for five days before they gave up. In October, twenty prisoners in Trenton's Wing 7 took hostages and barricaded the doors. Guards went in shooting machine guns, and the inmates surrendered, ending this riot quickly. The state commission eventually recommended that the old prison be closed and a new maximum-security prison constructed to replace it, but the recommendation was ignored. Trenton is still in use half a century later.

Similar riots occurred across America in the early 1950s. In one of the more shocking incidents, thirty-seven convicts of the Louisiana State Penitentiary at Angola slashed their Achilles' tendons to protest the conditions under which they were confined (the 1952 *Star-Ledger* headline would have fit Angola as aptly as it did Trenton Prison). The governor appointed an investigative commission that made a startling discovery: prisoners were telling the truth. *Collier's Magazine* labeled Angola "America's Worst Prison," and reform Governor Robert Kennon was elected in 1952 on his promise to "clean up Angola." This is perhaps the only time in American history a prison has had such an impact on state politics.

What was different about the prison uprisings of the 1950s was their explicitly political nature. They were not escape attempts or random assaults and vandalism. They were for the most part staged to draw outside attention to prison problems. Rioting often followed a pattern. After grievances had been continually ignored, a group of convicts would seize a housing unit or other building, taking hostages if they were available. They would destroy furnishings to make weapons and erect barricades, and convict leaders would present a list of demands or grievances to news media and government officials. Opposed by overwhelming force, the prisoners would surrender or, less often, be subdued, their demands ignored and with only partial promises, never kept, to show for their effort. The prison would be locked down, rioters beaten and put in isolation, and ringleaders indicted on new charges or sent to other prisons. More often than not, guards and staff hostages were released unharmed, except for the trauma of their ordeal and being used as pawns in the political struggle between convicts and prison administrators. When injury and death resulted, it was as likely to be done by armed guards or police quelling the riot as by the rioters. Most riots were resolved without serious injury or death.

This pattern was repeated many times in the early 1950s and sporadically since. The 1954 movie *Riot in Cell Block 11*, shot on location at California's Folsom Prison using convicts as extras, took a documentary approach in following the life of a fictional riot. When an investigative commission, appointed by the American Prison Association and headed by California Commissioner of Corrections **Richard A. McGee,** looked into the prison riots sweeping the country, it identified several major causes:

1. Inmate idleness
2. Severe overcrowding
3. Political neglect of prisons
4. Lack of public interest
5. Lack of educational and vocational programs
6. Poorly trained officers
7. Difficulty in managing huge prisons
8. Political interference in prison management
9. Anticrime crusades that promoted overcrowding[13]

To this list could be added chronic unresponsiveness of prison officials to convict grievances, though officials usually defended their inaction by blaming their political superiors. Clearly something needed to be done to move prisons forward out of the Big House era. But what could prison officials find to replace factory labor in their institutions?

REHABILITATION AND THE MEDICAL MODEL

In 1954, the American Prison Association voted to change its name to the American Correctional Association. The name change reflected the growing role of probation, parole, and other noninstitutional methods of supervising and helping criminals. But symbolically it gave prisons a new mission: rehabilitation. Over the next twenty years, prisons would offer an unprecedented number of programs designed to change the behavior of men and women in prison—to turn lawbreaking behavior into law-abiding behavior.

Today we use **reform** and **rehabilitation** as synonyms in their penal application. Both mean to change behavior. Early penitentiaries talked a lot about reformation but not at all about rehabilitation, a term that came along at the end of the nineteenth century as part of the social work movement. Prisons were intended to provide the opportunity for reform—to improve what is wrong, corrupt, or unsatisfactory. The prison provided the place, a dungeon that would move the prisoner to penance and reformation through meditation or contemplation in silence. Work was intended to develop a habit of industry that would be necessary for self-sufficiency on discharge, but reformation was a separate step. It was up to the individual to reform. Rehabilitation meant to restore to good condition or to return to a previous state, but most imprisoned criminals had no previous good state to which they might be restored. In the nineteenth century, as in the twenty-first, few prisoners had turned from productive, stable lives to lives of crime.

The birth of rehabilitation is usually tied to the creation of reformatories and juvenile training schools in the late 1800s. Reformatories in progressive states took in young adult criminals; ran them through a year or two of education classes, vocational training, moral and religious instruction, and physical conditioning; and then, relying on the new indeterminate sentence, released them on parole. The training schools did virtually the same thing with the new class of youthful criminals and misfits (soon to be called juvenile delinquents).

This approach was tied to the growing influence of the positivist school of criminology in this era. The positivists viewed criminality as a condition largely determined by biological and psychological factors. The medical model in corrections is considered a refinement of positivist thought.

Reformatories and training schools housed a very small percentage of people in custody; most prisoners did their time in penitentiaries built around hard labor. While some prisons did offer a few programs for inmates (New York prisons were offering literacy classes by the 1840s), most prisons did nothing. A prison might have a chapel or a library, but self-improvement under the reform model was up to the individual.

Rehabilitation, as it developed in the reformatory, changed this mode of thinking. Rehabilitation put the burden of change on the prison. Its mission was to carry to the prisoner the programs needed to promote change. Matching of programs to individuals could be enhanced through **classification,** which took place on the prisoner's entry into the system. Classification was critical to determining the background, capabilities, and needs of the criminal, which could then be met by assignment to particular prison programs. It was up to the prison to assess the inmate's rehabilitative potential and see that he or she was provided with the means to accomplish necessary changes.

As long as prisons followed the Big House model or the farm model, emphasizing hard labor, rehabilitation meant practically nothing to American prison inmates. It was only after the demise of the industrial prison that rehabilitation stepped to the forefront as a purpose of imprisonment. Some articles describing prison labor in World War II discuss the rehabilitative benefits of this work; convicts were being trained for work they could do after they got out of prison.

In the aftermath of the 1950s prison riots, rehabilitation moved front and center. Progressive states (progressive means not only a positive attitude toward changing criminals but also a willingness to spend money to bring about change) vastly expanded the programs their prisons offered. Education, job training, counseling and therapy, drug and alcohol treatment, religious services, recreation, and self-help organizations proliferated. Professional staff—teachers, social workers, psychologists, counselors, and case managers—entered the prison. New prisoners were processed through reception or classification centers to determine their needs. Progress of prisoners in programs was monitored closely. Convicts served indeterminate sentences, which meant they could be paroled when the prison determined they had reached the state known as rehabilitation.

Rehabilitation, or **treatment,** as it is often called, never dominated prison operations. Even in progressive states, 10 percent or less of the prison budget was spent on rehabilitation programs. In most states, it was much less. Security always ruled; rehabilitation was the stepchild. But the era from the mid-1950s through the mid-1970s did offer the hope of change through prison programming. It also gave inmates something to do with time they would otherwise have spent idle.

Federal prisons took rehabilitation a step further. **James V. Bennett,** director of the Bureau of Prisons from 1937 to 1964, believed that rehabilitation programs should be available to all inmates and that the programs should be matched to the individual's needs. The idea was that criminal behavior was a disease that had specific causes—biological, psychological, and sociological. Prison treatment, like hospital treatment, would identify these causes and tailor a rehabilitative program to cure them. The term for this individualized rehabilitation concept was the **medical model.** In the analogy, criminal behavior was a sickness, and prison was the hospital that treated it. The criminal was the patient who would be cured with treatment programs.

In the 1970s, rehabilitation came under simultaneous attack from two different directions. **Robert Martinson** and two of his colleagues, Judith Wilkes and Douglas Lipton, undertook a national study of rehabilitation for the New York State Governor's Special Committee on Criminal Offenders. Martinson's summary article on the research, titled "What Works? Questions and Answers about Prison Reform," appeared in *The Public Interest* in 1974. Martinson's answer to his question was, "**Nothing works,**" or, as he put it, "With few and isolated exceptions, the rehabilitative efforts that have been reported so far have had no appreciable effect on recidivism." He meant that no prison programs had been shown to achieve substantial, predictable reductions in **recidivism** (return to prison).[14] Some programs, such as intensive psychotherapy, were associated with *increased* recidivism.

Norval Morris, an attorney and criminologist who was then dean of the University of Chicago School of Law, criticized rehabilitation for a different reason. Treatment, as Morris saw it, was a coercive game. Because it was tied to release on parole, prisoners had to admit that they needed treatment, complete a program successfully, and adopt the properly respectful attitude of the healed patient to get out of prison. Authorities could never offer enough programs for all and could not precisely match prisoners to programs. Convicts who seemed to be rehabilitated were too often the slickest or most manipulative of the prisoner population. Recidivism rates had no connection to specific prison programs, completed or not completed. Failure and success were tied more to age, values, prior criminal history, family lifestyles, and other variables that had nothing to do with prison treatment programs.

The argument that rehabilitation was a waste of time and money or a mean-spirited, unpredictable charade had important effects. Rehabilitation's opponents and skeptics urged prisons to concentrate on locking criminals up and stop trying to change—or "help"—them. In 1975, the Federal Bureau of Prisons officially abandoned the medical model. Many state systems did the same with rehabilitation, cutting back on rehabilitation programming and reducing its ties to parole and release from prison. Participation became more voluntary than mandatory. Once again, rehabilitation or reform became an individual proposition.

THE REINTEGRATION ERA

One persistent criticism of rehabilitation was that it took place in *prison*, which is after all a completely artificial environment. Offering programs to teach prisoners how to be law-abiding citizens was said to be a bit like throwing non-swimmers onto desert sand and telling them to swim. They could go through the motions, but sand isn't water.

Prisons isolate, stigmatize, infantilize, and brutalize. No matter how proficient teachers, trainers, and social workers in prison might be, the argument went, their efforts were swallowed by the dominant security environment and indifferent bureaucratic atmosphere of modern prisons—not to mention the convict subculture that constituted an artificial society behind bars. Rehabilitation programming took place in groups, with few opportunities for individual treatment. Custody was 24/7, treatment was twice a week for two hours or, at best, maybe half a day five times a week for some educational and vocational training courses. Custody always took precedence over treatment; a prisoner making good progress in a class could be locked up for a few days for a minor disciplinary infraction and kicked out of the program, meaning that he would have to start all over again if he got another chance. Desirable programs never had enough slots available. Admissions priority was more likely to be based on proximity to release or seniority (or favoritism) than individual suitability.

Another frequent criticism of rehabilitation was that the people in the programs were prisoners. Many, especially the younger ones and some older career criminals as well, did not want to be rehabilitated. They just wanted out, as soon as possible, to return to previous habits. They made fun of programs and the prisoners who took them seriously.

For prisoners undergoing psychological treatment, one hazard was that rules about confidentiality and privacy applicable in society were ignored in prison. Prison officials had unfettered access to all treatment records, and sometimes prisoners could get into them, too. How would you like to admit in an admissions counseling session to fears of physical violence or doubts about your sexual orientation and then have this information become common knowledge among the guards or in the general prisoner population? Admissions in group therapy could be equally dangerous. Openness in admitting problems might be the first step to self-growth in society, but in prison, secrecy was a safer practice.

So if rehabilitation in prison was a bust, what could be done? Instead of bringing treatment programs into the prison, two alternatives were emphasized:

1. Keep as many criminals as possible under supervision in the community to avoid the negative effects of imprisonment
2. Send as many prisoners as possible out into the community to take part in real-world programs as opposed to inadequate prison programs

These ideas were influential during the 1970s, which is often called the **reintegration era** in penology. As a reaction to imprisonment and prison treatment programs, reintegration stressed the centrality of the community. Criminals leave it to go to prison, and almost all of them eventually return there. Programs for criminals in the community would be the same ones open to noncriminals. A greater diversity of programs would be available, and they would be more "normal" than those offered in prison.

Community-based alternatives to prison had been in use long before the 1970s, but this decade saw the expanded use of felony probation and the growth of halfway houses and prerelease centers. Prisoners also benefited from furloughs (weekend or holiday passes to their families), work release, educational release, and counseling and treatment in the community. The worst limitation for community-based programs was that prisons tended to be located in rural areas or small towns where program resources were often lacking. Prisons near cities were able to send their convicts home for family visits, to vo-tech schools for training, to colleges for higher education, to clinics for treatment, to prerelease centers for reentry preparation, and to halfway houses and work release to ease transition back into society.

Reintegration pushed community-based, nonsecure alternatives and treatment programs. Advocates argued that this approach was appropriate for the majority of convicted felons. Prisons ought to be reserved for the hard-core, dangerous few from whom society truly needed to be protected. Prison had its place, but it was not a very good place, and most criminals did not need to go there. If the ones who did go there needed programs, these should be provided in the community to the maximum extent possible.

WAREHOUSING

For a few years, especially after the decline of rehabilitation, reintegration was a dominant correctional model in many states. The number of people coming under correctional supervision was increasing, but most of the increase was in probation. Prison populations, which had been in decline through the early 1970s, even though the crime rate was rising, were increasing again. After the prison population doubled in the 1920s, the number of men and women in prison remained fairly constant for more than forty years, into the 1970s, staying within a range of 150,000 to 200,000 in state and federal prisons. The incarceration rate (the number in prison per 100,000 population) peaked at 139 in 1939, went down sharply during the war, and did not reach the prewar peak again until 1981. It seems clear that by the mid-1970s, part of what should have been a noticeable increase in prisoners was being temporarily diverted through reintegration.

In the early 1980s, the penal mentality took a hard right turn. The **War on Crime,** declared by President Lyndon Johnson in 1965 as part of his Great Society social program, was refocused to become a **war on criminals.** This meant that punishments would be made severe and that imprisonment would be preferred over other options, like probation. The politics of punishment flowered under Republican President Ronald Reagan, who held office from 1981 to 1989. His administration popularized the "get tough on crime" mentality that spread to state and local governments. New laws required mandatory prison sentences, abolished or restricted parole, and lengthened prison terms. Most significant, in its effect on prison populations over the next decade, was a new war—the **War on Drugs.**

A remarkable surge in the consumption of illegal drugs began in the 1960s and, though leveling off by the 1970s, continues at a high level today. For about twenty years, while large numbers of men and women with drug and alcohol problems entered prison for violent, property, and public order crimes, not many went to prison solely for possessing or distributing drugs—less than 10 percent of the prison population through the early 1980s. The perception was that only major drug dealers and habitual drug criminals went to prison.

Under Reagan, federal and state policies changed dramatically. Strict enforcement of drug laws swept huge numbers of men and women into the criminal justice system. The drug of emphasis, from about 1985 on, was crack cocaine. It was viewed as the most evil drug, for its addictive effect and for its relationship with inner-city gangs, turf wars, drive-by shootings, and other violence.

Overnight, the number of drug prosecutions skyrocketed. Tougher penalties for possession and distribution were enacted, especially for crack. More criminals of every stripe were going to prison during the terms of Presidents Reagan and George Bush (the elder), but the increase in the number of drug criminals in state and federal prisons was striking. The number of prisoners increased from 196,000 in 1972 (the last year of decline), to 305,000 in 1980, to 465,000 in 1985, to 713,000 in 1990, and to 1,033,000 in 1995. In the fifteen years between 1980 and 1995, the prison population more than tripled. Half of the increase was drug criminals.

From the 1970s to the 1990s, the percentage of violent criminals in prison decreased sharply, from 60 to 40 percent, while drug criminals flooded state and especially federal prisons. The number of drug criminals in jail and prison rose from 40,000 in 1980 to 453,000 in 1999, an increase of more than 1,000 percent in less than twenty years. By 1999, toward the end of the second decade of the War on Drugs, more people were in prison for drug crimes—320,000—than had been in prison, *period*, twenty years earlier.

Prisons were also pulling in violent criminals and property and public order criminals. How did the prison system respond to this massive influx, the likes of which had never before been seen in a democratic society? Most prisoners clearly suffered from drug and alcohol problems and from a panoply of social disadvantages—poverty, lack of education, unemployment, and more. Rehabilitation had been officially abandoned. Reintegration was too "soft on crime" and was now viewed as a threat to the communities where criminals would be supervised, housed, and treated.

So what role was prison to play? The most common term was **warehousing.** To warehouse is to place, deposit, or store in a controlled environment for a period of time and then to remove. To prisoners, this meant that their removal from society was solely for public safety. Nothing beneficial to them was expected to result.

The Federal Bureau of Prisons termed this view the **balanced model.** The bureau's position was that prison serves multiple objectives, including retribution, deterrence, incapacitation, and rehabilitation. Any of these—or all of these—might apply to the horde of men and women cramming state and federal prisons; or, as critics pointed out, none might apply. Prison might just be a place with no real purpose.

Under the balanced model, rehabilitation was the least important objective both because rehabilitation programs had been deemphasized and because sheer numbers overwhelmed programs that remained. The other purposes reflected society's interests and were compatible with the **icebox model,** which rationalizes warehousing. This model views prison as a large icebox in which "bad eggs" are stored (preferably for as long as possible) before being taken out for another look. If they do not smell too bad, leave them out in the fresh air and tolerate them. If the stink gets worse, put them back in storage until they rot away to nothing.

Such was the role of the American prison at the beginning of the twenty-first century. The prison population had increased every year since 1972 and at the end of 2001 stood at 1,330,000. The percentage of increase had slowed, from 8 percent annually in the 1980s to 1 percent by 2001. Politicians argued about the escalating costs of imprisonment and the long-term social consequences of warehousing America's social misfits, most of them young, poor, black, and Hispanic men. As the new century began, prison officials and policymakers were once again asking, "What are prisons for?"

SPECIALIZED CORRECTIONAL INSTITUTIONS

In the 1800s, the prison system was the penitentiary—a fortress that held prisoners in small cells under maximum security. Local jails held smaller numbers of prisoners but typically in larger cells, called "tanks," with up to ten or twenty men or women in each. The jail's detention function had not changed much in several hundred years, though the coming of liberal reforms and changing social mores had eliminated many of its old customers—debtors, runaway servants and slaves, and political and religious heretics. Jails were local lockups that fed convicted misdemeanants and felons into bigger state-operated penitentiaries. For most of the 1800s, this was the "corrections system."

Here and there, progressive states established specialized prisons as alternatives to the penitentiary. New institutions, founded on the argument that certain criminals deserved different treatment than ordinary criminals received in the penitentiary, were smaller and selective about their clientele.

Juveniles were targets for special treatment. Boston, New York City, and Philadelphia opened **houses of refuge** for boys (and smaller versions for girls) in the 1820s. These combination schools–shelters–workshops confined young criminals, runaways, orphans, abandoned children, and "wayward" children. As the house of refuge was the urban alternative to the jail (eventually evolving into today's juvenile detention center), the state-operated **training school,** also known as the industrial school or reformatory (not to be confused with the reformatory for adults), was the juvenile alternative to the penitentiary. Massachusetts opened the first training school for boys, the Lyman School, in 1847 and the first training school for girls, the State Industrial School for Girls at Lancaster, in 1856.[15] These special prisons spread through the Northeast and Midwest by the end of the 1800s.

Women also began to get separate, if not always better, treatment about this time. They were usually housed in their own wing or cell block of a men's penitentiary, but many reformers wanted separate prisons for women, run and staffed by women, and geared more toward the "place" of women in society. The **Indiana Reformatory Institute** for Women opened in 1873, before the first separate reformatory for men. Others followed in Massachusetts, New York, and elsewhere in the early twentieth century, culminating in the Federal Industrial Institution for Women at Alderson, West Virginia, which opened on November 14, 1928. These female prisons were generally smaller, were less security conscious (no walls), and provided dormitory or cottage housing. Alderson, for example, consisted of fourteen cottages (segregated by race), each holding about thirty women in separate rooms. The atmosphere was relaxed, and the program centered on providing domestic training for its predominantly white inmates.

Reformatories for young men, which came into common usage at the same time, generally looked like penitentiaries—Elmira in New York and Rahway in New Jersey, for example. Men, even young first-time felons, were considered more dangerous than women and more in need of cell confinement and strict discipline, including physical punishments. But reformatory prisoners also got the benefits of schooling, vocational training, religious instruction, physical conditioning, recreation, and inmate clubs. With the indeterminate sentence and parole, they also got out of prison faster than penitentiary prisoners. Later, reformatories would be built without walls and would serve as the model for the medium-security prisons that proliferated in the half century after World War II.

As the American prison population increased steadily in the early years of the twentieth century, the number of specialized prisons continued to grow. The diversity of prisons within a state depended on two key circumstances: the number of prisoners in custody and prison officials' and politicians' views on the need for different treatment for special populations.

As the more populous states faced increases in numbers of prisoners, they typically built penitentiaries in small towns and rural areas in different parts of the state. Pennsylvania's Eastern State Penitentiary in Philadelphia was balanced by the Western State Penitentiary in Pittsburgh. New York's Sing Sing, up the Hudson River from New York City, was balanced with Clinton in the center of the state, Auburn farther west, and Attica near Buffalo in the far west. Later, training schools for juveniles and reformatories for men and women were added to the institutional mix. Reception centers were needed to classify new prisoners.

After World War II, when rehabilitation programs became widely available, several states built separate prisons to provide treatment for certain types of criminals—the mentally ill, drug addicts, and sex criminals, for example. The federal prison system and several states built prison hospitals for old or sick inmates. States also began to build more medium- and minimum-security prisons—smaller in size and capacity, fences replacing walls, fewer security and more treatment staff, and dormitories and rooms replacing cell blocks. In the first half of the twentieth century, more than 90 percent of state and federal prisoners were held in maximum security. After the war, with most new prison construction tending toward the less costly lower-security designs, the shift to medium and minimum custody became more pronounced. Today, at least 75 percent of the total prisoner population live under less-than-maximum-security conditions.

Other small, separate prisons flourished during the reintegration era of the 1970s—work release centers, halfway houses, prerelease centers, and so on. These were usually located in urban areas to house men or women nearing the end of their sentences (or after release) and were classified as **open institutions,** meaning they had no armed guards or fences. A convict living there only had to walk away to escape. After recapture, the escapee was returned to a secure prison, likely to lockdown at the state penitentiary.

These small reintegration facilities should not be confused with the variety of **camps**—road camps, forestry camps, and "pea" farms—that were found in many states, particularly in the South and West. The role of these camps varied. Some held trusties in low security and were called "honor camps." Others were like tiny maximum-security prisons in a forest or on a farm. California and Michigan operated networks of forestry camps. The popular 1967 movie *Cool Hand Luke* was based on author Donn Pearce's recollection of his experiences in one of Florida's maximum-custody road camps after World War II.

While some states had large penitentiaries, small specialized prisons, and, possibly, camps as well, other states did not. Those with small prison populations, such as Montana, New Hampshire, and North Dakota, had only one small prison that held all convicted felons. Georgia, which Fred Haynes in the late 1930s said "probably has the poorest prison system in the country,"[16] turned most of its state convicts over to the counties. The 1931 film *I Am a Fugitive from a Chain Gang* was based on the best-selling memoirs of Robert Burns, who had twice escaped from Georgia prisons in the 1920s. South Carolina had a central prison, but most of its convicts were sent to county prisons. Other southern states operated plantation prisons. Louisiana and Mississippi operated penal systems centered on a huge prison farm—Angola in Louisiana and Parchman in Mississippi—with smaller satellite farms.

Louisiana, after World War II, had consolidated all prison operations at the Louisiana State Penitentiary (Angola), an 18,000-acre farm. Every adult felon, male or female, old or young, violent or nonviolent, short-termer or lifer, was confined there. Louisiana did not open its reformatory until 1957, its separate women's prison until 1961, and its first medium-security prison until 1976. Its simplified approach to penal management made its version of imprisonment different from that found in progressive industrial states.

STATE CORRECTIONS DEPARTMENTS

Prisons originally were independent institutions, each with its own warden or superintendent appointed by the governor, its own agenda, and its own management style. They were acknowledged to be political institutions. Officials were hired and fired as political administrations changed, and no civil service existed to protect the jobs of prison employees. Everything depended on political affiliation and personal relationships.

The warden's personality and beliefs gave each prison its style and, in states with multiple units, established each prison's ranking in the competition for political support and funding. Prisons were often in competition with each other. As businesses might market themselves today, prisons of the 1800s and first half of the 1900s tried to show that they were more productive, more efficient, more secure, or more reformative than other prisons within a state. Their continuity and future expansion depended on cultivation of favorable political contacts. Some of the better-known figures, such as Elam Lynds and Zebulon Brockway, achieved great successes and suffered equally great setbacks as their political power waxed and waned.

In the first part of the 1900s, political oversight of state prisons was usually vested in an intermediate controlling authority between the governor and the prison administration. This body was often called the board of control or prison commission, but its composition and authority varied considerably. Fred Haynes's 1939 chapter on "Penal Administration" lists six types of state penal authorities:

1. The ex officio organization, in which the governor and other elected or appointed officials oversaw the prison system

2. The institutional board of trustees, in which local boards of unpaid, appointed trustees oversaw each prison

3. The state prison commission, in which a central commission of paid officials (appointed or elected) administered the entire prison system

4. The board of control, very common in the progressive North and Midwest, in which an appointed board of professionals administered all charitable and correctional institutions

5. The New Jersey system, which was an attempt to take politics out of prisons and charitable institutions, relying on a group of volunteer citizens serving with the governor as a board of control, an appointed commissioner as the executive of the department, and a local board of trustees for each institution

6. The state department type, in which a cabinet-level official, called director, commissioner, or secretary, ran the prison system (and sometimes charitable institutions as well)[16]

These approaches to penal administration attempted to centralize control over prison policy and operations while limiting the governor's direct influence. After World War II, as the number of specialized prisons grew and probation and parole became more established, centralized corrections bureaucracies emerged as the dominant penal authorities in the states.

The new bureaucracy was most often called the state **department of corrections.** Two original models were Massachusetts and New York; each established a state department of corrections before World War II. Sanford Bates had been the Massachusetts prison commissioner in 1929, when he left to head the new Federal Bureau of Prisons.

Corrections departments could include adult and juvenile prisons, probation, and parole, though not all did. Probation often remained under the control of county judges. In some states, training schools and juvenile probation were put in a different agency or left under control of the welfare department. Other states grouped juvenile and adult corrections with mental hospitals and social service institutions—such as schools for the blind and deaf and homes for orphans, the mentally retarded, and pregnant girls—in departments of charities and institutions. In half a dozen less populous states, the corrections department also had responsibility for operating jails, a function of local sheriffs or police chiefs elsewhere.

The movement toward centralized corrections bureaucracies continued after World War II. California's Department of Corrections was established under Governor Earl Warren in 1944. Pennsylvania's Bureau of Correction, established in 1953, assumed authority over prisons from the Pennsylvania Department of Welfare. The bureau was reorganized and given cabinet-level status as the Department of Corrections in 1984. Tennessee's Department of Institutions underwent a name change, to Department of Correction, in 1955. Louisiana established a Department of Corrections in 1968. Wyoming's Department of Corrections was not created until 1991, when the state abolished its old Board of Charities and Reform.

Even following the unified department model, no two state systems are the same. American corrections today is fifty-one distinct systems, one for each state and one federal, not a unified national system. Local jails, probation, and juvenile justice complicate the picture. Most corrections departments have authority over all aspects of juvenile and adult corrections, but some split these functions. Wyoming, for instance, places juvenile corrections under the Department of Family Services. Louisiana's Department of Corrections was reorganized in 1981 as the Department of Public Safety and Corrections, overseeing not only corrections but also the state police, fire marshal, and other state-level law enforcement agencies.

THE CORRECTIONS SYSTEM TODAY

From its elementary origins 200 years ago, the modern prison has grown into the centerpiece of today's correctional system, an enterprise that provides diverse forms of social control never imagined by Enlightenment reformers. The American penal system once consisted of the jail and the penitentiary. One was for pretrial defendants in detention and minor criminals serving short terms and the other for all more serious criminals. The road to prison was short and straight (deliberately so to have the deterrent and reformative effect imagined for it): society to jail to prison.

The prison's place in society became more prominent even as its purpose became more diffused and murky, as evidenced by the incarceration explosion and political rhetoric of the past twenty years. The road to prison today is much longer and considerably more cut with side roads—diversion, probation, community corrections, and boot camp. State and federal prisons hold more than 1,300,000 men and women. Jails—mostly under city or county control but also state and federal—hold more than 650,000. Probation supervises 4 million misdemeanants and felons. More than 700,000 men and women are on parole. The juvenile justice system contains about a million youths—100,000 in detention centers and training schools, the rest in community-based facilities or on probation. This is a huge system. Three of every 100 Americans, juveniles and adults, are under correctional supervision at any given time.

To provide the supervision and the necessary administrative, treatment, and related functions, a vast network of correctional organizations has evolved. Agencies at four levels of government—federal, state, county, and city—with supporting roles played by many private businesses and individuals, employ a million people, including public employees, private contractors, and providers. This figure does not include the many private businesses that manufacture prison building components, equipment, and supplies. Estimates have put the economic cost of today's correctional bureaucracy—public and private—at upward of $60 billion per year, a huge expense that continues to grow as this network, already the largest of any on earth, continues to expand year by year. Many people, scholars and prison officials alike, question the role this system of formal social control has come to play in modern American society. It is surely far beyond the scope envisioned by the penitentiary's founders 200 years ago, but given the social and political conditions of today, it is difficult to imagine that any significant shrinkage will take place soon.

KEY TERMS

Big House	Sanford Bates	James V. Bennett	warehousing
scientific management	Hawes-Cooper Act	medical model	balanced model
hard labor	Ashurst-Sumners Act	Robert Martinson	icebox model
public account	Sumners-Ashurst Act	"nothing works"	houses of refuge
state account	Prison Industries Branch	recidivism	training school
convict lease	Richard A. McGee	Norval Morris	Indiana Reformatory Institute
contract	reform	reintegration era	open institutions
piece price	rehabilitation	War on Crime	camps
state use	classification	war on criminals	department of corrections
public works and ways	treatment	War on Drugs	

NOTES

1. Blake McKelvey, *American Prisons: A History of Good Intentions* (Montclair, N.J.: Patterson Smith, 1977), pp. 177–79.

2. Ibid., p. 283.

3. Christopher R. X. Adamson, *Hard Labor: The Form and Function of Imprisonment in Nineteenth Century America* (Ann Arbor: MI: UMI, 1982), p. 256.

4. Ibid., p. 93.

5. Fred E. Haynes, *The American Prison System* (New York: McGraw-Hill, 1939), p. 312.

6. Ibid.

7. Ibid., pp. 310–11.

8. Morgan O. Reynolds, "Restricting Work by Prisoners," in "Factories Behind Bars," National Center for Policy Analysis, September 1996, *www.ncpa.org/studies/s206/s206rw.html*.

9. "Wartime Production in State Prisons," *Monthly Labor Review* 59 (July 1944): 137–38.

10. John W. Roberts, *Reform and Retribution: An Illustrated History of American Prisons* (Lanham, Md.: American Correctional Association, 1997), p. 166.

11. Jon Blackwell, "1952: The Powder Keg Blows," *The Trentonian*, *www.capital century.com/1952.html*.

12. Ibid.

13. Roberts, *Reform and Retribution*, p. 169.

14. Robert Martinson, "What Works? Questions and Answers about Prison Reform," *The Public Interest* 35 (Spring 1974): 25.

15. Clemens Bartollas and Stuart J. Miller, *Juvenile Justice in America*, 3rd ed. (Upper Saddle River, N.J.: Prentice Hall, 2001), p. 244.

16. Haynes, *The American Prison System*, p. 173.

FURTHER READING

Bennett, James V. *I Chose Prison*. New York: Alfred A. Knopf, 1970.

Friedman, Lawrence M. *Crime and Punishment in American History*. New York: Basic Books, 1993.

Hallinan, Joseph. *Going Up the River: Travels in a Prison Nation*. New York: Random House, 2001.

Haynes, Fred E. *The American Prison System*. New York: McGraw-Hill, 1939.

McKelvey, Blake. *American Prisons: A History of Good Intentions*. Montclair, N.J.: Patterson Smith, 1977.

President's Commission on Law Enforcement and Administration of Justice. *Task Force Report: Corrections*. Washington, D.C.: U.S. Government Printing Office, 1967.

WEB AND VIDEO RESOURCES

The National Criminal Justice Reference Service, at *http:virlib.ncjrs.org/corrections.asp*, is the national repository for a huge collection of corrections publications and resources.

The Alcatraz Website is *www.nps.gov/alcatraz.*

The American Correctional Association Website is *www.aca.org.*

For a business and management focus, *The Correctional News Online* Website is *www.correctionalnews.com.*

COMMENTARY

3 The Drug War and Prisons

by Edmond Dantes

In December 2000, seventeen years into America's current "War on Drugs," state prisons held 251,100 drug criminals—21 percent of all state prisoners. The federal system held 73,389—57 percent of all federal prisoners. Why sentence so many drug criminals to prison?

History explains it. As the baby-boomer generation reached their teens in the 1960s, part of their typical youth rebellion against parental authority took the form of widespread drug use, especially marijuana. As the baby boomers aged into their twenties in the 1970s, they made marijuana and powder cocaine use fashionable. Young movie stars and rock idols wore coke spoons around their necks in films, on stage, and in real life. It drove older generations crazy, exactly as intended.

As the boomers reached their thirties, and as superstars started dying from drug overdoses—John Belushi, Jimi Hendrix, Janis Joplin, Jim Morrison—drugs didn't seem so attractive any more. Crack cocaine began to appear in urban black neighborhoods by the mid-1980s, soon turning them into war zones as black and Hispanic street gangs armed to the teeth fought savage turf wars to control crack distribution. Then, in June 1986, Maryland basketball star Len Bias collapsed in his dorm room and died of a seizure described as "cocaine-induced." It shocked the nation. President Ronald Reagan stepped up the national "War on Drugs" and his wife, Nancy Reagan, coined the phrase that would mark this era: "Just say no to drugs."

Politicians did just that, year after year passing increasingly tough penalties for drug offenses, starting with the Anti-Drug Abuse Act of 1988 and focusing especially on crack cocaine. Before the War on Drugs

became a national obsession, 75 percent of all arrests were for "public disorder" crimes—gambling, prostitution, vagrancy, shoplifting and other petty crimes. After a horde of politicians, including the president, defined drug abuse as a serious crime, police started picking up all the dope fiends and dealers (often one and the same) they could find, a task made easy because poor whites and ghetto blacks had to hit the streets to score. Hundreds of thousands were arrested each year and, during the "get tough" ambience of the eighties and nineties, many were packed off to prison to serve longer and longer terms—all the way up to life in prison for distributing Schedule I narcotics.

This, despite the fact that by the early nineties the crack wars were long over and crack use itself had plummeted. Like powder cocaine ten years earlier, it had run its course. "If you were raised in a house where somebody was a crack addict, you wanted to get as far away from it as you could," Selena Jones, a Harlem resident whose mother was a crack addict, told the *New York Times* in 1992. "People look down on them so much that even crackheads don't want to be crackheads any more."

After two decades of a futile $25- to $40-billion-a-year war against drugs, a rising number of public figures and politicians, including bedrock conservatives, began saying enough is enough. Several states—Arizona, Louisiana and New York among them, have reduced the penalties for many drug crimes. California's Proposition 36 mandates treatment instead of prison for most drug-possession crimes. Career cop and former San Jose, California, police chief Joe McNamara told the *Sacramento Bee* in December 2000, "We arrested everyone in sight, but it was clear nothing was getting any better. Prop 36 showed that the old easy slogans—that drugs are evil and drug users are evil people—are not being bought by the voters."

U.S. Representative Dan Burton, a longtime Republican conservative from Indiana, at a December 2002 hearing of the House Government Reform Committee raised the previously unthinkable prospect of legalizing dope: "Every time I have a hearing, I hear that people who get hooked on heroin and cocaine become addicted and they very rarely get off it. And the scourge expands and expands. There's no end to it. And we continue to build more and more prisons, and we put more and more people in jail. I hate drugs, and I hate what it's done to our society. But I have one question that nobody ever asks: What would happen if there was no profit in drugs? If they couldn't make any money out of selling drugs, what would happen?"

Why does America continue to sentence so many drug criminals to prison? Fear, institutional inertia, and lack of political leadership keep the drug war alive on the home front.

IDEOLOGIES AND SENTENCING

And if any mischief follow, then thou shalt give life for life, eye for eye, tooth for tooth, hand for hand, foot for foot, burning for burning, wound for wound, stripe for stripe.

— Exodus 21:23–25

Ye have heard that it hath been said, An eye for an eye, and a tooth for a tooth: But I say unto you, That ye resist not evil: but whosoever shall smite thee on the right cheek, turn to him the other also. . . . Love your enemies, bless them that curse you, do good to them that hate you, and pray for them which despitefully use you and persecute you.

— Matthew 5:38–39, 44

INTRODUCTION

We have thus far focused on the historical development of the prison and other components of the modern corrections system. This chapter looks at the choices we make in placing criminals within this system. This is the realm of sentencing—the judicial outcome of a criminal case. How do we match the individual criminal with the specific sentence? For the convicted criminal—felon or misdemeanant—sentencing is a critical event. It means the difference between freedom and confinement. It controls the future, often for many years to come. In a few cases, it means life or death. But, for many of us, including the political officials who make and enforce the laws as well as the ordinary citizens to whom the laws are applied, sentencing is a murky area, based more on ideology or personal feelings than any objective knowledge of cause and effect. After reading this chapter, you should be familiar with:

1. Principal objectives of punishment.
2. Sentencing models important in contemporary criminal justice.
3. Common sentencing options, from probation to imprisonment to death.
4. The sentencing decision.
5. Sentencing issues and reforms.
6. Impact of sentencing on corrections.

THE OBJECTIVES OF SENTENCING

What are we trying to accomplish through apprehending criminals and convicting them in court? The most common answer in American society today would probably be **punishment**, which has to do with the imposition of a penalty of some kind as a result of a rule or law violation. Punishment derives from the Latin *poena*, translated as "penalty" or "pain." Sentencing does not have to result in punishment. Just for theoretical purposes, we could have it result in the opposite, reward, if we were to give criminals a cash bonus or favorable recognition for each crime they committed; or, in the larger social context, if criminal behavior was recognized as a kind of disability (based on the kinds of disadvantages typically found in criminals), then the objective of sentencing could be assistance. Convicted criminals could be given monthly checks and provided with a broad range of social assistance, not unlike people (some of them former criminals) who receive such support based on various physical and mental disabilities. Indeed, some economic analysts have suggested that, with annual prison costs at $20,000 or $25,000 per adult and twice that for juveniles, it would be cheaper to subsidize criminals in the community, paying them regular salaries in hopes they would commit fewer crimes, and abolish prisons altogether except for the truly dangerous few.

Our policy, however, is "make war, not welfare"—we do not want criminals to be rewarded or subsidized. We want them to be punished except, occasionally, when someone commits an act that is technically a crime but so popular that the public approves rather than condemns the act, leading to celebrity status, books, movies, and collateral benefits. Vigilantes who take direct action against criminals are often in this category. Our notions of punishment as what is due the criminal derive from historical practice. The pre-Christian historical societies provided economic sanctions, slavery, banishment, corporal punishment, and death as sentences for guilty criminals. Early Christian societies continued the same punishments in their fight against sin. All these outcomes certainly qualify as punishment, and most of them were physically painful as well.

If we could ask people in those societies what they were trying to accomplish through punishment, they might well have looked at us in puzzlement, not understanding that punishment can have more than one purpose or objective. Punishment was something that was done—of necessity—to maintain balance and restore order in human relations or in the universe. Many wrongs in early times were considered violations of the natural order of humankind's relationship with the gods.

Legal scholars agree that punishment in ancient societies was based primarily on **retribution**, or **retaliation**, for the harm done by the crime. The concept of retribution is equivalence, returning to the victim what is due. The words of Exodus used to open this chapter are a well-known expression of this concept.

Punishment under *lex talionis*, the law of retaliation, was *limited* punishment. It was intended to replace the use of the blood feud and vendetta that had marked early family and tribal relations. Instead of revenge, which was personal and unbalanced and often led to extended conflict, as one party sought to gain the upper hand on another, retribution sought to bring about an impartial, equitable resolution of conflict. This applied to property loss as well as to physical harm.

It is important to note that once the criminal had been punished through economic or physical sanctions, he was square with the victim and with society. No further stigma was attached to him, nor was he in any way limited in his rights as a citizen. Philosophers such as Immanuel Kant and, more recently, Herbert Morris argued that the criminal should *demand* punishment not only to restore balance in society but also to regain his full standing as a citizen. Kant viewed punishment as a moral imperative, regardless of outcome—even if it made the criminal worse or more bitter. Blame, resulting in punishment, is useful because it is the right thing to do. Modern criminals have apparently forgotten this precept, as we rarely see anyone standing before the court demanding just punishment.

Retributive justice prevailed into the 1700s, when the ideas of the Enlightenment gave rise to **utilitarianism,** "the greatest good for the greatest number." Popularized in the writings of such scholars as Cesare Beccaria and Jeremy Bentham, utilitarianism emphasized the effects of punishment on the larger society. Three modern objectives of punishment grew out of utilitarian thought: deterrence, incapacitation, and reformation (later rehabilitation).

Deterrence, which in Beccaria's argument was to be achieved through the certainty of imprisonment, was the discouraging effect that punishment has on those who may contemplate committing a crime. We avoid the conduct or the criminal avoids its repetition because we know the consequences. We are restrained by our fear of punishment.

Incapacitation is the protective effect of punishment on society. A criminal who in the early days was banished or who is imprisoned today cannot harm society. Society is safer because criminals have been removed.

Reformation, in the twentieth century **rehabilitation,** posits that punishment reduces or eliminates future criminal behavior through individual change during confinement (reformation) or through programs designed to motivate law-abiding behavior (rehabilitation).

The utilitarian "goal of punishment is to prevent future harm."[1] Thus, punishment is a means to a social end. As primitive punishments tied to retribution were replaced by imprisonment and related sanctions, utilitarian objectives moved to the fore as purposes of penal confinement.

Which purpose is more important in comparison to the others? This becomes a matter of ideology. An **ideology** is a body of belief and doctrine that guides how an individual or a larger group sees the world. In America today, three contrasting ideologies are often compared to describe different philosophies of punishment. The **conservative ideology** is said to be "tough on crime." Conservatives want more severe criminal penalties and greater use of imprisonment. Think bigger, tougher prisons. The **liberal ideology** views most criminals as disadvantaged members of society. Liberals want more resources put into rehabilitation and crime prevention. Think nicer, more helpful prisons. The **radical ideology** takes an economic or class view of crime; the legal system is designed for social control. Radicals concentrate on attacking the ills of society—racism, poverty, materialism, and the overreach of the criminal law—and would significantly decrease (or abolish) the use of imprisonment. Think very tiny prisons filled with corrupt corporate executives and politicians and a few murderers and sex criminals.

SENTENCING MODELS

If an ideology is a way of thinking, then a **model** takes these beliefs or assumptions and turns them into a design for action. A model is a representation of a system based on what one believes and knows—it is a framework for putting ideas to work.

As criminal justice, described by the President's Crime Commission in 1967 as a "**nonsystem,**" has grown more systematic over the years, models have become more important in conceptualizing how the system ought to work. The **rehabilitation model** (as we discussed in chapter 3) was very important to prisons from the early 1950s through the 1970s. It emphasized institutional programs to correct the problems and disadvantages criminals needed to overcome if they were to live crime-free lives.

The **reintegration model** was particularly influential in the 1970s. Its emphasis on real-world programs, as opposed to rehabilitation programs offered within prison walls, and its preference for probation and other community-based forms of supervision were instrumental for several years in expanding noncustodial alternatives and holding down prison populations.

At the same time, concern with crime as a national problem had spurred debate over priorities. Herbert Packer's influential article "Two Models of the Criminal Process" (1964) and his book *The Limits of the Criminal Sanction* (1968) appeared just as the "War on Crime" was declared. Packer discussed criminal justice in America as incorporating two contrasting models: crime control and due process. The **crime control model,** which in this era focused more on efficient law enforcement and case processing leading to criminal conviction, emphasized the system's part in maintaining social order. Later, enlargement of the prison system would be argued as a necessity in housing those criminals who became persistent threats to the social order.

Packer contrasted crime control with the **due process model,** which emphasized the rights of criminal defendants in the legal system. Due process was very important at this time, as the U.S. Supreme Court under Chief Justice Earl Warren made many landmark decisions extending constitutional protection to state court defendants. No such federal protections had existed previously for defendants in state courts, although "due process" appears in both the Fifth and the Fourteenth Amendment to the Constitution.

Tension between the crime control and due process models is important—one focusing on the rights of the individual, the other on the greater good of society. Neither can completely dominate the other. As Frank Schmalleger has suggested, American criminal justice is *crime control through due process,*[2] incorporating individual protection within crime control. But, the emphasis on one or the other, particularly the critical role of the courts as intervening authorities, can change significantly over time.

In the 1970s, construction of an ideological framework for a new sentencing model (or the renovation of an old model) began. David Fogel's **justice model** was described in *We Are the Living Proof* (1975) and *Justice as Fairness* (1981). Fogel argued against rehabilitation and in favor of a rationalist, retributive approach that relied on a carefully constructed scale of crimes and punishments. Fogel's sanctions were on the lenient side. He believed, as Beccaria did 200 years ago and most criminologists do today, that certainty of punishment is more important than severity.

This idea of imprisonment as primarily retributive punishment was taken a step further by Andrew von Hirsch and other advocates of the **just deserts model.** Von Hirsch's 1976 book *Doing Justice* was more supportive of increased severity of punishment. Just deserts proponents tended to escalate the scale of penalties. Their views would be popular with politicians who demanded longer prison terms and more use of the death penalty to reduce the high level of crime in America during the 1970s and 1980s.

One aspect of American crime, high levels of illegal drug use, was a concern of the **neoclassical model** popularized in the 1980s. Drawing on Beccaria and Bentham and other members of the classical school of criminology of the late eighteenth and early nineteenth centuries, neoclassicists asserted the value of deterrence. They said an overreliance on probation had caused criminal penalties to lose their deterrent effect. What was needed, especially with drug criminals, was more extensive use of imprisonment. "Prison, not probation," was the neoclassic battle cry. President Ronald Reagan heard this cry, or perhaps he was the one standing at the front of the army shouting it. The cries to "lock 'em up," in the case of drug criminals, or to "lock 'em up and throw away the key," in the case of habitual and violent criminals, have resounded throughout our legal system since. The "War on Drugs," begun in Reagan's first term and perpetuated by succeeding presidents, became the prime force driving America's imprisonment rate upward.

Habitual criminals would soon have their own model, **selective incapacitation.** Deriving from the research of Peter Greenwood for the Rand Corporation in the 1970s (published as *Selective Incapacitation* in 1982), this model focused on high-risk or high-rate criminals. Looking not only at such obvious indicators as the numbers of arrests or convictions but also at work history (or lack thereof), criminal history of family members, and drug usage, this model sought to identify criminals fully committed to a criminal lifestyle. If our capacity to confine is limited, selective incapacitation argued, we do society the most good by imposing long prison terms on the criminals who commit the most crimes. Selective incapacitation inspired "three strikes" laws in many states over the next decade or so, resulting in the long-term incarceration of many habitual offenders (though whether these were the highest-risk criminals or merely the most inept remains uncertain).

Juvenile criminals were not immune from model changes. Juvenile justice, with its traditional emphasis on probation and community-based alternatives, was perceived as not being "tough enough" for violent juvenile delinquents of the 1980s and 1990s. Many juveniles, already habitual offenders at a young age, sneered at the system's puny punishments. "You can't do nothin to me," they said, expecting to get break after break after break. The **logical consequences** model was developed to tighten controls over juveniles who did not respond favorably to supervision. It emphasized discipline, accountability, and certainty of action. "If you do this, this will happen"—and then it had to happen exactly as promised. Restating deterrence in a form applicable to juveniles, logical consequences sought to bring a more adultlike management approach to young criminals. Its result was to put more juveniles behind bars and increase supervision over those who remained in the community.

The 1980s and 1990s saw more use of imprisonment and less concern with treatment. Due process rights were subordinated to crime control. State and federal courts, which twenty years before had taken a liberal view, became more conservative. Prison and jail populations increased dramatically, and the supervision of criminals in the community became more restrictive as well. On the scale of justice, the balance had shifted heavily to the right.

At the end of the twentieth century, a new justice model appeared on the scene. Called **restorative justice** or, awkwardly, the **balanced and restorative justice model,** its vision of justice was healing rather than punishment, a triangle of "three Cs"—community, crime victims, and criminals. The community needed to be more "interested" and involved. Crime victims, whose exclusion from the system had been at the heart of the politically aggressive **victims' rights movement** of the 1980s and 1990s, should be better informed and allowed more direct participation. Criminals—often themselves victims of other crimes—should be allowed to make amends for the harm they had done. The goal of restorative justice is to achieve a restoration to all parties, to repair the damage done. Its guiding principle was reconciliation (or redress, according to Willem de Haan, whose 1990 book *The Politics of Redress* advocates this political alternative to punishment).

While restorative justice has its proponents and is attracting more policy interest in many states, it remains a fuzzy and little-known model to many. All the dominant models relate to crime control. It is easy to visualize locking people behind bars but not so easy to imagine criminals, crime victims, and the community sitting in a big circle, discussing issues of guilt and harm, and working to reconcile their differences.

Models are important to justice in America, but they have to be seen in the context of a very disorganized and multilayered criminal justice system. In a system made up of federal, state, and local government agencies, each supplemented by many private organizations and individuals, many divergent models may be pursued at the same time, some of them often at odds or directly contradictory to one another. Harry Allen and Clifford Simonsen have referred to this **model muddle** as a defining characteristic of corrections in America. Corrections is often going not in any one direction but in several different directions at once, depending on where you happen to look. In this landscape, politics is more important than rationality.

The model muddle applies to the sentencing of individual criminals as well. Practitioners of sentencing apply different models or several models to different criminals. Take this scenario. A judge has before her four teenage defendants convicted of beating and robbing an old woman, supposedly as part of a gang initiation rite. The first one, the ringleader, she sentenced to ten years in prison. She said this was his "just deserts" for the harm done to the victim. To the second defendant, who had a couple of prior assault convictions, the judge also gave ten years. She said society would be safer with him tucked away in prison for several years. To the third defendant, who had gone to college as a scholarship athlete but dropped out, she gave an eight-year sentence. She said that she hoped others would be discouraged from following a life of crime by his example. To the last defendant, whose involvement in the incident was minimal, the judge gave a sentence of four years in prison. He had been a good student in high school and had just applied to college when he was arrested for the crime. She said that she hoped he would learn from this mistake and try to live a better life after his short term in prison.

There you have it—retribution, incapacitation, deterrence, and rehabilitation, as applied to four defendants for the same crime. A few weeks later, after they were processed through a classification unit, all four arrived at the same medium-security prison to serve their sentence. So no matter what models the judge might have had in mind at sentencing, the four defendants ended up in the same prison environment, sharing the same experience of confinement. What might we predict about outcomes?

This example illustrates Joycelyn Pollock's idea of prison as a "slippery fish." She has written, "What is probably most true about the penal enterprise is that is does not have one clearly defined, specific philosophy or rationale for existence. . . . Prison can be all things to all people."[3] The purpose of imprisonment, like beauty, is in the eye of the beholder.

SENTENCING OPTIONS: NONCUSTODIAL

Most criminals will never go to prison. Their crimes are not serious enough. Of the more than 10 million persons arrested each year in the United States, about 500,000 end up in prison. Five percent go to prison, and 95 percent go elsewhere (or nowhere, as half of all arrests are disposed of without a conviction).

Criminals can be divided into three offense types: traffic, misdemeanor, and felony. Traffic violators are most likely to get a fine. If an additional punishment is tacked on, it is likely to be community service or a suspended jail sentence. Traffic violators generally have to pay court costs as well, which in some courts can be substantial (like an extra "tax" on the criminal act). "Two hundred dollars, court costs, and ten days in jail suspended," the judge might say to someone convicted of excessive speeding or reckless driving. More serious violations, such as driving under the influence (DUI) or hit-and-run, often carry jail terms and larger fines.

Misdemeanor offenses call for a penalty of up to a year in jail and a fine prescribed for each offense. Misdemeanors include thefts, assaults, vandalism, possession of marijuana, disturbing the peace, and so forth. Convicted misdemeanants, like traffic violators, often get fines and suspended sentences. They may get probation if the court is able to provide active supervision; many courts at the municipal or county level are not. Repeat misdemeanants are more likely to get short jail terms. Community service, court costs, and probation supervision fees are also misdemeanor punishment options.

Special counseling ("treatment") programs have been developed for certain types of traffic and misdemeanor criminals in recent years. Involvement in domestic violence in many locales may result in referral to counseling. Traffic violators may be sent to driver improvement training. Persons involved in assaults and "road rage" incidents may be assigned to anger management classes. Huge numbers of persons convicted of alcohol and drug crimes are sentenced to substance abuse counseling. A growth industry of counseling minor criminals has developed in urban areas in recent years. Counseling sentences are almost always an "add-on," imposed in addition to any fines or other penalties.

Traffic violators and misdemeanants rarely end up in a state prison, with two exceptions. Some jurisdictions sentence selected criminals convicted of targeted offenses, such as domestic violence, DUI, or misdemeanor drug possession, to serve a short term in a state prison before returning to probation or other community-based sentence. This practice may be called shock probation or split sentence. Its intent is specific deterrence: to warn or scare the criminal by showing him where repetition of the crime will lead. Many authorities disapprove of this practice, not wishing to see minor criminals placed in a severe environment with convicted felons.

The other traffic or misdemeanor offenders who may find themselves in state prisons are probation or parole violators. Breaking the law is a violation of the general conditions of probation or parole. Even if the charge is a relatively minor one that would not carry a jail term, such as DUI, assault by fighting, or petty theft, it could serve as the reason to revoke the probationary or parole status and put the criminal behind bars.

Felons are the third type of criminals. In recent years, about a third of convicted felons have been sentenced directly to probation. These are predominantly first-time felons convicted of property and lesser drug crimes, though a few violent criminals, mostly those convicted of assault and battery, may also get probation. About 20 to 25 percent of felony offenders get a combination sentence—jail time followed by probation. These people are often held in jail pretrial until their case comes to court. They plead guilty, with credit for time served, and get released from jail directly to probation. In effect, they have served the incarceration part of their sentence *before* conviction; as soon as they plead guilty, they go free. The model for this process ("sentence first—verdict afterwards") can be found in *Alice's Adventures in Wonderland*.

SENTENCING OPTIONS: IMPRISONMENT

What Harry Allen and Clifford Simonsen have called "the correctional filter" takes most lesser criminals (and a good number of greater criminals against whom evidence is lacking) out of the system and returns them to the community from whence they came. For someone arrested for a felony in which the evidence is strong, the odds of imprisonment increase. If the charge sticks at the felony level, the defendant (particularly one who has a prior criminal history) has an even chance of going to prison.

A felony is generally defined as a crime for which the penalty is a year or more in a state or federal prison. The "or more" can range all the way up to a life sentence with or without parole (or finite terms of a hundred to several thousand years, used in some states to express the court's view that the defendant should never get out of prison). Felony sentences over the past decade have averaged about five to six years. Violent criminals get longer terms, while property, drug, and public order criminals get shorter terms. Repeat offenders in any category can expect longer sentences, up to a life term as a habitual offender.

According to state court records for 1998,[4] 928,000 adults were convicted of felonies. The great majority—94 percent—pleaded guilty, often as a result of **plea bargaining** (reaching a deal about the length of the sentence, the specific charge, or the number of charges). The other 6 percent were convicted at trial.

Conviction rates vary widely by crime. Sixty percent of adults arrested for murder are eventually convicted of a felony, but only 16 percent of aggravated assault arrests and 15 percent of auto theft arrests result in felony convictions. Oddly enough, the highest rate of felony convictions is not for murder but for drug trafficking, where 68 percent of arrests result in felony convictions.

Convicted felons drew three dispositions:

1. Probation—32 percent
2. Local jail term (often time served, with probation to follow)—24 percent
3. State prison term—44 percent

By categories, state court felons were convicted of the following:

1. Drug crimes—34 percent
2. Property crimes—31 percent
3. Violent crimes—18 percent
4. Public order crimes—18 percent

The likelihood of imprisonment varied considerably by crime of conviction:

1. Murder—94 percent
2. Robbery—76 percent
3. Rape—70 percent
4. Burglary—54 percent
5. Drug trafficking—45 percent
6. Auto theft—43 percent
7. Drug possession—36 percent
8. Fraud—35 percent

Federal courts sentenced 50,000 felons in 1998, the majority for drug trafficking (38 percent) or fraud (17 percent). Four out of five federal felons got prison time. Their average sentence was just over five years.

For state court felons, a sentence to imprisonment generally results in the transfer of the criminal from a local jail into the state prison system (though in some states, especially Louisiana, large numbers of state prisoners serve their time in the custody of local sheriffs). The sentencing court does not determine where the felon is sent. The prison system does this after running the new prisoner through a classification or reception center.

About two-thirds of felons entering state prisons each year are serving new sentences. The other third are parole or probation violators who have had their conditional status revoked and now have to serve their "old" prison sentence or the rest of it.

SENTENCING OPTIONS: DEATH

Death was once commonly applied to a wide variety of criminals. Under English common law, almost every felony eventually became a **capital crime.** Death sentences, liberally imposed, were society's way of saying, "We don't want you among us any more." Not all were carried out. Many were commuted. Many death-sentenced criminals were banished or later transported to the colonies. But, in all Western societies through the eighteenth century, death sentences were frequently imposed and executions were common public events.

No more. In August 2002, the United Nations and the Death Penalty Information Center identified 111 countries as abolitionist in law or practice: seventy-six for all crimes, fifteen for all but military crimes or crimes against the state), and twenty de facto (the penalty is on the books but never used).[5] About eighty-four countries are retentionist, still imposing death sentences, some sporadically, some frequently. Only a handful of countries—China, the Congo, Iran, Iraq, Saudi Arabia, and the United States—routinely carry out more than twenty to thirty executions a year. Strange company for the United States. The nations of western Europe, with whom we are culturally most similar, have all abolished the death penalty. Belgium, Italy, the Netherlands, and Norway have not executed anyone for a nonmilitary crime in more than 100 years. Even Russia, which used to execute considerably more criminals, both civil and political, than we did, imposed a moratorium on the death penalty in 1996 that remains in effect today.

Most Americans—from 60 to 70 percent—according to the most recent polls, support the death penalty. In the 1960s, public support was much lower. The number of executions in America had declined steadily from the 1930s on, slowing to a trickle by the 1960s. In 1966, only one man was executed, and a May 1966 Gallup Poll reported that more people were opposed to capital punishment than in favor of it. Six years later, the U.S. Supreme Court, in ***Furman v. Georgia*** (1972), declared that the death penalty as it was then being applied violated the Eighth Amendment's prohibition against "cruel and unusual punishment."

Opponents of capital punishment thought the death penalty had been abolished. However, four years later, in ***Gregg v. Georgia*** (1976), the Supreme Court approved reinstatement of the death penalty, provided that a structured process was followed. Today, thirty-eight states, the federal government, and the military follow the steps approved by the Court almost thirty years ago:

1. A narrow definition of the capital crime (which has come to mean that only some murders—murders committed during a felony such as robbery, rape, or kidnapping; multiple homicides; killings of police; and other specific circumstances, depending on state law—qualify for the death penalty). This crime is called first-degree, or capital, murder. Though some states have statutes allowing the death penalty for crimes other than murder (such as treason or child rape), only one person (in a Louisiana case that will test the death penalty for child rape) has gotten a death sentence for any crime but murder in the past thirty years.

2. A two-part trial, called a **bifurcated trial,** with a guilt phase followed by a separate penalty phase.

3. Presentation of **aggravating circumstances** and **mitigating circumstances** in the penalty phase. Aggravating circumstances, such as torture, prior criminality, victim impact, or future dangerousness, make the crime worse. Mitigating circumstances, such as the criminal's youth, family history, or mental disability, show that he may not deserve the death penalty.

4. Automatic appeal to the state supreme court, which reviews the trial record for errors and also to ensure **proportionality,** the concept that a similar crime elsewhere in the state might also have resulted in a death sentence.

The process is highly selective.[6] Over the past decade, as the number of homicides declined from 24,000 to between 15,000 and 16,000, death sentences averaged about 300 per year. For any single homicide during this time, the odds of getting a death sentence ranged from one in fifty to one in eighty. The number of executions ranged from a low of fourteen in 1991 to a high of ninety-eight in 1999, averaging about fifty per year for the 1990s. As the process works now, the odds on being executed, after receiving a death sentence, are about one in three or four, though this varies tremendously from state to state.

In the late 1990s, as the numbers of death sentences and executions had reached a static level, massive publicity about innocent men and women on death row undercut public and political confidence in the legal process. The number of death sentences dropped to 229 in 2000 and 155 in 2001. Executions also declined.

In June 2002, the Supreme Court, which had tended to take a hands-off approach and allowed states to do what they wanted so long as they followed the basic *Gregg* rules, announced two major decisions. *Atkins v. Virginia* prohibited the execution of mentally retarded criminals. *Ring v. Arizona* required the jury, after reviewing the aggravating factors, to impose (or recommend to the judge that he or she impose) the death sentence. In several states, judges had made the sentencing decisions in capital cases. The Court did allow the practice of executing juveniles as young as sixteen (at the time of the crime) to stand, although only seven states, all in the South, have actually done so in the past two decades.

In January 2003, Illinois Governor George Ryan, who had imposed a moratorium on executions in 2000 and established a commission to study the death penalty in his state (after thirteen defendants had already been sent home from death row as genuinely "innocent men"), used his executive clemency power to empty out Illinois's death row. Four inmates, victims of police torture and legal misconduct, were pardoned outright; another 167 had their sentences commuted to life imprisonment. Prosecutors and victim advocates screamed. Governor Ryan justified his action by sharply criticizing the quality of criminal justice in his state. These cases, he said, "are perfect examples of what is so terribly broken about our system. I believe a manifest injustice has occurred."[7]

The result of these judicial and political interventions has been to reduce the number of inmates under death sentence in America from a peak of 3,729 in 2002 to about 3,500 in early 2003. Is the death penalty finally on the way out? In all likelihood, not anytime soon. It remains popular nationally and hugely popular in the South, where about two-thirds of death row inmates are found and where about 90 percent of executions occur. Watt Espy, the death penalty historian, has recorded almost 20,000 lawful executions carried out by local, state, or federal authorities in America since colonial times. The practice appears so well ingrained culturally, particularly in the South, that America is not yet ready to join the rest of the Western world in letting go of this old-time punishment.

Reemergence of the death penalty in the 1970s, after it appeared so nearly dead, was about the politics of responding to violent crime. America, led by the local district attorneys who exercise the **gatekeeper function** in filing capital charges and bringing them to trial, reserves the right to almost randomly select a few scapegoats from a vast pool of murderers and eventually put some of them to death, just to show that we as a people have not lost our will in the war on criminal violence. These executions have no real impact on crime. Not even the most hard-line prosecutors talk much about the deterrent effect of the death penalty any more, unless they are complaining about the process taking so long that any possible deterrent effect is lost. Killing murderers is mostly symbolic—to show that we still mean business. We like capital punishment because it is tough, direct, and easy to understand. In the search for simple solutions to crime, the death penalty leads the way.[8]

THE SENTENCING DECISION

When the criminal has been convicted, who decides the sentence? Most people would probably respond, "the judge," because the robed figure on the podium is the one who imposes it. That used to be true, but today's judges face more constraints in imposing sentences.

Under English common law and European civil law, the **trial judge** was the sentencing authority. With possible sentences for common law felonies ranging from a minimal fine to the death penalty (or, in some instances, the discharge of a guilty defendant with no punishment), judges enjoyed wide discretion in deciding sentences. They listened to the evidence about the crime and what was known about the criminal's prior history, then imposed a sentence that was quickly carried out. Few cases were appealed or subject to the intervention of the king.

In the twentieth-century model of the American felony court, the sentence had to be more than a matter of judicial opinion. It was to be based on research. In this collaborative model, the judge did the sentencing based on research done by a **probation officer.** If the defendant was found guilty at trial, the judge would order a **presentence investigation report** to be prepared by the probation officer. This report was like a background investigation into the crime and the defendant. Prepared within a few weeks, it generally contained a sentencing recommendation (at least to the choice between prison and probation). The defendant would return to court for a hearing, and the "scientific" sentence would be pronounced.

Many researchers have questioned this model, particularly the role of the probation officer. Studies indicate that the judge tended to follow the recommendation of the probation officer 80 to 90 percent of the time. Was this because the judges trusted the probation officer's recommendations or because the probation officers tailored recommendations to suit judges' wishes? Probably some of both. As Clifford Dorne has suggested, it also suits the convenience of the court as a way of getting business done in a professional manner.

A greater flaw in the scientific sentencing model became apparent over the last half of the century. Trials decreased in number. Most convictions, 90 to 95 percent or more in virtually all courts, were obtained through plea bargaining. The plea bargaining model transfers sentencing power from the judge to the **prosecutor.** The prosecutor, as the representative of the public, negotiates an appropriate sentence for the defendant, who pleads guilty. The judge can ratify or reject this bargain (sending the case back for further negotiation if it is not acceptable), but the sentence is really the prosecutor's call. This compromise or **bureaucratic model**—involving prosecutor, defendant, defense counsel, and judge in a collaborative effort to impose punishment while avoiding costly and time-consuming trials—is a much more accurate representation of how sentencing works today.[9]

In the last twenty years of the twentieth century, as disparate and so-called lenient sentencing came under widespread attack, the influence of other actors on the sentencing decision attracted more attention. As every social studies fair judge across America knows, from having seen innumerable projects on how a bill becomes law, it is the legislature that makes the laws. Legislatures can—and in the late 1900s often did—affect sentencing decisions by changing penalties and removing certain options, particularly probation or parole, for certain crimes. Legislators also protested **judicial imperialism** in sentencing and then changed the laws to curtail it.

In about half the states, state **appellate courts** can review the sentence imposed by the trial court. They have the power to shorten the sentence if they believe an unduly severe sentence has been imposed. No appellate courts have the authority to increase the sentence given a defendant (except when a judge might give an improper sentence, such as probation to a defendant who is not legally eligible for it). Prosecutors and others criticize adjusting sentences downward only as being a clear-cut instance of due process subverting crime control, but this is how it stands at present.

The **governor** and two authorities that are part of the state's correctional system, the **parole board** and the **pardon board,** influence sentencing. The parole board has limited authority to allow the conditional release of the criminal from prison before his sentence is up. The pardon board can recommend to the governor a pardon to set aside a conviction or a commutation to shorten the sentence of someone in prison. Depending on state laws, the governor may or may not be bound by the pardon board's recommendation. In a few states, the governor also has to approve paroles.

Finally, the prison itself affects sentence length through its use of **good time,** time deducted from a prisoner's sentence for good behavior. This practice, which started as a way of reinforcing positive behavior at Auburn prison in 1817, was universal in American prisons throughout the twentieth century. State prisoners could often shorten their sentences by a third or a half; local jail inmates could get even more time off for good behavior. Good time today is often called **earn time** or **gain time** when it is tied to specific achievement on the prisoner's part, such as participation in vocational training or education programs rather than merely avoiding disciplinary misconduct.

To say that the judge decides the sentence ignores the significant impact of numerous other less visible participants. The judge is really just a stage actor in a much larger production. The producer, the director, the playwright, the supporting cast, and the stage crew are all watching his performance, along with the audience, and each of them may dump blame on him when critics attack the performance.

SENTENCING ISSUES AND REFORMS

The language of sentencing has become much more complex in the past thirty years. Many of the new terms in the sentencing vocabulary are geared to the political rhetoric of crime control—determinate sentencing, three strikes and you're out, habitual offenders, mandatory minimums, truth in sentencing, and public safety. A politician who wanted to sound "tough on crime" would work all these sound bites into his standard anticrime speech while directing unkind remarks at "lenient judges" and expressions of condolence to crime victims.

Before taking this turn, the method of sentencing used in the state and federal courts was called **indeterminate sentencing.** This model allowed for two forms of criminal sentencing. In some states, such as California, a defendant would be sentenced to an open-ended term, such as one to fifteen years for auto theft. In others, such as Louisiana, the judge would select a specific term, say five years, from a much longer range provided in the statute. The criminal would go off to prison to serve his term, but no one really expected him to stay for the full fifteen years in California or five years in Louisiana. His conduct after he got to prison, particularly his participation in rehabilitation programs, would determine how long he would serve. He would be eligible for both parole and good time, so the amount of time he would actually serve would range from a few months to perhaps five years tops in California or twenty to thirty months in Louisiana. The governor's liberal use of executive clemency to commute sentences was important in many states, further reducing actual time served. The only people who served their whole terms would be those who were denied parole or who lost all their good time for violence or escape, for instance.

It had not always been this way. Early penitentiaries used **determinate sentencing.** If you got two years for theft, you served every day of the two years. The advent of good time (adopted not to help inmates but to maintain order) changed this calculation, making it possible for well-behaved prisoners to get out early.

The rise of the reformatory in the late 1800s was equally important. In its practice of reformation (later rehabilitation), the reformatory used parole, determined at first by the institution's warden and later by a parole board—to release "new men and women" back into society. As parole spread gradually into the traditional penitentiaries in the first half of the twentieth century, the determinate sentence evolved into the indeterminate.

As Michael Tonry has written,

> Full-blown indeterminate sentencing existed in every American jurisdiction from the 1930s to the mid-1970s, at which point Maine and California became the first to reject core features such as parole release and the idea that probation ought to be available in nearly every case.
>
> "Individualization" was the fundamental idea behind indeterminate sentencing. At every stage officials needed broad authority to tailor dispositions to the treatment needs of individual offenders and the public safety risks they posed. Probation officers were to assert broad authority over probationers and to help them find jobs and overcome personal problems, and they were also to help judges make the best decisions by preparing comprehensive diagnostic presentence investigation reports. Judges needed broad authority to set appropriate sentences; parole boards needed authority to set release dates and release conditions; and prison managers needed authority to award and deny good time, grant furloughs, and move prisoners between institutions.[10]

When critics of sentencing came upon indeterminate sentencing in the 1970s, they acted as if they had overturned the rock they had been sitting on for years and discovered a deadly snake underneath it. The snake was named discretion. **Sentencing discretion** was essential to both English common law and

European civil law; the trial judge, tying his beliefs to the crime and the criminal, picked from a practically unlimited range of penalties. This led to widely varying punishments. In the old days, one thief might get a fine or a whipping. The next thief might be hanged. The one after him (e.g., a pregnant female) might be discharged without punishment. In modern times, one criminal might get a short prison term, while another might get a very long term for the same crime.

Consider the men in cells A-1 and A-2. In A-1, we find Bill and Bob. Both are young black men who robbed gas stations at gunpoint. This is the first felony conviction for both men. Bill got four years, and Bob got twenty years. Bob wonders why his crime was worth the extra sixteen years. The only distinction he can see is that he robbed a country store in an area that did not have much violent crime, while Bill committed his crime in a big city, where armed robberies are much more common.

In cell A-2 are Mack and Mike, two white men. Mike got twenty years for a convenience store robbery in which he threatened a clerk with a knife. Mike asked Mack one day, "What are you in for?" Mack replied, "Manslaughter." Mike asked, "What happened?" "I was watching a football game in a bar, and a guy changed the channel without asking. We got into a fight, and I beat him to death with a bar stool." "How much time did you get?" "Four years." "Four years," Mike thought, filing away the memory to always ask permission before he changed the channel on their TV. "He got four years for beating a man to death, and I got twenty for merely showing a knife to someone in a hundred-dollar robbery. It don't seem right."

Neither did it seem right to many critics of contemporary sentencing. Their argument was that discretion had become **disparity,** in which widely divergent penalties were applied to criminals convicted of similar crimes. Sometimes disparity resulted from **discrimination** based on race or other variables, but often it could not really be explained. It seemed a part of the sentencing culture that developed over time in a locale and was then applied by judges who differed sharply in particular cases. Some judges were tough on crime or on certain crimes, such as drug offenses, while others were lenient—and it was all perfectly legal as long as the sentence fell within the range provided by law, which was often very broad. For a long time in Louisiana, for instance, armed robbery carried a prison term of from five to ninety-nine years, while manslaughter carried a maximum penalty of twenty-one years in prison.

The way to attack disparity was to limit discretion, mostly judicial discretion but also discretion in the hands of other officials. The most direct way to reduce discretion in sentencing and correctional practice was to change the laws under which discretion was exercised, and this is what state legislatures and the federal Congress did during the 1980s and 1990s. The objective was to return to the old determinate sentence.

One of Beccaria's ideas about punishment was that to be a deterrent the penalty must be certain. In sentencing convicted felons, particularly for nonviolent crimes, probation had become the rule rather than the exception, so imprisonment had become a far from certain penalty. The probation option was one of the first attacked in the post-1970s era of sentencing reform. For several types of crimes—gun crimes, selling drugs, or sex crimes, for instance—probation was removed as an option. Conviction required mandatory prison terms, or what were more often called **mandatory minimum sentences.** These legal changes would send many more men and women to prison who had once benefited from probation.

On the other end of the spectrum—discharge from prison—the federal government and about fifteen states abolished discretionary release from prison on parole. This change could not be retroactive to prisoners held under prior sentences, but it could be made effective as of a certain date: from that date on, no convicted felons would be eligible for parole. Many other states also cut back on parole by eliminating eligibility for specific types of offenders—murderers, sex criminals, or repeat offenders, for instance—or by increasing the portion of the sentence that had to be served before the eligibility date was reached (such as from one-third to one-half the sentence).

Norval Morris had argued against the indeterminate sentence for different reasons in *The Future of Imprisonment* (1972). Convinced that rehabilitation, parole, and the indeterminate sentence were parts of a bogus design that promoted game playing by inmates and corrections officials, Morris proposed to narrow the span of indeterminate sentences and divorce "programming" participation from parole decisions.[11]

California and other states moved in this direction by adopting **presumptive sentencing.** This model, derived from just deserts, establishes a baseline sentence but allows a judge to give a greater or lesser sentence within a specified range based on specified aggravating or mitigating circumstances. The judge's reasons for deviating upward or downward have to be explained in writing and become part of the court record.

In 1993, Washington passed the first new **habitual offender enhancement** provision, commonly known as **three strikes and you're out,** which provided an automatic life term for the third serious felony conviction. All states already had habitual felon enhancement laws, but "three strikes" ignited crime-weary state legislatures to make these statutes more inclusive. Drawing on the baseball analogy, they aimed to selectively incapacitate repeat felons for long prison terms. California's three-strikes law, enacted in 1994, gave a mandatory sentence of twenty-five years to life to any violent felon convicted of two prior felonies of any type, violent or not, and doubled the sentence for the second felony conviction. It is the toughest in the country.[12]

Violent criminals were targeted as well by reduced good-time provisions. In new sentencing provisions that took effect in 1987, Congress mandated that all federal criminals had to serve 85 percent of their prison terms. Parole was abolished, and after good-time release, **supervised release** was added as a replacement. In the Violent Crime Control and Law Enforcement Act of 1994, Congress authorized funds for states to build new prisons and jails if they adopted the 85 percent standard for violent criminals. Twenty-eight states and the District of Columbia had done so by the end of the decade.[13]

The term commonly used for reducing good time is **truth in sentencing,**[14] the implication being that sentencing was previously a lie, that people were fooled into thinking that criminals were going away for a much longer time. Perhaps they were. But, members of the **courtroom work group**—prosecutors, defense attorneys, and judges—knew how good time and parole worked, and they agreed on sentences accordingly. The system worked well for those criminals who did reform (and for those who were slick enough to fake a veneer of reform over their evil hearts), and it established reasonable baselines for prison terms. As these baselines were destroyed by the changes to parole and good time in the 1980s and 1990s, actual time served grew substantially longer, particularly for those imprisoned for crimes of violence.

Another significant method of reducing discretion was the use of **sentencing guidelines** (or sentencing grids). The two most influential models were developed by Minnesota in 1980 and the U.S. Sentencing Commission in 1987. Sentencing guidelines set up a table arranging crimes from most serious to least serious on one side; across the top is a scale that considers the criminal's prior offense history. Where the two lines of crime and criminal history cross, a penalty is designated, usually a narrow range from within which the judge must choose. Sentencing thus becomes mathematical rather than a matter of discretion.

Minnesota's sentencing guidelines reflected a three-part strategy:

1. Creation of a permanent sentencing commission
2. Maintenance by the commission of a set of presumptive guidelines
3. Appellate sentence review to ensure that trial judges departed from guidelines only in appropriate cases[15]

The federal sentencing guidelines, based on a point scale, are highly technical, with points added and taken away depending on the many variables that may be involved in a particular criminal event. A long, very detailed manual, about the same length as the one a mechanic would read in repairing your motor vehicle, guides the federal probation officers who calculate sentences for federal judges.

By the late 1990s, "sentencing reform" had been ongoing for two decades, and the landscape of criminal sentencing in America was considerably altered. A 1996 survey conducted by the National Council on Crime and Delinquency (NCCD) for the Bureau of Justice Assistance reported these summary findings:

1. The predominant sentencing structure for most states is indeterminate (thirty-six states and the District of Columbia).
2. The vast majority of states, including those that have adopted determinate and sentencing guideline models, have retained some form of discretionary parole release and postrelease supervision.
3. All states employ some version of mandatory minimum sentencing laws, which target habitual offenders and the crimes of possessing a deadly weapon, driving under the influence of alcohol, and possessing and/or distributing drugs.
4. All states but Hawaii and Utah allow inmates to earn some form of good-time credits either to reduce a sentence or to advance a parole eligibility date.
5. Although most states have retained indeterminate sentencing structures, these laws are becoming increasingly determinate by greater use of mandatory minimums, truth-in-sentencing provisions, and reducing the amount of good-time credits an inmate can earn while incarcerated. In other words, states are using models other than sentencing guidelines to reduce sentencing disparity.[16]

The study gave this definition of determinate sentencing:

Sentences of incarceration in which the offender is given a fixed term that may be reduced by "good time" or earned time. Usually explicit standards specify the amount of punishment and a set release date with no review by an administrative agency (parole board). Postincarceration supervision may be part of the sentence.[17]

The contrasting definition of indeterminate sentencing was

sentences of incarceration in which an administrative agency, generally a parole board, has the authority to release an offender and determine whether an offender's parole will be revoked for violation of the conditions of release. In one form of indeterminate sentencing, the judge specifies only the maximum sentence length (a fixed term); the associated minimum duration is automatically implied but is not within the judge's discretion. In the more traditional form of indeterminate sentencing, the judge specifies maximum and minimum durations that are set by statute. The sentencing judge has discretion on the minimum and maximum sentences.[18]

The basic difference between the two definitions was parole. If a state retained parole, it was called indeterminate. If it abolished parole, it was called determinate. But even in the states maintaining parole, parole eligibility has been reduced. Some types of offenders (usually repeaters or those convicted of sex crimes or crimes of violence) may be parole ineligible, while others may be parole eligible later in their sentences (e.g., after one-half or later rather than one-third). Parole boards are more conservative, approving fewer prisoners for parole and these often later in their sentences rather than earlier, and parole supervision is tougher, resulting in more revocations and more people being returned to prison for parole violations. So even if the sentencing structure is called indeterminate, based on the continued use of parole, it is a very different form of indeterminacy in comparison to the early 1970s.

The 1996 NCCD survey discussed other sentencing reforms. Nineteen states and the federal government had established sentencing commissions. Seventeen states had adopted either presumptive or voluntary sentencing guidelines. Thirty states had adopted some form of truth in sentencing in which some offenders (usually violent or repeat offenders) were required to serve at least 85 percent of their sentence. Of the states that had abolished parole, the great majority (twelve of fourteen) had some form of postrelease supervision of inmates discharged at the end of their prison terms. It was not called parole, but it looked like parole's fraternal twin. Half the states, following Washington's 1993 lead, had enacted new two- and three-strikes laws (or expanded old laws) dealing with new crimes committed by persons previously convicted of a violent or serious felony offense. These laws usually required imprisonment, lengthened sentences, restricted parole, and reduced good-time credits.[19]

What did sentencing reforms accomplish? These reforms, aimed at eliminating discretion, often did not eradicate discretion at all. They only moved it around in the criminal justice system, particularly into the hands of prosecutors. Mandatory minimum sentences, three-strikes laws, and sentencing guidelines limited judicial discretion but passed it to prosecutors to decide the following:

1. To charge a defendant with a lesser crime (not the "true" crime that fit the facts) to avoid the mandatory minimum prison term
2. To not ask for the statutory enhancement for a repeat offender

Both were common practices in the past and continue to be used today to avoid what appear to be mandated penalties. "Charge" bargaining simply takes the place of "sentence" bargaining in plea negotiations. States have had habitual offender statutes on the books for ages but have applied them infrequently, using them more as a threat to induce guilty pleas. As judges lose discretion, prosecutors gain it, further shifting the balance of power in the legal system. Judges generally do not like the direction of the recent sentencing reforms that strip them of the discretion they have traditionally enjoyed. Prosecutors, who always knew they were running the show anyway, smile grimly as they gain even more power.

OTHER SENTENCING REFORMS

Before the movement to take away judicial discretion began, numerous other reforms had been offered to eliminate disparity by making the decision-making process more systematic or standardized. The **Model Penal Code** proposed by the American Law Institute in 1962 put forth a uniform set of criminal laws and penalties for the states to consider. Suggesting that imprisonment should be used as a last resort, it did not get a lot of attention in the post-1970 crime control era.

Sentencing institutes and sentencing councils for judges were also proposed as ways to reduce disparity. New judges, who in America usually come to office without prior training, were supposed to be sent off to **sentencing institutes** to learn how to sentence properly; this training was intended to at least expose these officials to the principles of proportionality and fairness. The National College of Trial Court Judges and other organizations do provide such training today, but it is not mandatory.

Sentencing councils were groups of judges who would review cases coming up for sentencing and share their views. Peer influence was supposed to result in sentences that would tend toward a norm rather than the extremes. Councils have been used in an advisory capacity but are no longer highly thought of today. Indeed, "discretion" in any form remains a bad word in the politics of sentencing today, except for the relatively hidden and totally unaccountable discretion of prosecutors. The crime is far more important than the criminal.

THE IMPACT OF SENTENCING ON CORRECTIONS

The corrections system has been profoundly affected by sentencing changes of the past thirty years. The obvious indicator is population growth. In 1972, America had 100,000 people in jail and 200,000 in prison. By 2002, the numbers had risen to 600,000 and 1,300,000. Our crime rate was not six times higher in 2002 than it was in 1972 (in fact, the best estimates suggest it was lower, particularly for violent crimes). The big change behind the incarceration explosion was the ideology of crime control, not crime itself.

California alone held 267,000 juveniles and adults in local, state, and federal correctional institutions in 2001, almost as many people as had been in confinement in the entire nation thirty years earlier. The majority of these, 160,000, were men and women confined in state prisons. Over a third of these inmates were sentenced under second- and third-strike provisions as repeat offenders. They will be a part of California's prison population for a very long time to come.[20]

Nationwide, we have far more people behind bars and under supervision in the community than we have ever had before. This condition is the result of several related changes in sentencing practices:

1. More convicted felons going directly to prison
2. Sharp increases in the imprisonment of drug criminals after 1980
3. Longer prison terms, particularly for violent criminals, habitual criminals, and drug traffickers
4. Criminals serving more of their terms, as parole and good time were cut back
5. More formal control of misdemeanants and felons under community supervision, imposing more conditions on them, and locking them up more often if they fail to comply

Some "time-served" statistics are deceptive because they combine "old" prisoners sentenced under previous laws and "new" prisoners sentenced under tougher current statutes. Prisoners discharged in recent years (termed "exit cohorts") are often people who were sentenced under older, milder laws. Punishment carries forward into the future. American prisoners of the early twenty-first century are serving the longest terms by far in the history of prison. As punishment for drug criminals has abated in recent years, punishment of violent criminals has become more severe.

Perhaps the best example of the overall trend toward greater punitiveness is the growth of **natural life sentences** in state and federal prisons—a punishment rarely used anywhere else in the world. Before the 1970s, there was no such thing as a true life sentence in American prisons. Only one state, Kentucky, had a natural life sentence on the books, and it was used very sparingly. All other life sentences were parole eligible, except for Louisiana's, where lifers were routinely pardoned by the governor and set free after ten and a half years in prison. "Parole eligible" did not mean that all lifers would be released one day; it meant they were *eligible* for release consideration. Some of them would stay in prison for life and die there, either because their crimes were so horrible or because they were "screw-ups" who kept making trouble in prison (or sometimes because they were simply lost in the system and forgotten).

In the 1970s, this began to change. Several states, led by Louisiana and Pennsylvania, enacted natural life sentences for serious crimes, Louisiana using it for first- and second-degree murder, aggravated rape, aggravated kidnapping, distribution of narcotics, and third-offense habitual offenders. After 1972, a life sentence in Louisiana suddenly meant imprisonment for the rest of the prisoner's natural life.[21]

The result has been the transformation of the Louisiana State Penitentiary into the model of a new prison unlike any other in the world—a "lifer's prison." Almost 3,400 of its 5,100 inmates are serving natural life sentences, and another 1,350 are serving "virtual" or practical life sentences, no-parole terms so long that the inmates will not live to complete them. Warden Burl

Cain has been frequently quoted, when asked what is distinctive about his prisoner population, "Eighty-five percent of them will die here."[22] No other prison in American history has had such a prognosis for its prisoner population.

This trend has spread to other states. The *2001 Corrections Yearbook* counted 117,000 lifers in American prisons on January 1, 2001, about 9 percent of the total prison population. Of these, 31,000 (or 26 percent) were natural lifers. Georgia had almost 6,000, Pennsylvania and Louisiana 3,600 each.[23] Texas, claiming no natural life sentence, requires recent lifers to serve forty years before reaching parole eligibility. This would take most criminals into old age, which is probably the point.

Is it necessary or a good idea to keep so many criminals locked up until they die, or has the attempt to remedy the disparities caused by discretion gone to the other extreme—a form of Draconian despotism in which redemption and individual differences do not matter? Is the crime the only thing that matters, even in some instances a crime in which no one was killed or injured and happened so long ago that no one even remembers what it was about? Only the label and the person serving the life sentence live on.

What is next for criminal sentencing? Many practitioners and corrections scholars would like to see a model of criminal sentencing that uses shorter sentences and more community-based alternatives. These goals may be unreachable in the short term. To whatever degree sentencing disparity has been reduced over the past three decades, the result has been the destruction of individualized sentencing. In the course of eliminating "leniency" by imposing sentences that are equally severe, we have driven our jail and prison populations to all-time highs. Many citizens and most politicians evidently want this trend to continue, even if the reasons for the policies are irrational or erroneous.

A recent report by The Sentencing Project found a curious relationship between public opinion, politics, and sentencing policy:

1. The public consistently misjudges trends in crime, thinking that crime is rising when it is in decline.
2. The public tends to underestimate the severity of sentencing, assuming that criminals are serving much shorter terms than they really are.
3. Public attitudes are strongly influenced by these mistaken beliefs, especially the beliefs that most criminals escape fair punishment and get out of prison much earlier than they do.
4. Political initiatives (such as the War on Crime) can have profound impact on public opinion unrelated to the reality of crime trends.
5. Politicians misjudge public attitudes, particularly those that would support moderation in criminal punishments.[24]

The result of this combination of ignorance, misjudgment, and political hoopla is a sentencing policy that is narrow-minded, excessive, and exorbitantly expensive in its economic and social impact on our nation and its people. There are signs in some states that sentencing policies may be changing—such as Vermont's use of reparative probation as a form of restorative justice and California's decision to push treatment rather than imprisonment for drug offenders—but overall more states have increasing than decreasing prison numbers.

KEY TERMS

punishment	due process model	proportionality	sentencing discretion
retribution	justice model	gatekeeper function	disparity
retaliation	just deserts model	trial judge	discrimination
lex talionis	neoclassical model	probation officer	mandatory minimum sentences
utilitarianism	selective incapacitation	presentence investigation report	presumptive sentencing
deterrence	logical consequences	prosecutor	habitual offender enhancement
incapacitation	restorative justice	bureaucratic model	three strikes and you're out
reformation	balanced and restorative justice model	judicial imperialism	supervised release
rehabilitation	victims' rights movement	appellate courts	truth in sentencing
ideology	model muddle	governor	courtroom work group
conservative ideology	plea bargaining	parole board	sentencing guidelines
liberal ideology	capital crime	pardon board	Model Penal Code
radical ideology	*Furman v. Georgia*	good time	sentencing institutes
model	*Gregg v. Georgia*	earn time	sentencing councils
nonsystem	bifurcated trial	gain time	natural life sentences
rehabilitation model	aggravating circumstances	indeterminate sentencing	
reintegration model	mitigating circumstances	determinate sentencing	
crime control model			

NOTES

1. Joycelyn M. Pollock, "The Philosophy of Punishment," in *Prisons: Today and Tomorrow* (Gaithersburg, Md.: Aspen Publishers, 1997), p. 9.

2. Frank Schmalleger, *Criminal Justice Today*, 6th ed. (Upper Saddle River, N.J.: Prentice Hall, 2001), p. 23.

3. Pollock, "The Philosophy of Punishment," pp. 21–22.

4. Matthew R. Durose, David J. Levin, and Patrick A. Langan, "Felony Sentences in State Courts, 1998," U.S. Department of Justice, Bureau of Justice Statistics Special Report, October 2001.

5. "The Death Penalty: An International Perspective," Death Penalty Information Center, *www.deathpenaltyinfo.org.*

6. Burk Foster, "How the Death Penalty Really Works: Selecting Death Penalty Offenders in America," in *Death Watch* (Upper Saddle River, N.J.: Prentice Hall, 2001), pp. 16–21.

7. "Commuting Sentences: The Controversy," *Corrections Forum*, January/February 2003, p. 26.

8. Burk Foster, "Why Death Is Different," in *Death Watch*, p. 11.

9. David W. Neubauer, *America's Courts and the Criminal Justice System*, 7th ed. (Belmont, Calif.: Wadsworth/Thomson Learning, 2002), p. 330.

10. Michael Tonry, "Reconsidering Indeterminate and Structured Sentencing," Papers from the Executive Sessions on Sentencing and Corrections, National Institute of Justice, September 1999, p. 3.

11. Norval Morris, *The Future of Imprisonment* (Chicago: University of Chicago Press, 1974).

12. James Austin, John Clark, Patricia Hardyman, and D. Alan Henry, "The Impact of Three Strikes and You're Out," *Punishment and Society* 1, no. 2: p. 131–62.

13. Paula M. Ditton and Doris James Wilson, "Truth in Sentencing in State Prisons," U.S. Department of Justice, Bureau of Justice Statistics Special Report, January 1999, p. 2.

14. Ibid.

15. Tonry, "Reconsidering Indeterminate and Structured Sentencing," p. 7.

16. National Council on Crime and Delinquency, "1996 National Survey of State Sentencing Struc-

tures," U.S. Department of Justice, Bureau of Justice Assistance, p. *xi.*

17. Ibid., p. 1.

18. Ibid., p. 2.

19. Ibid., pp. 16–17.

20. Criminal Justice Consortium, "Who Is Locked Up in California?," *www.idiom.com/ncjc/facts2001.html.*

21. Burk Foster, "What Is the Meaning of Life?," in Burk Foster, Wilbert Rideau, and Douglas Dennis, *The Wall Is Strong: Corrections in Lousiana,* 3rd ed. (Lafayette: Center for Louisiana Studies, 1995), pp. 80–89.

22. See "The Big House: Angola," The History Channel, 2000.

23. Camille Graham Camp and George M. Camp, *The 2001 Corrections Yearbook* (Middletown, Conn.: Criminal Justice Institute, 2002), p. 67.

24. "Crime, Punishment and Public Opinion: A Summary of Recent Studies and Their Implications for Sentencing Policy," The Sentencing Project, *www.sentencingproject.org.*

FURTHER READING

Currie, Elliott. *Crime and Punishment in America.* New York: Owl Books, 1998.

Durham, Alexis. *Crisis and Reform: Current Issues in American Punishment.* Boston: Little, Brown, 1994.

Mauer, Marc. *The Race to Incarcerate.* New York: Free Press, 1999.

Prejean, Sister Helen. *Dead Man Walking: An Eyewitness Account of the Death Penalty in the United States.* New York: Random House, 1993.

Tonry, Michael H., and Kathleen Hatlestad. *Sentencing Reform in Overcrowded Times: A Comparative Perspective.* New York: Oxford University Press, 1997.

WEB AND VIDEO RESOURCES

The most informative sentencing Website is *www.sentencingproject.org.*

Sister Helen Prejean's Website is *www.prejean.org.*

The American Civil Liberties Union's Death Penalty page is *www.aclu.org/DeathPenalty.*

The Clark County, Indiana, prosecuting attorney has a clearinghouse Website with thousands of links to all parts of criminal justice; the address is *www.clarkprosecutor.org/html/links/links.htm.*

COMMENTARY

4 Sentencing: Individualized and Standardized Justice

by Clifford K. Dorne and Donald J. Bachand

The ideal purpose of sentencing is to produce a just or fair case outcome for a convicted offender. This involves imposing some type of punishment upon the offender and at times also includes providing some service (e.g., rehabilitation) to the offender. Questions of justice or fairness in sentencing often refer to the extent to which the sentence's severity is proportionate to the seriousness of the offense within the bounds of constitutional law (due process and prohibition against cruel and unusual punishment).

Such questions may also be relevant to the degree that punishments are equitable across similar cases and are related to the issue of sentencing disparity. Can a sentencing system be just or fair if it results in case outcomes that are individualized, in which offenders convicted of similar crimes with similar prior records are sentenced differently? Should sentencing judges be given wide latitude in making sentencing decisions to the point of invoking their personal values and individual understanding of the case? Or is it more just or fair if a sentencing system treats offenders convicted of similar crimes with similar prior records as similarly as possible—a standardized approach? Such models are designed to reduce sentencing disparity and at least on the surface, may appear to increase justice and fairness when compared to the individualized approach, but these questions actually center on the issue of sentencing discretion.

In his classic treatise *Discretionary Justice*, law professor Kenneth C. Davis explained that an official has discretion "whenever the effective limits on his power leave him [or her] free to make a choice among possible courses of action or inaction." Davis' thesis was that legal discretion must be formally acknowledged, confined or limited, structured with training and education (the study of past case examples, etc.), and checked by a higher authority after the fact. Historically, American judges have enjoyed substantial sentencing discretion. Indeed, thirty years ago, Federal Judge Marvin Frankel observed in his famous book titled *Criminal Sentences: Law Without Order* that "the almost wholly unchecked and sweeping powers we give to judges in the fashioning of sentences are terrifying and intolerable in a society that professes devotion to the rule of law."

Back in 1973, Judge Frankel recommended the establishment of administrative sentencing agencies. Many states and the federal system developed sentencing commissions based on this idea and these tribunals put forth a variety of determinate sentencing models with the goal of standardizing justice primarily based on the idea of retribution or just deserts. Guideline sentencing and, in some states, presumptive sentencing, served to confine or limit judicial sentencing discretion. The guidelines tend to operate on a two dimensional matrix: instant offense and offender's prior record. Scores on these dimensions correspond to a type of sentence: probation or incarceration with indications of sentence length or ranges of length. In addition, there were attempts to standardize justice within corrections. This meant abolishing good time and parole, which a few jurisdictions did. Other jurisdictions severely restricted such discretion by tightening criteria for the issuance of good time credits and/or by implementing parole release guidelines.

Should we continue to move in the direction of standardization in criminal sentencing or revert back to the individualization that indeterminate sentencing models allowed? Perhaps this question should not be viewed as dichotomous but instead be perceived as a continuum. Some states now have voluntary sentencing guidelines, allowing judges to stray from the sentencing grid when they determine that individual variables need to be taken into account. The legislature enacts the guidelines and then the sentencing judge may follow them at his or her discretion. In many guideline sentencing states, if the judge diverges from the matrix or grid, the reasons must be written into the court record and the sentence is usually subject to appeal; the prosecutor would appeal if the judge opts for leniency and the defense may appeal if the judge imposes a sentence that is harsher than what is recommended in the guidelines. This arrangement represents a compromise between the standardization provided by guidelines and individual judicial discretion.

As Michael Tonry contends in his book *Sentencing Matters*, however, the two-dimensional guidelines so commonly linked to determinate or just deserts sentencing models may have led to needless harshness and rigidity. He calls for standard upper and lower limits on sentences within a jurisdiction, thereby permitting judges to retain enough discretion to individualize justice. Perhaps this is the best (most just?) way to address this issue: individualization of justice exercised within more general standardized parameters. This should be combined with training programs for judges focusing on criminal sentencing, effective sentencing commissions charged with continually reviewing sentencing structures, and active judicial involvement in the development of sentencing policies.

COMMENTARY

5   Would Jesus Pull the Switch?

by Sister Helen Prejean, S.J.M.

I was scared out of my mind. I went into the women's room because it was the only private place in the death house, and I put my head against the tile wall and grabbed the crucifix around my neck. I said, "Oh, Jesus God, help me. Don't let him fall apart. If he falls apart, I fall apart."

I had never watched anybody be killed in front of my eyes. I was supposed to be Patrick Sonnier's spiritual advisor. I was in over my head.

All I had agreed to in the beginning was to be a pen pal to this man on Louisiana's death row. Sure, I said, I could write letters. But the man was all alone, he had no one to visit him. It was like a current in a river, and I got sucked in. The next thing I knew I was saying, "OK, sure, I'll come visit you."

He had suggested that on the prison application form for visitors I fill in "spiritual advisor," and I said, "Sure." He was Catholic, and I'm a Catholic nun, so I didn't think much about it; it seemed right. But I had no idea that at the end, on the evening of the execution, everybody has to leave the death house at 5:45 p.m., everybody but the spiritual advisor. The spiritual advisor stays to the end and witnesses the execution.

People ask me all the time, "What are you, a nun, doing getting involved with these murderers?" You know how people have these stereotypical ideas about nuns: nuns teach; nuns nurse the sick. I tell people to go back to the gospel. Look at who Jesus hung out with: lepers, prostitutes, thieves—the throwaways of his day. If we call ourselves Jesus' disciples, we too have to keep ministering to the marginated, the throwaways, the lepers of today. And there are no more marginated, thrown-away, and leprous people in our society than death-row inmates.

There's a lot of what I call "biblical quarterbacking" going on in death-penalty debates: people toss in quotes from the Bible to back up what they've already decided anyway. People want to not only practice vengeance but also have God agree with them. The same thing happened in this country in the slavery debates and in the debates over women's suffrage.

Religion is tricky business. Quote that Bible. God said torture. God said kill. God said get even. Even the Pauline injunction "Vengeance is mine, says the Lord, I will repay" (Rom. 12:19) can be interpreted as a command and a promise—the command to restrain individual impulses toward revenge in exchange for the assurance that God will be only too pleased to handle the grievance in spades. That God wants to "get even" like the rest of us does not seem to be in question. One intractable problem, however, is that divine vengeance (barring natural disasters, so-called acts of God) can only be interpreted and exacted by human beings, very human beings. I can't accept that.

Jesus Christ, whose way of life I try to follow, refused to meet hate with hate and violence with violence. I pray for the strength to be like him. I cannot believe in a God who metes out hurt for hurt, pain for pain, torture for torture. Nor do I believe that God invests human representatives with such power to torture and kill. The paths of history are stained with the blood of those who have fallen victim to "God's Avengers." Kings, popes, military generals, and heads of state have killed, claiming God's authority and God's blessing. I do not believe in such a God.

But here's the real reason why I got involved with death-row inmates: I got involved with poor people. It took me a while to wake up to the call of the social gospel of Jesus. For years and years when I came to the passages where Jesus identified with poor and marginated people I did some fast-footed mental editing of the scriptures: poor meant "spiritually poor." When I read in Matthew 25, "I was hungry and you gave me to eat," I would say, "Oh, there's a lot of ways of being hungry." "I was in prison, and you came to visit me,"—Oh, there's a lot of ways we live in prison, you know."

Other members of my religious community woke up before I did, and we had fierce debates on what our mission should be. In 1980, when my religious community, the Sisters of St. Joseph of Medaille, made a commitment to "stand on the side of the poor," I assented, but only reluctantly. I resisted this recasting of the faith of my childhood, where what had counted was a personal relationship with God, inner peace, kindness to others, and heaven when this life was done. I didn't want to struggle with politics and economics. We were nuns, after all, not social workers.

But later that year I finally got it. I began to realize that my spiritual life had been too ethereal, too disconnected. To follow Jesus and to be close to Jesus meant that I needed to seek out the company of poor and struggling people.

So in June 1981 I drove a little brown truck into St. Thomas, a black, inner-city housing project in New Orleans, and began to live there with four other sisters. Growing up a Southern white girl right on the cusp of the upper class, I had only known black people as my servants. Now it was my turn to serve them.

It didn't take long to see that for poor people, especially poor black people, there was a greased track to prison and death row. As one Mama in St. Thomas put it, "Our boys leave here in a police car or a hearse."

It didn't take long to see how racism worked. When people were killed in St. Thomas and you looked for an account of their deaths in the newspaper, you'd find it buried on some back page as a three-line item. When other people were killed, it was front-page news.

Drug activity took place in the open, but when the sisters went to the mayor's office to complain, the officials would just shrug their shoulders and say,

"Well, you know, Sister, every city has a problem with drugs. At least we know where they are."

I began to understand that some life is valued and some life is not. One day a friend of mine from the Prison Coalition Office casually asked me if I'd be a pen pal to someone on death row in Louisiana. I said, "Sure." But I had no idea that this answer would be my passport to a strange and bizarre country. God is a mystery, but one of the definite characteristics of God is that God is sneaky.

When I began visiting Patrick Sonnier in 1982, I couldn't have been more naive about prisons. I wrote Patrick about life at Hope House in St. Thomas, and he told me about life in a 6-by-8-foot cell, where he and 44 other men were confined 23 hours a day. He said how glad he was when summer was over because there was no air in the cells. He'd sometimes wet the sheet from his bunk and put it on the cement floor to try to cool off; or he'd clean out his toilet bowl and stand in it and use a small plastic container to get water from his lavatory and pour it over his body. Patrick was on death row four years before they killed him.

I made a bad mistake. When I found out about Patrick Sonnier's crime—that he had killed two teenage kids—I didn't go to see the victims' families. I stayed away because I wasn't sure how to deal with such raw, unadulterated pain. I was a coward. I only met them at Patrick's pardon board hearing. They were there to demand Patrick's execution. I was there to ask the board to show him mercy. It was not a good time to meet.

Here were two sets of parents whose children had been ripped from them. I felt terrible. I was powerless to assuage their grief. It would take me a long time to learn how to help victims' families, a long time before I would sit at their support-group meetings and hear their unspeakable stories of loss and grief and rage and guilt.

I don't see capital punishment as a peripheral issue about some criminals at the edge of society that people want to execute. I see the death penalty connected to the three deepest wounds of our society: racism, poverty, and violence. The rhetoric says that the death penalty will be reserved only for the most heinous crimes, but when you look at how it is applied, you see that in fact there is a great selectivity in the process. When the victim of a violent crime has some kind of status, there is a public outrage, and especially when the victim has been murdered, death—the ultimate punishment—is sought.

But when people of color are killed in the inner city, when homeless people are killed, when the "nobodies" are killed, district attorneys do not seek to avenge their deaths. Black, Hispanic, or poor families who have a loved one murdered not only don't expect the district attorney's office to pursue the death penalty—which, of course, is both costly and time-consuming—but are surprised when the case is prosecuted at all.

In Louisiana, murder victims' families are allowed to sit in the front row in the execution chamber to watch the murderer die. Some families. Not all. Almost never African American families.

Ask Virginia Smith's African American family. She was 14 when three white youths took her into the woods, raped her, and stabbed her to death. None of them got the death penalty. Their fathers knew the district attorney, and they had all-white juries.

In regard to this first and deepest of America's wounds, racism, we'd have to change the whole soil of this country for the criminal-justice system not to be administered in a racially biased manner. The second wound is poverty. Who pays the ultimate penalty for crimes? The poor. Who gets the death penalty? The poor. After all the rhetoric that goes on in legislative assemblies, in the end, when the net is cast out, it is the poor who are selected to die in this country. And why do poor people get the death penalty? It has everything to do with the kind of defense they get.

When I agreed to write to Patrick Sonnier, I didn't know much about him except that if he was on death row in Louisiana he had to be poor. And that holds true for virtually all of the more than 3,000 people who now inhabit death-row cells in our country.

Money gets you good defense. That's why you'll never see an O. J. Simpson on death row. As the saying goes: "Capital punishment means them without the capital get the punishment."

I had to learn all this myself. My father was a lawyer. I used to think, "Well, they may not get perfect defense, but at least they get adequate defense." I tell you it is so shocking to find out what kind of defense people on death row actually have had.

Finally, the third wound is our penchant for trying to solve our problems with violence. When you witness an execution and watch the toll this process also takes on some of those who are charged with the actual execution—the 12 guards on the strap-down team and the warden—you recognize that part of the moral dilemma of the death penalty is also: who deserves to kill this man?

Patrick had tried to protect me from watching him die. He told me he'd be OK. I didn't have to come with him into the execution chamber. "The electric chair is not a pretty sight, it could scare you," he told me, trying to be brave.

But I said, "No, no, Pat, if they kill you, I'll be there." Then I remembered how the women were there at the foot of Jesus' cross, and I said to him, "You look at my face. Look at me, and I will be the face of Christ for you." I couldn't bear it that he would die alone. I said, "Don't you worry. God will help me."

And there in the women's room, just a few hours before the execution, my only place of privacy in that place of death, God and I met, and the strength was there, and it was like a circle of light around me. If I tried to think ahead to what would happen at midnight I came unraveled, but there in the present I could hold together and be strong. And Patrick was strong and kept asking me, "Sister Helen, are you all right?"

Being in that death house was one of the most bizarre, confusing experiences I have ever had. It wasn't like visiting somebody dying in a hospital, where you can see the person getting weaker and fading. Patrick was so fully alive, talking and responding to me and writing letters to people and eating.

I'd look around at the polished tile floors—everything so neat—all the officials following a protocol, the secretary typing up forms for the witnesses to sign afterwards, the coffee pot percolating, and I kept feeling that I was in a hospital and the final act would be to save this man's life.

It felt strange and confusing because everyone was so polite. They kept asking Patrick if he needed anything. The chef came by to ask him if he liked his last meal—the steak (medium rare), the potato salad, the apple pie for dessert.

When the warden with the strap-down team came for him, I walked with him. God heard his prayer, "Please, God, hold up my legs." It was the last piece of dignity he could muster. He wanted to walk. I saw this dignity in him, and I have seen it in the three men I have accompanied to their deaths. I wonder how I would hold up if I were walking across a floor to a room where people were waiting to kill me.

The essential torture of the death penalty is not finally the physical method of death: bullet or rope or gas or electrical current or injected drugs. The torture happens when conscious human beings are condemned to death and begin to anticipate that death and die a thousand times before they die. They are brought close to death, maybe four hours away, and the phone rings in the death house, and they hear they have received a stay of execution. Then they return to their cells and begin the waiting all over again.

The U.N. Universal Declaration on Human Rights states that there are two essential human rights that every human being has: the right not to be tortured and the right not to be killed. I wish Pope John Paul II in his encyclical "The Gospel of Life" had been as firm and unconditional as the U.N.

The pope still upholds the right of governments to kill criminals, even though he restricts it to cases of "absolute necessity" and says that because of im-

provements in modern penal systems such cases are "very rare, if not practically nonexistent." Likewise, the U.S. Catholic bishops in their 1980 "Statement on Capital Punishment," while strongly condemning the death penalty for the unfair and discriminatory manner in which it is imposed, its continuance of the "cycle of violence," and its fundamental disregard for human dignity, also affirm in principle the right of the state to kill.

In this last decade of the 20th century, U.S. government officials kill citizens with dispatch with scarcely a murmur of resistance from the Christian citizenry. In fact, surveys of public opinion show that those who profess Christianity tend to favor capital punishment slightly more than the overall population—Catholics more than Protestants.

True, in recent years leadership bodies of most Christian denominations have issued formal statements denouncing the death penalty, but generally that opposition has yet to be translated into aggressive pastoral initiatives to educate clergy and membership on capital punishment. I do not want to pass judgment on church leaders, but I invite them to work harder to do the right thing.

The religious community has a crucial role in educating the public about the fact that government killings are too costly for us, not only financially, but—more important—morally. Allowing our government to kill citizens compromises the deepest moral values upon which this country was conceived: the inviolable dignity of human persons.

I have no doubt that we will one day abolish the death penalty in America. One day all the death instruments in this country—electric chairs, gas chambers, and lethal-injection needles—will be housed behind velvet ropes in museums.

The death penalty is firmly in place, but people are beginning to ask, "If this is supposed to be the solution, how come we're not feeling any better? How come none of us feels safer?" People are beginning to realize that they have been duped and that the death penalty has not so much to do with crime as it has to do with politics.

The bottoming out that has to happen is kind of like in the 12-step program: the first step is to admit that as a society we have a problem and need help. People are capable of change, and the beauty and the power of the gospel is that when people hear it, they will respond to it.

When people support executions, it is not out of malice or ill will or hardness of heart or meanness of spirit. It is, quite simply, that they don't know the truth of what is going on. And that is not by accident. The secrecy surrounding executions makes it possible for executions to continue. I am convinced that if executions were made public, the torture and violence would be unmasked and we would be shamed into abolishing executions.

When you accompany someone to the execution, as I have done three times as a spiritual advisor, everything becomes very crystallized, distilled, and stripped to the essentials. You are in this building in the middle of the night, and all these people are organized to kill this man. And the gospel comes to you as it never has before: Are you for compassion, or are you for violence? Are you for mercy, or are you for vengeance? Are you for love, or are you for hate? Are you for life, or are you for death?

And the words of Jesus from the gospel kept coming to me that night: "And the last will be first" and "This too is my beloved son, hear him." On death row I grasped with such solidity and fire the grace of God in all human beings, the dignity in all human beings. I am not saying that Patrick Sonnier was a hero. I do not want to glorify him. He did the most terrible crime of all. He killed. But he was a human being, and he had a transcendence, a dignity. He—like each of us—was more than the worst thing he had done in his life. And I have one consolation: he died well. I hope I die half as well.

That night I walked with him, prayed with him through Isaiah 43, "I have called you by your name, you are mine." I played for him the tape "Be Not Afraid," which we had also played at the communion service we had before he died. In his last words he expressed his sorrow to the victims' family. But then he said to the warden and to the unseen executioner behind the plywood panel, "but killing me is wrong, too."

At the end I was amazed at how ordinary the last moments were. He walked to the dark oak chair and sat in it. As guards were strapping his legs and arms and trunk he found my face and told me that he loved me. His last words of life were words of love and thankfulness. I took them in like a lightning rod. I kept thinking of the execution of Jesus. I said to myself, "My God, how many times have I looked at that crucifix? How many times have we heard that story? How many times have we heard that Mary was there?"

I was watching a person being killed with an electrical current, in a few seconds. I couldn't imagine what it must have been for Jesus to be executed, hanging there on the cross, dying slowly. It gave me an entirely new awareness of what it means to have an executed criminal as a savior. What a scandal that must have been!

I held on to the Bible Pat had given me. I closed my eyes because I knew Pat couldn't see me any more. I heard them clank the switch. They pulled it three times. Then I looked up. One hand had grasped the chair. The fingers on the other were kind of curled. The doctor went in. They removed the mask. He was dead. And I began to pray to him.

I came out of the execution chamber that night having watched a man die in front of my eyes, whose last words were words of love. And when I turned to his Bible, thumbworn and underlined, I found that in the front of his Bible, where births, marriages, and deaths are recorded, he had written in his own handwriting the date of his own death.

It reminded me of Jesus' words: "You don't know the day and the hour." But when you die at the hands of the state of Louisiana, you do know the day and the hour very well.

Out of this experience has come a fire that has galvanized me and that cannot die in me. In the Catholic Church, when we receive sacraments, we say that an indelible mark is left on our souls. Being present at Pat's death has left an indelible mark on my soul. I think of it as a kind of second baptism in my life, for it forever committed me to pursuing the gospel as it relates to poor people and the quest for justice.

And it is this that has made me speak out about the death penalty ever since, and I will continue to do so to my dying day. I cannot not tell this story and proclaim the gospel message as I came to understand it that night. And it was this experience that led me to write the book *Dead Man Walking*. How the book got published, the movie got produced, and how both have been received—to me it's nothing short of a rip-roaring, Old-Testament, Yahweh-split-the-Red-Sea miracle.

I made a promise to Patrick before he died: "Patrick, I will tell your story across this land." I didn't know what I was saying. "Perhaps then your death can be redemptive for other people."

5   JAILS

Jail: An unbelievably filthy institution in which are confined men and women serving sentence for misdemeanors and crimes, and men and women not under sentence who are simply awaiting trial. With few exceptions, having no segregation of the unconvicted from the convicted, the well from the diseased, the youngest and most impressionable from the most degraded and hardened. Usually swarming with bedbugs, roaches, lice, and other vermin; has an odor of disinfectant and filth which is appalling; supports in complete idleness countless thousands of able bodied men and women, and generally affords ample time and opportunity to assure inmates a complete course in every kind of viciousness and crime. A melting pot in which the worst elements of the raw material in the criminal world are brought forth blended and turned out in absolute perfection.

— Joseph F. Fishman, *Crucibles of Crime*, 1923

INTRODUCTION

The jail is the entry point into corrections, the only correctional facility most criminals ever see. Jails hold an eclectic mix of adults (and a few juveniles) at all stages of the criminal justice process. After reading the material in this chapter, you should be familiar with:

1. The jail's place in corrections.
2. The jail's historical role.
3. The American jail system today.
4. The legal status of jail inmates.
5. A profile of jail inmates.
6. Jail design and architecture.
7. Jail problems.
8. Contrasts between urban and rural jails.
9. Proposals to improve the jail.

WHERE IS THE JAIL?

The telephone rings in the middle of the night. When you answer, your best friend says, "Hey, it's me. I was at that party last night, you know. I guess I had too much to drink. I was driving home and hit a parked car. The cops arrested me for DWI. I'm in jail. Can you come get me out in the morning? My bond is $1,000. They won't let me out for six hours." You can't help but notice the plaintive cry in your friend's voice. He is not a criminal, after all, and what he is really saying is, "Help, don't leave me here." You assure him that you won't forget, promising to go by the ATM early and withdraw the cash. You tell him to be cool, avoid the shower room, and get some rest and that you'll see him at eight o'clock. You hang up the phone and lie back in bed thinking, "Where is the jail?"

Scenes like this happen millions of time a year as freshly arrested persons call friends and family to come get them out of jail. Over 10 million people are booked into jails each year in America. Most of them stay there for twenty-four hours or less. Many wait in a holding cell until someone comes to get them or until a judge orders their release. They never get the "real experience" of being a long-term jail inmate, which in many respects (and in many jail facilities) may be a worse experience than being a prison inmate.

Most Americans have never been inside a prison, but practically all would know where to find the nearest jail. Most jails are downtown near the courts that do the processing of criminals arrested for traffic, misdemeanor, and felony offenses. Many early twentieth-century jails were incorporated into the courthouse building itself; this made moving prisoners back and forth to court a simple matter of going from one floor to another within the same building. As jail populations have increased over the past thirty years, new jails are more likely to be constructed as separate, free-standing buildings—sometimes built on open space away from downtown, sometimes built as multistory complexes near the court building. In larger urban areas, the jail is often several separate facilities decentralized by geography and clientele.

Although in a few states' jails are operated by state governments, jails in America are typically locally operated by county or city governments. American jails today are defined by extremes—from very small to huge, from primitive to ultramodern, from one short tier of cells to multistory high-rises, from isolated rural settings to downtown complexes, from no services at all to services equal to the best provided in state prisons. Jails run the gamut.

Jail inmates are a diverse group—felons, misdemeanants, transients and the mentally ill, drunks, drug addicts, and DWI offenders, juveniles in many jails, probation and parole violators under detainer, federal and state prisoners in many jails, material witnesses—anyone who can be locked up can be found in a jail. Most of the pretrial offenders who make up the largest single portion of the jail population get released on bail or other forms of pretrial release after spending a few hours to a few days in jail. But many offenders charged with felony offenses are kept in jail for months or years because they cannot afford to meet bail requirements. For them the presumption of innocence really does not apply; they simply start serving their sentences before conviction, often pleading guilty in bargains that count their jail time and turn them loose on probation.

Most people booked into jail are like your friend—relatively minor traffic and misdemeanor offenders who fall into that space between "too serious to write a ticket" and "not serious enough to do time." For them, the jail is just a brief encounter, not a life-changing experience. They will be out in a few hours, thankful to no longer be among the 2 million Americans behind bars.

THE JAIL IN HISTORY

The jail is the oldest correctional facility, though some would argue vehemently against the idea that the jail has ever had much of a correctional purpose. The jail's historical role was to hold prisoners awaiting trial or punishment. Today we call this role **detention,** the part of corrections that takes place before conviction and the imposition of sentence. The English institution that provided this function was called a **gaol.** The American pronunciation is the same, but the spelling is **jail.**

English jails trace their origins to legal reforms in the ninth-century reign of King Alfred the Great of England. But the real history of the English jail began with the provisions of the Assize of Clarendon of 1166. King Henry II required all sheriffs in English counties to construct jails to hold prisoners awaiting trial. The Catholic Church also maintained private jails, known as Bishop Prisons, during this time to hold church officials and private persons accused of violating ecclesiastical laws.[1]

The jail was nominally under the control of the sheriff, who was the king's chief administrative officer at the county level. Most sheriffs contracted the jail out to a **keeper** who was directly responsible for maintaining custody of inmates. Although the keeper was paid no salary, the contract was considered desirable in that it provided the keeper an income from fees charged inmates and the contract itself could be sold for an exorbitant price:[2]

> Jail operations were financed through a system of fees imposed upon inmates and paid to keepers. In addition to these fees, the keeper profited by selling goods produced by inmates or by selling their labor. While the contract was profitable for the keepers, their responsibilities towards inmates were minimal. Keepers were under no obligation to keep the jail clean or in repair. Nor were they responsible for providing adequate care to inmates. Their sole responsibility was to keep inmates from escaping.[3]

The **fee system** endured for several hundred years. It put the responsibility for financing the jail not on the government—local or national—but on the inmates or their families, friends, or charitable sponsors. As Linda Zupan discussed in *Jails: Reform and the New Generation Philosophy*, the pay-as-you-go philosophy made jail time a minor irritation for the rich and a dangerous deprivation for the poor.[4] Jails were divided into two sections: a master's side where the well-to-do inmates lived in privacy and comfort and a common side where penniless inmates lived in communal squalor.

Urban jails, then as now, were often overcrowded. Today we have tuberculosis, hepatitis, and HIV; early English jails had **gaol fever** (typhus), pneumonia, smallpox, starvation and a host of other ailments related to malnourishment, no medical care, and infectious diseases that spread rapidly in close quarters.

Women inmates and children, who were mixed in population, were subject to sexual exploitation by keepers and other inmates.

Zupan called the medieval English jail a **dumping ground** for social outcasts, misfits, and those for whom no care options existed at the time, such as the insane and the diseased, particularly lepers.[5] John Irwin's *The Jail* (1985) discusses the role of the early English jail in controlling vagrants, or, in his term, "detached persons," people cut loose from the land after the breakup of feudalism.[6] Irwin argues that the jail's role in controlling **rabble,** society's underclass, has always dominated its role in holding serious criminals. In most English jails, the majority of those confined were vagrants, debtors, the poor and unemployed, runaways, and the mentally ill; criminals awaiting trial or sentence were in the minority.

Jails proliferated across England for several hundred years until the first serious calls for reform were heard in the early 1700s. These reforms came to nothing until late in the century, when the tireless travels and meticulous writings of Sheriff John Howard of Bedfordshire attracted national attention to the shameful conditions of English county jails. In *The English Prisons* (1960), D. L. Howard lists John Howard's most important recommendations for reforming the jail in 1770s England:

1. Segregation of prisoners by age, sex, and severity of crime
2. Cells for prisoners to reduce moral and physical contamination
3. Salaried staff to prevent extortion by keepers
4. Appointment of chaplains and medical officers to promote the spiritual and physical well-being of prisoners
5. Prohibitions against the sale of liquor to prisoners
6. Provision of adequate clothing and food to prisoners to ensure their continued good health[7]

Howard's reforms, while popularly received, were put into practice long after his death in 1790.

Colonial American jails were based on the English model. They were under the control of county sheriffs, they charged prisoners fees for necessities and luxuries, and they were found as stone or wooden structures located downtown in the county seats. "The interior of such an establishment would probably be a series of small rooms, more like the arrangement of a house, and not like the typical jails of today with many cells in a row."[8] The best extant examples of these early jails are the ones in York, Maine, which date from 1653, and the colonial Williamsburg, Virginia, jail, erected in 1701.

The most influential colonial jail, Philadelphia's **Walnut Street Jail,** was closed in 1835 and eventually completely demolished. As Negley Teeters has pointed out in his book about this early jail,

> The jail, in its early days, was thought of as a temporary abode for the prisoners since, after his trial, he was either acquitted, fined, punished or, if guilty of a capital offense, executed. Since so many crimes were punishable by death, most of those convicted were summarily executed. Hence we see the early jail as only a temporary expedient in the penal practice of the colonies.[9]

While the American penitentiary developed as a state institution in the 1800s, the jail remained a local institution—primitive, understaffed, and poorly funded. Its only correctional motivation was avoidance: no one would want to come back. But surprisingly (and sadly) enough, however, many of its customers were regulars, the habitual drunks, riffraff, and petty troublemakers who lived on the fringes of modern urban society—John Irwin's "rabble."

The National Advisory Commission on Criminal Justice Standards and Goals offered this observation in 1973:

> Colonists brought to the new world the concept of the jail as an instrument of confinement, coercion, and correction of those who broke the law or were merely nuisances. In the early 19th century, the American innovation of the State penitentiary made punitive confinement the principal response to criminal acts and removed the serious offender from the local jail. Gradually, with the building of insane asylums, orphanages, and hospitals, the jail ceased to be the repository of some social casualties. But it continued to house the town's minor offenders along with the poor and the vagrant, all crowded together without regard to sex, age, and history, typically in squalor and misery.[10]

Attorney and author Ronald Goldfarb subtitled his 1976 book on jails *The Ultimate Ghetto* (he credits writer Jack Newfield with first using the phrase). In most parts of the country, the jail was still a single local institution, under the direction of the sheriff, serving the dual purposes of custodial confinement and misdemeanant punishment. For most of the twentieth century, its population typically included large numbers of drunks, vagrants (later the homeless), the mentally ill, and juvenile delinquents—"the most powerless people in society," in Newfield's description.[11]

Joseph Fishman said of his definition of the jail (used to open this chapter) that the only trouble with it was that it was not quite strong enough. An advisory report submitted to the National Commission on Law Observance and Enforcement (better known as the **Wickersham Commission**) in 1931 agreed, calling local jails "dirty, unhealthy, unsanitary—and ill-fitted to produce either a stabilizing or beneficial effect on inmates."[12] Forty years later, not much had changed, except that overcrowding was worse in the larger jails:

> The most striking inadequacy of jails is their abominable physical condition. The National Jail Census found that 25 percent of the cells in use in 1970 were built before 1920. And the chronological age of the facility is aggravated by the manner in which it is used. Jails that hold few persons tend to be neglected, and those that are overcrowded repeatedly push their equipment and fixtures beyond the breaking point. Given the fact that most jails are either overutilized, and hence overcrowded, or are using only a portion of their capacity, it is not surprising that most of the physical facilities are in crisis condition.[13]

This was the condition of the American jail in the early 1970s, when it held about 100,000 inmates. As the "War on Crime" got under way, these numbers would soar, to over 600,000 by 2001, aggravating jail problems that were centuries old.

THE AMERICAN JAIL SYSTEM TODAY

The structure of the jail system in America is not much different from what it was a hundred years ago (or from its origins in England a thousand years ago). The jail is a unit of local government. Most jails are operated by **county sheriffs;** indeed, although the sheriff may perform diverse law enforcement, civil, and court-related functions, more sheriffs' employees work in jails than in any other function.

A "jail" was defined by the "National Jail Census, 1970" as "any facility operated by a unit of local government for the detention or correction of adults suspected or convicted of a crime and which has the authority to detain longer than 48 hours."[14] This definition is still used today, except that it makes reference to detention after the first court appearance and increases the holding period from forty-eight to seventy-two hours.

Two types of facilities are excluded from this definition. **Lockups** are short-term facilities typically operated by local police under municipal authority. A lockup is most commonly a cell or group of cells in the back of a police station. An arrested person might be held there for a few hours or overnight pending questioning, release, or transfer to the county jail. Also excluded are **state-operated jails.** Six states—Alaska, Connecticut, Delaware, Hawaii, Rhode Island, and Vermont—operate combined jail-prison systems (Alaska also has fifteen locally operated jails) in which local, pretrial inmates are housed in state-run facilities.

The Justice Department's most detailed jail report, the "Census of Jails, 1999,"[15] counted 3,365 jails in forty-five states (including Alaska). They held 605,943 inmates, or an average of 180 inmates each, which on the surface appears to be a cozy, manageable number. An estimated 11 million persons were admitted to jail in 1999. By 2002, the jail inmate count was up to 665,475, an increase of 10 percent in three years.[16]

Most jails hold far fewer than 180 inmates; 63 percent in the 1999 survey had a capacity of under 100 inmates. The 2,100 jails in this category held only 71,000 inmates, or about thirty-four each. These were the jails that had the most empty beds, averaging about 71 to 85 percent of capacity. The 300 largest jails in America, on the other hand, housed 48 percent of the total inmate population, almost 300,000 inmates, under the most congested conditions. They were at 97 percent of capacity overall. Many of the large jails were at more than 100 percent of capacity, led by Las Vegas (Clark County) at 166 percent, Phoenix (Maricopa County) at 152 percent, and Philadelphia at 132 percent. The fifty largest jail systems, all of them in urban counties or cities, housed nearly a third of all jail inmates—209,847 as of June 30, 2002.[17]

In recent years, jails have tended to get bigger not only because of population growth but also because some smaller jails have been closed or consolidated to make larger regional facilities. The number of separate jail facilities had been in decline for a long time, as some city jails and small county jails were shut down or moved into the lockup category providing short-term detention only. This trend has reversed over the past decade as inmate numbers have forced jail construction, particularly in those urban areas where both crime and jail populations are highest.

So, if you are still looking for the jail where your intoxicated friend is sobering up, it is probably downtown, and it is probably operated by your local sheriff. Whether it is large or small depends primarily on the population of the jurisdiction for which the jail houses prisoners.

JAIL INMATES: LEGAL STATUS

Most arrested adults will be booked into jails—most of them locally operated but a few state or federal—as their entry point into the legal system. Juveniles are generally housed in separate **detention centers** or detention homes or halls, but some facing adult trials or living in rural areas where juvenile facilities are not available will be confined in adult jails.

According to the 1999 "Census," jails do the following:

1. Receive individuals pending arraignment and hold them awaiting trial, conviction, or sentencing
2. Readmit probation, parole, and bail-bond violators and absconders
3. Temporarily detain juveniles pending transfer to juvenile authorities
4. Hold mentally ill persons pending their movement to appropriate health facilities
5. Hold individuals for the military, for protective custody, for contempt, and for the courts as witnesses
6. Release convicted inmates to the community on completion of sentence
7. Transfer inmates to federal, state, or other authorities
8. House inmates for federal, state, or other authorities because of crowding of their facilities
9. Relinquish custody of temporary detainees to juvenile and medical authorities
10. Operate community-based programs with day reporting, home detention, electronic monitoring, or other types of supervision
11. Hold inmates sentenced to short terms (generally under one year)[18]

At midyear 2002, about 60 percent of jail inmates were held in pretrial detention. They were supposed to be detained and not punished, but it is not easy to tell the difference in many jails where they are mixed with other inmates serving sentences. Except for the ranks of what Harry Allen and Clifford Simonsen call **holdback inmates**—those felons serving state time—the sentenced inmates are misdemeanants, which means large numbers of people convicted of driving while intoxicated (DWI), theft, assault, and minor drug crimes. Many of these misdemeanants were originally charged with felonies, such as burglary, drug distribution, grand larceny, auto theft, robbery, and aggravated assault. They pleaded their crimes down to misdemeanors to avoid prison terms. Another category of jail inmates has been convicted but remain unsentenced or, if sentenced, not yet transferred to state or federal custody to begin serving the sentence. Jails also hold large numbers of probation and parole violators under **detainer,** meaning that they cannot be released until a revocation hearing is held. In the miscellaneous category, you might find a few material witnesses, a few people in contempt of court, and, more recently a growing number of people behind on their child support payments—so-called deadbeat dads. Finally, jails hold inmates awaiting transfer to other state prisons or to federal facilities, including alien deportation centers and military jails. Little wonder that the jail has been called the **bus terminal** to the rest of the corrections system. It is here that people make connections to wherever they are going.

As in a bus terminal, there is a lot of movement—people coming and going. An average jail stay in recent years is reportedly about twenty days, but like the average number of inmates per jail, this is a deceptive figure. Ninety percent or more of jail inmates turn over rapidly. They are in and out within a few hours. The other 10 percent stay longer. They are accused felons unable to make bail, misdemeanants serving short sentences, felons serving longer sentences in those states (such as Louisiana and Kentucky) where state prisoners have been housed in local jails, and probation and parole violators awaiting revocation hearings. So jails do have a semipermanent population, some of whom will be assigned **trusty** status to do the cooking, cleaning, and maintenance work. Trusties (not "trustees," who oversee financial or legal affairs) often live in better housing and are given more privileges; at one time they ran many jails.

JAIL INMATES: A PROFILE

Many minor offenders never go any farther than their one local jail, though they may go in and out of it many times during their lifetimes. Chronic drunks in the old days might have hundreds of arrests spread out over half a century. Linda Zupan's description of the jail as a "dumping ground," where police put people to get them off the streets temporarily, was highly appropriate until the due process revolution in the courts a generation ago. Included in this diverse group were drunks, the mentally ill, vagrants and derelicts (before they became "homeless people"), juvenile runaways, and anyone else the police wanted to detain until they could decide what to do with them. Even today, when other placements are more likely to be available for these categories of offenders, the life histories of jail inmates provide support for John Irwin's characterization: "rabble," "detached," "disreputable."

Jails today are more likely to house offenders formally charged with "real" criminal offenses, as opposed to the made-up and nuisance charges of the past. In urban areas especially, mental health clinics and crisis intervention centers deal with mentally disordered people who once would have ended up locked in jail. Homeless shelters house and feed people who once would have been confined or run out of town as vagrants. **Detoxification centers** have had great impact in removing habitual drunks and some offenders high on drugs from the drunk tank to the treatment ward. Rural jails with fewer resources often lack these options.

As some classes of offenders move out of the jail, others move in. When as local jurisdictions crack down on DWI and domestic violence offenders, more of them find their way into jail populations. Urban jails are now full of men and women arrested on drug charges—not drug dealing, necessarily, just simple possession of various illegal drugs. In addition, more homeless people are finding their way back into jail as police crack down on disorderly conduct in public places—trying to drive transients off the streets.

No matter what someone's underlying problems may be, if he or she is arrested for a real crime, the jail is the next stop. People with problems abound in jail. A few years ago, Sheriff James Dunning of Alexandria, Virginia, issued political officials this invitation: "I would like to invite you to come visit my neighborhood. It has a higher concentration of substance abusers and chronically mentally ill people than any other area of the city."[19]

The sheriff's statement about his "neighborhood"—his jail—is true for practically all jails. Sheriff Lee Baca of Los Angeles has pointed out that he was operating the largest mental institution in California—the county jail. In the 1980s, Dr. Linda Teplin of the Northwestern University Medical School in Chicago evaluated Cook County Jail inmates for three serious mental disorders: schizophrenia, severe depression, and mania. She found the prevalence of these disorders to be three times higher among jail inmates than among the population outside.[20]

Widespread substance abuse aggravates the mental and physical health concerns of jail inmates. If you went through the jails and eliminated the offenders without serious documented problems with alcohol and drugs and without a history of mental health issues, you would not have many people left in most jails. This is not to say that their crimes are excusable simply because they have other underlying problems. It does suggest that prevention and treatment programs may offer more hope of reducing criminality than repetitive processing through the legal system. Jails deal with many troubled people, as you see in jail death statistics—suicide trailing only natural causes as the leading cause of inmate deaths and AIDS deaths occurring at a rate several times higher than in the free world. Allen and Simonsen, in their analysis of recent jail inmates' criminal history, suggest that these inmates are a "marginal group of mostly male offenders who have had a lengthy but not necessarily serious involvement in criminal activity. They could best be seen as a group of high-need disadvantaged urban dwellers whose needs have not been adequately addressed by the social services agencies in their local communities."[21]

Recent reports by the Bureau of Justice Statistics provide this demographic overview of current jail inmates. They remain predominantly male—88.4 percent versus 11.6 percent female—although the number of female inmates has increased more rapidly than that of men over the past twenty years (since the "War on Drugs" began). At midyear 2002, nearly six in ten local jail inmates were racial or ethnic minorities. Whites made up 43.8 percent of the jail population, blacks 39.8 percent, Hispanics 14.7 percent, and other races (Asians, American Indians, Alaska Natives, Native Hawaiians, and other Pacific Islanders) 1.6 percent.[22] About 1.1 percent of jail inmates were under age eighteen, the majority of whom were charged with adult crimes. Inmates outnumber jail staff by about three to one (though keep in mind that only about two-thirds of the 210,000 jail employees are correctional officers, as opposed to other administrative, professional, and support staff, and that the correctional officers work shifts, so that on-duty ratios of inmates to correctional officers more often range from twenty-five to one to fifty to one).

Jails continue to evolve as the nature of their inmate population changes. Drug crimes have brought more women to jail. AIDS, tuberculosis, and hepatitis, all of which are strongly associated with drug usage and unhealthy lifestyles, have brought a lot more sick inmates into jails and have escalated the costs of jail medical care. Jails are still cheaper to operate than prisons because of lower guard-to-inmate ratios and the lack of rehabilitation and support services, but the cost differential is narrowing. Reform groups, such as the **John Howard Society** (or Association), named after the English sheriff, advocate a much broader role for the jail in dealing with criminal behavior. Jails touch far more lives than prisons do. As they continue to move further away from their original narrow detention function, they can begin to address more effectively the problems that direct the lives of their disparate clientele.

JAIL DESIGN AND ARCHITECTURE

Jails come in all types and designs, influenced most by age and intended capacity. Original jails "were simply comprised of one or more rooms, often lined with heavy wooden beams for security. From the outside, they looked scarcely different than other 17th- or 18th-century buildings."[23] Larger facilities built in the 1800s and 1900s were often found on the top floor or in the basement of the county courthouse. These jails featured what is now called the **linear/ intermittent surveillance design**—multiman cells arranged in long tiers like prison cell blocks. Guards walked up and down the corridors outside the cells observing inmates through the bars. These jails featured such cells as the **bullpen,** which might hold from half a dozen to twenty or more inmates in a single cell; the **drunk tank,** a foul, smelly cell where drunks were kept until they sobered up; a padded cell for mental cases; and separate cells or tiers for juveniles and women. These **first-generation jails** practiced little classification of inmates; a middle-age businessman arrested for traffic violations might be thrown into a bullpen with murderers and rapists who had been in jail for years.

In the 1960s, the **podular/remote surveillance design** was developed. Cells were arranged in sections commonly called **pods** (from podular), sharing a common floor space used for eating and other group activities; inmates spent most of their time in this common area, not locked in their individual (usually two-man or larger) small cells. These **second-generation jails** were designed to provide indirect surveillance of inmates by jailers who watched from glassed-in control booths. One jailer would typically be watching a pod that contained twenty or more inmates. Jailers were only in direct contact with inmates when they went into the pod:

> The primary problem with the first- and second-generation jail designs was that staff and inmates were separated. In essence, staff managed the hallways and control rooms, generally about 10 percent of the facility, while inmates ran the housing areas, roughly 90 percent. This unsatisfactory arrangement developed due to the divergent population categories that routinely flow through a jail. It allowed for maximum control through architectural barriers, but it proved to be an inefficient means of housing once minimum standards required staff to be within sight and hearing of all inmates.[24]

These problems were addressed in the construction of three model federal jails, called Metropolitan Correctional Centers, in the mid-1970s in Chicago, New York, and San Diego. These jails applied the **podular/direct supervision design** in which the correctional officer is placed inside each housing unit or pod with no bars or glass separating him from the inmates. The Martinez Detention Facility in Contra Costa, California, was opened in January 1981 as the first direct-supervision county jail in the United States.

Many of the newer, larger urban jails now apply the principles of direct supervision. They are called **third-generation** (or **new-generation**) **jails.** They look very different from the old jails laid out in cell blocks. In the third-generation design, the jailers are locked inside the pods with the inmates. The jailer mans a console or a desk where he can observe and talk to inmates directly at all times. This approach increases security and also promotes interaction between jail guards and inmates. Guards know much more about what is going on inside the jail. Many of these jails provide all routine services to inmates—visitation, recreation, food services, and medical care—in the pods, which reduces movement of inmates within the jail. The pods become minijails that stand alone within the larger facility. The podular cell design is now being supplemented by direct-supervision dormitories in many county jails, providing a less costly medium-custody environment for ordinary inmates.

JAIL PROBLEMS

The problems of the jail are diverse and enduring. Shocked by conditions he found in his own jail in Bedfordshire, Sheriff John Howard spent the last fifteen years of his life campaigning to improve English jails, but Howard had been dead a hundred years before most of his reforms were accomplished in the late 1800s. Many of the age-old problems of American jails have only been addressed seriously in the past thirty years, as increasing numbers have made old problems much worse.

When we look at *why* it has been so difficult to improve the jail, three aspects of the jail's operation stand out:

1. The jail is predominantly a local institution, meaning it often lacks the political and economic resources to better itself.
2. The jail's clientele—characterized as rabble, drunks, nuts, dopeheads, and losers—do not rate very far up the scale of social concern.
3. The short-term duration of the jail experience, in contrast to longer-term imprisonment, diverts attention away from jail conditions; the perspective is that even if jails are awful, most people will not be in them very long anyway.

Early American jails were much criticized on two counts: their deplorable physical conditions and their failure to segregate inmates by gender, age, and background. As we have already noted, early jails were small, single- or multiroom buildings that mixed criminals and noncriminals, men and women, boys and girls, murderers and runaways, insane and debtors, in the same room. The only segregation, as Zupan pointed out, was that based on ability to pay; the rich were separated from the poor.

Although jail conditions were thoroughly documented and publicized in the 1920s and 1930s by scholars,[25] by federal inspectors,[26] and by the Wickersham Commission, the President's Crime Commission wrote in its 1967 report on corrections, "Not only are the great majority of these facilities old, but many do not even meet the minimum standards in sanitation, living space, and segregation of different ages and types of offenders that have obtained generally in the rest of corrections for several decades."[27]

Six years later, the Corrections Task Force of the National Advisory Commission on Criminal Justice Standards and Goals was even more critical: "Outmoded and archaic, lacking the most basic comforts, totally inadequate for any program encouraging socialization, jails perpetuate a destructive rather than reintegrative process. Significantly it is in such facilities that the greatest number of persons have contact with the criminal justice system."[28]

Poor physical facilities often went hand in hand with poor staffing. Most jails were operated by county sheriffs or municipal police departments that considered the jail a nuisance function. Most jails were small, averaging fewer than twenty-five inmates with only one jailer on duty at any given time. The jailer was a police officer or deputy sheriff who was also the booking officer, dispatcher, and records clerk. Jail staff were often the newest officers in training or older men not fit for road duty. In many jurisdictions, even this minimal level of staffing was not a certainty. Jails were left unattended or in the care of trusties—inmates with the keys to the cells of other inmates.

Hans Mattick, who identified jails as the "cloacal region" of corrections in his influential research of the 1960s and 1970s, referred to jail administration in this era as guided by the principle of **custodial convenience,** defined as "everyone who can, takes the easy way out and makes only the minimal effort."[29] Jailers concentrated on preventing escapes and left inmates to work out their own internal order, not unlike conditions within English jails several hundred years earlier.

The jail was all about security—and much more about perimeter security, keeping inmates within the walls, than about the internal security that goes with a well-run institution. Treatment did not exist, medical care was not provided in most jails, work was not available except for the few inmates assigned trusty jobs, and recreation and visitation were haphazard. The jail environment was one of **enforced idleness,** meaning that inmates were kept in cells with no activities or programs. They could talk, smoke, play cards and dominoes, read, eat, and sleep; if you spent a day in jail or 180 days in jail, the routine was the same (and still is in many jails). As Harry Allen and Clifford Simonsen wrote recently, "A lot of 'doing time' is dead time."[30]

Daniel Glaser wrote in 1971,

> The major costs to society from jail conditions probably stem not from the clear violations of moral norms that the inmates suffer there, but rather, from the prolonged idleness of the inmates in highly diverse groups cut off from much communication with outsiders. In this inactivity and crowdedness day after day, those inmates most committed to crime "brainwash" the inexperienced to convert initial feelings of guilt or shame into smug rationalizations for crime. Also, jail prisoners become extremely habituated to "killing time," especially during pretrial confinement. Thus, deficiencies of ability to support themselves in legitimate employment, which may have contributed to their criminality, are enhanced at their release. While prison and reformatories are often called "schools of crime," it is a far more fitting label for the typical urban jail.[31]

Centuries of inattention and neglect would eventually come home to roost. Poor staffing, inadequate physical facilities, and the absence of programs were tolerable as long as jails were small and legally invisible. But when jail populations began to increase in the 1970s and jail **overcrowding** became a continuing problem, especially in urban jails, inmates began to file and win lawsuits in the federal courts. They attacked jail conditions as violating the "cruel and unusual punishment" provision of the Eighth Amendment. They sued for damages under the civil rights provisions of Section 1983, Title 42, U.S. Code. As they often pointed out, jail conditions were particularly deplorable given that most inmates held under these conditions had not yet been convicted of a crime. Inhumane confinement thus became a sort of punishment before conviction; many inmates were happy (or at least more relieved) to get on to prison where they could have more normal lives.

Overcrowding became a major problem for the largest jails by the early 1980s. In Ken Kerle and Dick Ford's influential 1982 report *The State of Our Nation's Jails*, a national survey asked jail administrators to list their five most serious problems. Their top five were the following:

1. Personnel
2. Modernization
3. Overcrowding
4. Recreation
5. Funding[32]

Among the 285 jails (10.7 percent of the total surveyed) that were under state or federal court order to improve jail conditions at the time, the survey asked why the jails were under court supervision. The most common reasons were the following:

1.	Crowded conditions	209
2.	Recreation	206
3.	Structure (modernization)	181
4.	Medical	164
5.	Visitation	158
6.	Fire hazards	111
7.	Other	104
8.	Staffing	102
9.	Food	94
10.	Health area	94
11.	Personal hygiene	93
12.	Mentally ill	47
13.	Suicides	26[33]

Kerle and Ford confirmed in their survey what a lot of jail administrators were already saying: many jails nationally were in a mess, and most of the impetus toward dramatic change was instigated by the courts.

Overcrowding would continue as a major concern of litigation into the 1990s, when the supply of jail cells (through new construction) began to catch up with the demand for space for new inmates. The number of jails under court order increased during the 1980s but has fallen off subsequently. Although inmate litigation, particularly civil rights litigation under Section 1983, has continued at a high volume, enough improvements have been made (and perhaps courts have become more conservative as well) that both state and federal courts less often find favor with inmate lawsuits and intervene in jail conditions than they did a few years ago.

Jail officials today continue to identify overcrowding and **staffing** as their two major problems. Even if they are no longer under court order, many large jails are always at or over capacity, which affects inmate medical care, food services, physical conditions, security, classification and segregation, and mental health services. Inmates in urban jails live together in jammed-together idleness, their existence defined by the culture of overcrowding.

Staffing remains a critical concern. Most people who work in American jails are deputies employed by local sheriffs. Most of them have no particular qualifications or interests in corrections. Many of them would rather be working in some other function within the sheriff's department; they will move on to do so when an opening comes up. Most jail employees are guards whose job is to maintain security. Jails do not provide nearly as many counselors or professional staff as prisons do; most jails provide minimal programs for which professional staff would be needed. The ratio of guards to inmates is lower, and fewer support staff are needed. Lower salaries, reduced staffing, and lack of professional services combine to make jails much cheaper to operate than prisons.

In most American jails today sheriffs are paid a **per diem** rate by county government (a descendant of the old fee system) for housing local prisoners. This rate is typically pitifully small; sheriffs use their own revenues, often supplemented by payments from state and federal authorities for housing their prisoners, to maintain decent living conditions. Many improvements have been made in the quality of jail staff, particularly in regard to training, but many jails remain both understaffed and badly staffed by employees who, like the inmates, would much rather be somewhere else.

Even persistent critics acknowledge that jails have improved over the past two decades. The population increases that created severe overcrowding in many jails resulted in lawsuits and court intervention that spurred several important changes. Jails are newer and bigger. Many of the most deteriorated old jails that were so vilified in the 1960s and 1970s have either been closed or renovated. Jail staff are better trained and more professional. The jail provides better services to inmates; larger jails now routinely provide job training, basic education, and at least minimal drug treatment programs. Medical care, which was responsible for many costly legal judgments against jails during the litigation boom period, is vastly improved. Jail architecture has changed away from the first-generation cell block design toward second- and third-generation podular designs that create a more open housing arrangement. Bigger jails are better able to classify and segregate inmates into different housing units.

But many of the longtime problems—understaffing, inadequate funding, inmate idleness, and a depressing environment—remain, and they are aggravated by more recent issues, particularly the physical and mental health concerns of jail inmates and the backlog of convicted felons accumulating in jails in several states as a result of prison overcrowding. These problems have affected jails large and small, though in many respects the largest jails—which are often better funded and better staffed—have been hit harder because they are more overcrowded. When jails are overcrowded, all the other problems are magnified, and the results are violence, disease, turmoil, and costly litigation.

BIG JAILS

The five largest jail systems in America—Los Angeles, New York, Cook County (Chicago), Maricopa County (Phoenix), and Philadelphia—held over 60,000 inmates at midyear 2002, about 10 percent of the nation's total jail population. These five cities each have more people in jail (more than 7,000) than eighteen states have in their prison systems. With the turnover rate for individual jails averaging 1,000 to 1,500 percent or even more annually, these jails regularly process from 100,000 to 300,000 inmates each year—the population equivalent of a large city flowing in and out of their doors.

The largest of these, Los Angeles County, has maintained an average daily inmate count of more than 19,000 for the past three years, which represents a decline from its peak years in 1991 and 1992, when it commonly held 21,000 to 22,000 inmates. Of the eight facilities that made up the Los Angeles County jail system in 2003, the largest unit, the Men's Central Jail in downtown Los Angeles, was not only the biggest jail but also the largest single correctional institution in America during the early 1990s, when it typically held 7,500 men in custody.

The Los Angeles County Jail, like other jails in California, saw its population increase during the mid-1990s as inmates charged with second- and third-strike crimes went to trial rather than pleading guilty and accepting long prison terms. This jail, as much as any other in the country, has been troubled by gang conflicts that are brought in from the streets. It began a program, "Operation Jail Safe," to isolate and pacify gang members—Bloods, Crips, and members of several Hispanic gangs—who were often involved in violent incidents within the jail.

Faced with increasing numbers of inmates testing positive for tuberculosis (TB), Los Angeles County began taking chest X-rays of inmates placed in population. Most jails use the tuberculin skin test for TB testing. Los Angeles County had so many inmates with TB, HIV, hepatitis, and drug addiction (often leading to multidrug-resistant TB, or MDRTB), that it resorted to the more expensive but also more thorough and more quickly available X-ray testing.

The jail also attracted attention late in 2001 by allowing an outside group, Correct HELP, to distribute condoms to about 300 gay inmates in the Central Jail. The sheriff's official policy was not that the department was condoning sex in jail (which is a felony under California law) but that high rates of HIV, syphilis, and other sexually transmitted diseases warranted the condom distribution program as a public health measure. "I don't believe you can stop people in jail from engaging in sexual activity because the law says it's forbidden," Sheriff Lee Baca said. "We just think that communicable diseases need to be controlled. That's all. That's what this is about."[34] Deputies pointed out that without the condoms, inmates had been using latex gloves—referred to in jail slang as "love gloves"—and Corn Nuts wrappers to protect themselves. Although AIDS activists urged the sheriff to make the condoms available in all jail housing units, he said he would not do so. Outside the gay unit, condoms would still be considered contraband. Only four other large jails were known to have policies providing condoms to inmates.

Journalist Jennifer Gonnerman spent time roaming New York City's jail complex, Rikers Island, for a *Village Voice* article in 2000. The population of Rikers

Island, which in the mid-1990s had grown to 20,000 inmates, larger than the Los Angeles County Jail at the time, was down to about 14,600. This jail complex is often called "the world's largest penal colony" because its ten jails make up a complex filling a small island less than one square mile. Rikers Island was a dumping ground even before it became a jail in 1935. From 1884 on, it was used as the city's trash dump, "the repository for what the city proper had no use for—broken boilers, old sofas, horse manure, garbage, tin cans, street sweepings, and earth from subway excavations."[35] The jail was built on top of this dump.

According to Gonnerman, Rikers Island was still a dump in 2000—a human waste dump, efficiently managed, and safer than in the past but essentially a "city-run superghetto kept out of the public eye" (only eleven miles from the Statue of Liberty):

> Statistics don't tell the whole story, but they do suggest that just beneath New York's media-hyped boom lies a world of poverty, suffering, and chaos: About 30 percent of prisoners report they were homeless at some point within three months before they were locked up. Twenty-five percent receive some mental health services. Twenty percent of the women and seven percent of the men are HIV-positive. And 90 percent are high school dropouts.[36]

She also found that three-quarters of the inmates were pretrial detainees held because they could not make bail; 42 percent of them had bail set at $1,000 or less, which they could not make. For a thousand dollars or less, they spent a year or two in Rikers awaiting trial or the opportunity to plead guilty.

The Cook County Jail in Chicago has a troubled past marked by violence and overcrowding, and a troubled present that looks much the same. A 1989 U.S. Justice Department study of the Chicago jail concluded that a more efficient criminal justice system could alleviate habitual overcrowding. Thirteen years later, the average daily jail population had more than doubled to over 11,000, in a facility with fewer than 10,000 beds (making the downtown jail at 26th and California officially the biggest single correctional institution in America for now), and the average length of stay had increased to 187 days, slightly over six months.[37] Overcrowding aggravates the gang problems that have traditionally marked this jail.

But not all jail gangs wear prisoners' uniforms. On February 24, 1999, according to *Chicago Tribune* investigative reports from February and March 2003, forty sheriff's deputies from the **Special Operations Response Team (SORT)** raided a maximum-security cell block for the sole purpose of beating and terrorizing gang members, then filed false reports to cover it up, according to Cook County sheriff's internal affairs documents, prisoner interviews, and sheriff's sources:

> As the unit's commander, Richard Remus, stood atop a table shouting, "SORT runs the jail," guards went from prisoner to prisoner examining them for gang tattoos. Anyone who looked away from the wall was struck with a wooden baton, prisoners said in interviews. Some prisoners were forced to lie on the floor, where they said they were stomped and kicked.[38]

At least forty-nine prisoners claimed they were beaten and then denied immediate medical attention. After an internal investigation that was delayed several times (amid accusations that sheriff's officials were trying to squelch it altogether), a report submitted three years and seven months after the incident cited one deputy, Remus, for beating inmates, nine officers for filing false reports, and four canine officers for bringing unmuzzled dogs into the cell block.[39] In the meantime, overcrowding has worsened, and investigators are looking into a July 29, 2000, incident in which jail guards are accused of beating five inmates after a disturbance in which several guards were injured.[40]

Maricopa County is more famous for its sheriff than its jail. The sheriff is Joe Arpaio, an ex-DEA (Drug Enforcement Administration) agent who is called "America's Toughest Sheriff," a nickname given him by the media (or possibly by himself) for hard-core anticrime and anticriminal practices. He is famous for his get-tough policies: housing 1,200 inmates in a tent city; chain gangs for men, women, and juveniles; only two meals a day (and these very cheap and plain); and banning smoking, coffee, movies, porn magazines, and unrestricted television in jail housing units. But he also stresses education and drug treatment programs, and he insists that he has reduced the recidivism rate among jail inmates (although an Arizona State University research study said otherwise).

Sheriff Arpaio is not well regarded by many of his jail inmates and by some of his employees as well. He runs a fabulous public relations campaign about himself and his conservative philosophy, but his jail continues to have many of the same problems other large jails have, including frequent lawsuits. In May 2003, a riot broke out in an Estrella Jail dormitory after a fight between two inmates over a doughnut. Two inmates were injured, and the rioters tore up their bunks and mattresses. The dorm held 130 inmates in space designed for sixty. Sheriff Arpaio said jail overcrowding and a shortage of deputies—caused by pay and other issues—contributed to the problem.[41] At the time of the disturbance, one deputy, a nineteen-year-old rookie, was on duty in the dorm.

At one time, the Philadelphia Jail was reputed to be one of the worst in America, a jail run by inmate gangs who routinely beat and raped new inmates thrown into the jail's tanks. Assistant District Attorney Alan Davis's research on sexual assaults in the Philadelphia jails concluded that at least 3 percent of the men who passed through the jail system were forcibly raped.[42] This was in the 1960s, but poor conditions in the jail persisted for many years, eventually resulting in a federal judge imposing a court order on the jail system. Jail population, once capped by the courts at 3,750, had risen to 7,695 by March 2003, partly as a result of new jail construction. Jail critics were concerned that old problems would begin to emerge again once federal court supervision was ended.

SMALL JAILS

At the opposite end of the scale from these huge complexes are the smaller jails that proliferate at the city and county levels. As the big jails' problems originate in high volume and overcrowding, the small jails' problems lie in meager resources and limited services.

The Kotzebue Regional Jail Facility in Kotzebue, Alaska, is an example of a modern small jail. Opened in 1995, the jail's capacity is twelve inmates in one pod and two individual cells. The one or two correctional officers on duty double as police and emergency dispatchers. Busy times often see well over 100 bookings per month, and the jail population has gone over thirty at peak times. Political officials have now prohibited overcrowding in the jail, so now any excess prisoners have to be taken to the Anvil Mountain Correctional Center in Nome, 200 miles away. The roads are closed in winter, when over-crowding is typically not a problem. The jail's Website proclaims,

> Overcrowding can be a problem. Stress levels rise quickly when 12–15 people, of-ten strangers, are in a relatively small area 24/7, and trying to decide which chan-nel to watch on the TV and sharing the use of 2 toilets! The meals are good and nutritious, but there is no choice of fare. The jail is a "No Smoking" facility.[43]

Overcrowding has also been a problem in 2003 for the Box Elder County Jail in Brigham City, Utah. The 150-bed facility, which opened in 1998, was intended to house about sixty county inmates, a dozen or so inmates from neighboring Cache County, and about sixty Utah state prisoners. Cache County and the Utah Department of Corrections paid Box Elder County $43 per inmate per day to house their inmates in the jail. But the number of local inmates has risen sharply, pushing out the paying inmates from out of county and causing county commissioners concerns about budget shortfalls. "We knew it was going to happen, but we didn't think it was going to happen as quickly as it did," said Sheriff Leon Jensen, in yet another example of the "if you build it they will come syndrome" that has prevailed in American jails and prisons the past thirty years.[44]

The Otsego County Jail in Michigan has had similar problems. In early 2003, the jail, with a capacity of thirty-four, housed forty inmates. Under Michigan law, when jail population stayed over capacity for ten straight days, the sheriff had to declare a state of emergency that allows early release of in-mates or transfer to other counties. Sheriff James McBride emphasized that the county's vulnerability to lawsuits substantially increases whenever the jail is overcrowded. The jail administrator, Lieutenant Brian Webber, said man-power is also a problem. His staff of ten has been reduced to nine, and he must have a minimum of two corrections officers on duty at all times. The jail, with a budget of less than $700,000 for 2003, is generating a lot of overtime costs as well as increased costs for food and medical care associated with over-crowding. Lieutenant Webber stated his personal belief that "the only long-term solutions are to build a new jail or expand the existing one."[45]

Small jails in Kentucky have been experiencing another problem common in local jails: inmate suicides. Jails still have a suicide rate estimated at four to five times higher than the free-world rate, though this has declined sharply in some jails with better screening and prevention procedures in recent years. The inmates in Kentucky apparently did not get the word, as seventeen of them killed themselves in a recent thirty-month period. An investigation by the *Louisville Courier-Journal* in 2002 found that employees in Kentucky's eighty-five county jails were not required to receive training in suicide pre-vention, and most inmates who committed suicide did so without having seen a mental health professional while in custody.[46] Kentucky's county jailers are elected directly by the people and have wide latitude on policy matters.

Lawsuits are common in jail death and injury cases. When fire swept through the Mitchell County Jail in North Carolina on September 5, 2002, eight inmates were killed, seven of them trapped in a second-floor holding cell. The county agreed to pay $2 million to families of the victims, and lawsuits were pending against the state, whose inspectors failed to detect safety violations in the jail.[47]

High operating costs and the possibility of a catastrophic legal judgment are on the minds of many local officials, according to Jillian Lloyd's article in the December 24, 1999, *Christian Science Monitor*. She reported from Colorado that "for a growing number of counties, the cost of operating a jail is prohibitive."[48] In rural Costilla County, the poorest county in Colorado, the solution was to shut down the jail. The dilapidated twelve-cell facility—last remodeled in 1964—posed health and safety risks to inmates and was chronically overcrowded. The sheriff's department had to begin transporting inmates to other county jails a hundred miles or more away. About forty of Colorado's sixty-two counties were struggling with the same problems: poor facilities, overcrowding, and budget constraints. Even in the wealthier counties, the public has been reluctant to spend money for jail improvements. Steve Ingley, the executive director of the American Jail Association, said; "Jails have been required to do a lot more, with a whole lot less. They have a huge responsibility, without the resources. If we're going to continue on this path of putting away people, we're going to have to deal with this."[49]

IMPROVING THE JAIL

How *do* you deal with this, particularly the fundamental problem of economics that has hampered local jails for a thousand years? Joel Thompson and Larry Mays, in *American Jails* (1991), provide a list of eight recommendations to improve the jail:

1. States should provide aid to local governments for jail construction and renovation.
2. States should develop mandatory jail standards.
3. Inspection and enforcement provision should be developed to compel compliance with standards.
4. States should support cooperative agreements to build regional jails.
5. Local governments should educate citizens about jail functions and conditions.
6. Local officials should develop long-term financial plans for the jail.
7. Jails should be required to have written policies and procedures.
8. Communities should explore alternatives to incarceration.[50]

How would these recommendations, if acted on, affect the jail, and how likely are they to become reality? State (and federal) funding for jail construction and renovation would allow local jurisdictions to replace the worst old jails and build new facilities reflecting modern design concepts. Federal funds for jail construction have been made available to local jurisdictions in most states under the Violent Offender Incarceration and Truth in Sentencing Incentive Grants in recent years. Under this grant program created by the Federal Violent Crime and Law Enforcement Assistance Act of 1994, the federal government pays up to 90 percent of the cost of new jail construction in states that add more beds for violent offenders and adopt the 85 percent "truth-in-sentencing" guidelines.

Mandatory jail standards accompanied by inspection provisions apply in about thirty-five states today. While these standards do get everyone "working on the same page" (in management lingo), critics point out that standards are set very low so as not to inconvenience the smaller rural jails that would have trouble meeting higher standards and that enforcement of inspection standards is often lax and haphazard. Rarely are jails shut down or penalized for failing to maintain standards. The most effective way of setting jail standards in the past generation has been through federal court orders, in which sheriffs could be threatened with contempt for failing to maintain standards. The threat of monetary fines or, even worse, being made a prisoner in their own jail was enough to encourage most sheriffs into compliance. But courts rarely take this step today.

The major indicator of high standards in jail operations today is the achievement of **accreditation** through the American Correctional Association (ACA). This process, which involves self-study according to national correctional standards and auditing by outside experts, is rigorous enough that few jails make the effort. By mid-2003, fewer than 100 (about 3 percent) of the more than 3,300 local jails were ACA accredited.

The other professional organization important to jails is the **American Jail Association** (AJA), formed in 1981 by the merger of two older organizations: the National Jail Association and the National Jail Managers Association. According to its Website, with a logo featuring the scales of justice, a lighted candle, and a flaming torch (these representing justice, knowledge, and truth in jail operations), AJA is dedicated to the following:

1. Banding together all those concerned with or interested in the custody and care of persons awaiting trial, serving sentences, or otherwise locally confined; to improve the conditions and systems under which such persons are detained.

2. Advancing professionalism through training, information exchange, technical assistance, publications, and conferences.

3. Providing leadership in the development of professional standards, pertinent legislation, management practices, programs, and services.

4. Presenting and advancing the interests, needs, concerns, and proficiency of the profession as deemed appropriate by the membership and their representatives.[51]

Many jail professionals have advocated the establishment of regional jails. These facilities typically serve multicounty areas. One big jail replaces several smaller jails, which become lockups or short-term facilities feeding long-term inmates into the regional facility. The Southwestern Virginia Regional Jail Authority began construction on three new jails in May 2003. These jails will eventually house 800 inmates from eight counties in southwestern Virginia. West Virginia has done the same thing, using bonds backed by court fees to build large general-use jails that are shared by several counties.[52]

Thompson and Mays's recommendations deal with the fundamental conditions underlying the jail's operation. They do not address other important issues such as jail staffing or services provided inmates. Probably the most difficult of their recommendations to accomplish is the one regarding educating citizens about jail functions and conditions. Most people accept the role of the jail as is. When sheriffs and political officials want to make improvements, if the improvements cost money that requires public approval (in the form of taxes or revenue bonds), the improvements are a hard sell. Even in well-off communities, jails are often given the most meager local resources to work with, which obliges them to look to higher levels of government for supplemental funds.

ALTERNATIVES TO JAIL

As overcrowding and other problems persist in local jails, authorities explore alternatives that would reduce jail populations. The easiest way to do this is to not put so many people in jail in the first place. Many minor offenders could be ticketed and released from custody without ever being booked into jail. If they are arrested, most misdemeanor offenders and many felons who are not dangerous could be discharged without having to post bail. This practice, formally called **supervised pretrial release** or release on recognizance, was first developed by the Vera Institute of Justice's Manhattan Bail Project in the 1960s. Using strong community ties as its guide, this project qualified low-income defendants for pretrial release without bail.

The **Pretrial Services Resource Center** in Washington, D.C., is a clearinghouse for information on pretrial release programs provided by private or public organizations. It sends consultants to work with local jails and courts in establishing guidelines to accomplish two objectives: diverting pretrial offenders from the jail into treatment and supervision options and making sure offenders show up for disposition or trial as scheduled.

The Dakota County Jail in Nebraska reduced its jail population by 70 percent by establishing a pretrial release program.[53] The Lafayette Parish Jail in Lafayette, Louisiana, an 800-bed jail, operates a Pre-Trial Monitoring Program that supervises between 400 and 500 pretrial defendants at any given time; without this program, the jail would be far above its lawful capacity.

Releasing pretrial inmates without bond runs head-on into the traditional and politically entrenched practices associated with **price-tag justice** in America. We tend to think that offenders with money or property should get out of jail on bail. Poor people, even those who are stable local residents not likely to flee, should stay in. After conviction, the same attitude prevails. "Ten days or a hundred dollar fine," judges used to say to misdemeanants. People with money paid their fines and went home; poor people went to jail, often repetitively, for drunkenness and other minor offenses. The image of the jail was—and is—that of the appropriate social institution for controlling poor people in the cities.

Special courts have been created in many localities to deal with certain types of offenders through diversion and treatment programs. The most prolific growth over the past decade has been in **drug courts,** which try to connect offenders with treatment and social services as an option to conviction and jail or prison time, but other special courts deal with domestic violence, mental health, juvenile, and traffic cases. The intent is to minimize the flow of new inmates into secure institutions.

For people sentenced to jail time, jails have explored such alternatives as intermittent sentences, in which offenders called **weekenders** spend weekends in jail and weekdays at home working, and performing **community service,** which obliges offenders to put in hours on charitable or public service projects. **Pretrial alternatives** and expanded sentencing options administered by a full-service community correctional center would provide increments of increased control over offenders, who could replace idle time with time spent more productively in the community.

The "Census of Jails, 1999" indicated that it was becoming more common for jails to supervise offenders outside of jail in programs such as community service, work release, weekend reporting, electronic monitoring, and other alternative programs. At midyear 1999, jail authorities supervised 82,030 offenders in such community-based programs, up from 25,174 in 1993. These nonconfined offenders were broken down by categories:

Community service	20,138	Day reporting	5,080
Weekender programs	16,089	Alcohol/drug treatment	4,044
Pretrial supervision	10,089	Home detention	516
Electronic monitoring	9,927	Other programs	8,367[54]

THE JAIL OF THE FUTURE

What will the jail of the future look like? Current trends suggest that it will be a larger, more diverse institution than the jail of a few years ago. In rural areas, it will be a regional jail shared by several counties. Many jails will offer a greater range of treatment programs and non-custodial alternatives. The jail might actually become the hub for many forms of correctional intervention at the local level, eventually evolving into the **community correctional center** that scholars and jail professionals have imagined for years. Some people would be locked up, pretrial and serving sentences, but far more people would be on pretrial release and work release, coming in to take part in diversion and treatment programs, performing community service, providing restitution to victims, and leading useful lives under supervision in the community.

The underlying difficulty, in imagining this expanded role for the jail, is its local nature. It is often difficult (or impossible) to get local authorities to work toward this model, especially when multiple jurisdictions are involved. County government officials in America are not famous for working together toward a common goal. The other obvious problem in pursuit of the "new jail" is money: who is going to pay for the facilities and staff needed to provide this higher level of service? Jail finances, as we have already seen, have been a problem from the beginning. Although we say the fee system is dead, inmates in many local jails today are charged fees for medical care, medications, and other basic needs.

Except in the few states with combined jail and prison systems, jail funding remains a patchwork—county funds, taxes for the sheriff's department, state funds, and occasional federal grants. Those jails holding large numbers of state and federal prisons (and inmates from other counties) have pioneered yet another form of supplementing their meager resources. The per diem rates sheriffs charge other jurisdictions are typically much higher than their own daily costs, so sheriffs get extra money to use in their own jail operations. Some sheriffs renting beds to outsiders have enjoyed an unprecedented economic boon. The flaw here is that the jail becomes a profitable enterprise in which the advantage is to house nonlocal prisoners. Thus, the jail abandons its function in serving the local community and becomes just another prison warehouse, ultimately undermining the community correctional center premise. The evolving role of the new jail remains uncertain.

In the meantime, your intoxicated friend in the holding cell should consider himself among the fortunate. He has someone with resources willing to help him out. Most of the men and women who would be his cell mates are not so lucky.

KEY TERMS

detention	holdback inmates	second-generation jails	supervised pretrial release
gaol	detainer	podular/direct supervision design	Pretrial Services Resource Center
jail	bus terminal	third-generation jails	price-tag justice
keeper	trusty	new-generation jails	special courts
fee system	detoxification centers	custodial convenience	drug courts
gaol fever	John Howard Society	enforced idleness	weekenders
dumping ground	linear/intermittent surveillance design	overcrowding	community service
rabble	bullpen	staffing	pretrial alternatives
Walnut Street Jail	drunk tank	per diem	community correctional center
Wickersham Commission	first-generation jails	Special Operations Response Team	
county sheriffs	podular/remote surveillance design	accreditation	
lockups	pods	American Jail Association	
state-operated jails			
detention centers			

NOTES

1. Anthony Babington, *The English Bastille: A History of Newgate Gaol and Prison Conditions in Britain 1188–1902* (London: McDonald and Company, 1971), cited in Linda Zupan, *Jails: Reform and the New Generation Philosophy* (Cincinnati: Anderson Publishing, 1991), p. 9.

2. Zupan, *Jails*, p. 10.

3. Ibid.

4. Ibid., p. 11.

5. Ibid., p. 13.

6. John Irwin, *The Jail: Managing the Underclass in American Society* (Berkeley: University of California Press, 1985), pp. 4–5.

7. D. L. Howard, *The English Prisons: Their Past and Their Future* (London: Methuen and Company, 1960), p. 9–10.

8. Negley K. Teeters, *The Cradle of the Penitentiary: The Walnut Street Jail at Philadelphia 1773–1835* (Philadelphia: Pennsylvania Prison Society, 1955), p. 9.

9. Ibid.

10. National Advisory Commission on Criminal Justice Standards and Goals, "Local Adult Institutions," *Corrections* (Washington, D.C.: U.S. Government Printing Office, 1973), p. 273.

11. Ronald Goldfarb, *Jails: The Ultimate Ghetto* (Garden City, N.Y.: Anchor Books, 1976), p. 9.

12. Ibid.

13. National Advisory Commission on Criminal Justice Standards and Goals, "Local Adult Institutions," p. 275.

14. Law Enforcement Assistance Administration, "National Jail Census, 1970," pp. 6–7.

15. James J. Stephan, "Census of Jails, 1999," U.S. Department of Justice, Bureau of Justice Statistics, August 2001, p. iii.

16. Paige M. Harrison and Jennifer C. Karberg, "Prison and Jail Inmates at Midyear 2002," U.S. Department of Justice, Bureau of Justice Statistics Bulletin, April 2003, p. 1.

17. Ibid., p. 10.

18. Stephan, "Census of Jails, 1999," p. 2.

19. Connie Fortin, "Jail Provides Mental Health and Substance Abuse Services," *Corrections Today* 55, no. 6 (June 1993): 105.

20. Bruce Bower, "Mental Illness Prevails in Urban Jails," *Science News* 137, no. 24 (June 16, 1990): 372.

21. Harry E. Allen and Clifford E. Simonsen, *Corrections in America: An Introduction*, 9th ed. (Upper Saddle River, N.J.: Prentice Hall, 2001), p. 177.

22. Harrison and Karberg, "Prison and Jail Inmates at Midyear 2002," p. 8.

23. David M. Parrish, "The Evolution of Direct Supervision in the Design and Operation of Jails," *Corrections Today* 62, no. 6 (October 2000): 84.

24. Ibid., pp. 84–85.

25. See Louis N. Robinson, *Jails: Care and Treatment of Misdemeanant Prisoners in the United States* (Philadelphia: John C. Winston, 1944).

26. See Joseph F. Fishman, *Crucibles of Crime: The Shocking Story of the American Jail* (New York: Cosmopolis Press, 1923). Fishman traveled the country as a federal jail and prison inspector and prison consultant.

27. Task Force on Corrections, President's Commission on Law Enforcement and Administration of Justice, *Task Force Report: Corrections* (Washington, D.C.: U.S. Government Printing Office, 1967), p. 75.

28. National Advisory Commission on Criminal Justice Standards and Goals, *Corrections* (Washington, D.C.: U.S. Government Printing Office, 1973), p. 309.

29. Hans W. Mattick, "Contemporary Jails in the United States: An Unknown and Neglected Area of Justice," in Daniel Glaser, ed., *Handbook of Criminology* (Chicago: Rand McNally, 1975).

30. Allen and Simonsen, *Corrections in America*, p. 446.

31. Daniel Glaser, "Some Notes on Urban Jails," in Daniel Glaser, ed., *Crime in the City* (New York: Harper and Row, 1971), p. 238.

32. Ken Kerle, "Introduction," in Joel A. Thompson and G. Larry Mays, *American Jails: Public Policy Issues* (Chicago: Nelson-Hall, 1991), p. *x.*

33. Ibid.

34. Beth Shuster, "Sheriff Approves Handouts to Condoms to Gay Inmates," *Los Angeles Times*, November 30, 2001.

35. Jennifer Gonnerman, "Roaming Rikers," *The Village Voice*, December 13–19, 2000.

36. Ibid.

37. Jeff Coen, "Cook Jail Crowding Fuels New Volatility," *Chicago Tribune*, March 3, 2003.

38. Steve Mills and Maurice Possley, "Mass Jail Beating Covered Up," *Chicago Tribune*, February 27, 2003.

39. Ibid.

40. Maurice Possley and Steve Mills, "Former Guards Allege 2nd Mass Beating," *Chicago Tribune*, February 28, 2003.

41. "Arizona Jail Disturbance Quelled," *http://database. corrections.com/news/results2.asp?ID=4914.*

42. Alan J. Davis, "Sexual Assaults in the Philadelphia Prison System and Sheriff's Vans," *Transaction* 6, no. 2 (December 1968): 8–16.

43. "Kotzebue Regional Jail Facility," *http://kotzpdweb. tripod.com/krjf.html.*

44. Kristen Moulton, "Local Crooks Crowding Box Elder's Jail," *Salt Lake Tribune*, October 16, 2002.

45. "Michigan Jail Overcrowding at Emergency State," *Gaylord Herald Times*, February 3, 2003.

46. Sara Shipley and Jim Adams, "Kentucky Did Not Draw Lessons from Suicides," *Louisville Courier-Journal*, February 25, 2002.

47. Tim Whitmire, "Nation's Jails Underfunded, Understaffed, Experts Say," *www.mapinc.org/drugnews/ v03/n549/a05.html?104.*

48. Jillian Lloyd, "Outdated Rural Jails Are Packed, Troubled," *Christian Science Monitor*, December 24, 1999.

49. Ibid.

50. Thompson and Mays, *American Jails*, pp. 244–46.

51. American Jail Association, "About AJA," *www. corrections.com/aja/about.html.*

52. David Fisher, "County Lockups Are Bursting at the Seams," *Seattle Post-Intelligencer*, September 28, 2000; "Funds in Hand, New Regional Authority to Start Building Jails," *http://database.corrections.com /news/results2.asp?ID=4844*.

53. Meghan Mandeville, "Examining Jail Overcrowding from a Pretrial Point of View," *http://database. corrections.com/news/results2.asp?ID=4610*.

54. James Stephan, "Census of Jails, 1999," p. 5.

FURTHER READING

Fishman, Joseph F. *Crucibles of Crime: The Shocking Story of the American Jail*. New York: Cosmopolis Press, 1923.

Goldfarb, Ronald. *Jails: The Ultimate Ghetto*. Garden City, N.Y.: Anchor Press/Doubleday, 1975.

Irwin, John. *The Jail: Managing the Underclass in American Society*. Berkeley: University of California Press, 1985.

Thompson, Joel A., and G. Larry Mays. *American Jails: Public Policy Issues*. Chicago: Nelson-Hall, 1991.

Wynn, Jennifer. *Inside Rikers: Stories from the World's Largest Penal Colony*. New York: St. Martin's Press, 2001.

Zupan, Linda L. *Jails: Reform and the New Generation Philosophy*. Cincinnati: Anderson Publishing, 1991.

WEB AND VIDEO RESOURCES

The American Jail Association Website is *www.corrections.com/aja*. Its journal is *American Jails*.

The National Juvenile Detention Association Website is *www.njda.com*.

The Pretrial Services Resource Center Website is *www.pretrial.org*.

COMMENTARY

6 A Day in the Awaiting Trial Unit

by Matthew Brady

It's the beginning of the work day, and I approach the double doors that are locked. I put my key in the opening and step into the Awaiting Trial Unit of the holding prison for women on North Street in Boston. This is considered a maximum security area, and I know that I'm in a place unlike anywhere else on this planet—the toughest section of a women's prison. I am welcomed to organized chaos and bed-lam.

The North Street Jail is what one would call the gray area of justice. The women here have been arrested and arraigned before a judge. They are struggling to pay bail so they can leave prison and attend their court hearings.

These women are victims of the sirens on the streets, and it is difficult to break the habits of street life and purge the blood of the poisoned lives they know best. They know the denizens of dope and where to buy it. They know where to sell and hustle their bodies without being arrested for prostitution. They maintain their contacts on the street even though the streets are their downfall and a very real part of their ongoing addictions.

These women have hit rock bottom, with things so bad that even their parents will not accept collect calls. Many of them cannot remember the names of the attorneys representing them. Almost all of these women have court-appointed attorneys, and they have little or no faith in them. This is the sad part; they feel defeated from the start.

The floor that I am working on is a floor that houses more than one hundred women awaiting their fates— by no means the most pretty or distinguished site in the world. Perhaps you could call this unit the "black and blue" version of prison life. I am hit by a pungent odor in the air. There is a sickening, ever-present smell of vomit, urine and feces. Some of the women getting ready for bail reviews still are dressed in the clothes they wore the night before.

As I enter the housing unit, many of the women yell my name repeatedly, hoping that I'll stop to speak with them. I must hear my name about one hundred times in a day. I'm bombarded by numerous questions and I respond to as many as I can.

One woman arrested the previous night is from Puerto Rico. She is dressed in her night gown, and speaks only in Spanish. Fortunately, I speak her language, and I am able to communicate with her. I help her locate some secondhand clothing donated by a local charity organization.

This morning, like every other morning, daily orientation is held for all women admitted the previous night. They will be given socks, underwear, and copies of the rules and regulations of the prison. Many are desperate for a cigarette. Others nearly fight over the free underwear. Their actions and behaviors are nearly panicked and primal, almost like sharks at a feeding frenzy. They are told to return to their rooms to get ready for lunch. Tired and unshowered, they look like a rag-tag army of embattled women. I try to be supportive, sympathetic and kind, no matter how tough and brazen some of these women are. They remind me of Dorothy in *The Wizard of Oz*. They have quickly and rudely been transported to a different form of existence, and they realize that they are not in Kansas anymore.

For those who are leaving here, there is very little time to prepare. They don't have cosmetics or anything decent to wear, and, overall, they look disheveled. They are packed into the backs of county transportation vehicles, where they will sit very close together with their hands cuffed. They are taken to courts allover the Boston area. Some will remain cuffed this way for hours until they see a judge in a crowded courtroom.

Some of these women have multiple warrants, so even after bailing from one case, they simply bail to another that is pending or in default. If there is enough money, the cycle will proceed until either a woman makes bail or gives up and awaits her court date. For some women, this can represent a turning point—a chance to leave the drugs, dope, and junk behind once and for all. For others, it marks a descent into a living hell.

Sometimes, the judge can reduce a woman's bail to as low as $50. Even at this price, many of these women still cannot afford bail, and the agony goes on. For the most part, their families and close friends have exhausted all their resources and will not pay the reduced amount. For many of their parents, their behaviors and predicaments have become accepted ways of life. They still love their daughters, but they have come to grips with the reality that heroin and cocaine now dominate their grown children's daily lives. They know all too well what it is like to be "burned" or suckered and deceived by their offspring. Over anguished and painful phone calls that reach desperate, frantic and panic-stricken tones, they ultimately must turn their daughters' cries away.

Some parents call the prison in hopes of finding daughters who have been missing for days on end. One distraught mother calls in search of her estranged daughter. Her voice cracks with emotion as she tells me of the stress she feels from taking care of her daughter's children. I dutifully relay the message to the daughter, who is detoxing from heroin. I tell her she can call her mother collect. Even with this courtesy extended to her, the daughter will not call. She lifts her head from her pillow and shakes it from side to side. Not interested.

After their hearings, most of the women return to the prison. So far, it's been a very busy day. I decide to go to lunch outside the prison because I need to get away from the tension. My breathing is heavy and strained, and I need a break from the routine and the misery. I eat a quick lunch, and I'm back at my desk in a half-hour. In my job, you need to be dedicated and devoted to remain steadfast and strong in the face of adversity. You need nerves of steel. You must become a rock of strength, and condition yourself to the crudeness and the profanities flying around you, becoming impervious to the women's harsh mockeries and banalities. If you don't, you'll never last.

In the afternoon, there is even more to do. Some of the women talk about receiving a TV or Walkman radio. These are very valued items in prison. And, there are calls to be made. I collect all the slips that have been submitted for a 5 p.m. attorney phone call. Some of the lawyers must accept the collect calls, while others will not. The end of the afternoon may bring a ray of hope and sunshine or a message of doom and despondency.

Patience is a virtue many of these women lack. They don't want to hear about the delay of gratification. One woman requests a phone call to her father to see if he will bail her out. She reaches him, but he is tired of her and insists on speaking with me. I try to extend my sympathy, but the father responds by abruptly saying that he doesn't need sympathy—just a little privacy. In other words, he wants to be left alone. He knows that his daughter is in prison for prostitution. His only response is that, if people have to go out and have sex anyway, what's wrong with selling it now and then? How very sad and callous his values are!

Another woman approaches me to share a letter she's received from her 10 year-old daughter. Written at the time of the Persian Gulf War, the child expresses concern about her mother's safety. The child doesn't understand where Iraq and Kuwait are located. She tells her mother about Scuds and Patriot missiles, then begs her not to go back to taking drugs. The letter is sincere, poignant and loving.

Later, I overhear a phone call at a pay phone a few feet from my office. A woman in the Awaiting Trial Unit for prostitution talks about a business transaction with a "john" or a "good trick"—a regular customer who will come up to the prison in the late afternoon and bail the woman. I learn that the catch is simple: He pays the bail, and she sleeps with him for the night. Of course, he will lose his bail money because she will not go back to court and thus default, with the court retaining his money, But, the "john" expects this to happen. He "takes it out in trade," as the saying goes. A month later, the same woman will be arrested for prostitution again, but she will call a different "john" or member of her clientele. Next time, though, she may not be as lucky, for she is burning all the bridges behind her.

So much is happening in the afternoon that the second half of the day seems to pass fairly quickly. I look at the clock and realize that I've worked past my shift and it's time to go home. I am relieved—especially since it's only been my first day on the job. I leave the building and pull the doors shut behind me. I find myself back in a different world. Away from the confines of the North Street Jail, I take a big breath of fresh air. I stand outside in the cool breeze.

STATE AND FEDERAL PRISONS

No matter what you call them, what color you paint them, or the scent of the disinfectant, a prison is still a place of confinement and limited freedoms and exceptional discipline. . . . Even under the best of conditions prisons are lousy places.

— W. J. ESTELLE, TEXAS DEPARTMENT OF CORRECTIONS

INTRODUCTION

Adults convicted of felony crimes may be imprisoned in one of the approximately 1,800 state, federal, local, or private prisons in America. Of the more than 1,300,000 felons in prison in 2003, the great majority were held in state prisons in various levels of security, from supermax to open. The Federal Bureau of Prisons confines felons convicted of federal crimes and houses pretrial defendants in federal jails in several large cities. At one time, the federal system was considered a model for state systems, but it has suffered from many of the same problems plaguing state systems in recent years, including an influx of drug offenders that has caused pervasive overcrowding and continuous expansion. After reading the material in this chapter, you should be familiar with:

1. The reasons for the growth of state prison systems in recent years.
2. The differing security levels in state and federal prisons.
3. Variations in the institutional makeup of state systems.
4. Close-ups of several state prison systems.
5. The history of federal prisons.
6. The different types of federal prisons.
7. Recent changes in the federal prison system.
8. The role of local and private prison systems.

THE GROWTH OF STATE PRISON SYSTEMS

Prisons confine felons serving sentences of longer than a year. They are operated primarily by state governments, although the Federal Bureau of Prisons confines federal offenders, three large cities operate their own prisons, county jails in several states now hold felons serving long sentences alongside pretrial defendants and sentenced misdemeanants, and private prisons hold contracts to house state and federal prisoners. Overcrowding, defined as housing inmates above the designed capacity, is a continuing problem in federal prisons and many state prisons. At year end 2001, state prison systems were operating between 1 percent and 16 percent above capacity, while federal prisons were 31 percent above their rated capacity.[1] Prisons are more difficult to manage when they are above capacity, and authorities agree that inmate (and staff) health and safety suffer when overcrowding persists.

Overcrowding persists despite the vast expansion of state and federal prisons since the 1970s. Over the past twenty-five years, as the baby-boom generation has matured, America's prison population has climbed to heights never reached before in our nation's history. Americans fear crime, and politicians turn fear into "get-tough" legislation that sends more people to prison and keeps them there for longer terms. The "War on Crime," particularly its offshoot the "War on Drugs," has tripled jail and prison populations since the early 1980s. For several years, through the early 1990s, almost half the increase was for drug crimes. In recent years, most of the growth in incarceration has come from increased confinement of violent criminals and parole violators. The prison population increase has slowed dramatically after 2000. Several states with big populations—California, New York, and Texas—have reduced the flow of inmates entering prison. Overall, the increase in the state prison population for the year ending June 30, 2002, was about 12,000 inmates, the equivalent of a 1,000-bed prison each month to keep up with the increase. This may sound like a lot, but a few years earlier the growth rate had required a 1,000-bed or 1,500-bed prison *each week*.[2]

The state prison systems of today were founded on the nineteenth-century penitentiary, which was itself based on the legal reforms of the eighteenth-century Age of Enlightenment. The scholars were looking for a more humane and reform-oriented alternative to death and the other corporal punishments of the day. What they got, over a half century of development, was the penitentiary. Sir Thomas Beever opened the **Gaol at Wymondham** in Norfolk, England, in 1785, incorporating principles of isolation, work, and penitence to change the nature of confinement. The Philadelphia Society for Alleviating the Miseries of Public Prisons, led by Dr. Benjamin Rush and other civic reformers, incorporated Beever's ideas into the design of the **Walnut Street Jail,** the first so-called penitentiary in America, which opened in Philadelphia in 1790.

Jeremy Bentham, the utilitarian philosopher, proposed his model **panopticon,** a huge prison with a glass top for improved lighting and better supervision of inmates. What developed in practice, however, was the **Pennsylvania model** or separate system and then the **Auburn model** penitentiary, which became the American prototype because of its cheapness and economic productivity. The northern and midwestern states perfected the model of the **industrial prison** that lasted into the Great Depression of the 1930s. The southern states of the post–Civil War era developed the model of the **agricultural prison,** the giant prison farm applying the plantation mentality to managing prison labor. States in the South and West also developed prison **work camps,** in which inmates worked on public roads, cleared forests, and completed other public works projects as "slaves of the state."

People borrowed ideas and then built institutions to try to apply the new ideas. The people who built the next generation of institutions tried to improve on the existing institutions of their time. Thus, what we have, in the prison system of today, is an ongoing social experiment in which men and women of "good intentions" use confinement of criminals as a principal means of controlling crime. Does it work? We cannot really say, but nothing else really seems to work either, so we keep on with current practices until the next new idea comes along. Then we incorporate it into the experiment too, looking for any kind of sign that anything we're doing is actually having the desired result when in truth we might be accomplishing as much, still whipping criminals and having mass hangings in the town square on Saturday afternoons, if only these practices were not so "uncivilized."

STATE PRISON SYSTEMS TODAY

Although both the federal government and several large cities operate prisons for sentenced felons, the bulk of America's convicted felons—well over 1 million men and women—are confined in institutions operated by state governments. The most common name for this network of prisons, as a state bureaucracy, is the "Department of Corrections." It usually consists of all prisons for adult felons as a core, and it may also include probation and parole for adults and juveniles, juvenile training schools, work release and halfway house facilities, juvenile group homes, and other special purpose facilities. In about half a dozen states with smaller populations, the state department of corrections also operates jails and juvenile detention facilities holding pretrial prisoners. In several other states, the state has assumed a greater role in promoting (and controlling) community-based alternatives through the passage of what are called "Community Corrections Acts," which prescribe a more comprehensive approach combining state, local, and private correctional agencies that provide a wide variety of nonsecure correctional services.

No standard model shows how a department of corrections should be structured or how the relationship of the various state, local, and private correctional agencies should be organized. Management and operational standards have been set by organizations such as the American Correctional Association, but no outcome-based performance measures exist. Private businesses rely on profit and loss statements (which as we know are not always above board); corrections most often relies on recidivism, defined as a former inmate returning to custody, as the standard measure of success or failure. But the definition of recidivism is so variable and the scope of violations so subjective (as in California, where most parole violators have failed drug tests) that it is nearly impossible to compare rates from one state to another.

The heart of the state's correctional system (and generally its most costly component) is its adult prisons. The number of prisons in each state ranges from three in North Dakota to well over 100 in Texas. Most states started their prison systems with one institution, a penitentiary based on the Auburn model, and then expanded the system by building additional prisons as the population increased and the need for special purpose facilities (such as those for women, younger offenders, or drug addicts) was accepted.

Early penitentiaries practiced maximum security; indeed, the enduring image of a "prison" is derived from the architecture of these institutions—high walls, guard towers, cell blocks stacked in tiers, and massive concrete and steel construction. The early American prisons not only maximized security but also practiced isolation and intimidation to a high degree. About sixty of these fortress-style prisons built in the 1800s remain in use today, including Sing Sing, the 1825 New York prison that institutionalized the features of the Auburn penitentiary model. It is these prisons—the oldest, largest, and most secure—that define imprisonment in America. It is these prisons to which Donald Clemmer applied the term **prisonization,** meaning the inmate's adaptation to the culture of the penitentiary. The more profoundly artificial and different the prison is from the outside society, the more the prison inmate is set apart from the values of conventional society. The prison culture becomes more important as inmates remain in prison to serve long sentences; prisonization becomes so complete that prisoners lose sight of the normal society beyond the walls.

Today prisons are graded according to security levels:

1. **Maximum-security prisons.** These are often the older, larger, walled penitentiaries with the most rigorous security procedures and the lowest ratio of inmates to guards. They hold about 12 percent of state inmates, almost entirely in one- or two-man cells. There is one step up from this level, the supermax prison, which is permanent lockdown—isolated confinement to a cell under the most restricted conditions in perpetuity.

2. **Close-high-security prisons.** In some states, these are considered a kind of maximum security, though the security measures are less restrictive and the ratio of inmates to guards may be higher. About 16 percent of state inmates are held in this classification.

3. **Medium-security prisons.** These are usually the smaller, newer prisons, with double fences instead of walls and dormitory or pod housing rather than cells. The inmate-to-guard ratio may be twice that of the maximum-security prison. About 35 percent of state inmates are held in this classification, which is now the usual starting place for new inmates who are not perceived as dangerous or escape risks.

4. **Minimum-security prisons.** These newer, smaller prisons have minimal perimeter security and fewer internal controls. The inmate-to-guard ratio is even higher, and inmates may live in rooms or dorms with more privacy and more amenities. About 31 percent of state prison inmates are held in minimum security. They have usually worked their way down from higher classifications; many are "short-termers" approaching release. The public and political fear of criminals has recently resulted in "cosmetic" security changes at some of these facilities, such as increasing perimeter fencing to make the public think they are safer, even though it remains very easy to escape from this type of facility. Many inmates are already outside the prison part of the time on work details or other assignments.

5. **Open-security facilities.** Not usually called prisons at all, these are non-secure facilities such as work release centers, prerelease centers, halfway houses, and other types of community-based facilities. They have no armed guards and no fences; to escape, all you have to do is walk away and not come back. When they catch up with you later, you will be put in maximum security as an escape risk. About 5 percent of state inmates are in the open classification.

Many state prisons are called **multilevel prisons** because they provide two or more of these levels of security within the same institution. Inmates can change from one grade to another without having to transfer to another prison. The general trend today is toward expanding the lower security grades, especially medium security, though now a greater number of prisoners are held in maximum and close security than were confined in all American prisons only twenty-five years ago.

In the 1990s, the term "supermax" entered the prison management vocabulary. Although Alcatraz, which opened in 1934, is often said to be the first supermax prison, the concept of a special prison or housing unit above maximum security became more prevalent during the continued expansion of the prison system in the 1980s. With the increase in the number of inmates overall, the number of inmates considered unmanageable, dangerous, or high-risk increased also.

Supermax refers to the highest level of security that can be applied to a prison housing unit. Inmates are kept in single-person cells, generally locked down twenty-four/seven. It is an earned status, based mostly on what the inmate does *after* he gets to prison rather than what he has done before. Most supermax inmates do not have work assignments, nor do they have access to ordinary prison recreation, inmate organizations, or programming. Visiting is restricted. Privileges are minimal. Contact with other people, including staff, is very limited. The inmate is isolated in his cell as much as possible, with brief outdoor exercise periods in a small, individual exercise yard. Supervision is very high, higher in many states than that provided inmates on death row. Some entire prisons are designated supermax; other prisons have cell block units so designated. The rules and procedures vary from state to state. Supermax refers as much to a type of inmate (who is perceived as a threat requiring control measures beyond maximum security) as it does to a particular prison architectural or management style. Less than 2 percent of the American prison population is confined in supermax housing.

Many prisons have a **special housing unit** with security conditions similar to supermax but housing disciplinary offenders for shorter periods rather than long-term security and control problems. Special housing would once have been called "the hole," where inmates were subject to physical punishments, restricted diets, and sensory deprivation. Some supermax prisons also have special housing units within them, and some special housing units use a level system where the worst-behaved inmates are kept on the lowest level. Scattered around the country, buried deep in the bowels of our supermax prisons and special housing units, are probably the few dozen "baddest" inmates in America; but they are so buried and isolated that even if we could identify them, we could not get to them to ask them just how bad they are.

We continue to build new maximum-security prisons today, including such supermax prisons as Pelican Bay in California and Florence, Colorado, in the federal system. However, most of the new prisons built in the twentieth century have incorporated lower levels of security—medium, minimum, and open. Once fences began to replace walls in defining prison perimeters, the look of prisons began to change. For one thing, people could actually *see* into the prisons, which had some effect on the traditional seclusion of inmates behind impenetrable walls. The mode of housing changed from cell blocks to dormitories and rooms. The ratio of guards to inmates was reduced, and the new prisons became more open, making it easier for inmates to move around. The absolute controls that were so much a part of the old-style penitentiary were relaxed, which tends to reduce the impact of prisonization on inmates. Medium- and minimum-security prisons also tend to be much smaller than the old penitentiaries, and because they are of more recent construction, they are much more modern in their design and amenities. Most corrections officials agree that only about 15 to 25 percent of prisoners require maximum security; the rest do fine with less.

State prison systems range in size from North Dakota, which has just over 1,000 people in prison, to the huge systems of California and Texas, each with more than 150,000 in prison. Rates of imprisonment vary greatly as well. They are highest in the South and lowest in the North. A vast gulf separates Maine and Minnesota, with imprisonment rates of 137 and 139 per 100,000, from Louisiana and Mississippi (and until last year Texas), with rates over 700 per 100,000. For the fifty states, the average was about 425 per 100,000 on June 30, 2001.[3]

North Dakota

North Dakota has the nation's smallest prison system—three prisons housing 1,168 inmates as of June 30, 2002. As recently as 1981, the system was small indeed, 280 inmates, which would hardly register as a blip on the prison radar screen today.

The system's Website is emblazoned with the image of a bearded cowboy wearing a wide-brimmed western hat; he is the symbol of "Rough Rider Industries," North Dakota's prison industry program, which uses inmate labor for the benefit of state and local governments. Inmates manufacture office furniture, traffic signs, metal products, and license plates.[4]

Two of the state's three prisons are located in Bismarck, the state capital. The North Dakota State Penitentiary was opened in 1885. It houses 520 maximum- and medium-security male inmates. Its stated mission is

> to protect the public by maintaining proper custody of the offenders sentenced by the courts; to provide a safe and healthy environment for staff and inmates; and to offer the best work, education, and treatment programs possible, encouraging inmates to make the needed changes to be law abiding and successful in society.[5]

The State Farm was established in the 1940s as a camp for penitentiary inmates. Located four miles southwest of Bismarck, it is now known as the Missouri River Correctional Center, a 150-bed facility for minimum-security males and females. Although agricultural work is still performed there, the more important purpose of this center is to reintegrate offenders into society by offering work release and community treatment programming.

North Dakota's newest prison is the James River Correctional Center. It opened in 1998 on the grounds of the State Hospital in Jamestown. This facility can house 160 male and 80 female medium-security inmates.

These three institutions make up the Prisons Division of the North Dakota Department of Corrections and Rehabilitation (DOCR), which was created in 1989 to replace the previous office of the Director of Institutions. The DOCR also consists of the Field Services Division, responsible for probation, parole, and community placements, and the Juvenile Services Division.

Although North Dakota's imprisonment rate (167 per 100,000 in 2002) is well below the national average and its prison population tiny in comparison to other states, the rapid growth of felons sentenced to imprisonment has been an important political issue over the past decade. The 2001 state legislature established an interim committee to study future prison needs. The average daily inmate population had nearly doubled in the previous eight years, from 567 in 1993 to 1,095 as of June 2001. The committee was to examine several key issues:

1. Relieving prison overcrowding, which required state prisoners to be housed in rehabilitation centers, local jails, and a private prison in Minnesota.
2. Rescinding mandatory sentences for drug crimes and other offenses. The average sentence for drug offenders had risen from forty months in 1993 to sixty months in 2000.
3. Providing more substance abuse treatment for prisoners. About two-thirds of North Dakota's inmates were alcohol or drug dependent, and few were able to get into treatment.
4. Building a separate prison for women. The number of women inmates had increased from twenty in 1990 to about 100 a decade later, presenting housing problems at the two men's prisons where they shared space.[6]

In 2003, the prison population was still growing, and these issues were otherwise unresolved. North Dakota was the last state without a separate women's prison, Corrections Director Elaine Little told the legislature as she sought funds to turn a hospital building into a new women's prison. State Penitentiary Warden Tim Schuetzle warned legislators that a proposed budget cut in corrections would sharply curtail treatment funds that had kept the state's recidivism rate low (20 percent, according to department figures). "What would end up happening is we would turn into South Dakota," the warden said. This reference apparently did not mean that North Dakota would disappear or that South Dakota was such a terrible place, only that both its prison population and the recidivism rate had increased dramatically. The legislators had no immediate response to this dire warning or to the warden's other concern that the state may be legally liable for failing to provide medical treatment for the majority of its prisoners who have hepatitis C (an estimated 10 percent of the prisoner population).[7]

California

On the opposite end of the scale from North Dakota are the nation's two largest state prison systems, California and Texas, which have often been engaged in an unenviable footrace to see who could lock up the most people in prison. For a while in the 1990s, it was Texas, then California took the lead, and now Texas has moved up again as California implements nonsecure options for drug criminals. Coming up on the outside to take the lead is the federal prison system, which by June 30, 2001, held 161,681 inmates and was adding inmates at a quicker pace, while California held 160,315 and Texas 158,131; Florida and New York were way back with 73,000 and 67,000 prisoners in custody.[8]

The history of the California prison system dates to the early 1850s, when inmates confined on the prison ship *Wapan* were put to work building a prison at Point Quentin in Marin County. When they had finished their new home, they moved from ship to shore into the prison, which came to be known as **San Quentin.**[9] It housed both male and female inmates until 1933, when the women's prison at Tehachapi was built. An early Barbara Stanwyck movie, *Ladies They Talk About*, is a prison romance set in San Quentin when the women were confined in their separate compound, officially known as Bayview, completely surrounded by the men's prison. The film is not a conventional prison romance, incidentally; Stanwyck's boyfriend is a crusading evangelist, not a male convict.

Tehachapi was shut down after it was struck by an earthquake in July 1952 (and reopened as a men's prison three years later), but San Quentin remains alive and thriving 150 years after its opening. Despite periodic schemes to shut it down—"the prison that would not die"—San Quentin held nearly 6,000 inmates in 2003. Folsom State Prison, California's second-oldest prison (dating from 1880), held 3,600.[10]

In the federal system and many international prison systems, the prevailing theory for a long time favored smaller prisons, following the reasoning that mass institutions made management more difficult and individualized treatment nearly impossible. Six hundred was often used as a maximum desirable prison population.

When you look at California's prisons today, you see just the opposite. California prisons are small towns behind bars. In 2003, California's correctional system consisted of thirty-three state prisons, twenty-eight camps, sixteen community correctional facilities, and five prisoner mother facilities. They held in total 160,000 inmates, the thirty-three prisons holding 148,000 of these—averaging about 4,500 inmates per prison. Most prisons are multilevel institutions, many of them broken up into entirely separate facilities practicing unit management. The two largest California prisons in 2003 were the Correctional Training Facility at Soledad and Avenal State Prison. Divided into South, Central, and North Facilities, Soledad held 7,000 men. Avenal held just over 7,000. The California Institution for Men (referred to in the system as Chino) held 6,300 men in four separate facilities. This was the prison that became famous as the "prison without walls," replacing the traditional high prison wall with fencing when it opened in June 1941.[11]

California prisons use five classification levels:

    I.   Open dormitories without a secure perimeter.

    II.   Open dormitories with secure perimeter fences and armed perimeter security.

    III.   Individual cells, fenced perimeters, and armed perimeter security.

IV. Cells, fenced or walled perimeters, electronic security, and armed officers inside and out.

V. Security Housing Unit, the most secure area within a level IV prison.[12]

The system also uses designations for special populations. *RC* is for men and women undergoing classification in reception centers. *Camps* designates the minimum-security inmates assigned to the system's forestry and firefighting centers; twenty such centers housing 2,200 male and female inmates operate out of the Sierra Conservation Center in Jamestown. *Condemned* is for the 560 male inmates on death row at San Quentin and the fourteen female inmates on death row at Chowchilla.

James V. Bennett wrote that in California of the late 1800s, the grim story of the American penitentiary reached its lowest levels. By the time of the rehabilitation era, however, from post–World War II through the 1970s, California was recognized as one of the most progressive state prison systems. It built special purpose facilities for treating drug offenders and sex offenders, a separate hospital facility, and classification centers employing the latest behavioral science methodology; it offered probably the widest variety of vocational and educational programming of any state prison system. These features are still around today, but the system is better known for its great success in locking people up than for its treatment effectiveness.

In 1981, California had 29,000 men and women in prison. Twenty years later, the system was five times larger. California built twenty-one new prisons and added housing units to existing facilities, never quite catching up with the demand for prison beds. Most of its thirty-three prisons in 2003 were filled well above their design capacities; Avenal State Prison, which opened in 1987, was designed for 2,320; fifteen years later, it held three times that number in the same physical space.

The mission statement of the California Department of Corrections on its Website in 2003 was, "Our mission is to develop and implement effective and innovative correctional policy, create a coordinated correctional system which is responsive to the citizen's right to public safety and governmental accountability, and maintain a reputation for excellence and integrity."[13]

With the flood of new inmates coming into the system under more punitive drug and habitual offender statutes, this has been a difficult mission. Prison costs have increased to the point that California has for the past decade spent more on prisons than on its famous system of higher education. Conditions in some of its institutions, particularly the supermax unit of the new Pelican Bay State Prison and the California State Prison at Corcoran, have generated lots of lawsuits and negative publicity. California's parole revocation rate, focusing on drug use by parolees, is the highest in the country. The state has recently changed its approach in dealing with drug criminals to promote more use of nonsecure treatment alternatives, but its prison population continued to grow in 2001 before declining in 2002. It has the same problem in common with Louisiana and several other states: a growing percentage of inmates have very long terms that will keep them behind bars until they are elderly or dead. The California prison system's reputation for progressiveness has been another casualty of the War on Crime.

Texas

When Fred Haynes visited Texas in his Depression-era travels through American prisons, he gave this report:

> The Texas prison system in 1928 consisted of a central receiving institution at Huntsville, twelve farms owned by the state with a total acreage of 77,910, and four farms of 5,500 acres leased by the state. The farms varied in size from 1,000 to 15,000 acres. They were widely scattered, and the problem of administration was difficult. At Huntsville were located the infirmary of the prison system and several industries that made products for use on the different farms.[14]

By 1934, one of these farms had been abandoned and sold, one was used for housing women, and another held men who were physically limited from doing farm labor. The nine active farms, each headed by a manager, supervised nineteen units or camps, headed by an assistant manager or "captain." Out of a prison population of 5,400, about 3,800 were actively engaged in farming.[15]

The central unit in **Huntsville** was established in 1849; the farms were spread around Houston and Huntsville up to a hundred miles or more away from "The Walls." Like many other old prisons, the Walls unit was the target of periodic political efforts to shut it down and replace it with a new industrial prison; like virtually all of these, it defied these efforts and, remodeled with a fresh coat of paint, continues to be used as a prison today. It is still the headquarters of the Texas Department of Criminal Justice, as the Texas prison system is called today, and it is now known around the world as the "capital of capital punishment," where it carries out more executions than any other prison in America (or possibly any other single prison in the world, though we cannot say this with certainty about China).

When George Beto became director of the Texas Department of Corrections (TDC) in 1962, it was still a loose confederation of maximum-security prison farms. When he left ten years later to head the Criminal Justice Center at Sam Houston State University, Beto had transferred power from the wardens to the central office of the TDC, creating what John DiIulio has called the control model in Texas prisons (more on this in chapter 7). This model emphasized farm work and strict discipline within a centralized bureaucratic environment.

Like many southern prison systems with a higher ratio of inmates to guards, Texas had relied on inmate trusties—called "building tenders" (BTs)—to maintain internal order. Unlike the other states, when federal courts began to abolish the practice of convicts controlling other convicts, Texas fought to keep its old-fashioned system intact. It lost. In ***Ruiz v. Estelle*** (1980, though this litigation was filed originally in 1972 and finally upheld on appeal in 1985), federal Judge William Wayne Justice ruled the Texas prison system was unconstitutional in seven major aspects:

1. Reliance on the building tenders
2. Staff brutality toward inmates
3. Prison overcrowding
4. Arbitrary discipline and grievance procedures
5. Inadequate classification of inmates

6. Violation of fire and safety codes
7. Lack of inmate access to attorneys and outside visitors[16]

The removal of the BTs, the induction of huge numbers of inexperienced security officers, and the abrupt collapse of the control model caused tough times in Texas prisons in the mid–1980s. Violence increased dramatically, and Texas prisons lost the sense of purpose forged under Beto's leadership. Prison populations soared. Texas went from third place, with 13,000 inmates in 1967 (well behind California and New York and just slightly ahead of Ohio), to first place, with 30,700 inmates, by 1980. By the early 1990s, its prisons were well over capacity, and another 30,000 inmates were being stored in county jails. The legislature got voter approval to sell bonds financing new prisons—forty-seven units holding 100,000 inmates. Problem solved.

Or was it? By early 2003, the system was nearing capacity again, with 158,000 inmates in prison, 10,000 of these in private prisons. Officials of the Texas Department of Criminal Justice were projecting the need for another 14,000 prison beds by 2008. Crime had dropped by a third from 1990 to 2001, but the prison system had continued its steady growth, leading legislators to consider five major options:

1. *Building more prisons.* The last-resort option, strongly opposed within the legislature
2. *Paroling more prisoners.* Reversing a sharp decline in the parole rate from earlier years
3. *Returning inmates to county jails.* A cost-saving measure of mixed benefits and liabilities
4. *Spending more on treatment.* Concentrating on community-based options to keep nonviolent felons out of prison
5. *Privatization.* Another cost-saving approach, not popular because of problems with private prison management in Texas[17]

While the legislature debates its options, the incoming tide of inmates rises higher. Texas will soon be passing California again.

Louisiana

Image-conscious state governments today seek a catchy slogan to represent their state in the public eye. Arkansas is "The Natural State." Oklahoma is "Native America." Louisiana has traditionally been "The Bayou State" or "Sportsman's Paradise." Today a better slogan would be "The Inmate State." Louisiana's rate of prison incarceration has held at about 800 per 100,000 from 2001 through 2003, and its jail incarceration rate has climbed to about 400 per 100,000. These two rates combined are the highest in the country. At any given time, one of every eighty people in Louisiana is behind bars, the highest rate of confinement in the world today (though apparently less than some totalitarian regimes of the past).

In 2003, to give you some basis for comparison, Louisiana, with a population of 4.2 million, held more than 50,000 people in jail and prison. Canada, with 30 million people, confined 36,000 people in 2001. Japan, with a population of 125 million, locked up 67,000.

A few years ago, a state senator warned his colleagues that if imprisonment trends continued, Louisiana would turn into (no, not South Dakota; they were long past that) a state in which everyone was either a convict or a prison guard—leaving no one to do the productive labor to support the state's vast system of jails and prisons. His speech was clearly intended as political rhetoric, but it was based on a factual trend. Over the thirty-year period from 1971 to 2001, Louisiana's prison population increased from about 3,500 to 35,000, a 1,000 percent increase that marked the most dramatic growth of any state prison system in the country.

In prison circles, Louisiana is best known for its state penitentiary at **Angola,** one of the largest and most enduring prison farms in America. Originally one of a cluster of private plantations along the Mississippi River northwest of Baton Rouge, Angola was used to house convicts under the private lease that prevailed in Louisiana after the Civil War. A prisoner population largely made up of ex-slaves and later their children and grandchildren did agricultural labor for the economic enrichment of the leaseholder, Major Samuel L. James, and his family.[18]

When the lease expired in 1901, Angola became a state-operated penitentiary. By the early 1920s, the state had purchased additional land to expand the size of "the farm" to 18,000 acres, or about twenty-six square miles, just slightly smaller than Miami, Florida, but slightly larger than Newark, New Jersey. For most of the twentieth century, Angola was the only real prison in Louisiana. Work camps were located in other parts of the state, and parish prisons held pretrial inmates, misdemeanants, and some short-term felons, but Angola was the destination of all the real felons—men and women, boys and girls—into the 1950s.

Several key features of the convict lease carried over to state operation of Angola—cheapness, hard labor, isolation, brutality, segregation, no rehabilitation, and the profit motive—making the prison a hard place to do time (or to stay alive) for much of the twentieth century.[19] The state opened an adult reformatory at DeQuincy in 1957 and followed by establishing a separate women's prison in an old trusty camp at St. Gabriel in 1961. Reforms at Angola during the 1950s built a new Main Prison complex to replace most of the camps scattered around the farm, and outside administrators were brought in to clean up the prison's worst abuses.

In the 1960s, Angola returned to its normal condition of benign neglect. Convicts were once more: "Out of sight, out of mind." A few years later, when prison populations began to climb, Angola was badly overcrowded. It had stopped using inmate guards but not yet hired free people to replace them. The result was a period of inmate-to-inmate violence that earned Angola the title of "the worst prison in the country." In June 1975, federal Judge Gordon West ruled that conditions at Angola were in violation of the Eighth Amendment's "cruel and unusual punishment" clause. Judge West ordered sweeping reforms: reducing the population; increasing security; renovating the physical plant; ending segregation; improving medical care, nutrition, and sanitation; and providing for more orderly discipline and for religious freedom—the court order went on and on.[20] Corrections in Louisiana has not been the same since.

The new corrections system that developed in Louisiana in the two decades following Judge West's court order is vastly improved from Angola's plantation-style prison, a system good enough to be called "the best in the South" by corrections officials—good enough that all state prisons have been fully accredited by the American Correctional Association and finally released from the consent decree through which the federal court regulated prisons and jails in Louisiana until 1997.

But, it is also a much more expensive system, a system that emphasizes long-term confinement of offenders rather than less drastic alternatives and a system that so far has not made much headway in selling its ideas of reform to hard-line, punitive politicians conscious that this is the "age of the victim," not the age of the criminal.

In Louisiana's new system, the majority of state prisoners are confined in medium-security institutions distributed in rural parishes across the state. Touring these prisons would take you to small towns not even most Louisiana natives have ever been to: Kinder, Winnfield, Cottonport, St. Gabriel, Jackson, Homer, Angie, and DeQuincy. These prisons, all except the one at DeQuincy, have been opened since the court order; they house about half of all convicts doing state time.

Of the remainder, most are held not in state prisons but in parish jails. They are serving state time, but they are in the custody of parish sheriffs who are compensated by the state—at a current rate of $22 per day—for keeping them. It is much cheaper for the state to pay sheriffs to keep state inmates in jail than for the state to care for them in a state prison. The number of state prisoners serving their time in parish jails continues to increase as sheriffs build larger jails to "help out the state"—and make more money for their own operations in the process.

In the new system, Angola is no longer the main prison. Only about 5,100 men, 15 percent of Louisiana's convicts are confined there. Its role is now that of the "long-termers' prison," confining 3,400 natural lifers and other inmates serving long sentences. Angola, as the national model of the lifers' prison now emerging in America, has the oldest inmate population of any major prison in the country.

Louisiana's state prisons are a part of the Corrections Services office of the Louisiana Department of Public Safety and Corrections. This mission statement is provided on the Corrections Services Website: "The mission of Corrections Services is to provide for custody, care, and treatment of adjudicated offenders through enforcement of laws and management of programs designed to insure the safety of the public, staff, and inmates and reintegrate offenders into society."[21]

The listed "Goals and Priorities" of Corrections Services include the following:

1. Public safety
2. Staff and inmate safety
3. Provision of basic services
4. Opportunity for change
5. Opportunity for making amends[22]

Many of its 50,000 jail and prison inmates—incarcerated for drug and property crimes—probably wish that opportunities for change and making amends rated higher on the list.

Minnesota

If Louisiana's prison system has the reputation of being a bloated system full of drug and property criminals, Minnesota's prisons have the opposite reputation—a small, rational system focused on locking up the most dangerous criminals. On June 30, 2002, Minnesota, with a population of 4.5 million, held just under 7,000 people in prison; its rate of 139 per 100,000 was the second lowest in the country behind Maine.

As a percentage of its state budget, Minnesota's prison system is the cheapest in the country. It relies heavily on probation to keep the numbers behind bars down, and it uses prison space to hold violent criminals. Its prison terms, following the sentencing guidelines adopted in 1980, have been among the longest in the country for this reason. Since 1987, sex offenders have made up the largest category of the inmate population, making up 19 percent of the population on January 1, 2001.[23]

The mission statement of the Minnesota Department of Corrections is one simple statement: "It is our mission to develop and provide effective correctional practices that contribute to a safer Minnesota."[24] The eight adult prisons are divided into a six-level custody classification system; some prisons have multiple custody levels:

1. One level 6 maximum-custody prison at Oak Park Heights
2. Two level 5 close-custody prisons—the old state prisons at St. Cloud and Stillwater
3. One level 4 close-custody prison at Rush City
4. Three level 3 medium-custody prisons at Faribault, Lino Lakes, and Moose Lake
5. One level 2 minimum-custody prison at Faribault
6. Three level 1 minimum-custody prisons at Willow River (a boot camp program), Lino Lakes, and Stillwater
7. One women's prison at Shakopee with all custody levels[25]

Minnesota's politicians and corrections officials take pride in having avoided the most extreme approaches of the "get-tough-on-crime" agenda of the past two decades—truth-in-sentencing and three-strikes-and-you're-out provisions, for example. But recently they have noticed that Minnesota is not completely immune from the punitive ethos. Its prisons are full, double bunking of single-person cells is under way in some prisons, and officials are discussing the need to build two new prisons by 2010.

The chief reason, according to Dennis Benson, Minnesota's deputy commissioner of corrections, is sentencing enhancements that have targeted certain criminals since the late 1980s. This list of longer sentences includes the following:

1. Felons caught with a gun
2. Felony drunk drivers
3. Lifers, whose minimum prison term was changed from seventeen to thirty years
4. Sex offenders
5. Drug offenders

Prison sentences were about eight months longer on average in 2003 than they had been fifteen years earlier, and the prison population was 1,600 people higher than it would have been if sentences had remained constant, according to corrections analysts.[26]

Most of this increase is attributed to drug offenders. In 1990, 219 offenders were in Minnesota prisons for drug crimes (7 percent of the total prison population); by 2001, this number had increased to 1,066 (17 percent). The state is exploring ways to deliver more effective treatment to both sex and drug offenders in community-based settings and in prison to reduce recidivism. It already proclaims a very low prison recidivism rate of about 20 percent, comparable to North Dakota.

Not all political officials want to keep the prison population down. The Republican governor and other conservatives are willing to pay more to keep more people behind bars, arguing that prison expenditures pay dividends by making communities safer. Chuck Samuelson, the executive director of the Minnesota Civil Liberties Union, said he found it ironic that Minnesota was moving toward the "Mississippi Model" of imprisonment (presumably meaning something like the South Dakota model but on a much grander scale), just as many states are moving toward Minnesota's model.[27]

THE BIRTH OF THE FEDERAL PRISON SYSTEM

The **Federal Bureau of Prisons** was created by an act of Congress signed into law by President Herbert Hoover on May 14, 1930. It was established as an office within the federal **Justice Department,** where it remains today. Before this legislation was enacted, there were federal prisons but no central office managing them; before the first federal prison was opened in the 1890s, there were federal prisoners, but they served their time in state and local institutions.

At one time, there were few federal crimes and few criminals serving federal prison time. After the Civil War, the numbers of both offenses and offenders began to climb. Many state prisons and local jails that had previously housed federal prisoners experienced overcrowding problems, and it became more difficult to place federal prisoners in these facilities. In response, Congress passed the **Three Prisons Act** in 1891. The first **U.S. penitentiary** was the old military prison at **Fort Leavenworth,** Kansas, which began to house federal prisoners in 1895. **McNeil Island,** Washington, an older prison already in use, was designated a U.S. penitentiary in 1907. The third penitentiary, **Atlanta,** was the first newly constructed federal prison. It opened in 1902. In the 1920s, Congress authorized a reformatory for young men at Chillicothe, Ohio, which opened in 1928, and the first federal prison for women at **Alderson,** West Virginia. In the year before its formal opening, on November 14, 1928, 174 women had already been sent to Alderson from state prisons and jails, two-thirds of them drug law violators and 70 to 80 percent suffering from "social diseases"—what we refer to as sexually transmitted diseases today.[28]

Institutions were being added one at a time, but no overall plan existed. Mabel Walker Willebrandt, an assistant attorney general in the Justice Department, had laid the groundwork for establishing a unified federal prison system in the 1920s. In 1929, Sanford Bates, the reform-minded director of the Massachusetts prison system, became federal superintendent of prisons. In the same year, the congressionally sponsored report of the Cooper Commission documented the horrors of the existing system and contained the seeds of the legislative proposals that gave birth to the Bureau of Prisons in the following year.[29]

Sanford Bates was appointed the first director of the new Bureau of Prisons, which quickly became known in corrections as the **BOP.** As defined by law, the director's post was a strong one. Bates consolidated control over the separate institutions in the new system and got rid of management and security staff who challenged his authority or committed acts of misconduct.

At the end of 1930, the new system was made up of fourteen institutions with just over 13,000 inmates. Bates oversaw the rapid expansion of the system over the next decade. The U.S. Penitentiary at **Lewisburg,** Pennsylvania, considered the most advanced institution of its kind in America, opened in 1933. The federal prison medical center at Springfield, Missouri, opened the next year. Federal prison camps to provide minimum-security housing and work assignments in forestry and road building began to open.

In 1934, the most famous of the federal prisons, **Alcatraz,** was opened, ironically against the wishes of the BOP central office, which considered the prison more trouble than it was worth. Bates and his aides in BOP headquarters were opposed to the establishment of Alcatraz, viewing it as an unnecessary political stunt in the high-crime Depression era, but J. Edgar Hoover of the Federal Bureau of Investigation, with the support of the attorney general and key congressional officials, got it created anyway. The old military prison on Alcatraz Island in San Francisco Bay was converted to confine civilian prisoners. Alcatraz is often identified as the first "supermax" prison (a title that more appropriately belongs to the U.S. Penitentiary at Marion, Illinois, which opened in 1963), though its reputation for both the meanness of its clientele and the impossibility of escape was always exaggerated. BOP management always viewed Alcatraz as a mistake and was pleased to shut it down in 1963.

DEVELOPING A MODEL SYSTEM

Throughout its history, the BOP has often been admired as a model system. Corrections officials in the states have looked enviously at the federal system in much the same way that the poor man walking to work looks at the rich executive being chauffeured to work in his limousine. "If only we had that kind of money to spend on our prisons." "When you only get the cream of criminals, it's easy to have a good prison system." "If we had as many staff that they do, we'd have good prisons, too." "No wonder the prisoners are happy; those federal prisons are all **country club prisons** anyway."

John DiIulio and others have discounted these conventional explanations based on more money and nicer prisoners. DiIulio believes that the federal prison system's success is due primarily to how the agency has been led, organized, and managed, both in the cell blocks and in the corridors of political power. "Management is the key," he has written.[30]

Since it was created in 1930, the BOP has had only seven directors:

Sanford Bates, 1930–1937

James V. Bennett, 1937–1964

Myrl Alexander, 1964–1970

Norman Carlson, 1970–1987

J. Michael Quinlan, 1987–1993

Kathleen Hawk Sawyer, 1993–2003

Harley Lappin, 2003 to present

Seven directors in more than seven decades—some state systems have had seven directors in one decade.

The early leadership of Bates and Bennett was critical. These men were professional leaders of vision and character. They also knew how federal politics worked. They were able to work with executive and legislative officials while minimizing the political intervention and instability that plagued many state systems, where philosophies and priorities underwent personality changes every time the governor's office changed hands. The BOP's employees, from prison guards up to wardens, enjoyed strong civil service protection; they were career people. Drawing on the stable financial resources of the federal government, the BOP could afford the facilities, equipment, programs, and staff necessary to a first-rate system. Its operation was much admired by state departments of corrections, which were always borrowing its ideas and trying to steal its people away.

If Mabel Walker Willebrandt laid the foundation and Sanford Bates built the framework, **James V. Bennett** completed the original construction of the BOP in his long tenure, which was marked by three important features:

1. **Federal Prison Industries, Inc.** Originally authorized by Congress in 1934, the BOP's industrial component has been a mainstay of the system since. Known since 1978 by the trade name **UNICOR,** this enterprise produces goods used by the military and the federal bureaucracy; since these goods are not sold directly to the public, they do not run afoul of the federal prison labor laws that so devastated state prisons in the 1930s. In 2002, about 18 percent of federal inmates worked for UNICOR producing goods ranging from clothes and Army helmets to office supplies, electronics, and furniture.[31] With wages ranging from 23 cents to $1.15 per hour, these prison jobs are comparatively well paying and highly sought after.

2. *The federal inmate classification system.* Bennett guided the development of a prisoner classification system intended to rationalize inmate management and promote individualized treatment.

3. *The medical model.* Reaching its peak in the late 1950s, this model was premised on providing inmates with the programs needed to change law-breaking into law-abiding behavior. Although it would later be officially abandoned as a policy, it did result in the expansion of educational, vocational, and treatment programs open to inmates.

Myrl Alexander, who succeeded Bennett, was a career BOP administrator and the first federal warden to rise to the director's position. In 1956, as president of the American Correctional Association, Alexander announced an "Inmate Bill of Rights" that included these provisions:

1. The right to clean, decent surroundings with competent attention to the inmate's physical and mental well-being

2. The right to maintain and reinforce the strengthening ties that bind inmates to their family and to their community

3. The right to develop and maintain skills as a productive worker in our economic system

4. The right to fair, impartial, and intelligent treatment without special privilege or license for any inmate

5. The right to positive guidance and counsel from correctional personnel of understanding and skill[32]

The application of these principles helped the federal system avoid much of the legal turmoil that engulfed state prison systems in the 1960s and 1970s.

The long tenure of **Norman Carlson** as director is noted for modernizing the management practices of the BOP. Under Carlson, the BOP was restructured into five (later six) regions, each with its own headquarters and regional director, to ensure control and accountability. The bureau also adopted a **master plan**—a set of principles establishing the direction in which it wished to be moving. In the 1970s and 1980s, the key components of the master plan included the following:

1. **Unit management.** Pioneered in the 1950s at the Ashland, Kentucky, federal prison, this approach broke larger prisons down into smaller units (based on housing units) in which security, treatment, and other staff were expected to work closely together within these autonomous units.

2. **Mandatory literacy.** Starting with the target of sixth-grade literacy in 1982 and increasing to high school equivalency in 1991, this program requires inmates to participate in literacy training to get better work assignments within the federal prison system.

3. **Gender-neutral employment.** Men and women are hired for all staff positions in every institution solely on their perceived ability to do the job.

4. *The* **balanced model.** After 1975, the BOP turned away from the **medical model,** which had been the brainchild of Director James Bennett, and adopted this composite model combining rehabilitation, deterrence, retribution, and incapacitation.

5. *The* **family culture.** Through seminars, agency meetings, expanded training, moves, and reassignments, the BOP sought to promote a close-knit relationship among its staff and their families.

6. **Legal standards.** Anticipating the prisoners' rights movement, the BOP provided higher standards of care and custody before being ordered to do so by the courts.

Carlson also presided over the beginnings of the expansion of the federal prison system, which had remained stable in size for forty years. In 1940, the BOP had twenty-four institutions with 24,360 inmates. In 1980, it had 24,252 inmates in forty-four institutions. The population had remained constant, while the institutional makeup had shifted from large prisons with mixed security levels to smaller, more cost-effective facilities that each confined inmates with similar security needs.

One of the new prisons that opened under Carlson was the Federal Correctional Institution (FCI) at **Butner,** North Carolina, which opened in 1976. Butner was designed to apply the postrehabilitation prison management ideas of criminologist Norval Morris. Butner

> featured an open, "normalized" environment, in which inmates were fairly free to move about within the secure perimeter during certain hours. It also offered a wide range of modern, innovative programs. However, apart from work assignments (which were mandatory, in part for purposes of inmate management), participation in these programs was voluntary. Butner attracted worldwide attention and was enormously influential.[33]

These new ideas about prison operations were soon to be overwhelmed by the press of incoming bodies. Tough new federal statutes, particularly those aimed at drug offenders, drove the federal prison population to 56,999 in 1990, more than double what it had been ten years earlier and 170 percent of rated capacity. Overcrowding, which had not been a serious problem in the federal system since the 1920s, became a concern once again.

J. Michael Quinlan, the attorney and warden who succeeded Carlson as director in 1987, had to keep building new prisons to house the influx of new inmates. Quinlan was welcomed to office by the two most destructive (though not the most deadly) prison riots in federal history. The two federal prisons at Oakdale, Louisiana, and Atlanta suffered major riots lasting several days in November 1987. In both institutions, Cuban inmates—at **Oakdale** those awaiting deportation and at Atlanta those serving federal prison sentences—rioted for a most curious reason: they wanted to stay in federal prisons rather than being sent back to Cuba. Many of the rioting inmates had come to the United States in the **Mariel Boatlift** of 1980. Involuntarily deported from Cuba as undesirables, many did not want to go home. Some of these Cuban prisoners, stuck in immigration limbo, have never been released from custody.

Kathleen Hawk Sawyer continued the rapid expansion of the federal prison system. By the time she retired in 2003, the system had grown to more than 100 institutions housing 140,000 inmates. In addition, another 15,000 prisoners were held in privately managed prisons, and another 11,000 were held in local jails or in open facilities in the community. By the time the current director, Harley Lappin, took over in 2003, the BOP had become the biggest prison system in America, and while many state systems are shrinking or at least stabilizing in size, the BOP is continuing to grow. During the twelve-month period ending June 30, 2002, the number of prisoners under state jurisdiction grew by less than 1 percent, while the number of federal prisoners grew by 5.8 percent.[34] The BOP had more staff in 2003, 34,000, than it had inmates twenty years earlier.

Despite its best efforts, the BOP has suffered the pains of too-rapid growth. Several institutions, especially the older, larger prisons, have been badly overcrowded for a long time. Drug offenders, many of whom are lower-class minorities, have brought their own brand of problems to the federal system. The BOP had wanted to close all three of its original penitentiaries but has so far been able to shut down only McNeil Island, which the State of Washington is now using as a prison. Atlanta and Leavenworth remain very much a part of the system—and are also very much overcrowded.

SECURITY LEVELS IN FEDERAL PRISONS

The BOP Website has this mission statement posted under "Protecting Public Safety":

> The Bureau protects public safety by ensuring that Federal offenders serve their sentences of imprisonment in institutions that are safe, humane, cost-efficient, and appropriately secure. The Bureau helps reduce future criminal activity by encouraging inmates to participate in a range of programs that have been proven to help them adopt a crime-free lifestyle upon their return to the community.[35]

Since 1979, the BOP has used a five-level security classification system for inmates. From lowest to highest, with inmate-to-staff ratios decreasing steadily up the line (from ten to one in minimum-security camps to two to one in the high-security penitentiaries), the levels are as follows:

1. **Minimum security.** These are the federal prison camps (FPCs), usually located adjacent to other federal prisons or military bases.
2. **Low security.** Called federal correctional institutions (FCIs), these prisons feature double fences and dormitory housing.
3. **Medium security.** These FCIs have stronger perimeters, cell housing, and greater internal control over prisoners.
4. **High security.** These are the U.S. penitentiaries (USPs), which look very much like everyone else's penitentiaries.
5. **Administrative security.** This category includes special purpose inmates, such as illegal aliens awaiting deportation and medical cases. The BOP operates federal jails called Metropolitan Correctional Centers or Metropolitan Detention Centers in several large cities. It also includes the 500 federal prisoners held in the **Administrative Maximum** unit at U.S. Penitentiary at Florence, Colorado. The ADX unit opened in 1996 to house the highest-security-threat inmates in the federal system, many of whom had previously been housed at the Marion prison. The BOP also operates the Federal Transfer Center (FTC) in Oklahoma City, whose job it is to move federal prisoners around the country. Its airline does not much resemble the one depicted in the movie *ConAir*.

The BOP's classification philosophy is to place inmates in the least restrictive security level in the institution closest to home. In mid–2003, inmates in BOP facilities were distributed among the five security levels as follows:

Minimum:	19.6 percent
Low:	38.8 percent
Medium:	24.6 percent
High:	10.8 percent
Administrative:	6.2 percent[36]

The BOP is responsible for convicted offenders who are not in federal prisons. One of the tenets of its master plan is that program alternatives should be available for offenders not in confinement. Offenders in this category are managed through twenty-eight **community corrections offices (CCOs)** spread across the country. Each CCO has a community corrections manager whose job it is to deal with contract agencies such as local jails, halfway houses, pre-release centers, and other organizations—both public and private—that provide services to federal offenders outside of prison. In comparison to state correctional systems, community-based alternatives have not been emphasized in the federal system over the years, and changes in sentencing practices since 1984 have restricted the authority of federal judges to use intermediate sanctions in lieu of confinement.

The sentencing guidelines adopted by the **U.S. Sentencing Commission** in 1985 have limited the use of probation for federal offenders and increased the length of sentences applied to many offenders, particularly those convicted of crimes of violence and drug offenses, by narrowing the sentencing discretion of federal judges. The **Sentencing Reform Act** (1984) dramatically changed good-time provisions; federal inmates now serve 85 percent of their actual sentence, getting no more than a 15 percent sentence reduction for good behavior. The same law abolished parole. Most federal judges now impose a new condition called **supervised release** on offenders after their discharge from secure custody. Supervised release, as an add-on period of supervision performed by federal probation officers, is practically identical in its effects to parole; it just happens to be imposed by the court instead of by a discretionary parole board.

WHAT'S DIFFERENT ABOUT FEDERAL PRISONS

When John DiIulio began to study federal prison management in the late 1980s, his first visit was to FCI Butner. He came away impressed:

> The quality of life inside Butner was amazing compared to what one could see in most State medium and high security prisons. . . . The prison staff was on top of things. Every unit sparkled. The food was excellent. The work areas hummed. No shouting. No aggressive horseplay. Little inmate idleness. In short, there were few of the unpleasant sights and sounds I had come to expect when observing life behind bars.[37]

DiIulio subsequently reexamined the four common assumptions he shared with many others about the BOP:

1. They had a very effective public relations machine.
2. They got "a better class of criminals."
3. They spent lots of money on criminals.
4. They had almost as many staff as inmates.[38]

What DiIulio found changed his mind about these assumptions (except for the first one; the feds are very good at public relations).

Federal prisoners are collectively hardly the **cream of criminals.** DiIulio found that in 1987, 45 percent had a history of violence, though they are on the whole much less likely to be confined for crimes of violence. Since the early 1970s, at least 25 percent of federal prisoners have been imprisoned for drug crimes: distribution or possession of illegal drugs. This percentage began increasing sharply in 1984, after the new War on Drugs policy took effect at the federal level. The percentage of drug criminals in federal prisons increased from 29 percent to its peak at 61 percent over the next decade, declining to about 55 percent by 2002. So most people in federal prisons are there for drugs. The next two leading categories are illegal possession or use of weapons or explosives and arson and immigration law violators, each making up more than 10 percent of the total population. Violent criminals convicted of murder, robbery, sex crimes, kidnapping, and felony assaults make up half the state prison population; in the federal system, they make up 11 percent.

A small number of federal prisoners, well under 10 percent, could be defined as **white-collar criminals** or **political criminals.** The four-term governor of Louisiana, Edwin Edwards, age seventy-five, serving ten years for racketeering, conspiracy, and other crimes related to casino gambling, is one of them. After sixteen years in the governor's mansion, Edwards's main work now in retirement as a prison inmate is cleaning the recreation area in his dormitory.

In a 2003 interview at the Federal Medical Center at Fort Worth, Texas, Edwards pointed out that his institution is not **Club Fed** and that he was not on vacation. His home is a medium-security prison. The closest companions of the man who dominated Louisiana politics for twenty-five years are convicted felons, most of them drug criminals. They all wear the same khaki uniforms. Edwards described a typical day: He gets up about 6:00 or 6:30 A.M., when he watches CNN. Breakfast is about 7:00. "Then I pick up my chemicals about 7:30 and go to work." Lunch is served about 11:00 A.M. In the afternoon, he works as a clerk, keeping track of room assignments for a corrections officer. Dinner is about 5:30, and after dinner he reads.[39]

"One thing I am not doing that I thought I would is watch a lot of television," Edwards said. There are three televisions in the recreation area. The inmates want to watch one of three things: MTV, the Hispanic channel, or wrestling. Edward is one of the few inmates interested in cable news or The History Channel. That's why he watches CNN in the morning. The books he reads must be sent in by an outside bookstore, such as *Amazon.com* or Barnes and Noble. Friends can send only letters, no other packages.

Edwards's roommate is a Los Angeles stockbroker with leukemia. Edwards's wife, Candy, age thirty-nine, comes to visit three weekends a month, prevented by a points system from coming more often. They are not allowed private or conjugal visits. They sit side by side in a prison visiting room under the eye of a correctional officer in a booth. Visits last for up to three hours at a time.

Edwards says he is healthy. He has lost twenty-three pounds in less than a year in prison. He said he misses foremost his family, then travel, then Louisiana food. Tops on his list of missed foods are: "seafood gumbo, crawfish, and fried shrimp." Gesturing with his hands to demonstrate, Edwards talked about prison cuisine. "They put some white rice on your plate, drop some sort of chicken chow mein on top of it, and that's what they call jambalaya. People down there [in Louisiana] don't realize how good they have it with their food."

He made another point at the end of the interview: "The main thing I want people to know, whether they like me or hate me or whatever, is to cherish their freedom because, until you lose it, you don't know how precious it is."[40]

The makeup of the federal prison population has changed significantly over the past twenty years. Three of every ten federal inmates are foreigners, most from Mexico, Colombia, Cuba, the Dominican Republic, and other Central and South America countries, but really from around the world. A visit to a federal prison is like attending a session of the "Criminal United Nations." Far more illegal aliens are held in detention awaiting deportation, some of them Marielito Cubans held in custody for more than two decades. The "war on drugs" has brought into the federal system a large number of drug users and street-level drug dealers who would once have gone to state prisons. These offenders bring with them their medical problems and the gang affiliations they had on the outside. As the profile of federal inmates has become more like that of state inmates, violence has become an increasing threat in federal prisons.

Federal prisons manage their inmate populations by better classification, not by having more correctional officers. The national average of prison inmates to correctional officers in 2001 was 5.4 to 1; in the federal system, the ratio was 9.7 to 1.[41] Salaries of federal correctional officers were above the national average but far below what some state systems, particularly in the Northeast and West, pay their correctional officers. Because less money in put into correctional officer salaries (which is always the bulk of the prison budget), more money is available for other staff—vocational, educational, medical, case management, and so on.

DiIulio found that federal prisons have a history of spending at about the national median per inmate. This remains true today. In 2000, the national average cost per inmate per day was $61.04; the federal cost was $59.02, about $2 per day less. The BOP did spend slightly above the national average on both food and medical care, two aspects of prison life that matter greatly to inmates.[42]

Several other features favor federal prisons. Federal prisons are newer, smaller (except for the old penitentiaries), and better designed than most state prisons. The physical settings are nicer, even without the tennis courts and picnic tables (which many state prisons have as well). UNICOR makes a huge difference. Having industrial jobs to keep 25 to 30 percent of inmates busy at full-time jobs is a great advantage to federal prison administrators. Work is supplemented by a broad range of programs—self-improvement (which typically means inmate-led organizations and clubs), substance abuse treatment, religious observance, parenting, anger management, counseling, and life skills.

Ex-prisoners used to give this advice to potential inmates: "If you have to choose between a local jail and a state prison to do time (length of sentence being equal), take the state prison. If you have to choose between a state prison and a federal prison, take the federal prison." Of course, most real inmates (as opposed to potential inmates) do not get to make these choices; the legal system chooses for them.

Changes in public policy enacted as changes in federal law have resulted in a 700 percent increase in the federal prison population in the past three decades. There is no end to this expansion in sight. Federal prisons remain well above 100 percent capacity at present, and new prisons are being built as fast as Congress appropriates the funds. The federal prison system is still looked to as a leader in the corrections field, but today it is driven by the same punitive mood that affects state corrections systems. Good management can only do so much to counterbalance hard sentencing. The BOP will be in an expansion mode for at least the next decade.

LOCAL AND PRIVATE PRISONS

Not all felons sentenced for state crimes end up in state prisons. In another of those historical anomalies, three large cities operate their own prison systems housing a portion of the felons their courts sentence to prison time. They supplement rather than replace state prisons. These are the following:

Cook County Department of Corrections

New York City Department of Corrections

Philadelphia Prison System

These cities operate prison systems larger than the systems of many states. They have jail systems for pretrial and misdemeanor inmates, but some of their convicted felons stay in local prisons rather than entering state custody. Until 1997, the Washington, D.C., prison system was also on this list, but Congress transferred the District of Columbia's felons into the BOP in that year, meaning that most of them would be sent to institutions much farther away from home.

It has also become much more common over the past decade for felons to serve state time in local jails, both in state and out of state. This practice is due primarily to overcrowding of state prisons and to the economic incentive for local sheriffs to house the overflow of state prisoners in their county jails. In 2001, local jails held almost 48,000 state prisoners. The practice is especially common in the South, where Kentucky, Louisiana, Tennessee, and Virginia each housed from 15 to 45 percent of their state prisoners in local jails. Louisiana has been doing this since the 1970s, resulting in a prison system that by 2003 housed almost as many felons (16,000) in local jails as it did in state prisons (20,000).

The past two decades have also witnessed the growth of privately operated prisons and jails in America. In 1983, when Corrections Corporation of America was chartered, no prisoners were held in secure institutions operated by private companies. Twenty years later, the approximately 160 private prisons and jails held about 140,000 inmates. Although the number of prisoners held in private facilities has leveled off from 1998 to 2003, these facilities have come to play an important role as a permanent part of some state systems and as a temporary measure to relieve overcrowding in others. When prisons are full, officials start calling around to locate private facilities where inmates can be stored temporarily, while politicians fix the problems that created overcrowding (which is always too many inmates coming into the system) in the first place. We will look at both of these issues—jails as prisons and privatization of jails and prisons—in greater depth in chapter 8.

ALTERNATIVES TO PRISON BUILDING

As we face a continuing influx of new prisoners, amounting to a minimum increase of 15,000 to 20,000 new state and federal prison beds annually, we have to ask about the wisdom of pursuing the bricks-and-mortar solution in corrections. Prisons are very expensive to construct. The more secure they are, the more expensive they are to build and to operate after opening. Furthermore, prison beds, once made available, are very difficult to empty. We continue opening new prisons, but we rarely shut down old ones—until they fall down from old age. The more we pursue building new prisons as the appropriate way to punish convicted felons, the more we commit to a future mind-set that encourages high rates of incarceration instead of alternative community-based programs or other crime prevention alternatives. If we have the prison beds available, we are highly likely to fill up the empty spaces first before we consider other options.

KEY TERMS

prisons
Gaol at Wymondham
Walnut Street Jail
Jeremy Bentham
panopticon
Pennsylvania model
Auburn model
industrial prison
agricultural prison
work camps
prisonization
maximum-security prisons
close-high-security prisons
medium-security prisons
minimum-security prisons
open-security facilities
multilevel prisons

supermax
special housing unit
San Quentin
Huntsville
Ruiz v. Estelle
Angola
Federal Bureau of Prisons
Justice Department
Three Prisons Act
U.S. penitentiary
Fort Leavenworth
McNeil Island
Atlanta
Alderson
Sanford Bates
BOP
Lewisburg
Alcatraz
country club prisons

James V. Bennett
Federal Prison Industries, Inc.
UNICOR
Norman Carlson
master plan
unit management
mandatory literacy
gender-neutral employment
balanced model
medical model
family culture
legal standards
Butner
Oakdale
Mariel Boatlift
minimum security
low security

medium security
high security
administrative security
Administrative Maximum
community corrections offices
U.S. Sentencing Commission
Sentencing Reform Act
supervised release
cream of criminals
white-collar criminals
political criminals
Club Fed
Cook County Department of Corrections
New York City Department of Corrections
Philadelphia Prison System

NOTES

1. Paige M. Harrison and Jennifer C. Karberg, "Prison and Jail Inmates at Midyear 2002," U.S. Department of Justice, Bureau of Justice Statistics Bulletin, April 2003, p. 1.

2. Ibid., p. 3

3. Ibid.

4. North Dakota Department of Corrections and Rehabilitation, *www.state.nd.us/docr/prison/prison_home.htm*.

5. Ibid.

6. Todd Dvorak, "Lawmakers Determining Future Prison Needs," Associated Press, August 20, 2001, *http://web.lexis-nexis.com*.

7. Deena Winter, "Officials Fighting for New Women's Prison," *Bismarck Tribune*, March 13, 2003, p. 1A.

8. Harrison and Karberg, "Prison and Jail Inmates at Midyear 2002," p. 1.

9. "San Quentin State Prison," California Department of Corrections, *www.cdc.state.ca.us/InstitutionsDiv/INSTDIV/facilities/ fac_prison_SQ.asp*.

10. "Folsom State Prison," California Department of Corrections, *www.cdc.state.ca.us/InstitutionsDiv/INSTDIV/facilities/fac_prison_FSP.asp*.

11. "California Institution for Men," California Department of Corrections, *www.cdc.state.ca.us/InstitutionsDiv/INSTDIV/facilities/fac_prison_CIM.asp*.

12. "California State Prisons," *www.psych-health.com/prisons.htm*.

13. California Department of Corrections, *www.corr.ca.gov/CDC/mission.asp*.

14. Fred E. Haynes, *The American Prison System* (New York: McGraw-Hill, 1939), p. 185.

15. Ibid., p. 186.

16. John J. DiIulio, Jr., *Governing Prisons: A Comparative Study of Correctional Management* (New York: Free Press, 1987), pp. 213–14.

17. Dave Harmon, "Prisons Nearing Capacity Yet Again: Solutions Include Paroling Prisoners, Relying on County Jails," *Austin American Statesman*, February 13, 2003, p. B1.

18. See Mark T. Carleton, *Politics and Punishment: The History of the Louisiana State Penal System* (Baton Rouge: Louisiana State University Press, 1971), pp. 29–31.

19. See Burk Foster, Wilbert Rideau, and Douglas Dennis, *The Wall Is Strong: Corrections in Louisiana* (Lafayette, La.: Center for Louisiana Studies, 1995).

20. Burk Foster, "Angola in the Seventies," in Foster et al., *The Wall Is Strong*, p. 57.

21. "Mission Statement," Louisiana Department of Public Safety and Corrections, Corrections Services, *www.corrections.state.la.us/Mission_Goals/mission.htm*.

22. "Goals and Priorities," Louisiana Department of Public Safety and Corrections, Corrections Services, *www.corrections.state.la.us/Mission_Goals/goals.htm*.

23. Minnesota Department of Corrections, "The State of the Prison Population: 2001 Commissioner's Report," p. 3.

24. "Mission Statement," Minnesota Department of Corrections, *www.doc.state.mn.us/mission.htm*.

25. "Custody Classification System," Minnesota Department of Corrections, *www.doc.state.mn.us/organization/adultservices/adult/custodylevel.htm*.

26. Patrick Howe, "Era of Get-Tough Laws Has Prisons Crammed," *Duluth News Tribune*, March 9, 2003.

27. Ibid.

28. Esther Heffernan, "The Alderson Years," *Federal Prisons Journal*, spring 1992, p. 22.

29. John J. DiIulio Jr., "Prisons That Work: Management Is the Key," *Federal Prisons Journal*, summer 1990, p. 9.

30. Ibid., p. 7.

31. Federal Prison Industries, "Fiscal Year 2002 Annual Report to the Congress of the United States," pp. 6–7.

32. John W. Roberts, *Reform and Retribution: An Illustrated History of American Prisons* (Lanham, Md.: American Correctional Association, 1996), p. 193.

33. Ibid., p. 198.

34. Harrison and Karberg, "Prison and Jail Inmates at Midyear 2002," p. 1.

35. "The Bureau in Brief," Federal Bureau of Prisons, *www.bop.gov/ipapg/ipabib.html*.

36. "Quick Facts," Federal Bureau of Prisons, *www.bop.gov/fact0598.html*.

37. DiIulio, "Prisons That Work," p. 8.

38. Ibid., pp. 8–9.

39. John Hill, "Edwards: Cherish Your Freedom," *Shreveport (La.) Times*, June 8, 2003, p. 1A.

40. Ibid., p. 3A.

41. Camille Graham Camp and George M. Camp, *The 2001 Corrections Yearbook: Adult Systems* (Middletown, Conn.: Criminal Justice Institute, 2002), p. 175.

42. Ibid., pp. 105–6.

FURTHER READING

Bates, Sanford. *Prisons and Beyond*. New York: Macmillan, 1936.

Bennett, James V. *I Chose Prison*. New York: Alfred A. Knopf, 1970.

Bruce, J. Campbell. *Escape from Alcatraz: A Farewell to the Rock*. New York: McGraw-Hill, 1963.

Jacobs, James J. *Stateville: The Penitentiary in Mass Society*. Chicago: University of Chicago Press, 1977.

Johnston, James A. *Alcatraz Island Prison—And the Men Who Live There*. New York: Charles Scribner's Sons, 1949.

Roberts, John W. *Reform and Retribution: An Illustrated History of American Prisons*. Lanham, Md.: American Correctional Association, 1997.

WEB AND VIDEO RESOURCES

The Federal Bureau of Prisons Website is *www.bop.gov*.

Each state department of corrections has a Website. The five referenced in this chapter are the following:

North Dakota: *www.state.nd.us/docr*
California: *www.corr.ca.gov/CDC*
Texas: *www.tdcj.state.tx.us*

Louisiana: *www.corrections.state.la.us*
Minnesota: *www.doc.state.mn.us*

The U.S. Justice Department's National Institute of Corrections (*www.nicic.org*) has a wealth of resources related to jails and prisons, including assistance for students writing research reports. This is a great site for exploring in corrections.

COMMENTARY

7 Seeing is Believing? The Depiction of Alcatraz in *Murder in the First*

by the Federal Bureau of Prisons

The Warner Brothers film *Murder in the First* claims to be "inspired" by the true story of Alcatraz inmate Henry Young (his first name is also written "Henri," apparently an alias). Although Henry Young was indeed an inmate at Alcatraz who was convicted in 1941 of involuntary manslaughter in the stabbing death of fellow inmate Rufus McCain, the events depicted in the motion picture are almost wholly fictional. In particular, the premise of the movie—that Young was a nonviolent inmate who was tortured on Alcatraz and was thereby driven to kill someone—is completely false.

Murder in the First claims that Young was a teenage orphan who was sentenced to Alcatraz for stealing $5 from a grocery store in order to feed his starving sister, and that he "never harmed or attempted to harm anyone" before entering Alcatraz. The true story is that he was a bank robber who had taken and brutalized a hostage on at least one occasion and committed murder in 1933—some three years before being incarcerated at Alcatraz. He had served time in State prisons in Montana and Washington before entering Federal prison for the first time in 1935 at the U.S. Penitentiary on McNeil Island, Washington (which is now a State prison).

Although Young did participate in a January 1939 escape attempt, he was not kept naked in a dark dungeon for 3 years as punishment, as the movie indicates. Instead, he was held in the disciplinary segregation unit in the main cellhouse as punishment for the escape attempt. He was confined to a normal cell—not a dungeon—with plumbing, an electric light, a cot, and other appropriate cell furnishings. Various events in the movie set in a dungeon—such

as scenes where the associate warden slashes Young's Achilles tendon to prevent future escapes—are fabrications.

The events surrounding Young's fatal attack on Rufus McCain are also portrayed inaccurately. In the movie, Young becomes a madman after three years in the dungeon, is then taken directly from the dungeon to the dining hall, and, moments later, stabs McCain to death with a spoon handle. The implication is that Young's homicidal behavior was a direct result of his inhumane confinement and that he had no control over his actions.

In reality, Young was released from his cell in segregation after only a few months. He was returned to the general population no later than autumn 1939. More than a year after that—in December 1940—he killed McCain in the industries building. The movie also implies that Young died on Alcatraz in 1942, evidently committing suicide after scrawling the word "victory" on the wall or floor of his cell. This is not true, either. Young remained at Alcatraz until 1948, when he was transferred to the Medical Center for Federal Prisoners at Springfield, Missouri. When his Federal sentence expired in 1954, he was turned over to the Washington State Penitentiary at Walla Walla to begin a life sentence for an earlier murder conviction. In 1972, he was released from Washington State Penitentiary, but he jumped parole and, according to Washington State authorities, his whereabouts are unknown. Far from committing suicide 53 years ago, therefore, Young might still be alive.

Many of the depictions of Alcatraz and its staff are completely inaccurate. *Murder in the First* portrays the warden as managing three prisons simultaneously: USP Alcatraz, and the California State prisons at Folsom and San Quentin. The movie further states that the warden visited Alcatraz only 24 times over a three-year period. In fact, no one has been warden of a Federal prison and a State prison simultaneously. James A. Johnston, the actual warden at Alcatraz and one of the most respected prison administrators of his generation, was warden at Folsom in 1912 and San Quentin from 1913 to 1924; he did not become warden at Alcatraz until 1934, and served in that position full-time. He lived right on the island, in a house just a few yards from the front door of the cellhouse.

Nor is there any validity to claims that FBI Director J. Edgar Hoover selected Johnston to be warden at Alcatraz, that Hoover and the Alcatraz management intimidated prospective witnesses in Young's trial, that inmates were being driven insane at Alcatraz, and that 32 were removed from the island in strait-jackets during a period of only a few years leading up to Young's trial.

Equally groundless and unfair is the depiction of officers at Alcatraz as sadistic brutes. The evil prison officer is one of the oldest and least imaginative movie cliches, and one of the most misleading.

7 MANAGEMENT AND CUSTODY

A major premise of traditional institutions is that, in order to minimize the danger to both the institutional staff and the community, security should be regarded as the dominant goal. Mechanical security measures are instituted, including the building of high walls or fences around prisons, construction of gun-towers, the searching of inmates as they pass through certain checkpoints, pass systems to account for inmate movement, and counts at regular intervals.

These measures also serve the idea that deterrence requires extremes of deprivation, strict discipline, and punishment, all of which, together with considerations of administrative efficiency, make institutions impersonal, quasi-military places.

An exaggerated concern for security and the belief in autonomous institutional responsibility for handling offenders combine to limit innovation and the development of community ties. Isolated, punitive, and regimented, the traditional prison and many juvenile training schools develop a monolithic society, caste-like and resistive to change.

— President's Commission on Law Enforcement and Administration
of Justice, *Task Force Report: Corrections*, 1967

INTRODUCTION

As a formal, complex organization, the prison presents unique management concerns, particularly in its efforts to balance the competing interests of custody and treatment. Although custody is the most important function of a prison or jail and more people work in security than in all other functions combined, administrative and treatment functions are also ongoing and require the services of significant numbers of staff. Correctional administrators of today recognize the impact their management styles have on their organizations; they look to the "free world" for direction on how best to manage the "unfree world" of prison. After reading the material in this chapter, you should be familiar with:

1. The prison warden's role today.
2. The evolution of management styles to the present.
3. The importance of custody (and the lesser role of treatment) in the correctional setting.
4. The influence of the prison environment on management and custody.
5. The important themes of correctional management.

6. The methods of secure custody in prison.
7. The problems of managing custody and treatment in prison.
8. Support staff common in the American prison.

THE PRISON WARDEN TODAY

The head of an American prison is typically called a **warden,** a title derived from an English term for a keeper of animals. In this view, the warden is essentially a gatekeeper. In any secure prison, the warden's chief objective is to maintain **secure custody** of prisoners, but secure custody involves much more than **perimeter security,** or merely keeping inmates confined within the walls and preventing escape.

Secure custody requires the maintenance of a safe, orderly internal environment in which inmates and staff interact with low levels of tension and conflict. Given the two-sided nature of prison life—the keepers and the kept, free people and convicts—this is not an easy balance to maintain. Secure custody is complicated by differences among inmates—racial and gang conflicts, age and cultural differences, and the prevalence of serious personality disorders—and by the public and political perception that prisons are already "too nice" or that prison life is "too easy." For many people, just putting convicts behind bars is not enough; they would like to see criminals "suffer," either for suffering's retributive benefit or for its deterrent effect. Thus, the contemporary warden's role has become one of balancing competing interests—the inmates, the staff, political officials, and the public—while maintaining physical and internal security, administering the prison, and providing positive programs to change behavior.

Elayn Hunt Correctional Center is located in St. Gabriel, Louisiana, fifteen miles south of Baton Rouge along the River Road. Hunt is a men's prison that opened in 1979. Its warden is **C. M. Lensing Jr.,** a native of northern Louisiana who went to work in corrections after completing a graduate degree in criminal justice at Northeast Louisiana University (now the University of Louisiana–Monroe) in 1975. After serving at other prisons and in corrections headquarters in Baton Rouge, Lensing was appointed warden at Hunt in 1989.

The prison provides this mission statement from Warden Lensing:

> It is the mission of Elayn Hunt Correctional Center (EHCC) to strive to provide a controlled correctional environment in a professional manner so as to protect the safety of the general public, the surrounding community, the staff, and the offender population. Each inmate is provided basic services relating to adequate food, clothing, health care and shelter. EHCC strives to provide an environment that enables positive behavioral change through educational and rehabilitative opportunities to allow offenders to become successful citizens upon release and to enhance the ability of the offenders to live lawfully in the community. All of this is accomplished through an assortment of assessment, diagnostic, work, educational, self-help, discipline, medical, mental health, and social programs. Inmates are also provided an opportunity to make restitution and to participate in restorative justice initiatives as a mechanism to compensate individuals and communities harmed by crime. Toward these ends, the warden formulates goals and objectives for the institution annually.[1]

When he speaks to college students about contemporary prison management, Warden Lensing often begins by asking if they know **Warden Norton.** Getting blank looks in response, he gives a big clue. "You know, the warden in *The Shawshank Redemption*." This time, most of the class raise their hands. This is a very popular movie among corrections students, with good reason. Warden Norton, as portrayed by Bob Gunton, was head of Shawshank, the fictional state prison in Maine (though based on the old, now demolished Thomaston Penitentiary) where Andy Dufresne spent the nineteen years from 1947 until 1966.

"That warden doesn't exist any longer," Warden Lensing points out. "He was the model of the autocratic warden of the past—the warden who had complete control over his institution. The warden of today operates in a very different environment—bureaucratic rather than autocratic."

Warden Lensing goes on to describe his role as warden as consisting of two parts: the traditional warden's role and the role of chief executive officer (CEO). The traditional warden's role—focused on institutional security—is now divided among several assistant wardens who oversee the prison's different operating units. Hunt is a multilevel prison housing inmates in maximum, medium, and minimum custody. It is four prisons in one: a maximum-security prison housing over 1,500 inmates; a boot camp program, IMPACT, for short-term offenders, holding 200 inmates; the Hunt Reception and Diagnostic Center, which processes and classifies incoming state prisoners for distribution to other prisons, holding about 400 inmates; and the Hunt Special Unit, a fifty-cell housing unit for severely mentally disordered convicts. The prison has also designed a 700-bed combined hospital/mental health facility that has not yet been built because of budget constraints. Hunt has practiced **unit management** (or unit team management) since 1994. This approach decentralizes management authority by housing units, breaking down the centralized control into smaller operating units. The goal is to get custodial, rehabilitation, and support staff working more closely together with the inmates they supervise.

Warden Lensing's remarks about his CEO role often draw surprised looks from students. Many people—convicts and civilians—often call his prison "Hunts," like the tomato corporation. "Hunts is catsup," Warden Lensing responds, and "Hunt Correctional Center's commodity is people." He points out that the budget of his prison in 2002 was over $40 million, over 80 percent spent on staff. The institution has 800 staff members, 582 of them correctional officers working in security. Turnover is a terrific problem for his prison, as it is in other Louisiana prisons and in most other state prisons and local jails. In one recent year, his prison hired 234 new correctional officers but lost 255 (abut 40 percent of his security staff), for a net decline of twenty positions. Most of the new hires are women. They are assigned to all security posts except those involving continuous supervision of shower and toilet areas. In the past few years, the percentage of women correctional officers at Hunt has increased from 18 percent to over 40 percent.

Students may think of wardens as scheming micromanagers who manipulate the details of their prisoners' lives. Perhaps officials like this still exist, but Warden Lensing indicates that he spends far more time with staff matters than with inmates—and that his staff cause him far more problems than the inmates do. At Hunt, every inmate has a job, a school assignment, or both. Inmates are busy or at least occupied. Levels of violence are very low. No inmates or staff have been killed at Hunt in the fourteen years that Warden Lensing has headed the prison; serious assaults and escape attempts are rare.

When students ask Warden Lensing about his management philosophy, he responds by listing several key elements: empowerment, safety, professionalism, secure resources, and unit management. **Empowerment** is the foundation (see commentary 10 at the end of this chapter). He defines it as "giving people control over their own work and lives." He applies this to inmates as well as to staff.

Safety has to do with the internal environment. People can go about their business without fear. Warden Lensing says he sees a difference in many prisons in other states when he visits as an auditor in the accreditation process of the American Correctional Association (ACA). Many prisons lack the internal order and stability for people living and working there to feel truly safe day to day.

Professionalism is a staff attitude. It is made up of several parts: standards, training, recognition, and commitment. With their utility uniforms, security officers wear Navy T-shirts with "Correctional Officer" emblazoned in big letters on the back. On the front is the prison's logo and underneath in small letters the phrase "Striving for Excellence." This might seem an odd slogan in a punitive southern state where new correctional officers earn less than $20,000 a year, but Warden Lensing emphasizes professionalism, particularly among his supervisory and management staff, as a necessary counterbalance to the high turnover rate among junior officers. Hunt Correctional Center is accredited by the ACA (as are the other state prisons in Louisiana), and Warden Lensing encourages his staff to become actively involved in ACA as he himself has been for many years.

Secure resources relate to the budget—the continuity of funding for staff and inmate programs from year to year. Warden Lensing stresses that Louisiana's wardens have more management authority than wardens in some other more centralized systems. He has direct control of his budget, which he uses to ensure that inmates have access to a wide range of programs and services and that his staff get the training and career-broadening assignments they want and the extra pay that goes with taking on added responsibilities.

Unit management fixes responsibility among supervisors and managers at the level of execution. It frees Warden Lensing to practice his version of "MBWA," **Management by Walking Around,** which takes him out of his office to visit each of the compounds that make up his prison. He deals with what he calls his "management team"—the deputy wardens who act as division heads and the assistant wardens who run the housing units—on a regular basis, but he makes it a point to get out and see people in the units most days that he is in his office.

The warden's role today is not simply a matter of running his own prison, Warden Lensing points out. He is a part of the corrections bureaucracy at the state level; as such, he is called to meetings, social events, and planning sessions relating to statewide corrections matters. He often meets with state legislators and members of the executive branch of state government regarding changes to laws and policies.

Warden Lensing says that the interest in rehabilitation and the individual criminal offender has turned around 180 degrees in recent years as victims have come to the forefront in criminal justice. Where attention was once focused on rehabilitation and recidivism, it is now directed more toward public safety and reducing victimization. The programs may still be the same in many instances, but the focus is less on their effects on the individual criminal and more on their outcomes once the criminal is back in society. Thus, everything related to rehabilitation has to be argued in the context of the criminal in the community.

Warden Lensing also deals with media representatives who are interested in particular inmates or prison programs. He has contact with family members, victims, and outside groups interested in particular inmates or in groups of inmates, such as clubs or religious organizations. He is always looking for more work assignments or charitable causes to involve his inmates in, first because it keeps them busy and, second, because it gives them a greater purpose than just "doing time." Finally, in his spare time, Warden Lensing is also a part-time faculty member at the Baton Rouge Community College, a growing junior college in downtown Baton Rouge. His specialty, as you might expect, is corrections.

PRISON MANAGEMENT THEN AND NOW

Correctional administrators draw from a wide range of sources as they manage their employees and perform their correctional functions. Correctional "institutions" run the gamut of size, purpose, and approach—from highly specialized treatment facilities where a handful of offenders live together to an old, overcrowded county jail to a maximum-security penitentiary holding 5,000 inmates, in effect a small town behind bars. There are as many different management styles in operating these several thousand separate organizations as there are personalities and philosophies of the people who run them. But management theory, as a science, is based on the construction of typologies in which approaches are grouped, compared, and contrasted. Management theory is always simpler than management practice because human beings constantly defy efforts to manage them scientifically—a characteristic that fits the people who work in prisons equally as well as it fits the people locked up there.

When management first began to develop as a science a century ago, one of the first major schools of thought was in fact called **scientific management.** As described in Frederick Taylor's *The Principles of Scientific Management* (1911), the ideal manager was a skillful manipulator of basically uncooperative, deficient human beings. (Sounds like the perfect job description of a prison warden, doesn't it?) His job was to arrange things to overcome human flaws and limitations in producing his organization's product. Human relationships were reduced to structure—the formal organizational chart. People needed to be constantly supervised, corrected, and time managed.[2]

The scientific management model, which still has influence in factory and assembly-line settings, was supplanted by the **human relations** movement of the 1930s. Human relations viewed human beings not as obstacles to be overcome but as social beings who wanted to work and produce; the manager's job was to do something not *to* them but *with* them. The human relations movement focused on the informal organization, on human relationships and morale as determinants of productivity.

Douglas McGregor's *The Human Side of Enterprise* (1960) proposed two contrasting theories of human behavior, Theory X and Theory Y.[3] **Theory X** assumed the following:

1. The average person has an inherent dislike of work and will avoid it whenever possible.
2. People must be coerced, controlled, directed, and threatened with punishment if they are to be motivated to achieve organizational objectives.

3. The average person prefers to be directed, avoids responsibility, has little ambition, and prizes security.[4]

Theory Y, in contrast, assumed that people are characterized by the following:

1. They are motivated by an inherent need to work.
2. They will voluntarily commit to working toward objectives without being subjected to external control and threat of punishment.
3. They will exercise self-direction and self-control if the work environment is supportive of these qualities.
4. They will accept and seek responsibility.
5. They have the ability to exercise a high degree of imagination, ingenuity, and creativity in the solution of organizational problems.
6. They have intellectual potentials that are only minimally utilized by Theory X managers.[5]

Another perspective on management approaches was found in Rensis Likert's *New Patterns of Management* (1961).[6] Likert suggested that organizations were either authoritative—in exploitative or benevolent ways—or participative—in consultative or group ways. Prisons, earlier and more recently, could be placed in the two authoritative models. Smaller, community-based programs and some treatment programs occurring within larger prison settings were more participative. Many correctional theorists today believe that small-group processes are far more effective in changing behavior than anything that is done in a mass setting. Some of the programs that have been identified as being most effective in reducing recidivism are those that create therapeutic communities, where like offenders are grouped together in pure, self-sustaining communities—controlling each other through internal forces rather than relying on external agents of control, such as guards or parole officers. Even with more openness in correctional management recently, the participative-consultative and participative-group models are rarely found in contemporary public corrections organizations.

Edgar Schein's *Organizational Psychology* (1965) described four views of people, each with a corresponding management style applicable to a correctional setting:

1. A rational and economic view, in which material rewards, incentives, and control provided the direction people need
2. A social view, in which human feelings and interaction were seen as the basis of making work satisfying
3. A self-actualizing view, in which management's task was to help workers achieve and find meaning in their work
4. The complex, or flux, view, in which the manager must constantly diagnose and adjust to meet different human needs and changing circumstances[7]

Prison managers refer to the **autocratic style** of earlier prison wardens. They were Theory X managers in the extreme. The dictionary definition of *autocrat* is "an absolute ruler." The warden of the 1800s and early 1900s had absolute authority if he chose to use it. He was not responsible to the courts or the public; his only allegiance was to the governor who appointed him and the state legislators who approved his budget.

The autocratic wardens were often not career prison officials. They came from other lines of work and sold themselves to political authorities on their ideology, leadership, and productivity. The prison was a factory, not a treatment unit, and it was the warden's job to see that the work got done. The autocratic warden practiced strict rules and strong discipline, and he demanded absolute obedience from people under his authority—both prisoners and staff. No civil service, no prisoners' rights, no court intervention, no reporters poking around—for a warden, these were the good old days.

The prototype of the autocratic warden was undoubtedly Captain **Elam Lynds,** the warden of both Auburn and Sing Sing prisons in New York in the 1820s. Lynds was a former military officer who used his political connections to become principal keeper at Auburn in 1818. He instituted a system of strict control (discussed in chapter 2) that emphasized three principles: "industry, obedience, and silence."[8] He built Sing Sing (originally called Mount Pleasant) on the same model.

Lynds's methods were not popular with inmates or with many reformers outside. His vigorous use of the cat-o'-nine-tails in imposing physical punishments in particular often generated dissent within the prison and criticism from without. By the time Beaumont and Toqueville arrived in 1831 to interview him for their penitentiary book, Lynds was no longer a warden. He was running a hardware store, his career in prisons done. Scott Christianson has written about this visit:

> Lynds was an archetypal autocrat, who in many ways resembled and modeled himself after the two "great men" of his age, Napoleon Bonaparte and Andrew Jackson. Like them, he was a military man, rigid and erect; he was extremely disciplined and he required discipline from everyone below him. He also demanded absolute authority to do whatever he deemed correct and fiercely resisted sharing any power whatsoever. He prided himself on being a self-made man, a man of determination and iron will, strength, and courage, and he was totally convinced of the moral rightness of his cause.
>
> When asked to explain his secret of prison discipline, Lynds replied, "The point is to maintain uninterrupted silence and uninterrupted labour; to obtain this, it is equally necessary to watch incessantly the keepers, as well as the prisoners; to be at once inflexible and just."[9]

In illustrating the meaning of "incessant" and "inflexible," the story was told of Lynds's order that three convicts be flogged. When three guards in succession refused the order, each was fired on the spot, until finally a fourth man was found to carry out the flogging.

If Lynds had read McGregor's *The Human Side of Enterprise* or *The Professional Manager*, he would likely have scorned the behavioral science approach to "persuasive" management. Many other early wardens would have agreed with Lynds about the need for absolute authority in running a prison. Even such a progressive reformer as Zebulon Brockway, the founder of the reformatory, believed in extreme discipline and regimentation as the basis of reform; as you may recall from chapter 2, he retired as Elmira's warden after criticisms of excessive use of physical punishments.

Not all early wardens were Theory X autocrats. **Thomas Mott Osborne,** who became warden of Sing Sing in 1914, was a prison reformer before he became warden. In the summer of 1913, he spent a week inside Auburn prison as an ordinary inmate, seeking, as he said at the time, to "break down the barriers between my soul and the soul of my brothers."[10] Warden Osborne ended the silent system at Auburn and inaugurated a plan of inmate self-government known as the Mutual Welfare League. He liberalized prison rules and established a token economy. The convicts apparently loved his Theory Y approach, but conservative political officials did not. He was indicted for neglect of duty and resigned his office in 1916.

Management historians commonly say that the autocratic management style of early penitentiaries yielded to the **bureaucratic style** of today after World War II. The change in styles was closely tied to the development of centralized state corrections bureaucracies and other changes outside of prisons that took away the independent authority wardens had previously enjoyed. This does not mean that autocratic wardens immediately went the way of the dinosaur.

James B. Jacobs's *Stateville: The Penitentiary in Mass Society* chronicles fifty years in the life of Stateville Penitentiary, Illinois's largest maximum security prison. From 1936 to 1961, Stateville was under the control of Warden **Joseph Ragen,** a former sheriff who became known as "Mr. Prison" in Illinois. Ragen had absolute autonomy in directing every detail of the Stateville routine, which Ragen bragged made it "the tightest prison in the United States."[11] Ragen's approach was charismatic, highly personalized, and authoritarian. He demanded complete loyalty from the people who worked for him, and he was well known for his distrust of "outsiders," which meant anyone who did not work directly for him.[12] But he was also highly aware of the role of the news media; his reputation as America's foremost prison warden was enhanced by a steady flow of positive articles written by journalists Ragen courted and favored with "inside" stories.

Robert Freeman has discussed the correctional manager as operating within both internal and external environments. The **internal environment** (what Warden Lensing refers to as the prison's personality) consists of three primary influences:

1. The inmate social culture
2. The prison's physical environment
3. The prison staff culture[13]

The contrasting **external environment** is made up of outside forces that interact with the internal environment. The principal external influences would include the following:

1. The department of corrections, which makes policies and requires accountability
2. The media, which influence public perceptions of the prison
3. The state political network, which includes the governor's office, key legislators, and other officials
4. The civil service department, which makes the rules for employees
5. Employee organizations and unions, which represent their members' interests
6. State and federal courts, which decide prison-based litigation
7. Rehabilitation advocates, such as those sponsoring particular behavioral science, educational, or religious interventions inside the prison

8. Victim and prisoner advocacy groups, who may take contrary positions on prison conditions and programs

9. Families of prisoners, who are interested in visitation and prison life issues

10. Representatives of special needs inmates, such as the mentally ill, the mentally retarded, or the elderly

In 1988, seven state and federal prison wardens gathered in Boulder, Colorado, at a National Institute of Corrections workshop to define the contemporary warden's duties. As reported in Warden Pamela Withrow's article "What Is a Warden?" the group identified 142 specific tasks in twelve major duty areas:

1. Manage human resources
2. Manage the external environment
3. Manage litigation
4. Manage change within the institutional environment
5. Manage the office
6. Manage inmates
7. Review/inspect institutional operations/physical plant
8. Maintain professional competence and awareness
9. Manage security processes
10. Develop long- and short-term goals and objectives
11. Manage emergencies
12. Manage the budget[14]

The twelve duty areas were arranged in no particular order, except they agreed human resources should be first, as the most complex responsibility. Withrow wrote, "The quality of staff and the training they receive are major factors in safe and effective prison management."[15]

The earlier autocratic wardens, through the tenure of Warden Ragen in Illinois, maintained their positions by maximizing their control over the internal environment and minimizing external influences. In effect, the prison was an island with the external influences flowing around it; everything entering the island flowed through the warden's office, and nothing entered without his permission. By the 1960s and 1970s, it was clear that the prison was no longer an insular institution. External influences became more dominant, and prison management became less of a one-man show and more of a team game.

Some people may imagine that contemporary wardens are hard-line conservatives—former guards who have been promoted because of their toughness and pessimistic views of human nature. This is not the case. Most correctional administrators today are college-educated professionals. Backgrounds in the behavioral sciences (criminal justice, sociology, psychology, and social work) predominate. Most wardens did not start as guards, or, if they did, their guard career was for a short time to finance their education or wait for a staff position to open up. Wardens are more likely to have held previous positions in case management, classification, treatment, administration, or probation and parole before moving into the prison managerial ranks.

Prison wardens today are usually products of the system, people who have moved around from one institution to another and have no particular ties to any institution. Their personalities and philosophies do not mean as much as they did at an earlier time. The centralized bureaucracy defines important policies, procedures, and practices; the state legislature and the governor's office provide political guidance; and the courts provide the customers.

The management of the contemporary prison is likely to be organized in a hierarchy. The formal structure has managers at the top, supervisors in the middle, and operating staff at the bottom. Management is more broad based and diffused, involving more specialists in different areas. The warden is more likely to see himself as a CEO who works with a large number of division managers and specialists on his management team than as a general commanding an army of privates, some of whom are inmates and some of whom are guards, as would have been the case in the nineteenth-century autocracy.

A 2002 ACA profile of over 2,000 wardens and superintendents in state prison systems provides this picture of top-level correctional managers today. The numbers of women are increasing steadily, about 25 percent in the most recent survey. Almost 20 percent of the wardens surveyed were black, and another 10 percent were Hispanic or other ethnic minorities. And about one in four wardens were cross-gender managers—no, not their style of dress but rather men managing women's prisons or, much more commonly, women managing men's prisons.[16]

In public policy circles, the prison wardens of today have often been accused of wanting to be invisible. They are rarely well-known public figures. They have tended to define themselves as administrators rather than leaders; they see themselves in primarily ministerial roles, as civil servants carrying out rather than making policies. They seldom speak out on issues, so we seldom hear what they have to say.

Why don't wardens assume a more visible role in society—write more, speak up more, and attempt to influence public policy more than they do? A few correctional officials have become both well respected by their peers and well regarded publicly as leaders of correctional reform. **George J. Beto,** the former Lutheran minister and college professor who in midlife became the director of the Texas Department of Corrections, was one such figure. Beto developed the "control model" of corrections, emphasizing work, discipline, and education in a rigorously controlled prison setting. This was an important transitional model between the autocratic and bureaucratic styles.[17] Although many elements of his model were later dismantled in the *Ruiz v. Estelle* federal lawsuit against the Texas prison system, his influence is still felt in many state systems today.

James V. Bennett, who headed the Federal Bureau of Prisons from the 1930s through the early 1960s, is another such figure. Bennett advocated "individualized treatment" of inmates, an idea that, if actualized, would mean that each prisoner would have his or her own personalized treatment regimen to guide the process of change that is supposed to take place in confinement. He built the federal prison system into a model that the states often borrowed from in trying to improve their own systems.

In Louisiana, **Ross Maggio** was called "Boss Ross" for the authoritative public style that characterized his two terms as warden of the Louisiana State Penitentiary at Angola in the 1970s and 1980s. Far from fighting against change, Maggio used the power of a federal court order to clean up Angola after a period of internal violence and disorder in the early 1970s. His straightforward, no-nonsense approach was reminiscent of earlier autocratic wardens, but he was instrumental in building a professional management team (with federal court support), something that previous wardens had been unable to do. He also minimized political intervention in prison affairs.

Correctional administrators are still struggling with the same problems they have always faced, aggravated by contemporary problems such as overcrowding, gangs, longer sentences, and violently unstable younger inmates. They are probably much better at managing their staff today; improved working conditions and more professional standards have made corrections a much better place to work. They remain uncertain, however, about what to do with inmates. Correctional administrators want to believe in change, and surveys indicate that they are far more understanding of criminals (and far more cognizant of the futility of much that goes on in their own prisons at present) than one might expect, but in the current climate it is not hard to understand why many of them would want to throw up their hands and ask, "Why bother?"

Perhaps surprisingly, a recent survey of wardens indicates high levels of career satisfaction. They like what they are doing and believe they are successful at it. This may be a good thing, or it may indicate only that their focus is so much *inside* the prison—on maintaining the secure custodial environment—that they are not much attuned to the problems of the criminal in the larger society.

TREATMENT VERSUS CUSTODY

Correctional administration has come a long way from the days of the early penitentiary. Remember that the reformers who met to found the National Prison Congress in Cincinnati in 1870 had to vote on a proposal to agree that "reformation and not vindictive suffering" should be the purpose of penal confinement. It took the lifetime efforts of such correctional administrators as Sanford Bates, the man who is called the father of modern penology for his work as director of the Federal Bureau of Prisons and other professional achievements covering half a century, to move prisons from the punitive to the rehabilitative era. The way has not always been clear. As Harry Allen and Clifford Simonsen have long pointed out, a "model muddle" has persisted for more than half a century, since the decline of the industrial prison, in regard to prison management. What is the prison supposed to do? How does the manager get the most out of the institution's staff? How democratic can prisons be in allowing participation by both staff and inmates? While custody must be maintained at a reasonable level, what can be done to enhance the effectiveness of treatment services within the prison setting?

We often use "treatment" and "rehabilitation" as synonymous terms. In the narrow definition, **treatment** would be the services—such as counseling, casework, and therapy—offered by the professional staff to change the behavior of prison inmates. Treatment is one part of rehabilitation, along with academic education, vocational training, recreation, religion, outside visitors, and inmate self-help activities. In its broadest definition, treatment can be anything positive that happens to an inmate in prison, even if neither the institution nor the inmate knows what it is or how important it is at the time. There has been a kind of skepticism about the effectiveness of treatment in the correctional setting for more than two decades. "What works?" Robert Martinson and his colleagues asked in reporting their research findings in 1974. "**Nothing works,**" they replied, or at least, "Nothing works consistently enough to apply it across the board with any reasonable expectation of success."[18]

We say that institutions then gave up on treatment, but in fact treatment had always been incidental to secure custody in prison. Treatment got what was left after custody, administration, and work programs took their share of the budget. This typically amounted to no more than 5 to 10 percent of the institution's budget, which is hardly a firm commitment to change, and even though we say we have given up on treatment, the portion of the budget devoted to rehabilitative services is greater in many prisons today than it was two decades ago. The medical model, as the most extreme form for the application of treatment, may be dead; correctional administrators' hopes for the possibility of changing criminal behavior into law-abiding behavior are far from dead. They are still seeking the right avenues for treatment, even if they do not talk about it as much as they once did.

Treatment is still custody's weak sister. Secure custody gets more resources and staff than all other functions added together. Security must be maintained at all times. You cannot shut down the guard towers that provide perimeter security just because you do not have enough guards or because there is a flu epidemic. You call in off-duty guards or extend the hours of guards already on duty to fill the essential positions, pay them overtime, and take the money out of treatment services. The inmates will never miss the transactional analysis sessions they did not have, the extra computer classes, or the job skills training for prerelease inmates. "You have to keep them in prison," the warden can point out, or nothing else matters, and the quickest way for him to get fired is to let some of them escape; no prison warden has ever been fired for failing to rehabilitate inmates. Indeed, after two centuries of locking up felons to serve prison terms, no one has a good idea as to whether prison wardens *can* rehabilitate inmates.

CLASSIFICATION AND ASSIGNMENT IN STATE PRISONS

In the complex, multilevel state prison system of today, incoming inmates usually go to a specific facility for classification on entry into the system. These facilities are called by various names—reception centers, diagnostic centers, reception and evaluation centers, or classification centers, for instance—but what they have in common is a process. Inmates are tested, interviewed, and monitored; their criminal history files are reviewed and prison records brought up to date. The prison attempts to determine the state of their physical and mental health, their educational and program needs, and any specific skills they may possess. Most of all, the **initial classification** is geared toward determining the level of security the inmate should be placed in. Is he an escape risk? A protection case? Is he dangerous to himself, to other inmates, or to staff?

Classification was originated as a tool to match the institution's programs to the needs of the prisoner, but it became over time more a device of security—to match the inmate to the **institutional needs** of the prison. Classification takes only a few weeks in most state systems (about four weeks in Warden

Lensing's Hunt Reception and Diagnostic Center (HRDC) at Elayn Hunt Correctional Center in Louisiana), but to the prisoner the outcome is tremendously important. It determines what prison he will be sent to, what security level he will be housed in, what his work assignment will be, and what programs he will be allowed to take part in. Classification determines which road you will be allowed to follow in prison; take a wrong turn, and it may be impossible to ever get back on the right track.

CUSTODY AS A WAY OF LIFE

From their origins as small, highly individualized institutions intent on salvation and humane penance, penitentiaries evolved into large, highly structured formal organizations intent on applying measures of bureaucratic control to hundreds or thousands of human beings. The modern prison is a prime example of Max Weber's characteristics of bureaucratic organization: hierarchical authority, job specialization, and formalized rules.

The person in charge of custody has long been the key figure in day-to-day prison operations. In some states, the deputy warden for custody was the mainstay of institutional continuity. Not only did he have more employees under his authority than any other prison official below the warden, but he was more likely to be a long-term employee. Wardens in several states, especially in the South, were considered **political hacks,** meaning that they were political appointees who got their jobs without any particular skills or interests or without any expectation that they would actually *perform* as wardens. They were paid to be figureheads. The security warden ran the prison. Wardens came and went; security was forever.

The custodial staff, then as now, relied on a variety of devices and techniques to maintain secure control of inmates. Among these measures are the following:

1. *The* **count.** The most important task of the custodial staff, most authorities acknowledge, is counting inmates to determine their whereabouts. The count goes in to a control center, and it must be verified. Until it is, prison life stops. The frequency of counting varies with the prison and the custody level.

2. *The* **sally port.** Basically a double gate, a sally port is used to control vehicle and pedestrian traffic into a prison. The sally port is like an airlock on a spaceship. Only one gate can be open at a time; in theory, prison security is always maintained.

3. *Prison rules.* Usually provided the newly arrived inmate in a handbook during classification or orientation, the rules define categories of offenses, disciplinary actions, and grievance procedures. Prisoners in violation of the rules may get a report, sometimes called a "write-up" or a "ticket." Serious incidents, such as "use of force" encounters involving physical confrontations, always warrant a report for the file.

4. *Control of* **contraband.** Contraband is anything not authorized by prison rules, including items that are allowed but of which the prisoner has too many: six spare batteries when only four are allowed or four cartons of cigarettes instead of two. Contraband may come in through the mail, or it may be carried in by visitors or other inmates. Most contraband comes into prison

through guards. Common contraband items smuggled in would include drugs, alcohol, pornography, weapons, and money.

5. *Searches.* Three basic searching techniques prevail in prisons. The **frisk search** is most common. It is a pat-down search of the inmate's outer clothing. The **strip search** requires the inmate to remove his clothing so that both his body and the clothing can be inspected more closely. Inmates suspected of hiding contraband in their rectum—a practice called "keestering," meaning to hide in one's keester—may be subjected to a **body cavity search,** which is supposed to be done by medical personnel rather than a guard with a fat angry finger. Some prisons have begun to use machines that do full-body scans to make these invasive searches, though if something shows up on a screen, it must still be retrieved.

6. *Tool and key control.* This prevents inmates from gaining access to items that could be used as weapons or as tools of escape. Inmate trusties or orderlies who once had keys, which allowed them to control access to other inmates and to supplies, no longer have them in the modern prison.

7. *Shakedowns.* A **shakedown** is a search of an area, such as a cell or tier of cells, a dormitory, a workplace, or a communal area, such as the library, the dining hall, or the chapel. Any contraband item can be hidden anywhere in the prison. Prisons have shakedown crews of guards whose job it is to carry out thorough searches. Shakedown crews do not find everything, but they do contribute a lot of useful anxiety to prisoners with contraband in their possession.

8. *Walls and fences.* Old prisons have walls, and new prisons have fences, usually double fences topped with **razor wire.** Guards armed with rifles man towers that surveil stretches of wall or fence. Several states, led by California, are using **electrified fences,** which can be as lethal as a rifle shot. This is called perimeter security to distinguish it from internal security within the walls.

9. *Lockdowns.* A **lockdown** means that one or more inmates, from a cell block to a dormitory to an entire prison, are confined to their living quarters for a period of time. This may often be done after an incident of violence or when trouble is anticipated. It is seen as a preventive measure, though with punitive consequences. Extended lockdown is used to hold the most troublesome inmates in long-term isolation.

Not on this list but of even greater importance to the old-style security warden were **snitches** and **trusties.** Snitches cultivated by guards were said to be the key to knowing what was going on in the old penitentiary. Wardens said that despite the credence given to the inmate code, virtually all inmates would snitch out other inmates in the right situation if the rewards were great enough. Trusty work assignments were one of these rewards. In most prison systems at one time, favored inmates were given direct control of other inmates, including making assignments, charging fellow prisoners fees for services and special favors, and, most commonly in the South, guarding them with guns.

For over half a century, Louisiana's Angola penitentiary relied on armed **inmate guards** (called "khaki backs" for their uniform shirts) to perform security duties. Former wardens from the 1950s and 1960s, such as Maurice Sigler and Murray Henderson, have told of their experiences arriving at the prison to take over as warden—and having their car searched at the front gate by inmates with guns. The prison had few free people employees; up to 20 percent of the inmates were trusties assigned to security duties (and living away from other inmates in relatively unsupervised dormitories).

In a contemporary prison, the security staff (free people only, inmates no longer given direct authority over other inmates) will be divided among shifts (usually three or four) and several types of job assignments:

1. Inmate living quarters, a critical assignment given experienced officers who get along well with inmates because it involves the most direct contact
2. Work sites, another assignment involving lots of direct contact with inmates
3. The **yard,** important as the site of the most open social interaction among inmates
4. **Towers and walls,** often viewed as a monotonous, undesirable assignment for new officers or officers who do not get along well with other officers or inmates (sometimes a disciplinary assignment)
5. **Gates,** which control movement within the facility
6. Visiting, important as an entry point for contraband
7. Dining hall, another important group congregation area
8. Hospital, treatment units, and recreation areas, all controlled access areas
9. **Escorts** and transports, which move inmates around or take them outside the prison for legal or medical visits
10. Training and administration, often assignments for officers believed to have management potential
11. Roving security patrols and **Corrections Emergency Response Teams** (CERT teams, like SWAT teams outside) that deal with uncooperative inmates, hostage incidents, riots, and other crises.

To the custodial staff, the two most serious events in prison are **assaults** and **escapes.** Assaults are serious for two reasons—first, someone may be hurt and, second, the notion of "secure custody" is threatened. According to *The 2001 Corrections Yearbook*, about 50,000 assaults of inmates and staff (two-thirds inmates, one-third staff) were officially reported in American prisons in 2000. About 19 percent required medical attention (at least an examination). In the same year, fifty-five inmates but no prison staff were killed in assaults by inmates.[19] The murder rate within prison, incidentally, was about 4.5 per 100,000 in 2000. This is considerably lower than the national homicide rate for the same year (5.6 per 100,000). Thus, prisoners are generally much safer from serious injury or death from assaults in prison than they were on the street; this is particularly true when prison violence rates are compared to the high-crime neighborhoods that prisoners come from on the street.

Escapes are also serious for two reasons—first, they reflect an obvious breach of security in some form, and, second, they reflect badly on the administration of the prison. Over 7,000 prison escapes were reported in 2000, but 90 percent of these were from open, nonsecure facilities, primarily involving work release, prerelease, and furlough inmates. These are often called **walkaways** rather than true escapes. Almost half of these escapes occurred in just three jurisdictions: Michigan, Missouri, and the District of Columbia.

Fewer than 800 escapes from secure prisons took place, and most of these were low-end institutions.[20]

In the old days, when there were fewer guards and inmate trusties were often involved in helping maintain security, prison escapes were common. They are not common now. About 65 to 70 percent of walkaways and escapees are recaptured quickly, picking up new criminal charges on recapture. If these inmates were in open- or low-security facilities before, their new home is almost certain to be a maximum-custody or lockdown unit.

THE SOCIAL SYSTEM AND CUSTODIAL MODELS

Prisons, especially maximum-security penitentiaries, are **total institutions.** They take away individual responsibility and autonomy, which is what we need to operate in the outside world, and attempt to make the inmate completely submissive to prison authority and totally dependent on prison routine. Prisoners enter most prisons naked, without any possessions of their own. They are as dependent as newborn babies.

The opening scene of the film *Escape from Alcatraz* vividly brings home this point. Clint Eastwood, as the newly transferred inmate Frank Morris, is brought over to Alcatraz at night through a rainstorm. No one is talking. He is examined, photographed and fingerprinted, stripped of his clothing, and issued his prison uniform. A guard then walks him naked down Broadway, the main corridor, to his cell. The door slams shut behind him, lightning flashes, and the guard speaks, "Welcome to Alcatraz." Morris looks out through the bars. Without the melodrama, welcome to prison, any prison, even today.

Babies grow and mature, but prisoners will still be treated like babies—like very bad babies—years later. This **infantilization** of inmates is a serious limitation of the custodial approach in corrections. Inmates do not progress much while they remain infantilized.

The inmate subculture, at whatever strength it remains today, divides the prison into the keepers and the kept. The subculture opposes the dominant culture imposed by custody; it tries to work around the rules and procedures and maximize the inmates' pleasure and control over their own lives. They seek through the subculture what they are denied by the formal organization.

The social system of the prison has been significantly affected in recent years by two circumstances. First, prisons in most states are at or over capacity. **Overcrowding** aggravates the natural conflicts that would occur in prison, it escalates tensions and the potential for violence, it gives prison officials fewer choices about how to place individual inmates (especially the ones who cause trouble), and it makes the task of keeping the prison safe and secure more difficult. Second, the rise of **prison gangs** has divided the social system into competing (sometimes warring) factions and further heightened the violence potential. Prison gangs are a problem mainly in the Southwest, where Hispanics are found in prison in greater numbers. The most influential gangs are the Hispanic gangs with such names as the Mexican Mafia, Mexikanemi, Texas Syndicate, and Nostra Familia. Whites, in the omnipresent Aryan Brotherhood, and blacks, in gangs typically associated with Crips and Bloods street gangs, often organize to protect their own interests in the conflict with the Hispanic gangs. Prison gangs demand a lifetime commitment, and death is said to be the only way out. Most prison violence occurs for personal reasons that have nothing to do with gang affiliation, but those states that have serious gang problems recognize that intergang and intragang conflicts make the problem of prison violence worse.

The history of custody in American prisons is the history of the paramilitary model. Guards wear uniforms and use military rank and like to imagine they are imposing military discipline. Of course, if the guards are the military force in charge of the prison, then what does this make the prisoners? One of the traditions of this model is that custodial staff remain separate and apart from inmates—the enemy forces. In American prisons, this has led to two enduring principles of prison operation:

1. *Custody rules.* All facets of prison life, including treatment, are subordinate to the custody function.
2. *Custodial staff only do custody.* They guard; they don't help, advise, counsel, treat, or express any interest in the inmate as a human being. To them, he is an alien with a number, and all they are interested in is the numbers adding up to the right total.

Contemporary prisons have explored different approaches to getting the custodial staff and the staff providing rehabilitation, recreation, and other programs to work more effectively together. One approach pioneered in the federal prison system and now used in one form or another in many state systems is called **unit team management** (comparable to the unit management approach used in Warden Lensing's Hunt Correctional Center). This approach breaks the prison up into quasi-autonomous parts, usually based around residential quarters. All the staff working in the unit report to one administrator. The idea is to break down barriers between specialists and get staff to take a broader role with inmates. Some correctional officers take well to this concept; many, schooled in the narrowest possible definition of their function, want no part of it. Custody and treatment remain more often adversaries than allies.

CORRECTIONAL OFFICERS

The people who work in security run the prison. Generally, the higher the security level of the prison, the lower the ratio of inmates to **correctional officers.** State averages of inmates to COs range from about 3.5 to 1 up to 8 to 1 (with a national average of 5.4 to 1 in 2000),[21] but these numbers have to be taken with a grain of salt. Some states include noncustodial staff, while others take out uniformed supervisory and management staff. The numbers of people in security are obviously influenced by the structure of security levels in the prison system—maximum, medium, minimum, and so on. In addition, because security is an around-the-clock operation, the number of officers is always divided among shifts. The basic mathematical calculation is that each security post requires from five to five-and-a-half people to man it continuously year-round because of sick days, holidays, training, and other assignments. Thus, if a big prison has a thousand security officers, about 160 to 200 would be scheduled to work at any given time (other than the day shift, which is top-heavy with administrative staff).

In the old days, the head of security was often called **the Captain** (see the films *Brute Force* and *Cool Hand Luke* for different representations of this figure). While the warden was a mythical political official on about the same level as God, the captain ran the prison day to day. He interacted with inmates, made assignments, disciplined and punished, and saw to it that the work got done. No one was sure what the warden did, but everyone saw the fruits of the captain's labor. Guards in the old-style prison had total power over inmates—and used it. The inmate nicknames for the guard—"screw," "bull," or "hack"—express the adversarial nature of the guard–inmate relationship in the maximum-custody penitentiary (and they express as well the contempt for the guards that marked the inmate subculture).

Prisons were typically located in rural areas. The guards were often farmers working in the prison to make ends meet. The convicts were most likely to be street criminals from the big city. These cultural differences were often heightened by differences of race and ethnicity as well. The old-style convict and the old-style prison guard were different in just about every way except for two points: they were both on the bottom level of society, and neither of them planned to end up in prison.

The correctional officer of today is a different kind of animal from the guard of a hundred years ago, at least in theory. Correctional officers are men and women, white, black, and Hispanic. In 2001, 23 percent of correctional officers were women, 21 percent black, and 6 percent Hispanic. These numbers are increasing steadily; of the new correctional officers hired in 2000, 35 percent were female and 39 percent minorities.[22] Two states, Mississippi and Arkansas, already have more women than men correctional officers, and several other southern states are moving in this direction. Men's prisons staffed (and managed) by women? Elam Lynds must be spinning in his grave.

More than 250,000 correctional officers worked in state and federal prisons in 2001. Their average starting salary was just under $24,000 per year; New Jersey's starting salary of $36,850, the highest in the country, was more than twice that of Louisiana, the lowest, at $15,324.[23]

Correctional officers in several states are unionized. Unionization has not been as strong in corrections as it has been in other public sector vocations, but it has thrown the fear of worker solidarity into prison administrators. Prison employee groups have sometimes used sick-outs or attacks of **blue flu** to support their demands for recognition or improved working conditions. Prison employees are not allowed to strike.

Prison administrators, for their part, want correctional officers to be better trained and more legally aware. They do not want to lose lawsuits and incur the wrath of politicians and public because of inept, brutal guards. Forty-eight of the fifty states have some requirement for preservice training for new correctional officers (the state average is 262 hours, more than six weeks), forty-seven have a probationary employment period averaging about ten months, and requirements for in-service training have increased steadily also, averaging almost forty hours per year.[24]

Despite the increasing professionalization of the correctional officer's role, the **turnover rate** for COs remains high. The simple truth is that the prison environment, while not as oppressive and dangerous as it once was, is still highly structured and closed in; many people cannot handle the work hours, the bureaucratic procedures, and the relationships with inmates or other staff.

A lot of new officers are fired or resign during their probationary periods. Others use the prison job as a stopgap. When a free-world job paying 5 cents per hour more comes along, they quit the prison.

The average annual turnover rate for prison custodial officers was about 16 percent in 2000, averaging between 12 and 16 percent for the decade of the 1990s. Massachusetts, Michigan, New York, and Pennsylvania had turnover below 5 percent (considered a desirable standard for private industry). Some states had much higher rates, led by Louisiana, Kentucky, and Wyoming with rates above 33 percent.[25] It is difficult to maintain a stable security force when turnover rates are this high, but such rates can actually be good news for correctional officers: the faster the turnover, the better the opportunity to move up. Advancement opportunities in corrections, with the comparatively high turnover rate and the continuing expansion of the system to deal with overcrowding problems, has made corrections an attractive career field for the time being.

Are today's correctional officers, with all their training, higher salaries, and professionalism, really different from the prison guards of earlier times? The prison guard of the past was **custody oriented.** His institution was the maximum-security penitentiary. He counted inmates, he worked them, he moved them around, and he beat them when necessary. An absolutely authoritative security force ran the early penitentiaries; later, as conditions of confinement became less severe, an alliance of guards and trusty inmates maintained order in the prison through most of the twentieth century.

The late twentieth-century and early twenty-first-century prison is a different environment. Only about one in four inmates is in maximum or close custody. Interaction with inmates and management of inmates are more important than authority and coercive power; lower security prisons strive for "normalcy." Some researchers have called attention to the more visible presence of female correctional officers from the 1970s on. They suggest that a more "feminine" or caring style has emerged in this era. Others suggest that this style is not gender based but simply a result of relaxing security standards—cooperation replacing compulsion.

Some management researchers argue that male officers can also talk to inmates and care about them as much as females might; their focus is not on a feminine correctional role but on a "human relations" role that applies equally to male and female officers. This role would expect that officers would be more empathetic with inmates, more interested in their problems, more involved in rehabilitation programs, and more suited to serving as role models. Prison guards saw prisoners as objects; correctional officers are supposed to see them as people. Most prison staff working in security today prefer to be known as correctional officers. "Don't call me guard," they say. But which are they? Is a correctional officer just a more politically correct term for a guard, or is there a genuine role difference?

PRISON: BASIC SERVICES

Prisons of all security levels, even maximum security in which custody is most emphasized, provide inmates with many services and activities beyond simply being locked up. Politicians and people on the street sometimes grumble about services provided inmates. Why are convicts entitled to these "special programs"? they ask, with images of "convict coddling" and "country club prisons" fresh in their minds. "They have it better in prison than they did on the street," they might add. Correctional managers have four ready responses:

1. Convicts are not on the street any longer. When they give up their freedom, the state assumes the responsibility for their welfare and safety.
2. Prisons are obligated to maintain constitutional living conditions. To do otherwise would invite costly lawsuits and court intervention.
3. Prisons at one time did not provide many of these services and activities, at least not at present levels. Inmates spent all their free time trying to exploit each other and escape. Giving prisoners more positive activities reduces their involvement in misconduct and makes the institution easier to manage.
4. The special programs may actually make inmates better human beings. Isn't it worth spending a little more if criminality is reduced as a result?

The level and quality of prison services to inmates varies greatly from one state to another, depending on the philosophy of corrections officials and how much the state is willing to spend to "help criminals." Some states have a tradition of doing a lot; others provide only minimal services. There are three basic services—medical, religious, and education and training—and a wide variety of staff positions allocated to provide these and other necessary and optional services. The custodial staff still dominate in numbers and in their influence on inmates (the influence of correctional officers in the housing units and on work sites is particularly important), but many inmates have been helped and redirected by a prison teacher, a counselor, a psychologist, a vocational instructor, or a chaplain. There is no formula that prescribes exactly how one person reaches another; in the prison environment, anyone, even the food service manager in the dining hall, may be the one responsible for starting an inmate down the road away from a criminal lifestyle.

All prisons must provide medical services to inmates. This has become an increasingly expensive obligation, with the sicker inmates of today (see the discussion of medical care in chapter 8). More inmates are substance abusers, more are elderly, more are mentally ill, and more come in with serious infectious diseases—HIV; hepatitis A, B, and C; rubella; and tuberculosis, including multidrug-resistant tuberculosis among inmates with other ailments.

Religion is an important prison activity. Some inmates fake it—to get to go to church and hang out with their buddies. Others who never took the time to seek out religion when they were running the streets find that prison religious programs change the whole direction of their lives. Many prisons have thriving religious communities, from Black Muslims to Eastern religions to every variety of Protestantism, Catholicism, and Judaism. Free-thinking prisoners are always inventing new religions and then demanding that prison authorities let them practice them (sometimes asking for such supplies as plastic inflatable dolls, altars, incense, and candles, all of which authorities deny). Inmates direct many of their own religious activities because it is hard to get free people to come into prison to work with inmate groups. The **prison chaplain** has been a staple of the institution since the days of the Walnut Street Jail. Some prison chaplains are dedicated, highly regarded men and women who have a special calling to work with prisoners; others are viewed as uninspired hacks who are little more than snitches for security.

The chaplain is one of many specialized careers required by prisons that people on the street rarely consider. People are aware of guards, administrators, and maybe the psychologists who work in treatment, but they fail to think of many other positions necessary for the day-to-day operation of the prison. These would include such positions as the following:

Facility manager. The person responsible for maintaining the prison's buildings and grounds. The director of the physical plant.

Food service manager. The person responsible for procuring food supplies and supervising the kitchen and dining facilities. Meal preparation is very important to inmates. This position is usually filled by a registered dietician.

Health system administrator. The manager of the institution's health care and medical programs. Usually, he or she is an administrator, not a physician.

Industrial specialist. The person who supervises the inmates working in a prison industry. Generally, this is someone who has special training or work experience in the specific work supervised.

Medical officer. A doctor licensed to practice medicine in the state, either a general practitioner or a specialist.

Ombudsman. A person who receives and investigates inmate (and sometimes staff) complaints. Only a few states have this position, though most have some type of grievance officer or investigator who looks into complaints.

Recreation specialist. A specialist in physical or other forms of recreational activities. Because most prisoners are young men, recreational programs are very important in prison.

Teacher. A person certified in education. Prisons need teachers with certifications from lower elementary through high school.

The role of the academic teachers and the vocational training instructors is particularly important. Education does not cure crime, but recidivism studies have found that better-educated ex-offenders (beyond GED or high school) are less likely to return to prison. Likewise, an inmate with no employment record and no job skills is more likely to recidivate than someone who can get and hold a good job.

Teachers are among the most numerous of the treatment staff working in prisons. It is not easy to teach in prison, where the students often have long records of failure at both school and work. About two-thirds of prison inmates lack a high school diploma. Many are functionally illiterate; a good number (ranging from 7 to 25 percent in different studies) are learning disabled. But some inmates make remarkable progress in making up for their educational deficiencies. A number of prisons have formed relationships with nearby colleges to provide college courses behind the walls; Project Newgate was the prototype of a prison college education program, starting in prison and then taking the offender out into the community to attend classes on campus. Some states continue to allow inmates to go out on educational furloughs to get vocational training or college courses, though, in the present political climate, furloughs are used much more cautiously than they once were.

Vocational training is more important in most prisons than academic education. Some prisons have so many types of job training for inmates that they resemble technical schools behind bars. One of the problems with giving inmates job training has been that since the decline of the industrial prison in the 1930s, real work for prisoners has been limited. Prison industries in the federal system and in most state systems concentrate on making products to be consumed by other units of government, such as state offices and institutions. If prisoners cannot do "real work," if they can only be trained and given busy work to do that does not make use of their skills, it is difficult to get them to see the connection between training and employment. Congress passed the Prison Industries Enhancement Act in 1979 to encourage greater private sector involvement with state penal industries. About twenty states have subsequently authorized private business to establish different types of business operations within prisons. The number of inmates participating in real-world work (and earning real-world wages) is very small; the prison remains a mostly untapped labor force.

The delivery of treatment services in the more narrow sense may involve the participation of several kinds of professionals from the behavioral sciences. These would include the following:

Psychologists, who do testing and measurement of inmates, construct personality profiles, and provide counseling.

Psychiatrists, who are few in number and not highly regarded in prisons. Their long-term therapies are often seen as being out of place in a secure-custody environment. They do more diagnosis and prescribing of medication than treatment in most prisons.

Sociologists, who do research and monitor the effectiveness of treatment programs rather than treating offenders directly.

Social workers, often called caseworkers, whose tasks include assessing needs, assigning and conducting programs, and evaluating progress.

Counselors, who are sometimes known by other titles within the prison job structure. This is a kind of generic job title for a person who often lacks the specific higher education in the behavioral sciences the other professionals possess. Counselors and other trained therapists do apply a number of treatment modalities—such as reality therapy, transactional analysis, behavior modification, and guided group interaction—in prison, but counseling in prison implies a more commonsense approach as opposed to a rigorously therapeutic treatment regimen.

Case managers or classification officers, usually assigned by housing units. Their job is to look after the inmates' overall welfare and progress through the prison system, paying attention to any personal matters that affect life in custody. The case manager is the inmate's intercessor in the prison bureaucracy.

IS PRISON TREATMENT POSSIBLE?

The greatest debate among treatment professionals over the past two decades or more is whether treatment, in the broadest sense, is either possible or desirable within the prison setting. The institutional model keeps large numbers of inmates locked up in secure institutions; treatment programs are built into the custodial routine. Many behavioral scientists would much prefer to see a reemphasis on the reintegration model, which sends offenders out into the community for treatment programs. They quarrel with the prison administrators of today who say they are following the reintegration model but strictly within prison walls. That is not reintegration, they say; it is just a slicker version of the old institutional model, and prisoners can tell the difference.

Treatment within prison is more likely to appear incidental to custody; treatment in the community is more likely to feel like the real thing. If the intent is to keep prisoners isolated and focused on the prison experience, we should continue as is; if we want them to look beyond the boundaries of the prison, we should explore every possibility of contact with the outside world. Treatment within prison can probably be improved, but it will always be under the domination of custody. Treatment in the community is much closer to how we want the offender to live for the rest of his life.

KEY TERMS

warden

secure custody

perimeter security

Elayn Hunt Correctional Center

C. M. Lensing Jr.

Warden Norton

unit management

empowerment

Management by Walking Around (MBWA)

scientific management

human relations

Theory X

Theory Y

autocratic style

Elam Lynds

Thomas Mott Osborne

bureaucratic style

Joseph Ragen

internal environment

external environment

George J. Beto

James V. Bennett

Ross Maggio

treatment

"nothing works"

initial classification

institutional needs

political hacks

count

sally port

contraband

frisk search

strip search

body cavity search

shakedown

razor wire

electrified fences

lockdown

snitches

trusties

inmate guards

yard

towers and walls

gates

escorts

Corrections Emergency Response Team

assaults

escapes

walkaways

total institutions

infantilization

overcrowding

prison gangs

unit team management

correctional officers

the Captain

blue flu

turnover rate

custody oriented

prision chaplain

ombudsman

counselors

case managers

NOTES

1. Elayn Hunt Correctional Center, *www.corrections.state.la.us/ehcc/mission/MissionStat.html.*

2. Frederick Taylor, *The Principles of Scientific Management* (New York: Harper and Row, 1947).

3. Douglas McGregor, *The Human Side of Enterprise* (New York: McGraw-Hill, 1960).

4. Robert Freeman, "Management and Administrative Issues," in Joycelyn M. Pollock, *Prisons: Today and Tomorrow* (Gaithersburg, Md.: Aspen Publishers, 1997), p. 283.

5. Ibid., pp. 284–85.

6. Rensis Likert, *New Patterns of Management* (New York: McGraw-Hill, 1967).

7. Edgar Schein, *Organizational Psychology* (Englewood Cliffs, N.J.: Prentice Hall, 1965).

8. Scott Christianson, *With Liberty for Some: 500 Years of Imprisonment in America* (Boston: Northeastern University Press, 1998), p. 14.

9. Ibid., pp. 127–28.

10. Ibid., p. 207.

11. James B. Jacobs, *Stateville: The Penitentiary in Mass Society* (Chicago: University of Chicago Press, 1977), p. 41.

12. Ibid., pp. 30–34.

13. Freeman, "Management and Administrative Issues," p. 274.

14. Pamela K. Withrow, "What Is a Warden?" in *A View from the Trenches: A Manual for Wardens by Wardens* (Lanham, Md.: American Correctional Association, 1999), p. 1.

15. Ibid., pp. 1–3.

16. American Correctional Association, "Adult Correctional Wardens and Superintendents and Cross-Gender Supervision on September 30, 2002," in *The Adult Correctional Administration Directory, 2003* (Lanham, Md,: American Correctional Association, 2003), p. 42.

17. See John J. DiIulio Jr., *Governing Prisons: A Comparative Study of Correctional Management* (New York: Free Press, 1987), pp. 195–231.

18. Robert Martinson, "What Works? Questions and Answers about Prison Reform," *The Public Interest* 35 (spring 1974): 25.

19. Camille Graham Camp and George M. Camp, *The 2001 Corrections Yearbook: Adult Systems* (Middletown, Conn.: Criminal Justice Institute, 2002), p. 42.

20. Ibid., pp. 33–34.

21. Ibid., p. 175.

22. Ibid., p. 165.

23. Ibid., pp. 168–69.

24. Ibid., p. 166.

25. Ibid., pp. 170–71.

FURTHER READING

Conover, Ted. *Newjack: Guarding Sing Sing*. New York: Random House, 2000.

DiIulio, John J., Jr. *Governing Prisons: A Comparative Study of Correctional Management*. New York: Free Press, 1987.

Hawkins, Gordon. *The Prison: Policy and Practice*. Chicago: University of Chicago Press, 1977.

Lombardo, Lucien X. *Guards Imprisoned: Correctional Officers at Work*. 2nd ed. Cincinnati: Anderson Publishing, 1989.

WEB AND VIDEO RESOURCES

The North American Association of Wardens and Superintendents' Website is *www.corrections.com.naaws*.

Correctional News (*www.correctionalnews.com*) is a useful entry into the business end of corrections, calling itself "the online source for design, construction, management, and operations" in corrections.

The American Correctional Association Bookstore provides a good collection of training, management, and learning materials at *www.aca.org/store*.

8 Management and the Organizational Culture

by C.M. Lensing, Jr.

Nothing is more important to the successful operation of a prison or jail than management. Poor inmate quality of life, use of excessive force, unsafe living conditions, deficient education and rehabilitative programs, disturbances, and escapes are all products of poor prison management. I have never believed that a warden could shift blame for a poorly run institution to internal or external factors, such as gangs, "politics," budget constraints, architectural designs, and/or overcrowding. These factors—difficult, fatiguing and thankless—are limiting, but never impossible to manage.

To manage a prison, the warden *must* come to terms with its organizational culture. Culture is to an organization what personality is to an individual. Like human culture, organizational culture is generally passed from one generation to the next. It is there when you arrive, and it will be there when you leave. Your objective, as a leader, is to make it better than you found it. If you do not want to try to make it so, you should not be in a leadership position.

A strong management culture within an institution is one that is persistent with a patterned way of thinking about the tasks to be accomplished. I have on numerous occasions referred to a correctional operation as a "people business," meaning that I think human relationships are the core of the culture. If you create the right organizational culture, combining correctional leadership with the institutional make-up, certain interlocking patterns will become apparent. John DiIulio's *No Escape: The Future of American Corrections* (1991) discusses these patterns at greater length.

How do correctional managers go about the task of leading? One accepted definition of leadership is "the ability to influence people to work willingly and enthusiastically towards the achievement of established goals." Today we understand that people should be guided and motivated, not coerced and threatened, into pursuing our goals.

Leadership within a correctional facility is relatively simple. It is the establishment of a very clear direction that is designed to continuously improve the culture of the facility. This direction has to be principle-centered, and it must emphasize a commitment to values and respect for other people. Good correctional leaders are men and women with posi-

tions of influence who work primarily in the pursuit of one objective; to these leaders, principles and respect for others mean more than power and authority. Stress is inherent in the correctional setting; it need not be compounded by gossip and unprofessional behavior. Substitute a strong social and moral workplace for these poor practices. Leadership should strive to bring people together to create a positive environment.

My approach has been one of empowerment with an emphasis on listening. Empowerment requires people to make decisions. In the correctional setting, it means including the right people at the right levels of the organization in decision making. It reinforces the fundamental team concept. A prison can be strengthened by applying the best that each employee can contribute towards improving its operation. To successfully use the concept of empowerment, you must constantly encourage and challenge the staff. This will leave a culture that reaffirms that good ideas come from every level within the operation.

The warden does not have all the answers. Empowerment closely relates to listening. To empower, you must be willing to ask for input. I have seen too many managers within a correctional facility believe that the quality of management is measured by how loud they can yell. They believe they aren't really doing their duties unless they are screaming at someone or chewing someone out. I believe, to the contrary, that good managers are good listeners and that listening behaviors should be reflected by all good executives. In my own management approach, I have always believed that prison executives should be fair, avoid playing favorites, expect rejection, be consistent, and keep promises. Loyalty to the organization, as opposed to certain individuals, has always been a keen point with me. Acknowledging the importance of staff, a good follow-through mechanism, giving credit, and taking responsibility are all areas that make a corrections executive fulfill his or her potential.

This cannot be done from an office. I must be out walking around, asking questions, discussing issues with staff, watching them doing things right (and wrong) and giving constructive criticism. It is my culture, and I have to see it to know it. This is my formula for success in correctional management.

Finding Her Place

by Michele D. Buisch

A third-generation migrant worker, Elaine White began picking fruits and vegetables from fields throughout Florida, Michigan, New York, and North Carolina when she was just six. Her family moved from place to place in pursuit of available work, staying no more than four months in one location, which made it difficult for White, as it is for most migrant children, to develop roots and a sense of place.

During her childhood, White was exposed to the depressed, substandard conditions that are rampant among migrant camps. Living in a world largely forgotten by society, she was surrounded by despair. Many people drank alcohol and took drugs to keep themselves going; others were in and out of jail. Education was not required, nor important, and workers were not held accountable. It was a difficult life in which they were at the mercy of the weather and the landowners, who at times, did not pay the migrant workers.

However, White's mother wanted something better for her family. Although no one was checking to ensure migrant children attended school, she enrolled her children in the local schools each time they arrived in a new town—even if it was for just a week. "Most migrant parents would say, 'Oh we're only here for two or three weeks,'" says White. "My mom would say, 'You're going.'"

As a result, White—the seventh of 13 children kept up with her studies and was the first in her family to go to college. A straight-A student, she graduated from Haines City High School in Florida in 1976 with a four-year academic scholarship to Florida State University, where she studied correctional management. Upon graduation, White put her degree to work and searched for a correctional agency that was actively seeking women and minorities. What she wanted most, however, was a permanent place to call her own. She longed for what many take for granted: stability and a retirement, which no one in her family had ever had. "When I graduated from college, I was looking for an opportunity to belong to something," explains White. "On a migrant camp, there is always a feeling of worthlessness and diminished self-esteem."

White got her start in corrections when she was hired by the Hillsborough County Sheriff's Office in Florida as a deputy sheriff. She has been with the agency ever since—nearly 20 years. Throughout her distinguished career, White, now a major, has worked her way through the ranks, holding every supervisory position in the department, and was promoted five years ago to division commander of the Orient Road Jail, which is the largest facility in the system, with 1,714 beds.

White is a hands-on supervisor, preferring to handle things directly, bypassing memos for face-to-face interactions. To her, the most important aspect of her job is ensuring that staff are well-trained. From her migrant days, she also understands the importance of teamwork and expressing to staff how important they are to her and the successful operation of the jail. "I try to remember every day that my staff make me look good. It's not just 'me' thing."

White is a leader both at work and in the community. Two years ago, she created an Orient Road Jail fund—raising committee to involve her staff in projects that benefit the community as well as promote the sheriff's office. Together, they sponsor a number of projects each year, one of which is called Foster Angels. During the holiday season, the committee compiles a wish list from children living in area foster homes or orphanages and puts the information on the back of blue angels for boys and pink angels for girls and hangs them on a Christmas tree at the jail. Staff pick one or two angels, buy the gifts, wrap them, and deliver them to the children. Several months ago, they hosted a fund-raiser to benefit a 14-year-old girl with terminal cancer. And in October, they participated in a benefit breakfast in conjunction with a local church to support an aftercare program for women recently released from the Hillsborough County jail system.

White's passion is people. She likes to be out in the community, interacting with people and positively representing women in the sheriff's office. To that end, White tries to give about 50 speeches per year to different community groups, including schools and churches, and conducts tours of her facility. With everything she does, White includes her staff. "We're proud of our facility and I also want the staff to always know that they are important," she says.

In addition to helping the community, White hosts seminars for staff, such as smoking cessation and financial planning workshops. Using her connections in the community, she provides a seminar for staff approximately every six weeks. White also started a chapter of the public speaking group, Toastmasters International, at her facility to help improve staff's communication skills and, ultimately, their self-esteem. Further, she and the fund-raising committee organized a job fair last spring, which included facility tours, application materials, information about each position and mentor assignments to help prospective employees work through the hiring process.

White also is a migrant advocate and helped develop the Professional Migrant Advocates, a 15-year-old private organization for professionals who come from migrant backgrounds. In that capacity, she has been involved in several projects statewide to help generate public understanding of the plight of migrant children.

Several months ago, one such project was held in Hillsborough County called, "Project Zapatos," which is Spanish for shoes, and successfully collected new shoes for migrant children. After nine months of hard work, White, who started and has been running a similar program for 10 years, gathered 2,000 pairs of new shoes. Instead of just giving out the shoes, the organizers, which included some staff, set up a makeshift store at the YMCA, complete with racks for the shoes, greenery for decoration, and cashiers. The children picked out their shoes, "paid" with a voucher and received a shopping bag and a receipt that read, "Believe in yourself."

"It was magical for me," says White, who received her first pair of shoes when she was in the eighth grade. "It was overwhelmingly successful....; I wanted the kids to come into a store setting, something most of them never have an opportunity to do."

Although her mother did not understand White's decision to go into corrections when she graduated college, and for a time, was even disappointed because of the experiences she had had with law enforcement as a migrant worker, White could not be happier with her career or the way her life has turned out. "I love the people, the interaction. I love the fact that although I'm the only black person on the sheriff's staff, the only woman, and the only tall person, I'm just accepted. I work with about 25 of the top supervisors in the sheriff's office, including the sheriff. I'm kidded and the whole nine yards like everybody else," says White. "Had I not taken this job, I know my family's path would have been different."

White thinks about how far she has come every day. A lot of people in her family, people with whom she grew up, people with whom she went to school, are dead, in prison or living on the streets, never having experienced the luxury of a stable job or the feeling of belonging. "I was looking for acceptance when I took the job," she says, "and I got more than I ever expected."

Correctional Shock: Ten Rules for Therapists in Prison

by Steve Rybolt

Way back when, I was a therapist in the country's first adolescent heroin treatment center (Riverside Hospital, North Brother Island, New York City). It's been a circuitous route to my present work with the Missouri Department of Corrections. For two years now, I've been engaged in developing chemical dependency services in the correctional system for maximum- and medium-security offenders.

What a change in perceptions the intervening years have brought. The concern I'm addressing to "outsiders" who are trying to provide services in the criminal justice system is what I'll call "correctional shock." Here are ten factors that need to be addressed, matters that you outsiders must pay attention to if you intend to provide effective addiction treatment services to the nation's correctional systems.

1. First and foremost, you're going to be dealing with a complicated system dedicated to security, control and punishment. That's because modern prisons—places where we pretend to rehabilitate people without souls—have revolving doors and no space. One in, one out.

2. Decision-making and getting a task accomplished often require many layers of review until a final judgment is rendered. Remember, you are dealing with a system with goals of confinement, control, security, and punishment. Every level expects to have a say in the outcome of anything that changes the operation of the institution.

3. Addiction and the disease model are foreign to most persons who deal with offenders. You often

will hear responsible persons say, "Well, if he only would use a little willpower," or, "They simply have no morals"—statements indicating no comprehension of the complexities of working with persons in trouble with chemical dependency.

4. Addictive drugs are available, for a price, for those in prison who want them. Even those who believe in what you're trying to do will tell you that until you can stop the drugs from coming into the institution, you'll always have a problem.

5. Violence, fights and threatening behavior accompany prison drug usage. An addict who buys in prison must pay dearly for his habit; when he gets in debt over his head he will be dealt with severely. He can even be reached if he "turns himself in" to protective custody.

6. Where seldom is heard a rehabilitative word, you'll wonder if there are any people who support your efforts. You may discover that those who are most encouraging are those who somehow get "clean and dry."

7. You may experience more program resistance from the staff than from inmates.

8. Parole violations for substance use only reinforce the correctional system's cynicism.

9. Your professional credentials will not matter much to offenders. Your own recovery will mean a great deal, however. It's the phenomenon of "until you've walked in my moccasins."

10. Finally, don't look for or expect commendations from the system. The rewards of your effort and competence will have to be found in the outcomes of the lives of those persons who manage to turn things around.

The lines seem to be drawn in our system: stiffer penalties, more prisons, longer sentences. There are those of us who believe in the humane treatment of offenders in trouble because of chemical dependency. But much of the corrections community remains resistant to change.

It will be difficult in the short term to demonstrate convincing evidence that chemical dependency programs will work, that they can and do make a difference. But those who intend to serve the nation's prisons must address these issues professionally, believing firmly in rehabilitation. They must be able to demonstrate that change can produce results—that's the bottom line.

8

CORRECTIONS POLICIES

AND ISSUES

Prisons do not exist in a vacuum; they are part of a political, social, economic, and moral order.

— James B. Jacobs, *Macrosociology and Imprisonment*, 1977

INTRODUCTION

The most consequential issue in American corrections since the early 1980s has been the extent of use of incarceration itself as a crime control measure. Is America better off in 2003 with more than 2 million behind jail and prison bars than it was in 1980, when that number was about 400,000? We will come back to this issue in the international context in chapter 16 at the end of this book. In this chapter, we will look briefly at several other issues that have dominated policy debates regarding institutional corrections in the past decade. After reading the material in this chapter, you should be familiar with:

1. Professionalization and the accreditation movement in corrections.
2. Prison health care.
3. Responding to population increases.
4. Privatization.
5. Race and imprisonment.

PROFESSIONALIZATION AND ACCREDITATION

Professionalization and accreditation have become important terms in correctional administration in the past two decades. **Professionalization** has to do with gaining professional status for persons working in corrections, while **accreditation** seeks comparable status for their employing organizations.

"Professional" is a commonplace term in America today. In its simplest forms, it means one who follows an occupation as a means of earning a living—a professional baseball player as opposed to someone who just plays ball for the fun of it—or merely someone who is an expert at what he does—such as an experienced plumber. In its higher form, "professional" refers to the learned professions—such as medicine and law—which have high standards of education, training, ethics, and responsibility. It seems odd that people working in corrections, a field that has probably ranked lower in public esteem than either baseball or plumbing, might aspire to the same status as doctors or lawyers; how do they propose to make this giant upward bound?

The first step is to define the characteristics of the status they are seeking. In her discussion of professionalism in the first edition of *Comparative Criminal Justice Systems*, Erika Fairchild identified six key indicators:

1. Merit hiring, which has to do with the qualifications and selection process used to bring new employees into the field
2. Training, which consists of preservice, in-service, and supervisory and management training for employees at all levels of the organization
3. Advanced technology, which has to do with the equipment resources available to employees
4. Incorruptibility, which requires employees to avoid selling favors to their clients
5. Equal treatment of citizens, which means avoiding discrimination for or against on the basis of personal or cultural biases
6. Close adherence to the law, which means following the law closely in performing one's daily work[1]

Some would doubtless criticize Fairchild's choice of indicators, arguing particularly that preservice education, ethical standards, public service orientation, and the public's view of the occupation's practitioners should also be on this list. But her six indicators (which were part of a discussion of international policing standards) do give us a baseline for discussion. Where does corrections stand on the professional scale?

Corrections is a very large field of work. Well over half a million public employees work in jails and prisons for adults and juveniles; perhaps half that number work in nonsecure supervision alternatives, such as probation and parole, and an untold number as full-time, part-time, and contract private sector workers performing corrections-related duties. Would most of these meet Fairchild's indicators? Not by any stretch of the imagination. There is movement in that direction, but several big steps remain between where they are and where they aspire to go.

Merit hiring means that most entry-level corrections workers have a high school diploma or GED; degreed positions in administration, probation, or parole do attract college graduates in criminal justice and other behavioral science disciplines, but they also attract many applicants with no prior education in the field. If they can pass a civil service test and have no serious criminal record themselves, they have a good chance of employment.

Training for both operational- and management-level positions has increased steadily in recent years. Starting with virtually no formal preservice training requirements in most states thirty years ago, in 2000 at least forty-six of the fifty states required an average of six and a half weeks (262 hours) of recruit training, ten months of probationary status, and a week (thirty-eight hours) of annual in-service training for new correctional officers in operational positions.[2] Probation and parole staff training requirements varied more widely from state to state in 2000, but forty-six of the fifty states required an average of about four weeks (170 hours) of preservice training and a week (thirty-seven hours) of annual in-service training.[3]

Advanced technology has surely made an impact on institutional corrections and nonsecure supervision in recent years. The annual meetings of organizations such as the American Correctional Association and the American Jail Association seem dominated by technology. They have become huge trade shows for companies selling the latest in corrections technology and equipment. Modular jail cells, electrified fences, drug testing kits, computerized control monitors, flame-resistant pillows, electronic monitoring bracelets, laptops, indestructible cell furniture—a jail or prison manager can find anything he needs, from a single plastic razor to a fully equipped 1,000-bed prison, for sale at these meetings. As managers search for ways to improve monitoring and security and hold down personnel costs, the application of technology in corrections has advanced dramatically, sometimes to the point that equipment receives more emphasis than staff or that technology is emphasized while human deficiencies are ignored.

Fairchild's last three indicators—incorruptibility, equal treatment of citizens, and adherence to law—are more difficult to evaluate in their correctional context. One need not search very hard to find examples of corruption, discrimination, and illegal conduct in corrections. Indeed, the front page of the leading corrections Website, *www.corrections.com*, lists links to recent news articles about misconduct by corrections staff, operational and administrative, some of it resulting in litigation. But there is a general sense among people who have worked in corrections for thirty or forty years that both the ethical standards of corrections staff and the legal framework within which they operate are much stronger today than they were a generation ago. Not all of this advance has been voluntary; much of it has to do with federal and state court orders demanding higher standards of accountability in care, custody, and control. But over time, however, these standards, once set from outside, have become internalized: corrections workers now seek their own standards rather than those set for them by outsiders.

The leading advocate of corrections professionalism today is the **American Correctional Association** (ACA), which originated in the National Congress on Penitentiary and Reformatory Discipline meeting in Cincinnati in 1870. Known as the National Prison Association and the American Prison Association until it adopted its present name in 1954, the ACA now represents the professional interests of the corrections field.

The ACA's **Professional Development Department** takes its direction from Article 7 of the 1870 Declaration of Principles:

> Special training, as well as high qualities of head and heart, is required to make a good prison or reformatory officer. Then only will the administration of public punishment become scientific, uniform and successful, when it is raised to the dignity of a profession, and men are specially trained for it, as they are for other pursuits.[4]

The Professional Development Department consists of four sections:

1. Grants, Contracts, and Cooperative Agreements
2. Conference Programming
3. Training and Technical Assistance
4. Educational and Training Products

This last section includes a range of products used in individual or group training, including correspondence courses, lesson plans, videos, workbooks, and Internet-based instruction.[5]

Since 1999, this section has also provided a professional certification program leading to four different levels of **certification:**

1. Certified Correctional Executive—for individuals at the highest institutional level
2. Certified Correctional Manager—for those who work with other staff and have some contact with inmates
3. Certified Correctional Supervisor—designed for individuals who work with both staff and inmates
4. Certified Correctional Officers—for individuals who work primarily with inmates[6]

Certification is viewed as a way of teaching a standardized body of professional knowledge to individuals who enter corrections work at different levels with very divergent backgrounds.

The ACA also promotes professionalism through hundreds of topical seminars conducted at its annual conference each summer and a winter meeting each January. It publishes the monthly journal *Corrections Today*, which all its members receive; one of the regular features of the magazine is a **"Best in the Business"** section that highlights the accomplishments of corrections workers at all levels. The ACA also publishes the bimonthly refereed journal, *Corrections Compendium*, presenting scholarly research articles.

The other major advance in corrections promoted by the ACA over the past twenty-five years is known as accreditation. What professionalism is to individuals working in the field, accreditation is to organizations—a movement toward higher standards. Accreditation began more than thirty years ago with a critical vote of the ACA executive committee during Maurice Sigler's term as president (1971–1972). Sigler recalls that some were opposed to the idea, arguing that corrections organizations were not yet ready to meet the standards accreditation would demand. The vote resulted in the establishment of the **Commission on Accreditation in Corrections** (CAC), which developed the national standards to be used in granting organizations accredited status.

Accreditation officially began in 1978. Jointly administered today by the ACA and the CAC, the accreditation program offers public and private organizations performing correctional functions the opportunity to evaluate their operations against national standards, to remedy deficiencies, and to upgrade the quality of correctional programs and services. According to the ACA, the recognized benefits from such a process include the following:

1. Improved management
2. Defense against lawsuits through documentation and the demonstration of a "good faith" effort to improve conditions of confinement
3. Increased accountability and enhanced public credibility for administrative and line staff
4. A safer and more humane environment for personnel and offenders
5. Establishment of measurable criteria for upgrading programs, personnel, and physical plant on a continuing basis[7]

Correctional accreditation is an ongoing process. In essence it measures the organization's compliance with nationally accepted standards in the field, as maintained by the CAC. An organization seeking accreditation follows a prescribed sequence of steps:

1. *Preaccrediation assessment.* This is a confidential evaluation of the organization's prospects for accreditation before the formal application.
2. *Application status.* The contract is signed, and fees are determined.
3. *Correspondent status.* Using the applicable ACA standards, the organization completes a self-evaluation report.
4. *Candidate status.* Awaiting the official audit, this period lasts for up to a year.
5. *Standards compliance audit.* Using several outside consultants to make up the Visiting Committee, the organization is audited for compliance with hundreds of mandatory and nonmandatory standards.
6. *Accreditation hearing.* The formal review of the audit report, resulting in a decision to grant or deny accreditation.
7. *Accredited status.* This is good for three years.
8. *Reaccreditation.* This involves going through the audit and hearing again, for an additional three years.[8]

Accreditation started slowly but really accelerated by the 1990s. Today, the ACA publishes standards manuals for twenty-one different types of correctional functions, each prepared by a subcommittee of members with expertise in the specific function, from prison and jails through probation and boot camps to such specialized functions as health care, training academies, and juvenile day treatment centers. By 2003, the ACA indicated that more than a third of all state prisons but less than 5 percent of local jails were accredited. All state corrections agencies (or private corrections organizations housing state offenders under contract) had been accredited in two states, Louisiana and Ohio. Louisiana's corrections secretary, Richard Stalder, emphasized accreditation as an obvious method of pulling corrections in his state out of the mire it had sunk into in the 1970s.

Critics point out that accreditation in and of itself is no guarantee of organizational performance, any more than familiarity with the Ten Commandments is a guarantee of moral conduct. The military has a term, "pencil whip," which means that a problem is shown on paper as having been solved whether in fact it has been solved or not. Accreditation's critics, while generally not opposed to national standards in the field, point out that a big gap often exists between what is written down or what an organization says it is doing and what it is actually doing in practice. In the corporate world, look at Enron for illustrative examples. In corrections, it is not hard to find accredited institutions where systematic mistreatment of prisoners has occurred. Critics also point out that standards may be set too low in many instances (the "lowest common denominator" concept), and that no real enforcement mechanism exists, except for the denial of reaccreditation, which is virtually unheard of.

The Suffolk County Jail in Boston, Massachusetts, passed its accreditation audit in 2000 with a score of 98.96. The next year, seven jail officers were indicted on federal charges of abusing inmates, and the sheriff was accused of absenteeism and systematic mismanagement. The Tallulah Correctional Center for Youth, a privately operated juvenile training school in Louisiana, looked great on paper and in videos. It was accredited in 1996 and remained accredited even after it was sued in federal court, taken over by the state, and finally ordered shut down by the legislature because of its inability to control violence—staff to inmate and inmate to inmate—within the facility. The Northeast Ohio Correctional Center in Youngstown, a privately operated adult prison, was accredited in 1998. In that year, two inmates were stabbed to death, six inmates escaped from the facility, and dozens of inmate assaults were reported. The next year, the prison paid $1.65 million to inmates and agreed to a series of reforms as part of a class-action suit against guards for brutality.[9]

"I'm embarrassed sometimes when I'm called to go to some of these facilities and I see ACA certificates hanging on the walls," said Dale Sechrest, a criminologist who directed the ACA's standards program from 1975 to 1984. "The process could be far more rigorous than it is," he said. "If it's not a rigorous process, what good is it?"[10]

Accreditation's adherents, including upper-echelon officials of the ACA, take a contrary view, pointing out that corrections is obviously much better off because of accreditation than it would have been without it. They also cite the importance of professional national standards available to practitioners, something that is particularly important in the decentralized American corrections system. The standards establish baseline practices that apply across geographic boundaries—common goals to guide future development. In this view, accreditation is one of the important forces driving correctional organizations forward.

CORRECTIONAL HEALTH CARE

Long before their populations began to count large numbers of older inmates, jails and prisons were known for their unhealthy living conditions and poor medical care. Jail inmates were long subject to malnutrition, cramped living quarters, disease, and lack of medical attention. John Howard, the English sheriff, reported in the late 1700s that jail inmates were far more likely to die of disease in jail than they were to be executed for their crimes. Howard himself died of typhus, "gaol fever," on a visit to Russian prisons in 1790.

In 1884, a writer for the *New Orleans Daily Picayune* looked into mortality rates at the Angola plantation prison in Louisiana and then in the midyears of the Samuel James convict lease. He reported,

> The remorseless cruelty of the present management has been more fatal to the lives of the convicts than the percentage of losses of the two armies during the late civil war. This is a startling statement, but we have reliable authority for making it. The average convict life is six years. It would, therefore, be more humane to punish with death all prisoners sentenced to a longer period than six years.[11]

Mortality rates were 10 percent or higher in the last decade of the lease, which expired in 1901, and were as high or higher in many other southern prison farms and camps during the same era. The best thing convicts had going for them in this era was the brevity of their sentences. Convicts rarely served terms of the length routinely imposed today. If they stayed longer than five years, the odds were good that they would die from overwork, disease, malnutrition, misadventure, or brutality.

In Louisiana and elsewhere, more humane treatment of convicts and improved health care reduced prison mortality rates in the 1900s. Indeed, the old Eastern State Penitentiary in Philadelphia was proud to note that toward the end of the nineteenth century, its mortality rate was lower than that of the city as a whole.

This points to one of the persistent problems of prison health care: the prison draws its population from the least healthy part of the general population—the urban poor, often referred to today as the underclass. As James Marquart and his colleagues have noted,

> Research shows marked variations in health status and access to health care by socioeconomic status. The poor exist in "triple jeopardy," for they are typically uninsured, generally live in medically underserved areas, have difficulty obtaining needed health care services, and continue to have higher mortality rates than higher income persons.[12]

The largest single demographic group in the jail and prison population in 2003 is black males, who have higher rates of cancer, hypertension, stroke, syphilis, cirrhosis, diabetes, arthritis, **AIDS,** and chronic mental disorders than other demographic groups. Hispanic males, another significant minority group in prison, also had higher rates of heart disease, cancer, chronic liver disease, cirrhosis, and AIDS than did white non-Hispanic males.[13]

The concentration of large numbers of unhealthy, poor minorities in prison provides a foundation of concern. In the most recent survey of prison inmate health status, "Medical Problems of Inmates, 1997," Laura Maruschak and Allen Beck reported that nearly a third (31 percent) of state inmates and a quarter (23.4 percent) of federal inmates reported having a physical impairment or mental condition. Most of the impaired inmates said that they suffered from multiple impairments or that they were limited in the kind or amount of work they could do.[14]

About one in five prison inmates reported being injured since admission, most of these injuries occurring in accidents. About 10 percent of state inmates but only 3 percent of federal inmates reported being injured in a fight. More than one in five (21 percent) of both state and federal inmates reported treatment or surgery being required since admission; inmates over age forty-five and those who had been in prison longer than six years had the highest rates of injury and treatment for medical problems.[15]

This survey of prison inmates' general medical problems, while providing a useful overview, does not reveal the extent of serious medical conditions among prisoners. The National Commission on Correctional Health Care, a nonprofit group that works for improved health care in prisons, issued a report on serious, contagious diseases among inmates over a three-year period in the mid-1990s:

1. An estimated 34,800 to 46,000 inmates (about 2.0 to 2.5 percent of the jail and prison population at the time) were infected with **HIV,** with an estimated 9,000 with full-blown AIDS.

2. An estimated 98,500 to 145,500 HIV-positive inmates were *released* from prisons and jails back into society during this time.

3. As much as one-fifth of the prison and jail population of 2 million could be infected with hepatitis C.

4. There were an estimated 1,400 active cases of **tuberculosis** (TB) in jails and prisons in 1997, and as many as 12,000 inmates carrying the disease were released that same year.[16]

Even people who could not care less about what happens to prisoners ought to be concerned about the flow of sick inmates back into society. "There's a misconception on the part of the general public that people behind bars are a separate population," said Jonathan Shuter, who was director of inmate health at the Rikers Island jail complex in New York City during the 1990s. "Inmates cycle in and out of these places. They're not staying there."

Shuter saw a dramatic increase in TB and HIV cases at Rikers Island. Women in custody are much more likely to be HIV positive than men (3.6 to 2.2 percent, according to the Bureau of Justice Statistics in 2000), and New York has by far the highest rate of HIV-positive inmates in the country (8.5 percent). One-fourth of the women admitted to Rikers Island when Shuter was there had the virus, half of them unaware that they were infected. "It was astonishing," Shuter said. "That approaches the worst African countries."[17]

Although HIV and AIDS have been in decline in American prisons since about 1995, they remain at least four times more prevalent in prison than in the general population; some authorities argue that the lack of testing for HIV in most jails and prisons underrepresents this figure significantly. The primary reason for the increased prevalence of HIV behind bars in the 1980s and 1990s was the increased confinement of intravenous drug users; although injecting drugs and practicing unsafe sex behind bars can spread HIV infection, the great majority of prisoners (such as the drug-addicted prostitutes Dr. Shuter was seeing on Rikers Island) were already infected on admission. By 1997, over half of all incoming state prisoners reported using drugs in the month before their arrest, many of them using needles to do so.

Drug users who inject drugs are often infected with multiple diseases: blood borne, such as hepatitis and HIV, and airborne, such as TB. Inmates who are in and out of custody often stop taking their drugs after release, so their symptoms may be alleviated, but they are not completely cured. This is particularly important for inmates with TB, who may develop what is called **multidrug-resistant tuberculosis** (MDR-TB), which has been on the upswing in poor parts of several large American cities—Washington, D.C., New York City, and Los Angeles—with large concentrations of intravenous drug users. As they go back and forth from confinement to the street, they magnify the risk of harm to the outside population.

With HIV in decline at present and TB concentrated in urban areas, the greatest health care threat behind bars has become hepatitis, the term for several viral infections affecting the liver. At one time, the focus in prisons was on the **hepatitis B virus** (HBV), which is spread by sexual contact and blood. It has a long incubation period and can cause serious long-term liver damage. The past decade, attention has shifted to the apparently much more widespread **hepatitis C virus** (HCV), a blood-borne virus spread by intravenous drug use or blood transfusions before improved screening began about 1990.

Less than 2 percent of the free-world population in the United States is HCV infected. Among the prison population, the infection rate is estimated at 18 percent, ten times higher, because of the concentration of intravenous drug users in prison. Many of the estimated 360,000 prisoners infected with HCV contracted the infection twenty, thirty, or even forty years ago. Hepatitis C causes liver disease in 20 percent of its victims and eventually kills 5 percent of those infected.[18] Many people who contract it suffer few ill effects. For others, liver failure, long-term debilitation, and death result.

Vaccines exist to treat hepatitis A and B. Hepatitis C requires lengthy treatment—at least one full year—with expensive medication, costing $10,000 to $25,000 annually per patient, with uncertain success rates. Some states provide no treatment for HCV inmates; others are treating small groups of infected prisoners to determine the effectiveness of treatment regimens.

Prisoners in several states are suing to demand HCV treatment. Edward McKenna, a fifty-five-year-old New Yorker in prison for shooting his brother to death in an argument, is one. McKenna, who says he contracted hepatitis C injecting drugs in the military in the 1960s, is among 10,000 New York prison inmates estimated to be HCV positive. Ninety-five were being treated in 2001. McKenna was denied treatment. "In a roundabout way, they're telling me I'm going to die and that's the way it is," he said in an interview with the *New York Times* in 2001. "They won't treat me." He expected to live only two more years at best.[19]

The controversy over treating HCV-infected inmates raises larger questions about the quality of medical care jails and prisons provide. What standards must correctional institutions meet in providing health care to inmates? The standards of today are very different from those of yesterday. Jails and prisons of the past enjoyed poor reputations as health care providers. If you had asked a convict of a generation or two ago, "What happens to you when you get sick in prison," the answer would be, "You die."

Prison medical services were minimal, and jail services were subminimal. Staffed by underpaid, underqualified, often part-time doctors and nurses (and often by inmate orderlies who were good people to know if you needed drugs), correctional infirmaries were viewed as being little more than first-aid stations and terminal wards; any serious medical work required transportation to a free-world hospital where "real doctors" did treatment. Hospitals behind bars were too often the province of recent immigrants, incompetents, drunks, and the "professionally impaired" (and, occasionally, really good people who were totally committed to their work). The conscience of the 1947 *film noir* prison classic *Brute Force* is the alcoholic physician, Doc Walters, who needs a couple of shots of whiskey before he attends morning staff meetings.

This image began to change in the 1960s and 1970s. Litigation attacking poor conditions in confinement often put medical care near the top of the list, usually just below overcrowding and poor security. One of the early landmark prisoners' rights cases, ***Estelle v. Gamble*** (1976), established a standard that remains in effect today: prisoners are entitled to **adequate medical care.** What does "adequate" mean? It does not mean the best, excellent, superior, or even good. It means suitable for people in their circumstances with two circumstances being particularly important: they are poor and they are locked up. Thus, what prisoners get is a minimalist standard of medical care—public health for the poor as modified to fit prison.

Michael S. Vaughn and Leo Carroll discussed prison health care standards in their excellent article "Separate and Unequal: Prison versus Free-World Medical Care" in *Justice Quarterly* in 1998. They point out the two sides to the argument over standards. One side is occupied by health care professionals, prisoner advocates, some correctional administrators, and sick prisoners. They argue the

principle of equivalence, the notion that with respect to medical care, no distinction should be made between inmates and citizens of the free world.[20] The contrasting view, more popular with the public and political officials who pass laws and make policies, is the **principle of less eligibility.** Drawing on George Rusche's analysis of punishment from the 1930s, this principle asserts that prison conditions must always be "a step below the minimum standard of living of people working or on welfare" in the free world.[21] This makes the prison the least attractive place in society for poor people to live, and it argues that prisoners must be treated worse than the lowest law-abiding citizens outside.

The courts, as part of the political system shaping the application of punishment, recognize that prisoners are entitled to some level of medical care, while the public outside is entitled to a higher standard. One prisoner put it this way, using the luxury hotel as his metaphor: "Rich people get the penthouse, the middle class gets the upper floors, poor people get the lobby, and prisoners get the basement."

Prisoners are entitled to less, and when mistakes happen, it is more difficult for them (or their survivors) to collect damages for bad medical care. *Estelle v. Gamble* established the standard of **deliberate indifference** in federal courts dealing with prison medical malpractice litigation. As Vaughn and Carroll point out in their article, this is a much higher standard, amounting to gross negligence or recklessness, than the standard of negligence that would apply in free-world medical malpractice claims. Not only is the liability standard much higher and thus more difficult for prisoners to meet, but when prisoners take medical care litigation to trial and win (which happens nationally an average of only seven to ten times each year), the median damages awarded them, from the 1970s into the 1990s, was less than $20,000. The comparable figure in free-world malpractice cases that went to trial was $400,000.[22] On this scale, medical harm to a free person was worth about twenty times that of comparable harm to a prisoner.

Prisoners typically have fewer options than free-world patients. They are often denied access to medical specialists, to the latest medication and drug therapies, to timely delivery of medical services, to technologically advanced diagnostic techniques, to second opinions, and to alternative therapies. Some prisoners do luck into these options because of their proximity to superior free-world medical facilities or their ties to better-connected medical authorities, but overall they remain low on the priority list.

When prisoners complain about deficient medical care, some political official is sure to respond, "What have they got to gripe about? They're getting better care than a lot of people in society, and they don't have to pay for it" (which is not true in most prison systems any longer, as prisoners are charged basic fees for medical attention and medication). The fact is that being in prison takes away the prisoner's right to make a lot of basic choices, including those about medical decisions. If you choose to ignore a cancerous growth until it is too late to treat it and you die, that was your decision. A prisoner can make the same choice, and some do. But if the prisoner seeks treatment and it is denied because of cost or he gets only the cheapest treatment or the most minimal treatment because that is all the prison is required to provide, then we should acknowledge that we consider suffering and death as deserved corollaries of penal confinement.

The **penal harm** advocates of today do just that. They argue that prison life should be made harder or tougher; making prisons too comfortable reduces the deterrent effects of the harsher criminal penalties adopted since the 1980s. The members of this school view medical care as an amenity rather than a necessity—like having a house doctor in the prison resort where convicts go to vacation from the stress of the real world. One Louisiana state senator, in a recent discussion of the medical problems of older inmates, argued that the state was not responsible for meeting the needs of this costly group. His policy would be to confine them securely, ignore their complaints, and let nature take its course. Many people in politics and society agree with him.

Prison medical care, focused on a population that is both older and more prone to serious illness than earlier populations, is an expensive proposition. The budget of the Louisiana State Penitentiary at Angola is $100 million for a population of 5,100 inmates. Twelve million dollars of this (12 percent) is dedicated to medical care. Other states report similar expenditures, in the range of 10 to 15 percent, for medical care in their prison systems. Jails, which house shorter-term offenders, have generally spent much less on inmate health care, but this has changed in some areas. Urban jails that get a lot of sick, debilitated drug users, homeless people, and mentally ill have had to lay out large sums to upgrade their medical and mental health services. Prison officials, who know that medical care is one of the aspects of prison life most important to inmates, generally want to provide more and better services, but when they need more money, they have to turn to political officials who are prioritizing budget cuts in tough economic times. The officials outside are looking for even more wiggle room within the legal definition of "adequate."

RESPONDING TO POPULATION INCREASES

The expansion of the prison and jail system since the 1980s has been managed within two limiting factors: money is tight, and prisoners are a valuable commodity. Some states have fared better than others economically, and the federal government always seems to have money to throw at whatever causes it deems worthy, but as economies falter, the cost of housing prisoners becomes more troublesome. In all states, the percentage of state budget expenditures devoted to corrections has increased faster than state revenues, meaning that the percentage of the budget devoted to corrections has increased steadily. If you were using a pie chart, in the early 1970s, corrections' piece of the pie would have been a thin slice, less than 2 percent. Three decades later, the slice would have been much larger, two and a half to three times larger in most states. Revenues are finite. Every additional dollar spent on corrections is one less dollar spent on something else—education, transportation, social services, or the environment. Alida Merlo and others have discussed at length the significant impact of prison expansion on California's support for higher education; the huge increases in prison costs were funded in large measure by reducing support for colleges and universities.

Prisons cost money in two ways:

1. Capital outlays for construction
2. Annual operating costs, which are primarily (75 to 90 percent) personnel costs

Average construction costs for new prisons vary from $10,000 per bed to over $100,000 per bed, depending on the security level of the institution, prevailing construction wages, and other costs. Thus, a new 1,000-bed prison might cost anywhere from $10 million to $100 million, depending on where it was located and whom it was designed to hold.

Likewise, average operating costs vary widely depending on salaries, the distribution of inmates in various custody levels (maximum or supermax costing two or three times as much as minimum), and the provision of medical care and rehabilitation programs. Alabama's average cost of $25.19 per inmate day in 2001 was the cheapest in the country, followed by South Dakota, Louisiana, and Missouri. Alaska's daily cost of $111.89 was the highest in the country, though Massachusetts, Rhode Island, and Hawaii were not that far behind. The national average per inmate day in 2001 was $61.04, or $22,279 to keep one inmate in prison for a year. The federal prison system was slightly cheaper, averaging $59.02 per day, or $21,542 annually.[23]

As the emphasis in prison management has shifted from rehabilitation and reintegration to warehousing, corrections officials have looked for ways to reduce prison costs—both construction and operation. Most of the new prisons built since 1980 have been medium- to minimum-security facilities that cost less to construct. Design and construction techniques emphasizing modular components have reduced costs also. Any prison remains an expensive cathedral to public safety, and state policy has consistently been not to build new prisons (the **bricks-and-mortar solution**) in anticipation of growth; instead, they wait until existing prisons are full and then build new facilities to relieve overcrowding. Many states have been in the same predicament as Mickey Mouse playing the sorcerer's apprentice in *Fantasia*—constantly searching for new receptacles to put the overflow spilling out of existing containers.

We have traditionally defined three principal options open to states in managing the flood of convicted felons passing through the courts and into the corrections system:

1. Front-end solutions
2. Double bunking
3. Back-end solutions

The **front-end solutions** emphasize probation and community-based alternatives to imprisonment. Some states hold down prison populations by supervising more criminals, particularly drug and property offenders, in nonsecure settings—which is usually the criminal's home but can also be different types of correctional facilities in the community. The states with high incarceration rates tend to be those that keep more nonviolent criminals behind bars rather than in these front-end placements.

Double bunking has to do with making more "efficient" use of existing space. If you take a sixty-man cell block or dormitory and replace single beds with bunk beds, you can easily increase the capacity to ninety or 120 prisoners in the same space. The 1,000-bed prison becomes the 2,000-bed prison overnight, with no new construction costs. If you maintain the same level of staffing (say, two officers always on duty in the dorm or cell block), you can double the capacity without increasing costs much. The quality of prison life will probably deteriorate, as overcrowding and reduced supervision generate health and safety problems, but it is definitely cheaper in the short run.

At one time, the prisoner's best friend was the federal judge who, using "cruel and unusual punishment" to define unconstitutional prison conditions, prevented prisons from using double bunking to create permanent overcrowding. As the courts have backed away from intervening in such matters in recent years (or, through the Prison Litigation Reform Act, had Congress limit their bounds of intervention), the prisoner's new best friend has become the state fire marshal, who sets limits for safe housing in institutional settings. Without the fire marshal and other health inspectors (and to lesser extents the ACA's minimal standards and the residual intervention authority of the courts), most prisons today would be much more overcrowded than they already are.

The other option in dealing with overcrowding lies in the so-called **back-end solutions.** This means that when prisons get badly overcrowded, some inmates are released to bring the numbers down. The mechanisms for early release are most often early parole or enhanced good-time calculations, most often applied to nonviolent criminals. Some states, such as Texas and Florida, have relied on formulas. When the prison reaches a certain percentage of capacity, these pressure-release measures kick in, allowing the discharge of inmates to bring the numbers down. Jails have often done the same thing, especially when they were under court orders to relieve overcrowding. The principle is the same: you turn the best of the worst loose to accommodate the new inmates, making sure that everyone gets to taste the joy of imprisonment.

By the 1990s, as warehousing had settled in as the dominant purpose of imprisonment, prisons developed a fourth option: **alternative storage.** Included in this option are private prisons (in state and out of state), prisons in other states, and jails (usually in state but sometimes in other states also). The theory here is that the prisoner is a commodity to be stored. The preference is to store him (or her) in your own state prisons to the maximum extent possible. When limits are reached and breached, you turn to other secure facilities as temporary measure, waiting for one of two things to happen:

1. The population goes down.
2. New institutions open to hold what had been the excess.

The rapid growth of private prisons in the decade from 1987 to 1998 is discussed at length in the next section of this chapter. Private prisons promised economy and efficiency, but to many states their most attractive feature was the availability of emergency bed space at no start-up cost (if the private corporation built the prison) and no long-term commitment. The private corporation, wagering that it would keep its contract long enough to make a profit, assumed all the risk. At the end of 2002, 73,500 state prisoners, about 5.8 percent of the total state prison population, were held in private facilities.[24]

A much smaller number of state prisoners, estimated at about 5,000, were held in the prisons of another state. According to newspaper accounts, the greatest number of these were housed in the state of Virginia, which has been capitalizing on prisoner population growth by renting out its prison beds to other states and the federal government. In 2001, out-of-state inmates, some from as far away as Hawaii, were expected to fill 3,380 of Virginia's 32,100 prison beds. This would generate $78 million in revenues. Virginia's jails were also housing another 1,163 federal inmates, estimated to bring in over $20 million in revenues.[25]

"It's extraordinary—it's like they've become a private prison corporation, almost. It seems like they're in the business of taking in everybody's spare prisoners," said Jenni Gainsborough, senior policy analyst with The Sentencing Project in Washington, D.C. She said having cells available to other states makes it too easy to incarcerate inmates far from home, making it more difficult for them to maintain family ties or even communicate with their lawyers.[26]

The other alternative storage facility, beyond the private prison and the prison in another state, is the local jail. By the end of 2001, over 5 percent of all state prisoners, 67,760 inmates, were housed in local jails, either temporarily or permanently through contractual arrangements with local sheriffs. Six states—Alabama, Kentucky, Louisiana, New Jersey, Tennessee, and Virginia—each held more than 3,000 state prisoners in local jails.[27] Virginia was pursuing an interesting policy—temporarily delaying transfer of its own felons into state custody while it rented out jails cells more profitably to other states.

Kentucky held a quarter of its state prisoners—4,200 out of 16,500—in county jails at the end of 2002, paying the counties $28 per day plus medical and transportation costs to confine the state inmates. This is much cheaper than Kentucky's prison cost of $46 per day per inmate. Most of the inmates held in local jails are Class D felons—inmates convicted of nonviolent, less serious crimes and sentenced to one to five years in prison.

Kentucky state officials often repeat the *Field of Dreams* mantra, "If you build it, they will come," referring not to a baseball field but to a prison or jail cell. "We have too many people in jail and prison," said Kentucky Senator Gerald Neal. "We need to rethink that policy." Representative Rob Wilkey, who wrote the 1991 legislation that allowed felons to be stored in local jails, said, "I do think there is a better, cheaper, more humane, and more efficient way to house people outside of incarceration."[28] State legislators are alarmed at the amount of new jail construction going on at the county level. Sheriffs are building new jails—borrowing money and selling bonds to finance construction costs—for the specific purpose of housing state inmates. The result is that the increase in beds is outpacing the supply of inmates eligible to serve their sentences in jails. Sheriffs may be in a heap of financial trouble if they build new jails and then cannot fill the beds—or maybe they can just rent out the empties to Virginia if the price is right.

If Kentucky officials want to see what the logical progression of their policy leads to, they should take a trip south to Louisiana. Beginning in the 1970s, when its state prison at Angola was placed under federal court order to improve conditions and reduce overcrowding, Louisiana started storing its excess inmate population in parish jails. This was considered a temporary measure. State prisons were under construction that would house the backlog of convicted felons building up in jail. Between 1976 and 1990, Louisiana opened seven new prisons for men and added bed space at Angola and other facilities, increasing the number of state prison beds to 18,799; but the backlog of state prisoners in jails had grown apace, increasing to 4,720.

Louisiana's parish sheriffs, who are very influential local political officials, had protested mightily when they were first obliged to hold state inmates in their jails. But over time, certain accommodations were made. The sheriffs, who were originally paid $4.50 per day for each state inmate, lobbied the legislature to raise this per diem rate, to $8.50, to $13.50, to $18.25, and eventually to $22.39. The sheriffs who had fought the housing of state prisoners in their facilities tooth and nail began to sing a new song when the rent went up. They could make a tidy profit from housing state inmates, while the department of corrections could house state prisoners one-third cheaper ($22 per day versus $32 per day) in local jails than in state institutions.

What started as a stopgap measure became a **parallel universe.** Shorter-term inmates ("short" is a relative term, in Louisiana meaning anything under twenty years) were housed in parish jails. Long-term inmates, lifers, physically and mentally ill inmates, and parole violators were to go into the state prisons. After 1990, the state stopped building new prisons (although it did add beds in existing institutions); all the new facilities built in the next decade were parish jails, most of them designed to hold not local pretrial inmates or misdemeanants but state or federal prisoners. The federal prisoners, who were pretrial detainees and illegal aliens, were even more valuable tenants than the state inmates because the federal government paid better rates, in the range of $40 to $45 per day, for their housing.

The result of carrying out this policy over the long term was apparent in the numbers of 2003. Of the 36,000 convicted felons in Louisiana, 17,000 were held in state prisons, 3,000 were held in two private prisons, and 16,000 were held in local jails. Louisiana is the only state to hold less than half its state prisoners in state-operated institutions. Its focus on reducing costs has taken it further along the alternative storage path than any other state.

How is this alternate universe plan working? How does the incarceration of convicted felons in parish jails compare with incarceration in prison? When the first penitentiaries were proposed 200 years ago, the contrast was made with existing jails: reformers did not want prisons to turn into jails. Jails were not prisons. They were local institutions providing short-term confinement of pretrial inmates. They could not provide anywhere near the same level of care, custody, and control that prisons could.

Jails—even the bigger, modern jails of today—are still not prisons, and most cannot provide the level of services or supervision that prisons can. The Louisiana Department of Corrections, recognizing that a **double standard** of living existed in jails and prisons, came up with "Basic Jail Guidelines" that sheriffs have to follow in housing state prisoners. A report by the state legislative auditor criticized these guidelines as being "inadequate to meet the needs of the prisoners being held in the system." Among the concerns were the following:

1. Screening services to identify the rehabilitative, medical, and mental health needs of prisoners were being entirely omitted.
2. Rehabilitation services at local jails were either minimal or nonexistent.
3. Security at local jails is not as stringent as at state prisons.
4. Almost no oversight exists for the department of corrections to regulate the housing, care, and rehabilitation of the inmates.[29]

From the point of view of inmates serving state time in the parish jails, local time is pretty much dead time. While a handful of jails are ACA accredited and offer reasonable medical care and programming, most inmates spend practically all their time sitting in dorms or cell blocks doing nothing. They eat, they sleep, they play cards and dominoes, they watch TV, and they "recreate" on the yard. They do not work, take classes, attend training, get any kind of counseling or therapy, or do anything else that might change them for the better during confinement. Security is more lax, so the jails have greater problems with escapes, assaults, and minor misconduct than the prisons do. They also have much greater problems with contraband; some jails are notorious within the prison system for allowing inmates access to marijuana, crack cocaine, other illegal drugs, and alcohol—while they are locked up serving felony sentences.

The alternate universe plan has now been in effect for such a long time that it would be difficult to dismantle it. It has changed the landscape of jailing in Louisiana, particularly in rural parishes. The longtime sheriff of Avoyelles Parish, Bill Belt, who was one of the first to see the future of housing state prisoners, would in time operate five jails with a capacity of over 1,300 inmates. Tensas Parish, with a population of fewer than 7,000 residents, operated two jails with a combined capacity of 860. East Carroll Parish, a poor parish in northeastern Louisiana, with a population of fewer than 10,000, a few years ago had one parish jail with a capacity of thirty-seven inmates. By 2002, it had four parish jails and a privately operated prison farm with a total capacity of more than 1,300 inmates. When you visit some of these facilities, you see metal buildings or prefab buildings with fences around them, inmates sitting in idleness in dormitories, and nothing much going on. They perfectly fit the definition of warehousing. In these parishes, jailing has passed from being a function to an industry. The sheriff's department has grown from a small public safety organization to a commercial enterprise—in several rural parishes the largest employer in the local economy.

The 1990s were boom times for Louisiana's sheriffs. No one really knows how much "profit" they made from jail operations because they are not required to show how much they spent on the state prisoners they were housing. Their per diem is based on head count, not on their actual cost, so the assumption is that some made lots of money. Many sheriffs and private entrepreneurs have joined together to plan and build more new jails over the next decade. But times are changing. State officials are attempting, through legal and policy changes, to rein in the prisoner population. Their goal is to hold down the annual increase in the number of state prisoners, eventually matching inflow to outflow to reach a level of stasis. It will not happen for several years (if at all), but it has already slowed growth enough that some sheriffs are in trouble. Sheriffs built new jails anticipating an uninterrupted supply of state prisoners. For the first time, the state has more local jail beds than it has state inmates to fill them.

The surplus of jail beds has sheriffs worried. Sheriff Belt, who had to close one of his Avoyelles Parish jails for lack of inmates, said, "I will admit, we are in a jam right now. There has been a proliferation of jail beds in the state. Everyone built for capacity when they had the budget and now they can't get the prisoners."[30]

Kentucky (and other states) take note: the financial problems brought on by overbuilding are expected to get worse. Quite apart from whatever sheriffs are not doing for prisoners, their financial precariousness, built on human trafficking, threatens them with ruin in the years ahead—unless, of course, their marketing people can sell their empty beds to prisons in other states, which is exactly what many of them are trying to do at this moment.

PRIVATIZATION

Warehousing prisoners for profit is closely related to another important issue in corrections over the past two decades: the role of private corporations in corrections or, more specifically, the private operation of secure prisons and jails. In 1980, no secure, privately operated jails or prisons existed in America. By 2001, about 150—100 prisons and fifty jails—were open for business, holding about 120,000 prisoners, or 6 percent of the jail and prison population. What is responsible for this sudden development?

The most obvious circumstance is that the corrections system itself has gotten huge in the past twenty-five years. Starting in the late 1970s, corrections has become a major growth industry. If you had bought corrections stock three decades ago, your investment would have multiplied several times over by now. Most of the growth of corrections has occurred in the public sector, and it has taken place without any apparent effect on the crime problem in America. This has focused attention on two major corrections related issues: cost and management effectiveness. Why does corrections cost so much to accomplish so little? The American people are constitutionally very skeptical about services provided by government, and they believe just as strongly in the superiority of private enterprise.

It seems natural that corporations, many of which were already involved in selling equipment and security technology to correctional facilities, and private investors, many of them former political officials and corrections officials with expertise in the field, would come forth to argue in favor of privatizing jails and prisons. Corrections Corporation of America, the world's largest private corrections company with sixty-three prisons and jails in the United States and several new facilities overseas, lists these top ten reasons for privatization:

1. Privatization can allow new prisoner housing capacity to be brought "online" more swiftly.
2. Privatization can achieve economies in the area of construction costs.
3. Privatization frees up scarce government resources for other priorities, such as education, health care, and other concerns.
4. Privatization can achieve economies in the area of everyday operating costs.
5. Privatization introduces competition. The existence of privatized correctional facilities in a jurisdiction often encourages improvement in the public facilities of that jurisdiction.
6. The quality of services and programs in privatized facilities can be superior to what otherwise would have been provided.
7. Public agencies can often manage the delivery of correctional services more cost effectively when they deal with independent contractors rather than groups of public employees.
8. The considerable legal liability costs associated with operating jails and prisons can be substantially reduced by privatization.
9. Changes in the nature and scope of various types of programs for prisoners can be made more easily and more swiftly in privatized settings.
10. A combination of contracts that set forth detailed performance requirements on on-site government contract monitoring make private management firms more accountable than traditional government agency operations.[31]

Advocates of privatization attacked corrections as an inefficient public bureaucracy, arguing that they could save the public 10 to 20 percent in the operating costs of jails and prisons. Critics of privatization, including political officials, corrections officials, and social scientists, were quick to respond. Their initial objection concerned transferring secure custody—for a long time a public responsibility—to private corporations motivated by economic concerns: cost and profit. They most often attacked the ideology of **punishment for profit** and cited the danger of a **correctional/industrial complex**—a network of private corporations, politicians, and corrections officials—that would promote public policies to continue the growth of the corrections industry. How does corrections grow? By bringing more people into the system. How does it operate more cheaply? By cost-cutting measures, particularly those that have to do with the levels of services and staffing, which are the most significant parts of the correctional budget. In much the same way that the military/industrial complex is blamed for the perpetuation of the Vietnam War, the correctional complex is blamed for the continuation of the "War on Crime." War is always good for business.

Critics sometimes conjure up images of a **corporate demon** (the term used by Charles W. Thomas, a leading academic consultant to private corrections), scheming in the boardroom to keep the public afraid of crime, to keep politicians constantly passing new laws getting tougher on criminals, to keep widening the net of offenders brought under formal control, and to keep locking up more offenders in secure facilities. Robert Lilly and Mathieu DeFlem, in their article "Profit and Penality: An Analysis of the Corrections-Commercial Complex," warn of the monetary colonization of criminal justice. Profit supersedes human values, and economic interests drive justice decisions.

Joseph Hallinan, author of *Going Up the River: Travels in a Prison Nation* (2003), describes the close relationship between private prison owners and state and local politicians. Private corporations make big contributions to influential politicians who then approve the contract necessary for private prison operations. The politicians (or their kin) take jobs as lobbyists for the prison corporations. Public policy—expensive public policy—emerges from this symbiotic relationship.

Hallinan provides examples of "prison millionaires"—the corporate investor or executive (often a former public prison administrator) whose salary and stock options have made him rich—from incarcerating criminals. That this wealth has resulted from dubious political connections seems no bother whatsoever. Prison beds are just one more commodity to be sold on the market, and ethics does not stand in the way of performing a lucrative public service, even as the millionaires shape the policies that will put money in their pockets. Public prison administrators can get pretty cynical about the connections between private prison entrepreneurs and politicians.

The proponents of privatization strongly resist efforts to portray them as the "dark side of the force." They point out the following:

1. It is government and not private entrepreneurs who establish corrections priorities, and government controls private corrections with a detailed **contract;** fail to live up to the contract, and you get fired or sued or both.

2. Private corrections is only an alternate means to achieving public goals. "It's worth a try," they would say. "Let's experiment to see if private corrections can operate better than public corrections." Though some may argue that the

involvement of private contractors looking for public bucks drives net widening, placing minor offenders under greater social controls, no one has seriously attacked the role of private corrections in providing community-based noncustodial services or specific called-for services within institutions. What the opponents of privatization focus on is the private operation of secure prisons and jails.

The involvement of the private sector in corrections is far from a new idea. In the community, private persons and organizations have operated residential facilities for both juveniles and adults and have provided other nonresidential services, such as counseling, monitoring, treatment, and medical care. Private involvement has taken three main forms:

1. **Private for-profit**. A few halfway houses and many drug and alcohol treatment facilities are operated for the profit of their owners. Many individual service providers—such as therapists and counselors—simply contract or bill for their services, often at an hourly rate.
2. **Private nonprofit**. This is a corporation organized to perform a specific function, such as operating a work release facility for inmates completing state prison sentences. The corporation is managed by a board of directors that gets no income from their civic work.
3. **Charitable organizations**. Often a branch of a larger national organization, such as the Salvation Army or Boys Town, this organization usually has a broader funding base and operates a network of elated programs.

Above the community level, many other individuals and organizations are corrections **contractors.** They contract with jails or prisons to provide services the institutions either cannot or do not want to provide—often because the service is only part time or because no one at the institution is able to provide it. Examples would include medical care, psychiatric treatment, specific types of counseling, education and vocational training, and food service. Public funds have been used to pay people in the private sector for their corrections services for many years.

The role of the private sector in corrections has not always been a happy story. Early English sheriffs and their wardens were essentially profiteers who operated their jails to make money from the fees charged inmates. Entrepreneurs transported indentured servants from English jails to hard labor in the American colonies. In the United States, as long as we have had penitentiaries, we have had people trying to make a profit from prison labor. Private businesses once operated factories within prison walls and contracted for prison labor. This is a practice similar to the so-called **employer model** of today, in which businesses move production centers to prisons and hire prisoners to work in them. **Convict leasing,** primarily in the South, rented out convicts to private lessees who in effect owned the convicts lock, stock, and barrel. Convict leases—in which mostly black inmate populations labored as **slaves of the state** (from *Ruffin v. Commonwealth*, an 1871 Virginia case) at agricultural labor, railroad building, levee building, cutting trees, building roads, indeed any form of labor they were directed to by the private businessmen who owned them—lasted into the early years of the twentieth century. Local jail inmates labored on private property at the direction of their sheriffs until very recently. The exploitation of prison labor for the profit of prison officials, politicians, and sharp businessmen is a principal reason for the poor image of privatization in corrections today.

In recent years, privatization has been argued mostly as an issue in its application to secure custody, especially medium- and maximum-security jails and prisons. There has been an increase in private operation of facilities at these levels of security. As Harry Allen and Clifford Simonsen have pointed out, however, the principal impact of privatization in corrections has been felt in other applications, most notably the following:

1. Treatment programs
2. **Low-security custodial facilities** and nonsecure residential settings
3. **Surveillance technologies** for offenders not incarcerated

Private sector treatment programs can be either residential or nonresidential. Many are directed at chronic substance abusers. Adolescents are most often the targeted clientele, particularly for those "life experience" programs that remove young offenders from familiar environments and place them in wilderness areas.

Many of the programs for adults feature a combination of job training, social skills, and a practical treatment modality, such as transactional analysis or reality therapy. By contracting with public agencies, these programs can, in theory, be precisely matched with the perceived needs of the offenders who are referred to them for treatment.

Low-security custodial facilities are the greatest part of the institutional business of private corrections. Private management firms have concentrated on low- and minimum-security prisons; they have also targeted other short-term residential facilities providing work release, prerelease, and other functions in the community.

Private contractors have also moved quickly into the application of surveillance and control technologies. Private drug-testing labs support many community-based corrections programs. A number of electronics firms offer **electronic monitoring** devices—everything from bracelets to home video monitors with breath-testing capabilities—to suit many levels of supervision. In some jurisdictions, the monitoring itself is done by private firms that contract with the courts and work under the direction of the local probation and parole office.

The foundation for private operation of secure prisons was laid in 1983 with the formation of **Corrections Corporation of America** (CCA) in Nashville, Tennessee. CCA made a bid to take over the operation of the Tennessee prison system, which the state rejected. CCA went ahead with its plans to operate secure prisons, if not a whole system, then one prison at a time. Two decades later, it remains the largest private prison operator in America. With a capacity of 62,000 inmates in its sixty American jails and prisons in 2001, CCA houses just over half of all adult prisoners in private secure institutions. Its nearest competitor, **Wackenhut Corrections Corporation** (WCC), while concentrating more on the overseas market, maintains a 21 percent share of the American market with 26,000 beds. Together, CCA and Wackenhut control 75 percent of the private prison beds in America. CCA bought out its second-largest competitor, U.S. Corrections Corporation, in 1998. Among the dozen other private corrections corporations in the United States, only two—Cornell

Corrections and Management and Training Corporation, controlling about 8,500 and 10,500 beds have developed into major players in recent years.

Private prisons grew rapidly in their early years. In 1987, the number of inmates incarcerated in privately operated correctional facilities worldwide was 3,100; by 1998, the number had risen to 132,000[32]—117,000 of these in the approximately 150 private jails and prisons in the United States. Thirty-one states had at least one privately operated jail or prison by 1998, led by Texas with forty-three and California with twenty-four. By the end of 2002, several states in the South and West, led by New Mexico (43 percent), Wyoming (30.3 percent), Alaska (30.9 percent), Montana (29.3 percent), and Oklahoma (27.7 percent), held more than a quarter of their prison population in private facilities.[33] Private prisons have tended to make the most headway in states without strong public employee unions to oppose their acceptance at the state level. About 7 percent of state prisoners were held in private prisons by the end of 1998.

What was behind this rapid growth? Many of the state and local governments that turned to private companies were in a position comparable to a heroin addict suffering withdrawal pains—they were looking for a **quick fix.** In the case of prisoners, the attraction of the private companies was based on their ability to bring new prisons online quickly without investment of public funds in capital outlay. The slightly cheaper per diem costs promised were an additional benefit. The lack of long-term commitment was also important; if the number of prisoners declined or if the level of services provided by the private company failed to meet expectations, the contract would not be renewed. For about fifteen years, then, private jails and prisons were one of the stopgap measures used to reduce some of the financial burdens of pursuing the bricks-and-mortar solution to criminal sentencing—the massive expansion of the jail and prison system. The number of inmates in jail and prison increased from 645,000 at the end of 1983 (the year CCA was founded to promote private imprisonment) to more than 1,800,000 by the end of 1998. The system expanded by about 1,200,000 million beds, 10 percent of these in private prisons and jails.

How has the experiment with private incarceration worked out? The first few years looked like the same sort of euphoria that the owners of new restaurants often experience as people flock to their establishments for something "new and different." Then the new wears off, business declines, customers move on, and, within a couple of years, the majority shut their doors.

Private corrections companies are far from being out of business, but their business has certainly leveled off after 1998. The number of state prisoners in private prisons has declined by about 10,000 over the past five years (to 2002), reducing the percentage of state inmates in private custody to 5.2 percent, which is about what it was in the mid-1990s. Texas, for example, has reduced its placement of inmates in private prisons by several thousand, mostly as a result of contract differences with CCA. Only the rapid increase in the number of federal inmates in private prisons (to almost 14,000 by 2002, with another 6,700 federal inmates in nonsecure private facilities) has enabled private prisons to maintain a total head count of around 120,000 inmates. The Bureau of Prisons has been in a real jam for prison beds as it has continued to expand the federal prison system.

The longer private prisons operate, the more they look like public prisons. In their early years, private prisons effected most of their savings in salaries and benefits, where 75 to 90 percent (or more) of a prison's budget typically goes. Private prisons said they relied on more multitasking—combining several specialized functions in one person—and fewer management-level staff to achieve more "streamlined" administration while devoting approximately the same staff resources to security and rehabilitation. They also paid lower salaries in general and provided fewer fringe benefits. Part of the lower salary package was based on the newness of the prisons—new staff starting at lower pay grades. But over time, however, the once-new staff have acquired seniority and more benefits comparable to those paid in public institutions.

James Austin and Garry Coventry, in their February 2001 monograph *Emerging Issues on Privatized Prisons*, undertook a general review of the progress of private prisons to date. Their summary, "The Diminishing Returns on Privatization," is most enlightening:

> This report supports the basic premise that private facilities appear to perform at the same level of efficiency as public facilities. Although they tend to house a higher proportion of minimum-custody inmates in relatively new facilities, private facilities tend to have the same staffing patterns, provide the same levels of work, education, and counseling programs for inmates, and have the same rates of serious inmate misconduct as public facilities. The few credible impact studies show more similarities and fewer differences between the two methods of operation.
>
> What seems to have evolved in the United States is a privatization model that essentially mimics the public model but achieves modest cost savings, at least initially, by making modest reductions in staffing patterns, fringe benefits, and other labor-related costs. There is no evidence showing that private prisons will have a dramatic impact on how prisons operate. The promises of 20-percent savings in operational costs have simply not materialized. Even if they had, the limited market share of less than 5 percent for private prisons would have had a limited impact on prison budgets. For example, assume that 10 percent of a state's prison system become privatized and that each private prison produced a 10-percent savings in operational costs. Even at this level, the overall impact on a state prison budget would be only 1 percent (10 percent of 10 percent = 1 percent). This amount of savings will not revolutionize modern correctional practices.
>
> Today it appears that achieving even a 10-percent market share will prove to be increasingly difficult for several reasons. The growing number of well-publicized stories of poor performance is growing (e.g., Colorado, Louisiana, Oregon, South Carolina, and Texas). The problems associated with the CCA-operated Northeast Ohio Correction Center in Youngstown, Ohio, have dramatized how badly a privatized prison can be operated. In this facility, 17 inmates were stabbed, 2 were murdered, and 6 escaped in the first 15 months of operation. Operational flaws were linked to inexperienced staff, inadequate training, and a willingness on the part of prison authorities to accept inmates who should not have been transferred to the facility. If nothing else, the private sector has shown that it is as equally capable of mismanaging prisons as the public sector.
>
> These problems suggest that the sales division of the private sector may well be outperforming the production division. It may well be that the difficulties private prisons are experiencing may increase simply because they, like prisons in the public sector, are finding it increasingly difficult to recruit competent staff.[34]

A few years ago, private corporations were bullish on their future in prisons. Today they are facing a bear market. Political officials, except at the federal level, seem more skeptical of their sales pitches. The numbers of inmates in custody are growing very slowly or declining in most states; the sense of crisis in needing new beds has passed in most places. The major private corporations, CCA and Wackenhut, are looking to expand their overseas operations, though it remains to be seen if American prisons, like American cigarettes, are easily exportable. Some private corporations, such as CiviGenics, which has long been active in nonsecure treatment alternatives, are convinced that the future of private corrections (read: *continuing revenues*) lies in community-based programs, not secure prisons. Perhaps the one great advantage of private corrections is flexibility; if the venture into running medium- and maximum-security prisons does not work out, then write off your losses and move in another direction. A decade from now, private corporations may be as bullish on intermediate sanctions as they were on prisons and jails twenty years ago.

RACE AND IMPRISONMENT

As the current generation of prisoners has aged and become less healthy, their skin color has darkened as well. By 2002, about two-thirds of state and federal prisoners were minorities—blacks, Hispanics, Indians, Asians, or others. Black inmates alone made up 45 percent of incarcerated felons at year end 2002, compared to 34 percent white, 18 percent Hispanic, and 3 percent all others. If you visit virtually any prison in America, you will be struck almost immediately by the overrepresentation of racial and ethnic minorities in the population. Why do race and ethnicity play such a big part in imprisonment? Let's look at the current picture of race and imprisonment first, then look at the historical influences and recent legal changes affecting this picture, then speculate about underlying causes, and then close with a consideration of the long-term consequences for American society (and the people who make it up).

Two recent Bureau of Justice Statistics reports describe prisoners and trends in imprisonment in detail. "Prisoners in 2002" provides the following figures for rates of imprisonment by race and gender. These numbers represent the number of sentenced prisoners per 100,000 in the American population in each category:

	Male	*Female*
White	450	35
Black	3,437	191
Hispanic	1,176	80 [35]

These figures indicate that in comparison to white males, the imprisonment rate for Hispanics is about two and a half times higher, while the rate of black imprisonment is eight times higher. For females, the comparable rates are two and a half and five and a half times greater. Black males are 100 times more likely to be incarcerated than white females. Some of the more detailed breakdowns by age within race and gender categories are startling. The highest imprisonment rate for any group was for black males age twenty-five to twenty-nine—10,376 per 100,000, meaning that more than 10 percent of young black men in their late twenties were in prison in 2002. We know that overall the imprisonment rate for women has increased sharply since the 1970s (from 4.0 percent in 1979 to 6.8 percent in 2002), but changes within certain categories are even more striking. The imprisonment rate for black females age thirty to thirty-four (662) and age thirty-five to thirty-nine (566) is higher than the imprisonment rate for white men under twenty or over age forty-five. This is the first time in history that any group of females has been incarcerated at a rate higher than a group of men.

The second report, "Prevalence of Imprisonment in the U.S. Population, 1974–2001," describes trends in imprisonment over the past three decades and estimates long-term statistics based on current practices. At year end 2001, about 5.6 million adults in the United States were in prison or had previously served prison terms, which is about 2.7 percent of the adult population. But the lifetime likelihood of going to prison has increased sharply since the 1970s—from 1.9 percent in 1974 to 5.2 percent in 1991 to 6.6 percent in 2001—as imprisonment rates have climbed. Of the children born in 2001, one in sixteen would go to prison at least once in their lifetime if current rates of imprisonment hold.

Men are imprisoned at rates much higher than females, though the lifetime likelihood of imprisonment has increased far more dramatically for women since the 1970s. For women, the chances of going to prison were six times greater (1.8 percent) than in 1974 (0.3 percent); for men, the chances of going to prison were over three times greater in 2001 (11.3 percent) than in 1974 (3.6 percent).[36]

The current rate of ever having gone to prison among adult black males (16.6 percent) was over twice as high as among adult Hispanic males (7.7 percent) and over six times as high as among adult white males (2.6 percent). The long-term projections, for males born in 2001, are even more extreme. About one in seventeen white males, one in six Hispanic males, and one in three black males (32.2 percent) will do prison time during their lifetime if current incarceration rates remain unchanged.[37] This is *imprisonment* in a state or federal prison, mind you, not just a felony conviction that might carry only a short jail term or probation. If we add this group to the total, then the majority of black males born in 2001 will be convicted of a felony at some time in their lives. The comparable figure for white males would be about 10 percent. With the increased processing of women criminals, the projected percentage of felony convictions for black females is only slightly lower than that for white males.

The projection for white males (and black females) is bad enough; the projection for black males is truly awful. What is responsible for this dismal prediction, made all the worse in its disparity? Much of the research compares the influence of race and socioeconomic class, particularly the long-term relation of poverty to criminality. Scott Christianson's *With Liberty for Some: 500 Years of Imprisonment in America* emphasized the historical linkage between the lower class and imprisonment. From colonial times through the 1960s, indentured servants, slaves and free people of color, immigrants, ex-slaves and their descendants, and the urban poor who make up the bulk of the present day **underclass** have dominated jail and prison populations. Crime and imprisonment have been a part of the normal life of the urban poor since the founding of the republic.

America's minorities—blacks, Indians, and Hispanics—have always been overrepresented in the population held behind bars. The first annual report of the Boston Prison Discipline Society cited the "degraded character of the colored population" as the foremost cause of crime in America. In support of this conclusion, they offered official prison statistics: blacks made up only one in thirty-five of the population of New York State but one in four state prisoners (of the 637 convicts of that time); in Massachusetts, one in seventy-four and one in six; in Connecticut, one in thirty-four and one in three; in New Jersey, one in thirteen and one in three; and in Pennsylvania, one in thirty-four and one in three.[38]

Slavery had been abolished in these northern states by this time, and freed blacks were increasingly finding themselves behind bars. After the Civil War, which historian Mark T. Carleton has called "the most decisive event in the history of Southern penology," the same thing happened in the South. Blacks replaced whites as the majority population in prisons overnight, as prisons replaced slavery as a means of social control. In Louisiana at the end of Reconstruction, blacks made up 85 percent of the prison population, about ten points higher than today. When Hans von Hentig studied the growth of imprisonment during the Depression years of 1930 to 1936, he observed that the white incarceration rate had decreased slightly, while the black incarceration rate had increased to a level about three times greater than that of whites.[39] Gunnar Myrdal, the Swedish researcher who was studying race relations in America at about the same time, noted that Americans viewed crime and punishment as the outcome of personal defects of "badness" rather than in their relation to social conditions.[40]

The gap between white and minority imprisonment rates continued to widen into the 1970s, and then it began to accelerate again, particularly for Hispanics, who began immigrating to this country from Mexico and other Latin American countries in great numbers from the 1960s on. In the early 1970s, the overall percentage of men who had done prison time was 2.3 percent—1.4 for whites, 8.7 for blacks, and 2.3 for Hispanics. By 2001, the white percentage had almost doubled (to 2.6 percent), the black percentage had likewise almost doubled (to 16.6), but the Hispanic percentage had more than tripled (to 7.7 percent).[41]

What is responsible for the persistence of this wide gap between white and minority imprisonment rates? Some would argue that it proves the continuing importance of racism in the criminal justice system, this despite the civil rights movement and such superficial changes as including more minorities and women in decision-making positions within the system. Others suggest the influence of other factors, including social disadvantages and high crime rates among the poor, the persistence of a significant subculture of poverty in the United States, and, particularly in regard to drug crimes, the politics of selectivity in bringing offenders into the system.

William Julius Wilson has argued that although racial oppression was important earlier, the problems of blacks in the modern industrial world are more directly associated with economic class. As the significance of race in American life has declined, Wilson has suggested, "class has become more important . . . in determining black life-chances."[42]

Marc Mauer, assistant director of The Sentencing Project in Washington, D.C., has written as much about criminal sentencing policies and consequences as anyone else in America over the past decade. He has pointed out that a significant portion of the increase in minority imprisonment is related to the concentration of drug law enforcement in poor minority neighborhoods where drugs, particularly crack cocaine, are sold. Seventy-five percent of drug users in America are white, but 75 percent of criminals in prison for distributing or possessing drugs are black and Hispanic, most of them from poor urban neighborhoods targeted for concentrated enforcement.

To some commentators, blacks have become the contemporary criminal "bogeyman." Mauer has contrasted our crime control policy with our policy in dealing with AIDS, which he has described as a more compassionate and public health–oriented response:

In examining the crime problem, though, the public perception of the "criminal" has become predominant in determining the direction of the policy. Just as various waves of European immigrants were viewed as the source of the crime problem in the early years of the twentieth century, so too have African Americans now become the public image of the "criminal." As this perception has become more pervasive, the policy response that has developed has been one that emphasizes punishment and incarceration over an approach that engages the nation in a search for causes and cures.[43]

Darrell Steffensmeier and his colleagues over the past several years have researched the **focal concerns theory** of judicial decision making in Pennsylvania courts. This theory emphasizes three "focal concerns" in sentencing: the offender's blameworthiness, protection of the community, and practical considerations, such as cost and family effects. He found initially that young black males received more severe sentences than any other race, age, and gender combination. In follow-up interviews with judges, he found five key themes underlying this philosophy of sentencing:

1. The criminal records of young black males were viewed as being more serious and more indicative of future criminal behavior.
2. Some judges were reluctant to sentence white offenders to prison for fear of victimization in the majority black inmate population.
3. Women and older offenders were defined as less dangerous, lesser risks to community safety, and less blameworthy (because of mitigating factors) than young black males.
4. Women and older offenders were also seen as potentially presenting greater costs and problems for the correctional system to bear in terms of health care and child welfare.
5. Women and older offenders were seen as having more ties to the community, more likely to be supporting a family, and more likely to have a steady job now or in the future, while young black males were seen as lacking the social bonds that would reduce the likelihood of future criminality.[44]

Steffensmeier's original research contrasted blacks and whites. In more recent research, he divided the study population into three groups—Hispanic, black, and white—and found that Hispanics, who were increasing in number as defendants in Pennsylvania courts, were given harsher penalties than either blacks or whites.[45]

Other researchers are less certain that blacks and Hispanics are punished more harshly than whites in terms of both the in/out decision to incarcerate and the length of the prison term. They offer two general responses. The first acknowledges the selectivity of crime control policies. From the 1980s through about the mid-1990s, the "War on Drugs" brought far more minorities than whites into prison for drug crimes; since then, violent crimes, particularly homicide, robbery, and assault, have continued to bring much greater numbers of blacks and Hispanics than whites into prison. Two-thirds of all arrests for homicide and felony assault and three-quarters of all arrests for robbery are of black and Hispanic offenders. These crimes, except for armed robbery, typically involve victims of the same racial or ethnic group as the offenders.

The second response looks at the variables influencing sentencing decisions in the criminal courts. Even when the severity of the crime and the defendant's prior criminal history are held constant, as measures of comparison, other more subjective variables come into play, including the following:

1. The defendant's work record (or school record, if still of school age)
2. The defendant's family "connectedness," including the support of family members in court proceedings
3. The defendant's suitability for alternative programs not requiring incarceration
4. The court's perception that the defendant needs "treatment" in some form rather than punishment through incarceration

Coming from more dysfunctional social environments with fewer resources to fall back on and perceived as being culturally less inclined to change, black and Hispanic criminals are less likely to be dealt with leniently by the justice system—to get nonincarcerative sentences and shorter terms behind bars. Researchers who have looked at the processing of youthful offenders through the juvenile courts have stressed the importance of the concept of **beyond rehabilitation,** meaning that a juvenile is much more likely to be punished severely or transferred to the adult court for processing if he or she is perceived to no longer be amenable to rehabilitation. The court looks at specific circumstances—family involvement, performance in school, gang ties, extracurricular interests, and "attitude"—in deciding whether to keep working with the juvenile or give up and deal with him as an underage but almost certain future adult criminal.

In 1975, Steven Spitzer used the term **social dynamite** to describe those members of the deviant population in society who are viewed as particularly threatening and dangerous; people so labeled tend to be more youthful, alienated, and politically volatile. Regarded as more in need of formal social control, they are more likely than less volatile offenders to be formally processed through the criminal justice system.[46]

The consequences of this formal processing, as Marc Mauer has often pointed out, have to do with both image and reality. In the 1990s, the image of the **superpredator**—the violent inner-city teenager and young adult, often a gang member heavily involved in drug dealing, and almost always black or Hispanic—proliferated in music and film, culturally popularized in the term **thug life.** Although there were not many of them and they were concentrated in the poorest parts of a few large cities, the superpredators' image—and their popularity with American youth in general—was enough to scare the hell out of the political system.

The real consequences are important, too. *Invisible Punishment: The Collateral Consequences of Mass Imprisonment,* by Marc Mauer and Meda Chesney-Lind, details the many disqualifications attached to persons with a criminal record, especially a felony conviction. Four to five million convicted felons are unable to vote; if only half their number voted in national elections, they would be a potent force in politics in several states. About twenty states ban drug felons from receiving welfare or food stamps. Drug felons may also be denied public housing and student loans for higher education. A felony criminal record is a serious impediment in finding better-paying jobs or self-employment where licensing is required.

For many felons leaving prison, even those with a mind-set to follow the law and stay out of trouble, the barriers to entering mainstream society are formidable. They make it difficult for ex-cons to get a good job, to get the assistance they need to get out of poverty, to maintain stable family lives as spouses and parents, and to live productive lives in their communities. A generation ago, the term **self-fulfilling prophecy** was often used to mean a consequence that came about because it was expected or predicted. An example would be black children not doing well in school because they were said to be not as smart or not trying as hard as white children, which was used to explain why many minority-dominated schools were deficient and also to justify avoiding serious efforts to make them better.

Today, with criminals, the concept is more like a **cycle of doom,** in which young black males (and, to a lesser extent, young Hispanic males) are foretold to live unproductive lives of crime and poverty on the fringes of society. When we think of America as the land of equal opportunity for all, we should also think of the young black boy babies being born in America this year, more than half of whom will grow up to be convicted felons.

KEY TERMS

professionalization

accreditation

American Correctional Association

Professional Development Department

certification

"Best in the Business"

Commission on Accreditation in Corrections

AIDS

HIV

tuberculosis

multidrug-resistant tuberculosis

hepatitis B virus

hepatitis C virus

Estelle v. Gamble

adequate medical care

principle of equivalence

principle of less eligibility

deliberate indifference

penal harm

bricks-and-mortar solution

front-end solutions

double bunking

back-end solutions

alternative storage

parallel universe

double standard

punishment for profit

correctional/industrial complex

corporate demon

contract

private for-profit

private nonprofit

charitable organizations

contractors

employer model

convict leasing

slaves of the state

low-security custodial facilities

surveillance technologies

electronic monitoring

Corrections Corporation of America

Wackenhut Corrections Corporation

quick fix

underclass

focal concerns theory

beyond rehabilitation

social dynamite

superpredator

thug life

self-fulfilling prophecy

cycle of doom

NOTES

1. Erika Fairchild, *Comparative Criminal Justice Systems* (Belmont, Calif.: Wadsworth, 1993), pp. 92–93.

2. Camille Graham Camp and George M. Camp, *The Corrections Yearbook 2001: Adult Systems* (Middletown, Conn.: Criminal Justice Institute, 2002), p. 166.

3. Ibid., p. 224.

4. Diane Geiman, "Invest in Corrections' Greatest Asset . . . Your Staff," *Corrections Today* 61, no. 8 (December 1999): 110.

5. Ibid.

6. James A. Gondles Jr., "Professional Development: Meeting the Challenge of Change," *Corrections Today* 61, no. 8 (December 1999): 6.

7. American Correctional Association, "Introduction to Accreditation," *Standards of Adult Local Detention Facilities,* March 1991, p. xvi.

8. Ibid., pp. xvi–xxi.

9. Francie Latour, "Suffolk Jail Audit Group Is Faulted," *Boston Globe,* June 20, 2001.

10. Ibid.

11. Burk Foster, "Slaves of the State," *The Angolite,* July/August 2000, p. 50.

12. James W. Marquart, Dorothy E. Merianus, Stephen J. Cuvelier, and Leo Carroll, "Thinking about the Relationship between Health Dynamics in the Free Community and the Prison," *Crime and Delinquency* 42, no. 3 (July 1996): p. 334.

13. Ibid., p. 335.

14. Laura Maruschak and Allen Beck, "Medical Problems of Inmates, 1997," U.S. Justice Department, Bureau of Justice Statistics Special Report, January 2001, pp. 1–2.

15. Ibid., pp. 1–3.

16. Jim Oliphant, "When Prison Cells Breed Disease," *Legal Times,* December 9, 2002, p. 1.

17. Ibid.

18. David Rohde, "A Health Danger from a Needle Becomes a Scourge behind Bars," *New York Times,* August 6, 2001. See also Lane Nelson, "Silent Scourge," *The Angolite,* November/December 2002, pp. 28–35.

19. Ibid.

20. Michael S. Vaughn and Leo Carroll, "Separate and Unequal: Prison versus Free-World Medical Care," *Justice Quarterly* 15, no. 1 (March 1998): 3.

21. Ibid.

22. Ibid., p. 24.

23. Camp and Camp, *The Corrections Yearbook 2001,* pp. 105–6.

24. Paige M. Harrison and Allen J. Beck, "Prisoners in 2002," U.S. Justice Department, Bureau of Justice Statistics Bulletin, July 2003, p. 6.

25. Frank Green, "Inmates Boost Virginia's Revenue: Housing Other States' Prisoners Yields Millions," *Richmond Times-Dispatch,* February 25, 2001.

26. Ibid.

27. Camp and Camp, *The Corrections Yearbook 2001,* p. 14.

28. "State Rethinks Paying Counties for Jails," *Ashland (Ky.) Daily Independent,* December 2, 2002.

29. C. J. Schexnayder, "Empty Beds, Empty Pockets," *The Times of Acadiana (Lafayette, La.),* October 16, 2002, p. 25.

30. Ibid., p. 27.

31. Corrections Corporation of America, "Frequently Asked Questions," *www.correctionscorp.com/overview/faq.html.*

32. James Austin and Garry Coventry, *Emerging Issues in Privatized Prisons,* U.S. Justice Department, Bureau of Justice Assistance, February 2001, p. iii.

33. Harrison and Beck, "Prisoners in 2002," p. 6.

34. Austin and Coventry, *Emerging Issues in Privatized Prisons,* p. 59.

35. Harrison and Beck, "Prisoners in 2002," p. 9.

36. Thomas P. Bonczar, "Prevalence of Imprisonment in the U.S. Population, 1974–2001," U.S. Justice Department, Bureau of Justice Statistics Special Report, August 2003, p. 1.

37. Ibid.

38. Boston Prison Discipline Society, *First Annual Report* (Boston, 1826), as cited in Scott Christianson, *With Liberty for Some: 500 Years of Imprisonment in America* (Boston: Northeastern University Press, 1998), p. 141.

39. Christianson, *With Liberty for Some,* p. 229.

40. Ibid., p. 228.

41. Bonczar, "Prevalence of Imprisonment in the U.S. Population, 1974–2001," p. 1.

42. William Julius Wilson, *The Declining Significance of Race: Blacks and Changing American Institutions* (Chicago: University of Chicago Press, 1980), p. 150.

43. Marc Mauer, "The Social Cost of America's Race to Incarcerate," *Phi Kappa Phi Forum,* winter 2002, p. 29.

44. Darrell Steffensmeier, Jeffrey Ulmer, and John Kramer, "The Interaction of Race, Gender, and Age in Criminal Sentencing: The Punishment Cost of Being Young, Black, and Male," *Criminology* 36, no. 4 (November 1998): 775.

45. Darrell Steffensmeier and Stephen Demuth, "Ethnicity and Judges' Sentencing Decisions: Hispanic-Black-White Comparisons, *Criminology* 39 (February 2001): 145–79.

46. Steven Spitzer, "Toward a Marxian Theory of Deviance," in Henry R. Pontell, *Social Deviance: Readings in Theory and Research,* 2nd ed. (Upper Saddle River, N.J.: Prentice Hall, 1996), pp. 114–18.

FURTHER READING

Irwin, John, and James Austin. *It's About Time: America's Imprisonment Binge.* 3rd ed. Belmont, Calif.: Wadsworth, 2001.

McCall, Nathan. *Makes Me Wanna Holler: A Young Black Man in America.* New York: Random House, 1994.

Mauer, Marc. *Race to Incarcerate.* New York: New Press, 1999.

Shicor, David. *Punishment for Profit: Private Prisons/Public Concerns.* Thousand Oaks, Calif.: Sage Publications, 1995.

Wright, Richard A. *In Defense of Prisons.* Westport, Conn.: Greenwood Press, 1994.

WEB AND VIDEO RESOURCES

A good Website for keeping up with topical national news in corrections is *www.prisonsandjails.com.*

The two largest private prison corporations, Corrections Corporation of American and Wackenhut Cor-

rections Corporation (now known as The GEO Group, Inc.), have Websites at *www.correctionscorp.com* and *www.wcc-corrections.com.*

COMMENTARY

11 Race, Class, and Prison

by Edmond Dantes

Do race and class determine who goes to prison? Look at the numbers. Half of all prisoners are black, while blacks are only 13 percent of America's population. Whites, the dominant demographic, provide a little over a third. Of the more than 1.3 million prisoners at year end 2001 (the latest figures available), the U.S. Bureau of Justice Statistics informs us that about 600,000 were black, 450,000 white, 200,000 Latino, and the rest other ethnicities. An estimated 441,700 were black males between the ages of 20 and 39. At the same time, 10 percent of all black males age 25 to 29 were in prison, compared to 2.9 percent of Latino males and 1.2 percent of white males in the same age group.

Neither the states nor the federal government track the class of their prisoners. If they did, they would confirm what is common knowledge among penal professionals. Nearly all prisoners come from blue-collar or impoverished families and neighborhoods, with a sprinkling of middle-class embezzlers, molesters, rapists, and wife (or husband) killers. The upper class, represented by the likes of Edwin Edwards and Michael Milken, is so few in number they don't register on the radar. One wag, paraphrasing the Gospel of Matthew, put it this way: "It is easier for a rich man to pass through the eye of a needle than to enter the kingdom of prison."

This is not an anomaly of the justice system; it's supposed to work this way. It began in 1215, when England's barons rebelled against King John and forced him to sign the Magna Charta. That document guaranteed their rights, set procedures for trials, and standardized penalties for felonies. Ever since, criminal law has been written and used to control the teeming lower classes. Prisons, since their invention, have been repositories for the unruly poor, rowdy immigrants and, after the Civil War, blacks.

At this point someone will shout, "Wait a minute. Blacks are overrepresented in prison because they commit more crimes." Yes, many impoverished blacks are criminally active, but not to the extent they populate prisons. Several studies have found that young blacks commit crimes at a slightly but not significantly higher rate than young whites, and continue committing crimes somewhat longer than their white counterparts. This falls far short of explaining why most prisoners are black, as many as 80 percent in Southern prisons.

The *2000 Sourcebook of Criminal Justice Statistics* (the latest available) states 9,100,050 people were arrested in 1999—6,283,294 were white and 2,600,510 black. From those arrests flowed 997,970 felony convictions.

Of those convicted, 538,904 were white and 439,107 black. So, if whites are arrested at two- and-a-half times the rate of blacks and convicted at a 23-percent greater rate, why aren't whites the majority in prison? Because their charges were reduced to misdemeanors (or dropped altogether), they went to pretrial diversion programs, or they're on probation. At the end of 1997, according to the *Sourcebook*, 1,448,241 whites were on probation, compared to 777,974 blacks—nearly twice as many.

Think of the manner in which police do their job. They target ghettos, barrios and "white trash" areas for enforcement and patrol tonier neighborhoods to deter marauders. William Chambliss, professor of sociology at George Washington University and past president of the American Society of Criminology, writes in *Power, Politics, and Crime:*

> "To be perceived as effective and useful, the police must operate in a narrow space. An arrest is organizationally effective only if the person arrested is relatively powerless. Put quite simply, if police treat the middle or upper class [cocaine-snorting college students or Wall Street lawyers] the same way they treat the lower class [ghetto-dwelling crackheads], they are asking for trouble from people in power. Arrests of poor black men, however, result in nothing but gains for the [police] organization and the officer. Organizations reward members whose behavior maximizes gains and minimizes strains. If they focus their law-enforcement efforts on the lower classes, they are praised and supported by the "community," that is, by the middle- and upper-class white community."

In other words, equal justice for all is impossible in a class society.

9   MALE AND FEMALE PRISONERS

Individual offenders differ strikingly. Some seem irrevocably committed to criminal careers; others subscribe to quite conventional goals or are aimless and uncommitted to goals of any kind. Many are disturbed and frustrated boys and young men. Still others are alcoholics, narcotics addicts, victims of senility, or sex deviants. This diversity poses immense problems to correctional officials, for in most institutions or community treatment caseloads a wide range of offender types must be handled together.

— President's Commission on Law Enforcement and Administration of Justice, *Task Force Report: Corrections*, 1967

INTRODUCTION

This chapter is about people behind bars—the more than 2 million men and women in America's prisons and jails. What are they like? What kinds of paths did they follow to get locked up? What are their problems? What are their similarities and differences? How are they different from the 99 percent of Americans who are not behind bars at any given time? Even with increased incarceration rates in recent years, an estimated 75 percent or more of Americans will never spend a night in jail, much less a day in prison. What is different about those who do, especially those who make a lifetime out of being locked up—some in one continuous stretch, others serving "life on the installment plan," as some inmates describe their own life history? After reading the material in this chapter, you should be familiar with:

1. The background of men in prison.
2. The profile of a "typical" state prisoner.
3. The background of women in prison.
4. The profile of a "typical" female prisoner.
5. How state and federal prisoners differ and how jail and prison inmates differ.

MEN IN PRISON: CRIMINAL HISTORIES

Prisons hold two-thirds of America's prisoners, jails the remaining third. If we look closely at the more than 1.3 million people in state and federal prisons as of 2003, what commonalities do we see? No one would likely set out in childhood to become a criminal—have you ever heard a child respond to the question,

"What do you want to be when you grow up," by answering, "A convict"? But imprisonment does become a predictable outcome for many young people growing up in America today. Being locked up can become more a matter of "when" than "if," and when the criminal gets to prison, friends and family who know him (or, less often, her) say that this outcome is what they had anticipated for a long time. Imprisonment is rarely a surprise.

James Welch's *The Indian Lawyer* is a novel about prison life and politics in Montana. The protagonist is Sylvester Yellow Calf, a Montana lawyer who is a Blackfoot Indian and potential congressional candidate. As a member of the Montana Parole Board, he crosses paths with a prisoner named Jack Harwood, who involves his wife, Patti Ann, in a scheme to seduce Yellow Calf and blackmail him to spring Harwood from the pen. Harwood is not your typical inmate. He is a graduate of the University of Montana with a degree in economics. He was working as an accountant when he committed his first felony, a burglary, at the age of twenty-four. He did not have a troubled childhood. He has no alcohol or drug problem. He just likes to hang around criminals and commit armed robberies, which is how he landed in the state prison at Deer Lodge as a repeat offender. Yellow Calf thinks back on Harwood's appearance before the parole board: "He very seldom forgot an inmate of Harwood's caliber.... Bright, educated, clean-cut, good-looking, a mystery, maybe even a flake. He committed crimes because he was fascinated by crime."[1]

Jack Harwood, afraid of being killed by Indians trying to extort money from him in prison, on the surface resembles the mass of prison inmates in two main aspects: he is male (the gender differences of prisoners to be discussed later in this chapter), and he is a repeat offender. Most prisoners have been in trouble before, many of them consistently since early adolescence. Research by Marvin Wolfgang and others has supported the **chronic offender** concept. Following birth cohorts—people born in a locale in a given year—Wolfgang found that a relatively small number of persons in society, perhaps 5 or 6 percent, was responsible for the majority of all arrests and an even greater majority of violent crime arrests.

About one in three boys and one in seven girls will be arrested as juveniles (under age eighteen) according to current estimates, which on the flip side means that most juveniles (even many caught in an act of wrongdoing) will never be formally taken into custody. Of the ones who are, most will be arrested only once or twice and will be dealt with leniently by being warned and sent home or through the use of deferred adjudication, diversion, referral to community programs, or probation. But a juvenile with three or more juvenile arrests becomes a high-risk offender more likely to be viewed as a serious threat by the system. Three arrests is also an important marker for predictability—most juveniles arrested three or more times will also be arrested as adults. Although they get a fresh start in that their juvenile record does not carry over into the adult criminal court, no one would pretend that the system does not know they are habitual offenders. The black marks they accumulate, as juveniles and adults, begin to add up, and in time the legal decision makers—prosecutors, probation officers, and judges—will decide that the criminal is out of chances: it is time for imprisonment.

Criminal history studies suggest that prisoners like the fictional Jack Harwood are relatively rare in the system. Harwood turned to crime at age twenty-four out of apparent boredom or from making new friends who were already experienced criminals. The great majority of adult criminals not only have committed felonies but also been arrested at least once by age twenty-one. After age twenty-five, arrest rates fall off sharply, even for people who have been arrested previously. Those offenders who are arrested for the first time in middle age or older have a higher probability of being arrested for a crime of violence or a sex offense, often involving a relative or someone they know, more of a situational offense than one that grows from the criminal lifestyle that is far more typical of younger criminals.

Among state prisoners in 1997, 23 percent were in prison as first offenders, 32 percent had one or two prior felony sentences, and 42 percent had three or more prior felonies.[2] The number in prison as first offenders (we should remember that **first offender** means first time caught and processed as a felon, not first time actually committing a crime or being arrested; "first felony convictee" is probably a more accurate term) had increased from 19 percent in 1991, most likely as a result of reduced sentencing discretion in the courts. But essentially about three in four people in state prisons in the 1990s had prior felony convictions involving either probation or imprisonment.

Among federal prisoners in 1997, 38 percent were incarcerated as first-time felons, while 31 percent had one or two previous felony convictions, and 29 percent had three or more. The higher rate of incarceration of first-time felons in the federal system is attributed to stricter federal sentencing guidelines that limit the use of probation. The 1997 rate had fallen off sharply since 1991, when 49 percent of federal prisoners were first offenders.

For most of the offenders with previous sentences, that sentence had been within the recent past; the usual range is about 90 percent within the previous five years. For most of these, the criminal sentence is not only recent but contemporaneous: 46 percent were on probation or parole when they were arrested on the felony charge for which they were sent to prison.

Imprisonment is a status directly related to criminal violence and prior conviction record. The "Survey of State Prison Inmates, 1991" indicated that 94 percent of inmates had been convicted of a violent crime or had a previous sentence to probation or incarceration; this would mean that only 6 percent of the prison population was made up of nonviolent first offenders in for drug, property, or public order crimes.[3] Of the 6 percent who were nonviolent neophytes, the majority (61 percent) were in prison for drug trafficking or possession, while 12 percent were imprisoned for burglary.

The crimes for which people have been imprisoned have shifted over the years. In the 1970s, when incarceration rates were much lower and prison systems much smaller, persons convicted of crimes against persons made up about 60 percent of the state prison population, property criminals 30 percent, and drug and public order criminals together the remaining 10 percent. These numbers underwent a remarkable change during the 1980s after the "War on Drugs" was declared. By the mid-1990s, the number of persons imprisoned for violent crimes had declined to about 40 percent, property and drug offenders were about 25 percent each, and public order criminals (including such crimes as weapons and explosives violations, driving while intoxicated [DWI], escape, commercialized vice and morals offenses, and other regulatory crimes) made up the remaining 10 percent. These percentages are based on the actual head counts of who was in prison at any given time. Because violent criminals were usually serving longer sentences than criminals in the other categories, the turnover rate of prisoners in other categories was significantly higher. In most states and the federal system from the mid-1980s to the mid-1990s, more criminals were coming into prison for drug crimes than for any of the other three categories. After the mid-1990s, the number of drug criminals began to decline, and the number of violent criminals went up again.

By 2001, this was the breakdown of sentenced inmates in state prison systems by category and offense:

Total	1,208,700
Violent offenses	596,100 (49.3%)
Murder	159,200
Manslaughter	16,900
Rape	30,900
Other sexual assault	87,600
Robbery	155,300
Assault	118,800
Other violent	27,400
Property offenses	233,000 (19.3%)
Burglary	104,700
Larceny	45,500
Motor vehicle theft	18,000
Fraud	33,700
Other property	31,100
Drug offenses	246,100 (20.4%)
Public order offenses	129,900 (10.7%)
Other/unspecified	3,600 (0.3%)[4]

By specific crimes, offenders convicted of murder and robbery appear most numerous, followed by those convicted of assault and burglary; these four crimes account for 45 percent of the prison population. But the construction of the table obscures one important fact. The single largest group of convicted felons, greater in number than either murders or robbers, is drug traffickers. About two-thirds of the 246,100 drug felons (or more than 160,000) were convicted of various crimes related to drug distribution, and in over 70 percent of these cases, the drug was either crack or powder cocaine. In many state prison systems today, even as the War on Drugs supposedly wanes, the number one category of new admissions remains people convicted of distributing cocaine.

Paige Harrison and Allen Beck, the Bureau of Justice Statistics researchers who conducted the most recent prisoner survey, point out that the both the rate and the direction of imprisonment have changed since 1995. Annual increases have slowed, and most of the growth (63 percent) comes from violent offenders. Of the remainder, 2 percent comes from property offenders, 15 percent drug offenders, and 20 percent public order offenders.[5]

The sentences that imprisoned offenders are serving have grown longer over the past two decades. The following table, adapted from the *Sourcebook of Criminal Justice Statistics 2001*, shows the mean (or average) sentence length and mean time served until first release from prison for inmates discharged in 1990 and 1999:

	Mean Sentence Length (in months)		Total Time Served (in months)		Percentage of Sentence Served	
	1990	*1999*	*1990*	*1999*	*1990*	*1999*
All offenses	69	65	28	34	38.0	48.7
Violent offenses	99	87	46	51	43.8	55.0
Murder	209	192	92	106	43.1	53.1
Manslaughter	88	102	37	56	41.0	52.5
Rape	128	124	62	79	45.5	58.3
Other sexual assault	77	76	36	47	43.8	57.0
Robbery	104	97	48	55	42.8	51.6
Assault	64	62	30	39	43.9	58.7
Property offenses	65	58	24	29	34.4	45.6
Burglary	79	73	29	36	33.9	44.3
Larceny/theft	52	45	20	24	35.5	46.9
Motor vehicle theft	56	44	20	25	33.1	52.5
Fraud	56	49	20	23	33.2	41.7
Drug offenses	57	59	20	27	32.9	42.8
Possession	61	56	18	25	29.0	42.4
Trafficking	60	64	22	29	34.8	42.0
Public order offenses	40	42	18	23	42.6	51.1[6]

This table does not show sentence lengths and time served for earlier periods. If it did, what it would show is a steady increase in the length of the official sentence from the 1970s through the early 1990s. Then as truth-in-sentencing policies, tougher parole standards, and the abolition of parole began to kick in among the states and at the federal level, sentence lengths leveled off overall or declined slightly, while the length of time served before release increased sharply—by about ten percentage points, or six months overall, for all offenses. You should also keep in the forefront of your mind, as prison commentator (and lifer) Douglas Dennis has often pointed out concerning release statistics, that these are the figures for inmates *released*, not the figures for inmates remaining in prison. The ones still in prison have done more time and served more of their sentences than the ones getting out; the new ones coming in now will serve terms perhaps twice as long (in real time) on average as the ones who came in back in the 1970s. Thus, regardless of whether they are destined to be recidivists or law-abiding citizens on their release from prison, it will take them twice as long to get to that critical juncture of choice.

MEN IN PRISON: PERSONAL DEMOGRAPHICS

In chapter 8, we looked at issues relating to two key demographic variables on prisoners: race and age. The most recent comprehensive profile of state prisoners, conducted in 1997, reported these statistics on race and age:

Race		Age-Group	
White	33.3%	Under 25	19.8%
Black	46.5%	25–34	38.1%
Hispanic	17.0%	35–44	29.4%
Other	3.2%	45+	12.7%[7]

Federal prisoner statistics show more Hispanics and others in population (and fewer blacks and whites), and federal prisoners are a few years older. If the median age of state prisoners now is about thirty-three, the median age of federal prisoners is about thirty-seven. In the 1970s, whites outnumbered blacks in the prison population, but continuing high rates of violent crime (murder, assault, and robbery) among blacks and the antidrug focus on crack cocaine have driven the numbers of blacks in prison much higher since then. As the number of Hispanics living in the United States has shot up since the 1960s, the number of Hispanics in prison has increased at a rate even higher than that of blacks.

The gender of prison inmates is a frequent topic in the news, with commentators often pointing out that "women are the fastest growing segment of the prison population." (If only two genders exist, the choice here is limited.) Although in absolute numbers the number of women in prison has increased sharply—from fewer than 10,000 in the early 1970s to nearly 100,000 thirty years later—the fact is that state and federal prisoners remain overwhelmingly male. Males made up 93.7 percent of state prisoners in 1997 (down from 94.5 percent in 1991) and 92.8 percent of federal prisoners in 1997 (up from 92.2 percent in 1991).[8] Thus, although the media and some researchers have focused on increased arrest and imprisonment rates among women, fewer than seven of every 100 prison inmates are women. As the legal system nationwide has begun to shift its attention away from punishing drug offenders and toward increasing punishments for violent criminals over the past decade, there is some indication that the percentage of women in prison (*not* in jail) is leveling off. Between 1995 and 2002, the total number of male prisoners grew 27 percent, and the number of female prisoners grew by 42 percent.[9] Women remain much less likely to be arrested for the violent crimes that are growing in statistical prevalence among prison inmates.

For young people seeking to avoid imprisonment as they grow up, avoiding arrest until after age twenty-one has been a long-standing predictive variable. Another sage bit of wisdom has always been "get married." Only one in six state prison inmates and three in ten federal prison inmates are married. Most state prison inmates have never been married. In 1997, 68 percent of black inmates, 54 percent of Hispanic inmates, and 43 percent of white inmates had never been married. Before you rush out to the altar to avoid imprisonment, you should keep in mind that marriage does work both ways; about 15 percent of people in prison for homicide and assault are there for crimes against their spouses or family members. But all in all, as a purely scientific proposition, the benefits of marriage appear to outweigh the risks.

Another predictor of avoiding prison is higher education. Only about 13 percent of state prison inmate have any college education, and very few could match fictional Jack Harwood's college degree (in economics, no less). The 1997 education breakdown by categories was as follows:

Less than high school	39.7%
GED	28.5%
High school graduate	20.5%
More than high school	11.3%[10]

Almost 70 percent of state prisoners did not graduate from high school, compared with about 18 percent of adults not in prison. Many of the inmates with GEDs got them in jail or prison. Federal prisoners were better educated; 51 percent graduated from high school or had some college. Prisoners have often done poorly in school before they dropped out, so they often test much lower than the last grade attained. Prisons are full of high school dropouts who begin prison life functioning at elementary school literacy levels. These inmates are said to be **functionally illiterate.**

One other important predictor of avoiding incarceration is holding a full-time job. Prisoners have long been notoriously underemployed. The surveys of state prison inmates going back into the 1980s indicate that in general about two-thirds were working in the month prior to their arrest, while one-third were not. In 1997, these figures were 67 and 31 percent. But not all the ones working were employed full time—55 percent were full time and 12 percent part time. At a time when national unemployment rates have been in the 5 to 6 percent range, prisoners were about six to eight times more likely to be unemployed or working only occasionally, often at transient labor jobs.

The 1997 survey did not include statistics on income as earlier surveys had done. The surveys from 1986 and 1991 demonstrated what we might expect about the preprison income levels of inmates, influenced as they would be by low-paid, sporadic work; lack of high school education; and criminal histories. If you were setting your sights on a modest income at which you could sustain yourself, without a spouse or children to support, $25,000 per year would be a basic figure providing for a minimal, no-frills life just above the poverty level. In the 1986 and 1991 surveys, only 11 percent (1986) and 15 percent (1991) of prisoners were earning $25,000 or more annually before they came to prison. Twenty-seven percent (1986) and 22 percent (1991) were earning less than $3,000 per year before they came to prison. Well over half in both surveys had annual incomes of less than $10,000, below even what a college student living on loans and a part-time job can live on.[11]

How would a grown man (or woman) keep alive on such an income, and of what use would he be as a provider to his family, especially his spouse and children? About two-thirds of prisoners do have at least one child, though they are not likely to be married to the mother. If a prisoner's lawful income is this low, it is easy to see that crime, especially selling drugs, becomes a covert "hustle" to pick up the money needed to meet basic necessities of life.

MEN IN PRISON: LIFE HISTORIES

Thus far, we have established that most prisoners are young to middle-age men, predominantly lower-class minorities, with lengthy criminal histories and poor education and employment records. What other disadvantages might they have? The most significant burden many of them are carrying around is a history of substance abuse. The drug histories of prisoners are replete with statistical examples that set them apart from nonprisoners; the extent to which alcohol and illegal drugs influence their lives is perhaps the main feature setting prisoners apart from mainstream society.

Prisoners drink alcohol and consume a variety of drugs way out of proportion to what other people not in prison do. Although most drug criminals are in prison for crimes related to powder or crack cocaine, their **substance abuse histories** and those of other inmates not in prison for drug crimes are diverse. They start earlier in life, drink alcohol to excess and use drugs more often, and experiment with a greater range of hard drugs than nonprisoners, right up to the time of their arrest. For many prisoners, time spent in jail is the first time they have been sober in years.

About half of all prison inmates claim to have been under the influence at the time of the crime leading to their arrest. The surveys from 1986 and 1991 showed these results:

	Percent of inmates	
	1991	*1986*
Under the influence of		
Alcohol only	18	18
Drugs only	17	17
Both alcohol and drugs	14	18
Total	49	54[12]

In the 1997 survey, alcohol was the single most influential drug by itself (36.5 percent), followed in descending order by marijuana (14.8 percent), the "other drugs" category (8.4 percent), crack cocaine (8.3 percent), powder cocaine (7.4 percent), and heroin (5.5 percent).[13] The inmates who were drinking immediately before their crimes, which has consistently been about a third of all prisoners, had consumed on average about three six-packs of beer or two quarts of wine, drinking for a median time of about six hours, before going out to commit their crimes.

When you finish the experiment suggested in chapter 2, the one in which your friend locks you in the closet for a year to simulate life in solitary in the Auburn prison, you can try this one. Sit down and drink three beers per hour for the next six hours, ideally with two or three ex-fraternity boys who have been kicked out of the frat for uncivilized behavior and bad grades. The simulation would be improved if you would smoke a couple of joints and perhaps eat a few of those brightly colored pills (of unknown effect) that your friends offer you. Then at the end of six hours, see how you feel and in what direction your thoughts have turned. Then do the same thing tomorrow and every day for the next month. Warning: do not try this experiment alone, and do not attempt to drive when it is over; you would definitely be over any state's DWI threshold. In fact, do not try this one at all. It is too dangerous, and you would be a menace to society. It does, however, approximate the befuddled state of mind of from one-third to one-half of all prisoners at the time they committed their imprisonment offense.

Over the past twenty years, the majority of prison inmates have indicated that they were using at least one illegal drug, most likely marijuana (but with crack and powder cocaine counted together as one drug close behind in second place), in the month before their arrest. About 80 percent of inmates reported using illegal drugs at least once in their lives, and 60 percent or more identify themselves as **regular drug users** at some point in their lives. These figures do not include alcohol. A lot of people in society have smoked marijuana or experimented with cocaine, but for most of them, drug abuse stops at that level. Prisoners take it a lot farther. About one in four prisoners has used heroin or other opium derivatives, and about one in four has used a needle to inject drugs, most often heroin, cocaine, or crank. This explains most of the hepatitis and HIV among prison inmates.

The composite effect of drugs and alcohol on imprisonment is profound (if not absolutely startling). In percentages, it breaks down this way:

Inmates under the influence of drugs or alcohol at the time of the imprisonment crime—50 percent

Inmates in prison for drug and alcohol crimes—22 percent

Inmates committing their crime to get money for drugs—17 percent

These categories overlap, obviously, but even so it is apparent that if substance abuse could be prevented or treated more effectively, the numbers of people in prison would be reduced substantially. Slightly more than half these inmates (56 percent in 1997) have ever participated in a drug or alcohol treatment program. Most who have participated did so outside of prison, as the availability of substance abuse treatment and relapse prevention programs in prison has declined over the past decade.

Prisoners drink and use drugs. So what else is new? "Happy families are all alike; every unhappy family is unhappy in its own way," Tolstoy began *Anna Karenina*. Most prisoners belong in the "unhappy family" category, or the **broken family,** at a minimum. The 1997 inmate profile gave these statistics:

Person lived with while growing up:

Both mother and father—43.7 percent

Mother only—38.5 percent

Father only—3.6 percent

Grandparents—8.2 percent

Other—5.1 percent[14]

The mother and father category probably appears more conventional than it really is because it would include parents who were not married to each other, stepmothers or stepfathers, and live-ins who acted as surrogates. Most prisoners, perhaps three out of four, did not grow up living continuously in a stable household with their two natural, married parents.

Family fragmentation is most noticeable among black inmates. The decline of marriage in the black community over the past forty years has resulted in two generations of black children growing up in single-parent households. By 2000, far more black inmates were products of single-mother households than two-parent households. This trend has become more pronounced among younger Hispanic and white inmates as well but not to the same degree as among blacks. About one in six inmates had lived in a foster home or in some other state or private institution at some time, and about the same number had lived with grandparents, other relatives, or friends while growing up.

The influence of parents on youngsters growing up to become criminals in America today is in decline, and some of the remaining parental influences are bad. About one in three state prisoners in 1997 grew up in a household where a parent abused alcohol or drugs or both (leaving it up to the prisoners being surveyed, who are often overly kind to their parents, to define "abuse").

About 15 percent of state prisoners identified themselves as childhood victims of physical or sexual abuse in 1997.[15] This estimate is again determined by how inmates choose to define "abuse." It appears unrealistically low to many authorities in the field. In her research into the connection between childhood abuse and adult criminality, Cathy Spatz Widom used the phrase **cycle of violence** to suggest that a childhood history of physical abuse predisposes the survivor to violence in later years. She found that documented abuse or neglect as a child increased the likelihood of arrest as a juvenile by 53 percent, as an adult by 38 percent, and for a violent crime by 38 percent.[16]

In research involving men and women inmates in a large urban jail in the early 1990s, two-thirds of the men and almost half the women reported serious domestic violence in their childhoods. The most significant finding was the following:

> Both violence and non-violence tend to be continuous. If you had a violent family life as a child, you are very likely (in the range of 90 percent) to have a violent adult family life as well. If you had a non-violent family life as a child, your adult family life is likely to be non-violent also, unless you happen to hook up with a spouse (more likely a male than a female) who proceeds to give your life a violent turn.[17]

Patrick Fagin, senior fellow at the Heritage Foundation, has explored the social influences on crime and violence in his writings for more than a decade. His recurring theme is summed up in a policy article he wrote in 1995, "The Real Root Causes of Violent Crime: The Breakdown of Marriage, Family, and Community." Fagin summarizes two contrasting bodies of research. One set considers the increase in crime since the 1960s:

1. Over the past thirty years, the rise in violent crime parallels the rise in families abandoned by fathers.
2. High-crime neighborhoods are characterized by high concentrations of families abandoned by fathers.
3. State-by-state analysis indicates that a 10 percent increase in the percentage of children living in single-parent homes leads typically to a 17 percent increase in juvenile crime rates.
4. The rate of violent teenage crime corresponds with the number of families abandoned by fathers.
5. The type of aggression and hostility demonstrated by a future criminal often is foreshadowed in unusual aggressiveness as early as age five or six.
6. The future criminal tends to be an individual rejected by other children as early as the first grade who goes on to form his own group of friends, often the future delinquent gang.[18]

He then offers a set of contrasting findings:

1. Neighborhoods with a high degree of religious practice are not high-crime neighborhoods.
2. Even in high-crime inner-city neighborhoods, well over 90 percent of children from safe, stable homes do not become delinquents. By contrast, only 10 percent of children from unsafe, unstable homes in these neighborhoods avoid crime.
3. Criminals capable of sustaining marriage gradually move away from a life of crime after they get married.
4. The mother's strong affectionate attachment to her child is the child's best buffer against a life of crime.
5. The father's authority and involvement in raising his children are also a great buffer against a life of crime.[19]

Whereas others tend to focus on race or socioeconomic variables in explaining crime, Fagin sticks to a family structure explanation. He identifies seven family conditions leading to crime:

1. Fatherless families
2. The absence of a mother's love
3. Parental fighting and domestic violence
4. The lack of parental supervision and discipline
5. Rejection of the child
6. Parental abuse or neglect
7. Criminal parents[20]

These family conditions lead to higher rates of juvenile delinquency and in time adult criminality, which, when concentrated in a specific geographic locale, such as a minority lower-class urban ghetto, can destroy the sense of community necessary to sustain the neighborhood. Although we may use poverty or race as the markers, the real **"root cause" of crime** in these areas, as Fagin sees it, is broken families.

How do inmates see their own family lives? In a survey conducted among prisoners at the Louisiana State Penitentiary in 1996, inmates were asked to rank the influences on their criminal behavior. Among seven possible influences, they most strongly rejected family life as influencing their imprisonment. The two most important influences to them were, first, drugs and alcohol, and, second, their friends and associates. Although more than 40 percent of this group of prisoners had immediate family members in prison and many agreed that their family lives as children and adults were troubled, most of them did not blame their families for their imprisonment; they pointed instead at their friends on the street and their own bad habits in abusing alcohol and drugs.[21]

We are very aware today that crime runs in families. Do you have an immediate family member who has served prison time? About 95 percent of us do not, but about four in ten prisoners do, which is one of the more striking features of their background. Among young black inmates, given the increased likelihood of imprisonment among blacks, the chance of another family member having been in prison is almost even. Most commonly it is a brother (31 percent), followed by a father (6 percent), and a sister (4 percent), with mom (God bless her!) coming in last (2 percent). But with the increasing numbers of young black women in prison over the past twenty years, this is changing also. It is no longer far-fetched to find entire black families—father, mother, sons, and daughters—who have done prison time or are sometimes even locked up in different prisons at the same time. In this context, family reunions take place in halfway houses when everyone gets out.

MEN IN PRISON: A SELF-PROFILE

In the 1996 survey of prisoners at the Louisiana State Penitentiary, the participants were asked to comment on their lives and the choices that had brought them to prison. Most of the participants in this survey were lifers, and the median length of time served was already more than ten years, so this group may appear more reflective than many younger, shorter-term prisoners in other institutions. This is what they had to say:

> "I had just got out of Angola from doing 12 years. I try to get me a five day a week job but the only thing I could find was working for job services every now in then."
>
> "I grew up with a feeling of hopelessness, without any positive direction."
>
> "There was no 'real' father figure due to alcohol and financial problems."
>
> "My family didn't have love for each others. I never was loved by my mother, because of the way my father treated her. She took it out on me. I didn't know anything about life. Until I got here for life."
>
> "My family was there for me, but I led another kind of life."
>
> "I did not want to do the right thing in school. Thats how everything happen buy not going to school."
>
> "I went out with people that never finished school, and never worked, 'just always stood in the neiborhood with nothing to do.'"
>
> "It turned me on to be around people just as crazyer then me. I enjoyed brother-folly."
>
> "My (friends?) were people whom I knew in bars. Drinking (friends?). I never really had a true friend."
>
> "I never had a job to keep me off the street most of the day. I feel as though if I had a job I wouldn't be in this situation I'm in."
>
> "I never had a problem working. My problem was getting a job that paid enough to get by. This is a problem when you stay in the low-income community."
>
> "My friends all like to use drugs so I used them on the day I committed the crime. I think if I wasn't using drugs and drinking I wouldn't be in here."
>
> "I agree 100 percent that drugs is the cause of my action and the reason I'm in prison today. As a young man I didn't even think about my life or responably. Today drugs has taken over the world to the extend where they don't even care about anything at all."
>
> "If I would have put more faith into God when he was offering me opportunities I will not be sitting here writing this."
>
> "I became powerless to control myself during the use of drugs and alcohol. I also became powerless to avoid doing them, because I never knew I had a problem, until it was too late."

"All I needed was a 9-to-5 job and I would be out right now."

"No work, no money but still loved to drink."

"With an education I would have been equiped to bypass negative situations (my own like of drive in school would be my answer)."

"Because my family don't really care about me now. I never hear from them at all. I don't know what it is to be loved. Know one never showed me love before, but my sister and she's locked up now."

"Drugs and alcohol was my downfall and I would half to say 70% of people in prison that also was the problem."[22]

The profile of prisoners that emerges from the statistical surveys and from personal interviews is a bleak one. Men in state and federal prisons suffer from a broad range of social disabilities and personal limitations. Many come from unstable and abusive families. A much higher percentage of prisoners than nonprisoners have long-term histories of alcohol and drug abuse; half or more say they were high when they committed the crime that got them sent to prison. Use of hard drugs—cocaine, heroin, and methamphetamine—is much higher among prisoners than in the general population. Most prisoners have not graduated from high school; a good portion are functionally illiterate. Many prisoners have personality or "attitude" problems that make it difficult for them to get along with people. They used to be called **sociopaths;** today the more common term is **antisocial personality disorder,** meaning that they exhibit such characteristics as impulsiveness, poor self-control, lack of remorse for wrongdoing, lack of empathy with others, manipulativeness, irresponsibility, superficial charm, exaggerated sense of self-worth, and disregard of the consequences of their behavior—one important consequence being imprisonment. They have problems staying attached to people in the free world, and then they enter into the even more highly filtered world of prison, where virtually all their neighbors are convicted felons with similar background and problems.

Prisoners are predominantly poor minorities with limited prospects. When they are not in prison, they are likely to be found living in the densest, poorest urban neighborhoods where crime and substance abuse flourish. They live there because that is where their families and friends live; most of them lack the resources to move somewhere else even if they wanted to separate themselves from underclass culture and start new lives. If America had a **caste system,** prisoners would be on the bottom level, even without one final impediment to moving upward toward mainstream society: a felony record. Many job opportunities that are open to others will be closed to them because of their criminal records. Would you hire an armed robber to work in your store? A man convicted of sexual assault to do maintenance work in your apartment complex? A drug addict to work in a hospital? A murderer to work in a child care center or a nursing home? When you look at where prisoners came from and what they have to return to when they get out, the interesting thing is not that half of them end up back in prison within five years, either on new convictions or as parole violators. The interesting thing is that half of them do not come back. We should probably spend more time looking into the successes of ex-prisoners (or at least at how half of them manage to avoid reincarceration) rather than continuing to reexamine the failures of the ones who keep returning to prison. For most of these men, prison is a normal life experience.

WOMEN IN PRISON: PERSONAL FEATURES

Jean Harris published her first book, the autobiographical *Stranger in Two Worlds*, in 1986. The first world in her story was the world she was born into as Jean Struven in 1923 and lived in until she was middle aged. As a school-teacher and divorced mother of two sons, Jean Harris became a school administrator. She also became the girlfriend of Dr. Herman Tarnower, the New York cardiologist who wrote one of the first best-selling diet books, *The Complete Scarsdale Medical Diet*. In this world, she eventually became head-mistress of the exclusive Madeira School in McLean, Virginia, while continuing an often difficult relationship with Dr. Tarnower. Stressed out with crises at school, taking strong antianxiety medication, and worrying that her lover was dumping her for a younger woman, she came to the gate of her second world—the Bedford Hills, New York, women's prison—in 1981, convicted of murder. She had gone to confront Dr. Tarnower and commit suicide, she told the jury at her trial. She said she had shot him accidentally when he tried to take the gun from her. The jury found her story unconvincing, particularly since her lover had been shot four times. They convicted her of second degree murder, and the judge sentenced her to fifteen years to life.

Jean Harris actually did have a college degree in economics (like the fictional Jack Harwood in *The Indian Lawyer*); she earned hers *summa cum laude* from Smith College. But she felt as much like a fish out of water among the women inmates of Bedford Hills—the thieves, drug addicts, habitual criminals, and vice offenders—as Jack Harwood did among the Indians in the Montana penitentiary. Her education did not prepare her for life in the women's prison; nothing in the first world prepared her for the second. Although she despised how the prison's staff and administration treated her, she at least understood them and had more in common with them than she did with her sisters in crime. Harris wrote, in *Stranger in Two Worlds*,

> The chasm between me and the other women was wide and deep when I came to Bedford. In some ways I have bridged the gap. In many others I have not and never could. I am almost 40 years older than the other women here, and I am considered "rich" because I am white, and because I have been widely publicized as "social."[23]

Even as a woman who had murdered her lover, a not uncommon crime in the women's prison, she knew that she was not like the others. Her education, her culture, her values, and even her reaction to the experience of imprisonment set her apart from the other inmates.

Who were the prisoners of Jean Harris's second world? In their demographic description, they are not radically different from men prisoners. Joycelyn Pollock, who has written about women in prison for twenty-five years, has made this observation:

> The typical female prisoner has changed little over the years. Women in prison are increasingly members of minority groups; they are more likely to be older than in previous years; and they continue to be undereducated and underemployed or unemployed before incarceration. They are more likely to be unmarried than in

years past. Most women in prison are mothers of young children. They are increasingly in prison for drug crimes and admit to having drug problems.

Compared to men in prison, women in prison tend to be slightly older, slightly more educated, and more likely to be unemployed prior to incarceration (60 percent compared to 40 percent for men in prison). They are more likely than men to have been primary caregivers of their children. They are also more likely than men to admit to drug problems, although men are more likely to report problems with alcohol. The profile of women in prison is roughly similar whether one utilizes large national samples or smaller state samples.[24]

The characteristics of women in state and federal prisons in 1998 were reported as follows:

	State Prisons	Federal Prisons
Number of prisoners	75,200	9,200
Race/ethnicity		
White	33%	29%
Black	48%	35%
Hispanic	15%	32%
Other	4%	4%
Age		
24 or younger	12%	9%
25–34	43%	35%
35–44	34%	32%
45–54	9%	18%
55 or older	2%	6%
Median age	33	36
Marital status		
Married	17%	29%
Widowed	6%	6%
Separated	10%	21%
Divorced	20%	10%
Never married	47%	34%
Education		
Eighth grade or less	7%	8%
Some high school	37%	19%
High school graduate/GED	39%	44%
Some college or more	17%	29%[25]

In this survey, two in three women in prison were estimated to have children under age eighteen. The average was about 2.3 children each, or a total of 128,000 minor children with mothers in prison.

Women in prison tend to have less serious criminal histories than do men in prison. About 65 percent of women in prison had prior felony convictions, compared to 77 percent of men. Male inmates were twice as likely to have had a juvenile history—38 versus 19 percent. Male inmates had also acquired more convictions than women. Of women prisoners, 32 percent had three or more prior convictions, compared to 43 percent of men.[26]

Crimes of imprisonment also vary by gender. Seventy-five percent of women's felony convictions in state court in 1996 were for property crimes (mostly fraud and larceny) and drug crimes. Of women passed along to imprisonment in state prisons in 1998, the leading category of offenses was drug crimes (34 percent), followed by violent crimes (28 percent), property crimes (27 percent), and public order crimes (11 percent). Thus, while half of all men are in prison for crimes of violence, over 70 percent of women are in prison for nonviolent crimes and generally with a less prominent criminal history than men sentenced to imprisonment.[27]

Although news accounts often give the impression that women of today are more violent, the number of women convicted of homicide and robbery has fallen off steadily in recent years. The most common violent crime for which women are arrested is the misdemeanor simple assault, typically against an acquaintance, friend, or family member. Women are much less likely to commit or be charged with predatory violent crimes against strangers. Of the 60,000 murders committed by women between 1976 and 1997, over 60 percent were against an intimate or family member; among the 400,000 murders committed by men over the same period, 20 percent were against family members or intimates. The female murder rate in 1998 (1.3 per 100,000) was less than half what it had been in 1976 (3.1 per 100,000).[28] The male murder rate was 11 per 100,000, about nine times the female rate.[29]

Most of the researchers into women's criminality have found two distinctive features marking the lives of women prisoners: abuse and drugs. Joycelyn Pollock has reported,

> Studies consistently show that a substantial percentage of incarcerated women have been abused, both sexually and physically, as children. For instance, Chesney-Lind and Rodriguez reported that half the women sampled had been raped as children, and 63 percent had been sexually abused. . . . A study conducted by the Oregon Department of Corrections (1993) found that the incidence of physical and sexual abuse of women inmates was considerably higher than in the general population. In a study of Oregon female prisoners, 45 percent reported physical abuse, 66 percent reported sexual abuse, and 37 percent reported abuse before 18.[30]

Similar research in Oklahoma found that about two-thirds of women inmates reported being abused at some point in their lifetimes. The Oklahoma study was notable in showing the continuity of abuse: women who were physically or sexually abused as children were likely to be abused as adults as well.[31]

A recent Bureau of Justice Statistics report also explored abuse and reported these findings:

1. Male prisoners were more likely to report abuse only as children; women reported abuse as children and adults.
2. The abuse of men was by family members; the abuse of women was by family members and intimates.
3. Abuse is associated with foster care, parental abuse of drugs or alcohol, and criminal history.

4. Abused prisoners are more likely to be serving sentences for violent crimes.

5. The use of drugs and alcohol is higher among those who have been abused.[32]

This last finding is particularly important in the life histories of women prisoners: physical and sexual victimization is often tied to alcohol and drug abuse. Joycelyn Pollock reports,

> The most recent figures indicate that about half of women in prison had been regularly using drugs or alcohol; and about 40 percent of women (compared to 32 percent of men) had been under the influence of drugs at the time of the offense. Women evidently are more likely than men to abuse drugs, while men are more likely to abuse alcohol. According to this same report, 60 percent of women said they used drugs in the month before the offense, 50 percent were daily users, 40 percent were under the influence at the time of the offense, and nearly one in three committed an offense to get money for drugs. Women were also more likely to have been through treatment programs (56 percent compared to 41 percent for men).[33]

The prevalence of drug abuse in the background of women prisoners is important in one other regard. Women are sicker than men, at least partly because of intravenous drug use. Women prisoners are much more likely to be HIV positive and to be infected with hepatitis B and C than men are. At year-end 2000, 3.6 percent of all female inmates were HIV positive, compared to 2.2 percent of males.[34] Hispanic female inmates reported the highest HIV infection rate of any group in prison.

The personal histories of women prisoners, in comparison to men, seem even more filled with sadness and misfortune. The 1993 Oregon study of its female prisoners gave this summary:

> This survey presents a picture of women inmates characterized by low achievement, early delinquency, and high experience of abuse. The women have generally low education levels, worked at unskilled jobs as teenagers, and a high percentage used alcohol and drugs as teenagers. A third grew up without their natural father in the family, and a third had some experience in foster care or living with caretakers other than parents. Families of origin tended to be large (average 5.6 children). Two-thirds of the women ran away from home at least once while growing up, and half were arrested at least once. Two-thirds had parents or siblings who had been arrested.[35]

Barbara Owen, who wrote *In the Mix: Struggle and Survival in a Women's Prison*, based on research and intensive interviews in the Central California Women's Facility, offered this observation: "The offense profile also suggests that women tend to commit survival crimes to earn money, feed a drug-dependent life, and escape brutalizing physical conditions and relationships."[36]

WOMEN IN PRISON: THEORIES OF CRIME AND PUNISHMENT

After steady increases in the number of women going to prison since the War on Drugs began in the early 1980s, women now make up between 6 and 7 percent of the total prison population. Although the percentage remains small, it does reflect consistent growth since the early 1970s, when women made up just over 4 percent of felony prisoners. Women actually make up about 22 percent of arrestees and 16 percent of convicted felony defendants but only 10 percent of all prison admissions each year because their crimes are generally less serious than those of men. In the "most equal" index crime category, women make up exactly a third of all arrestees for larceny. In the "least equal" category, women make up only about 10 percent of arrestees for murder and robbery and less than 2 percent of arrestees for sexual assault. Women's prison terms, again tied to the crimes they commit, are generally shorter, and with the number of men already in prison so much greater, the representation of women in the total population of imprisoned offenders remains small.

In the history of the penitentiary, which is to say the modern history of punishment, why have so few women been imprisoned? Many scholars of the criminology of women believe that women once received **preferential treatment**—translated as leniency—within the legal system. There were several reasons cited for this favorable treatment:

1. The nonviolent nature of women's crimes, except for murder, which, when committed by females, usually involved family members or loved ones as victims.
2. The lack of serious prior criminal histories among most women offenders.
3. The presence of a man to put the blame on.
4. The condition of motherhood, still prevalent today; about 80 percent of women in jail and prison are mothers, the great majority of these with minor children still living with them.
5. The role of males with conventional middle-class values as the prime decision makers in criminal justice—as police, prosecutors, judges, and prison officials. The paternalistic attitude of judges toward women is often cited, though you can just as easily point out that judges are also paternalistic toward juveniles, drunks, and sometimes even male felons.

Otto Pollak suggested in *The Criminality of Women* (1950) that the legal system practiced **chivalry**, meaning that the male-dominated system treated women protectively. Pollak also suggested that much of women's crime was **hidden crime** in that it involved victims who were family members or friends of the offender. They would presumably be less likely to call the crimes to the attention of the system (or demand punishment) because of their relationship with the criminal.

The early biophysical criminologist Cesare Lombroso said the only crime to which women were well suited was **prostitution**, not only because it was so prevalent at the time but also because it was passive and required little skill. He ranked women criminals at the bottom of the scale of evolutionary development. The early English and American criminal justice systems spent a lot of time trying to punish and correct prostitutes and make them into moral, law-abiding wives and mothers. We do not know if this worked or not; we suspect not.

The early women's prisons, which were only separate wings of larger men's prisons, were full of women who were whores, thieves, and consorts of criminal men. Many correctional reformers of the 1800s, such as the English Quaker **Elizabeth Gurney Fry**, advocated dealing with these women in special facilities, run for and in some cases by women (though usually under the direction of men). The more progressive states began to establish separate prisons for women by the end of the 1800s.

The first all-female prison was the Indiana Reformatory Institute, which opened in 1873 and applied Zebulon Brockway's reform methods. The first federal prison for women, at **Alderson,** West Virginia, opened in 1927. The woman sometimes identified as the first female warden (though other women held other titles as heads of other early women's prisons), **Mary Belle Harris,** was its head. These and other prisons set the tone of women's corrections—the idea that women prisoners were immoral beings unduly influenced by men who needed to be reformed but did not present much of a physical threat to safety and security. Women offenders were capable of evil, but they were not really dangerous, professional criminals.

Prostitution remains an important criminal offense today, though generally not a felony for which the offender is put in prison. But many practitioners of prostitution get in trouble for other crimes—for crimes of violence related to their work, for drug-related offenses, and for other crimes related to their hustling lifestyles. As one of the service-related or victimless crimes, prostitution remains at the center of an unsavory, often dangerous lifestyle. Careers in prostitution run the "professional" gamut, from the oldest to the newest, from the streetcorner hooker who might perform oral sex ten or twenty times a night, to the crack whore who has unprotected sex for a rock or two of crack cocaine, to the "pretty woman" courtesan who might have a six-figure income, at least for a while.

A 1979 General Accounting Office report assessed the impact of prostitution on female criminality:

> Studies have shown that most women enter prostitution for pressing economic reasons and see it as a viable alternative to scraping by on welfare or poverty level wages. It also tends to be self-reinforcing. Once the woman has a prostitution conviction on her record it becomes more difficult for her to get another job. In addition bail demands are often so high that the prostitute must get money from her pimp to get her freedom. Consequently recidivism is high.
>
> The woman incarcerated for prostitution suffers more serious consequences than a record. She generally acquires other criminal skills during her confinement. Though many prostitutes spend little time in prison for prostitution, they spend a lot of time in jail. Over 30 percent of the inmates in most women's jails are convicted prostitutes, and they serve longer sentences than other misdemeanants. For these women, long jail terms become schools for crime; seven out of every ten women in prison for committing a felony were first arrested for prostitution.[37]

The best-known former prostitute in recent years was likely Aileen Wournos, the Florida serial killer executed on October 9, 2002. After a long history of commercial sex, sexual promiscuity, mental illness, heavy drinking, and drug abuse, Wournos began killing men who picked her up for sex. She killed seven before she was arrested in January 1991. On Florida's death row, Wournos maintained that she had been defending herself from criminals attacks and suffering from flashbacks at the time of the killings. Then she abruptly dropped her appeals and asked to be put to death as soon as possible. This was her final statement before execution: "I'd just like to say I'm sailing with the Rock and I'll be back like Independence Day with Jesus, June 6, like the movie, big mothership and all. I'll be back."[38] Wuornos did return, in a manner of speaking. Her life and crimes were the subject of a critically acclaimed 2003 film, *Monster*, for which actress Charlize Theron won an Academy Award for her portrayal of Wuornos.

The differential treatment of women did not always mean better treatment, particularly once a woman actually ended up in prison. Women's prisons might be smaller, less restrictive, and less secure, but they were also typically more demeaning to women offenders and less inclined to offer support services and rehabilitation programs.

Liberation theory, which is based on analysis of the changing roles of women in society as exemplified in the impact of the women's liberation movement, suggests that women are not as likely to be given preferential treatment or differential treatment today. They are more likely to be viewed as the criminal equals of men in a system where women are moving more into important decision-making roles as well. Laws that treat all offenders equally, particularly drug laws, have greatly reduced the likelihood that women, even the mothers of small children, will get favorable treatment by the system.

Despite these professions of **equal opportunity imprisonment,** the plain truth is that the prevalence of women in the prison population would not have increased significantly over the past three decades were it not for the War on Drugs. In the early 1970s, when fewer than 10,000 women were in prison in America, about a thousand were drug criminals and the rest about equally divided between violent and property crimes. Thirty years later, at the end of 2002, 97,500 women were in state and federal prisons. The two leading crimes among women inmates were drug trafficking and drug possession, accounting for one-third of the women in state prisons and two-thirds of the women in federal prisons.

In California, the state the with largest number of women in prison, the 1983 female inmate population was divided 42 percent crimes against persons, 41 percent crimes against property, 13 percent drug crimes, and 4 percent other. By 1999, the female inmate population was 43 percent drug crimes, 29 percent crimes against property, 24 percent crimes against persons, and 4 percent other.[39]

If the incarceration of women for drug crimes in America had held at the 1970s rate, 20,000 fewer women would have been behind prison bars in 2002, and the percentage of women in the prison population would be around 5 percent, about what it has averaged historically. The War on Drugs has been fought on many fronts, but the pitched battles have been fought against the urban underclass, mostly blacks and Hispanics who traffic in and consume crack cocaine. Large numbers of drug users who have dealt and used crack cocaine have found their way into America's prisons over the past twenty years. Drugs are at the heart of the upsurge in women's imprisonment today.

Imprisonment for drugs has particularly affected the numbers of minority women in prison. Recent Bureau of Justice Statistics estimates suggest that about eleven of 1,000 women will go to prison in their lifetime. This likelihood varies by race—five out of 1,000 white women, fifteen out of 1,000 Hispanic women, and thirty-six out of 1,000 black women. What is most interesting here is that the projected imprisonment rate of white males, forty-four per 1,000, is not that much higher overall than that of black females. At current imprisonment rates and life expectancies, black females have almost the same lifetime prospect of imprisonment as white males.[40] As the number of women in prison has increased so rapidly in such a short time, the number of women's prisons has also increased quickly. California alone has gone from one women's prison holding a thousand inmates in the early 1970s to five prisons holding more than 10,000 in 2002. The two largest women's prisons in America, Valley State Prison and the Central California Women's Facility, both located outside Chowchilla, hold more than 7,000 inmates; these two prisons could have housed every female felon imprisoned in America thirty years ago.

The states that imprison men at high rates tend to do the same with women. The five states with the highest overall incarceration rates at the end of 2002 were the following:

Inmates per 100,000

	Population
Louisiana	794
Mississippi	743
Texas	692
Oklahoma	667
Alabama	612[41]

The five states with the highest incarceration rates for women in 1998 were the following:

Inmates per 100,000

	Women Residents
Oklahoma	122
Texas	102
Louisiana	94
Mississippi	77
California	67[42]

The 1980s was the biggest single decade in the history of building prisons for women; thirty-four new prisons for women were built in this decade. Many of the new prisons are designed with more maximum-security features to house a "deeper-end," more long-term and hard-core population. There is still a perception in corrections that women's prisons are "nicer" than men's prisons, but women in prison are still routinely described as harder to manage and more difficult to deal with day to day than men in prison. Correctional officials do not mean that the women are more violent or escape prone, but they say that women complain too much, get involved in too many petty disputes, and do not adapt as well to prison routines. The women inmates, who almost universally are addressed as "ladies," for their part complain that they are treated like children and written up for petty violations that would be ignored in a men's prison. The title of Jean Harris's second book, more detailed in her observations on prison life, was *They Always Call Us Ladies*.

Incarceration is a different experience for women (this will be discussed at length in the next chapter). Women in American society are not used to being locked up, to living in the congregate (such as men in the military), or to being sent "away" and separated from their families. About a fourth of women are either pregnant or have infants when they arrive in prison. They cannot keep their children with them. Pregnant inmates have to give their children to someone—usually the prisoner's mother or sister, less often the baby's father—or turn them over to the state for foster care or adoption within a few days after giving birth.

About 80 percent of women in prison are mothers. It is no surprise that women prisoners report that separation from their children and family outside ranks as the greatest pain of imprisonment. Women's prisons are often located far away from the urban population centers the women come from, and most family members lack the resources for convenient travel. Visiting is often limited or restricted, with little opportunity for prisoners to meet privately with their children, their mothers, and their sisters. The security environment of prison also discourages many mothers from wanting their children to visit. Who wants to see her four-year-old "assume the position," hands on wall, while a security officer frisks him? Some prisons are much more open to visiting than others, and new programs allowing mothers to spend more time with their children are always being established, but much more needs to be done to promote family cohesion as a prison policy rather than just a collection of incidental programs.

Jean Harris resolved, shortly after she entered Bedford Hills, not to let the prison—either the administration or the inmates—beat her down. Influenced by the writings of psychiatrist Viktor Frankl, Auschwitz survivor and author of *Man's Search for Meaning*, her credo became; "No matter what they do to me I will decide how I will react to what they do." She determined not to serve her prison time in idleness and self-pity. She writes,

> It took time, but I have finally come to understand that the only way for me to be useful to the women in here, and for us to reach one another, is through their children, and that is the route I have finally taken. I should add quickly that it was not altruism that led me there. I was looking for a reason to be alive.[43]

Harris began working in the prison's Children's Center, where visiting took place. The center's director, Sister Elaine Roulet, suggested that Harris teach a parenting class. In a 1998 interview, she described her reaction: "I had never heard the word—**parenting**—before I went to prison," Harris said. "I thought it was prison jargon."

She spent months reading the latest pediatric studies and observing mothers with their children. "That's one of the things I'm really grateful for about the prison. It was just an eye-opening experience."

Yet what she saw often broke her heart.

"It was the lack of gentleness toward their children that struck me first, even though they were loving mothers. They had been smacked when they did something wrong and now they were doing the smacking. . . . One young woman in my class was totally deaf in one ear and partially deaf in the other and it was from her mother smacking her in the head."

"Gentle is what we've got to teach them," Harris told herself, and she found a creative visual prop to help her. To every member of the class, she gave a color reproduction of Michelangelo's Sistine Chapel, of God reaching out "to touch life into Adam."

"God looks very powerful," she told them. "He could have smacked life into Adam, but what he did was reach out and just barely touch life into Adam. And that's what you have to do. . . . They loved that picture. They always asked for an extra copy to send home to a friend."[44]

Jean Harris was granted clemency by New York Governor Mario Cuomo in 1983 and released from prison. She has continued to write and lecture on prison issues in the years since. In her public appearances, she sets out this agenda for her audiences:

1. Higher education for prisoners.
2. Preschool care for the poor children most likely to fall into criminality.
3. Church members going into prison to teach, "not just the Bible but whatever talent they have—art, music, writing, poetry, civics and economics, basic things like the importance of voting."
4. Church-operated day-care centers; "the greatest thing you can do for prisons, trying to save the next generation from going to prison."[45]

The money that Harris raises from her appearances and her books goes to the Children of Bedford Fund, which pays for boarding school tuition, books, and tutoring for children of inmates.

STATE VERSUS FEDERAL, PRISONS VERSUS JAILS

America has three types of secure custody institutions for adult criminals: state prisons, federal prisons, and local jails. Just as the role of each type of institution is different, so is its inmate population. State prisons hold convicted felons, about half of whom are in prison for crimes against persons. The other half are predominantly repeat offenders convicted of crimes against property, drug crimes, and public order offenses. An "average" prison term is about five to six years; an "average" length of stay is about two and a half to three years. The average sentence length and the average length of stay would be longer for crimes against persons than for the other offenses; truth-in-sentencing provisions and parole ineligibility have made it more difficult for persons convicted of violent crimes to get out of prison early over the past decade.

If you were an inmate in a state prison, you would most likely be confined in a medium-custody institution with other criminals who are about equally likely to be locked up for a violent or nonviolent crime. More of the violent criminals serving long-term sentences or those criminals who have been involved in violent incidents or serious disciplinary infractions since coming to prison will be passed up the chain to the maximum-security or close/high-security institutions. They will cross paths with other inmates who have been in higher-security institutions but are no longer considered management problems. The modern state prison system, built around classification and multiple security levels, moves inmates up and down the security ladder according to its perception of their behavior—good or bad—in confinement.

As a state inmate, your environment at any given time—the housing, the staff, and the other inmates—is determined by the institution's assessment of what level of custody you require. Special needs, such as physical or mental health, protection concerns, or treatment needs, may be important in particular cases. The management theory is to move the inmate through the system through progressively lower levels of security until he or she reaches an open security status—nonsecure placement in a work release or prerelease facility—shortly before discharge. Because most states do not have that many open beds available, however, most prisoners continue to discharge directly from secure prisons, some from the highest-level institutions because of misconduct or security threat status within the prison. When the sentence ends, generally, the inmate has to be discharged, unless he is facing other charges or sentences or civil confinement as a sex offender or mentally ill person.

The same concepts guide the placement of inmates within the federal system, except the federal system is now larger than any single state system and has a lot more prisons to move inmates around in if it wishes to do so. Some inmates tour the country in the course of a federal prison term (though what they see from inside prison walls and fences looks pretty much the same no matter where they are). The two most distinctive features of federal criminals are, first, that most are drug criminals, and, second, that many are citizens of other nations.

In 2001, about 55 percent of federal prisoners were convicted of drug crimes. Immigration offenses (10.5 percent) and weapons crimes, such as possession of a firearm by a convicted felon (8.8 percent), were the second and third most common offenses, followed by robbery (7.2 percent) in fourth place. Although, as John DiIulio has pointed out, many federal prisoners have some kind of violent history, the great majority of them—88 percent—are in prison for nonviolent crimes.[46] Louisiana has more murderers in just one prison—2,500 in the state penitentiary at Angola—than the Bureau of Prisons has in its entire prison system.

Almost a third of the federal prison population is made up of foreign nationals, mostly from Mexico and other Latin American countries. If you plan to either work in or become an inmate in the federal prison system, you should definitely learn to speak Spanish before you get to prison. Federal prisoners are also in general a few years older than state prisoners, more likely to be married, and substantially better educated. These variables, while not necessarily making them "nicer" inmates, do make them in general easier to manage. The makeup of the population (supplemented by a good classification scheme) has a lot to do with the generally lower-security environment that prevails throughout the federal system.

Jails are another matter. The most correct way to think of the jail population is to think of two different groups, a short-term population, the ones who will be here today, and a long-term population, the ones who will still be here in ninety days. When the National Jail Census took its last one-day census in 1999, it found that about 35 percent of inmates had been in jail a week or less. Most of these newcomers would have been recently arrested, joining the category of pretrial inmates who made up 60 percent of the total jail population in 2002. Many in this group turn over rapidly. Although no recent national breakdown of jail inmates by level of offense exists, perhaps half of these confined pretrial inmates are misdemeanants whose stay in jail is brief, from a few minutes to a few days; about 75 percent of all arrests are for misdemeanor and traffic offenses. Bail for these crimes is low, and even if they lack the financial resources to make bail, many qualify for the no-bail release on recognizance programs that flourish in many urban areas with large jail populations.

Some of these short-term inmates are working-class, middle-class, and upper-class citizens arrested for such crimes as driving under the influence, domestic violence, possession of drugs, and theft. Far more are lower class—the urban poor, adolescents and young adults, homeless street people, prostitutes, alcohol and drug abusers, and the mentally ill—who make up John Irwin's **rabble** (as discussed in chapter 5). Their minor crimes and nuisance public behavior—fighting, public drunkenness, theft and petty property crimes, and drug use—often result in arrest, sometimes dozens or even hundreds of arrests over a lifetime. They may not stay in jail very long on any particular charge, but when you examine their life history, some have spent more time behind bars than most felony offenders. These habitual misdemeanor offenders are often assigned to trusty positions in the jail doing the cooking, the laundry, the cleaning, and maintaining the sheriff's vehicle fleet.

The long-term inmates in the jail population are of several types. Some are misdemeanor criminals given fairly long sentences, from ninety days up to a year, in jail. Some are probation and parole violators held in jail under a detainer until revocation hearings are held to determine if they should be set free or sent to prison. Many are felony arrestees whose crime and prior record make them good prison candidates; if their bail is set at more than a few thousand dollars, most of them sit in jail until their case is over. Some will have the charges against them dismissed, some will plead guilty to get released with credit for time served and probation, and some will go straight to prison from jail on conviction.

In recent years, the greatest change in the long-term jail population has been in the number of felony state prisoners serving their terms in local jails. In 2002, about 71,000 state and federal felons were confined in local jails; this is just over a quarter of all sentenced inmates held in jails.[47] Housing state felons in local jails to save money has become most common in the South, where Louisiana (45 percent of state prisoners in local institutions), Tennessee (27 percent), Kentucky (23 percent), and Mississippi (20 percent) have come to rely more and more on jails to hold their prison overflow. These numbers continue to increase around the country as states delay deciding their future prison policies—whether to expand, which means building new prisons, or to push decarceration, which would result in closing existing prisons.

The jail itself does not divide its inmates into short and long term according to how long they are expected to remain behind bars. If it is a larger jail, it may place offenders in housing units—either cell blocks or pods—by level of dangerousness; in a smaller jail, everyone may be mixed together. If you are a middle-class offender stuck in a jail for a few days waiting for someone to come up with the money to get you out, this represents a chance for you to make new friends with people whose lifestyles are far different from your own. The 300 large jails, mostly in big cities, with a capacity of 1,000 inmates or more hold half of all jail inmates in America; a week in one of these facilities is an excellent way to sample our country's diverse cultural experience.

Primarily because of the number of misdemeanants in jail, the demographics of jail inmates differ slightly from those of prison inmates. The percentage of women in the jail population is higher—11.6 percent, compared to 6.7 percent in prison.[48] The numbers of whites (43.8 percent) have climbed again recently so that they are now more numerous than blacks (39.8 percent) or Hispanics (14.7 percent).

The jail is closer to the street than the prison is; it gets a lot of inmates who are still high on drugs or alcohol when they come in. It also gets more inmates who are mentally ill, some of them dangerously so. About one in six jail inmates held in jail at any given time is estimated to have a serious mental illness—between 600,000 and 1,000,000 admissions a year. Jails now hold more people receiving psychiatric treatment than public psychiatric hospitals do. More than thirty years ago, Dr. Marc Abramson, a California psychiatrist, originated the term **criminalization of the mentally ill** to describe what he saw as people who had been held in state hospitals were turned loose and entrusted to the care of community mental health clinics. Many of these former mental patients ended up homeless, psychotic, arrested, and in jail.[49] Today we often call this process **transinstitutionalization,** referring to the transfer of mental patients from hospitals to jails. In 1999, about 9 percent of jail inmates were taking some type of psychotropic medication, about the same number who were receiving some kind of mental health therapy or counseling.[50] No one who works in a jail would say that every inmate who needs medication or treatment gets it.

Although jail suicide rates have fallen by more than 50 percent in the past twenty years, jails still have more suicides each year than prisons do. About 35 percent of inmate deaths in jail in 1999 (324 of 919 total) were by suicide (the rate was fifty-four per 100,000 inmates), compared to 11 percent of prison deaths (twenty-six per 100,000 inmates).[51]

Jail inmates are also sicker than prison inmates, coming off the streets with diseases such as hepatitis, tuberculosis, and HIV that require immediate treatment. Many jail inmates get good treatment while in jail (or at least better treatment than they were getting on the street), only to discharge before they complete treatment. Back on the street, they fail to continue treatment, symptoms recur, and treatable diseases get worse and more resistant to further treatment. The people the sick former inmates interact with also come to share their diseases.

Much of this is related to the high incidence of substance abusers in the jail population. People whose lives are dominated by the consumption of alcohol and drugs have trouble sticking to a plan—a work plan, a family plan, a treatment plan, any kind of plan. When sheriffs say they are treating more mentally ill people than community mental health clinics are, they can also say they are treating far more substance abusers than all community facilities combined. The problem is, as we noted previously with mental health treatment, that this treatment is far from inclusive. More than half of all jails (which would be mostly the larger jails) provided some type of alcohol or drug treatment or counseling program in 1999, but these programs were available to only a small percentage of those identified as substance abusers and qualifying for treatment.

In comparison to prisons, the greater diversity (and more rapid turnover) of the inmate population is one of the jail's two most striking features. The other is the almost complete absence of anything purposeful to do. "Jail time is dead time," observers have said for a century, and the statement remains just as true in virtually all jails today. When you go through any jail and look at what the inmates are doing, you see people sleeping, playing cards and dominoes, watching TV, listening to music on headphones, reading, or just sitting around talking, killing time. About 15 percent of jail inmates have some sort of work assignment; perhaps a smaller number participate in various rehabilitative programs—literacy, GED, life skills, job skills, parenting, or anything else. In practically all jails (even before the advent of so-called faith-based initiatives), the most pervasive program was religious services, which usually drew a big congregation of inmates seeking any kind of relief from the terminal boredom that otherwise prevails in the jail.

Thus, if you're planning to become a federal prisoner, practice your Spanish; if you're planning to become a habitual jail inmate, practice doing nothing for long periods of time. We will look further at life behind bars in the next chapter.

KEY TERMS

chronic offender

first offender

functionally illiterate

substance abuse histories

regular drug users

broken family

cycle of violence

"root cause" of crime

sociopaths

antisocial personality
  disorder

caste system

Jean Harris

preferential treatment

chivalry

hidden crime

prostitution

Elizabeth Gurney Fry

Alderson

Mary Belle Harris

liberation theory

equal opportunity
  imprisonment

parenting

rabble

criminalization of the
  mentally ill

transinstitutionalization

NOTES

1. James Welch, *The Indian Lawyer* (New York: Penguin Books, 1991), p. 223.

2. These contrasting state and federal profiles in 1991 and 1997 are from the report of the General Accounting Office (GAO), "State and Federal Prisoners: Profiles of Inmate Characteristics in 1991 and 1997," U.S. General Accounting Office, May 2000, pp. 20–22, 25–26, 27–29, and 32–34.

3. Allen Beck, Darrell Gilliard, Lawrence Greenfeld, Caroline Harlow, Thomas Hester, Louis Jankowski, Tracy Snell, James Stephan, and Danielle Morton, "Survey of State Prison Inmates, 1991," U.S. Department of Justice, Bureau of Justice Statistics Report, March 1993, p. 11.

4. Paige M. Harrison and Allen J. Beck, "Prisoners in 2002," U.S. Department of Justice, Bureau of Justice Statistics Bulletin, July 2003, p. 10.

5. Ibid.

6. This table is adapted from one appearing in *Sourcebook of Criminal Justice Statistics 2001*, U.S. Department of Justice, Bureau of Justice Statistics (Washington, D.C.: U.S. Government Printing Office, 2002), p. 505.

7. GAO, "State and Federal Prisoners," p. 20.

8. Ibid., pp. 20 and 27.

9. Harrison and Beck, "Prisoners in 2002," p. 4.

10. Caroline Wolf Harlow, "Education and Correctional Populations," U.S. Department of Justice, Bureau of Justice Statistics Special Report, January 2003, p. 1.

11. Beck et al., "Survey of State Prison Inmates, 1991," p. 3.

12. Ibid., p. 26.

13. GAO, "State and Federal Prisoners," p. 21.

14. Ibid., pp. 20–21.

15. Ibid., p. 21.

16. Cathy Spatz Widom, "The Cycle of Violence," U.S. Department of Justice, National Institute of Justice, Research in Brief, October 1992, p. 1.

17. Burk Foster, Craig J. Forsyth, and Stasia Herbert, "The Cycle of Family Violence and Criminal Offenders: A Study of Inmates in One Louisiana Jail," *Free Inquiry in Creative Sociology* 22, no. 2 (November 1994): 1–5.

18. Patrick F. Fagan, "The Real Root Causes of Violent Crime: The Breakdown of Marriage, Family, and Community," *Backgrounder*, no. 1026 (March 17, 1995), p. 1.

19. Ibid., pp. 1–2.

20. Ibid., pp. 4–9.

21. Burk Foster and Francis Green III, "'Where Did I Go Wrong?' What the Inmates Said," unpublished paper, 1997, p. 6.

22. Ibid., pp. 7–9.

23. Jean Harris, *Stranger in Two Worlds* (New York: Macmillan, 1986), p. 262.

24. Joycelyn M. Pollock, *Women, Prison, and Crime*, 2nd ed. (Belmont, Calif.: Wadsworth Thompson Learning, 2002), pp. 53–55.

25. Lawrence A. Greenfeld and Tracy L. Snell, "Women Offenders," U.S. Department of Justice, Bureau of Justice Statistics Special Report, December 1999, p. 7.

26. Ibid, p. 9.

27. Ibid., pp. 5–6.

28. Ibid., p. 14.

29. Ibid., p. 4

30. Pollock, *Women, Prison, and Crime*, p. 57.

31. Beverly R. Fletcher, Garry L. Rolison, and Dreama G. Moon, "A Profile of Women Inmates in the State of Oklahoma," *Journal of the Oklahoma Criminal Justice Research Consortium* 1 (August 1994): 6.

32. Caroline Wolf Harlow, "Prior Abuse Reported by Inmates and Probationers," U.S. Department of Justice, Bureau of Justice Statistics Selected Findings, April 1999, pp. 2–3.

33. Pollock, *Women, Prison, and Crime*, pp. 60–61.

34. Laura M. Maruschak, "HIV in Prisons, 2000," U.S. Department of Justice, Bureau of Justice Statistics Bulletin, October 2002, p. 1.

35. As reported in Pollock, *Women, Prison, and Crime*, p. 65.

36. Barbara Owen, *"In the Mix": Struggle and Survival in a Women's Prison* (Albany: State University of New York Press, 1998), p. 11.

37. As reported in Harris, *Stranger in Two Worlds*, pp. 245–46.

38. "Aileen Wuornos: Killer Who Preyed on Truck Drivers," *www.crimelibrary.com/notorious_murders/women/wuornos/1.html*.

39. Center on Juvenile and Criminal Justice, "California Prison Growth," May 29, 2003, p. 2, *www.cjcj.org/cpp/ccf_growth.php*.

40. Greenfeld and Snell, "Women Offenders," p. 11.

41. Harrison and Beck, "Prisoners in 2002," p. 1.

42. Greenfeld and Snell, "Women Offenders," p. 9.

43. Harris, *Stranger in Two Worlds*, pp. 262–63.

44. Nan Cobbey, "Jean Harris: A New Life after 12 Years' Prison Education," Episcopal Life Selections, *http://gc2003.episcopalchurch.org/episcopal-life/JeanHarr.html*.

45. Ibid.

46. Harrison and Beck, "Prisoners in 2002," p. 11.

47. Ibid., p. 6

48. Paige M. Harrison and Jennifer C. Karberg, "Prison and Jail Inmates at Midyear 2002," U.S. Department of Justice, Bureau of Justice Statistics Bulletin, April 2003, p. 8.

49. Spencer P. M. Harrington, "New Bedlam: Jails—Not Psychiatric Hospitals—Now Care for the Indigent Mentally Ill," *The Humanist* 59 (May 1999): 12.

50. James J. Stephan, "Census of Jails, 1999," U.S. Department of Justice, Bureau of Justice Statistics, August 2001, p. 40.

51. Ibid., p. 8.

FURTHER READING

Archer, Jeffrey. *A Prison Diary*. New York: St. Martin's Press, 2003.

Archer, Jeffrey. *Purgatory: A Prison Diary Volume 2*. New York: St. Martin's Press, 2004.

Harris, Jean. *Marking Time: Letters from Jean Harris to Shana Alexander*. New York: Charles Scribner's Sons, 1991.

Pollock, Joycelyn M. *Women, Prison, and Crime*. 2nd ed. Belmont, Calif.: Wadsworth Thomson Learning, 2002.

Stohr, Mary K., and Craig Hemmens. *The Inmate Prison Experience*. Upper Saddle River, N.J.: Pearson/Prentice Hall, 2004.

WEB AND VIDEO RESOURCES

The Canadian *Journal of Prisoners on Prisons* is what it says—prisoners writing about prisoners but with an "academically oriented" approach. Its address is *www.jpp.org*. It has been inactive lately, but articles from old issues remain available online.

National Public Radio's *Prison Diaries* series—a radio documentary of life behind bars in two state prisons—is available at *www.npr.org/programs/atc/prisondiaries*.

The Other Side of the Wall (*www.prisonwall.org*) is a clearinghouse with a huge collection of prison writings and links to other prison-related sites, including music and films. It emphasizes California prisoners.

Inmate Classified (*www.inmate.com*) is organized around a "Pen Pals" page and a "Prison Links" page.

Prison Talk Online (*www.prisontalk.com*) is a Web community of about 20,000 members supporting prisoners.

The film *Monster* (2003) is based (not always precisely) on the story of serial killer Aileen Wuornos.

12 Who Should Be Behind Bars?

by James A. Gondles, Jr.

Statistics show that drug and alcohol abuse are significant problems within our nation's prisons. Eighty percent of inmates in state prisons report histories of drug and/or alcohol abuse. More than half of state inmates report that they were using drugs or alcohol when they committed the crimes that led to their incarceration.

These numbers are staggering. Although no part of our society is immune to the problems associated with alcohol and drugs, the connection between substance abuse, crime, and corrections is particularly remarkable. And there is no simple way to deal with those who commit crimes while under the influence of drugs or alcohol.

Individuals should not be allowed to use drug or alcohol abuse as an excuse for their actions. Those who break the law must expect to pay the price for their crimes. Often, this price includes time within our nation's correctional system.

If we are to fight crime effectively, we must do more than punish it. We need to address the factors that cause individuals to commit crime. Far too often, one of the major causes of crime is a dependence on drugs or alcohol. Alcohol is associated with the majority of violent crimes, and the desire for drugs is what pushes many offenders into criminal lifestyles because stealing money and property supports their expensive habits.

Prison and jail populations have skyrocketed during the past two decades, spurring new construction and often generating crowded conditions in our institutions and facilities. Substance abuse is directly and indirectly responsible for a large portion of this population increase. The high number of incarcerated substance abuse offenders exhausts shrinking budgets and strains scarce correctional resources.

Corrections has many objectives: punishment, retribution, deterrence, incapacitation and rehabilitation. The severity of a crime has much to do with the punishment, and officials must always consider public safety when deciding what to do with a convicted offender. However, correctional experts have long agreed that corrections' objectives often can be met by using the least restrictive environment that is reasonably possible. That is, not all offenders need to be locked up behind bars.

Finding different ways to punish some offenders helps to relieve crowding and reduce costs. It also places many offenders in situations in which they are more amenable to rehabilitation. This has not been lost on our political leaders or on the public. Public support for alternative sentencing is especially strong for programs that divert nonviolent offenders from incarceration into other forms of punishment and rehabilitation, especially when programs are combined with treatment and/or restitution.

In California, under Proposition 36, petty drug offenders are now being sent to community-based treatment in lieu of incarceration, and most probationers and parolees who violate a drug-related condition of community release receive treatment rather than reincarceration. Spurred by the success of this program and Arizona's 1996 Proposition 200, there are additional sentencing reform proposals on the ballot in Florida, Michigan and Ohio this November.

These are all steps in the right direction. Dangerous offenders should be locked up. But with many nonviolent drug offenders, there are effective alternatives. We can continue to place these individuals into our nation's prison system, but unless we do more to help cure their addictions, more crimes will be committed, there will be more victims and more people will be returned to our prisons and we will have done nothing to solve the problems of substance abuse that plague our society.

10 PRISON LIFE

The prisoner's world is an atomized world. Its people are atoms interacting in confusion. . . . Its own community is without a well-established social structure. Recognized values produce a myriad of conflicting attitudes. There are no definite communal objectives. There is no consensus for a common goal. The inmates' conflict with officialdom and opposition toward society is only slightly greater in degree than conflict and opposition among themselves. Trickery and dishonesty overshadow sympathy and cooperation. . . . It is a world of individuals whose daily relationships are impersonalized. It is a world of "I," "me," and "mine," rather than "ours," "theirs," and "his." Its people are thwarted, unhappy, yearning, resigned, bitter, hating, revengeful. Its people are improvident, inefficient, and socially illiterate. . . . Except for the few, there is bewilderment. No one knows, the dogmas and codes notwithstanding, exactly what is important. . . .

It is into this complex maze of the prison world that the newly-committed inmate comes.

— DONALD CLEMMER, *THE PRISON COMMUNITY*, 1958

INTRODUCTION

This chapter looks at life behind bars as it is lived by men and women serving terms in prison. Each year, 600,000 or more men and women enter prison as newly convicted felons or parole violators. Imprisonment is a hard, life-altering experience for the men and women sentenced to "felony time." Everyone who enters prison experiences "prisonization," in Donald Clemmer's term, but the experience depends on what kind of prison the criminal is sent to, how he or she is classified, where he or she lives and works within the prison, and many other circumstances, some of which the inmate brings to prison, such as gang affiliation or family support, and others waiting on arrival, such as enemies waiting to get even or rehabilitation programs that might change the direction of the prisoner's life. After reading the material in this chapter, you should be familiar with:

1. The evolution of prison life.
2. Sociological views of prison life.
3. Prison life today.
4. The life of women in prison.

5. Prison violence.

6. Sex in prison.

7. Prison gangs.

8. Death in prison.

9. Perspectives on prison life.

PRISON LIFE: WELCOME TO PRISON

The steel prison door slides shut behind you. The sound is more a solid metallic click than the old-fashioned heavy clang you had expected. This is your cell in the state's newest maximum-security prison. You look around the space that will be your home for the next few years. You hold your arms out to the side—you can touch both walls. Six feet across, maybe nine feet deep, appearing to be poured out of some hi-tech metal alloy that gives off a dull gray shine under the recessed fluorescent lighting. Two wall-mounted bunk beds on the left, with two metal footlockers underneath the bottom bunk. Opposite are two metal desks, also attached to the wall, with three shelves above and a molded metal chair pushed underneath. In the back left corner are two metal cabinets. Probably the closets, you think. In the middle of the back wall is a shiny metallic sink with a metal mirror above it. The toilet sits in the open in the right rear corner of the cell. Privacy was apparently not an issue in the design of this cell: bathroom functions are to be performed within three feet of whoever would be working at the rear desk.

The cell is cold and appears to be indestructible—a stainless-steel cocoon in which the Terminator would feel right at home. Well, you think, it can't get any worse than this. The door clicks open behind you. A huge figure stands in the doorway. My God, you think, it *is* the Terminator. He is over six feet tall and must weigh at least 300 pounds. He has to turn sideways to get through the door. His head is shaved. His eyes are, well, beady under a jutting brow. He has tattoos that run up both arms. He looks you over without smiling before he speaks. "You're the new fish? I'm Bubba, your cellie. Do what I say, and we'll get along just fine. Don't mess with my stuff. Cross me, and there'll be trouble. I hope you like to play dominoes. Can we get along?" You nod, grateful that his accent is southern and not Teutonic, and he lies down on the bottom bunk. You turn to look out through the bars at the concrete wall ten feet away. You feel many things, but mostly what you feel is out of place, like a character in a science fiction novel you started but never finished in a high school English class. The title was *Stranger in a Strange Land*. You wonder how it turned out.

Bubba has fallen asleep on his bunk. He is snoring, and then he farts softly and sighs, like he is in a happy place. The cell smells of stale sweat and smoke. You would like to climb up on the top bunk to rest also, but you are not certain about the risk of waking up Bubba. So you sit down in a chair and stare out through the bars. You think about your past, particularly the fistfight you had with the deputy sheriff in jail—what was it about, how long you'd been talking on the phone?—that got you classified as maximum custody and put you in this cell with your new pal Bubba. I wish I hadn't messed up on probation, you think, I wish I was in a dorm. I don't really belong in prison, yet here I am. You try not to think about the future.

Welcome to prison, or to the middle-class American's worst nightmare of imprisonment: life in a cell with a roommate like Bubba. The views of most Americans about the experience of imprisonment—"doing time"—probably run to extremes. On the one hand, you have prison life as depicted in *The Shawshank Redemption*. Captain Hadley, the warden's sadistic, foul-mouthed enforcer, inflicts a severe beating on a new inmate known only as "Fat Ass," whose offense was complaining that he did not belong in prison. Fat Ass dies untreated in the prison hospital; no one knows his name or even seems to care. The hero, Andy Dufresne, is harassed, beaten, and raped by a gang of predatory homosexuals known as "the Sisters." The prison administration is corrupt and completely arbitrary. Both guards and other inmates hold life-and-death power over the prisoners like Andy and his best friend, Red Redding. Prisoners struggle to hold on to hope and humanity in a world where terrible things can happen to anyone at any time. This is the view of prisons as they used to be.

The modern contrasting view is that of the "country club prison," a sort of prison resort where white-collar criminals and politicians—and maybe gangsters and other rich and lucky inmates—do easy time. The prisoners do pretty much what they want. Their rooms are private and nicely furnished. The staff is there to serve their needs. In the absence of work, all forms of recreation abound. Prisoners play tennis, swim, play a round or two of golf, and then retire with their spouses or girlfriends to the prison motel for conjugal visits. They cannot leave, of course, except for the frequent furloughs they are allowed to go to town, but all in all life in the country club prison is comfortable.

Two views of prison life; which one is more real today? The Big House view of prison life on which *Shawshank* is based is surely more realistic, particularly for its time, 1947 to 1966, than the country club view ever has been. Indeed, in prison circles, the country club prison is often compared to the Loch Ness monster—a creature that is the object of much speculation and controversy but that no one can establish has ever really existed. Prisons have always come much closer to the sense of dread and terror implicit in the Big House than to the notion of comfort and relaxation associated with the country club prison.

THE EVOLUTION OF PRISON LIFE

For the convicted felon, prison life has changed as the nature of the institution itself has changed. Some changes reflect social trends or developments; many have to do as much with prison management philosophy and public policies as they do with the inmates. We can trace the evolution of ordinary prison life through five stages, from the end of the eighteenth century to the beginning of the twenty-first:

1. The prepenitentiary jail
2. The penitentiary
3. The Big House
4. The correctional institution
5. The contemporary prison warehouse

In the late 1700s, life in confinement was life in jail waiting for trial, sentencing, or punishment. Prisoners of all sorts were mixed together; the only ones who got better treatment were the ones with money who could afford to pay for nicer quarters. Jail conditions were primitive and close. Jails were dirty and unhealthy. Epidemics and malnutrition were common problems. Prisoners had no activities and no recreation. Violence and exploitation of women and younger inmates were commonplace. The themes of life in this institution, the predecessor to the penitentiary, were degradation and idleness. Even for temporary housing of the rabble of society, jails were beneath the standards of civilized men and women.

The jail's replacement as the repository for serious criminals was the penitentiary. The penitentiary of the early to late 1800s was intended to be an improvement over the worst features of the jail. For most inmates, penitentiary life was better. Inmates had work to do, either individual craft work or labor in groups. They were better fed and cared for, and isolation in individual cells made incarceration physically safer. The most undesirable features of inmate life were isolation, brutal punishment for disciplinary violations, and extreme regimentation in the daily routine. From the inmate's point of view, the good things about imprisonment in this era were that rates of imprisonment were low (well under 100 per 100,000 population in all states throughout the 1800s) and sentences were short. The penitentiary was a dreadful place (though its conditions were no worse than those in the urban slums from which most prisoners came), but not many people went there, and if you could deal with the isolation, silence, and monotony, you would not do a lot of time.

As the reformative ideals of the penitentiary yielded to the more practical objectives of economic productivity and efficient management, the Big House model emerged by the early 1900s. Many of these older fortress prisons are still in use a century later. This prison was a bureaucratic, high-walled, maximum-security factory in which most prisoners worked long hours six days a week. Regimentation and routine remained the order of the day, but the more repressive measures of earlier institutions, such as silence and the lockstep, were relaxed or abolished altogether—so, unfortunately for prison officials, was prison labor, whose abolition during the 1930s left prisons full of idle, angry men who became increasingly difficult to manage. Prisons were no longer so isolated from society, and prison wardens were no longer absolute despots who could run their institutions without concern for what the public or politicians might think.

The quandary of what to do with 200,000 increasingly idle state and federal convicts was dramatized by the prison riots of the early 1950s. If work was no longer the main focus of imprisonment (and we should stress that in the federal system and in the southern prison farm states, hard labor continued uninterrupted during this era), what other activities could be found to take its place? Over the next two decades, three principal types of activities developed as answers to this question:

1. **Rehabilitation.** Prisons began to offer a much broader range of programs— vocational training, educational, religious, and treatment oriented—open to far more inmates than previously.
2. **Recreation.** Sports, movies, arts and crafts, and free-time activities proliferated.
3. **Self-improvement.** Inmates were allowed more time and resources to read and study on their own and to form clubs and other organizations devoted to particular interests—twelve-step, literary and political discussion, civic (both internal or prison-improvement and external benefiting specific

groups, such as juvenile delinquents, or society as a whole), dramatic and performing arts, social, and religious.

Whatever value these activities may have in prison, the main reason for their advancement (or toleration) by prison officials was to fill the time no longer devoted to work. They were intended to give inmates something to do. How well did this scheme work? Perhaps satisfactorily in a few prisons but not in most.

Ex-convict Malcolm Braly, the author of *False Starts: A Memoir of San Quentin and Other Prisons*, wrote of doing time in the 1950s:

> The hardest part of serving time is the predictability. Each day moves like every other. You *know* nothing different can happen. You focus on tiny events, a movie scheduled weeks ahead, your reclass, your parole hearing, things far in the future, and slowly, smooth day by day, draw them to you. There will be no glad surprise, no spontaneous holiday, and a month from now, six months, a year, you will be just where you are, doing just what you're doing, except you'll be older.
>
> This airless calm is produced by rigid routine. Custody doesn't encourage spontaneity. Walk slow, the Cynic says, and don't make any fast moves. Each morning you know where evening will find you. There is no way to avoid your cell. When everyone marched into the block you would be left alone in the empty yard. Each Monday describes every Friday. Holidays in prison are only another mark of passing time and for many they are the most difficult days. Most of the outrages that provide such lurid passages in the folklore of our prisons are inspired by boredom. Some grow so weary of this grinding sameness they will drink wood alcohol even though they are aware this potent toxin may blind or kill them. Others fight with knives to the death and the survivor will remark, "It was just something to do."[1]

Piri Thomas, the author of *Down These Mean Streets* and *Seven Long Times*, writes of his routine as a prisoner in New York at about the same time:

> Every day at Great Meadows Correctional Institute was the same. Our lives were regulated by the sound of a trumpet. It blared at 7:30 A.M. every morning to get us up for breakfast and work. It blared again at 12:00 noon for lunch, and at 3:30 P.M. it signaled the end of the workday and time for supper. There was also yard recreation, and then around 5:00 P.M. it sounded for lock-in time. We remained in our cells from fourteen to sixteen hours to await another day of the trumpet.
>
> Saturdays and Sundays we were off and had yard privileges most of the day, until 5:00 P.M. In summertime, we had movies on Sunday; in wintertime, we had them on Saturday and Sunday. You could either go to the movies, stay in the yard, or keep to your cell. You couldn't go home.[2]

This period is often called the rehabilitation era, although it is clear that rehabilitation was not the dominant theme. But other changes were taking place in society that had their effects within prisons. Prisoners were not only more interested in society—society was more interested in them. Activists of many stripes, from traditional religious groups to political revolutionaries, found it easier to visit men and women in prison. The civil rights movement, which broke down the barriers separating the races in society, did the same in prison a few years later. Black convicts who had been kept in segregated and subordinate status—not only in the Old South, where they had made up the majority of the prison population since Reconstruction, but in the North and West as well—became a greater force in prison society, and prisoners as a whole began to get greater access to the courts. Prisoners who had previously enjoyed few legal rights began to find, during the due process revolution of the 1960s, that the courts would listen to their complaints, define their rights in confinement, and intervene to deal with bad living conditions and abuses of power by prison officials.

These important changes—social, racial, and legal—undermined the remnants of the old social order in prisons. Most prisons went through periods of extreme internal instability at some point during the 1960s and 1970s. The symptoms of instability were easy to see—murders and assaults, strikes and riots, litigation, scandals and inquiries, and changes of administration. The causes of instability were harder to define. Too few resources were made available to prison officials, perhaps, especially as they related to understaffing. This resulted in the shift of more power into inmate hands, aggravating internal relations between prisoners and custodians. Overcrowding was becoming a problem as prison populations increased after the early 1970s. Lack of classification and inadequate mental health housing intensified conflict between inmates who did not mix well in the volatile prison environment. Some prison officials blamed outside reformers and the political radicalization of inmates for stirring things up.

The relaxation of internal controls made it easier for inmates—either as individuals or in groups—to engage in violence against other inmates or guards or to draw attention to their political causes; or perhaps, as some critics have suggested, this period of turmoil simply exposed the bankruptcy of the entire penitentiary-based theory of punishment—the notion of imprisonment resulting in the betterment of the criminal and society. These critics would say that all the problems that became so visible in American prisons in the 1960s and 1970s, highlighted in such works as Jessica Mitford's *Kind and Usual Punishment: The Prison Business* (1974) and Leonard Orland's *Prisons: Houses of Darkness* (1975), had been there all along; they had been minimized only by rigid structure and hidden by the high walls. Once the absolute controls were relaxed and people were allowed to see what was going on, the complete futility of the prison as a social institution became apparent.

SOCIOLOGICAL VIEWS OF PRISON LIFE

Most of the early accounts of prison life were written either by inmates or prison officials. Prisons were closed institutions. Occasionally, distinguished visitors, such as Dickens or Beaumont and Tocqueville, would be allowed inside, but objective outside views of prison life were rare. Scholars began to take a strong research interest in the maximum-security prison around the middle of the twentieth century. The most influential (and in many respects still the most comprehensive and interesting to read) of the sociological studies of prison life was Donald Clemmer's *The Prison Community*. In the early 1930s, Clemmer had worked as a sociologist at the Illinois State Prison at Menard, a typical maximum-security prison of its time with 2,300 inmates and 230 employees. In 1940, Clemmer combined his research and observations into the first edition of *The Prison Community*. He updated the text in 1958, and it continues to influence thinking about prison life today.

Clemmer writes about the prison as a social organization. He observes the prisoners' culture and demographics; the prison's organization, social groups, social relations, and social controls; and what the inmates do—leisure time, work, and sex. His premise is that prison is a microcosm of society—a particularized setting in which inmates create a social system based on life outside of prison but within the limitations imposed by the prison environment. He compares the new prisoner to the immigrant entering American society. Immigrants undergo assimilation, while prisoners undergo **prisonization,** defined as "the taking on in greater or less degree of the folkways, mores, customs, and general culture of the penitentiary."

Clemmer wrote about prisonization,

> Every man who enters the penitentiary undergoes prisonization to some extent. The first and most obvious integrative step concerns his status. He becomes at once an anonymous figure in a subordinate group. A number replaces a name. He wears the clothes of the other members of the subordinate group. He is questioned and admonished. He soon learns that the warden is all-powerful. He soon learns the ranks, titles, and authority of various officials. And whether he uses the prison slang or argot or not, he comes to know its meanings. Even though a new man may hold himself aloof from other inmates and remain a solitary figure, he finds himself within a few months referring to or thinking of the keepers as "screws," the physician as the "croaker" and using the local nicknames to designate persons.[3]

The conduct of prisoners in the penitentiary was measured against the **convict code:**

> The fundamental principle of the code may be stated thus: Inmates are to refrain from helping prison or government officials in matters of discipline, and should never give them information of any kind, and especially the kind which may work harm to a fellow prisoner. Supplementary to this, and following from it, is the value of loyalty among prisoners in their dealing with each other.[4]

The rules of the code could be expressed like commandments:

1. "Do your own time."
2. "Don't be a rat."
3. "Be a man."
4. "Don't interfere."
5. "Don't talk to the guards."

The concept was that each inmate was responsible for himself and for maintaining solidarity with other inmates in opposition to the values of the dominant culture, in prison represented by the guards and the administration. Men who followed the code often called themselves **convicts;** those who did not or who obviously identified with the values of the **free world** were called **inmates.** Calling a convict an inmate was a fistfighting insult.

One aspect of Clemmer's research was the compilation of common words of the **prison argot**—the language of imprisonment, shared by prisoners and staff. Clemmer compiled a "dictionary" of 1,063 slang words and terms used in prison conservation or writing; he includes an entire appendix made up of the most common words of the prisoner's vocabulary, from which this selection is adapted:

Big house: a penitentiary

Bug: an insane person

Bug doctor: a psychiatrist

Croaker: the prison physician

Dozens: a series of vulgar and profane epithets, usually about the inmate's parentage

Fish: one newly arrived in prison

Jocker: the male role in homosexual behavior

Junk: any narcotic

Kid: a young male prostitute

Rat: a stool pigeon

Screw: a guard

Shiv: a knife, usually hand fashioned and contraband

Sister: a male homosexual[5]

Syndicate: a group of convicts in prison which by means of bribery of officials or other sinister methods control the better jobs and privileges among the convicts

Prison society was often viewed as being shaped like a pyramid or, more correctly, a diamond. At the top were the professional criminals, assisted by their lieutenants in the second level. The bulk of ordinary cons made up the bulge around the middle. Squares, rats, and bugs made up the lower level. At the very bottom were the child molesters ("baby rapers"), who as the lowest of the low often got paid back in kind in prison for what they had done outside.

Clemmer pointed out that every inmate was subject to the **universal factors of imprisonment**—acceptance of an inferior role, the facts concerning the prison's organization, new habits of daily life, the local language, the idea that the environment should minister to his needs, and the desire for a good job to make it easier for him to "do his time and get out." He pointed out that several other factors also shaped the extent of the individual's degree of prisonization:

1. The length of sentence
2. The prisoner's personality and relationships before imprisonment
3. His relations with persons outside the walls
4. The extent of his integration into prison groups
5. The prisoner's cell mate, cell block, and work assignments
6. The prisoner's willingness to participate in gambling, sex, and other illicit prison activities[6]

Inmates were not all of one type, Clemmer recognized. He discussed four different modes of affiliation:

1. *The complete "clique man."* The man who is a member of a group of three or more men who are all close friends. The group is permanent, and the association is very strong.

2. *The "group man."* A man is friendly with several others but the association is not as strong; he may also associate with others not in the group.

3. *The "semi-solitary man."* His social contacts are casual and he has no close friends.

4. *The "complete-solitary man."* He is generally alone, keeps constantly to himself, and shares nothing with other inmates.[7]

Forty percent of the inmates in Clemmer's prison were not part of any group. He recognized that men could be of one type at one time in their incarceration and another type at another time.

To contrast possible modes of prisonization, take two inmates. One is serving a short sentence. He had lived with his family outside, and his family members continue to visit him in prison. He keeps to himself in prison, spends a lot of time reading and writing letters to his girlfriend outside, and avoids getting in debt or crossing paths with inmates who might take advantage of him. He is cautious and always alert to danger. He does not want to do anything that would jeopardize his return to the free world.

The other inmate is serving a long sentence after having served two previous prison terms. He has lost touch with his family. His only friends are other convicts and ex-convicts. He is a member of one of the more influential prison **cliques,** or social groups, that control gambling and the sexual exploitation of younger inmates. Others might say that he is **institutionalized,** but as far as he is concerned, he is doing easy time. For him, prison is normal life. Although everyone talks about getting out of prison and the fun things they want to do on the street, the prospect of being released scares him; he knows that he enjoys a higher status in prison than he would have in the free world.

Clemmer was one of many scholars becoming interested in the subculture of the prison during this time. Hans Reimer had given a presentation, "Socialization in the Prison Community," at the American Prison Association meeting in 1937. In their 1940 article "The Prison as a Community," University of Washington sociologists Norman Hayner and Ellis Ash made a strong argument that the Big House subculture indoctrinated inmates more completely into criminal behavior. The 1930s "get tough on crime" approach advocated by FBI director J. Edgar Hoover's "machine-gun school of criminology" made it difficult to propose prison reforms.[8] They suggested that more prisoners should be housed in less expensive minimum-security institutions where they could better be prepared to reenter their own communities.

The penitentiary was commonly viewed as an arena in which two conflicting subcultures confronted each other. Hayner and Ash referred to the constant hostility between guards and inmates, like the relations between lions and their trainer. But as the old methods of control in the penitentiary broke down, the lions were growing more powerful, and the trainer was ever more on the defensive.

The time period—the late 1930s and 1940s—was important here. This was the end of the era of the factory prison, when industrial productivity—the reason for being of the Big House—was killed by restrictive federal legislation. As prisoners were left with little work to do and no immediate substitute activity to occupy their time, the difficulties of controlling idle inmates in huge prisons became obvious. The lion tamers were badly outnumbered, their whips no longer had the sting of old, and the lions had too much room in which to roam about. Observers had already noticed that only the support of the leading lions—their co-optation into the prison power structure—allowed their trainers to maintain the functioning of the Big House into the mid-twentieth century.

In the penitentiary, a long-term process was at work. Robert Johnson has suggested that while the early penitentiary offered a life essentially devoid of comfort or even distraction, the Big House routine was the culmination of a series of humanitarian milestones that made these prisons more accommodating.[9] Among these milestones were the replacement of corporal punishment by the use of solitary confinement (in "the hole"), the introduction of tobacco, and a general movement toward allowing internal freedom of association within the prison. Big House prisoners still worked hard, typically long hours six days a week, and they lived (and often worked as well) under strict racial segregation, but they were beginning to have more free time, and they were allowed to spend this time with other inmates—in multiman cells, in recreation, and particularly in the center of prison social life, **the yard,** the open space in the middle of the quadrangle of prison buildings.

Inmate trusties had been incorporated into the Big House workforce as prison populations had grown and pressures to hold down costs had increased in the years before the Great Depression. Jobs that had been performed by free people earlier were now assigned to inmates. In several southern states, this was most noticeable in the gun-toting convict guards who worked other inmates in the fields. But even in the more progressive states, inmates were given responsible work positions—as office clerks, work foremen, cell block runners and supervisors (such as Texas's "building tenders"), and hospital orderlies. This was not a new concept, exactly; even the warden of Eastern State in the 1830s had used an inmate as his butler, and prisons had always used inmates to cook, clean, deliver food, and run errands. In the later Big House years, however, inmates assumed more full-time responsibilities as part of the prison administration, and, more important, they assumed direct control of other inmates. They made work and housing assignments; maintained records; dispensed medicine, food, and property; and provided special favors with or without the supervision of prison staff. Trusties took orders from staff, and they also took orders—and bribes—from other inmate leaders whose authority was independent of the prison administration.

In *The Society of Captives* (1958), Gresham Sykes wrote about the evolution of the prison social system from absolute to shared authority. His book was based on three years of research at the New Jersey State Maximum Security Prison at Trenton, one of the oldest, best-known prisons in America and the scene of three riots in 1952. Sykes wrote about custody that "to understand the meaning of imprisonment, we must see prison life as something more than a matter of walls and bars, of cells and locks. We must see the prison as a society within a society."[10]

Relations between the custodians and the prisoners make up the heart of Sykes's analysis of prison life; "the prison exists in an uneasy compromise of liberty and restraint," he writes. The custodians, who in theory have absolute power to compel prisoners to do anything they want, cannot accomplish this total control throughout a major prison in which they are completely outnumbered by the inmates, in which inmate labor is a part of the institution's daily life, and in which inmates must be managed according to civilized standards. Why don't guards just carry clubs and mercilessly beat into submission every inmate who crosses them, or why don't guards carry guns and shoot down inmates for serious disciplinary violations? The obvious response is that these actions would lead to one of two extreme scenarios: (1) the prison would operate under martial law, and virtually all prisoners would be locked down all the time, which would be very expensive and a lot of trouble, or (2) the prisoners would take the clubs and guns away, riots would ensue, and we would revert to the first scenario.

Sykes refers to the accommodation of custodians and prisoners within prison walls as **corruption of authority**—"the imperfect enforcement of the organization's regulations and orders with the tacit acceptance of the officials"—and he sees it not as an evil but as a necessity to the prison of this era:

> The custodians to the New Jersey State Prison, far from being converted into brutal tyrants, are under strong pressure to compromise with their captives, for it is a paradox that they can insure their dominance only by allowing it to be corrupted. Only by tolerating violations of "minor" rules and regulations can the guard secure compliance in the "major" areas of the custodial regime. Ill-equipped to maintain the social distance which in theory separates the world of the officials and the world of the inmates, their suspicions eroded by long familiarity, the custodians are led into a *modus vivendi* with their captives which bears little resemblance to the stereotypical picture of guards and their prisoners.[11]

The struggle between prison guards and inmates, Sykes argued, is in part due to the practice of **deprivation** in prison operations. Deprivation means "the removal or withholding of something," usually something that the person would otherwise be entitled to. The **pains of imprisonment** result from several important deprivations:

1. Liberty, or freedom of movement
2. Goods and services, particularly their material possessions from the free world
3. Heterosexual relationships (more on this later in this chapter)
4. Autonomy, or the freedom to make choices
5. Security, or the safety of his person and property (Sykes quotes one New Jersey inmate who said, "The worst thing about prison is you have to live with other prisoners.")

In the absence of money (still contraband in many prisons today), an alternate economy developed. The principal medium of exchange was **cigarettes.** Want to get in on the football pool? Two packs. Want to get someone beat up? Two boxes (cartons). Want to get that cute seventeen-year-old boy assigned to your cell? Five boxes. Or you could borrow cigarettes to smoke, but be careful to repay your debts on time, or something physical may happen to you in return.

Like Clemmer, Sykes was interested in prison language, or argot, pointing out that it provided "a map of the inmate social system." Criminal argot, he argued, was not about secrecy (because the guards understood it as well as the inmates did) or symbolic membership in the underworld; it was a way to structure the prison experience. Sykes reported several argot terms that are still often used in discussing prison life by both prisoners and outsiders:

> **Rat** or squealer: one who betrays the inmates to the guards because it benefits him or because he identifies with the guards
>
> **Center man:** an inmate who shares the viewpoint of the guards

Gorilla: an inmate who takes what he wants by force or intimidation

Merchant or peddlar: an inmate who sells material goods to other inmates

Wolf: a masculine, aggressive homosexual

Punk: an inmate who may not appear feminine but who becomes a passive homosexual in prison

Fag: a feminine homosexual who engages in homosexuality because he likes it ("Punks are made, but fags are born.")

Ball buster: a rebellious inmate who challenges the authority of the guards unnecessarily

Real man: the standard of the code, the convict who endures imprisonment with dignity

Tough: a touchy, unstable inmate who "won't take anything" from other inmates

Hipster: an inmate who talks toughness or leadership but is hollow at the core[12]

Sykes discusses the interaction of inmates and guards within the unstable prison social system and the corruption of authority that occurs over time, "finally reaching a point where the inmates have established their own unofficial version of control. The custodians, in effect, have withdrawn to the walls to concentrate on their most obvious task, the prevention of escapes."[13] When something happens to upset this balance of power—scandal, investigation, political change, or a change of prison administration—the prisoner leadership becomes more unstable and proceeds toward the moment of explosion, the riot, such as those occurring in Trenton in 1952. Order is restored, reforms are made (or not), and the cycle begins anew.

In his book *Asylums: Essays on the Social Situation of Mental Patients and Other Inmates* (1962), sociologist Erving Goffman defined a **total institution** as a "place of residence and work where a large number of like-situated individuals, cut off from the wider society for an appreciable period of time, together lead an enclosed, formally administered round of life."[14] He described the features of total institutions:

A basic social arrangement in modern society is that the individual tends to sleep, play, and work in different places, with different co-participants, under different authorities, and without an over-all rational plan. The central feature of total institutions can be described as a breakdown of the barriers ordinarily separating these three spheres of life. First, all aspects of life are conducted in the same place and under the same single authority. Second, each phase of the member's daily activity is carried on in the immediate company of a large batch of others, all of whom are treated alike and required to do the same thing together. Third, all phases of the day's activities are tightly scheduled, with one activity leading at a prearranged time into the next, the whole sequence of activities being imposed from above by a system of explicitly formal rulings and a body of officials. Finally, the various enforced activities are brought together into a single rational plan purportedly designed to fulfill the official aims of the institution.[15]

If the inmate stays too long within this system, Goffman suggests that **dis-culturation** occurs. By this he means that the inmate undergoes an "untraining" that makes him temporarily (or permanently) incapable of managing certain features of daily life on the outside, if and when he gets back to it. The more common term for this experience is **institutionalization.** A prime example would be Brooks Hatlen, the librarian at Shawshank Prison, who chooses suicide after he is paroled into a world with which he has lost touch.

The concept of a monolithic prison social system, developed within the isolated prison in response to the deprivations of prison life and training new "fish" in its values, was challenged by the research of John Irwin in California prisons in the 1960s. Irwin, a former prisoner who had done five years in prison before becoming the first of the "convict criminologists," wrote "Thieves, Convicts, and the Inmate Subculture" (1962) with Donald Cressey and then continued his study of the inmate subculture in *The Felon* (1970). In contrast to the deprivation model, Irwin suggested an **importation** model, in which convict norms, status, and roles are brought into the prison from the outside world. The premise would be that most convicts are already criminal, sharing "age-old criminal norms and values," long before they get to prison. As opposed to an egalitarian prison society with roles defined by the code, Irwin offers eight criminal identities defining world views *before* people get to prison—the thief, the hustler, the dope fiend, the head, the disorganized criminal, the **state-raised youth,** the lower-class man, and the **square john.**[16]

Irwin saw the prison social system as a mix of all these identities, a mix further complicated by the prisoner's mode of adaptation to prison life. He identified three principal modes:

1. **Jailing.** cutting yourself off from the outside world and attempting to construct a life within prison.
2. **Doing time.** making no effort to change your life patterns, but trying to live comfortably in prison while maintaining outside contacts.
3. **Gleaning.** looking outside the prison and trying to improve yourself using the resources the prison has to offer.[17]

Irwin's view in *The Felon*, focused on California prisons, was that the prison is not a separate, isolated world but a part of a larger world whose members move in and out of prison taking their external values, behaviors, and norms with them into prison life. You can speak of a "prison society" if you wish, meaning all the people who live and work within the walls of the prison, but what you really have is a large number of primary groups, often in competition or conflict with each other, rather than making up a cohesive whole:

> The convict population in California tends to be splintered. A few convicts orient themselves to the prison social system and assume roles in regard to the prison, and a few others withdraw completely, but the majority confine their association to one or two groups of convicts and attempt to disassociate themselves from the bulk of the population. These groups vary from small, close-knit primary groups to large, casual groups. They also vary greatly in the basis of formation or focus. Many are formed on the basis of neighborhood and/or racial ties, others on the basis of shared criminal identities, especially in the case of thieves, dope fiends, heads, and hustlers, but the great majority of the groups are formed on a rather random basis. Many convicts who cell together or close to each other, who work or attend school together, maintain friendship ties which vary greatly in strength and duration.[18]

The prison Irwin observed was a prison in transition, the Big House being transformed by modern ideas on rehabilitation, classification, and management into something that was less than the sum of its parts—a greater institution broken down into its components without the dominant ethos that had once marked its life. The old, maximum-security penitentiary had been supplanted by its successor, the modern "correctional" institution, which would in turn be replaced by the contemporary prison warehouse.

PRISON LIFE TODAY

Changes over the past twenty-five years have limited the most destructive features of prison life, particularly as they affected the physical safety of inmates. After 1980, when the prison population boom really took off, most of the new prisons that were built were medium- or minimum-security facilities where inmates are not housed in cells. Today about three of every four prison inmates live in less-than-maximum- or high-security housing. Classification is used to separate out those inmates who are dangerous to other inmates or staff; they go to higher-security prisons. Inmates who commit violent or disruptive acts can expect disciplinary action, including being transferred to a higher-security prison or being locked down in their own. The vast expansion of the prison system gives authorities a lot more options in what to do with troublesome inmates. Supermax prisons are one of these options. Whatever bad things critics may say about supermax prisons—in terms of their conditions or effects on the human spirit—they do give officials a place to put the bad actors in prison, making prisons safer for the rest of the inmate population and the staff.

While both inmates and staff agree there is such a thing as an inmate social system or subculture, particularly in the older, maximum-security prisons that are least susceptible to unit management, they recognize that it is not as strong as it once was. Some old cons, in their writing and interviews, sound mistily nostalgic for the "good old days" of the code, when real men (often using themselves as examples) set the standard for prison conduct. Yeah, you might ask this old fellow, but what about the time you snitched out Shorty Smith so you could get his cushy job and take over his young punk? What about that time? Well, that was personal, he might say, and besides, he had it coming. The code, like morality, was always applied more strictly to others than to oneself.

Prisoners today are far from isolated unless they choose to be. Through the entertainment and news media and through liberal visitation policies, they are more in contact with the outside world. Levels of staffing are much higher in most state systems than they were in the Big House days, and inmate trusties no longer have direct control over other inmates. Court intervention, which was associated with some of the instability in prison operations through the 1970s, eventually resulted in improvements; prisons were forced to become better to meet the constitutional standards set by the courts.

In determining the nature of life in the contemporary prison, some researchers, most notably John J. DiIulio Jr., are more likely to study prison administrators than relations among inmates. DiIulio's 1987 book *Governing Prisons: A Comparative Study of Correctional Management* sets out what he calls a **governmental perspective** on prisons. DiIulio looks back to the early views of Beaumont and Tocqueville, who believed that inmate societies were neither inevitable nor to be welcomed. The French observers

> anticipated much of the sociological literature on prisonization by arguing that where inmates are permitted to associate freely, they are bound to think and act in ways that make them less manageable and "still more corrupted." They did not believe in what we would term rehabilitation and were certain that prison could do little to effect "the radical change of a wicked person into a honest man—a change which produces virtues in the place of vices." But they did believe that in an orderly, well-administered prison where the convict is governed not by other convicts but by disciplined, honorable, and caring officials, he may contract "honest habits" and become "at least more obedient to the laws; and that is all which society has a right to demand."[19]

DiIulio acknowledges that his governmental perspective on prisons does not provide practical solutions to particular correctional problems:

> Rather, it is a way of thinking about and studying prisons that may lead us to such knowledge. From this perspective, the key actors in any prison setting are the prison administrators, from the director to the warden to the most junior correctional officer in the cellblock. They are the government of the prison, and it is assumed that the quality of prison life will depend mainly, if not solely, on what they do or fail to do. It is the government of keepers, not the society of captives, that is of primary importance. A governmental perspective on prisons asks whether, given the lawless and uncivilized character of their citizens, inmate societies ought not to be subject to strong official controls and a tight, mandatory regime of work and programs. In essence, it admits the possibility, so long foreclosed by prison sociology and its minions, that given appropriate checks on the authority of the keepers, those prison managers may govern best who govern most.[20]

The central concept of the governmental perspective is that the prison administration, not the inmate population, really determines the prison's environment. A safe, orderly, well-run prison is one with a good administration that has the resources to carry out its mission; an unsafe, disorderly, chaotic prison is one with a poor administration lacking such resources (or mismanaging the resources if it has them). In the latter institution, power passes into the hands of the inmates (see Sykes's discussion of corruption of authority), and living and working in prison become high-risk endeavors once again. Or, as the old cons say, "If the warden wants to run the prison, he can. If he doesn't, we will."

Putting aside discussions of sociological and political perspectives for now, what is prison life like for most inmates in American prisons today? For the prisoner, the basic conditions of life are determined by the institution in which he or she is confined. In intake or classification, the staff looks at several key indicators—age, length of sentence, security threat, history of violence in custody, treatment needs, enemies in custody, and where bed space is available—in making this assignment. When the inmate arrives at the new prison, he or she is assigned a housing unit based on these same criteria. In a sense, then, as a newly arrived inmate, your placement is always partly determined not so much by what you need as by how you compare with others who are already there.

Despite our perception of prisons as high-walled fortresses (or Gothic monoliths, as Harry Allen and Clifford Simonsen have long described the old maximum-security penitentiaries), most inmates live in much newer, lower-security facilities. In 1972, about 600 state and federal prisons held 200,000 inmates. Three decades later, the number of institutions had almost tripled, to about 1,700, while the population had increased more than sixfold, to about 1,300,000. Does this mean that prisons have gotten bigger or more overcrowded in the past thirty years? While overcrowding has been a persistent problem since the 1980s and virtually all prisons are at or slightly above capacity, prisons are not severely overcrowded at present.

Prisons have grown larger, but they have also grown smaller. The diversification of security levels has had both effects on size. Before the 1970s, the old Big House prisons often held between 1,000 and 3,000 men. In several southern states and some less populated states, prisons were much smaller, averaging 200 or fewer inmates, but maximum security prevailed among both large and small.

Most of the new prisons built to house the 1,000,000-plus additional convicts in the prison system over the past thirty years have been medium-, minimum-, and open-security facilities. Part of this is cost related. To build a new maximum-security prison, the national average per bed cost is about $100,000. For a minimum- to medium-security prison, the average is about $40,000 to $50,000 per bed. The other major reason for decreasing custody over time is that prison officials generally agree that no more than 15 to 20 percent of the prison population needs to be confined in cells under more labor-intensive high security.

Inmates under lower security are generally confined in smaller institutions, while those in higher-security levels are often placed in larger institutions. Many prisons today are multilevel, meaning they hold inmates in two or more different security levels. Some have been built new with this idea in mind, while others are old prisons in which new wings have been added. California's prisons, which are by far the largest in the world, averaging 4,000 to 5,000 beds each, are built on this model. One warden is in charge overall, but the prison applies unit management to each of several smaller housing units. The several thousand inmates are never all in one place at one time.

This is the breakdown of prisons by type, by capacity, and by average population in 2001:

Type	Number	Capacity	Average Population
Open/community	194	46,128	238
Minimum	325	141,771	436
Medium	327	275,417	842
High/close	92	76,234	829
Maximum	95	120,357	1,267
Multilevel	302	270,006	894[21]

The maximum category includes most of the old Big House prisons still in use, including such famous names as Auburn, Sing Sing, San Quentin, Trenton, and Leavenworth. About fifty of these old penitentiaries dating back to the 1800s remain open today, according to recent reports. Some of the old prisons were merely functional architectural monstrosities, while others—especially those built at the end of the 1800s—were grand architectural models. The lower-security prisons built in the building boom of the 1980s and 1990s tend to be more functional than striking; the prevailing design, as one inmate said, is "late Lego," by which he meant blocks assembled to house people as cheaply as possible, with little attention to aesthetics.

In the old prisons, inmates were housed in cell blocks. Ted Conover's *Newjack: Guarding Sing Sing* recounts the year he spent as a rookie guard in New York's second-oldest prison. The main housing is two enormous cell blocks, stacked in tiers five high, each holding several hundred men. The new prisons are typically one- or two-story dormitories in which fifty to 100 inmates live in bunk beds, rooms, or cubicles with a common dining area and recreation area built into each dorm. They resemble low-rise versions of college dormitories built during the same period. They have the normal amenities, including electricity, running water, central heating, and cable TV, though some prison systems, such as Louisiana, view air conditioning as a luxury and restrict the channels inmates can watch on TV. ESPN and crime shows are always popular choices.

Life in the new prisons is pretty much lived in the congregate; one of the rights you give up as an inmate—perhaps the one right those of us who are not imprisoned would miss the most if we were locked up—is the right to privacy. It is difficult to impossible in most prisons ever to be completely alone, to get away from everyone else—to have your own "space." A general rule of supervision in a medium- or maximum-security prison is that each prisoner is to be either in his cell or in the line-of-sight supervision of a staff member at all times. While this works well for security (if it is actually practiced), it does not do much for one's sense of privacy. The only way to be completely alone in most prisons is to be in lockdown, which is not a desirable status because of its duration. You might want to be alone for a day or two, but not for thirty, sixty, or ninety days and not with the loss of privileges that usually accompanies lockdown status.

As an inmate, when you are not working, you have three other common places to be:

1. At home, which is your bed, your room, or your cell
2. In the housing unit common area, which might include a dayroom, recreation area, hobby shop, or TV room
3. On the yard, an outdoor area where inmates gather to talk and sometimes play sports

The one place you do not want to be is in another inmate's home without permission. To enter another person's room or cell without permission, whether the inmate is at home or not, is disrespectful. It invites a response that will cause trouble and result in disciplinary action.

Prisons were not made for shy people; if you cannot go to the bathroom or take a shower with other people around looking at you, you should avoid prison life. At least in the Big House, inmates could retreat to their cells when they wanted privacy; inmates in many of today's new prisons have no such option. Headphones plugged into a CD player or radio make music the only private world available to them.

Modern prisons are filled with light, which makes it more difficult to get away with misbehavior; if the administration tolerates it, prisons are also full of noise—continuous noise. If you are a light sleeper, you are in for a prolonged period of sleep deprivation. Someone or something is always banging, clanging, talking, or singing. Much of the conversation is R-rated. Jean Harris, writing about the Bedford Hills women's prison in New York, had this observation:

> The rule book, handed to me the day I entered prison, says, under General Rules, rule 1: "Obscene language will not be tolerated." In fact, obscene language is one thing that is always tolerated. I sit in my cell sometimes and jot down the sounds of the corridor verbatim. "You tell that motherfucker somebody fuckin' with you and he don't give a fuck." "That ain't no fuckin' way to talk to no fuckin' body. You ain't got no fuckin' discretion." The language of Bedford isn't White English or Black English or pigeon Spanish. It's Fuck-Speak with the volume on high.[22]

Regardless of security level, prisons run on routine. Malcolm Braly's observations on "rigid routine" apply as much to lower-security prisons today as they did to San Quentin in the 1950s. The day is highly structured: three meals (two hot, one cold), work in the morning and afternoon (about two-thirds of prisoners have some kind of work assignment, with food services, dorm orderlies, groundskeeping, the laundry, the warehouse, and maintenance the most common), half a day of class or training if you are in school, visitation in an assigned block of time, usually once a week, and club meetings, church, sports, TV, hobby crafts, and free time evenings and weekends—all of this taking place within the same circle of people grouped together by the institution's choice.

As an inmate, you are told what to do by correctional officers wearing uniforms. Your position, expertise, or status before you came to prison do not matter: the correctional officer gives orders, and you follow them. Remember, as you read, that Edwin Edwards, who served four terms as governor of Louisiana, is mopping the rec room of a federal prison today. If the correctional officer, who is a high school graduate who spent four years in the Army before getting into prison work, looks at the floor and says, "Hey, Edwards, you missed a spot," what does the former governor of Louisiana reply? "Yes, sir," and he goes over to correct his mistake.

Prisons today are very big on rules. When you enter prison as a new inmate, you are given the institution's rule book. Inmate misconduct is usually divided into two levels—less serious and more serious or major and minor. Fighting is minor; fighting with a weapon or resulting in serious injury is major. Disrespect to an officer is minor; disobedience in failing to respond to an order is major. Inmates who break the rules are subject to being written up. Inmates often call it "getting a ticket." Inmates average about 1.5 to 2.0 disciplinary tickets a year. Some inmates get none, while some get many. Some states write a lot, while some write many fewer. Disciplinary rates tend to be higher for younger inmates, inmates convicted of nonviolent crimes, women (in some states), and inmates with a history of narcotics usage.

Inmates who are written up will face a disciplinary hearing before one officer or a board of up to three members, depending on the seriousness of the offense and the institutional practice. Inmates face minor punishments, from loss of privileges or visitation to extra duty, or major punishments, such as loss of good time, lockdown, or reassignment from one housing unit to another or to another prison. If you were caught in the act having sex with your homosexual sweetheart, for example, you should probably think in terms of finding a new sweetie; in most prisons, you are never going to be near or perhaps even see this one again. End of romance.

Most inmates prefer to be in population, or **general population,** a status that is least restricted and that allows the most freedom of movement. Most large prisons have **special management** housing units. The American Correctional Association uses these terms to define four types of housing:

1. **Administrative segregation.** an inmate removed from general population as a threat to security or to the safety of other inmates and staff (This is a long-term status but it is not a punishment for a disciplinary violation.)
2. **Disciplinary detention.** (or disciplinary segregation): an inmate removed from general population for committing serious violations of institutional rules
3. **Protective custody.** an inmate removed from general population who requests or requires separation from other inmates for his own safety
4. **Mental health housing.** an inmate removed from general population because of serious mental disorders that make it impossible for him to mix with other inmates in open housing

Different states use different terms for these statuses. California, for instance, uses the Special Housing Unit for administrative segregation and Ad Seg for disciplinary detention. The status is the same; only the name is different. An estimated 6 to 8 percent of the prison population nationwide is in special management housing at any given time, most often for either administrative segregation or disciplinary detention.

Besides the lack of privacy and the need to maintain subservience to the guards (if you need to be reminded that in a real prison you cannot beat "the man," watch the last half hour of *Cool Hand Luke*, the classic 1967 film in which Paul Newman plays a rebellious inmate who just cannot make himself conform to the rules), the other aspect of prison life that you would notice is that you do not have to think a lot. You do what you are told, you stay out of trouble, you pass the time as best you can, and the days go by until you get out. Obviously, this does not work for everyone, as we will look at more closely later in this chapter, but some prisoners do talk about doing time in today's nicer prison (the "humane prison," Robert Johnson calls it) as entering into a mindless zone where time passes without your active participation. Life is not so painful, but neither is it very productive. Prison time is a lot of time sitting around talking with other people who are in pretty much the same boat as you—a boat becalmed on an empty sea. You are drifting slowly toward your release date, waiting for some strong wind to spring up and drive you in a more definite direction, whether toward a lawbreaking or a law-abiding life you really cannot say. Despite what you might tell the parole board (if your state still has one granting discretionary release), you would be hard pressed to say exactly how prison has changed you or how you are better for the experience.

Some of the important features of the American prison have not changed much since the origin of the penitentiary 200 years ago. They remain almost entirely monosexual institutions for inmates, though staffing is now more mixed. Felons are still sent away to serve their sentences, often to remote locations far from home and family; they serve their whole sentence in a secure facility, ineligible for community contact until the very end of the sentence. They are locked up with hundreds or thousands of other felons, perpetuating their identification with the criminal underclass. In these mass institutions, they forfeit their civic responsibilities, and their individual features are ignored by their custodians. They lose their individuality, and they lose the right to expect to have other people listen to them as equals. Prisoners often say they are suffering from diminished status, which is why they have to shout to be heard.

THE LIFE OF WOMEN IN PRISON

Is the prison experience for women different than it is for men? Today we simply assume that it is and begin to explore the differences. But it is fair to say that until little more than a generation ago, no one really looked inside women's prisons to find an answer to this question. On the one hand, reformers argued—as early as Elizabeth Gurney Fry in the early 1800s—that women criminals should be dealt with through a regimen particularized for them in institutions separate from men's prisons. This became the norm in the more populous prison states in the first half of the 1900s. But on the other hand, outside observers and researchers did not make serious inquiries into women's imprisonment until much later—in the 1960s and 1970s.

The sociological studies of women's prisons began with David Ward and Gene Kassebaum's *Women's Prison: Sex and Social Structure* (1965). In their research at the California Institution for Women in Frontera, Ward and Kassebaum compared the social roles of women in prison with those of men in prison, as described in the other literature of the time, and found that the common convict roles of the men's prison did not have their equivalent in the women's prison. Instead of a cohesive subculture, the women's prison was divided into small, intimate family groups centering on homosexual relationships. Ward and Kassebaum suggested that women prisoners suffered from **affectional starvation.** Their emotional and sexual needs for men led to the creation of a prison culture of **dyads** (or two-person relationships) based on male and female roles.[23]

Rose Giallombardo spent a year researching the women's prison community at Alderson. Her book *Society of Women: A Study of a Women's Prison* (1966) argues against the deprivation or pains-of-imprisonment thesis and for the Irwin and Cressey importation thesis, suggesting that the social order of the women's prison is based on identities brought in from the outside world. Much of *Society of Women* is concerned with the explication of the **prison family** or **kinship** networks. These are groups, small or large, similar to families in the free world but based on females playing all the parts—husbands and wives, sisters and brothers, grandmothers and grandfathers, aunts and uncles, and so on. Nothing comparable to this had been found to exist in men's prisons.

Giallombardo looks at social roles and sex roles in detail. She describes such roles as the "snitcher," the "square" and the "jive bitch," the "rap buddy" and "homey," the "connect" and the "booster," and the "pinner" (important as the lookout in homosexual liaisons). She defines several sex roles in what she calls the "homosexual cluster," particularly the roles of **femme** and **stud broad,** who are the female and male roles in a homosexual relationship.[24] (Barbara Owen, in her 1990s research, makes a case for using the term "same-sex relationship" as opposed to "homosexual relationship" to avoid the negative sexual denotation of homosexual; she points out that many of the intimate relationships among the women in prison that she studied were not sexual but rather emotionally intimate.[25] This is probably even more true in many of the women's prisons of today where sexual contact is more closely regulated than it was previously.)

Giallombardo collected prison **kites,** or letters between inmates, many of which were love letters. She also included a glossary of prison terms in use by Alderson inmates at the time. Many of these terms are the same as terms from the argot of men's prisons. They focus on sex, drugs, the legal system, and criminal careers. Among the most distinctive terms related to sex and relationships are these:

Bull dyker: a lesbian

Cash register: a vagina

Dozens: vulgar and profane epithets with regard to one's mother; questioning one's parentage

Drop the belt: to switch from a male role to a female role

Fay broad: a white inmate, especially one who hangs out with blacks

Flagging: an older inmate attempting to involve a younger inmate in homosexuality

Found a home: to find prison life congenial

My people: partner in a homosexual relationship

Suede: a black inmate, usually "suede broad"

Whorehouse: a prison cottage where all inmates are paired off in homosexual couples[26]

In *Making It in Prison: The Square, the Cool, and the Life* (1972), Esther Heffernan found, as had previous studies, that the substitute family (in other settings also known as the play family or make-believe family) was a critical element to the social order of the women's prison.[27] Her analysis of prison identities was comparable to that of John Irwin; she defined three basic orientations to prison life:

1. **The life:** the habitual deviant criminal, often with a background in prostitution and drug abuse, who settles comfortably into the internal life of the prison
2. **The cool:** the professional criminal who tries to control the prison environment while maintaining contacts with the outside world
3. **The square:** the noncriminal tied to conventional norms and values[28]

Another book from this time period is Kathryn Watterson's *Women in Prison: Inside the Concrete Womb,* originally published in 1973. Watterson is a journalist rather than a sociologist, and her work was based on visits and interviews in women's prisons and jails all over the country. Thus, instead of a sociological study of life in a particular institution, what emerges is a picture of women in prison in America, often in the words of the women prisoners themselves. Watterson updated *Women in Prison* in 1996, after a period of explosive growth in the imprisonment of women. Her observations on prisons then and now, based on interviews with nearly a thousand inmates and prison officials, make for highly informative reading. We get a vivid sense of the enduring elements of the prison life of women, and we can see how this changed as women's prisons have changed from small to mass institutions.

In the 1960s, when the early sociological studies of women's prisons were completed, fewer than 10,000 women were in prison in America. By 2002, the number of women in prison had increased to more than 97,000. Two states, Texas and California, and the federal prison system *each* have more than 10,000 women in their prisons—more women than were imprisoned in the entire country only a generation ago. The two largest women's prisons in America (perhaps the two largest in the world) are California's Valley State Prison for Women (3,500 inmates) and the Central California Women's Facility (3,100 inmates). These two new prisons, "sister institutions" each located on one square mile of land outside Chowchilla, California, alone would have held every female state and federal prisoner in the country as recently as 1973, when 6,004 women were in prison at the end of the year.

We have looked earlier in this text at reasons for the rapid increase in the numbers of women in prisons, emphasizing changes in sentencing, legal decision making, and the "War on Drugs." But how has prison life changed for women as the system has been flooded with new inmates?

Several scholars, most notably Barbara Bloom, Meda Chesney-Lind, and Joycelyn Pollock, have written extensively about policies and practices in imprisoning women over the past two decades. The best recent book to focus on the "new" culture of the big women's prison is Barbara Owen's *"In the Mix:" Struggle and Survival in a Women's Prison* (1998). Based on three years of observation, interviews, and research in the Central California Women's Facility (CCWF), Owen's work describes the culture of imprisoned women in a big contemporary prison.

What did Owen see in CCWF? She saw mostly women from the economic and social margins of American society, women whose lives were shaped by the overlapping dimensions of drug use, crime, and often violence.[29] For these women, crime is a survival skill. The prison they were sent to is a tough, impersonal place. One woman who had been in prison several times compared the old California Institution for Women (CIW) to CCWF: CIW was more like a college, was more settled, and provided more privacy for inmates. She said, "CCWF is bigger, more attitudes, personality. . . . CCWF is harder time but this teaches me more. I guess CIW didn't teach us a hard enough lesson—when I was there I forgot that I was in prison and I had to be reminded that I was in prison."[30]

The women in CCWF believe that their prison is less violent than a men's prison, with less allegiance to a convict culture (though they say that some states, like New York, when Jean Harris was imprisoned, do have problems with violence in their women's prisons). Race and security classification are not considered barriers to inmate interaction, and the inmates described fairly cooperative relationships with prison staff, about two-thirds of whom were men.

Some states have very few men working as correctional officers in their women's prisons. In 2001, Louisiana had eight in their one women's prison, Arkansas had three, and Mississippi had one.[31] Other states, such as California, Illinois, and New York, have hundreds. Despite lower rates of violence and fewer escape attempts, women are often perceived as being more difficult to manage in prison, at least in part because they do not like the impersonal setting and want to be treated more as individuals. One recent study of women convicts in Illinois prisons in the 1800s uses a title that many staff and administrators would find applicable to their work today: "One female prisoner is of more trouble than twenty males."[32] But some researchers (and many women inmates, in interviews) say women follow the rules better in institutions where male staff predominate. Disobedience to the rules, as measured by disciplinary reports, tends to be higher in female-staffed institutions.

The last chapter of Owen's book is titled "The Mix: The Culture of Imprisoned Women." **The mix** is behavior that causes trouble and conflict with staff and other inmates. "A variety of behaviors can put one in the mix. The most frequently mentioned issues were related to 'homo-secting,' involvement in drugs, fights, and 'being messy,' that is, being involved in conflict and trouble."[33] The mix is centered on the prison yard, as the scene of the most open interaction among inmates. Thus, to avoid the mix, inmates stay to themselves—in their own housing or, even better, in their own rooms. They associate with a few trusted others who are also "out of the mix."

Several circumstances contribute to the problems of women in prison. Eighty percent or more of women in prison are mothers, most with custody of minor children immediately before entering prison, so child custody, the welfare of their children, and visitation are major concerns. Women in prison overwhelmingly report that their children or their own mothers are the most important people in their lives; only 10 percent identified a husband or a man in this status.[34] Men in prison worry about themselves, while women in prison worry about their children, their families, and themselves (even though, as some skeptics point out, many women in prison become better mothers *during* imprisonment than they were before).

Women in prison are said to be in an even more subservient relationship to authority than men are. Scholars of prison history point out that women in custody were often viewed as being morally and intellectually inferior to men—less redeemable and more stupid. Because they had fallen so far from the proper place of women in society, they were invariably talked down to by their keepers, shamed like bad children. This point of view persists today, as Kathryn Watterson recently pointed out: "Inmates had repeatedly told me, 'They treat us just like children. They think we're four years old. They think we can't think for ourselves. They call us girls, but we're women.'"[35] Watterson sees the analogy of inmates in total institutions as infants, subject to forced dependency on their keeper (like parents) for everything they need. If they resist this kind of control and try to retain their autonomy, they risk being labeled "problem prisoners" and placed in more restrictive housing—in the contemporary prison, administrative segregation, or lockdown. Such housing is more readily available and more often used in the contemporary prison. Prime candidates are said to be younger, minority, repeat offenders who are said to be both leaders and troublemakers.

Women in prison have traditionally suffered from fewer opportunities to work and participate in programs than men enjoyed. "Women's work" in the penitentiary meant three things: laundry, cooking, and sewing. As Joycelyn Pollock has pointed out, vocational training meant, first, the domestic model of necessary household skills if the woman was to get out of prison and become a wife, or, second, the traditional skills of lower-class women in the workplace: sewing, food services, cosmetology, and office skills. When rehabilitation programs became more plentiful in prisons, many of these programs did not filter down to women's prisons. Part of the explanation was said to be ideological, that women were not as important or as deserving of attention as men (which is also often said to be a reason for the delay in studying women's prisons because almost all the researchers were men); part of it, especially in explanations provided by corrections officials, is attributed to the small numbers of women in prison before the drug-induced burst of the 1980s. The typical state prison for women before the 1980s held only about 100 to 200 women, hardly enough to offer a wide range of rehabilitative programs.

Women have also not fared well when it comes to treatment—in many forms. Women have particular medical concerns and see themselves as needing more regular and intensive medical care than men do. Men rarely come to prison pregnant. Women often do (5 percent or more in the jail and prison population at any given time); they have to deal with prenatal care, giving birth, and placing their children after birth, all while dealing with the greater experience of imprisonment. Women in prison have more serious drug abuse histories than men do, and women are much more likely to be HIV positive than men are. Prisons are not well regarded for providing any of these forms of treatment—gynecological, substance abuse, or HIV.

For these reasons and more, women often indicate they have a harder time "doing time" than men do. They do adapt to imprisonment, but they think of the prison experience as being harder on them than it is on men. This is particularly true as prison systems today adopt the policy that Meda Chesney-Lind calls **vengeful equity**.[36] Advocates of improvements in women's prisons were said to be seeking equal treatment or parity. Chesney-Lind defines vengeful equity as the dark side of the equity or parity model of justice—one that emphasizes treating women offenders as though they were men, particularly when the outcome is punitive (as in imprisonment), in the name of equal justice.[37]

Among both staff and inmates, the perception is that prison life for women has changed noticeably since the early 1980s. In some respects, such as the greater availability of rehabilitative programs, the changes are for the better. In most other respects, such as longer sentences, more formal disciplinary procedures, stricter rules on visitation, overcrowding, and other features relating to the increased size of women's prisons, the changes have been for the worse. Women are not men, and they do not or probably will not in the future attack other inmates and staff, try to escape, or riot as men do. In the entire eighty-year history of the Alderson federal prison for women, the only riot reportedly occurred the day after the violent suppression of the inmates at Attica in 1971—either as a show of sympathy with those who had been killed and injured or as an expression of disgust with how authorities handled the matter.

Security is still generally less of a concern in women's prisons, but this is changing. Sometimes you can better see how this is happening if you focus on one institution over time. The Louisiana Correctional Institute for Women (LCIW) opened at St. Gabriel, Louisiana, in 1973, to replace an older prison nearby. The prison had a capacity of 198. All the women were housed in one dormitory. Each woman had a separate room to which she kept the key. Women wore their own clothes. The environment was laid back and informal. After work hours, the inmates (who were called "ladies" by the staff) gathered in the central quadrangle (the "yard") to socialize. The atmosphere was very relaxed; usually no guards were in sight, and physical contact between inmates, short of overtly romantic physical actions such as kissing or fondling body parts, was allowed. Punishment was confinement to your room for a period of time. The grounds was referred to as "the campus," and it much resembled a small vocational school. It had a chain-link fence around it but no other obvious security measures.

Thirty years later, the prison looks very different. A thousand women now live within the same physical confines that held 200; another 1,500 state prisoners are dispersed among parish jails because there is no room for them at LCIW. The prisoners share the same yard, which is now more densely populated. New dorms have been built. All rooms now hold two or three women, and the residents no longer have their own keys. The women wear color-coded uniforms that identify their status, including some security risks in black-and-white striped jumpsuits. Noise levels are much higher, and some inmates (by no means all) speak more rudely in the direction of visitors. There seems to be more commotion; someone is always yelling. Guards are more visible. Any physical contact between inmates is a write-up. Serious disciplinary violators are locked down in Capricorn Unit—three blocks of segregation cells in the back of the complex. Prison officials and inmates say the women today have tougher attitudes and present more management problems. A new maximum-security cell block is under construction. The fences are higher and topped with razor wire. Aside from the fact that it remains more open on the interior, as opposed to being divided off through internal fences, and lacks a tower from which an armed guard could surveil the perimeter and shoot escapees (the warden asked to build one a few years ago, but the legislature turned him down), LCIW looks very much like what a present-day medium-security men's prison looks like in Louisiana. The bigger it gets, the more it moves in this direction. The women of LCIW are now split in their opinions. Some say the prison treats them like children; others say the prison treats them like men. Not many would say they are treated as women ought to be treated.

PRISON VIOLENCE

Although violence is less common today than a generation ago, it remains a part of the prison experience. Scholars who study prison violence have divided it into five types:

1. Self-violence, in the form of suicidal gestures and attempts. We will look at suicide in prison later in this chapter.
2. Staff-to-inmate violence, which was once the norm for running a tightly disciplined prison. Most prisons had their guard **goon squads** to administer physical punishment to inmates until recently (in some prisons, perhaps yesterday). Today the preferred term is **SORT,** for Special Operations Response Team, used most often to subdue uncooperative inmates without inflicting extraneous damage.
3. Inmate-to-inmate violence, in the form of assaults and homicides.
4. Inmate-to-staff violence, in the same form.
5. Collective violence against authority, in the form of disturbances and riots.

Some may argue that prisons today are more violent than ever, but that is not what the statistics say. Fifty-five state and federal prisoners were homicide victims in the year 2000.[38] No prison staff were homicide victims. The number of prisoners killed in homicides was thirty fewer than the number executed and far fewer than deaths from AIDS, suicide, and natural causes. Most states experienced no homicides; forty-one of the fifty states had either zero or one inmate homicide. California had nine, and Texas had eight.[39]

The prison homicide rate overall was 4.49 per 100,000. The national homicide rate in 2000 was 5.6 per 100,000, so even on the surface, prisoners were less likely to be murdered in prison than on the street. If we make adjustments for the demographics of the prison population—predominantly male, minority, urban, and younger—prisons look even better as a safe haven.

Prisons were much more violent in the good old days, when inmates ran the joint, as John DiIulio, Bruce Jackson, and others have reported. To illustrate, the Louisiana State Penitentiary at Angola averaged one to two homicides a month during one bloody period in the mid-1970s. California, which had an average prison population in the 1970s of about 25,000, averaged about twenty inmate homicides per year, or a rate of about eighty per 100,000. The comparable rate in the year 2000 was 5.6. Texas was considered the safest big prison system in America through the mid-1970s, when it averaged one inmate homicide per year. But as the population grew and the control model broke down, by the early 1980s homicides were averaging ten per year.[40]

Physical violence is more of a threat than a daily occurrence in most prisons today, and when it occurs, it is at a much lower level than in the past. A huge gulf exists between a dormitory fistfight and gangs of inmates fighting with knives in the yard, as often happened in California prisons in the 1970s.

Other than by counting dead bodies, it is difficult to get a precise grasp on the seriousness and extent of inmate violence in prison today, even with modern techniques for counting and reporting. *The Corrections Yearbook 2001* reported about 50,000 assaults in state and federal prisons in the year 2000. About a third were against staff, the other two-thirds against inmates.[41] Most of these were simple assaults—basically fights not involving weapons. Fewer than 10,000 of the assaults required medical attention (in several states, all parties involved in assaults get a medical exam unless they decline). About 4,200 of the total number of assaults (split 45 percent against staff, 55 percent against inmates), or less than 10 percent of the total reported, were referred for prosecution as criminal offenses.[42] How do these numbers compare with the street? It is hard to say. If we count only the incidents referred to prosecution as serious assaults, the rate is about 323 per 100,000. The FBI's *Uniform Crime Reports* gives a rate of aggravated assault (crimes reported to the police) of 318.5 per 100,000. Again prisons do not show up as being significantly more violent than the free world, given that what statisticians call the "dark figure of crime," unreported crime, is as important in prison as it is on the street.

What are the causes of violence in prison? What are the causes of violence on the street? Many people assume that prisons are tinderboxes in which psychotic inmates fueled by racial, ethnic, gang, political, and various other animosities attack people as targets of symbolic hatred. First, few prisons are tinderboxes, and, second, most violence is personal and has nothing to do with larger issues. Inmates fight with other inmates they don't like for personal reasons—conflict has nothing to do with politics, culture, or race and in most states very little to do with gangs. The nature of prison life surely aggravates violence. In the free world, we do have some choice of our associates, and if certain people annoy us, we try to avoid them. Prisoners may have no such freedom of choice. It would be easy to hate Bubba but not so easy to avoid him or get rid of him.

Ron Wikberg, a prison journalist and inmate at the Louisiana State Penitentiary during the turbulent early 1970s, said most of the violence was rooted in one of three primary causes: stealing, debts, or sex. Not on his list but likely also important were snitching—an inmate getting back at someone he thought had gotten him into trouble—and disrespect, which was as often expressed by the taking of property or invasion of space as it was by directly rude remarks. In the relative absence of internal security within the prison at this time, personal disagreements between inmates often erupted into knife fights that left inmates dead or seriously injured. In the same prison today, the same disputes are still there, but the knives are not, and the fivefold increase in the number of security officers results in a much different atmosphere.

Individual acts of violence against staff or other inmates are one concern; prison disturbances and **prison riots** against the authority of the institution are another. Collective prison violence pre-dates the penitentiary. Prison historians often cite a rebellion in the underground Simsbury, Connecticut, prison in 1791 as the first prison riot in America. In this abandoned copper mine, prisoners confined in a long room belowground rioted. A report blamed "violence, poor management, escapes, assaults, orgies, and demoralization" while noting that overcrowding was also a problem.[43] The Auburn prison experienced major rebellions against the authoritarian rule of Warden Elam Lynds in 1818 and 1820. The military had to be called out to put down the first riot, and prisoners burned down a new cell block in the second.

These collective acts continued through the history of the penitentiary and Big House. Gresham Sykes, in *Society of Captives*, described a "cyclical rhythm from order to disorder to order" in prisons; in this view, a riot is "a logical step in a pattern of repeated social change."[44] Prison riots often did occur in clusters where news of one riot might inspire rebellion in another institution. But many prison disturbances, from the early 1800s through World War II, were not so much political demonstrations as they were escape attempts. A major disturbance would erupt on plan, either to seize control from the guards or to provide a diversion so that some prisoners might escape. After prisoners got more collective freedom to plan and act together, some of these events were very successful. Over 200 inmates ran away from California's new San Quentin prison in the Great Escape of 1862. Seventeen prisoners attacked their guards and escaped from Leavenworth prison in 1898. In the biggest prison break of the twentieth century, thirty-six convicts, led by trusty guards who turned their guns on other guards, fled Arkansas's Cummins State Prison Farm on Labor Day 1940. The Battle of Alcatraz in 1946 began as an escape attempt. Six would-be escapees took an entire crew of guards hostage. When the escape broke down, for want of an exterior door key, a three-day gun battle ensued, leaving three convicts and two guards dead and at least thirteen other guards wounded.

The disturbances of the early 1950s were a different matter, as we have already discussed. Escape was not an end. These actions were about calling attention to prisoners' complaints. Whether spontaneous or planned, they followed a pattern: inmates seizing a building, taking available guards hostage, presenting a list of demands, publicizing their complaints about the prison as much as possible, and then capitulating when their demands were met or when the use of overwhelming force appeared imminent. This pattern was followed time after time in this era.

Investigations into these riots were conducted at the state level and nationally by the American Prison Association (APA). Some had proposed a **mass rebellion** theory, which the APA report rejected. It divided riot causes into seven categories:

1. Inadequate financial support and official and public indifference
2. Excessive size and overcrowding of institutions
3. Substandard personnel
4. Enforced idleness
5. Unwise sentencing and parole practices
6. Lack of professional leadership and professional programs
7. Political domination of management[45]

The 1950s riots were captured on film in the quasi-documentary *Riot in Cellblock 11* (1954), filmed on location at California's Folsom Prison and closely following the events of the 1952 riot at Jackson, Michigan. The reality of this film makes a strong contrast with another film of only seven years earlier, the film noir classic *Brute Force* (1947), which follows the riot-as-mass-escape plot.

Strikes, disturbances, and riots that focused on media attention and political demands recurred in another cycle at the end of the 1960s, leading up to the most famous and most deadly prison riot in American history, the **Attica riot** of September 9 to 13, 1971. After a period of increasing tension and conflict in the New York prison, a gate failure in Times Square, the control center, on September 9 allowed inmates to take over an entire section of the prison, including about fifty hostages. After three days of negotiations over lists of demands, practical proposals, and points, the state broke off negotiations and sent in an assault force of state police and guards—rifles, shotguns, and pistols blazing—to recapture the prison. Forty-three people died, thirty-nine of them (ten hostages and twenty-nine inmates) killed by the assault force during the attack; three inmates apparently were killed as snitches by other inmates; and one guard, William Quinn, died of injuries sustained in the inmate takeover of Times Square; about another 100 men received gunshot wounds, and an untold number suffered other injuries.[46] Tom Wicker, a *New York Times* editor who was one of thirty-seven observers allowed inside the prison to attempt to mediate the takeover, wrote *A Time to Die* (1975) about the riot. Attica became known as the classic example of how not to handle a prison riot, especially in the general rampage of shooting that brought it to an end.

If Attica was the political riot, then the riot at the New Mexico State Penitentiary in February 1980 was the "apolitical prisoner" riot or some said the "prison code" riot. In the **Santa Fe riot,** prisoners took over the control center and held hostages, some of whom were tortured and brutalized. But the rioters vented their greatest rage on other inmates, particularly snitches and weaker inmates in protective custody. The riot lasted only thirty-six hours, and all hostages were rescued alive. Prison officials, happy at ending the riot, entered the cell blocks to see what damage had been done—and found a scene of carnage out of the most obscene horror movie. "New Mexico entered the history books as the most savage (on the part of the inmates, at least) prison riot in American history. Thirty-three men had been hideously killed and mutilated, and hundred of others were raped, beaten, tortured, or terrorized."[47] Roger Morris's *The Devil's Butcher Shop: The New Mexico Prison Uprising* (1983) is a graphic account of this riot.

The most economically destructive riot in American history destroyed the old Oklahoma State Penitentiary at McAlester in 1973. Inmates took over the prison, nicknamed "Big Mac," on July 27. Badly overcrowded, with ill-trained guards, almost daily violence, and convict bosses running the inmate subculture, the prison had been in trouble for years. Prison officials, anxious to avoid another Attica, kept negotiations going even after the prisoners burned the prison down, at an estimated cost of $20 million. The inmates took twenty-four hostages and held the prison two days before surrendering. Three inmates were killed by other inmates, three escaped in the confusion, and several inmates and guards were injured, but the prison avoided the major cataclysm many expected. The state rebuilt the prison in a smaller version and began restructuring its prison system into smaller units spread around the state.

The last "famous" riots in American prison history were the November 1987 riots of Cuban inmates who seized the two federal prisons at Oakdale and Atlanta to demand that they not be sent back to Cuba. Both riots resulted in great property damage but no loss of life. Other disturbances and smaller-scale riots have occurred in the years since but nothing of first-level magnitude. Does this mean that riots are a thing of the past? Hardly. Prison officials know that in theory a riot can occur in almost any prison at any time. The only way to keep it from happening is to lock down inmates individually, maintain high security, never allow groups of inmates to congregate, and hope no one makes a mistake.

This is a very costly and tedious approach and practically impossible to maintain long term. What officials are more likely to do is to isolate in administrative segregation or supermax housing those inmates believed to be most likely to instigate disturbances and to punish anyone involved in a real disturbance the same way. Prison officials want to ensure that inmates thinking of leading a planned riot or jumping into one just taking off ask themselves one important question: what is in it for me? In recent years, though we have more prisons and more prisoners than ever before, prison administrators have been able to avoid the major riots that have erupted periodically in the past.

SEX IN PRISON

There is no sex in prison—or that's what the rules say. A prisoner described sex as a suit of clothes: you check it at the gate when you enter prison, and you get it back when you check out. We know that it does not really work that way, but that is the official line. Officials do not pass out condoms to promote safe sex in prison because they do not want to give the appearance of sanctioning what is officially not permitted. Prison sex is generally divided into three types:

1. Self-sex, or masturbation
2. Heterosexual sex, involving male and female inmates or staff
3. Homosexual sex, involving either male or female inmates or staff

Other scenarios involving animals, inflatable dummies, and other objects are possible, but we won't go there.

Of the three types, masturbation is by far the most common and widespread, with more than 90 percent of men and women inmates admitting in surveys that they practice it in prison. Masturbation is not an approved prison practice. If an inmate should be observed playing with himself (or herself) in the shower or with busy fingers under the blankets at night, this is a disciplinary write-up—some states call it "unsanitary practices." The defense that it is just clean fun and does not harm anyone else does not work. Prison life is not only **monosexual,** the inmate would be reminded, but also **asexual.**

Heterosexual sex in the days of the old jail and the penitentiary typically meant sex between a male custodian and a female prisoner. It was criticized as coercive or an abuse of the guard's authority but not illegal, and it was recognized as commonplace.

Sex between prison staff and inmates is illegal in about forty-six states today, although guards who cross the line are most often fired or asked to resign and not prosecuted. Prison officials suggest that sex between male staff and female inmates is the lesser concern today; as more women go to work in men's prisons, sex between male prisoners and female staff is a much greater problem. This sex is most often not coercive but rather voluntary—described as romantic, seductive, or recreational. Its problem is not just the sex, which is a serious disciplinary violation and a crime; it also creates compromised relationships between those maintaining security and those affected by it. Sex is a wedge in the door to a world of greater privilege.

Heterosexual sex can also take place between male and female inmates if they happen to be among the few American prisoners held in so-called **co-correctional prisons** that allow regular interaction between inmates of opposite genders. These co-ed prisons are usually small, special purpose facilities. They combine males and females in the same population for treatment, pre-release, work release, education, or some other specific function. They have also been used as a stopgap measure to relieve overcrowding in other facilities, particularly women's prisons, when no other immediate housing was available. Co-correctional facilities allow interaction; they do not encourage or allow sex between inmates; the surest way to be transferred out of such a facility is to be caught in a sex act.

Political and public opposition to mixing males and females behind bars has worked against the co-correctional prison in recent years. Critics see this kind of prison as too "normal." Prisons are supposed to be painful, and deprivation of sex is one of the expected pains. Pregnancy and other complications can also occur. The federal government and several states were once moving toward greater use of co-correctional prisons, but their prevalence has declined of late (to about eighty smaller low-security and open prisons holding less than about 1 percent of all prisoners) as prison officials acknowledge their unpopularity and cite problems with managing inmates in such facilities. It is "easier" (and less commotion) to operate conventional same-sex prisons.

When most people think of prison sex, they think of homosexual sex, usually between men (unless they have been watching *Women in Chains* or other such lurid prison flicks involving—or perhaps requiring as part of the genre—extensive lesbian sex), and commonly violent and coerced. To outsiders, the typical prison sexual encounter is the **gang rape,** in which sexual predators beat a younger inmate into submission and force him into anal sex. In prison movies, the victim then either commits suicide or becomes the sexual play-thing of other inmates to whom he turns for protection from future assaults.

How prevalent is this scenario in real prison life today? The honest answer is that no one can say exactly. Estimates range from virtually nonexistent to minimal to frequent, depending on who is doing the estimating and what prison they are referring to. Stop Prison Rape, Inc., the most important national activist group interested in this issue, gives what it calls a "conservative" estimate of 300,000 males sexually assaulted behind bars annually.[48] Several of the leaders of this group, including the late Stephen Donaldson, Thomas Cahill, and Hope Hernandez, were rape victims in custody, though none of the rapes actually happened in a prison. The two men were gang raped in jails long ago, and Hernandez was raped by a guard outside of jail.

Most prison officials are in total disbelief at this estimated number of sexual assaults. In the December 2000 *Prison Journal,* an issue devoted to the topic of "Prison Sexuality," Cindy Struckman-Johnson and David Struckman-Johnson reported their research on sexual coercion in midwestern men's prisons. They noted other research reporting prison rape rates varying from less than 1 percent to as high as 14 percent, with a much greater number of men reporting other unwanted sexual pressures or touching. In their research, involving 1,788 inmates and 475 security officers in seven state prisons, they found that 21 percent of inmates had experienced at least one incident of pressured or forced sex while incarcerated in their state.[49] Seven percent of the inmates had been victimized in circumstances that would meet the legal definition of rape: forced sex and penetration.[50] The great majority of these were one-to-one encounters, not group attacks.

Several other findings from this research were notable. In about 20 percent of the incidents, the sexual aggressor was a male or female staff member. In six of the seven prisons, the staff estimates of inmates coerced into sex were much lower than the inmate estimates. Several factors were identified by the inmates as creating a climate in which sexual coercion was more likely—large prison population, a high percentage of inmates incarcerated for a crime against persons, barracks housing, racial conflict (involving black aggressors and white victims), and lax security (including a "permissive" environment in which staff allowed sexual exploitation to occur).[51] Bigger prisons that were understaffed generally had more problems than smaller prisons with adequate staffing.

The findings from this contemporary article compare with Louisiana prison journalist Wilbert Rideau's 1979 article "Prison: The Sexual Jungle." Rideau writes about sex—coerced and voluntary—in the Louisiana State Penitentiary at Angola and in other southern prisons historically. In these understaffed institutions, sexual exploitation was taken for granted. The guards allowed older inmates to turn young inmates into **galboys** to maintain order within the prison. Sexual favors were also used as currency to settle debts and earn cash for the cons who pimped out their "kids."

Rideau's article focuses on several inmates, one of whom, James Dunn, came to Angola for burglary at age nineteen in 1960. He was raped and became the "wife" of the convict who raped him. Dunn took care of his old man, who once sold him to another convict for two bags of heroin and $100. "Two weeks later," Dunn recounted, "he bought me back because he was loving me."[52] When Dunn's old man was released from prison, other inmates moved in. Dunn fought back, finally killing one inmate trying to take him over. Dunn got a life sentence for murder, and everyone left him alone—for a while.

Rideau also interviewed other inmates who were more comfortably settled into prison homosexuality. Some had been homosexual before imprisonment, while others—**jailhouse turnouts**—adopted homosexuality as a way of dealing with the oppressive climate of fear within the prison. Some were in lockdown because they had been caught in sexual acts or because security staff had identified them as needing protective custody; others were in general population.

Rideau wrote that prison rape was an act of "violence, politics, and an acting out of power roles," an act of conquest and demasculation, stripping the male victim of his status as "man."[53] The aggressor reinforced his sense of manhood and personal worth by dominating the weaker inmate, and the prison of that time either could not or would not do anything about it.

Perhaps times have changed with this generation of prisons, prison administrators, and political officials. On September 4, 2003, President George W. Bush signed into law the **Prison Rape Elimination Act of 2003.** The statute had four major provisions:

1. The gathering of national statistics about the problem
2. The development of guidelines for states about how to address prisoner rape
3. The creation of a review panel to hold annual hearings
4. The provision of grants to the states to combat the problem[54]

In focusing on sexual deprivation as one element in the problem, some authorities have advocated greater reliance on such methods of approved sexual contact as **furloughs** and **conjugal visiting.** Furloughs for home visits are used extensively by prisons in many foreign countries, but they have been out of fashion in the United States since the 1980s. Conjugal visiting, sometimes called family visiting to indicate that it is about more than just sex in a trailer, is allowed in only six states—California, Connecticut, Mississippi, New Mexico, New York, and Washington—and then only to married inmates with good disciplinary records in certain levels of custody. A very small percentage of inmates qualify for and make use of conjugal visits.

For practically all prisoners, including those in the conjugal visiting states, prison remains the asexual place it has been since the creation of the penitentiary. This is obviously not to say that sex does not go on, only that it is repressed and covert rather than openly acknowledged. Most prisoners today (and most prison officials) believe that most prison sex is consensual rather than coerced, even if it occurs for reasons that fall short of pure ideals and even if most participants would not call themselves homosexual outside of prison. Malcolm Braly, in *False Starts*, described the process of seduction—playing on fear, emotional longing, property needs, or various other personal needs more psychological than physical—in which inmates turned to other inmates for same-sex sex. In the abnormal world of prison, Braly wrote, sex between men in time seemed no more abnormal than anything else.[55]

PRISON GANGS

Once prisoners were allowed to congregate together in housing units and on the yard in their idle time, men and women began to form primary groups.

Donald Clemmer called them cliques. In other prisons, they were known as tips. In women's prisons, they were most often called families. In their most extreme form in the contemporary prison, they are called **prison gangs** or, in the argot of prison officials, **security threat groups** (STGs). A gang would be a street term for a group of people who hang out together, commit crimes together, socialize together, and consider a particular geographic area their home turf. The STG designation is reserved for a group of inmates who belong to a tightly knit organization that attempts to manipulate the internal life of the prison to the benefit of the organization's members.

Most authorities agree that prison gangs are directly connected to street gangs outside. When street gang members go to prison, they find other members of their gang already in prison. The membership of the street gang becomes the core of the membership of the prison gang. Members flow back and forth over time; whether in prison or on the street, they are always affiliated with the same group of people involved in criminal enterprises. James Jacobs has written,

> The presence of powerful prison gangs sporting their colors, tattoos, and insignias sends a signal to inmates that the staff do not control the prison and that antisocial norms and values prevail there as in the inner city. For inmate gang members, the prison is not a "time out" from the gang life of the streets. It provides an opportunity to perform in front of some of the gang's legendary leaders; rank and status are won and lost, criminal careers are shaped.[56]

The official view is that prisons gangs are collectively similar organizations. They have a structure with one person designated as the leader who oversees a council of members who make the group's final decisions. The rank and file form a hierarchy, making these groups look more similar to organized crime than their counterparts on the outside. The U.S. Department of Justice suggests that leaders and hard-core members are some 15 to 20 percent of a gang's membership and that the majority of members do not have a vested interest in the organization leadership.[57]

Prison gangs, like some street counterparts, have a creed or motto, unique symbols of membership, and a constitution prescribing group behavior. Absolute loyalty to one's gang is required, as is secrecy. Violent behavior is customary and can be used to move a member upward in the prison hierarchy. Prison gangs focus on the business of crime generally through drug trafficking.[58]

Prison gang members typically do not give detailed interviews to scholarly researchers or publish their secrets in their memoirs, so it is hard to know if this view of the gang as a formal, highly structured organization is generally correct. Some gang members suggest that gang activities are more informal and uncoordinated—that the gang is more of a confederacy of small groups and individuals acting in their own interests without strong, centralized, controlling authority. While the prison gang experts may see everything as a grand conspiracy orchestrated by a few powerful leaders, prison gang members shrug and say, "Things just happen." Their view is more akin to the view expressed in Clemmer's remarks used to introduce this chapter: no one really knows what is important or what is going on.

The dominant prison gangs in America are Hispanic. They include the following:

1. The **Mexican Mafia** *(La Eme)*. Said to be California's first prison gang, it formed in the 1950s among Chicano teenagers in the custody of the California Youth Authority, later expanding to Folsom and San Quentin. It was composed primarily of Mexican Americans from the Los Angeles area. Its life and influence are traced in the excellent (if brutal and graphic) Edward James Olmos film *American Me*, in which Olmos portrays Santana Montoya, the gang's founder and resident "philosopher."

2. The **Nuestra Familia.** Founded in the 1960s in Soledad prison, its members were Hispanic inmates from northern California who organized to protect themselves from the Los Angeles–based Mexican Mafia.

3. The **Texas Syndicate.** Appearing at Folsom and San Quentin in the 1970s, its membership consisted of Texas Mexican Americans who hung together to reduce harassment by the California-based gangs.

4. The **Mexikanemi** (or Texas Mexican Mafia). Organized in the early 1980s, this is the largest gang in the Texas prison system.[59]

Numerous other Hispanic gangs were active in the prisons of the Southwest, from Texas across to California, by the 1990s. By names, these include the Nortenos, the Surenos, the New Structure, the Border Brothers, the Nuestro Carnales, the Hermano de Pistoleros Latinos, and the Raza Unida. Although the new gangs were smaller, they were often said to be more violent and aggressive, seeking alliances with the older, established "corporate" gangs to enhance their own influence.

In opposition to the Hispanic gangs of the Southwest were several other gangs with ethnic origins. These include the following:

1. The **Aryan Brotherhood.** This is the leading white supremacist prison gang, organized in San Quentin in the 1960s to oppose the growing dominance of Hispanic and black gangs. It is the most widespread white gang in American prisons today, with branches in several states and the federal system.

2. The **Black Guerilla Family.** Revolutionary inmate George Jackson is credited with uniting several black groups into this California supergang of the late 1960s. Politically charged and belligerent, it was the prison contemporary of the Black Panthers on the street. It later disintegrated.

3. The **Bloods** and **Crips.** Offshoots of the Los Angeles street gangs, these groups formed in California prisons in the 1980s and were exported to other states as their members were imprisoned there.[60]

Prison gangs are most influential in the Hispanic Southwest, but their influence has been felt in several other states or in particular state prisons at certain times. During his year as a guard in the New York prison system, Ted Conover found that the Latin Kings, a New York City Hispanic gang, was the dominant gang. James Jacobs discussed the dominance of four Chicago street gangs—the Black P Stone Nation, the Devil's Disciples, the Conservative Vice Lords, and the Latin Kings—in Illinois's Stateville prison after 1969. These four supergangs were estimated to have at least 50 percent of the inmate population of Stateville as members by 1972; they were also highly involved in urban politics in Chicago.[61] Illinois continues to have the most gang-dominated prison system in America today; more than half its inmates, concentrated in high-security prisons, are reportedly gang members.

By January 1, 2001, thirty-seven states and the federal prison system reported monitoring and managing prison gangs (as security threat groups) within their prison systems. About 5.1 percent of inmates were identified as having had some type of gang affiliation (through self-admission, criminal history, or tattoos), while about 1.7 percent were classed as prison gang members.[62] These numbers are somewhat speculative, as systems for classifying gang members vary widely from one state to another, and Illinois does not make an official report of its statistics. The challenge of the security threat groups is said to be most daunting in states with big cities and long-established gangs, such as Illinois, California, New Jersey, and Texas. In other states, only a small fraction of inmates are known gang members, although even small groups have been violently disruptive at times.[63]

The winter 2001 issue of *Corrections Management Quarterly* is devoted to prison gang issues. One of the most basic is how to manage gangs within institutions. Several popular strategies have emerged, including the following:

1. *Segregation.* This places gang members in administrative segregation, which is costly and perceived by many prison officials to be ineffective.
2. *Isolating gang leaders.* This more targeted kind of segregation focuses on key inmates. This method also relies on **bus therapy,** an old practice of transferring inmates to other prisons or shipping them out of state.
3. *Jacketing.* This is a form of labeling gang members by putting intelligence information (which may come from snitches or other sources) into an inmate's file to be sure gang members are recognized as such.
4. *Gang databases.* This involves compiling computerized records systems on gang members that can be shared by different prison systems and law enforcement agencies.
5. *Deprogramming.* This is often used with segregation as a strategy to get gang members to renounce the gang and return to general population.
6. *Concentrating gang members in high-security prisons.* This approach tries to leave most of a state's prisons gang free by concentrating gang members in a few institutions.[64]

Prison gangs are an important part of the environment of several state prison systems. Their attempts to control drug trafficking and other contraband, their ties to outside criminal activities, and their efforts to neutralize the work of security officers (through corruption and intimidation) are important to maintaining control of the prison. But most gangs are relatively small in number and view themselves as primarily defensive in purpose—their principal role, they say, is protecting their members from *other* prison gangs. Except in the very worst prisons, most inmates are not gang members. They go out of their way to avoid gangs and especially to avoid conflict with gang members that might result in violence to themselves.

Prison officials have been successful in reducing the numbers of assaults and homicides attributed to gangs in recent years, but it is not reasonable to expect that they can wholly eradicate gangs from their prisons. The permanent street gang, with lifetime membership, has become a part of the criminal culture of many American cities. When its members are concentrated in the volatile environment of a high-security prison, it seems logical to expect that the intense, "blood-in, blood-out" philosophy of the ethnic prison gang would develop. The prison management strategy becomes one of containment, not eradication.

DEATH IN PRISON

Death in prison once meant sudden death—from guard violence, inmate violence, epidemic, overwork, or suicide. Death in prison in the twenty-first century is a different matter. It is increasingly death from old age or death from the diseases of substance abuse.

The Corrections Yearbook 2001 reports this distribution of inmate deaths in the year 2000:

Type	Total	Average per State
Natural causes	2,509	48
Suicide	201	4
AIDS	195	4
Unknown/other	118	2
Execution	85	2
Homicide	55	1
Accidental	39	1
Escape	1	0
Total deaths	3,203	62[65]

AIDS became statistically significant enough to be counted as a separate category about fifteen years ago, but the number of deaths in prison from AIDS has declined sharply since its mid-1990s peak of over 1,000 per year. Included in the natural causes category are deaths from hepatitis, which is now responsible for more deaths in prison than AIDS.

The steady increase in the number of natural causes deaths in prison over the past decade is attributed to two main causes: the general aging of the inmate population and the increasing use of long sentences, including natural life sentences, since the early 1980s. There really are lots of old men and women in prison, as we will see in the next chapter, and more of them are dying in prison because they are not eligible for release. Deaths from heart disease, cancer, stroke, and other ailments associated with aging have increased accordingly.

The suicide rate in prisons nationwide has averaged about fourteen to sixteen deaths per 100,000 for the past decade. The overall suicide rate for men in the United States in 1999 (according to the World Health Organization) was 19.7 per 100,000, so, in general, men in prison have *lower* suicide rates than men in the free world—whether because they are tougher, happier, more closely watched, lethal weapon deprived, or getting better mental health care we cannot say.

Douglas Dennis, writing on suicide in prison in *The Angolite* magazine, discussed research into prison suicides in Maryland: "They found that prisoners aged 15 to 34 had a greater risk of killing themselves, and that mentally disturbed or psychotic inmates are at the highest risk. They also confirmed previous studies that found prisoners serving life are more likely to commit suicide."[66]

When the number of suicides at Dennis's prison increased in the early 1990s, prison authorities responded with better training for correctional officers, more rapid EMT response, and training of inmates in the housing units as first responders in suicide attempts. Suicides in prison are predominantly hangings, followed by drug overdoses (often on prescription medication) and opening veins. Increased attention to would-be suicides and quicker response to attempts can be highly effective in reducing opportunities for successful suicides by these means in prison.

Angola has been successful in reducing the number of suicides to none or one in a typical year, but it cannot protect its mostly long-term inmate population from the effects of chronic disease and aging. Angola is one of three prisons in the country with **prison hospices** licensed by the American Hospital Association. Begun in 1998, Angola's hospice provides end-of-life care for up to six inmates at a time. The hospice volunteers are a group of about fifteen to twenty inmates, mostly lifers who know that they will one day be likely candidates for hospice care themselves. Tanya Tillman, the prison nurse who oversees the hospice, says that most hospice patients die from cancer or complications related to hepatitis C.[67] In a prison where more inmates die than get paroled each year, hospice provides more attention than dying inmates could expect in the past.

Prisons like Angola also have to deal with the disposition of the bodies of inmates who die in custody. Many prisoners are from out of state or are older and separated from their families or have poor families that cannot afford to pay for their burial expenses. These prisoners have to be buried at public expense somewhere. Angola has its own cemetery, called Point Lookout II (after the original Point Lookout became filled to capacity), where inmates are given a dignified funeral. Until a few years ago, inmates were stuffed in packing crates and unceremoniously dropped into the ground. Now, through the efforts of the Angola Human Relations Club—an inmate organization—and the full support of Warden Burl Cain, the body of the inmate in placed in a handmade wooden coffin, loaded onto a horse-drawn wooden hearse, accompanied by inmate pallbearers and any family who attend (and an inmate honor guard of military veterans for prisoners who were veterans), and taken to the grave site, where an inmate choir sings gospel songs before the burial service. Each prisoner's grave is marked with its own cross.[68] Some say his life sentence is over; others say he will spend eternity in prison.

PERSPECTIVES ON PRISON LIFE

In trying to understand prison life today and how it has changed over time, we can look to various sources from inside prison walls and from outside. Many accounts of prison life through the Big House era were written from inside the walls by prisoners, prison guards, and prison administrators. Lewis Lawes, who was warden of Sing Sing in the 1920s and 1930s, wrote five books during this period—*Cell 202–Sing Sing, Life and Death in Sing Sing, Twenty Thousand Years in Sing Sing, Invisible Stripes*, and *Man's Judgment of Death*. Collectively, these volumes present the most coherent articulation of penal philosophy ever published by an American prison official. Lawes explains his views on criminals and the causes of crime, his thoughts on what society might do to reduce the prison population—through changing the law, improved family life, education, religion, and better training of youth—and why he changed from supporting to opposing capital punishment.

Soon after Lawes published *Twenty Thousand Years in Sing Sing*, Victor F. Nelson, an ex-convict, published *Prison Days and Nights*, one of the best accounts of life in the Big House industrial prisons. Nelson was in and out of prisons in New York and Massachusetts for more than twenty years, a prisoner with potential who kept "messing up." Dr. Abraham Myerson, the Massachusetts prison psychiatrist who encouraged Nelson to write down his experiences and helped him find a publisher, called him "a thief and a drunkard" but also a man of "subtle and surging intellect."[69] The chapters give a vivid picture of prison life in this era: "Prison Days" and "Prison Nights" on the routine of prison life, "Men without Women" on sex in prison, "Drugs and the Criminal" about drug addiction, "Prison Ethics and Etiquette," and half a dozen more, including a final chapter titled "The Prisoner Speaks to the Psychiatrist," in which Nelson cautions "bug doctors" against reading too much into what convicts tell them.

Prisoners' autobiographies would continue to be popular in the prison reform era of the 1960s and 1970s. Among the most enduring are these:

1. *The Autobiography of Malcolm X* (1964), by Malcolm X with the assistance of Alex Haley, a powerful account of the transformation of Malcolm Little, black Harlem and Boston street hustler, pimp, drug addict, and convicted burglar, into Malcolm X, leader of Black Muslims in and out of prison.

2. *Soledad Brother* (1970), George Jackson's political letters, written at the peak of the prison political movement in the late 1960s. Jackson writes as a black revolutionary prisoner trying to stir others to action. Jackson was shot to death in San Quentin in what officials called an escape attempt (and what political activists called a deliberate murder) in August 1971. His death and the reaction to the Attica prison riot that occurred the next month are often cited as the beginning of the end of political radicalism in prison.

3. *In Constant Fear* (1975), Peter Remick's account of Walpole Prison in Massachusetts in the early 1970s, when reformers were trying to modernize the state's prison system. As Remick points out, in his description of day-to-day life in the prison, these reforms left inmates in charge of the prison and resulted in high levels of violence, chaos, and fear among both inmates and staff. Remick wrote the book in lockdown, where he had been placed for his own safety at his request. He wrote in the introduction that he was not sure he would leave the prison alive, that he lived under constant threat of murder—"my murder."[70]

In the 1950s, Caryl Chessman became a best-selling author while awaiting his execution on California's death row. Jack Henry Abbott's prison letters to Norman Mailer, written while Abbott was in maximum security in the Utah State Penitentiary and published as *In the Belly of the Beast* (1981), represent the point of view of the hard-core convict; Robert Johnson called Abbott the poster child of the "state-raised" convict so prevalent in prisons today. Wilbert Rideau and Ron Wikberg, convict editors of *The Angolite* magazine at the Louisiana State Penitentiary, published *Life Sentences: Rage and Survival Behind Bars* (1992) about the transformation of Angola into a lifers' prison. Jean Harris's three books, written in the 1980s while she was an inmate at New York's Bedford Hills women's prison, offer exceptional observations on the prison life of women.

Among the more noteworthy recent commentaries on prison life written by outsiders are these three:

1. *Living in Prison: The Ecology of Survival* (1975), Hans Toch's analysis of prison life featuring detailed interviews of inmates discussing survival strategies
2. *The Hot House: Life Inside Leavenworth Prison* (1992), in which journalist Pete Earley looks at the inmates and the administration of the federal penitentiary in the late 1980s
3. *Hard Time: Understanding and Reforming the Prison* (3rd ed., 2002), Robert Johnson's historical perspective on living and working in prison—and the prospects for prison reform

More recently, several other new books have been published to present inmate perspectives on imprisonment. Among the most informative and readable are these three:

1. *Behind a Convict's Eyes: Doing Time in a Modern Prison* (2004), by K. C. Carceral, a life-sentenced convict who has been locked up for more than twenty years. Four academics helped him edit his stories of prison life.
2. *About Prison* (2004), by Michael G. Santos, provides the author's perspective as a convict traveling through the institutions of the federal prison system. He had served sixteen years and earned a bachelor's degree and a master's degree by the time his book was published.
3. *The Fellas: Overcoming Prison and Addiction* (2003), by Charles M. Terry, one of the "ex-convict criminologists" who have moved from prison to graduate school to academia, is a study of twenty heroin addict/convicts in and out of prison.

These books, written at different times and reflecting varying viewpoints on imprisonment, can illuminate the darkness of our ignorance as we seek to learn more about prison life. A word of caution, however: each work, especially if it speaks about prison from inside the walls, has to be put in its time and place. No work speaks for all prisoners in all prisons, particularly not in the highly differentiated prison system of today. Watch a prison movie from the Big House era and then relate it to what you see when you visit a medium-security state or federal prison today. The environments are radically different. The text that provides the best general guide to contemporary prison life is *Behind Bars: Surviving Prison* (2002), by Jeffrey Ian Ross and Stephen C. Richards. Both are PhD criminologists; Ross worked in prison for four years, and Richards served eleven years in prison and on parole as a convicted drug dealer.

In their introduction, Ross and Richards write, "Prison bears little resemblance to what you've seen in movies or read about in books."[71] Their point is well made: public perceptions of prison life are shaped by the most popular accounts, which are often the most extreme and sensationalized. The most violent, sociopathic inmate who tells the most depraved stories of his prison experiences in maximum security and supermax may get all the attention because his stories are the most *interesting*—murders, rapes, escapes, riots, brutality. The prison film that tells the biggest lies and most distorts the truth, particularly if it shows a convict who triumphs over an unjust legal system and lives happily ever after, is the one that gets all the attention (and often wins the awards). The ordinary prisoner in the predominant low- to medium-security prison of today leads a much less interesting life. The account of his days looks like the diary of a house cat: "ate, slept, peed, and looked out the window." Who would buy his story? Thus, outsiders, seeing the movies and reading the popular books, tend to think that all prisoners live the lives of the two extremes—either the very worst or the very best—when in fact the lives of most prisoners in confinement are characterized by humdrum monotony, boredom, and dead time strung out for years on end. What can prisons do to make prison time less of a waste to both prisoner and society?

KEY TERMS

rehabilitation
recreation
self-improvement
prisonization
convict code
convicts
free world
inmates
prison argot
bug
fish
screw
shiv
universal factors of
 imprisonment
cliques
institutionalized
the yard
corruption of authority
deprivation
pains of imprisonment
cigarettes
rat

center man
gorilla
merchant
wolf
punk
fag
ball buster
real man
tough
hipster
total institution
disculturation
institutionalization
importation
state-raised youth
square john
jailing
doing time
gleaning
governmental perspective
general population
special management

administrative segregation
disciplinary detention
protective custody
mental health housing
affectional starvation
dyads
prison family
kinship
femme
stud broad
kites
the life
the cool
the square
the mix
vengeful equity
goon squads
SORT
prison riots
mass rebellion
Attica riot
Santa Fe riot

monosexual
asexual
co-correctional prisons
gang rape
galboys
jailhouse turnouts
Prison Rape Elimination
 Act of 2003
furloughs
conjugal visiting
prison gangs
security threat groups
Mexican Mafia
Nuestra Familia
Texas Syndicate
Mexikanemi
Aryan Brotherhood
Black Guerilla Family
Bloods
Crips
bus therapy
prison hospices

NOTES

1. Malcolm Braly, *False Starts: A Memoir of San Quentin and Other Prisons* (Boston: Little, Brown, 1976), pp. 181–82.

2. Piri Thomas, *Seven Long Times* (New York: Praeger Publishers, 1974), pp. 83–84.

3. Donald Clemmer, *The Prison Community* (New York: Rinehart and Company, 1958), p. 299.

4. Ibid., p. 152.

5. Ibid., pp. 330–36.

6. Ibid., pp. 301–2.

7. Ibid., p. 118.

8. Norman S. Hayner and Ellis Ash, "The Prison as a Community," *American Sociological Review* 5 (August 1940): 577.

9. Robert Johnson, "Race, Gender, and the American Prison: Historical Observations," in Joycelyn M. Pollock, *Prisons Today and Tomorrow* (Gaithersburg, Md.: Aspen Publishers, 1997), p. 40.

10. Gresham M. Sykes, *The Society of Captives: A Study of a Maximum Security Prison* (Princeton, N.J.: Princeton University Press, 1958), p. xii.

11. Ibid., p. 58.

12. Ibid., pp. 84–108.

13. Ibid., p. 127.

14. Erving Goffman, "Characteristics of Total Institutions," in *Asylums: Essays on the Social Situation of Mental Patients and Other Inmates* (Chicago: Aldine Publishing, 1962), p. xiii.

15. Ibid., pp. 5–6.

16. John Irwin, *The Felon* (Englewood Cliffs, N.J.: Prentice Hall, 1970), pp. 7–35.

17. Ibid., p. 68.

18. Ibid., p. 66.

19. John J. DiIulio Jr., *Governing Prisons: A Comparative Study of Correctional Management* (New York: Free Press, 1987), pp. 46–47.

20. Ibid., p. 47.

21. Compiled from Camille Graham Camp and George M. Camp, *The Corrections Yearbook 2001: Adult Systems* (Middletown, Conn.: Criminal Justice Institute, 2002), pp. 79–84.

22. Jean Harris, *They Always Call Us Ladies: Stories from Prison* (New York: Charles Scribner's Sons, 1988), p. 139.

23. Discussed in Barbara Owen, *"In the Mix": Struggle and Survival in a Women's Prison* (Albany: State University of New York Press, 1998), p. 5.

24. Rose Giallombardo, *Society of Women: A Study of a Women's Prison* (New York: John Wiley & Sons, 1966), pp. 123–29.

25. Owen, *"In the Mix,"* p. 193.

26. Giallombardo, *Society of Women*, pp. 200–209.

27. Discussed in Owen, *In the Mix*, p. 7.

28. Ibid.

29. Ibid., p. 61.

30. Ibid., p. 69.

31. Camp and Camp, *The Corrections Yearbook 2001*, p. 156.

32. L. Mara Dodge, "One Female Prisoner Is of More Trouble Than Twenty Males: Women Convicts in Illinois Prisons, 1835–1896," *Journal of Social History* 32 (summer 1999): 907.

33. Owen, *In the Mix*, p. 179.

34. Ibid., p. 120.

35. Kathryn Watterson, *Women in Prison: Inside the Concrete Womb* (Boston: Northeastern University Press, 1996), p. 78.

36. Meda Chesney-Lind, "Women in Prison: From Partial Justice to Vengeful Equity," *Corrections Today* 60, no. 8 (December 1998): 68.

37. Ibid.

38. Camp and Camp, *The Corrections Yearbook 2001*, p. 42.

39. Ibid.

40. DiIulio, *Governing Prisons*, pp. 54–56.

41. Camp and Camp, *The Corrections Yearbook 2001*, p. 53.

42. Ibid.

43. American Correctional Association, *The American Prison: From the Beginning . . . A Pictorial History* (Gaithersburg, Md.: American Correctional Association, 1983), p. 26.

44. Sykes, *Society of Captives*, p. 110.

45. Peg and Walter McGraw, *Assignment: Prison Riots* (New York: Henry Holt, 1954), p. 217.

46. Tom Wicker, *A Time to Die* (New York: Quadrangle/ New York Times Book Co., 1975), p. 301.

47. Scott Christianson, *With Liberty for Some: 500 Years of Imprisonment in America* (Boston: Northeastern University Press, 1998), p. 273.

48. Stephen Donaldson, "Can We Put an End to Inmate Rape?" *USA Today Magazine*, May 1995, p. 40, and "Prison Rape Elimination Act Becomes Federal Law," September 4, 2003, *www.spr.org/en/ pressreleases/2003/0904.html.*

49. Cindy Struckman-Johnson and David Struckman-Johnson, "Sexual Coercion Rates in Seven Midwestern Prison Facilities for Men," *Prison Journal* 80, no. 4 (December 2000): 383.

50. Ibid., p. 385.

51. Ibid., p. 379.

52. Wilbert Rideau, "Prison: The Sexual Jungle," *The Angolite*, November/December 1979, p. 54.

53. Ibid., p. 52.

54. Donaldson, "Prison Rape Elimination Act Becomes Federal Law."

55. Braly, *False Starts*, p. 227.

56. James B. Jacobs, "Focusing on Prison Gangs," *Corrections Management Quarterly* 5, no. 1 (winter 2001): vi.

57. Mark S. Fleisher and Scott H. Decker, "An Overview of the Challenge of Prison Gangs," *Corrections Management Quarterly* 5, no. 1 (winter 2001): 3.

58. Ibid.

59. Ibid., pp. 4–5.

60. Ibid.

61. James B. Jacobs, *Stateville: The Penitentiary in Mass Society* (Chicago: University of Chicago Press, 1977), pp. 138–46.

62. Camp and Camp, *The Corrections Yearbook 2001*, pp. 77–78.

63. Ann Scott Tyson, "Prison Threat: Gangs Grab More Power," *Christian Science Monitor*, July 15, 1997.

64. Fleisher and Decker, "An Overview of the Challenge of Prison Gangs," pp. 7–8.

65. Camp and Camp, *The Corrections Yearbook 2001*, p. 42.

66. Douglas Dennis, "Suicide in Prison: The Hanging Game," *The Angolite*, March/April 1993, p. 25.

67. Brett Barrouquere, "Death and Redemption: Inmate Volunteers Help Dying Fellow Prisoners at Angola's Prison Hospice," *Sunday Advocate* (Baton Rouge, La.), December 21, 2003, p. 4B.

68. Ibid.

69. Abraham Myerson, "Introducing the Prisoner," in Victor Nelson, *Prison Days and Nights* (New York: Garden City Publishing, 1936), p. xvii.

70. Peter Remick and James B. Shuman, *In Constant Fear* (New York: Reader's Digest Press, 1975), p. xi.

71. Jeffrey Ian Ross and Stephen C. Richards, *Behind Bars: Surviving Prison* (Indianapolis: Alpha Books, 2002), p. ix.

FURTHER READING

Any of the books mentioned by author and title in this chapter would be useful resources for learning more about prison life. The ones listed here are highly recommended.

Braly, Malcolm. *False Starts: A Memoir of San Quentin and Other Prisons*. Boston: Little, Brown, 1976.

Clemmer, Donald. *The Prison Community*. New York: Rinehart and Company, 1958.

Earley, Pete. *The Hot House: Life Inside Leavenworth Prison*. New York: Bantam Books, 1992.

Harris, Jean. *They Always Call Us Ladies: Stories from Prison*. New York: Charles Scribner's Sons, 1988.

Nelson, Victor. *Prison Days and Nights*. Garden City, N.Y.: Garden City Publishing, 1936.

Owen, Barbara. *"In the Mix": Struggle and Survival in a Women's Prison*. Albany: State University of New York Press, 1998.

Remick, Peter, and James B. Shuman. *In Constant Fear*. New York: Reader's Digest Press, 1975.

Rideau, Wilbert, and Ron Wikberg. *Life Sentences: Rage and Survival behind Bars*. New York: Times Books, 1992.

Ross, Jeffrey Ian, and Stephen C. Richards. *Behind Bars: Surviving Prison*. Indianapolis: Alpha Books, 2002.

Ross, Jeffrey Ian, and Stephen C. Richards. *Convict Criminology*. Belmont, Calif.: Wadsworth/Thomson Learning, 2003.

Santos, Michael G. *About Prison*. Belmont, Calif.: Wadsworth/Thomson Learning, 2004.

Watterson, Kathryn. *Women in Prison: Inside the Concrete Womb*. Rev. ed. Boston: Northeastern University Press, 1996.

Wicker, Tom. *A Time to Die*. New York: Quadrangle/New York Times Book Co., 1975.

WEB AND VIDEO RESOURCES

PrisonerLife.com (at *www.PrisonerLife.com*) describes itself as "an open and uncensored forum networking prisoners, prisons, and the world."

Cell Door Magazine is an online journal written by prisoners for the free world. Its address is *www.celldoor.com*.

The Stop Prisoner Rape Website is *www.spr.org*.

13 Convict Criminology

by Stephen C. Richards and Jeffrey Ian Ross

The dramatic increase in prison populations in the United States created the opportunity for a growing number of former prisoners to study criminology and become professors. As a result of their experience with arrest, trial, and years of incarceration, many have unique insights that inform what we know about crime and corrections.

Since 1997, a handful of ex-convict criminology and criminal justice professors have organized sessions at annual meetings of the American Society of Criminology, Academy of Criminal Justice Sciences, and American Correctional Association. These presentations draw large audiences and feature provocative discussions about the academic response to and responsibility for deteriorating prison conditions.

The conference presentations were used to build a working group of ex-convict and non-convict critical criminologists to contribute to "The New School of Convict Criminology" (Richards and Ross, 2001; Ross and Richards, 2003). This is a "new criminology" led by ex-convicts who are now academic faculty. These men and women, who have worn both prison uniforms and academic regalia, are the primary architects of the movement. As ex-convicts now employed at universities, the convict criminologists openly discuss their personal history and distrust of "mainstream" criminology.

Regardless of criminal history, all the group members share a desire to go beyond "managerial" and "armchair" criminology by conducting research that includes ethnography and "inside perspective." In contrast to normative academic practice, the "Convict Criminologists" hold no pretense for value-free criminology and are partisan and proactive in their discourse. This includes merging convict, ex-convict, and critical voices in their writing.

The ex-convicts can be described, in terms of academic experience, as three distinct cohorts. The first are the more senior members, full and associate professors, some with distinguished research records. A second group of assistant professors is just beginning to contribute to the field. The third, only some of which have been identified, are the graduate student ex-convicts.

While all these individuals provide Convict Criminology with unique and original experiential resources, some of the most important contributors may yet prove to be critical scholars who have never served prison time. A number of these authors (e.g., Bruce Arrigo, James Austin, Mary Bosworth, Preston Elrod, Burk Foster, Marianne Fisher-Giorlando, Barbara Owen, Jeffrey Ian Ross, Michael Welch) have worked inside prisons or conducted extensive research on the subject. The inclusion of these "non-cons" in the new school provides the means to extend the influence of the new school while also supporting existing critical criminology perspectives. For example, Convict Criminology speaks to the use of criminal justice machinery to oppress the underclass, working class, racial and ethnic minorities, and women.

Convict Criminology specializes in "on site" ethnographic research where their prior experience with imprisonment informs their work. The exconvicts are comfortable interviewing in penitentiary cellblocks, in community penal facilities, or on street corners. Their method is to enter jails and prisons and converse with prisoners. This may include a combination of survey instruments, structured interviews and informal observation and conversation. As former prisoners they know the "walk" and "talk" of the prison, and how to gain the confidence of the men and women who live inside. As a result, they have earned a reputation for collecting quality and controversial data.

The Convict Criminologists all share an aversion to the language used in most academic research writing on crime and corrections. Typically, researchers use words like "offender and "inmate." In comparison, Convict Criminology prefers to use convicts, prisoners, or simply men or women. The distinction is important as it illustrates the different point of view of researchers and authors that have never been incarcerated with those that have. Offender and inmate are "managerial words" used by police, court officials and criminal justice administrators to deny the humanity of defendants and prisoners. To the ear of a former prisoner, being referred to as an offender or inmate, is analogous to a man being called a boy, or a women a girl. Clearly, the struggle feminists fought to redefine how women were addressed and discussed taught an important lesson to the Convict Criminologists: words are important.

Our text *Convict Criminology* suggests several policy recommendations. First, the group advocates dramatic reductions in the national prison population through diversion to probation or other community programs. Today, many men and women are sentenced to prison for nonviolent crime. These people should be evaluated as candidates for early release, with the remainder of their sentence to be served under community supervision. A prisoner should have an opportunity to reduce his or her sentence by earning "good time credit" for good behavior and program participation.

Second, Convict Criminologists support the closing of large-scale penitentiaries and reformatories, where prisoners are warehoused in massive cellblocks. Over many decades, the design and operation of these "big house" prisons have resulted in murder, assault, and sexual predation. A reduced prison population housed in smaller institutions would be accomplished by constructing or redesigning prison housing units with single cells or rooms. Smaller prisons, for example, with a maximum of 500 prisoners, with single cells or rooms, should become the correctional standard when we begin to seriously consider the legal requirement for safe and secure institutions. As a model, we should look to European countries that have much lower rates of incarceration, shorter sentences, and smaller prisons.

Third, we need to listen carefully to prisoner complaints about long sentences, overcrowding, double celling, bad food, old uniforms, lack of heat in winter, no air-conditioning in summer, inadequate vocational and education programs, and institutional violence. The list grows longer when we take a careful look at how these conditions contribute to prisoners being poorly prepared for returning home and the large number that return to prison.

Fourth, we have strong evidence that prison programs are under-funded, since administrators and legislators continue to emphasize custody at the expense of treatment. Prisoners should be provided with opportunities for better paid institutional employment, advanced vocational training, higher education, and family skills programs.

We need to ask convicts what services and programs they want and need to improve their ability to live law-abiding lives rather than assume and then implement what we believe is good for them. At the very least, all prisons should have a program that supports prisoners to complete college credit course by correspondence.

Fifth, Convict Criminology advocates voting rights for all prisoners and felons. The USA is one of the few advanced industrial countries that continues to deny prisoners and felons voting rights. We suggest that if convicts could vote, many of the recommendations we advocate would become policy because the politicians would be forced to campaign for convict votes. State and federal government will only begin to address the deplorable conditions in our prisons when prisoners and felons become voters.

Sixth, we advocate prisoners released from prison have enough "gate money" that would allow them to pay for three months worth of rent and food. All prisoners exiting correctional institutions should have clothing suitable for applying for employment, eye glasses (if needed), identification (social security card, state ID or driver's license, and a copy of their institutional medical records).

Seventh, our most controversial policy recommendation is eliminating the snitch system in prison. The snitch system is used by "guards" in old-style institutions to supplement their surveillance of convicts. It is used to control prisoners by turning them against each other, and is therefore responsible for ongoing institutional violence. If our recommendations for a smaller population, housed in single cells or rooms, with better food and clothing, voting rights, and well-funded institutional programming were implemented, the snitch system would be unnecessary.

Finally, we support the termination of the drug war. Military metaphors continue to confuse our thinking and complicate our approach to crime and drug addiction. For example, the theory of judicial deterrence, discussed as a rationale for sentencing in nearly every criminal justice textbook, is derived from the "Cold War" idea of nuclear deterrence. This idea evolved into mutually assured destruction (MAD), which was the American rationale for building thousands of nuclear bombs to deter a possible Soviet nuclear attack. The use of deterrence and war has now bled over from the military strategic thinking to colonize criminal justice. The result is another cold war, this one against our own people. We advocate an end to the drug war, amnesty for drug offenders, and a reexamination of how our criminal justice priorities are set.

Convict Criminology is a new way of thinking about crime and corrections. The alumni of the penitentiary now study in classrooms and serve as university faculty. The old textbooks in criminology, criminal justice and corrections will have to be revised. A new field of study has been created, a paradigm shift occurred, and the prison is no longer so distant.

14 Humane Prisons: A Call for Decency in Conservative Times

by Robert Johnson

Americans sink a lot of money into prisons these days, and they want a return on their investment. National opinion surveys routinely show that most Americans want prisons to punish and reform criminals, thereby doing justice and reducing crime. The popular view that criminals should take their medicine (punishment), get well (with the help of correctional programs) and then move on to law-abiding lives shows a wisdom that belies the angry conservative sentiments we hear about in the media.

Prisons are, first and foremost, settings of punishment where criminals are sent to serve hard time for the harms they've done. The lives of inmates are mostly lives of deprivation and pain. Though some offenders are embittered and made more dangerous by imprisonment, confinement need not be a destructive experience. The mainstream of public opinion is correct in supposing that hard time can be constructive time—that decent prisons provide a rehearsal for responsible living in the free world.

It is a measure of our conservative times that the very notion of a decent prison seems naive. Today, among a vocal and influential minority, the term "hard time" has become a euphemism for harsh—even brutal—prisons and a clarion call for gratuitous suffering through the restriction of recreation, the imposition of more cell time and even the escalation of the pace of executions and reinvention of such degrading practices as the chain gang. In many ways, we are attempting to roll back prison history—a history that is in no small measure one of modest but important efforts to develop humane prisons.

Attempts to make hard time harder amount to political rhetoric. Few restrictive proposals have been implemented, though no doubt more will be put in place over the coming years. These proposals are troubling because they are mean-spirited and wrong-headed. Inmates are not asked to trade off creature comforts for correctional programs—television time for program time; barbells and basketballs for computers and books. Instead, programs are to be thrown out with such luxuries as regular exercise and daily showers.

If brutal prisons deterred, one might well support them. But the futility of inhumane punishments is a matter of long historical record. The experience of abuse, on the streets and in prisons, renders people less, not more, capable of managing their lives. To deter criminals, we must discourage crime and encourage conventional living. We must inspire fear of punishment while providing options for noncriminal living. Fear alone never is enough to deter crime; the likely result is a cornered and desperate criminal who is a profound danger to society. Sending offenders to decent prisons is not only the humane thing to do, it is the effective thing to do because it can promote rehabilitation.

Much of today's get-tough mania is the product of misguided nostalgia. Politicians in Mississippi recently bemoaned the passing of the days when convicts "smelled like convicts" because they didn't have the privilege of regular showers. These sentiments appear to be shared by politicians in states as disparate as North Carolina, Virginia, and California.

Some politicians favor the return of chain gangs, and indeed chain gangs have emerged in Alabama, Florida, and Arizona in a limited form. Once again, our political leaders appear to have forgotten the real nature of the chain gangs that have traversed many of our southern and western states over the years. The smell of slavery always was a feature of these grotesque operations. So, too, was the smell of death; death rates on chain gangs were incredibly high. No one mentions dead black men and women convicts today when they applaud the rebirth of chain gangs, hailing them as perhaps the ultimate antidote to today's alleged country club prisons.

It is against the backdrop of country club prisons and soft time that some citizens and politicians raise their voices in favor of hard time and a dramatic end to the supposed coddling of inmates. The comments of Charles Smith, a Mississippi state representative, are typical: "It used to be you'd pick cotton, and people weren't too crazy about going to prison. Nowadays, if you want to lead a life of luxury, sit around and watch TV, you can go to prison."

Although such comments are sincere, the claim that our prisons are country clubs is ludicrous. While it is true that some prisons offer comforts, these generally are modest. The real problem is warehousing—the storage of inmates in penal environments that offer them little or nothing constructive to do. Ironically, warehouse prisons viewed from the outside may look inviting. Idle time prevails in a warehouse prison, and idle time can look like easy time. Outsiders are taken in by appearances, and citizens begin to imagine convicts lolling about in orgies of leisure, assuming this to be the norm. In the absence of tangible evidence of punishment—such as the work, pain, and visible suffering obvious with chain gangs—the public infers contentment and even a country club lifestyle.

But appearances to the contrary, our prisons are not country clubs: the guests are involuntary, the conditions spartan and the routine deadly dull. Little can be found that can pass for luxury; even less occurs to lift the human spirit or mend broken lives. Most inmates spin out empty days and kill time by napping in their cells, walking the yard with their buddies, exercising, or slouching semi-comatose before incessantly blaring televisions.

Corrections professionals know better than to think of prisons as country clubs, but sometimes we have trouble spelling out exactly what we think prisons are or should be. My vision of prisons is premised on the notion of decency. Decent prisons should be suitable for human habitation and responsive to basic human needs.

Decent prisons are "good enough" institutions—prisons good enough for the job of housing offenders under humane conditions. However, they do not offer inmates the right to an easy or comfortable time behind bars. Inmates must serve hard time, but hard time also can be constructive time. Inmates can learn something worthwhile during their confinement.

The most valuable lessons inmates can learn are those that enable them to cope maturely with the pains of imprisonment. Mature coping, as I have defined the term, has three elements: (1) dealing directly with one's problems, using resources legitimately at one's disposal; (2) refusing to employ deceit or violence other than in self-defense; and (3) building mutual and supportive relationships with others. Mature coping means dealing with life's problems responsibly.

Inmates who cope maturely are the solid citizens of the prison community. Lessons in mature living learned in prison are valuable because, though it may not be obvious, there are parallels between the pains of prison and the pains of life in general. Imprisonment is painful because it deprives a person of liberty, goods and services, heterosexual contact, autonomy and security. It puts an enormous strain on relationships with loved ones outside and suspends or even ruins the possibility of a conventional occupational career. Yet all of us suffer these pains to some degree. Most of us are not as free as we would like, do not have all the goods and services we'd like,

don't feel completely satisfied by our sexual outlets, or don't feel as autonomous or secure as we'd like. We all must live with restrictions and deprivations of one kind or another.

The correspondence between general life problems and prison problems is especially salient for the lower-class men and women who make up the vast bulk of our prison populations, Indeed, we know that many of these offenders come from urban slums that arguably are as harsh and depriving as prisons themselves. "Doing time" in a ghetto is a familiar if uncongenial experience in the lives of these men and women. The inmate who learns to cope maturely with the stresses posed by confinement is learning to cope maturely with the stresses of life.

All inmates retain a right to conditions of confinement that show consideration and respect for their humanity, but they still are responsible for their crimes and deserve punishment. Offenders must be treated as persons who deserve to suffer the deprivation of freedom inherent in imprisonment, as well as the loss or attenuation of many of the comforts and privileges that attach to freedom in our society. Our modern understanding of this arrangement is that offenders are sent to prison as punishment—loss of freedom and associated privileges—not for punishment that might be meted out behind bars. Earlier prisons were settings of corporal punishment, but modem prisons are settings of deprivation.

A decent prison, then, should have a bare-bones, Spartan quality to it. The regime is one that is short on amenities but long on autonomy—it need not entail the elimination of choice. The hallmark of personhood is self-determination, which brings with it the potential for personal growth and self-actualization. Self-determination requires that a person deal directly with problems, the first step in mature coping. No just punishment—and hence no decent prison—can take away the inmate's capacity for self-determination. Persons have the moral right to make choices that influence their lives and the moral obligation to bear responsibility for the consequences of these choices. One can argue that inmates have chosen the punishment of prison as a consequence of their crimes, but prison need not be a human wasteland. Prisons must promote autonomy, even as they limit freedom. Inmates should be free to make choices within the prison world that have meaningful implications for the quality and character of the lives they will lead behind bars and upon release.

11 SPECIAL NEEDS PRISONERS

The prison, above all others, should be the most human of institutions.

— EUGENE V. DEBS, 1927

INTRODUCTION

Prisoners have often been called "special people" not because they are so beloved but because they suffer from so many disabilities or limitations that make it difficult for them to succeed outside prison—even without the curse of a felony conviction. We have touched on these issues earlier as part of the background of men and women behind bars. This chapter looks at special needs prisoners in custody, focusing on their problems in confinement and how the prison system responds to their needs. After reading the material in this chapter, you should be familiar with:

1. Juvenile prisoners.
2. Mentally ill prisoners.
3. Substance abusing prisoners.
4. Mentally retarded or developmentally challenged prisoners.
5. HIV/AIDS prisoners.
6. Sex criminals.
7. Protective custody prisoners.
8. Older prisoners.

We will look in depth at juvenile prisoners, spending less time on the other categories as we try to get an overall understanding of the complications added to prison life by these special needs inmates.

JUVENILE CRIMINALS

For a very long time, juvenile criminals were dealt with by the same courts and under the same terms as adult offenders: age made no legal difference in processing or punishing offenders, except whatever human feelings a judge might have for an offender of tender years. The origins of American juvenile law can be traced to English common law, which divided children into three categories: under age seven, seven to fourteen, and fourteen and over. Children under seven could not be held criminally responsible. With seven- to fourteen-year-olds, the issue was whether they understood right from wrong; if they understood their act was wrong, they were punished as adults. Anyone fourteen or older was subject to adult punishment.[1]

As the common law developed, a special civil court called the **chancery court** was created. One of its functions was to provide for the welfare of minor children, in particular those left orphaned or abandoned. The doctrine of *parens patriae,* meaning "the state as parent," gave the king, as the father of the country, authority to manage the affairs of dependent children through the courts. Such a child was called a **ward** of the state. Thus, the concept of state intervention in the lives of children was established long ago, though it was not until the 1800s that modern behavioral scientists defined the concept of **juvenile delinquency;** reformers argued that youthful offenders should be handled by a separate court following civil procedures, not the criminal procedures of the adult court. The modern juvenile court represents a merger of the old authority of the chancery court and more contemporary ideas about causes of behavior.

Today we take the existence of the juvenile court for granted. If you are a juvenile—meaning that you are under the age of adult criminal responsibility, which in the majority of states is eighteen—you will be dealt with by a separate system that processes only juveniles, under special rules and procedures. The only exceptions would be those persons legally juveniles who are waived or transferred to the adult courts for prosecution, usually either as habitual offenders or as defendants charged with the most serious violent crimes.

The juvenile justice system of today is often criticized as being ineffective in dealing with crimes committed by young people, particularly a perceived outburst of juvenile violence. Juvenile criminality does strongly influence our crime statistics. Each year, about one-third of arrests for the FBI's Index crimes and one-sixth of arrests for the index violent crimes were of persons under age eighteen. The arrest rate, which is the likelihood that a person of a certain age will be taken into custody, is highest for persons in the fifteen-to-eighteen age-group and declines substantially over the next few years into the mid-twenties, where it declines even further. Present estimates are that about one in six boys and one in twelve girls will be referred to juvenile court before their eighteenth birthday. Juveniles are our most active criminals, though social historians tell us this has been true in earlier cultures as well—societies with lots of young people tend to have high rates of antisocial behavior, including criminal behavior.

The perception that today's juveniles are meaner than those of even a few years ago has led to calls to "get tougher" on juvenile crimes, with the usual prescriptions—more court referrals, longer sentences, more juveniles behind bars, and more juveniles subject to transfer to adult court—to ensure that hardcore juvenile criminals do not "slip through the cracks." In the 1990s, our political vocabulary began to include such terms as "predator" and **superpredator,** usually referring to a violent, inner-city minority youth who is also a gang member, to define our fear of juvenile criminality.[2] Statistics say otherwise, showing that juvenile violence has dropped sharply since 1994, but policymakers are perfectly willing to ignore the facts when public opinion dictates.

Juveniles not only commit violent crimes but also are victims of violent crime at higher rates than are adults. Juvenile violence is often associated with gangs that now exist in many inner-city and suburban areas. The victims of violence are often members of other gangs or people who get in the way of intergang conflict. Much juvenile violence takes place at school; many schools have become high-security fortresses in an effort to control violence by students and nonstudents on school property. As **juvenile gangs** have become more involved in drug trafficking, particularly crack cocaine, they move into a world where the three Rs, formerly "reading, 'riting, and 'rithmetic," are now rip-offs, retaliation, and riddance of the opposition, namely, other intrusive, drug-dealing gang members, in neighborhood turf battles that center around schools.

The greater accessibility of firearms to juveniles and the enhanced cultural support for the use of deadly force to resolve disputes make life in the poorest parts of many large cities much like living in a war zone. Edwin Sutherland's influential 1930s social learning theory of criminality, **differential association,** suggested that juveniles learn criminality from their peers and reject the more conventional values of middle-class society. The youngsters of today's urban underclass have been exposed to so much violence in their environment—being around such a high concentration of both criminals and victims their entire lives—that violence for them is just a fact of life. What values will they teach their own children?

The juvenile court stepped into the lives of the young urban poor at the very beginning of the twentieth century. **Juvenile** comes from the Latin *juvenis*, meaning young, and it applies to children under the age of adult majority. The role of the state, through the juvenile court, was to provide protection or salvation, which developed over time into the contemporary idea of rehabilitation. We think of the juvenile court as handling criminals, but in fact a sizable number of juvenile court cases deal with juveniles not charged with crimes. The historical evidence suggests that the juvenile court was really intended to deal more with petty criminals and noncriminals, especially the children of the **dangerous classes**—poor immigrants and minorities who were flooding American cities by the end of the 1800s.

The juvenile court was designed to apply civil law procedures to the lives of young persons who required state intervention, whether they were criminals or merely troubled young people who seemed likely to grow into unproductive adults. The court would in time divide its clientele into three main types of cases:

1. A **delinquent juvenile** is a minor who has committed a crime for which an adult could be arrested. Technically, a juvenile is not a delinquent until he has been to court and in a hearing before a judge has been "adjudicated delinquent." Delinquency is in this sense a legal label. In the broader social sense of delinquency, we call young people delinquent who engage in all sorts of inappropriate behavior, whether it is criminal or not. Delinquents are one category of young people processed through the juvenile court.

2. This category is made up of what are called **status offenders,** who have engaged in acts that are specifically wrong for underage youth but not against the law for adults. Such acts typically include running away, curfew violations, truancy and school misconduct, disobeying or threatening parents,

sexual promiscuity (emphasized much more for girls than boys), and under-age drinking. Status offenders may be referred to in the statutes as **incorrigible juveniles.** In the terminology of the juvenile court, they are often identified as **PINS** (persons in need of supervision), CHINS or CINS (children in need of supervision), or MINS (minors in need of supervision). Some states have broadened this concept to FINS (families in need of services) to recognize that the status offender's problem is usually part of a larger family context. The whole family often needs intervention rather than just one problem child.

3. This category of children subject to juvenile court intervention is made up of what the Uniform Juvenile Court Act—a legal model drawn up by the American Bar Association in the juvenile court reform era of the 1960s—calls "deprived, neglected, or dependent children." These children have not done anything wrong, or at least they are not in court because they have. Their problems lie with their parents' failure to provide for them. These children are usually termed either **neglected,** meaning their parents are at fault for not taking proper care of them, or **dependent,** meaning that the parents, through no fault of their own (such as sickness or mental illness or extreme poverty), have failed to provide a proper home environment. Children in either category can end up wards of the state under *parens patriae.*

The original **juvenile court** was deliberately different from the adult criminal court of the time. The first American juvenile court began operating in Chicago (Cook County), Illinois, in 1899. Its principal features were the following:

1. Traditional courtrooms were not used; all that was actually required were a table and chairs where the judge, the child and his or her parents, and probation officers could sit together and discuss the case.
2. Children could be brought before the court on the basis of complaints of citizens, parents, police, school officials, or others.
3. The children's hearings were not public, and their records were kept confidential because children coming before the court were not considered criminal.
4. Proof of the child's criminality was not required for the child to be considered in need of the court's services.
5. The court had great discretion in determining what kind of services the child required and had wide latitude in determining a disposition.
6. Lawyers were not required because the hearings were not adversarial.
7. The standards and procedures long in use in adult courts were missing in the juvenile courts; the standard of proof beyond a reasonable doubt was not required, and hearsay was permitted.[3]

The juvenile court system today continues to use different terminology and operates (at least in theory) under a premise different from the adult criminal court. Juveniles brought into the system are screened through a process called **intake.** The majority of all juveniles taken into police custody are released or handled through other informal alternatives at this point; the more serious or chronic offenders will have a petition filed. The **petition** is the legal document that specifies the basis for juvenile court action. The juvenile who goes to court is entitled to two hearings, though they are often collapsed into one. The first is called **adjudication,** which proves guilt, like an adult trial; the second is **disposition,** which determines the proper sentencing alternative—most often some form of probation.

The juvenile court was founded on the hope of **rehabilitation.** Its broad authority is captured in *Commonwealth v. Fisher*, a 1905 Pennsylvania Supreme Court decision:

> To save a child from becoming a criminal, or from continuing in a career of crime, to end in maturer years in public punishment and disgrace, the legislature surely may provide for the salvation of such a child, if its parents or guardian be unable or unwilling to do so, by bringing it into one of the courts of the state without any process at all, for the purpose of subjecting it to the state's guardianship and protection. . . . The act is but an exercise by the state of its supreme power over the welfare of its children, a power over which it can take a child from its father, and let it go where it will, without committing it to any guardianship or any institution, if the welfare of the child, taking its age into consideration, can be thus best promoted.[4]

The juvenile court was intended to help, embracing a broad range of young people, more noncriminals than criminals at first but gradually mixing large numbers of each indiscriminately, within its loving arms. Acting through the kindly, paternal figure of the juvenile court judge, who represented the authority and discipline believed to be missing from the young person's life, the court was to push the juvenile along into the institutional or noncustodial setting, where he or she could get the assistance needed for the problem behavior.

Despite its good intentions and optimistic start, what happened over time was that juvenile justice became the most neglected part of the criminal justice system. It was the worst funded and least supported. It operated outside the visible adult system, and few people really knew what it was doing. The legal process in the juvenile court was highly informal, lacking any relation to due process, and the sanctioning authority of juvenile court judges was unchecked as long as they remained within statutory age limits. A murderer could be put on probation, whereas a habitual runaway could be locked up until he turned eighteen or twenty-one. Criminals and noncriminals were dealt with as if they had similar problems and needs and were equally deserving of confinement. A generation ago, you could go to a secure juvenile training school in most states and find large numbers of status offenders and neglected children—as well as the mentally retarded, handicapped, orphans and abandoned children, pregnant girls, and any other juveniles for whom the state lacked placement alternatives—confined with delinquents who had committed serious crimes. This mix gave rise to the frequently stated notion that what were intended to be "reform schools" became **crime schools,** which made their young residents much worse. The recidivism rates of training schools, which were much higher than the rates for adult prisons, tended to support this notion.

In the 1960s and 1970s, the courts, the federal government and many state governments began to address the problems a half century of neglect had created in the juvenile courts. The first two in a series of important U.S. Supreme Court decisions, ***Kent v. United States*** (1966) and ***In re Gault*** (1967), addressed the legal rights of juveniles. *Kent* was an important background case, although in substance it dealt only with the issue of waiving juveniles to adult courts for trial in that it reviewed the history of second-rate juvenile court operations.

The *Gault* case was much more important, applying adult standards of due process to what had previously been a very informal legal environment. With *Gault*, juveniles got the right to counsel, to notice of charges, to an adversarial proceeding, and to the privilege against self-incrimination that had been lacking previously. Other cases over the next decade further clarified the juvenile's legal rights, moving juvenile courts toward the more formal **due process** standards of adult criminal courts.

In 1974, Congress passed the **Juvenile Justice and Delinquency Prevention Act.** This important piece of legislation had great impact on the states, requiring several important changes of direction in juvenile justice if the states wished to continue receiving federal crime control money:

1. Noncriminal status offenders and other noncriminals were not supposed to be mixed with criminal delinquents in secure custodial settings.
2. Juveniles were not supposed to be mixed with adult offenders in jails and prisons.
3. A policy of **decarceration,** often called **deinstitutionalization,** in its application to noncriminal juveniles, which involved reducing the number of young people held in secure custody, was to result in larger numbers of young people being dealt with through community-based alternatives rather than in secure settings.
4. **Decriminalization** of deviant behavior was to result in the removal of noncriminals from the juvenile court and particularly from secure institutions such as detention homes and training schools. Criminals should be dealt with formally, according to the emerging concepts of juvenile due process, but noncriminals should be handled informally outside the system as much as possible.

Officials at the state level and in many local jurisdictions tried to go even further. **Jerome Miller** in Massachusetts closed his state's juvenile training schools in the early 1970s, trying to work with almost all delinquents, including violent offenders, in community-based programs. Miller rejected the **custody philosophy,** which suggests that some juvenile offenders on a scale of seriousness must always be locked up. He believed that for rehabilitation, secure custody did far more harm than good.

Other jurisdictions pushed diversion programs designed to take lesser offenders and noncriminals out of the process early on. Seeking to avoid the effects of labeling, **diversion** allows the offender to avoid a conviction by participating in a program providing treatment, community service, or some other alternative disposition. Diversion programs in local courts continue to siphon off a good percentage of young people who a few years ago would have been passed along to formal adjudication in the juvenile court. Diversion programs are sometimes accused of **net widening,** that is, pulling minor offenders into supervision within the system (because the recourse for a person who fails in diversion is to be returned to the formal system for routine processing), but such alternatives remain very popular with local officials who are often very discouraged at the results of more formal juvenile court processing.

The overall picture of the operation of the juvenile courts and juvenile corrections systems looks like this. It starts with juvenile arrests. Howard Snyder reports,

> In 2001 law enforcement agencies in the United States made an estimated 2.3 million arrests of persons under 18 (the accepted age of adult status, though in some states it is a lower age). According to the Federal Bureau of Investigation, juveniles accounted for 17 percent of all arrests and 15 percent of all violent crime arrests in 2001. The substantial growth in juvenile violent crime arrests that began in the late 1980s peaked in 1994. In 2001, for the seventh consecutive year, the rate of juvenile arrests for violent crime index offenses—murder, forcible rape, robbery, and aggravated assault—declined. Specifically, between 1994 and 2001, the juvenile arrest rate for violent crime index offenses fell 44 percent. As a result, the juvenile violent crime index rate in 2001 was the lowest since 1983. From its peak in 1993 to 2001, the juvenile arrest rate for murder fell 70 percent.[5]

About 70 percent of arrested juveniles were sent on to juvenile court. The remainder were dealt with through dismissal of charges, diversion, or referral to adult court. Juvenile courts processed about 2 million petitions—about 1.7 million delinquency cases based on arrests, the other 300,000 involving either status offenders or dependent and neglected children. The majority of these cases are handled informally through screening and adjustment. In 1999, 639,100 juveniles (about one in every four juveniles arrested) were formally adjudicated delinquent.[6]

The four common dispositional alternatives used in these cases were divided as follows:

Probation: 62 percent

Out-of-home placement (placement in a residential treatment center, juvenile corrections facility, foster home, or group home): 24 percent

Other disposition (restitution, fines, community service, or other referral): 10 percent

Release without sanction: 4 percent[7]

Juvenile Offenders and Victims: 1999 National Report counted nearly 106,000 juveniles under the control of the juvenile courts in public and private residential placement facilities on October 29, 1997, the date of the most recent census. The great majority (93.5 percent) were delinquents; the rest were status offenders. Over 70 percent of those in placement facilities had already been to court and been adjudicated; the rest were in detention. About 74 percent of juveniles were placed in public facilities, the other 26 percent in private facilities.[8]

If placement is made to what are called **staff-secure facilities,** meaning nonsecure or no locked doors or gates to keep juveniles in custody, four basic options are available:

1. **Group homes.** Mostly privately operated by nonprofit, for-profit, or religious organizations; often used for status offenders
2. **Treatment centers.** Many also privately operated but some public; the focus is on juveniles with substance abuse and mental health problems

3. **Experiential programs.** Also often privately operated; includes wilderness programs, such as Outward Bound, and other programs that remove juveniles from their home environment for enriching experiences

4. **Shelters.** Both private and public, housing short-term populations of neglected and abused children, runaways, and other juveniles, predominantly noncriminals

Two main types of publicly operated **locked facilities** house about two-thirds of all juveniles in placement:

1. *The* **detention center.** This facility, sometimes called by such names as the detention home or juvenile hall, is the jail for juveniles. It is typically a smaller, locally operated facility housing juveniles precourt and those awaiting transfer to other facilities. It is the descendant of the **house of refuge,** historically used to house poor children in the cities.

2. *The* **training school.** This facility, sometimes called the industrial school, reform school, or training institute, is the juvenile prison. It developed as a state-operated alternative to the penitentiary for younger criminals in the latter part of the 1800s. Various facilities that go by other names, including farms, ranches, boot camps, and reception centers, are similar to training schools if they hold committed juveniles behind locked doors.

Since the guiding principle of juvenile placement is supposed to be **the least restrictive alternative,** juvenile authorities pay close attention to the demographics of placement, especially with regard to the juveniles committed to state training schools. These facilities have such high long-term recidivism rates that a staff member long ago suggested that all juveniles sent home should be given little blue jackets like high school farm boys used to get when they were inducted into the FFA (Future Farmers of America). Only the training school jackets would read "FCA," for Future Convicts of America.

Juveniles placed in staff-secure facilities are about equally likely to be white or minority. They tend to be younger than those in locked facilities, and girls—who made up 14 percent of the juveniles in residential placement in 1997—are more likely to be placed in private or staff-secure facilities. The staff-secure facilities are used to place most status offenders (since in theory they are not supposed to be locked up) and many lesser delinquents on their way up. The farther along the scale of placement alternatives you go, from private to public, from staff secure to locked, the more the population resembles the population of the adult prisons in a given state. This means minority males who are repeat offenders; they are younger versions of the adult prison population. Status offenders, females, whites, middle-class juveniles, and those from two-parent families are more likely to be held in the private and staff-secure facilities that Clemens Bartollas and Stuart Miller have referred to as the **hidden system,** existing to process the more amenable-to-treatment middle-class juveniles. Lower-class male minorities from more dysfunctional environments and with fewer resources at hand get their shot at rehabilitation in the public, locked facilities.

We should keep in mind that at any given time, fewer than 10 percent of juveniles under correctional supervision are in secure custody, compared to about 30 percent of adults under correctional supervision. With its guiding principles of leniency, community-based alternatives, and second chances (principles bruised but still in place as the crime war abates), the juvenile justice system uses secure custody much more narrowly. Although custody was once frequently applied to disobedient and troublesome children—whether they were criminals or not—today it is focused on those serious criminals and habitual offenders who, if they were adults, would almost surely be locked up.

What is life like in the public juvenile facilities? Detention centers hold juveniles between arrest and disposition or placement. Most of them are small, holding fewer than fifty boys and girls (in separate housing), though some large city centers may hold 100 to 200 or more in a single facility. The juvenile courts tend to move more rapidly than the adult courts, so the average length of stay in custody is short. An average stay is about two weeks; 86 percent of juvenile in detention stay less than sixty days.[9] The increase in juvenile crime through the early 1990s resulted in overcrowding of detention facilities; in 1995, half of them—particularly the larger urban facilities that held about three-quarters of all juveniles in detention—were operating above their design capacity.

Many of the same criticisms that would be directed at small jails also apply to small detention centers. Even though they typically have more staff proportionately than jails do, they generally lack programs or purposeful activities for their residents, in part because of the short-term stays and high turnover. Like jails, detention centers have a much higher rate of suicide attempts than do institutions for committed offenders. In 1997, an estimated 9,100 youths under age eighteen were held not in detention centers but in adult jails. This practice, common at one time, was strongly discouraged by a provision of the Juvenile Justice and Delinquency Prevention Act of 1974 requiring **jail and lockup removal.** Short-term exceptions were allowed if the jail met **sight and sound separation** requirements—basically housing any juveniles in a separate unit where they had no contact with adults. These requirements were directed toward the old practice of throwing youths into cells with older prisoners where they were subjected to physical and sexual abuse.

The great majority of the youth in adult jails in 1997—over 75 percent—fall into one of two categories. In about ten states, the adult age of criminal responsibility is less than eighteen (either seventeen or sixteen). In these states, persons who would be juveniles in other states are considered adults for criminal processing. In all states, juveniles can be passed along to the criminal court for prosecution as an adult in certain circumstances. This action, called **waiver,** transfer, or certification, is generally based on a combination of two circumstances—age and serious criminality—such as a fourteen-year-old who commits a rape and murder or a sixteen-year-old who is an habitual burglar. Procedures for waiver vary from state to state. Sometimes it is required by law, sometimes the judge holds a hearing to decide, and sometimes the prosecutor has direct filing authority to decide which court the case will be processed in. The prosecutor, in deciding what charge to file, is really the dominant figure here, just as she is in the adult court.

The court assignment is an either/or decision; the juvenile can be processed in only one court, not both. Processing in the adult court makes the juvenile liable for the adult penalty, which is typically more severe than what he or she would face in the juvenile court. The case of Lionel Tate, a twelve-year-old Florida boy who got life in prison as an adult when he was convicted in the beating death of a younger playmate (after his mother insisted that he turn down a plea bargain for three years in prison), attracted national attention. When Tate's life sentence was overturned, he agreed to the original three-year sentence for second-degree murder in a plea bargain in January 2004.

One of the "get tough" proposals in response to rising juvenile crime in the 1990s was to send more juveniles upward. Laws were changed allowing this to happen, and for a while in the mid-1990s, a spike of waivers occurred, but for the most part not much has changed. Fewer than 1 percent of juveniles processed to court after arrest have been waived into the adult courts; in 1990, the total was 8,300; in 1999, 7,500.[10] These cases are not necessarily only the most heinous or violent. Researchers have established that the juveniles sent up to be punished as adults are most often those whom court officials find to be **beyond rehabilitation,** meaning that they have been through the system several times and show little sign of changing.[11] Research has also established that juveniles convicted as adults generally are punished more leniently than adults would be, sometimes more leniently (because this is their first adult conviction) than they would have been punished it they had stayed in the juvenile system. The big difference is that they are getting a head start on their adult criminal record: a first felony conviction at age sixteen has more long-term significance than a first felony conviction at age twenty.

Youths convicted as adults go into the adult prison system, not to juvenile training schools. About 7,000 juveniles fit into this category in 1996. The typical offender in this category is a seventeen-year-old minority male convicted of robbery, aggravated assault, or drug trafficking. Most prison systems make some effort to keep younger prisoners in separate institutions or housing units until they get older (although the older prisoners may claim that it is they who need protection from the young thugs of today rather than vice versa).

Most youths kept in locked facilities as delinquents go to state training schools. Training schools have been described as miniprisons with schools. Bartollas and Miller have suggested a maximum population for these facilities of fifty (along with a maximum of thirty for detention centers) to individualize attention and promote rehabilitation, the theoretical purpose of placing the juvenile in custody.[12] Most state training schools are not this small. Training schools average about 100 to 200 residents each, though several of the older institutions are larger, and many special purpose facilities are smaller.

Training schools were formerly referred to as "campuses," emphasizing their educational functions, and they did resemble campuses. Two models prevailed: the **cottage style** with several small residences grouped around a hub of administrative buildings and a **dormitory style** similar to a military barracks. Juveniles were rarely housed in cells, though this has changed in the new training schools built in the past two decades. Cell blocks have been added to house the disciplinary problems and older inmates who are said to require higher security. The numbers of security officers have also been increased in most states. The result is that the newer institutions often look more like real prisons.

The routine of training school life is similar to imprisonment. Incoming juveniles go through a form of classification in a reception center. They are assigned to a housing unit. They have daily chores to do. Unless they are already high school graduates, which is unlikely because of their admission age in most states, they go to school in levels—preliteracy, literacy, pre-GED, and GED or the preferred high school diploma. Most training schools have an abundance of recreational programs—the less they have of other activities, the more they rely on sports to keep their residents busy. Others follow a variety of **treatment modalities,** from one or two sessions of group therapy a week to daily substance abuse counseling to highly structured behavior modification programs. Days can be highly structured and intense. Boys and girls do not stay as long in training schools—the average was about six months in 1997—so days have to be full to get everything in. **Boot camp** programs, which proliferated at the end of the twentieth century, are particularly regimented; they cram a lot of discipline, physical fitness, and behavior therapy into a ninety- to 180-day program.

Sentences to training school are still generally indeterminate. In most states, the juvenile court judge has the authority to shorten sentences on the recommendation of training school officials. Most juveniles are released early, to **aftercare,** the juvenile version of parole. However, part of the changing nature of juvenile confinement in the 1990s was to keep more juveniles locked up longer until they were well into adulthood. The California Youth Authority can keep persons convicted as juveniles in custody until age twenty-five. Louisiana keeps a few delinquents given "juvenile life" locked up until their twenty-first birthday.

Until a generation ago, most training schools were low- to medium-security facilities: no walls, no armed guards visible, sometimes no fences at all, and a more open and casual environment. It looked "nice" to visitors, but to residents it was an ominous, threatening environment that allowed the strong to prey on the weak. Many accounts of life in these institutions suggest that victimization and exploitation were at least as high if not higher than in adult prisons. Many juvenile institutions had more internal disorder, more assaults, and a much higher rate of escapes than adult prisons did. They were tough places to do time in and to work in. Staff brutality, or at least physicality, was commonplace.

Many juvenile facilities today have adopted **zero-tolerance policies** on the use of violence by residents and staff and anger management classes are a standard part of the inmate and staff curriculum. They do not always work. Louisiana's newest juvenile facility, the privately operated training school at Tallulah, which once held more than 500 juveniles in boot camp and long-term placement, was taken over by the state and is due to be completely phased out as a juvenile institution in 2004, in large part because of continuing problems with internal violence involving both residents and staff.

Training schools are supposed to provide rehabilitation—education, vocational training, counseling, and treatment. These alternatives are offered to a much larger percentage of residents than is true in adult institutions, requiring a much greater number of professional staff with degrees than is common in adult facilities. More professional staff and a higher ratio of security officers to residents equate to much higher personnel costs than in adult prisons. Juvenile institutions are expensive. States calculate that on average it costs about twice as much per day to keep a juvenile in a locked facility as it costs to keep an adult in prison. This means that the national average *per diem* cost to keep at juvenile in a public institution ranges from $100 to $200 per day. Critics point out that you could send the kid to Harvard for this, which is true but ignores the fact that an Ivy League education is not a realistic alternative for most delinquents.

Juveniles in locked facilities are a stubbornly intractable population. Few are first offenders; most have been through the courts and other noncustodial placements several times. Many are state raised, with a lengthy history of living in foster homes. They have done poorly in school; many have dropped out or been expelled for disruptive behavior. Their families are disorganized or completely nonfunctional. They have no job or social skills. Their principal influences are their criminal peers with whom they spend most of their time hanging out. Many of them have personal and family histories marked by violence and physical and sexual abuse, aggravated by their own abuse of drugs and alcohol. They do not deal well with authority; they have "attitude problems" to the nth degree. The only thing they are really good at is doing time, which is great training as preparation for lives as adults in prison.

Training schools have two goals: to manage this population in custody and to get them to participate in programs to remedy their deficiencies. The management part is easier than the participation part: you remember the old saying that you can "lead a horse to water, but you can't make him drink." The training school in principle tries much more actively than the adult prison to change behavior, but it is dealing with an adolescent population that is actively opposed to the notion that it ought to have its behavior changed. The typical five-year recidivism rates (as measured by return to secure custody) for juveniles is in the range of 70 to 80 percent, the highest of any age-group. Some private facilities do better (though some do worse, too) because they are dealing with deviants rather than hard-core criminals, but on the whole juveniles placed in institutions are predisposed to failure. This is not to say that the system should give up, but it does explain the frustrations of the security and professional staff working with this population. It also suggests why the preference in juvenile justice is to work with salvageable cases outside of secure placement. Putting a juvenile in a locked institution seems mostly to accomplish the confirmation of criminal status.

The premise of juvenile justice is that no child should be consigned to a wasted life before he reaches adulthood; the people who work in this system continue to advocate the goal of rehabilitation, and to some extent they are successful. Most juveniles will get in formal trouble (arrest and court referral) only once or twice, and they are less likely to end up behind bars as adults. But at three or four arrests and court referrals, the odds of the juvenile going on to acquire an adult criminal record are better than even. These are the criminally active "failures" who make working with juvenile delinquents so discouraging.

Sometimes success can be defined in different terms: Sure he's still a criminal, but maybe he's not quite as violent as he was before, or maybe he can read a little better. Maybe he won't change now, but maybe he will change earlier than he would have otherwise. The people who work in juvenile justice are often their own worst critics. Considering the clientele society gives them to work with, they say, failure comes with the territory. Most still believe, however, that our system of juvenile justice works better with young people than the alternative, often discussed today, of abolishing the juvenile court and simply treating all juveniles as adults, including punishing them with adult sentences. That was the old way of dealing with juveniles, before the 1800s, and it failed to deter or prevent the emergence of juvenile delinquency as the growth of the city defined a new social order.

The impression is that today's juvenile courts have turned more punitive than previously, though it is a selective punitiveness directed at the more hard-core juvenile criminal—the urban minority youth with the long criminal record and the absence of family or other resources to intervene on his behalf. While small numbers of juveniles are waived to adult courts for trial, most continue to be handled by a juvenile justice system committed to two principles: helping is more purposeful than locking people up, and promoting change is a higher goal than punishing failure. Most juveniles will outgrow their criminal behavior before they become adults. The ones who are punished least are the ones most likely to avoid adult criminality.

MENTALLY ILL PRISONERS

To discuss the handling of the mentally ill in corrections, we should make two splits at the start. First, we should separate civilly mentally disordered from the criminally disordered; second, we should separate the legally insane from the ordinary mentally ill prisoner. The mentally ill or mentally disturbed have been placed in social institutions since the 1500s, when the **asylum** first appeared in Europe. London's St. Mary of Bethlehem Hospital (pronounced "bedlam" by local people and coming to mean a place of noisy, chaotic uproar) became a kind of tourist attraction after its founding in 1547; visitors would pay to watch the inmates' strange behavior. Committing the seriously mentally ill to the asylum became a standard practice of modern society. State-operated asylums—holding civil patients, not criminal—grew plentiful and huge, many of them larger than modern penitentiaries.

Historically, mental illness, like age, made no difference to the criminal court. Before the 1800s, it was really of no consequence if a criminal was mentally disordered. He still got the same punishment that a right-thinking offender got or sometimes a little extra. Reflecting notions of good and evil that have prevailed in different guises throughout history, insane criminals were often subjected to special tortures to drive out the vile demons that possessed them. Celus, the first-century Roman physician, proposed that hunger, chains, and fetters should be used to chastise the insane person who did or said anything wrong—and this proposal was considered benevolent for the time.

Thus, in the early modern era, the mentally ill who had committed no crime were locked in asylums or left in the care of family and community, while the mentally ill who committed crimes were punished right along with ordinary criminals. This began to change in the 1800s, when legislatures and courts began to develop modern legal practices for dealing with mentally ill criminals. At the core of these practices is **insanity,** a legal term for a mental condition. The most influential definition of insanity was the **M'Naghten rule,** established in 1844 after delusional Englishman Daniel M'naghten tried to assassinate Prime Minister Robert Peel, the former home secretary historically recognized as the creator of the first modern police force in London in 1829. M'naghten, who did not know Peel on sight, killed Peel's male secretary by mistake. The jury found M'Naghten not guilty by reason of insanity. When the law lords of the British House of Lords reviewed the case, they gave this definition of insanity:

> To establish a defense of insanity, it must be proved that at the time of committing the act, the party accused was laboring under such a defect of reason, from disease of the mind, as not to know the nature and quality of the act he was doing, or if he did know it, that he did not know what he was doing was wrong.

Today the states use several different specific definitions of insanity, but all of them center around the person's ability to know **right from wrong** and behave accordingly. The **insanity defense** is used infrequently, generally in only a fraction of 1 percent of criminal cases, most commonly in crimes of violence led by assault and murder. Colorado, as part of a legislative review of treatment of the mentally ill in its prisons in 2003, found that in a typical year, about 4,500 men and women were admitted to prison. The insanity defense was used in only about twenty-six cases, with an actual **not guilty by reason of insanity** (NGRI) verdict returned in about ten cases per year.

When the insanity defense is used, the defendant must typically have a fairly well-documented history of mental disorders for it to be used successfully. The defendant enters a plea of NGRI and then must prove that he did not know right from wrong at the time of the crime. Extreme anger or **temporary insanity** does not work here, though this defense was allowed in a few jurisdictions until recently. The court will almost always hear testimony from mental health expert witness, such as psychologists and psychiatrists—who often offer completely opposing opinions, testifying for the prosecution and the defense, as to the defendant's mental state at the time of the crime.

Some defendants do not deny they were sane when they did the crime but argue that they have subsequently gone insane—they are **incompetent to stand trial,** typically because they do not understand the proceedings against them and cannot aid their lawyer in the defense. These defendants can be stuck in limbo indefinitely, their criminal charges pending while they undergo mental treatment—most often in a secure facility that may look a lot like a prison. Someone who was incompetent and regains competency after treatment can then be tried on the original criminal charges. Thus, sometimes it is better to stay incompetent as long as possible and wait for everything to die down.

A person who is found NGRI at trial is not convicted of a crime; he or she has no criminal record. Such a person is rarely discharged and sent home; he is much more likely to end up in secure confinement within a state or private mental hospital. His discharge from custody becomes a medical decision, subject to the court's approval.

The process for dealing with mental illness in court has been strongly criticized in the past two decades, and some changes have occurred as a result. If one attempted political assassination is said to have created the insanity defense, another resulted in major limitations being put on its use in this country. In March 1981, John Earl Hinckley attempted to assassinate President Ronald Reagan, seriously wounding Reagan and three other men in the attack. Hinckley's motivation for the crime was to prove his love for actress Jodie Foster, whom he had been bombarding with love letters for months. At his trial in June 1982, Hinckley was found not guilty by reason of insanity. Many people were outraged that Hinckley had "beaten the system."

In the decade that followed the crime and the insanity verdict, the federal courts and several states abolished the insanity defense and created the optional verdict of **guilty but mentally ill** (GBMI). Offenders get an ordinary sentence but serve it in a prison treatment unit—if space is available—or a regular prison if it is not. They are prisoners first, patients second. After its legislative study in 2003, Colorado moved to join the states adopting this verdict not because politicians wanted to punish the mentally ill but rather to provide a more uniform system for treating the mentally disordered who commit crimes. The view was that few discernible differences existed between the handful of NGRI offenders and a much greater number (100 or more per year) of other seriously mentally ill offenders entering the prison system. About a third of the states had adopted the GBMI verdict through the end of 2003.

The question psychiatrists are often called on to answer is, "Will this person commit another crime if he or she is released after treatment?" Psychiatrists cannot predict potential dangerousness with any degree of certainty. There is evidence that insane offenders after discharge have a lower recidivism rate than sane offenders, but the public in large measure looks on insane offenders as either dangerous persons or con artists and at the insanity defense as a way of cheating justice.

After twenty-two years in a hospital in the Washington, D.C., area, John Earl Hinckley was court approved for unsupervised visits with his family late in 2003. The uproar was mild but immediate: critics said he should never be allowed outside. But this is a civil process, not a criminal process, and the law requires the judge to listen to the recommendation of psychiatric experts in deciding when the mentally ill person is ready to return to society. Daniel M'Naghten died in a mental hospital twenty-two years after he attempted to kill Sir Robert Peel.

Studies have shown that people judged insane often serve *more* time in custody before release than they would have served had they been convicted of criminal charges. Lawyers tell clients considering insanity pleas that it is harder to free yourself from a mental hospital than a prison. This makes some sense: the level of proof for insanity is so high that the people who are so adjudicated— as not understanding right from wrong in their own behavior—would likely become long-term patients.

Some people in prison, then, are mentally ill, not legally insane. They are serving finite sentences (except for the lifers) and will eventually be returned to society in whatever mental state they are in at the time of discharge.

Correctional and mental health authorities estimate that about 15 percent (one in six) prison inmates is mentally ill; the percentage among jail inmates, who are closer to the street, is estimated to be even higher. In its 2003 report *Ill-Equipped: U.S. Prisons and Offenders with Mental Illness*, Human Rights Watch provides this overview:

> Somewhere between two and three hundred thousand men and women in U.S. prisons suffer from mental disorders, including such serious illnesses as schizophrenia, bipolar disorder, and major depression. An estimated 70,000 are psychotic on any given day. Yet across the nation, many prison mental health services are woefully deficient, crippled by understaffing, insufficient facilities, and limited programs. All too often seriously ill prisoners receive little or no meaningful treatment. They are neglected, accused of malingering, treated as disciplinary problems.
>
> Without the necessary care, mentally ill prisoners suffer painful symptoms and their conditions can deteriorate. They are afflicted with delusions and hallucinations, debilitating fears, extreme and uncontrollable mood swings. They huddle silently in their cells, mumble incoherently, or yell incessantly. They refuse to obey orders or lash out without apparent provocation. They beat their heads against cell walls, smear themselves with feces, self-mutilate, and commit suicide.[13]

Recent estimates suggest that prisons hold about three times as many mentally ill persons as do civil mental hospitals and that the prevalence of severe and chronic forms of **mental illness** (defined as serious impairments in everyday functioning) is from two to four times higher among prisoners than among the free-world population, depending on which state (geographically, not of mind) you happen to be in.

The number of mentally ill prisoners has increased dramatically over the past thirty years. Among the reasons commonly cited are these:

1. Mental hospitals have been downsizing. Community health centers were supposed to provide the therapy and medication that those with serious mental illnesses needed, but the centers generally have not been effective. Either support is lacking or the mentally ill don't use them.

2. Those who are mentally ill are likely to be alienated from family and friends. They have a hard time getting and holding a job. Over time, many of them will stop taking their medication and turn to criminal behavior to meet their needs.

3. Other than prison, judges have few, if any, sentencing alternatives in the community for mentally ill offenders.

4. Judges tend to give the mentally ill longer sentences, and because of the increased risk of reoffending, parole boards are reluctant to parole them.[14]

Human Rights Watch suggests that the increased incidence of mental illness in prison is an unintended consequence of the convergence of two separate public policies:

1. The punitive anticrime effort, particularly the "War on Drugs," since the early 1980s

2. The failure of community health systems to replace the large public mental health hospitals shut down as part of the deinstitutionalization effort that began in the 1960s[15]

Correctional officials, especially those who run jails, often emphasize the importance of the second policy. When the role of the big state mental hospitals in providing long-term confinement for large numbers of mentally ill patients came into serious question in the 1960s, the response was the adoption of the **Community Mental Health Act** of the 1970s. Only the nonfunctioning and dangerous (to themselves and others) inmates were to remain hospitalized. The others were to be **deinstitutionalized**—returned to the community and treated through clinics on an outpatient basis.

What was wrong with this scenario? It certainly sounded good, and it was protective of the rights of the confined, but it turned loose on the streets many thousands of mentally dysfunctional former patients—people who weren't directly dangerous but who were also not very productive and not playing by other people's conventional rules. Many of them are today's homeless people, marching the streets to their different drum, and many of them, in the process called **transinstitutionalization,** have left the asylum for the jail and prison. Left on their own, they keep messing up enough to stay in trouble with the law. In the late 1950s, the per capita rates of confinement in mental hospitals averaged over 300 per 100,000 population, almost double the combined jail and prison incarceration rates, which were averaging about 170 per 100,000 during this time period. Forty years later, at the end of the twentieth century, the mental hospital rates had declined to about thirty per 100,000, while the jail and prison rates had increased to almost 700 per 100,000. Where did the missing 90 percent of the late 1950s mental hospital population go?

Many circumstances were involved in this huge transformation, but it is clear that the population of mentally ill inmates in corrections increased as the population of the asylum declined. Texas federal Judge William Wayne Justice, in the district court case of *Ruiz v. Johnson* (1999), wrote this opinion:

> It is deplorable and outrageous that this state's prisons appear to have become a repository for a great number of its mentally ill citizens. Persons who, with psychiatric care, could fit well into society, are instead locked away, to become wards of the state's penal system. Then, in a tragically ironic twist, they may be confined in conditions that nurture, rather than abate, their psychoses.[16]

Human Rights Watch places the mentally ill prisoner within the context of the secure custodial population:

> Doing time in prison is hard for everyone. Prisons are tense and overcrowded facilities in which all prisoners struggle to maintain their self-respect and emotional equilibrium despite violence, exploitation, extortion, and lack of privacy; stark limitations on family and community contact; and a paucity of opportunities for meaningful education, work, or other productive activities. But doing time in prison is particularly difficult for prisoners with mental illnesses that impair their thinking, emotional responses, and ability to cope. They have unique needs for special programs, facilities, and extensive and varied health services. Compared to other prisoners, moreover, prisoners with mental illness also are more likely to be exploited and victimized by other inmates.[17]

Most states have established special **treatment units** for the more troublesome mentally ill in their prisons; the larger states have entire separate prisons for this purpose. But most mentally ill prisoners are managed in population as long as they can interact safely with other inmates and staff; the key is their ability to function and follow the prison's daily routine. The report "Mental Health Treatment in State Prisons, 2000" provides this breakdown of treatment options:

1. Twenty-four-hour care: 1.6 percent of inmates were housed in special units for the most seriously mentally ill, where they were continuously monitored and provided intensive treatment.
2. Therapy/counseling: 12.8 percent of inmates participate in some type of regular therapy or counseling sessions, most often group counseling. Some of these participants may be attending for reasons other than mental illness, such as substance abuse or sex offender treatment.
3. **Psychotropic medication:** 9.7 percent of inmates were taking one or more mood-altering drugs—antidepressants, stimulants, sedatives, tranquilizers, or other antipsychotic drugs—designed to alter their mental state.[18]

As there is overlap between categories (an inmate taking medication who is also in therapy), the estimation is that no more than about 15 percent of inmates are getting any form of regular mental health treatment. Whether these are the 15 percent said to suffer from serious mental illness is anyone's guess. The business of prisons and jails is custody, not treatment. For the mentally ill in population, treatment is usually daily meds with occasional visits with a social worker or psychologist who asks such deep questions as "How are you feeling?" and then wishes the prisoner "Good luck" and moves on, no matter what the answer is.

Colorado's San Carlos Correctional Facility (SCCF) is a 250-bed prison for male inmates with serious mental illnesses. This facility, which has almost as many staff as it has inmates, is considered a model for its individualized treatment approach. It is also a very expensive facility, costing about $59,000 per inmate per year in 2003. Despite the expense, Colorado plans to double the size of the facility to treat more of the seriously mentally ill in its prison system—estimated at more than 10 percent of its 18,000 state prisoners.

One of SCCF's wings is a thirty-two-bed **therapeutic community** unit for substance-abusing inmates who are also mentally ill. The therapeutic community views the prisoners, under staff supervision, as being the primary therapists for one another. In an institutional treatment unit or in a community-based setting, therapeutic communities have been successful in providing intensive treatment to alcoholics and drug addicts where less drastic approaches have failed.

Bill Groom, the author of a *Corrections Today* article about the SCCF, refers to its prisoner-patients as examples of a **triple whammy**—serious mental illness, substance abuse, and criminal behavior.[19] The trio make a potent combination. About 25 to 30 percent of prisoners, in self-reports, define themselves as mentally ill, a rate ten to fifteen percentage points higher than that suggested by mental health experts. Part of this higher self-report could be an excuse for their criminal behavior, but part of it is also recognition that their drug and alcohol problems—treated or untreated—were closely tied to their criminal behavior. While therapists may see the substance abuse as a problem related to mental illness, the prisoners see it *as* mental illness, something they absolutely need treatment for if they hope to avoid criminal behavior when they return to the streets.

SUBSTANCE-ABUSING PRISONERS

In looking at the preprison background of prisoners in chapter 9, we saw that perhaps the most pervasive aspect of the lives of both men and women prisoners is the influence of substance abuse. If you took a group of 100 prisoners and asked them, "How many of your lives have been significantly affected by your use of alcohol or drugs," about eighty would raise their hands. If you took this group of eighty and asked them this follow-up question, "How many of you would cite alcohol or drugs as being directly involved in the crime that brought you to prison," about forty to forty-five would raise their hands. Alcohol tends to be more important for men, while drugs are more of a problem for women, but for the majority of prisoners, substance abuse is closely linked to criminal behavior.

The "Just Say No" proponents take a simpler view. While acknowledging evidence linking genetics and addiction, they reject the notion that substance abuse *causes* criminal behavior. We all have free will, they might say—anyone can refrain from using alcohol or drugs that would get him or her in trouble. Substance abuse is a "moral weakness." This same concept would apply to a great number of other problems in American society, including obesity, smoking, domestic violence, infidelity, debt, gambling, and materialism. We can all say no to food, cigarettes, physical force, sexual adventurism, credit cards, risking money, and greed; we would be better off, as people and as a society, if we did so. But as a practical matter, people do not cease unhealthy or troublesome behavior merely because it is bad for them and hurts others. Many prisoners have made alcohol and drugs so much a part of their daily lives that they cannot separate substance abuse from life itself—from friends and family, from recreation and social interaction, from coping with the stresses of daily life, from filling empty time, or from avoiding pain and misery. For most of the habitual abusers of alcohol and drugs who wind up behind bars, self-control is only part of the answer to adopting a different way of life—one in which substance abuse is not the dominant force—after discharge.

You might think that prisons would be inclined to help prisoners prepare to avoid falling back into old habits when they leave prison, particularly because returning to the use of alcohol and drugs has been identified as the number one reason criminals return to prison after release. (In the short term, more criminals are returned to prison for violating release conditions than for committing new crimes.) If you do think so, you would be wrong. Prisons officially ascribe to the moral weakness philosophy. Other than allowing inmates to participate voluntarily in self-help groups, such as **Alcoholics Anonymous** or **Narcotics Anonymous,** most institutions do very little to educate prisoners about substance abuse or to help prevent the use of drugs and alcohol in the future.

This oblivious approach to substance abuse in prison has three principal causes:

1. *People are no longer high in prison.* They may have been high when they first came into jail several months before (more than half of arrestees have alcohol or drugs in their system), but they have sobered up by now (unless they are in a bad prison where contraband alcohol and drugs are readily available). As a total institution, the prison has the theoretical capacity to remove alcohol and drugs (along with interpersonal violence, the two most destructive forces in its prisoners' lives) from daily life within the institution. Many prisons fail to do this, resulting in the black market distribution of drugs and alcohol (often imported by staff) within institutions. Some prisoners give accounts of becoming drug addicts *after* they got to prison.

2. *It's like the weather; what can you do about it?* Substance abuse history is so pervasive that it becomes part of the prison environment that people acknowledge but do not try to do anything about. You cannot really tell who has a substance abuse problem and who does not: they do not wear scarlet As for "alcoholic" or DAs for "drug addict" around their necks. You assume, in fact (an assumption based on reality), that most of the people around you have problems with alcohol or drugs.

3. *Prisoners first, patients second.* Prisons are for punishment, not treatment. The institution's human and fiscal resources are directed toward secure custody rather than future behavior. The prison is far more interested in what you do *in* prison than what you might do later *out* of prison.

The long-term prospect on dealing more actively with substance abusers in custody as special needs inmates is not encouraging. The **Center on Addiction and Substance Abuse** (CASA) completed a three-year study of the prison population in 1997. It reported,

A CASA survey of state officials estimated that about 70 to 85 percent of inmates need some level of substance abuse treatment. But in 1996, only 13 percent of state inmates were undergoing any such treatment. The Federal Bureau of Prisons (BOP) estimates that 31 percent of federal inmates are addicted to drugs, but only 10 percent were in treatment in 1996. The proportion of jail inmates who need treatment has not been estimated, but given the similar alcohol and drug abuse profiles of state prison and local jail inmates, it is likely to mirror the state estimate of 70 to 85 percent. Only 8 percent of jail inmates were in treatment in 1992, the last year for which statistics were available.[20]

Although the perceived need among prison officials for increasing substance abuse treatment grew with the rapid surge in drug offenders in prison in the 1980s and early 1990s, not only the percentage of inmates in treatment but also the actual numbers went down—partly for philosophical reasons but partly for economic reasons as well: money was shifted from treatment to security as the prison population increased steadily during this period. About half the increase was drug criminals, most of whom were substance abusers.

By the early years of the twenty-first century, there were signs that drug treatment was being emphasized once again, especially through the growth of drug courts at the local level. But most of the treatment emphasis was focused *outside* prison, on persons not in custody, rather than inside. Participation in prison drug treatment programs at the beginning of 2001 was broken down as follows:

1. **Separate unit:** about 48,000 inmates lived in a prison housing unit with other prisoners getting stepped-up treatment.
2. **Addiction groups:** about 54,000 inmates took part in regular therapy as a member of a group being treated for drug addiction.
3. Counseling only: about 41,000 received individual or group counseling only.[21]

After deductions for overlap, the total number of inmates receiving drug treatment in the forty-five reporting states totaled about 120,000, or 12.9 percent of all inmates in custody. Many of the treatment programs deal not only with drugs but also with alcohol as part of a generic approach to substance abuse.

CASA called the absence of drug treatment for the prison population a "missed opportunity":

> Preventing drug and alcohol abuse and providing effective treatment for drug- and alcohol-abusing inmates hold the promise of significant savings to taxpayers and reductions in crime. CASA estimates that it would cost approximately $6,500 per year, in addition to the usual incarceration costs, to provide an inmate with a year of residential treatment in prison and ancillary services, such as vocational and educational training, psychological counseling, and aftercare case management.[22]

The study observed that reducing drug and alcohol abuse and addiction is the key to the next major reduction in crime in America. It recommended a series of policy changes focusing on the substance-abusing prisoner population—preprison, in-prison, and postprison. The in-prison recommendations include the following:

1. Train correctional officers and other personnel in substance abuse and addiction so that they can better prevent the use of alcohol and drugs in prison and better assist inmates in the recovery process.

2. Keep jails and prisons tobacco, alcohol, and drug free. This means enforcing prohibitions against alcohol and drugs, promoting smoke-free prisons and jails to enhance the health of inmates, and eliminating the free distribution of tobacco products to inmates.

3. Expand random testing of inmates, deter drug and alcohol use, refer inmates for substance abuse treatment, and monitor their progress.

4. Provide treatment in prison for all who need it—alcohol- or drug-involved offenders, including property offenders, violent offenders, and drug sellers. Tailor treatment to the special needs of inmates, such as women and children of alcoholics and drug addicts.

5. Encourage participation in literacy, education, and training programs. Such programs should be widely available, and inmates should be encouraged to enroll in them to increase their chances of obtaining employment on release from prison and avoid returning to lives of crime and imprisonment.

6. Provide substance-abusing inmates with a range of support services, including medical care; mental health services; prevention services, including confidential HIV testing; counseling; and other services.

7. Increase the availability of religious and spiritual activity and counseling in prison and provide an environment that encourages such activity.[23]

These recommendations to date remain more a set of ideals than a program for action, though a number of states have moved to provide more focused treatment, especially what is called **relapse prevention** to inmates immediately before discharge.

MENTALLY RETARDED PRISONERS

In *Justice for All*, her study of the mentally retarded in California prisons, Joan Petersilia introduces us to inmate Duane Silva:

> Duane Silva sits today in a California prison cell serving 25 years to life, having been convicted of stealing a VCR and jewelry in a 1994 residential burglary. Silva is mentally retarded, with an IQ of 70, the mental age equivalent to that of a 10- or 11-year-old. Silva was one of the first offenders to be sentenced under California's Three Strikes Law, having had two previous "strikes" for arson, one involving a fire he started in a trash can and another involving a fire that began in a parked truck where it appears he was playing with matches.[24]

Recent estimates suggest that about 4 to 10 percent of a state's prison population is mentally retarded, which is considerably higher than the 1 to 2 percent of the population outside prison. The definition of **mentally retarded** is an IQ of below 70; an IQ in the range of 70 to 85 is said to be **borderline mentally retarded.** The problem with placements in these categories is that test scores may vary by several points from one time to another and on different scales—verbal versus cognitive—within the same test, so it is hard to make precise judgments based on test scores.

Many experts say you have to look at the person in the social context. Petersilia suggests that mentally retarded persons have a childlike quality of thinking, coupled with slowness in learning new material. Mentally retarded persons have little long-term perspective and little ability to think in a causal way to understand the consequences of their actions. They are not insane. Though some of them may also be mentally ill, they do know right from wrong. They are often referred to as **developmentally challenged,** meaning that they function at a lower mental age, often a preadolescent age. They are usually followers, easily manipulated, and often used by others with more intelligence and/or experience.[25]

Although the most notable recent publicity about the mentally retarded in the legal system has been in regard to the death penalty, no evidence suggests that mental retardation is associated with violent crime. They are disproportionately represented among nonviolent offenders—easy for the police to catch and often eager to confess (sometimes to acts they did not do) to please the police or make themselves look more important.

Most mentally retarded do not "look" retarded in the sense of having a physical deformity. They are not fluorescent mutant dwarfs. They appear normal (sometimes far more normal than people appearing on TV reality shows), they move around normally, and their verbal communication skills allow them to interact with other people. Prison systems might pick up on retardation during classification if it is careful enough or involves testing, but for many retarded prisoners, the system will not notice their intellectual disability until *after* they get in trouble in prison.

In the landmark case of *Ruiz v. Estelle* (1976), officials estimated that about 10 to 15 percent of the Texas prison population was retarded. These inmates were observed to be more abnormally prone to prison injuries and more likely to be found guilty of disciplinary infractions.[26] Other research in different systems has found that mentally retarded prisoners suffer from other adjustment problems:

1. More frequent physical abuse and victimization
2. Economic exploitation and theft of property
3. Greater involvement in fights as a response to victimization
4. Adjustment problems that often result in lockdown, higher security classification, and, for victims, protective custody
5. Lack of participation in and completion of programs
6. Lower rate of selection for parole and early release options

Petersilia says, "In sum, it appears that offenders with mental retardation do more time, do harder time, get less out of their time, and are more likely to be returned to prison after release than persons who are not mentally handicapped."[27] California will spend close to a million dollars protecting the public from Duane Silva if he stays in prison for the next twenty-five years, but it may have more difficulty protecting Silva from other inmates in the prison system.

Within the past decade, attention has been devoted to the prison's management of the mentally retarded out of two general concerns. First, many of them are relatively low-risk criminals who pose little threat to public safety. When prison systems focus on locking up more dangerous criminals, many mentally retarded can be moved to community-based residential centers that can better accommodate their needs. Expensive prison beds should be used to best protect the public, not merely to house those for whom alternative placements have not been developed.

The second concern is litigation—on two fronts. The **Americans with Disabilities Act** (ADA), passed in 1990, prohibits discrimination based on disability, including the intellectual disability implicit in mental retardation. States have been sued on behalf of mentally retarded inmates. Prisons have been required by the courts (or have voluntarily changed their policies) to screen inmates and make certain that prison programs are open to eligible inmates with disabilities.

The second front—which ought to be embarrassing if Americans were more concerned with world opinion—is in regard to the death penalty for the mentally retarded. In *Atkins v. Virginia* (2002), the U.S. Supreme Court ruled that severely mentally retarded murderers cannot be executed. This judgment would involve an estimated 150 to 200 of the 3,500 defendants on death row. The problem with the response to this decision is that the states have set up different definitions of retardation and different procedures for making the determination, including, in the broadest possible discretionary situation, letting the jury decide, after hearing experts testify in the penalty phase of the trial, whether the defendant is retarded. This is really no different from what we were already doing. In the meantime, Virginia inmate Daryl Renard Atkins, whose IQ has been reported to be as low as 59, sits on death row, facing a prosecutor who says she will make it as difficult as possible for him to leave death row and get a life sentence. While other death penalty nations at least pay lip service to the idea that the retarded should not be executed, American prosecutors have no such compunctions. "Even children should be punished if they know right from wrong," they say, "and when the crime is murder death is the appropriate punishment."

HIV/AIDS PRISONERS

The first reports of **AIDS**—Acquired Immune Deficiency Syndrome—in American prisons were among drug-injecting inmates in New York and New Jersey in 1981 and 1982. By the end of the 1980s, as medical knowledge of **HIV,** the human immunovirus resulting in AIDS, increased, the vast increase in the numbers of intravenous drug users coming into prison made AIDS not just the "gay disease" but also the "prisoners' disease." The number of **HIV-positive** prisoners and the number of prison deaths from AIDS increased steadily until 1995, when about 25,000 known HIV-positive inmates were held in custody (2.3 percent of state and federal prisoners) and over 1,000 state prisoners died of AIDS. By 2000, the number of HIV inmates was holding steady at just over 25,000 (the percentage decreasing to 2.0), while the number of deaths had declined sharply to 174.[28] When prisoners complain about medical neglect, prison health officials point to the rapid decline in the AIDS death rate in state prisons, from 100 per 100,000 in 1995 to fourteen per 100,000 in 2000, as evidence that this is not true. (So then the prisoners say, "Oh yeah, well what about Hepatitis C," and the argument heads off in a different direction.)

In any case, HIV infection remains much more prevalent, about four to six times so, according to recent estimates, than HIV infection in society. HIV rates are higher in certain states and certain prisons than in others. New York,

Florida, and Texas together hold about 45 percent of HIV-positive prison inmates. New York has the greatest number—about 6,000—of HIV-positive inmates and also the largest percentage of its prison population—8.5 percent—infected. AIDS is more of a problem where large numbers of poor drug users are in custody; rates are also higher for women (3.6 percent) than men (2.2 percent) and higher among minorities than whites. The truly staggering infection rates were not in prisons but jails in certain urban areas; among females booked into Washington, D.C., and New York City jails, about 40 and 25 percent of inmates were HIV positive. (As a travel tip, if a prostitute in either of these cities offers to inject drugs into you using her needle, this is one time when you should definitely follow Nancy Reagan's "Just Say No" advice.)

The states of the Northeast, dominated by New York, have the highest overall prevalence of HIV in prison, over 5.0 percent, but even in this locale some states have few HIV inmates—New Hampshire with seventeen, Vermont with fifteen, and Maine with nine. In other parts of the country, numbers are even lower. Wyoming has only eight HIV inmates, South Dakota five, and North Dakota two.[29]

In forty-eight of the fifty states and the federal system, HIV inmates are generally distributed throughout all prisons in the system. Two states, Alabama and Mississippi, segregate HIV-positive inmates in special housing units comparable to protective custody. Medical privacy laws prohibit authorities from identifying HIV inmates to other inmates and staff. Indeed, the majority of the states do not know who is HIV positive among their inmates because they do not test them to find out. Twenty states test everyone entering their system, and eleven more test designated "high-risk" groups. The states with the largest HIV populations do not employ mandatory testing.

The result is that as a prison inmate, you do not know who among your fellow or sister inmates is HIV positive unless they tell you directly or unless you are so informed by a third party. If you are a prisoner in an institution that provides hospital care, the percentage of inmates around you who are HIV positive is likely to be higher. HIV prisoners with AIDS and other diseases (such as MDR-TB) that require more continuous medical attention than other prisons can provide are more likely to be assigned to hospital facilities. Employees, except those providing medical care who have access to patient records, are also ignorant of HIV status.

Thus, if you live or work in prison, you know that somewhere between 1 and 5 percent of the inmates around you are HIV positive, but you don't know for sure who they are. Staff are trained to be cautious, especially with inmate contacts that involve exchange of bodily fluids, such as treating an inmate with a bleeding wound. Security officers doing searches wear gloves to offer some protection from sticks by hidden needles. Over the past twenty years, the incidence of prison staff HIV infection from performing job-related functions has been minimal and related mostly to providing medical care; most prison staff who are HIV positive got it from sex and drugs, just like the inmates did.

Sex and drug-using behavior in American prisons is complicated by the presence of HIV-positive inmates; it is further complicated by policies denying that such behavior occurs. Many state prisons have education programs about HIV and AIDS, warning inmates of the dangers of prison sex and drug use involving needles. These prevention programs—generally following the "Just Say No" model—often fall on deaf ears. Most jails and virtually all prisons refuse to take the more practical course of giving inmates condoms for sex or bleach for needles used to inject drugs because that would constitute de facto recognition that inmates in the prison are having sex and using drugs.

What flows from this is an **environment of risk.** If inmates choose to inject drugs or have sex with other inmates, these at-risk behaviors, besides resulting in the possibility of disciplinary action, can also result in HIV infection. Most prisoners are not completely self-destructive. They may even ask the ultimate personal question—"Are you HIV positive?"—before engaging in anal sex or sharing a needle. But not everyone who answers the question knows their status, and some who do would not tell the truth. The risk is always there.

Some prisoners really do not care what happens to them or anyone else. One of the members of the Louisiana State Penitentiary's Peer Education Team, which gives HIV education talks to inmates and health care groups, spoke of the difficulty of getting long-term inmates motivated to protect themselves. Andrew Joseph said,

> A lot of people would prefer to die having their fun, rather than lay here knowing they will never get out. With no family, no friends, just prison, they get off into homosexual activity. Some even know their sex partners are HIV-positive. Perhaps in their thinking this may be the best way out for them. In turn, they pass the virus to short-termers coming through, and those short-timers go back into society adding to the already devastating problem.[30]

Some prisoners care a lot (or too much), taking out their hostilities on possibly or openly HIV-positive inmates who happen to be around them in population. Some are homophobic or AIDS-phobic; others simply do not want to have contact with "sick" prisoners, even if the inmates still appear healthy enough on the surface. Michael F. Haggerty, the former director of the Correctional HIV Consortium, has reported,

> Inmates have been attacked and killed for being perceived as gay and/or HIV positive in prison. HIV is still largely considered a "gay disease" inside. If an inmate becomes too interested in treatment or education, he or she may be labeled as gay, adversely impacting health, housing, and life.[31]

In addition to the problems relating to the interaction of HIV-positive inmates with other inmates and staff, prisons also have to worry about the special needs of inmates with AIDS. About one in four HIV inmates has confirmed AIDS. The medical care and medication needs of the estimated 6,500 prison inmates with AIDS set them apart from other inmates. Medications alone used in some AIDS regimens may cost $10,000 to $20,000 per year, without factoring in other costs of medical care and security.

While only Alabama and Mississippi group HIV positives together, states tend to cluster their AIDS inmates for medical convenience and to enhance medical expertise in combating AIDS-related illnesses. Twenty-five prison hospital facilities housed about 2,000 AIDS patients, almost a third of the total in prison, at midyear 2000. The two largest facilities, the Stiles Unit in Texas and the Broad River Correctional Institution in South Carolina, held 452 and 217 confirmed AIDS patients.[32] Prisons grouping inmates in this fashion have to be prepared to deal with questions about segregation—whether inmates are being isolated as punishment—and access to work, programs, and other normal inmate activities. Prisons have been able to justify their management of AIDS inmates; separation of HIV inmates is seen as a less defensible practice, though Alabama and Mississippi have so far (through 2003) remained committed to the policy.

SEX CRIMINALS

Fewer than 10 percent of American prison inmates are imprisoned for crimes involving sex acts—about 2.5 percent for forcible rape, 6.0 percent for other sexual assaults, and a lesser number for other nonviolent sex crimes. How many of these are sex offenders? The answer is all of the above. Anyone who commits a sex crime can be labeled a **sex criminal,** though under the laws of most states certain types of sex criminals are singled out for particular attention.

Broadly defined, a **sex offense** can be any criminal act of a sexual nature. On one end of the scale is the violent offense of forcible rape; on the other end are such minor crimes as window peeping, indecent exposure, and prostitution. In between are lesser sexual assaults, child molestation, incest, and offenses in the **crimes against nature** category rarely prosecuted today—sodomy, buggery, and bestiality. Sodomy refers to any sex act other than conventional penis-to-vagina sex between a man and a woman. Buggery refers to anal sex between a man and another man, a woman, or an animal. Bestiality refers to sex between a human and an animal. There are many other older sex offenses, such as fornication and adultery, that are rarely prosecuted any longer, unless you happen to be a member of the armed forces, where such acts remain court-martial offenses.

Sex offenses may be heterosexual or homosexual, they may be violent or consensual (as in carnal knowledge or statutory rape where one participant is underage), they may involve strangers or people in the same family, they may be one-time events or involve the same people in relationships that go on for years (as in family incest), and they may involve offenders who are otherwise apparently normal (like athletes or fraternity boys) or who are so twisted and perverted that their whole lives are wrapped around their criminal acts (like serial rapists or the sex fiends of lore).

A **sex offender** is by definition anyone convicted of a sex offense. What imprisoned sex offenders have in common is that most are men and that most are there for heterosexual acts. There is a popular perception that sex offenders are stigmatized within the inmate subculture. While it is true that child molesters and other offenders convicted of sex crimes against family members may be looked down on as being slimy and weird, these offenders are probably less likely to be systematically victimized today than they once were. The hierarchy is not as rigid and the stigma not as strong; among today's inmates, there is more of an "anything goes" attitude.

Comparatively few sex offenders are in institutions designed specifically for treating their behavioral problems; comparatively few sex offenders are taking part in any regular treatment program. Of the ones who are in treatment, most are young men with a lengthy history of involvement in a variety of sex offenses, not necessarily violent but often directed at children or family members. Many of them may be seeking self-understanding or enlightenment, and many may be seeking ratification of treatment—the proof they need that they have been "cured" so they can get out of prison faster. Treatment modalities often involve a combination of topics, including sex education, social skills, anger management, and avoiding risks. Some treatment programs also involve the participation of victims of sex crimes to discuss their feelings with offenders.

Robert Gladhill is a forty-two-year-old Minnesota sex offender who was first interviewed in 2002 for a National Public Radio (NPR) series on life after prison. Minnesota's corrections system in known as one of the "leanest" in the country in its use of imprisonment but also the system in which sex offenders are the number one category among prisoners. "I'm here on first- and second-degree criminal sexual conduct, against two victims," Gladhill told NPR. "One's my daughter and the other is a next-door neighbor girl. I assaulted her (his daughter) between the ages of 9 and 11 from '91 to '93. The next-door girl, it was a one-time thing. I touched her, and got arrested in May of 1995."[33]

In his seven years in prison, Gladhill went through intensive therapy, said Steve Huot, who heads sex offender treatment programs for the Minnesota Department of Corrections. The Lino Lakes prison, where Gladhill was held, holds 1,100 men, all of them sex offenders sent there for treatment. Some get the short course and some the full course lasting two years or more and including chemical dependency treatment. The treatment moves through a number of steps, culminating in what is called a "reoffense" or "relapse prevention" plan. Huot said,

> In a cycle, there are certain points. . . . Many times, the child molesters identify that the start of their negative behavior was in some sort of negative emotions, like feeling depressed, or loneliness or feeling ostracized and inadequate. What they do with that feeling in very important. If they isolate and don't talk about it, if they start looking through catalogs with pictures of kids in them, that's negative. Instead, what you want is them talking to their support system. You want them going to a counselor, you want them realizing that they can't keep going down the negative road.[34]

When Gladhill was released from prison to his home in Faribault, Minnesota, he left prison with $159 in his pocket. He got a motel room for $185 per week and went looking for work. He was on intensive supervision, meaning at least four contacts a week with his corrections agent (parole officer). In two weeks, Gladhill could not find a job. He was running out of money, frustrated, and upset, and he looked briefly at some child pornography Websites on a computer in an employment office. He knew that he was in trouble—"going into my cycle," he called it—and he should have asked for help, but he didn't. He returned to the same computer. Gladhill said,

> I made the decision that I wanted to go back to prison, because I knew I didn't have a place to go. I was giving up on myself, so instead of telling my sponsor and my PO, I decided to go into the workforce center that day to sit there and wait until I got caught on the Internet, which I did.[35]

When he was caught viewing pornography on the computer, his parole was revoked for a technical violation. He was not charged with another sex crime. The day he was arrested, he was finally offered a job making over $400 a week. But he was already on his way back to prison—to more treatment and at least another year in prison before he would be again eligible for release. Gladhill admitted that he needed more treatment. He said, "I need to learn more so that when I go out again, if I ever do, I can let people know they can be safe, although they can worry, and that's all right. I can show people I can change."[36]

Offenders who sexually victimize children have been targeted for close scrutiny recently. The general trend over the past generation or two has been to deal more severely with **child abusers,** who physically abuse children; incidents that had previously been viewed as private family matters or punished minimally in court are now viewed very differently. **Child molesters** have fared even worse under the law of late. Even though the reported short-term (three-year) rate of new convictions for offenders convicted of sex crimes other than forcible rape is the lowest of any category of offenders, public support for the imprisonment, identification, regulation, and treatment of sex offenders victimizing children is very strong—and likely to remain so.

In the decade after Megan Kanka was murdered by a paroled sex offender in New Jersey, all states adopted some form of "Megan's Law" requiring sex offender registration; almost all have a community notification requirement as well. A number of states have passed laws giving prisons the authority to keep dangerous sex offenders locked up even after their prison term expires, in effect holding them in extended quarantine as if they were mentally ill.

These **sexually violent persons** (SVP) laws tend to focus on criminals who have served prison terms after victimizing multiple victims—adults or children. At the end of their prison term, those criminals deemed at high risk to reoffend, through a formal review process, are civilly committed to a state-run treatment program—in a locked facility—until the treatment staff recommend their release. The committing judge, as in mental health commitments, has the final release authority. When the Supreme Court, by a five-to-four vote, approved Kansas's Sexual Predator Treatment Program in its June 1997 decision in *Kansas v. Hendricks*, the ruling cleared the way for other states to adopt similar procedures. On April 25, 2002, the California Supreme Court issued an important twofold ruling on that state's SVP law in the case of *People v. Superior Court (Ghilotti)*:

1. For those civilly committed criminals, the mental health evaluator can recommend continued incarceration (for treatment) even when the criminal is believed to have less than a fifty-fifty chance of recidivism.
2. The judge who reviews the evaluator's recommendation for release can reject the findings and order continued incarceration if he finds the evaluator failed to meet the proper legal standards for release.[37]

All current SVP programs use the **stage concept** of treatment. Austin DesLauriers, who had been clinical director of the Kansas Sexual Predator Treatment Program since 1995, offered this description of his program in 2002:

> These stages, or levels, offer a concrete way for each person to gauge his movement through the program and to understand the expectations the program will have of him at any particular point. Each level provides an increasing number of privileges for a resident as further motivation to continue his work.[38]

Level 1 is the entry phase. It is intended to famililiarize the resident with program rules and expectations and give him time to work through the belief that he is a victim of the system. It allows staff to gather information and assess him. Level 2, the core phase, lasts a year. It teaches critical concepts that allow residents to identify their thought and behavior patterns before, during, and after their crimes. Level 3, the advanced phase, teaches the resident to apply in his daily life the concepts learned in the core phase. The resident also has to draft a relapse prevention plan. Level 4, the honor phase, fine-tunes the relapse prevention plan. Residents are monitored to ensure their intellectual grasp of key concepts and their ability to apply these concepts in their daily living. Level 5 is the awaiting transition phase. The residents have completed all inpatient requirements and are awaiting transition to a structured environment, such as a halfway house.[39]

Statutes regulating SVPs are applied to a small percentage of sex offenders released each year, reflecting an attempt to balance community protection and due process. We will look at sex offender registration and civil commitment laws in more depth in the next chapter on the legal rights of offenders.

States have also intensified research into in-prison and out-of-prison treatment programs for sex offenders trying to find more effective control models. Most follow traditional therapy models, using a progression through levels over time. A few courts have allowed offenders to volunteer for **castration,** which involves surgical removal of the testicles. A handful of states require—and several others allow—chemical castration through the use of the drug **Depo-Provera,** a birth control hormone that kills or sharply reduces a male offender's sex drive (see commentary 16 at the end of this chapter).

The other inmates may not care as much now what you are in prison for today, but the legal system, reflecting society's concern, does. Particularly in the cases involving children and multiple victims, sex offenders have been held to a higher standard of accountability.

PROTECTIVE CUSTODY PRISONERS

Protective custody (PC) is both a status and a housing, a label and a place. To a prisoner, PC means that he has been identified as a likely victim and cannot remain in general population; he will thus be removed from population and placed in a housing unit—a dormitory or cell block—populated by other inmates like himself. While supermax has often been cited as a "prison within a prison," so is PC.

Who are the people most likely to end up in PC? Writing in the late 1980s, convict journalists Ron Wikberg and Wilbert Rideau said that PC units house "what most prisoners perceive and refer to as snitches, queers, punks, rats, faggots, and gal-boys." But this perception of PC inmates as either sexual deviants or violators of the convict code was affected by other growing concerns, Wikberg and Rideau observed, including "overcrowding, violence developing from debts, drugs, a growing number of sex offenders, prison informants, a more youthful and violent offender coming into the prison system, and the growth of gangs."[40]

The steady increase in the number of inmates placed in PC during the 1970s and 1980s can be attributed to one basic rationale: PC was safer than general population. Inmates who had been victimized, sexually or physically; who lived in fear of victimization; or whom prison authorities identified as likely victims requested PC (or were assigned directly with no choice) to avoid the violence and exploitation expected to result if they remained in population. PC was sanctuary, and many inmates sought it.

By the 1990s, the prison's management of PC inmates had undergone important changes. Classification was used more effectively to separate **protection cases** as they entered the system. The increased number of prisons gave classification teams more choices about where to send particular inmates. Enemies could be sent to different prisons, for example, instead of being mixed in population in one big penitentiary where they were more likely to cross paths. As lower-security prisons became commonplace, many inmates afraid of the inmates held under maximum security found a safe home in their more open environments—they stopped asking to be placed in PC—and prison officials, when inmates asked to be put in PC, developed a standard response: "Give me a good reason why." PC became something that had to be earned rather than something given to anyone who asked (if space was available), as had been the case in many prisons previously.

The American Correctional Association (ACA) has established the following model policy on PC:

> It is the policy of the Department of Corrections to provide specialized housing for inmates who require protection from other inmates in order to ensure their personal safety when no other reasonable alternative is available. This is typically done by affording them protective custody status in the facility's administrative segregation unit.[41]

ACA guidelines stress that PC is not a punitive measure, and it must be based on factual needs, not a reaction to stress or a "feeling" that something bad might happen. An inmate asking for PC would be placed in administrative segregation while an investigation was conducted to determine the validity of the request; he would then either be placed in PC or returned to other housing, depending on the outcome of the investigation. Inmates can also be placed in PC involuntarily (in effect a reclassification), provided they are given the right to an internal hearing first. They remain in PC subject to periodic status reviews—such as every thirty or ninety days—with the goal of returning as many inmates as possible to general population.[42]

How many inmates are in PC today? Most prison authorities say far fewer than in the old days, though the numbers are hard to pin down. *The Corrections Yearbook 2001* estimates that only about 1.2 percent of inmates in the states responding to their survey were held in PC.[43] But about three times that number were held in ad seg; many of these were on their way to PC and would be sent along when space was available. In real numbers, the range would be from a minimum of about 15,000 inmates to a maximum of possibly 50,000 inmates. In all but the largest states, the number of PC inmates would be a few hundred at most—enough for a separate prison or two or three specific PC housing units.

Most prisoners know that life in PC is not a piece of cake. Although ACA policies specify that PC conditions—including visitation, correspondence, food service, recreation, and programs—should approximate those provided to the general population, it is often impossible to maintain comparability in a small locked unit. Wikberg and Rideau pointed out,

> The conditions of life within the PC units make up the largest consistent complaint expressed by those assigned to it. Because of the more restricted and isolated

environment, prisoners with PC at the Louisiana State Penitentiary have little or no social activities, organized sports or recreation, and they are prohibited from any academic or vocational training despite a great number of them being relegated to protection status for many years.[44]

A prisoner they interviewed in PC had this observation on being shut off from the mainstream of prison life:

> They put all the whores here so they can keep an eye on them and keep them separated from the rest of the population, and they are weak, so what are they going to do. . . . All I do is run the yard, do some legal work, and read. That is all there is to do. . . . In effect, we are being punished for opting for protection. If you are weak and can't live anywhere else, they are going to send you to a place that has sub-standard conditions and you are going to have to stay there.[45]

Other than the restrictions placed on daily life, PC has two further complications. First, prisoners cannot be completely protected. Prisoners are placed in PC for different reasons, some of which are not compatible with others. A child molester who has been beaten up by other inmates might be placed in the same unit with a former gang member who has snitched out gang leaders. Just because the snitch turned against his own gang does not mean that he will find living with child molesters tolerable.

A good example of what can happen in PC was the killing of defrocked pedophile priest John J. Geoghan in Massachusetts's Souza-Baranowski Prison in August 2003. Geoghan, who had been convicted of groping a ten-year-old boy and was accused of molesting almost 150 boys, had been in the prison's PC unit for four months. He had been transferred from another Massachusetts PC unit, at his lawyers' request, after prison guards urinated and defecated on his bed and encouraged other inmates to kill him.

Geoghan was killed by another PC inmate, Joseph Druce, who had been in prison for fourteen years for strangling a man he believed was gay. Druce had been in trouble in other prisons before being transferred into the same PC unit where Geoghan was placed. Prison authorities said the attack was carefully planned. Druce followed Geoghan into his cell when they were putting up their lunch trays. Only one guard was on the unit. Druce jammed the cell lock, tied up Geoghan, strangled him with a ligature tied around his neck, and then jumped off the bed onto the ex-priest's chest several times to finish the job. Because the cell door was jammed from the inside, guards who responded to the scene could not get inside to render assistance. Geoghan's lawyers called the killing a "classification failure," saying there was no way that Druce, with his homophobic history, should ever have been allowed near Geoghan.[46]

The second complication with PC has to do with leaving it to reenter population. Once they find out where you've been, other inmates assume there is something wrong with you—physically, sexually, psychologically, or in combination—and they often want to find out what it is. A former security officer once suggested that the most effective way of discrediting a convict leader—better than putting him in supermax—was to put him in PC or, even better, to move him from one PC unit to another. Frequent housing changes in prison are often a sign that the inmate is being persistently harassed or victimized by the inmates he lives with. After a few such moves, enhanced by gossip spread over the prison grapevine, the former leader would have lost his status—and might actually need PC for his own safety.

OLDER PRISONERS

When we think of the crime problem in America, we think of young men. Crime remains a young man's game for the most part. Arrest rates for both violent and property crimes peak out in the late teen years and decline sharply after the early twenties. This remains as true today as it did in the 1930s, when researchers Sheldon and Eleanor Glueck suggested that declining arrest rates were related to the process of maturation.

Punishment rates or, more specifically, imprisonment rates have always lagged behind arrest rates, primarily because we are more lenient on younger offenders, often giving them one or sometimes several chances to stop committing crimes (the official term is desistance) before we resort to imprisonment. Thus, a gap of several years often occurs between the time a young man (or woman) begins getting in serious trouble and the first sentence to imprisonment. The teenage thug, even if he has been in trouble as a juvenile, gets a fresh start when he turns eighteen, then gets charges dropped a time or two or reduced to misdemeanors, and then gets probation (or jail time and probation) for a felony or two before he first finds his way into the prison system in his mid-twenties. Harry Allen and Clifford Simonsen have called this phenomenon the **commitment lag.** It applied to many ordinary criminals, excepting the most violent and the most active (or most unlucky) who used up their second chances more quickly.

When you looked closely at adult prisons until recently, the great majority of the population were between ages twenty and forty-five—a few teenagers and a few old men on the extremes but mostly young adults to early middle-age men making up the mass of prisoners. In the 1970s, the average age of state prisoners was reported as twenty-six or twenty-seven. It has increased steadily since then, reaching 34.7 by 2001.[47] This is an average increase of seven to eight years, within a relatively short period of time. What is responsible for the aging of America's prison population?

Researchers have cited four major reasons for this effect:

1. *The aging of the general population from which prisoners come.* The **baby-boom generation** (referring to children born from 1946 through 1960), which is widely cited for its impact on crime rates in the 1960s and imprisonment rates in the 1970s, is now middle age. The big population bulge in America is now between ages forty-five and fifty-five, whereas thirty years ago it was late teens to mid-twenties. The "criminal pool" contains more older fish, even if the younger fish are more active.

2. *The accumulation of men and women who have aged in prison while serving exceptionally long sentences.* This has to do with the proliferation of natural life, life with parole after twenty or twenty-five years in prison, and other long finite sentences from the 1970s on, combined with reduced parole eligibility and declining used of executive clemency in commuting long sentences.

3. *The focus on career criminals with previous incarceration histories.* Through the application of "three strikes and you're out" laws and other statutes aimed at

repeat offenders, middle-age criminals get longer sentences not because their crimes are getting worse but because they failed to mature out of crime as they were supposed to.

4. *The introduction of more older first-time offenders into the prison system.* As the legal system concentrates on homicide, drug distribution, and sex offenses, more middle-age and elderly criminals are entering prison as first-time felons but with sentences long enough to keep them in prison until they are dead or nearly so.

The result of this combination of circumstances is twofold: the prison population as a whole is nearly a decade older than it was a generation ago, and the number of inmates over age fifty-five has grown dramatically, increasing tenfold from 1979 to 2001. In most states, it is the fastest-growing segment of the inmate population. Camille Camp and George Camp, in their *Corrections Yearbook* annual, indicate that by 2001, 7.9 percent of the prison population was age fifty or older. In five states and the federal system, the percentage is already above 10 percent.[48]

Two questions come to mind. First, what age should be used as the entry point into senior citizen status in the prison population? Some states use fifty, while others use fifty-five. Other authoritative sources (McDonald's, movie theaters, and the airlines) typically use fifty-five or sixty or even sixty-five; the Social Security Administration is gradually raising the age for full benefits to sixty-seven. People in general may not be considered old when they turn fifty or fifty-five (especially those of us who are already there and striving to stay healthy and fit), but prisoners tend to age more rapidly than free people. Many prisoners are physically much older than their chronological ages.

Kathleen Auerhahn, in an article on simulation modeling and prison populations of the future, gave several reasons why. "Prisoners are a population characterized by generally poor health status," she wrote. They are disproportionately drawn from groups that have the poorest health status in the free society—low income, minorities, and urban dwellers. Prisoners are more likely to engage in unhealthful risk behaviors such as drug and alcohol use, particularly the increasing proportion of prisoners incarcerated for drug crimes. "Additionally, crowded prisons present ideal conditions for the spread of infectious diseases."[49] This means that in general, prisoners are sicker, weaker, and less likely to have been treated for chronic conditions than people outside. The result is that they enter old age a decade or more ahead of the rest of us. Thus, fifty or fifty-five is used as the boundary line for older inmates.

The other question is why the number of inmates over age fifty matters. Two of the experts on the subject of aging in prison are themselves inmates, Douglas Dennis and Lane Nelson, longtime staff writers for *The Angolite*, the prison magazine of the Louisiana State Penitentiary at Angola. This prison has the largest collection of lifers of any prison in America; Angola has become the prototype of the "lifers' prison." The average age is past forty, and 400 of its 5,100 inmates have already been in prison more than twenty-five years. They are eligible to attend the annual "Longtermers Day" held at the prison each summer—an event described not as a celebration of growing old in prison but as an opportunity to reflect and lament years lost forever.

The feature articles Dennis and Nelson have written for *The Angolite* often describe the experiences of inmates growing old in prison. In addition to their physical and mental health problems, these older inmates are often isolated from their families and the outside world. The prison world is no piece of cake, either, especially when your companions are thugs two generations younger than you. Preferences in food, music, television, recreation, and conversation are different. Older inmates complain about the youngsters' disrespectful attitudes, lack of cleanliness, and noise level—or, to put it in the perspective of the younger inmate, you might like to visit your grandfather, even spend a few hours talking together; but how would you like to live in a six-by-eight cell with him or be in the next bed in a dormitory—permanently?

The cultural conflicts between younger and older inmates have led many prisons, including Angola, to set up residential units for older inmates. At Angola, Camp F is a trusty camp for middle-age and older inmates, including Walter Culbreath, nicknamed "Daddy-O," who at age ninety-three in 2003 was one of the oldest inmates in America. Culbreath, who is living proof that not all people mature out of criminal behavior as they age, came to prison at age thirty-nine for the first time for aggravated assault. Discharged on parole, he returned at age forty-seven for three counts of theft. Discharged again, he moved to New Orleans, where he was convicted of manslaughter at age fifty-five for shooting a woman in the projects. Paroled after seven years, he was free for six more, then stabbed his former girlfriend to death on the street in New Orleans. He was sixty-nine. Culbreath was tried, found guilty, and sentenced to death. When the Louisiana Supreme Court overturned the sentence, he left death row for Angola's general population. Every able-bodied Angola inmate has to work, even a nonagenarian. Culbreath has tended the coffee pot in Camp F's security office and trimmed bushes in front of the building in recent years. He walks six miles per day to stay fit. Culbreath is a familiar sight to security officers patrolling the roads that lead from one camp to another on the farm—Daddy-O trudging along after fifty-five years in and out of prison, still hoping for one more chance in the free world.[50]

Management in population is not the only problem caused by the increase in older inmates. Cost is a major concern. Various studies indicate that elderly inmates cost two to three times as much to house as younger inmates, primarily because of more costly medical care and medication. A California study found that the cost of younger inmates was about $21,000 annually, while it was $60,000 for inmates over the age of sixty. The primary reason for the high cost of older inmates is medical care. Those over age sixty-five are likely to spend twice as much time in medical facilities and have three times the health care costs of younger inmates.[51]

Florida, whose percentage of prison inmates over age fifty is projected to rise from 8.6 percent in 2001 to almost 14 percent by 2011, is among those states looking at alternatives to reduce the cost of keeping them in prison. In its *2001 Annual Report*, the Florida Corrections Commission noted that it already had one facility, the River Junction Work Camp, housing 355 "generally healthy" elderly inmates who work at the neighboring Florida State Hospital. The commission has recommended to the governor and legislature that a "special needs" facility for infirm or disabled **geriatric inmates** also be opened soon. It expects to have over 12,000 elderly inmates by 2011, many of whom will need placement in such a facility.[52]

California, which is trying to cut prison costs in the face of growing state budget deficits, is experiencing similar cost and population projections. Interestingly,

California has no general rule for handling elderly inmates, who are mixed in with the regular prison population. It is not among the sixteen states, such as Florida and Louisiana, with separate facilities designated to house older inmates. But Corrections Secretary Robert Presley indicated in 2002 that he thought it best to put old inmates in one prison.

Louisiana's **geriatric prison,** Forcht-Wade, opened in 1998 as a branch of a larger prison in northern Louisiana. It operates as a nursing home for the elderly and disabled, holding about 400 minimum-custody inmates who require extra care in reduced-custody status.

As more prisons move into the nursing home business, coping with older inmates will be a huge problem for cash-strapped state governments in the years ahead, says Ronald Aday, a professor at Middle Tennessee State University and author of the 2003 book *Aging Prisoners: Crisis in American Corrections*. "In addition to health care issues, work assignments, [Medicare] co-payments, nutritional requirements, concerns for victimization, end of life issues, and appropriate staffing are concerns that will have to be addressed. The task is a daunting one."[53]

Dying in prison is an issue in itself, requiring corrections officials to act as funeral directors, cemetery operators, and grief counselors. At the Louisiana State Penitentiary, thirty-four inmates died in prison in 2002, most of them among "the first generation of lifers to reach their twilight years behind bars," according to prison journalist Wilbert Rideau.

It seems almost too obvious to raise one possible way of alleviating part of the problem of housing older inmates—turn some of them loose. Research has found lower recidivism rates for inmates released from prison after age forty-five (typically in the range of 10 to 20 percent being convicted of new crimes) and even lower rates for offenders released after age fifty-five (reconviction rates of less than 10 percent). So why not turn more of them loose, especially those who have good conduct records in prison? Two common objections are raised:

1. It is not fair to give some people a sentence break (by turning them loose early) just because of their age.
2. The crimes they have committed—particularly the homicides, drug crimes, and sex offenses that are common among elderly inmates—warrant full punishment, not leniency.

Both California and Louisiana have looked at legal changes that would release more elderly inmates. California's proposal would have released more nonviolent seniors to parole, and Louisiana's would have made lifers parole eligible after a combination of years in prison and age was reached. Despite the low recidivism rates, neither proposal was adopted. "So the costs of imprisonment go way up at the same time the benefits of imprisonment, in terms of public safety, go way down," commented Franklin Zimring, a law professor at the University of California at Berkeley.[54]

A WORD ON SPECIAL NEEDS PRISONERS

This discussion of prisoners as people with special needs is not intended to promote sympathy for criminals or excuse their criminal conduct. It is intended to make three specific points about prisoners and prison life:

1. The conventional profile of the convict as a young male sociopath who "chooses" crime for adventure or economic gain is not all-inclusive. While it does describe the stereotypical prisoner, it fails to consider many other prisoners of divergent backgrounds who become convicted felons for many different reasons. We tend to think of criminals as a group when we ought to be seeing them as individual human beings instead.

2. The management of special needs prisoners in population creates complications both for them and for prison managers. Many special needs prisoners cannot hold their own with other inmates in the repressive, closed-in environment of prisons; they are more likely to be victimized and exploited, to "cause trouble" that is often not of their own making.

3. The **one-size-fits-all** approach to imprisonment—downplaying individuality and emphasizing uniformity—that prevails today fails to take into account the differences among prisoners with special needs; many of these inmates do their time without ever having their special problems addressed in meaningful treatment programs that would help them avoid future criminal behavior after they get out of prison.

We should also consider that special needs are not distributed one per inmate. A juvenile criminal may also be both mentally retarded and mentally ill; a sex criminal may be isolated as a protection case not because he is a pervert but because he is HIV positive. In the prison environment, these special needs—making their bearers targets for victimization—can be even more defining than they are on the street.

KEY TERMS

chancery court
parens patriae
ward
juvenile delinquency
superpredator
juvenile gangs
differential association
juvenile
dangerous classes
delinquent juvenile
status offenders
incorrigible juveniles
PINS
neglected
dependent
juvenile court
intake
petition

adjudication
disposition
rehabilitation
crime schools
Kent v. United States
In re Gault
due process
Juvenile Justice and
    Delinquency
    Prevention Act
decarceration
deinstitutionalization
decriminalization
Jerome Miller
custody philosophy
diversion
net widening
probation
staff-secure facilities

group homes
treatment centers
experiential programs
shelters
locked facilities
detention center
house of refuge
training school
the least restrictive
    alternative
hidden system
jail and lockup removal
sight and sound
    separation
waiver
beyond rehabilitation
cottage style
dormitory style
treatment modalities

boot camp
aftercare
zero-tolerance policies
asylum
insanity
M'Naghten rule
right from wrong
insanity defense
not guilty by reason of
    insanity
temporary insanity
incompetent to stand trial
guilty but mentally ill
mental illness
Community Mental
    Health Act
deinstitutionalized
transinstitutionalization
treatment units

psychotropic medication

therapeutic community

triple whammy

Alcoholics Anonymous

Narcotics Anonymous

Center on Addiction and Substance Abuse

separate unit

addiction groups

relapse prevention

mentally retarded

borderline mentally retarded

developmentally challenged

Americans with Disabilities Act

Atkins v. Virginia

AIDS

HIV

HIV-positive

environment of risk

sex criminal

sex offense

crimes against nature

sex offender

child abusers

child molesters

sexually violent persons

stage concept

castration

Depo-Provera

protective custody

protection cases

commitment lag

baby-boom generation

geriatric inmates

geriatric prison

one-size-fits-all

NOTES

1. Clemens Bartollas and Stuart Miller, *Juvenile Justice in America*, 3rd ed. (Upper Saddle River, N.J.: Prentice Hall, 2001), p. 4.

2. Ibid., p. 57.

3. Ibid., p. 97.

4. *Commonwealth v. Fisher*, 213 Pennsylvania 48, 62A, pp. 198–200.

5. Howard N. Snyder, "Juvenile Arrests 2001," U.S. Department of Justice, Juvenile Justice Bulletin, December 2003, p. 1.

6. Charles M. Puzzanchera, "Juvenile Court Placement of Adjudicated Youth, 1990–1999," U.S. Department of Justice, Fact Sheet, September 2003, p. 1.

7. Ibid.

8. Howard N. Snyder and Melissa Sickmund, *Juvenile Offenders and Victims: 1999 National Report*, National Center for Juvenile Justice, Office of Juvenile Justice and Delinquency Prevention, September 1999, pp. 186–88.

9. Ibid., p. 201.

10. Puzzanchera, "Juvenile Court Placement of Adjudicated Youth, 1990–1999," p. 1.

11. Joseph B. Sanborn Jr., "Certification to Criminal Court: The Important Policy Questions of How, When, and Why," in Ralph A. Weisheit and Robert G. Culbertson, *Juvenile Delinquency: A Justice Perspective*, 3rd ed. (Prospect Heights, Ill.: Waveland Press, 1995), p. 117.

12. Bartollas and Miller, *Juvenile Justice in America*, p. 268.

13. Human Rights Watch, *Ill-Equipped: U.S. Prisons and Offenders with Mental Illness*, 2003, p. 1, *www.hrw.org*.

14. Bill Groom, "Handling the Triple Whammy: Serious Mental Illness, Substance Abuse and Criminal Behavior," *Corrections Today* 61, no. 4 (July 1999): 115.

15. Human Rights Watch, *Ill-Equipped*, p. 5.

16. *Ruiz v. Johnson*, 37 F. Supp. 2d 855 (S.D. Texas, 1999).

17. Human Rights Watch, *Ill-Equipped*, p. 2.

18. Allen J. Beck and Laura M. Maruschak, "Mental Health Treatment in State Prisons, 2000," U.S. Department of Justice, Bureau of Justice Statistics Special Report, July 2001, p. 6.

19. Groom, "Handling the Triple Whammy," pp. 114–19.

20. Steven Belenko, Jordan Peugh, Joseph A. Califano Jr., Margaret Usdansky, and Susan E. Foster, "Substance Abuse and the Prison Population: A Three-Year Study by Columbia University Reveals Widespread Substance Abuse among Offender Population," *Corrections Today* 60, no. 6 (October 1998): 85.

21. Camille Graham Camp and George M. Camp, *The Corrections Yearbook 2001: Adult Systems* (Middletown, Conn.: Criminal Justice Institute, 2002), pp. 136–37.

22. Belenko et al., "Substance Abuse and the Prison Population," p. 87.

23. Ibid., p. 89.

24. Joan Petersilia, "Justice for All? Offenders with Mental Retardation and the California Prison System," *Prison Journal* 77, no. 4 (December 1997): 358.

25. Ibid.

26. *Ruiz v. Estelle*, 503 F. Supp. 1265 (S. D. Texas 1980).

27. Petersilia, "Justice for All?," p. 361.

28. Laura M. Maruschak, "HIV in Prisons, 2000," U.S. Department of Justice, Bureau of Justice Statistics Bulletin, October 2002, p. 1.

29. Ibid., p. 2.

30. Lane Nelson, "Educating the Educated," *The Ango-lite*, November/December 1994, p. 52.

31. Michael F. Haggerty, "Incarcerated Populations and HIV," *CRIA Update*, summer 2000, p. 3, *www.thebody.com/cria/summer00/prison.html*.

32. Maruschak, "HIV in Prisons, 2000," p. 6.

33. Cathy Wurzer, "Life after Prison: Robert Gladhill's Story," Minnesota Public Radio, March 4, 2003, p. 1, *news.mpr.org/features/2003/03/05_wurzer_prisongladstone*.

34. Ibid., p. 2.

35. Ibid., p. 5.

36. Ibid., p. 6.

37. "California: Sex Offenders May Be Held beyond Sentence," *Organized Crime Digest*, July 5, 2002, p. 7.

38. Austin T. DesLauriers, "Kansas' Sex Offender Treatment Program," *Corrections Today* 64, no. 6 (October 2002): 119.

39. Ibid., pp. 119–20.

40. Ron Wikberg and Wilbert Rideau, "Protective Custody," *The Angolite*, July/August 1989, p. 39.

41. American Correctional Association, "Protective Custody Operations," *Guidelines for the Development of Policies and Procedures* (Laurel, Md.: American Correctional Association, 1991), p. 263.

42. Ibid.

43. Camp and Camp, *The Corrections Yearbook 2001*, pp. 38–39.

44. Wikberg and Rideau, "Protective Custody," p. 54.

45. Ibid.

46. Fox Butterfield, "Prison Policy Put Priest in Unit with His Killer," *New York Times*, August 29, 2003, p. 14.

47. Camp and Camp, *The Corrections Yearbook 2001*, p. 63.

48. Ibid., pp. 34–35.

49. Kathleen Auerhahn, "Selective Incapacitation, Three Strikes, and the Problem of Aging Prison Populations: Using Simulation Modeling to See the Future," *Criminology and Public Policy* 1, no. 3 (July 2002): 353–87.

50. Douglas Dennis, "Ages," *The Angolite*, March/April 1994, pp. 22–27.

51. Laura Gater, "Correctional Healthcare Special Needs Populations," *Corrections Forum* 11, no. 4 (July/August 2002): 12.

52. Florida Corrections Commission, *2001 Annual Report*, August 30, 2003, *www.fcc.state.fl.us/fcc/reports/final01/4eld.htm*.

53. Patrick McMahon, "Aging Inmates Present Prison Crisis," *USA Today*, August 11, 2003.

54. "California Struggling with Growing Numbers of Elderly Prisoners," June 9, 2002, *globalaging.org/elderrights/us/CAprisons.htm*.

FURTHER READING

Bartollas, Clemens, and Stuart J. Miller. *Juvenile Justice in America*. 3rd ed. Upper Saddle River, N.J.: Prentice Hall, 2000.

Braithwaite, Ronald L., Theodore M. Hammett, and Robert M. Mayberry. *Prisons and AIDS: A Public Health Challenge*. San Francisco: Jossey-Bass, 1996.

Feld, Barry C. *Bad Kids: Race and the Transformation of the Juvenile Court*. New York: Oxford University Press, 1999.

Santamour, Miles B., and Patricia S. Watson. *The Retarded Offender*. New York: Praeger Publishers, 1982.

WEB AND VIDEO RESOURCES

The Center on Juvenile and Criminal Justice Website is *www.cjcj.org*.

The National Council on Crime and Delinquency is available online at *www.nccd-crc.org*.

The federal Office of Juvenile Justice and Delinquency Prevention Website is *www.ojjdp.ncjrs.org*.

The American Bar Association's Juvenile Justice Center is available at *www.abanet.org/crimjust/juvjus/home.html*.

An interesting reference is *Juvenile Justice Magazine Online* at *www.juvenilejustice.com*.

Two good resources on substance abuse are the National Institute on Drug Abuse (*www.nida.nih.gov*) and the Addiction Resource Guide (*www.addictionresourceguide.com*).

15 "Juveniles in Adult Prisons: A Very Bad Idea"

by David W. Roush and Earl L. Dunlap

Although certain juveniles require extensive and secure incarceration, the incarceration of juveniles in adult prisons is wrong for both children and society. There are significant differences between adults and children (persons under 18 years old), and public safety is best served by correctional efforts that restore youths to healthy, law-abiding lifestyles. The mission of adult corrections, as defined by politicians, the public, and the courts, is at odds with these principles.

Myth #1 The adult system is more effective for juveniles. The adult system is overworked, overcrowded and overwhelmed, and there is no evidence that it is more effective for juveniles. Research indicates that youths in the adult system have higher rates of recidivism than youths incarcerated in the juvenile system for the same offenses. Placing juveniles in adult prisons does not restore the victim, the community or the offender, nor does it express concern for anyone's future. It simply reinforces the popular notion of "out of sight, out of mind."

Myth #2 The juvenile system is ineffective. The placement of juveniles in adult prisons mistakenly assumes the failure of the juvenile justice system. Juvenile justice has spent too much time making excuses and apologizing instead of debunking the "nothing works" fallacy with empirical findings. Evidence underscores the differences between the juvenile and adult systems in all areas of effectiveness and public safety. Sending juveniles to the adult system denies the juvenile system the chance to address young offenders' needs.

Myth #3 The best model of justice eliminates discretion and shifts the basis for decisions to the nature of the offense and away from the individual. The placement of juveniles in adult prisons is an outgrowth of the offense-based decision-making system. Offense-based decision-making eliminates the discretion needed for individual justice, which is a principle at the very heart of juvenile courts. We have seen a nationwide lowering of the age at which juveniles can be tried as adults. If this continues, juvenile courts may be reduced to handling only dependent and neglect issues. An offense-based system for juveniles denies the individual characteristics of each child and overgeneralizes by enforcing a "one-size-fits-all" strategy. It also compounds the empirically demonstrated racial bias already present in our system.

Myth #4 Public opinion is trustworthy. Advocates of placing juveniles in adult prisons often claim that it reflects public opinion when it may only reflect the preference of those setting forth policy. Some of the most prominent public opinion research regarding juvenile offenders indicates a desire that they be held to the same legal standards as adults. Yet when asked about how that treatment should be implemented, more than 75 percent believe that incarceration of juveniles should be for rehabilitation purposes.

Myth #5 A punitive approach can be made effective by increasing its intensity. The placement of juveniles in adult prisons reflects a disregard for history, which is replete with examples of how "get tough" approaches fail. When sanctions are swift and certain, they need not be lengthy or severe to be effective. Punishment suppresses behavior; it doesn't change it. Our comparatively longer periods of imprisonment have not made us one of the world's most violence-free societies. Because punishment inevitably fails to achieve retribution, we slowly increase the severity until we are desensitized to how much like an offender we have become. The desire to "get tough" is a thinly veiled desire to "get even."

Myth #6 Treating children like adults is right. Housing children in adult prisons is simply wrong, regardless of the evils they've committed. Research indicates that juveniles are five times more likely to be sexually assaulted and two times more likely to be beaten in prison than in a juvenile institution. Placing them in adult prisons constitutes deliberate indifference to their well-being and dehumanizes them. In addition to being costly in terms of time and resources, it prevents reconciliation and healing.

Transferring the problem of the most serious juvenile offenders to an even more overwhelmed and less effective system makes no sense. We must challenge political leadership to provide the resources necessary for both systems to develop a proactive strategy for dealing with this situation and to articulate a policy direction that is collectively supported. Archbishop Desmond Tutu best expressed our opposition in his response to a question about our moral and ethical obligation to rehabilitate troubled youths. He said, "If we don't do all we can to salvage [them], it is almost like spitting in the face of God."

16 "Kinder Cut: A Limited Defense of Chemical Castration"

by Craig Turk

Last year, the California legislature became the first state to mandate "chemical castration"—the temporary and reversible suppression of sex drive through hormone shots—for several classes of convicted sexual predators. And sometime next year, a California court will almost certainly strike down the law.

The court will likely say that the law is too vague, that the treatment may not always work and that the measure as written is "cruel and unusual punishment." In all of this, the court will be absolutely correct. But lawmakers in Florida, Michigan, Massachusetts, Missouri, Texas and Washington should not abandon their efforts to pass similar laws just yet. In at least some cases, injections of medroxyprogesterone acetate (more commonly called Depo-Provera) can function as a sexual appetite suppressant, keeping convicted molesters from harming again. Moreover, when administered as part of a broader psychological treatment regimen, the shots can actually help in rehabilitation.

California erred mainly by passing a law that applied the treatment so indiscriminately. A more carefully tailored measure—one that invoked chemical castration in more limited circumstances—would not only be an effective crime deterrent and rehabilitation tool, it is also more likely to pass constitutional muster.

Under California's law, which took effect in January, state courts can force anyone convicted of molesting children younger than 13 to undergo, as a condition of parole, Depo-Provera shots, which reduce testosterone to prepuberty levels and are supposed to prevent sex offenders from molesting again. After a second conviction, injections are mandatory.

The concept of chemical castration is not new. Though not quite as effective as surgical castration—an option California graciously offers, presumably for felons who really hate needles—physicians have used drugs like Depo-Provera for over twenty years. Published data strongly indicate that very low testosterone levels correlate with low sexual libido for men, and several studies have shown such treatment works in controlling the sexual behavior of certain types of pedophiles.

Some of the most striking results, frequently touted by proponents of the California legislation, come from studies in Denmark and Switzerland, where voluntary chemical castration reduced recidivism rates from 50 percent or higher to substantially less than 10 percent. In a widely cited statement, one Danish sex offender raved, "My sex fantasies, which once made me a criminal, are gone. Watching a pornographic movie is like watching the evening news."

But if California had bothered to check the details of these studies, it would have known better than to mandate chemical castration for such a broad class of sexual criminals. For starters, the European studies used small samples and lacked adequate control groups. Everyone who underwent the treatment did so voluntarily, which suggests the participants at least wanted to be treated and raises questions about whether Depo-Provera would work for offenders less eager to be reformed.

What's more, sex offenders are not a homogeneous group: even among those who prey only upon children, there are numerous types. Some individuals cannot attain sexual or emotional satisfaction with adults at all; others, such as the mentally retarded, sometimes turn to children because they cannot deal successfully or maturely with adults. There are those whose crimes are the product of impaired judgment—one study recently concluded that as many as 76 percent of sex offenders abuse alcohol, and that half of their crimes are committed while the offender is intoxicated. And there are also sadistic offenders motivated by malice.

Depo-Provera may help control the trenchcoat-wearing, candy-toting playground stalker, yet the evidence suggests it will do little to prevent crimes against children by predators who act for reasons other than sexual gratification, who harm children out of rage and emotional imbalance, or whose gratification for their crimes may not be wholly sexual. The only way to keep these criminals from molesting again, experts say, is to keep them in prison, or through intensive treatment and counseling. The California Psychiatric Association, which like most medical groups has opposed the California law, concluded: "While we support efforts in finding effective methods of stopping sex offenders from reoffending, psychiatrists fundamentally believe that not all offenders would necessarily benefit from this type of treatment intervention and that treatment is most effective when the person agrees to try to change their behavior."

For practical purposes, this might not seem like a fatal flaw, given that the safety of children is at stake. "Nothing's 100 percent," says Assemblyman Bill Hoge of Pasadena, who introduced the bill after being sickened by a story of a child rape in Texas. The courts, however, will probably see things differently.

There is, first, the question of whether chemical castration amounts to "cruel and unusual punishment," as prohibited by the Eighth Amendment. Although jurisprudence in this area is somewhat muddled, it generally involves evaluations of how a punishment was viewed historically and how it meets modern standards of decency.

Given the nature of the crimes at issue, the high-tech elegance of the procedure and its considerable political popularity, courts are unlikely to strike down Depo-Provera injections as cruel and unusual—if they are used in cases in which the treatment works. But, because the California law applies the punishment indiscriminately, it is constitutionally vulnerable: it may seem like we cannot be cruel enough to child molesters, but the Constitution makes no allowances for pure vindictiveness. Forcing weekly injections of a hormone—particularly one not FDA-approved for such purposes—on criminals who will not be controlled or rehabilitated by it is precisely the kind of severe and random punishment the Eighth Amendment sought to prohibit.

Another legal issue concerns the Fourteenth Amendment, which prohibits deprivation of life, liberty or property without due process. Although the Supreme Court has not recognized a right to a libido, it has declared—in a 1942 decision striking down involuntary sterilization for habitual felons—that procreation is a "basic civil right of man." While chemical castration is reversible, and while it does not necessarily impair functioning to the point of making intercourse or procreation impossible for men, it does make procreation temporarily impossible for women. Indeed, for women Depo-Provera is a form of birth control—and it does not dampen their libidos.

To justify this infringement upon a fundamental right—the right to procreate—the state must show that it has a compelling interest, "narrowly tailored" to the situation involved. Controlling convicted child molesters through hormone suppression is likely to satisfy the "compelling state interest" test: sex crimes against children are a serious public problem, and Depo-Provera treatments can help redress it in some cases. But California's program fails the "narrowly tailored" test: Depo-Provera's temporary sterilization of women has nothing to do with the professed goal of lowering offenders' sex drives. And, even if it had been limited to men, the California law does not ensure that only those who can be helped by the process are chemically castrated.

This is not a case of unjustified public rage, but of legislative pandering subverting a potentially effective solution to a barbaric problem. Proponents of California's law claim their measure is better than nothing, but lawmakers elsewhere should realize that nothing is not the only alternative.

12   PRISONERS' RIGHTS

Judges are not wardens, but we must act as wardens to the limited extent that unconstitutional prison conditions force us to intervene when those responsible for the conditions have failed to act.

— U.S. Seventh Circuit Court of Appeals, *Harris v. Flemming* (1988)

INTRODUCTION

The convicted felon in confinement exists in a legal world much different from that of free people outside prison. Prisoners give up many rights on conviction, and the rights they retain are constrained by the nature of confinement. The loss of citizenship rights is not limited to felons serving prison terms. Anyone convicted of a felony, including those persons who never go to prison, may lose any number of citizenship rights and face other restrictions because of the criminal conviction. After reading the material in this chapter, you should be familiar with:

1. The historical legal status of the convicted felon.
2. Recent developments in prison litigation.
3. Leading cases in prisoners' rights, including those involving legal access, discipline, medical care, and personal rights.
4. Effects of litigation on jail and prison administration.
5. Alternatives to litigation.
6. Postrelease consequences of a criminal conviction.
7. Civil rights commonly denied felons.
8. Registration and civil commitment of ex-offenders.
9. Methods of erasing criminal records and restoring offenders' rights.

THE CONVICTED FELON IN HISTORY

Nine California prisoners file a class-action lawsuit accusing the state prison system of providing poor medical care to over 160,000 prisoners. Federal prison inmates sue for the return of *Playboy* and *Penthouse* magazines, banned for their sexually explicit pictures by a new act of Congress. Two Wisconsin inmates file suit over restrictive conditions in the state's supermax prison. A state prisoner sues to be allowed to send his semen to his wife outside, maintaining that imprisonment without conjugal visiting denies his right to procreation. Attorneys for a psychotic death row inmate sue to stop his forced medication, arguing that the state only wishes to keep him stable enough to be executed on schedule. A Chicago jail inmate complains in his lawsuit that his personal privacy and "Christian modesty" are violated because women guards watch him shower and use the bathroom. An HIV-positive inmate sues a gossipy prison guard for damages, claiming that his heart was broken when his fiancée broke off their relationship after the guard revealed the prisoner's HIV status to mutual friends.

What two important common features do these recent (and real) lawsuits share? They are all part of the category of prisoners' rights litigation, and if they had occurred fifty years ago, none of them would ever have seen the light of day, much less the focus of media and court attention. Fifty or a hundred years ago, if you had posed the question, "What are the rights of the convicted felon," the simple answer would have been, "None," and this chapter would be over. This was the legacy of the convicted felon—a person to whom the rights of ordinary citizens did not apply.

For hundreds of years under common law, a felon had no commonly accepted legal status. When the final guilty verdict was pronounced, the convicted offender became a dead man in the eyes of the law, or he at least entered the realm of legal purgatory. The concept was called **civil death,** meaning that the felon no longer had the civil rights of other persons. Whatever happened to him after conviction, including death, was legally fitting. The convicted felon became an **outlaw,** no longer a member of society. He lost the rights of citizenship, becoming the equivalent of what the later Soviet system would call a **nonperson.**

This legal status (or lack of legal status) attached to the convicted felon continued from the early days of common law into the modern era—well into the days of the penitentiary. The case most often cited as representative of the status of the convict in the penitentiary is the 1871 Virginia appellate court decision *Ruffin v. Commonwealth,* which declared, in part,

> A convicted felon, whom the law in its humanity punishes by confinement in the penitentiary instead of with death, is subject while undergoing that punishment, to all the laws which the Legislature in its wisdom may enact for the government of that institution and the control of its inmates. For the time being, during his term of service in the penitentiary, he is in a state of penal servitude to the State. He has, as a consequence of his crime, not only forfeited his liberty, but all his personal rights except those which the law in its humanity accords to him. He is for the time being the slave of the State. . . .
>
> The bill of rights is a declaration of general principles to govern a society of freemen, and not of convicted felons and men civilly dead. Such men have some rights it is true, such as the law in its benignity accords to them, but not the rights of free men. They are the slaves of the State undergoing punishment for heinous crimes committed against the laws of the land.

This case, in describing the condition of **penal servitude** and defining the prisoner as the **slave of the state,** seems authoritative in restating the "convict-as-social-outcast" principle that had endured for centuries. Donald Wallace has taken a different perspective. He has pointed out that the Virginia appeals court judges were overstating their opinions on a case that was not really about hard labor or prison management. Woody Ruffin had killed a private guard attempting to escape from a work detail. After he was condemned to hang, he argued that his trial should have been held where the crime was committed rather than in Richmond, where the prison was located. The appellate court, after appearing to say that he had no rights, in fact reviewed his claim and said that holding the trial in Richmond was allowed, as this was Ruffin's "vicinage," his lawful residence. If Ruffin had no legal rights, the court would not have been required to review the merits of his case.[1]

Wallace goes on to cite other cases from this era that illustrate his theme that not all courts viewed prisoners as civilly dead or without legal standing. He argues that "the slave of the state view was not generally held, if it was ever held by any court."[2] A Georgia Supreme Court case from 1909, *Westbrook v. State*, found that the prisoner was owed some affirmative obligation from the state:

> The convict occupies a different attitude from the slave toward society. He is not mere property, without any civil rights, but has all the rights of an ordinary citizen which are not expressly or by necessary implication taken from him by law. While the law does take his liberty, and imposes a duty of servitude and observance of discipline for the regulation of convicts, it does not deny his right to personal security against unlawful invasion.[3]

Wallace reviews other cases from the late 1800s and early 1900s relating to the physical conditions in jails and prisons and the administration of discipline in these institutions, particularly the use of physical punishments that were then common practice. Although in this era state and county institutions were considered legally immune from damages in prisoner lawsuits, municipalities and individual jail and prison officers were occasionally held liable for injuries to inmates. The Kansas Supreme Court, holding custodians liable for damages in *Topeka v. Boutwell* (1894), wrote of the duty of custodians to treat prisoners "humanely":

> . . . keepers of city prisoners have no warrant authority in law to be harsh and brutal in the management of those in their custody.
> . . . the constitution of the state forbids cruel or unusual punishments, and the courts have ample power to prevent such punishments from being inflicted. In making arrests and in the treatment of prisoners, in or out of city prisons, no police or other officer is justified in using unnecessary harshness or excessive violence.[4]

If you accept Wallace's view, which runs contrary to much of the general commentary on the prisoner's legal status during this era, the convicted felon, if not exactly a dead man, was surely on a legal frontier—a remote place where the rules that applied to everyone else did not generally apply to him. Perhaps he might find an attentive court to listen to his arguments, but more likely not. No general doctrines defined his legal standing. And the fact that he was in the physical custody of a warden with complete control over his body tended to limit his access to the courts free people would have access to (though we know that poor people, even when free, have never found it easy to get the courts to pay attention to their legal problems).

Convicts were lost in the penitentiary's dark womb. If anything happened to them, if they fell sick and died from neglect, if they were harmed by another inmate, or if they were killed by a guard, no explanation was necessary. The state was not liable for any misadventure that befell a felon in prison, nor was it required to meet standards of decent care. Bad management or deliberate abuse of prisoners had no legal consequences.

By the 1940s and 1950s, the widespread legal philosophy was that the courts left prison operations alone. Court officials acknowledged that they lacked the expertise to tell prison officials how to run their institutions. This concept, called the **hands-off doctrine,** allowed prison wardens to run their institutions with legal impunity. Prison officials were not accountable in either state or federal courts for their actions or for conditions within their institutions. Donald Wallace calls this a step back, or retrenchment, from an earlier time when courts might have been more inclined to step into matters relating to the administration of jails and prisons; other scholars view the hands-off era as the logical position of the courts in avoiding intervention on behalf of unpopular complainants.

Whatever explanation one accepts, the result was that in general state and federal courts did not intervene in prison and jail operations, and prisoners were not entitled to damages resulting from injuries sustained while in custody. One often-cited case from 1944, *Coffin v. Reichard*, appears to run counter to this doctrine. In *Coffin*, the U.S. Sixth Circuit Court of Appeals held that "a prisoner retains all the rights of an ordinary citizen except those expressly, or by necessary implication, taken from him by law." Four years later, in reviewing a petition by an Alcatraz inmate to appear in person to argue his appeal, the U.S. Supreme Court ruled in *Price v. Johnston* (1948), "Lawful incarceration brings about the necessary withdrawal or limitation of many privileges and rights, a retraction justified by the considerations underlying our penal system."

This typically was interpreted to mean that constitutional rights invariably had to give way to expressed (but rarely documented) corrections concerns about the administering of prison systems—problems and needs relating to custody, security, rehabilitation, discipline, punishment, and resource limitations.[5] Not until the 1960s, when social and legal changes shook up the existing order of American society, would the hands-off doctrine be abandoned and prisoners begin to find courts more concerned about their rights as citizens in confinement.

LEGAL ACTIONS OPEN TO PRISONERS

While we probably should not say that courts in the penitentiary era completely ignored prisoners as human beings, it is fair to say that prevailing doctrines worked against prisoners getting their issues into court and getting a fair review once there. Here and there exceptions occurred, but the rule was that prisoners could expect little consideration from both state and federal courts. From the 1960s on, prisoners would experience two important changes in their previously diminished standing as litigants:

1. A wide variety of legal avenues leading into the courts would open to prisoners.
2. State and federal courts would extend to prisoners constitutional rights not previously acknowledged.

We are going to concentrate on two of the most important legal channels that were opened to prisoners between the 1960s and the end of the twentieth century—the "cruel and unusual punishment" clause of the Eighth Amendment and the civil rights provisions of Section 1983 of Title 42 of the U.S. Code—but we ought to review other legal routes as well.

Christopher Smith has provided an overview of legal actions that may be filed in state and federal courts:[6]

1. **Appeals.** Anyone convicted at trial (a small percentage of all convictions in comparison to guilty pleas in which appeals are less readily available) has the right to appeal the conviction into higher state and federal courts. The great majority of appeals result in decisions against the convicted criminal.

2. **Torts.** Based on negligence or intentional actions, a tort suit is simply a lawsuit for damages filed in the state or federal court that would have jurisdiction over the place of confinement. If the roof of a prison dorm collapsed during a rainstorm, injured prisoners could sue for damages just as college students could if a dorm roof fell in on them.

3. **Criminal charges.** Inmates or prison staff who commit crimes against prisoners could have criminal charges filed against them if the prisoner can convince a local district attorney or U.S. district attorney with jurisdiction over the prison to accept charges. This was rarely done in the past but is more common today, particularly in cases related to sexual assault and victimization.

4. **Writ of mandamus.** Mandamus is another old common law legal action. A person asks a court to order a public official to perform his or her lawful duty. If, for instance, prison policies provided that inmates were to receive three hot meals per day and prison officials because of budget cutbacks went to one hot meal and two cold meals, a prisoner could file a writ of mandamus to require officials to comply with their own policies.

5. **Administrative appeals.** Applying mostly to internal actions within the prison such as disciplinary hearings, classification, and transfers, these appeals would be carried forth into a court when they could not be resolved within the internal workings of the prison or corrections bureaucracy. These appeals grow out of the administrative remedies set up after the litigation of the 1970s required some structure to process prisoner grievances.

6. *Other legal actions.* This category would include a broad range of other civil and administrative actions that a prisoner might be involved in because of events *outside* prison. This would include such legal matters as divorce, child custody, inheritance, real estate transactions, Social Security, veterans benefits and other financial matters. The prisoner retains the citizenship rights of ordinary persons in these actions.

State and local prisoners, who make up over 90 percent of all prisoners in custody, have two common means available to litigate their confinement in the federal courts:

1. *Habeas corpus* **petitions**
2. **Civil rights lawsuits**

Habeas corpus is an old English legal remedy. As it was used in English and American courts for a long time, it allowed a court to review the legality of a prisoner's confinement. After the appeal was over, prisoners could file *habeas corpus* petitions in a state court or a federal court asking the judge to review constitutional issues related to the legal process and conduct of the trial. They typically sought an order granting a new trial, a sentence reduction, or discharge from custody. Such an order was itself subject to appeal. Because it typically took a long time, *habeas corpus* was associated more with long-term sentences, such as life sentences and death sentences, when appeals of these sentences became common after World War II. Indigents who would have the legal right to appointed counsel for the appeal (at least through state court appeals) have no such right in filing *habeas corpus* petitions; they must file the actions themselves or find paid or unpaid legal assistance.

Habeas corpus, its use defined in Section 2254 of Title 28 of the U.S. Code, was initially available only to challenge the basis or duration of imprisonment, but in time the courts allowed these petitions to challenge the nature as well as the fact of confinement. In *Coffin v. Reichard* (1944), the U.S. Sixth Circuit Court of Appeals ruled,

> A prisoner is entitled to the writ of *habeas corpus* when, though lawfully in custody, he is deprived of some right to which he is lawfully entitled even in his confinement, the deprivation of which serves to make his imprisonment more burdensome than the law allows or curtails his liberty to a greater degree than the law permits.

A state prisoner who files a *habeas corpus* petition is likely to be asking the federal courts to review his conviction, but he could be asking for a review of the conditions under which he is serving his prison term.

Over the past forty years, most of the litigation attacking prison conditions or treatment has arisen in the federal courts under the Federal Civil Rights Act (Section 1983 of Title 42 of the U.S. Code). Several reasons exist for prisoners' preference for pursuing civil rights litigation:

1. It was a comparatively simple form of action to use.
2. It potentially covered a multitude of prison conditions and procedures.
3. It offered a wide range of possible remedies (including monetary damages) for violations of prisoners' rights.
4. Many states did not have legal remedies available to challenge prison conditions.
5. In civil rights cases, state remedies did not have to be exhausted first before a federal claim could be made.
6. Prisoners found federal courts more objective and receptive to their claims, primarily because the judges were not part of the state political system that the prisoners blamed for their legal problems.[7]

THE EIGHTH AMENDMENT: CRUEL AND UNUSUAL PUNISHMENT

The **Eighth Amendment** to the **Bill of Rights** of the U.S. Constitution contains these provisions: "Excessive bail shall not be required, nor excessive fines imposed, nor cruel and unusual punishments imposed." For almost two centuries, the **cruel and unusual punishments** clause had no application to prisoners. The Bill of Rights, adopted to limit the power of the federal government and its officials, had no application to state prisoners—only federal prisoners—as originally applied. The Supreme Court looked at very few cases relating to the issue of cruel and unusual punishment prior to the 1970s. The phrase "cruel and unusual punishment" had originally appeared in the English Bill of Rights in 1689, apparently directed against punishments not authorized by law or beyond the jurisdiction of the sentencing court. In including it in the Bill of Rights, the draftsmen of the American Constitution were more concerned with torture and other physically excessive means of punishment.

In this era, the death penalty was an accepted punishment. In *Wilkerson v. Utah* (1879), the Supreme Court unanimously held that execution by shooting was not a prohibited form of execution. The Court said that "it is safe to affirm that the punishments of torture . . . and all others in the same line of unnecessary cruelty, are forbidden by that amendment to the Constitution." When the Court was asked to rule on New York's new electric chair in *In re Kemmler* (1890), it held the Eighth Amendment inapplicable to the states and added the following comment: "Punishments are cruel when they involve torture or a lingering death; but the punishment of death is not cruel within the meaning of that word as used in the Constitution. It implies there something inhuman and barbarous, something more than the mere extinguishment of life."

In 1910, the Court ruled in *Weems v. United States* that a sentence could be cruel and unusual when it was disproportionate to the crime committed—in this case, twelve to twenty years at hard labor in chains and perpetual loss of civil rights for the crime of accessory in falsifying public documents. However, in the well-known death penalty case of *Louisiana ex re. Francis v. Resweber* (1947), the Court ruled it permissible to "reexecute" Willie Francis after a malfunction short-circuited the first attempt to electrocute him: a second electrocution was not cruel and unusual punishment.

Smith and Dow have commented on the next important case in this chronology:

> The seminal case that shaped the meaning of the Eighth Amendment was *Trop v. Dulles* (1958), which concerned an unusual circumstance regarding an American soldier who was convicted of desertion during World War II. He received a dishonorable discharge and served a sentence in a military prison. Years later, he learned that he had also lost his citizenship under the requirements of the congressional statute governing wartime desertion. The Supreme Court examined the case and declared that the forfeiture of citizenship in these circumstances, which render a native-born American "stateless" and without rights and protections from any nation in the world, constituted cruel and unusual punishment in violation of the Eighth Amendment.
>
> The most important aspect of the decision was the test announced by Chief Justice Earl Warren for defining the Eighth Amendment—a test that continues to govern the Cruel and Unusual Punishments Clause more than 40 years later. According to Warren, "The words of the amendment are not precise . . . and their scope is not static. The amendment must draw its meaning from the evolving standards of decency that mark the progress of a maturing society." As indicated by this test, the Eighth Amendment has no fixed meaning. Instead, the meaning of "cruel and unusual punishments" will change as society changes and as judges assess whether specific "punishments" are consistent with evolving society values. In sum, individual judicial officers must make their own judgments about whether the Eighth Amendment has been violated.[8]

None of this yet meant anything to state prisoners, whose state constitutions, not the U.S. Constitution, defined their rights, but this would soon change abruptly. In the 1960s, the Supreme Court, through the more frequent application of a legal doctrine known as **incorporation,** began to apply the provisions of the Bill of Rights to the states, including local jurisdictions within the states. The mechanism for incorporation was the **Fourteenth Amendment** to the Constitution, adopted in 1868 after the Civil War. Section I provides, in part, "No State shall make or enforce any law which shall abridge the privileges or immunities of citizens of the United States; nor shall any State deprive any person of life, liberty, or property, without due process of law; nor deny to any person within its jurisdiction the equal protection of the law."

The **due process** and **equal protection** provisions of the Fourteenth Amendment made citizens subject to state laws—such as criminal defendants and convicted criminals—also subject to federal constitutional standards. The Bill of Rights applied as much to state cases as it did to federal cases. In landmark cases such as *Mapp v. Ohio* (1961), *Gideon v. Wainwright* (1963), *Miranda v. Arizona* (1966), *In re Gault* (1967), *Brady v. Maryland* (1968), and dozens of other cases in this decade and the early part of the next, the Court moved to set consistent national standards where only widely varying state standards had existed previously. Most of the early decisions dealt with criminal suspects pretrial and at trial, not in confinement after conviction. However, as the **Warren Court** undertook what is called the **due process revolution** at the national level, federal district judges began to accept lawsuits filed by state prisoners alleging unconstitutional prison conditions in state prisons.

The most important Eighth Amendment lawsuits complaining of bad living conditions were filed or adjudicated during the 1970s. Some of these were individual suits in which one prisoner claimed that he or she had been mistreated or made to suffer because of a prison's bad living environment. The most influential of these cases were **class-action lawsuits** filed by a small group of inmates but on behalf of a much larger group—such as all inmates in a treatment unit, all inmates in a jail or prison, or sometimes all inmates in all the jails of a particular county or the prisons of a particular state.

During the 1970s, virtually every state prison system and most urban jails would be hit by inmate lawsuits arguing that confinement in these institutions constituted "cruel and unusual punishment" under Eighth Amendment standards. The South was hardest hit. In state after state across the South, federal district judges heard Eighth Amendment and Fourteenth Amendment suits charging that prisons were overcrowded, dilapidated, violent, and failing to provide needed care, particularly in regard to medical care and mental health services.

Federal judges responding to inmate lawsuits would hold fact-finding hearings and conduct inquiries into the allegations made. The suits often became **totality of conditions** actions in which several different lawsuits with different complaints would be rolled into one megacase examining the whole prison or, in several states, the entire prison system. Then the federal judge would issue a court order for prison reform in the name of the lead case. In Arkansas, it was *Holt v. Sarver* (1970); in Alabama, it was *Newman v. Alabama* (1972); in Mississippi, it was *Gates v. Collier* (1972); in Louisiana, it was *Williams v. McKeithen* (1975); and in Texas, it was *Ruiz v. Estelle* (1980).

Holt v. Sarver was the first state-level totality-of-conditions Eighth Amendment case. The federal court found in *Holt* that the Arkansas prison system was in violation of the cruel and unusual punishments clause in several key aspects:

1. The prison was run largely by inmate trusty guards who breeded hatred and mistrust.

2. The open barracks within the prison invited widespread physical and sexual assaults.
3. The isolation cells were overcrowded, filthy, and unsanitary.
4. There was a total absence of any program of rehabilitation and training.[9]

The court commented,

> It is one thing for the State to send a man to the Penitentiary as a punishment for crime, it is another thing for the State to delegate the governance of him to other convicts, and to do nothing meaningful for his safety, well being, and possible rehabilitation. . . . However constitutionally tolerable the Arkansas system may have been in former years, it simply will not do today.[10]

When prison officials acknowledged their problems but argued they could make no improvements until the state legislature appropriated the funds to make improvements, the court was unsympathetic:

> Let there be no mistake in the matter; the obligation of prison officials to eliminate existing unconstitutionalities does not depend upon what the Legislature may do, or upon what the Governor may do, or indeed upon what prison officials may actually be able to accomplish. If Arkansas is going to operate a Penitentiary System, it is going to have to be a system that is countenanced by the Constitution of the United States.[11]

In Louisiana, four inmates filed a class-action lawsuit about conditions at the Angola penitentiary in 1971. After a federal magistrate investigated the allegations and found most of them to be substantially true, efforts were made to settle the case without judicial intervention. These efforts failed, and on June 10, 1975, Federal District Judge Gordon West issued a twenty-page "Judgment and Order." In signing the order, Judge West observed that conditions at Angola "not only shock the conscience" but also flagrantly violated basic constitutional requirements. Among the more important provisions of Judge West's order were these:

1. The prison was to hire 400 more correctional officers to bring the staff up to a minimum of 950.
2. Two guards were to be placed in each living unit twenty-four hours per day to maintain a safe living environment.
3. Overt and aggressive homosexuals were to be removed from the general population.
4. Violent inmates were to be separated from the general population.
5. Temporary housing must be used to deal with overcrowding.
6. Medical care must be dramatically improved.
7. Incoming inmates must get physical exams.
8. The psychiatric unit (also known as "PU" and called a "hellhole") must begin providing real therapy to mentally ill inmates.[12]

When Louisiana officials dragged their feet responding to the order for over a year and appealed to a higher court—losing the appeal—Judge West tightened the screws. He put a population limit on Angola of 2,640 inmates—its official capacity—though it then held 4,000 inmates in custody. This forced the system to make immediate changes and to begin storing state prisoners in parish jails, leading to the state's split system of today. Judge West and his successor, Judge Frank Polozola, kept the court order in *Williams v. McKeithen* in effect for twenty-one years, until April 1996, eventually expanding it to include all adult prisons, all parish jails, and all juvenile training schools in the state. Even after the court removed the general order in 1996, it retained provisions relating to prison medical care, which had still not been brought up to adequate standards, and to the juvenile institutions, which had been plagued by internal violence and disorder.

SECTION 1983: CIVIL RIGHTS LITIGATION

Although the Eighth Amendment and Fourteenth Amendment litigation had the more profound impact in accomplishing broad institutional reform during the 1970s and 1980s, the most common form of prisoners' rights litigation during this era (and continuing today) is through what is commonly called a **Section 1983 lawsuit.** Section 1983 of Title 42 of the U.S. Code provides,

> Every person who, under color of any statute, ordinance, regulation, custom or usage, of any State or Territory, subjects of causes to be subjected, any citizen of the United States of other person within the jurisdiction thereof to the deprivation of any rights, privileges or immunities security by the Constitution and laws, shall be liable to the party injured in an action at law, suit at equity, or other proper proceeding for redress.

This statute was enacted in 1871 during Reconstruction after the Civil War. For almost a century, it lay dormant in its application to local or state criminal justice officials until 1961, when it was first applied to police officers. Section 1983 actions proliferated by the early 1970s. From about 200 filings in 1966, the number of Section 1983 suits jumped up to 5,000 in 1972, and the numbers increased steadily for the next twenty-five years, roughly paralleling the increase in state prisoner population, to more than 40,000 in 1996. The premise of these actions is that a state or local government official acting **under color of state law** has deprived a prisoner of a constitutional right. These actions normally name a specific person or persons as defendants. Supreme Court decisions have established that while neither states nor state agencies (such as the department of corrections) can be sued as entities, municipalities and counties can be if the alleged violation in part of local government policy.

Hanson and Daly, in their review of the issues in Section 1983 prison lawsuits filed in 1992, provided this summary of the principal cause of action cited:

1. Physical security (prisoner attacked by other prisoners or by corrections officers)   21 percent
2. Medical treatment   17 percent
3. Due process (internal transfers or disciplinary action without following proper procedures)   13 percent
4. Challenges to conviction (prisoners mistakenly raising *habeas corpus* issues in a Section 1983 action)   12 percent

5.	Physical conditions in prison	9 percent
6.	Access to courts, lawyers, and communication with others	7 percent
7.	Living conditions (denied access to recreation or programs)	4 percent
8.	Religious expression	4 percent
9.	Assault by arresting officer	3 percent
10.	Other	11 percent[13]

Of the approximately 25,000 Section 1983 lawsuits filed in 1992, 74 percent were dismissed by the court based on the prisoner's complaint. Another 20 percent were dismissed after the individual and government unit being sued responded to the complaint. This left about 6 percent of the total filings, or 1,500 cases, still alive. Four percent were dismissed with the prisoner's agreement, sometimes because of a settlement. Two percent went to trial; prisoners won less than half the cases that went to trial. Thus, out of 25,000 lawsuits filed, prisoners won outright less than 1 percent and settled to their advantage another small percentage, totaling perhaps fewer than 1,000 out of 25,000 filed. Hanson and Daly divide outcomes into three categories: win nothing, win little, and win big. For prisoners, win nothing was by far the most common; win big was like winning the lottery, and even there the winnings were usually small, no more than a few thousand dollars.[14]

Hanson and Daly identified the principal reasons for dismissal of these suits:

1.	Prisoner failed to follow court rules in filing case	38 percent
2.	No evidence exists of constitutional rights violation	19 percent
3.	Issue is frivolous (no basis for claim in fact or law)	19 percent
4.	Issue presented is not covered by Section 1983 (mistakenly raises *habeas corpus* issues about the basis of the conviction)	7 percent
5.	Defendant is a judge or prosecutor and therefore is protected by law against lawsuits	4 percent
6.	Defendant does not work for the government	3 percent
7.	Other	9 percent[15]

Each of these cases would have been under review in the federal courts for an average of five to nine months prior to its dismissal, some with complex issues more than twice this long. In the decade of the 1990s, Section 1983 lawsuits made up more than 10 percent of all civil cases filed in the federal courts. In some districts with lots of prisoners, the suits were the most common filings in the district courts.

FEDERAL COURT INTERVENTION

In less than ten years, "hands off" had been transformed into a very definite "hands on," and so it went in many other states and hundreds of county and city jails across America during the 1970s and into the early 1980s. New York City's old jail, the Tombs, was shut down by federal court order on November 15, 1974, the only major institution actually closed as a result of judicial intervention, but hundreds of other state and local facilities were under court order, some for years at a time, during this era.

The intervention process typically followed steps similar to those described previously for Louisiana. The federal district court with jurisdiction over the institution would get a Section 1983 lawsuit or a *habeas corpus* petition filed by inmates proceeding pro se (without counsel) or with counsel, often pro bono (unpaid) or legal aid attorneys interested in prisoners' rights litigation. The court would appoint attorneys to represent the inmates' legal interests if it found merit to their initial claim. If the litigation could not be resolved through negotiation, over a period of months or years, the court would hold a formal hearing and announce its judgment. This ordinarily involved the imposition of a **court order** giving the court controlling authority over some aspect of the institution's operations and requiring that certain steps be taken to eliminate unconstitutional conditions. Sometimes the court granted an **injunction,** a legal order to stop an action or a practice that was ruled improper.

If the intervention was broad based and would go on for an extended period, the court would appoint an official usually termed a **court master** or **monitor** to oversee the institution's response to the order. The master, someone outside the system but experienced in corrections, did the legwork for the judge. Thus, while the correctional institution was working within its own governmental bureaucracy to effect change, it was also being monitored by a representative of the federal court to ensure that progress was being made. If population limits were set, for instance, and the master found that the institution had exceeded these limits, this would be reported to the court, and the judge would schedule a hearing to determine why this violation of the order occurred.

The court's authority ultimately resided in its **contempt power,** its ability to impose a jail term or a monetary fine on officials who violated its order. Because the orders came from a federal district court, where some judges might be considered too "liberal" or **activist,** meaning that they were siding with the prisoners against the administration, it was common for prison officials to appeal unfavorable rulings to the federal appeals courts and eventually to the Supreme Court. These legal battles were often protracted struggles that went on for decades. Improvements were being made, new prisons being built to relieve overcrowding, and prisoners getting better care than they had previously, but the details were hashed out in court—the federal court imposing its authority to umpire the adversarial relationship between the prisoners and prison administrators. The goal of the court order was to achieve a formal agreement, called a **consent decree,** in which both sides agreed (through their attorneys) on the actions to be taken to resolve the litigation. When the court determined that the institution had met the requirements of the court, as written down in the consent decree, the court order was terminated. The institution could operate on its own again without federal court supervision.

Some individual institutions worked their way through this process fairly quickly, while statewide systems confronting totality-of-conditions rulings often worked much more slowly, particularly if state officials contested the details of intervention. Prison systems were compared to a longtime alcoholic: you could cooperate, take your treatment immediately, and try to reform, or you could fight treatment, try it on your own, fail, try again, fail again, and eventually accept what you had rejected when it was first offered. The long-running Texas case of *Ruiz v. Estelle*, which brought sweeping reforms to the Texas prison system and created chaos when it broke down the old control model of Texas prisons in the process, began in the courts in 1972 and was not finally resolved until 1986.

Let us now take a closer look at several key areas of federal court intervention, most of these the subject of Section 1983 lawsuits but some initiated through habeas corpus petitions. The topics we will focus on include the following:

1. Access to courts
2. Discipline and due process
3. Medical care
4. Personal rights

PRISONERS' RIGHTS: ACCESS TO COURTS

In the "good old days" of the penitentiary, prison officials had complete control over the prisoner's contact with the outside world. If the warden did not want a letter or legal document complaining of prison conditions to get out, he simply destroyed it and locked the prisoner in "the hole" for daring to criticize the prison. All the prisoner's other rights thus depend on this first right of **access to courts**—to bring a complaint to the attention of authorities who will require prison officials to follow the law.

In one of the earliest prisoners' rights cases decided by the Supreme Court, *Ex parte Hull* (1941), the Court examined a Michigan prison regulation that required "all legal documents, briefs, petitions, motions, habeas corpus proceedings, and appeals . . . to be submitted to the institutional welfare office and . . . the legal investigator to the Parole Board." Parole board investigators forwarded the documents to the court if they believed they were properly written, but they sent them back to prisoners if they believed the documents did not comply with court regulations. In effect, state officials had the power to determine which communications from prisoners would actually be sent to the courthouse. The Supreme Court rejected the Michigan regulation, ruling that a prisoner's right to petition a federal court for a writ of *habeas corpus* could not be abridged or impaired.

Prisoners would argue later that the right of access was meaningless if they did not have legal assistance and access to legal resources in preparing writs and briefs and submitting materials to the courts. Two cases defined these rights to legal assistance and legal materials. The Supreme Court, in *Johnson v. Avery* (1969), was asked to consider the case of a Tennessee prison inmate who was transferred for acting as a **jailhouse lawyer,** assisting other inmates with legal matters. Since prisoners were not entitled to professional attorneys, the district court ruled, "for all practical purposes, if such prisoners cannot have the assistance of a 'jail-house lawyer,' their possibly valid constitutional claims will never be heard in any court." The Supreme Court ruled that the state could not enforce a regulation barring inmates from furnishing assistance to other prisoners.

A few years later, the issue of research materials was addressed in the North Carolina case of *Bounds v. Smith* (1977), often called the **law library** case. The Supreme Court held that "the fundamental constitutional right of access to the courts requires prison authorities to assist inmates in the preparation and filing of meaningful legal papers by providing prisoners with adequate law libraries or adequate legal assistance from persons trained in the law." Some states provided attorneys—either paid or pro bono—or law students to provide legal assistance; most relied on prison law libraries staffed by inmate paralegals (the more dignified term for jailhouse lawyer). A later ruling in this same case (*Smith v. Bounds* [1987]) defined an "adequate" prison library as consisting of the following:

1. Photocopy materials without charge
2. Inmates trained as paralegals
3. The availability of prison law libraries for all inmates

After the original *Bounds* decision, law professor Barry Nakell and others established North Carolina Prisoner Legal Services (NCPLS) as a nonprofit organization to provide legal assistance to prison and jail inmates. NCPLS has refined its operation several times since its founding in 1978, but it has continued to assist prisoners in basic rights cases and grievance resolution, including filing lawsuits when necessary. In 2003, as it celebrated its twenty-fifth anniversary, NCPLS had a staff of thirty-four, including fourteen lawyers and ten paralegals, to assist prisoners in both civil (including Section 1983) and postconviction (*habeas corpus*) legal matters. It operates through a contract with the North Carolina Department of Corrections. Many other states do not provide this level of assistance to inmates, providing inmate-staffed law libraries as the basic alternative.

The requirement of access to legal materials by all inmates has often been a problem for prisoners held in special housing units, such as segregation or mental health. It has also been an issue for inmates whose first language is not English. In a later case reviewing the intervention of an Arizona district court into these issues—*Lewis v. Casey* (1996)—the conservative Supreme Court of the 1990s overturned the detailed requirements the lower court had established for prison library operations to serve specific targeted populations. It said that without showing that these inmates were actually being harmed by inadequate legal resources, the court should defer to the judgment of prison authorities. In basketball terms, "no harm, no foul."

Justice Clarence Thomas, in a concurring opinion in *Lewis*, wrote,

> I agree that the Constitution affords prisoners what can be termed a right of access to the courts. That right, rooted in the Due Process Clause and the principle articulated in *Ex parte Hull*, is a right not to be arbitrarily prevented from lodging a claimed violation of a constitutional right in the federal court. The State, however, is not constitutionally required to finance or otherwise assist the prisoner's efforts, either through law libraries or other legal assistance. Whether to expend state resources to facilitate prisoner lawsuits is a question of policy and one that the Constitution leaves to the discretion of the States.[16]

This case is an important recent example of the deference doctrine (akin to hands off) that we will discuss later.

PRISONERS' RIGHTS: DISCIPLINE AND DUE PROCESS

As prison officials once had complete control over prisoners' contacts with the courts, so they once had complete authority in internal disciplinary and punishment matters. The key Supreme Court case to address procedures in imposing punishments for violating prison rules was *Wolff v. McDonnell* (1974). Prior to this decision, jails and prisons typically relied on informal internal procedures in dealing with inmates who violated the rules. Inmates might be locked down, transferred, given extra duty, have privileges taken away, or have good-time credits canceled by the order of prison officials—all of these done verbally without a formal hearing or creation of a record for the action.

It was only six years before *Wolff*, in *Jackson v. Bishop* (1968), that the U.S. Eighth Circuit Court of Appeals had finally struck down corporal punishment of prisoners in Arkansas. Three years before, the federal district court had allowed Arkansas to continue its old practice of beating prisoners with a leather strap, as had been done in numerous other states into at least the 1950s. The earlier decision in *Tally v. Stephens* (1965) provided that whipping could continue to be used so long as safeguards were followed to prevent abuse:

> It must not be excessive; it must be inflicted as dispassionately as possible and by responsible people; and it must be applied in reference to recognizable standards whereby a convict may know what conduct on his part will cause him to be whipped and how much punishment given conduct may produce.

Jackson said essentially, "This is not working, so it is time to quit." Justice Harry Blackmun, who wrote the *Jackson* opinion for the court of appeals before he was appointed to the Supreme Court, said that the use of the strap violated the Eighth Amendment (the cruel and unusual punishment doctrine). The ruling said no rule or regulation could prevent abuse. Sounding like the Enlightenment philosophers who had advocated the abolition of whipping two centuries before, the court wrote,

> Corporal punishment generates hate toward the keepers who punish and toward the system which permits it. It is degrading to the punisher and the punished alike. It frustrates correctional and rehabilitative goals. This record cries out with testimony to this effect from the expert penologists, from the inmates, and from their keepers. . . . In any event, the testimony of the two expert penologists clearly demonstrates that the use of the strap in this day is unusual and we encounter no difficulty in holding that its use is cruel.

In *Wolff v. McDonnell*, Nebraska prison inmates sued over the informality of prison misconduct proceedings that could result in the loss of good-time credits. The Supreme Court ruled that prisoners were protected by the Fourteenth Amendment's due process clause even though the prison environment is far different from the free-world environment, as Justice Byron White noted in the opinion:

> Prison disciplinary proceedings . . . take place in a close, tightly controlled environment peopled by those who have chosen to violate the criminal law and who have been lawfully incarcerated for doing so. Some are first offenders, but many

are recidivists who have repeatedly employed illegal and often very violent means to attain their ends. They may have very little regard for the safety of others or their property or for the rules designed to provide an orderly and reasonably safe prison life. . . . Guards and inmates co-exist in direct and intimate contact. Tension between them is unremitting. Frustration, resentment, and despair are commonplace. Relationships among the inmates are varied and complex and perhaps subject to the unwritten code that exhorts inmates not to inform on a fellow prisoner.

The Court then ruled that the prison must extend basic elements of due process to prisoners in these proceedings (specifically if they involve a possible **liberty interest,** such as loss of good time or punitive segregation). The required safeguards included the following:

1. Advance written notice of the charges must be given to the inmate no less than twenty-four hours prior to his or her appearance before the committee.
2. There must be a written statement by the factfinders as to the evidence relied on and reasons for the disciplinary action.
3. The inmate should be allowed to call witnesses and present documentary evidence in his or her defense if permitting him or her to do so will not jeopardize institutional safety or correctional goals.
4. Counsel substitute (either a fellow inmate or a staff member) will be permitted when the inmate is illiterate or when the complexity of the issues make it unlikely that the inmate will be able to collect and present the evidence for an adequate comprehension of the case.
5. The prison disciplinary board must be impartial.[17]

Some prisoners' rights advocates thought this decision did not go far enough. They wanted such additional safeguards as the right to confront and cross-examine witnesses and right to counsel, which would have turned these proceedings into "minitrials" similar to outside courtrooms. The Court was not willing to go this far, and, while it has never really gone further than this decision in defining rights in disciplinary cases, *Wolff* had a great impact on prison and jail operations. Imagine—say, as a parent—what the effect on discipline would be if, each time you wanted to punish a child for misconduct, you had to schedule a hearing, notify participants, and assemble a board to hear the case.

Just the mechanics of following the rules work to reduce arbitrariness and personal abuses—and likely reduce as well the number of such violations that might be written up and forwarded to the disciplinary board. The **DB Court** (for disciplinary board), meeting on a regular schedule, has become a standard part of the internal disciplinary system of all secure custodial and community residential facilities since *Wolff*.

PRISONERS' RIGHTS: MEDICAL CARE

As we discussed in chapter 8, access to medical care and the quality of care provided are important issues to prisoners who suffer from a broad range of health problems related primarily to poverty and substance abuse. Prison health care before the reform era was inconsistent and often "shockingly substandard," in the words of law professor Sheldon Krantz.[18] Several of the whole-prison or whole-system lawsuits of the 1970s included descriptions of deficient medical care. In *Newman v. State of Alabama* (1972), for instance, the federal district court had found the general quality of medical care within the Alabama prison system to be "barbarous" and "shocking to the conscience" and therefore in violation of the Eighth Amendment.[19]

Not until the Texas case of *Estelle v. Gamble* (1976) did the Supreme Court address medical care by itself as an Eighth Amendment issue. J. W. Gamble was a prisoner who was injured when a bale of cotton fell on him while he was unloading a truck. He was provided with medical treatment but maintained that he was still in too much pain to return to work. When he was subjected to disciplinary action based on refusal to work, he filed a Section 1983 lawsuit.

The Supreme Court reviewed the history of Gamble's medical treatment and determined that his case did not rise to the level of **deliberate indifference** to the serious medical needs of inmates: "the unnecessary and wanton infliction of pain." The Court went on to say that not all claims of inadequate medical treatment would be covered by the Eighth Amendment's cruel and unusual punishment provisions. An inadvertent failure to provide adequate medical care would not qualify, nor would an accident, simple negligence, or disagreement as to treatment options. The Court denied Gamble's claim, suggesting that if he had a claim at all, it was a medical malpractice claim that should be filed in state court as a tort suit for damages.

Gamble lost, but the Court established the deliberate indifference rule that became the foundation of later Section 1983 litigation of all types, not just medical care. Deliberate indifference, which is comparable to gross negligence or recklessness, focuses on the motives or thoughts of prison officials responsible for the injury, which in medical cases results from the bad care provided. Justice John Paul Stevens, who dissented in *Estelle v. Gamble*, objected to the decision's focus on the "subjective motivation" of prison officials, which meant that a prisoner had to show bad intentions or shameful neglect to fix responsibility. Justice Stevens argued that "whether the constitutional standard has been violated should turn on the character of the punishment rather than the motivation of the individual who inflicted it." (A similar example would be hate crimes, in which the penalty is increased because of the motivation rather than the harm done.)

Justice Stevens used the example of the Confederate Civil War prison at Andersonville, where thousands of Union troops died of disease and starvation as prisoners of war. The prison's commandant, Captain Henry Wirz, was the only southerner hanged by federal authority after the war ended. Wirz claimed he was not responsible for the conditions and had tried to fix them but lacked the resources. According to *Gamble*, Wirz's situation would be comparable to a doctor who completely misdiagnosed an inmate's case of cancer and refused to refer him to a specialist for treatment, saying, "Here, take two aspirin three times a day and come see me if you don't get better." If the inmate sued because his cancer became terminal, the doctor would respond, "I tried to do what I could. I just made a mistake," and the inmate would lose his Section 1983 lawsuit because no constitutional violation occurred.

Several years later, the Supreme Court reiterated this point in *Whitley v. Albers* (1986), a use-of-force case:

After incarceration, only the unnecessary and wanton infliction of pain . . . constitutes cruel and unusual punishment forbidden by the Eighth Amendment. To be cruel and unusual punishment, conduct that does not purport to be punishment at all must involve more than ordinary lack of due care for the prisoner's interests or safety. . . . It is obduracy and wantonness, not inadvertence or error in good faith, that characterize the conduct prohibited by the Cruel and Unusual Punishments Clause, whether that conduct occurs in connection with establishing conditions of confinement, supplying medical needs, or restoring official control over a tumultuous cellblock.

Estelle v. Gamble is said to have established a general right to "adequate" medical care in prisons, meaning that the medical needs of prisoners cannot be completely ignored or botched. Prisoners do have a right to treatment, even if it is not constitutionally protected at the same level as the right of private citizens. But what of the opposite right, the **right to refuse treatment?** Terry Castleberry, a death row inmate at the Louisiana State Penitentiary, suffered from several ailments, including progressive kidney failure. He could undergo dialysis, if he wished, at state expense in the prison hospital, but he would continue to be housed on death row. Castleberry expressed his wish to refuse treatment, which would result in his death. Should he be allowed to decline treatment that would keep him alive?

Treatment of prisoners against their will often ventures into the subject area of mental incompetence. If a patient—free or in prison—is mentally competent, he or she has the right to refuse treatment. This is a right to privacy decision called the **informed consent** doctrine. People have the right to decide what will and will not be done to their bodies. That includes the right to decide whether to take medication or permit surgery.[20]

Like many rights, this right is not absolute. The state may have an interest in requiring treatment for someone who is suicidal, for instance, or who has a contagious disease. In prison, this issue of compelling treatment comes up most often with prisoners who are mentally incompetent either because of mental illness or serious medical conditions such as dementia or Alzheimer's. The leading Supreme Court case in this area is *Washington v. Harper* (1990). Harper was an inmate in a Washington prison who was suffering from a manic-depressive disorder. He took his medication voluntarily and then stopped. His physician wanted to continue the medication and took the issue to a special committee described in a prison policy. Harper was found to be a danger to others, and the committee allowed his involuntary treatment with antipsychotic drugs. When he was transferred out to another prison, he briefly stopped taking the drugs, then started again—involuntarily—on his return. He sued under Section 1983.

This case considered two questions:

1. Can a prisoner be treated with antipsychotic drugs against his will?
2. Can the review by an internal committee take the place of a judicial hearing?

To both questions, the Court answered yes. The medication was necessary, given Harper's history of violent behavior when he was off his medication, to reduce the danger he posed to other persons. The committee review satisfied the liberty interest of the inmate, in the Court's language, "perhaps better . . . by allowing the decision to medicate to be made by the medical professionals rather than a judge." The Court was satisfied that the State of Washington had provided due process to the inmate.[21]

This issue has come up again recently in connection with inmates on death row. The 1986 decision in *Ford v. Wainwright* had ruled that to be executed, inmates must be mentally competent—at least to understand their crime and the punishment. Can inmates be medicated against their will to remain functional enough to be processed along toward their execution date? Does the state have the authority to **medicate to execute?** Some states do not allow this, but thus far no Supreme Court ruling prohibits the practice. Some borderline types, such as Scott Panetti—a schizophrenic who was hospitalized fourteen times prior to his conviction for the murder of his wife's parents in 1992—have faced execution while on medication on death row; Panetti's scheduled 2004 execution was delayed indefinitely while the courts consider whether he is mentally competent to die. As for Terry Castleberry, his decision to opt out of waiting for execution in Louisiana was allowed. He died in the prison hospital of kidney failure in April 2002.

PRISONERS' RIGHTS: PERSONAL RIGHTS

A Buddhist prisoner is placed in solitary confinement on a bread-and-water diet for sharing religious materials with other inmates. Journalists and inmates are prohibited from conducting face-to-face interviews. Prisoners object to the institution's seizure of magazines on a "forbidden" list, including *High Times* (about drug use) and *Guns and Ammo* (about firearms). Jail inmates are denied contact visits with their families. Prisoners want to form a labor union to promote better working conditions for inmates.

These are real cases related to the **personal rights** of prisoners, rights commonly placed under the **First Amendment** of the Bill of Rights. It reads, "Congress shall make no law respecting an establishment of religion, or prohibiting the free exercise thereof; or abridging the freedom of speech, or of the press; or the right of the people peaceably to assemble, and to petition the Government for redress of grievances."

Religion is very important to many prisoners, the center of their prison life. Some of the most important early prisoners' rights cases in the 1960s dealt with the right of inmates to practice an established religion, in these cases the **Black Muslim** faith in Illinois and California prisons. One of the leading cases—the first Section 1983 case decided in a prisoner's favor—was *Cooper v. Pate* (1964), a lawsuit filed by Thomas X. Cooper, a former Catholic turned Black Muslim in Illinois's Stateville Prison. While the prisons saw the Muslims as an adversarial political group, the courts ruled that prisoners had to be allowed to practice their faith and not be punished for doing so.

Cruz v. Beto (1972) dealt with a Buddhist prisoner in the Texas prison system. Cruz was not allowed to use the prison chapel, nor to correspond with his religious advisor in the Buddhist sect. He was also placed in solitary on a restricted diet for allowing other inmates to read his religious materials. When he filed suit under Section 1983, the Supreme Court agreed that the Texas Department of Corrections had discriminated against Cruz by denying him reasonable opportunity to practice his Buddhist faith, comparable to opportunities offered to other inmates of conventional religious beliefs.[22]

This case has been used since by numerous individuals and groups as a "foot in the door" to new religions and religious practices in prisons. Later cases have generally been less tolerant of new, "prison-founded" religions and religious practices that conflict with "legitimate penological interests," a term defined in the case of *Turner v. Safley* (1987), discussed later in this chapter. A New Jersey case, *O'Lone v. Estate of Shabazz* (1987), involved Muslim inmates who said they were denied participation in religious services because of work assignments. The court sided with prison officials, basically saying that security was more important than the prisoners' religious rights.

The free exercise of religion is an important issue in American society. Congress passed a new law, the **Religious Freedom Restoration Act of 1993,** which was intended to force the government to provide compelling justifications for insisting that any law or policy was more important than people's religious practices.[23] This law was not about prisoners' religious rights, but Congress did allow prisoners to be included within its protective provisions. This law was declared unconstitutional by the Supreme Court in 1997 on the basis that Congress lacked the authority to enact such legislation.[24] Several states have adopted or considered the adoption of similar laws since. State corrections departments generally oppose including prisoners among the groups granted religious freedom in legislation, arguing that this tends to promote frivolous lawsuits by oddballs and splinter groups who want to practice new religions they have made up. Let's say that the inmates who wanted to form a chapter of the new prison religion, the Church of the New Song, were not allowed to do so by prison authorities and that a journalist from a major religious magazine wanted to interview them in prison. Do journalists have the right to interview particular inmates in prison? This was the issue in *Pell v. Procunier* (1974) and *Houchins v. KQED, Inc.* (1978). These two California cases established two important standards:

1. A state prison regulation prohibiting media interviews with specific inmates does not violate the constitutional rights of the media or the inmates as long as alternative means of communication are available.
2. The media have no right of access to inmates and prisons beyond that given to the general public.[25]

In *Pell*, prison officials argued that interviews make inmates "famous" (or notorious) and give them influence over their fellow inmates that can be a threat to security. As long as alternative forms of communication such as correspondence and visitation remained available, prisoners had no rights to direct media access except as might be permitted by prison officials. A popular 2003 film, *The Life of David Gale*, about a former professor awaiting execution in Texas, was premised on a series of last-minute interviews of inmate Gale by outside journalists—lengthy, individual, face-to-face paid interviews that the prison system would very likely not have allowed in the first place (but that's showbiz).

In *Houchins*, a television station that wanted to tour the county jail was prohibited from doing so by the sheriff except within limits specified in a departmental policy. The TV station wanted more access than the sheriff was willing to give. The Supreme Court sided with the sheriff. It cited other alternatives that, though not as convenient as going on location to shoot live footage, were also available to get the story. The secure operation of the jail took precedence over the media's right to gather information to present to the public.

If prisoners do not have the right to meet directly with journalists, what general rights do they have to communicate with or visit with other persons, including family and friends? One of the defining qualities of imprisonment is separation from the outside world. Prisoners are not simply convicted criminals. They are also husbands and wives, fathers and mothers, sons and daughters, sisters and brothers, and friends to people in the outside world. As a result, they are eager to maintain contact with outsiders.[26]

Prisoners who want to maintain family and friendship ties face severe limits on the frequency, duration, and type of contact allowed in visiting. Many prisons (and even more jails) still enforce rules on noncontact visits, and in many institutions the display of any kind of personal affection is a write-up. Sex is absolutely forbidden except in the six states that allow conjugal visits for at least a portion of the inmate population, usually trusties or medium-security inmates who are married and have good conduct records. As Christopher Smith has pointed out,

> Communication with the outside world . . . can cause problems. Visitors and mail are primary methods for bringing illegal items, especially drugs, into a prison. In addition, prisoners may use letters and telephones to plan escapes, harass people outside the prison, and even carry out significant criminal activities, such as fraud schemes. Thus, prison officials have good reason to monitor and regulate some aspects of inmates' communications.[27]

Until a generation or so ago, prison authorities routinely censored prison mail—outgoing and incoming. Mail censors marked out objectionable parts or simply threw offensive correspondence away. Today, mail can be opened and inspected but is generally not censored. Publications must be on an approved list (or not be on the disapproved list, such as porn magazines). Books and periodicals must be sent directly from the publisher or a bookstore and not from a private person.

The two leading cases regarding correspondence and publications received by inmates are *Turner v. Safley* (1987) and *Thornburgh v. Abbott* (1989). *Turner* dealt with a Missouri prison regulation that allowed prisoners within its system to communicate with other family members in prison and other inmates about legal matters but prohibited general correspondence between inmates in different prisons. The Court asked whether the prison regulation was related to **legitimate penological interests** of the prison. Several factors were to be considered in determining the reasonableness of a regulation:

1. Whether there is a valid, rational connection between the regulation and the legitimate government interest put forward to justify it
2. Whether there are alternative means of exercising the right that remain open to prisoners
3. The impact that accommodation of the asserted right will have on guards and other inmates and on the allocation of prison resources generally
4. The existence of ready alternatives to the regulation[28]

Because mail could be used to plan escapes, arrange violent acts, or expand gang activity, the regulation was valid. Prisoners could communicate with lots of other people but not other prisoners.

The focus in *Thornburgh* was a Federal Bureau of Prisons regulation on the books or periodicals inmates could receive. Publications determined to be "detrimental to the security, good order, or discipline of the institution" or that might "facilitate criminal activity" were targeted, but amplification of those standards was provided in the following language:

> Publications which may be rejected by the Warden include but are not limited to publications which meet one of the following criteria:
>
> 1. It depicts or describes procedures for the construction or use of weapons, ammunition, bombs, or incendiary devices.
>
> 2. It depicts, encourages, or describes methods of escape from correctional facilities, or contains blueprints, drawings, or similar descriptions of Bureau of Prisons institutions.
>
> 3. It depicts or describes procedures for the brewing of alcoholic beverages, or the manufacture of drugs.
>
> 4. It is written in code.
>
> 5. It depicts, describes, or encourages activities which may lead to the use of physical violence or group disruption.
>
> 6. It encourages or instructs in the commission of criminal activities.
>
> 7. It is sexually explicit material which by its nature or content poses a threat to the security, good order, or discipline of the institution, or facilitates criminal activity.[29]

The Court, applying the four-part test developed in *Turner*, determined that this regulation was constitutional. It provides general guidance to state and local officials, who often use it to restrict inmate access to certain publications, including magazines such as *Playboy* or *Penthouse*, that correctional officers might find objectionable—if, for instance a prisoner papered his cell wall with nude photos and then made suggestive remarks to women officers. The institution could react by punishing the individual inmate for a disciplinary violation, or it could establish a blanket rule that would prevent all inmates from gaining access to such materials in the first place. Some prison administrators find it easier to think in general terms—"Ban all magazines with sexual content"—than individual cases—"Punish inmates who abuse their privileges." Although court decisions generally allow jails and prisons broad authority to censor incoming publications, some institutions do so to a much greater degree than others. Practices within states vary considerably.

With regard to visitation, the courts have long allowed prison officials to define visitation as a privilege rather than a right. This gives officials the authority to restrict visitation to certain places and times; to monitor visitation; to prohibit physical contact, even between married couples or parents and minor children; to bar visitors with criminal records or histories of violating visitation rules, as in smuggling contraband; to require strip searches of inmates after visits (even in some instances where the visits were through glass where no contact was possible); and to move inmates far away from home, making it nearly impossible for would-be visitors to get to them. Under the restrictions sometimes imposed, visiting can become more of an obstacle (a "pain in the ass," one inmate described it in explaining why he would not allow people to visit him) than a delight.

The two leading visitation cases are *Block v. Rutherford* (1979), which held that Los Angeles jail inmates could be denied contact visits with spouses, children, relatives, and friends on security grounds, and *Bell v. Wolfish* (1979), which defined jail inmate search standards before and after receiving a visit (and is also viewed as the source of the deference doctrine discussed later). Inmates have also sued for conjugal visits for reproductive purposes (denied) and for homosexual as well as heterosexual conjugal visits (also denied). It is instructive to note that the *Block* decision also dealt with shakedown searches of cells in the absence of their inmate occupants; courts have consistently ruled that the Fourth Amendment's search and seizure provisions do not apply to prisoners in custody (and are limited in their application to probationers and parolees as well). Institutional security again prevails over individual rights.

The last example given at the opening of this section involved the formation of a prisoners' labor union. Though the very idea of such an organization would probably cause Captain Elam Lynds to rise up from his grave and begin cracking his whip, it is in fact based on *Jones v. North Carolina Prisoners' Labor Union Inc.* (1977). About 2,000 North Carolina prisoners had joined this union by 1975. Its principal purposes were to represent prisoners' interests in work-related issues and assist in resolving inmates' grievances. Prison regulations allowed membership in the union but made it impossible for union members to meet or conduct business. It was obviously more political than recreational in its purpose. The Court agreed with prison officials that the union would be detrimental to "prison order and security" in that it would encourage "adversary relations" within the prison system. The Court also rejected the inmates' arguments under the equal protection clause of the Fourteenth Amendment—basically that the union had as much right to exist as other organizations that the prison did allow to function for other purposes.

PRISONERS' RIGHTS: WOMEN IN PRISON

Equal protection is not used nearly as often in prisoners' rights cases as are cruel and unusual punishment and due process. When it has been used successfully, it has been applied to race (as in segregation of prison housing, job assignments, or programs) and indigency (as when poor inmates would get lower-quality services, such as medical care or mental health treatment, than other inmates or sometimes free people would get from other state-supported service providers).

Equal protection has sometimes been an issue in regard to a third class of prisoners: women. Men prisoners have been much more numerous than women prisoners in the past. This remains true today, when 93 percent of state and federal prisoners and 88 percent of jail inmates are male. This has led women prisoners and their advocates to make two general claims about the management of women in prison:

1. Women generally have fewer programs and treatment options open to them than men do.
2. The programs and options that do exist are not gender specific; they are designed for men rather than for women.

The basic argument is that the focus of prison management is so much on men that women are incidental, not deserving of equal attention. This deals with the concept of **gender equity.**

Several courts have found **differential treatment** of male and female prisoners in the recent past. The landmark case here is *Glover v. Johnson* (1979 and 1987). In this Michigan case, a U.S. district court found that female inmates were offered educational and vocational programs that were markedly poorer than those offered to male prisoners.[30] The court found that women were educationally disadvantaged by having fewer courses made available to them and that these were offered on a more limited schedule so that it was more difficult to complete them while in custody. While men had access to twenty different vocational programs, women had access to five, and "the male versions of those programs . . . were often more extensive and more useful to the inmates." The court said, "The women inmates have a right to a range and quality of programming substantially equivalent to that offered the men, and the programs currently offered do not meet this standard. . . . Institutional size is frankly not a justification but an excuse for the kind of treatment afforded women prisoners."

An earlier case from New Mexico, *Barefield v. Leach* (1974), had used this language in its decision: "What the equal protection clause requires in a prison setting is parity of treatment . . . between male and female inmates with respect to the conditions of their confinement and access to rehabilitative programs." If **disparate treatment** had marked the imprisonment of women to this time, **parity of treatment** became the subsequent goal.

Many of the scholars who write about the imprisonment of women are not certain that the **parity model** is a good idea in practice. The women's prison system for a long time no doubt did treat women not only as being different from men but also as being inferior or less important, likely because of both numbers and status. The parity model that evolved from 1970s litigation treated women prisoners *as if they were men* (to use Barbara Bloom and Meda Chesney-Lind's emphasis), applying a male standard to women at sentencing and in prison.[31] From differential treatment, which often disadvantages women prisoners through neglect, the prison system has moved to **vengeful equity,** in which women are treated exactly as men are.

The official line would go something like this. You want to come to prison pregnant? Okay, you can go outside to have the baby, but you come back to prison the next day without the baby, and someone else gets to raise your infant. You want to go through a short-term program? We have the boot camp, in which your head will be shaved and you will be run ragged and yelled at, just as if you were in the military (or an abusive relationship, which a lot of the women were). Oh, and since we have men on chain gangs, to show there's no discrimination, we have to put women there, too. So guess what you will be doing in your striped suit tomorrow?

The argument about policy goals in managing the imprisonment of women today is often said to come down to a contrast between the **equal treatment** model and the **special needs** model: "Equality is defined as rights equal to those of males, and differential needs are defined as needs different from those of males."[32]

A few cases have supported the special needs model, particularly with regard to medical care and visitation with their children, but in general the equity model is more prevalent. The huge increase in the numbers of women in jail and prison over the past thirty years—from about 15,000 to approaching 200,000—has also provided an impetus to treat female prisoners as a clientele more deserving of equitable attention.

PRISONERS' RIGHTS: THE EFFECT ON JAIL AND PRISON ADMINISTRATION

Before the due process revolution, incarceration was a closed, internal world. When federal courts, in the Warren Court era, began to look into this world, they saw conditions—in individual cases and often with entire institutions— that did not meet standards of how civilized prisons ought to operate. Using the Constitution as the framework to define their intervention, the courts opened up jails and prisons to outside review. Prisoners, accustomed to being ignored by guards and officials, found they had access to officials who would at least listen to their complaints and occasionally order corrective action.

As James B. Jacobs wrote about the origins of federal court intervention in prisons,

> The Supreme Court's first modern prisoners' rights case, *Cooper v. Pate* (1964), was an appeal from a lower court ruling upholding the discretion of prison officials to refuse Muslim prisoners their Korans and all opportunities for worship. The Supreme Court's decision was narrow: the Muslim prisoners had standing to challenge religious discrimination under Section 193 of the resurrected Civil Rights Act of 1871. But for the prisoners' movement it was not the breadth of the decision that mattered but the Supreme Court's determination that prisoners have constitutional rights; prison officials were not free to do with prisoners as they pleased. And the federal courts were permitted, indeed obligated, to provide a forum where prisoners could challenge and confront prison officials. Whatever the outcome of such confrontations, they spelled the end of the authoritarian regime in American penology.[33]

Forty years later, how do we assess the impact of the prisoners' rights movement on corrections? Jacobs, writing in 1980, when this movement was at (or already past) its peak, offered several hypotheses about the effects of legal changes on prisons:

1. The prisoners' rights movement has contributed to the bureaucratization of the prison. Prisons are governed much more by policies, procedures, and regulations than they were previously.

2. The prisoners' rights movement has produced a new generation of administrators. The new generation of wardens is much better able to deal with external influences, including the courts, and to operate the prison as a bureaucracy.

3. The prisoners' rights movement expanded the procedural protections available to prisoners. Prisoners not only have greater access to state and federal courts but also benefit from grievance procedures to provide dispute resolution within the prison.

4. The prisoners' rights movement has heightened public awareness of prison conditions. Media attention to prison litigation made the public and public officials more responsive to correctional needs.

5. The prisoners' rights movement has politicized prisoners and heightened their expectations. Prisoners developed an *attitude*, expecting the courts to intervene on their behalf.

6. The prisoners' rights movement has demoralized prison staff. As prisoners gained legal standing, correctional officers and administrators likely felt they

were losing authority and status. This would be particularly true for institutions under court order—in effect supervised by the courts for past failures.

7. The prisoners' rights movement had made it more difficult to maintain control over prisoners. Past use of informal, physical punishments was replaced by a rulebook approach. Prisoners are also better able to sue for damages when physical force is used.

8. The prisoners' rights movement has contributed to a professional movement within corrections to establish national standards. One way of avoiding criticism is to make your operation better. Accreditation as promoted by the American Correctional Association is a prime example of this approach.[34]

Court intervention and its corollary—the need to avoid intervention—did all of these and more. It resulted in huge budget increases for correctional institutions, particularly in those states where corrections had been cheapest. Malcolm Feeley and Roger Hanson have discussed the costs of correctional intervention in the South, in such states as Arkansas, where the correctional budget increased sixfold after *Holt v. Sarver* and was credited with breaking loose money for prison improvements.[35] In Louisiana, the operating budget for the state penitentiary at Angola increased from less than $10 million in 1975—the year of *Williams v. McKeithen*—to nearly $100 million in 2000.

Most of the initial budget increases in prisons and jails went to hire new staff, especially in those institutions that had relied heavily on inmate trusties as workers and guards. Free people were more costly than unpaid prisoners. Capital expenditures were also necessary to renovate old facilities and build new housing to alleviate overcrowding, a frequent circumstance in the totality-of-conditions cases. Rehabilitation programs, medical care, and mental health treatment were costly new additions in many states. Then, as prison and jail populations really exploded after 1980, correctional systems were obliged to build new institutions to house the new inmates instead of just cramming then into existing facilities as they would have done in the past.

Corrections became a higher priority because it was the subject of expensive and often embarrassing litigation. No state official wants to have his prison system described as "brutal and inhumane"; private citizens would hardly take pride in having a local jail described as "one of the worst in the country." You can almost hear people in decision-making positions saying, "Well, we have to do something about corrections, even if we would rather not." In Louisiana, this recognition did not come about until more than a year after Judge West's court order to reform Angola. While the state appealed the order, the legislature appropriated money that could have been used to start reforms to instead begin construction of a new upper deck on the Louisiana State University football stadium. It was then that the judge closed the prison to new admissions, forcing corrections officials to place prisoners elsewhere and the governor to call a special session of the legislature to consider prison reforms. Real change started at this point.

Court intervention also had a major impact in defining correctional standards, as Jacobs mentioned previously. Each state's prison system is different from the others, and local jails vary even more widely. How do we determine what standards these institutions should meet in their operation? Litigation forced comparison. What does this state have? What does this jail do that this one does not? The process of gaining compliance with court orders forced officials to meet with the court masters and monitors appointed by the court to oversee implementation of the orders. The objective was to realize a consent decree that would result in the termination of the court order. But this would be done only when correctional officials, outside experts, and the court were satisfied with the new standards that had been set.

Jails and prisons were obliged to find new ways to deal with prisoner complaints so that every minor issue did not end up the subject of a federal court lawsuit. Discipline and complaint procedures were formalized. Prisoners were given rule books explaining their rights in custody, classifying disciplinary infractions as major and minor, and providing channels for complaints. Institutions established **grievance procedures** for inmates to follow. Several prison systems established the position of **ombudsman,** based on a long-established position in Scandinavian countries, to receive, investigate, and act on complaints—sometimes from staff as well as inmates. This puts the institution in the posture of being self-critical, which is a major step in actually trying to learn from your mistakes rather than just cover them over.

Most correctional administrators who were active in the period of the most intensive court intervention, from about 1970 through the mid-1980s, would agree that this was a difficult time for them. They were often caught between opposing forces—prisoners seeking their "rights," politicians who for the most part could not have cared less, and federal courts trying to define constitutional conditions. How do they view the effects of intervention long after the fact? Although they may find fault with the details of some of the consent decrees, most agree that the prisoners' rights movement speeded up the process of change and brought positive results, making correctional management if not easier, then more professional.

Ross Maggio, nicknamed "Boss Ross" by the inmates in his two stints as warden of Angola prison in the 1970s and 1980s, said in a February 2000 interview that the prison was "underfunded, overcrowded, dirty, run-down, and dangerous for inmates and employees alike" when he arrived to work there in the late 1960s. Sexual predators preyed on weaker inmates, most prisoners carried knives for protection, killings were commonplace, and inmate cliques and guards ran Angola.[36]

Twenty-five years later, "the basic system in our state adult prisons is a good one because of the 1975 court order," Maggio said. "The court order gave us the resources for physical plant construction and hiring new staff. At the same time, we developed a philosophy that didn't exist before: that the administration was going to run the prison and not share power with inmate cliques and strong-armers."[37] Noting trends to reduce the authority of federal judges to intervene in prison matters, he said that criticisms of federal court intervention overlooked two basic facts: the urgent need for reforms in the 1970s and the positive effects of those reforms that had lasted through the end of the century. Many correctional administrators at the local and state levels would agree with his opinions.

PROBATION AND PAROLE

When we think of "prisoners' rights" as applicable to persons confined in jails and prisons, we should remember that the term also applies to persons on probation and parole. A sentence to probation, in lieu of imprisonment, or release on parole, after serving a portion of a sentence in confinement, both require supervision, both impose conditions on the convicted person, and both involve a reduced-rights status in comparison to the rights enjoyed by law-abiding citizens. Although probationers and parolees are free in the community, their freedom is conditional, and the people who supervise them have considerable authority over them.

In *Griffin v. Wisconsin* (1987), the Supreme Court ruled that the search of a probationer's home without a warrant was legal. Usually, the search of a home would require probable cause and a warrant, but in the case of Griffin, who was on probation, the Court allowed the warrantless search of his home by a probation officer, acting on information from police that Griffin had a gun, to stand. One of the conditions of probation is that the probationer not be in possession of a firearm. Griffin had a gun, he was caught with it, and he picked up a new sentence of two years in prison as a result. In another search and seizure case involving an offender on parole, *Pennsylvania Board of Probation and Parole v. Scott* (1998), the Supreme Court ruled that the **exclusionary rule,** which bars improperly obtained evidence in criminal proceedings, does not apply to parole revocation hearings. Parole officers used weapons found in a warrantless search of Keith Scott's home as part of the basis for revoking his parole. The weapons were not used to bring new criminal charges. Scott argued the search was illegal and that the weapons could not be used to revoke his parole. The Court rejected his argument: "We therefore hold that the federal exclusionary rule does not bar the introduction at parole revocation hearings of evidence seized in violation of parolees' Fourth Amendment rights."

The parolee's basic rights in revocation hearings were established in the landmark case of *Morrissey v. Brewer* (1972). The Supreme Court ruled that parole revocation represents a "grievous loss" of liberty to the parolee to which the parolee is entitled to due process. The Court discussed a two-stage parole revocation process: a preliminary hearing to establish the probable cause of the violation and the revocation hearing itself. In these hearings, the parolee is entitled to the following due process rights:

1. Written notice of the claimed violations of parole
2. Disclosure to the parolee of the evidence against him
3. Opportunity to be heard in person and to present witnesses and documentary evidence
4. The right to confront and cross-examine adverse witnesses (unless the hearing officer specifically finds good cause for not allowing confrontation)
5. A "neutral and detached" hearing body, such as a traditional parole board, members of which need not be judicial officers or lawyers
6. A written statement by the fact finders as to the evidence relied on and reasons for revoking parole[38]

The following year, the Supreme Court applied these same six due process rights to probationers in *Gagnon v. Scarpelli* (1973). Probationers were entitled to a hearing, the Court ruled, but not to have an attorney represent them.

Both *Morrissey* and *Scarpelli* clarified what had previously been highly variable revocation and often informal proceedings leading to the revocation of parole and probation. But the courts have not done much to go beyond these basic rulings since. Parolees have tried, in particular, to get more rights in regard to parole release hearings, but the Supreme Court has consistently held that parole is a privilege, not a right; that parole is an option up to the state to define in practice (including abolishing parole altogether); and that parole release hearings do not have to meet due process requirements—the difference being that release relates to a liberty that one desires, not a liberty one has.[39]

THE POLITICS OF "MODIFIED HANDS OFF": AEDPA AND PRLA

Although both prisoners and jail and prison officials would agree that prisoners' rights litigation resulted in positive changes in corrections in the last decades of the twentieth century, you would find sharp differences of opinion about the need for that litigation to continue at high levels into the indefinite future. Many jail and prison inmates would prefer to see *more* litigation for several reasons:

1. It is their way of challenging the system that put them behind bars. Because most prisoners hold state or local authorities responsible for their confinement, they turn to the federal system for relief—in effect using one legal system to get back at the other.
2. Legal actions, large and small, give them something to do while serving time. Some judge, somewhere, some day, may find merit in a *habeas corpus* petition or a Section 1983 suit. Maybe you will get some money, a little relief, or at least a couple of trips to court out of it to break the monotony. Jay D. Jamieson has called this the "blind pig" theory of litigation, based on the premise that even a blind pig finds an acorn sometime.
3. They may see no other effective way to resolve valid problems. Grievance procedures, ombudsmen, and other remedies are all part of the corrections system. Prisoners want someone outside the system looking at their complaints.

Correctional officials would like to see *less* litigation for contrasting reasons:

1. Improvements have been made to bring prison and jail conditions up to reasonable levels. Prisons are nice enough places to live. Further litigation over basic conditions is pointless.
2. **Frivolous lawsuits.** defined as those lacking in factual merit or of such a trivial nature they are not worth the court's time—by jailhouse lawyers or inmate "writ writers" take up a lot of time on the part of corrections officials and officers of the court, including the attorneys who must defend such cases and the judges and magistrates who must review legal briefs and hear the cases. Prisoners may have a lot of dead time to fill with doing legal research and writing out their lawsuits, but the public officials have other work they could be doing if they were not tied up dealing with litigation.
3. A high percentage of inmate-filed litigation (an estimated 95 percent plus) are simply badly prepared gripes, grievances, and crank letters that waste the court's time. Much of it is filed by chronic complainers who have no other purpose in mind than messing with the system.

The public and political perceptions that inmates have won enough rights, that much litigation is frivolous, and that federal judges have been too intrusive into state affairs have led to important legislative changes in recent years. In 1996, the U.S. Congress passed two major pieces of legislation, the **Anti-Terrorism and Effective Death Penalty Act** (AEDPA) and the **Prison Litigation Reform Act** (PLRA), both aimed at prisoners' rights litigation in the federal courts.

The AEDPA had several features intended to limit the number of habeas corpus petitions filed in U.S. district courts:

1. Placing a time limit of one year from the date their conviction becomes final (after the appeal is over) to file a *habeas corpus* petition in federal court
2. Restrictions on second or successive *habeas corpus* petitions (already ruled on by the Supreme Court in the death penalty case of *McCleskey v. Zant* [1991])
3. Requirements that state remedies be exhausted before the federal petition is filed
4. A presumption of correctness for state court findings that limits the intervention authority of federal judges

By imposing time limits and other restrictions, the political intent of the AEDPA was to speed up the processing of *habeas corpus* petitions, specifically reducing the time spent processing death penalty cases. Some had predicted that the average length of time spent between sentencing and execution could be reduced from ten to twelve years, in ordinary cases, to perhaps five or six years. This has not yet happened.

The PLRA was much more significant to prisoners' rights issues in general because of the much higher volume of Section 1983 lawsuits, almost three times as many (42,000 to 15,000) as *habeas corpus* petitions in 1995. Christopher Smith has written about the PLRA:

> The Prison Litigation Reform Act represents a political reaction to judges' involvement in prison administration. Stated another way, prison litigation reform has produced a political backlash that has imposed limitations on both judges and prisoners. Some of the statute's most significant provisions include the following:
>
> 1. The establishment of specific requirements for findings that judges must make before relief can be granted or consent decrees can be imposed.
>
> 2. A reduction in judges' authority to order the release of prisoners in response to overcrowding.
>
> 3. Short time limits on the effective period for judges' remedial orders.
>
> 4. A new requirement that prisoners must exhaust administrative remedies before filing civil rights lawsuits.
>
> 5. Increased influence by corrections officials over the appointment of special masters to supervise the implementation of remedies.
>
> 6. The definition and limitation of special masters' powers.
>
> 7. The imposition of the special master's costs upon the court rather than on the state whose officials were sued in the case.
>
> 8. Stricter procedures for filing fees by requiring partial payment of fees by prisoners with very limited resources instead of the waiver of fees, as usually occurred in the past.[40]

The PLRA was intended to limit prisoners' opportunities to file civil rights lawsuits and to restrict the large-scale intervention of federal judges who might be so inclined. The number of civil rights suits filed by prisoners has fallen off sharply since the law took effect, so it appears to be having the desired result.

PRISON LITIGATION TODAY

In a 1995 article titled "The Supreme Court and Prisoners' Rights," Jack Call divided the history of prisoners' rights into three periods:

1. The hands-off era (before 1964)
2. The rights era (1964–1978)
3. The deference era (1979 to present)[41]

In the hands-off era, prisoners had minimal legal standing. The courts took the abstention approach, saying that it was up to the executive and legislative branches of government to provide for the care of prisoners. The federal courts viewed prisoners as the domain of the states and rarely intervened in these cases.

The **rights era** reflected a dramatic reversal of the hands-off approach. The Warren Court's due process revolution applied the Fourteenth Amendment and the Civil Rights Statute (Section 1983) to create national standards applicable to all prisoners. Call suggests that several forces were at work during the 1960s and 1970s:

> First, prisoners, perhaps reflecting society as a whole at the time, became more militant and aggressive in asserting their rights. Second, the legal profession developed a cadre of "public interest lawyers" who were willing to take on these cases, either *pro bono* or with financial support from government and private foundation grants. Third, the judiciary as a whole seemed to become more responsive to the legal arguments advanced by politically disadvantaged groups. Fourth, judges were often presented with cases that involved such horrible conditions of confinement that they cried out for some sort of remedial order.[42]

In little more than a decade—most of the important Supreme Court decisions were made in the 1970s, after the intervention precedent was established in the 1960s—prisoners became citizens of America with constitutional rights guaranteed by the federal courts. The prisoners might have thought that this trend would continue in their favor until the rights of prisoners and correctional administrators achieved some kind of balance. But the time of expanding rights had quickly run its course.

The official origin of the **deference era** is traced to *Bell v. Wolfish* (1979), a lawsuit filed over conditions in the new federal Metropolitan Correctional Center in New York City. Inmates submitted a laundry list of complaints, including double bunking in one-man cells, overcrowding, improper searches, inadequate staffing, and lack of recreational and rehabilitative activities. Justice William Rehnquist wrote the majority opinion rejecting the inmates' legal claims:

> There was a time not too long ago when the federal judiciary took a completely "hands-off" approach to the problem of prison administration. In recent years,

however, these courts largely have discarded this "hands-off" attitude and have waded into this complex arena. The deplorable conditions and Draconian restriction of some of our Nation's prisons are too well known to require recounting here, and the federal courts rightly have condemned these sordid aspects of our prison systems. But many of these same courts have, in the name of the Constitution, become increasing enmeshed in the minutiae of prison operations. Judges, after all, are human. They, no less than others in our society, have a natural tendency to believe that their individual solutions to often intractable problems are better or more workable than those of the persons who are actually charged with and trained in the running of the particular institution under examination. But under the Constitution, the first question to be answered is not whose plan is best, but in what branch of the Government is lodged the authority to initially devise the plan. This does not mean that constitutional rights are not to be scrupulously observed. It does mean, however, that the inquiry of federal courts into prison management must be limited to the issue of whether a particular system violates any prohibition of the Constitution or, in the case of a federal prison, a statute. The wide range of "judgment calls" that meet constitutional and statutory requirements are confided to officials outside of the Judicial Branch of Government.

Or in other words; "back off." Rehnquist's call for **judicial deference** to corrections and legislative officials was made in 1979. Twenty-five years later, Chief Justice Rehnquist presides over a Supreme Court that has grown more conservative in the exercise of federal authority in state matters, including jail and prison operations. Long before Congress enacted the AEDPA and the PLRA to restrict prisoners' access to the federal courts, Supreme Court decisions had made it clear that prisoners' rights went only so far—that in a federal system, the states retain primary authority for the confinement of prisoners. The core of cases defining judicial deference would include the following:

Gregg v. Georgia (1976). State death penalty statutes that contain sufficient safeguards against arbitrary and capricious imposition are constitutional.

Rhodes v. Chapman (1981). Double celling of prisoners does not, in itself, constitute cruel and unusual punishment.

Hudson v. Palmer (1984). A prison cell may be searched without a warrant or probable cause because a prison cell is not protected by the Fourth Amendment.

Turner v. Safley (1987). A prison regulation that impinges on inmates' constitutional rights is valid if it is reasonably related to legitimate penological interests.

Wilson v. Seiter (1991). "Deliberate indifference" is required for liability in conditions of confinement cases. In conditions of confinement cases under Section 1983, "deliberate indifference" means a "culpable state of mind" on the part of prison officials.

Farmer v. Brennan (1994). A prison official is not liable under the Eighth Amendment for injury inflicted on an inmate by other inmates "unless the official knows of and disregards an excessive risk of harm to an inmate." It is not enough for liability that "the risk was so obvious that a reasonable person should have noticed it."

Lewis v. Casey (1996). The constitutional right of court access is violated only if a prisoner's attempt to pursue a legal claim is hindered by prison officials.

Inadequacies in state's delivery of legal services to inmates is insufficient as a basis for such claim.[43]

If *Bell v. Wolfish* announced the message in 1979, *Turner v. Safley* provided the philosophical doctrine in 1987. Its creation of the "legitimate penological interests" rule allows judges to defer to corrections officials provided that officials can explain the reasons for their actions and policies. When prison policies and prisoner rights are in conflict, *Turner* applies the **reasonable relationship** test. All prison authorities have to do is prove that a prison regulation is reasonably related to a legitimate penological interest in order for that regulation to be valid even if a constitutional right is infringed.[44] It is conceivable (and in fact has happened) that two states could have policies completely contradictory to each other and that both policies could be allowed to stand as legitimate when officials provide a reasonable explanation for them. Serving as the basis for a new conservative perspective on confinement, *Turner* limits constitutional rights and expands state power.[45]

Does this mean that prisoners have given up or that we are about to reenter the hands-off era? Neither, actually. Prisoners continue to file federal *habeas corpus* petitions and Section 1983 lawsuits as well as other legal actions in both state and federal courts. While the number of *habeas corpus* petitions had remained fairly constant, in the range of about 2,000 to 2,500 new filings per month through 2000, the numbers of Section 1983 filings had declined to about the same range, 2,000 to 2,500 new filings per month, three years after the PLRA took effect. Recent research suggests that the filing of *habeas corpus* petitions continues to roughly parallel the numbers of state prisoners, while Section 1983 filings have dropped by almost half.[46]

A *Corrections Compendium* survey completed in June 2003 indicated that the great majority of the states reported sharp declines (averaging 69 percent) in federal lawsuits between 1996 and 2003; in about half the reporting states, the numbers of state court lawsuits had increased over the same period. The forty-two states in the survey estimated approximately 20,000 federal lawsuits pending in 2002. Eleven of these states reported paying no damages to prisoners in lawsuits concluded in 2002. California lost the only suit—for bad medical care—in which an inmate received more than $1 million. Texas, which used to routinely have more than a thousand lawsuits pending at any given time, reported about 400 in 2002. It paid damages in a total of fifteen suits:

Six for use of force, averaging $8,350

Five for failure to protect inmates, averaging $6,464

Three for personal injury, averaging $108,226

One for cruel and unusual punishment, settled for $2[47]

This survey also indicated that as the number of lawsuits has declined, the number of inmate grievances has increased sharply. The thirty-six states that maintain grievance statistics reported 769,000 grievances filed in 2002, or about one per inmate. Texas alone reported 212,000 grievances in 2002, indicating that prisoners, although less litigious, still find aspects of imprisonment worthy of formal complaint.[48]

The PLRA dealt not only with inmates, remember, but also with the intervention authority of federal judges. The intent was to free jails and prisons from federal court supervision. This has apparently happened as well, as the number of states with at least one prison under federal court order had declined from thirty-six in 1987 to fewer than half that number in 2002. The survey noted that twenty-one state systems had successfully sought termination of previous court orders or consent decrees affecting their prisons between 1996 and 2002, while new orders or decrees were issued in eight states. The issues covered in the new legal orders include overcrowding, medical and mental health care, grooming standards for religious purposes, equitable relief in earned good-time credits, visitation rules, inmate classification in high-security facilities, reading materials that may be considered threatening to security, and the use of canines to search visitors. In responding to a question about the reasons for the decline in litigation, the state systems listed the number one reason as the requirement that inmates exhaust all available administrative remedies before filing lawsuits; other reasons given were speedier access to trial calendars, requirements that inmates pay filing fees, and the reduction in the percentage of fees awarded to attorneys representing inmates in litigation.[49]

We should note that the outcome of grievance procedures is critically important to litigation long term. If the grievance procedures work and the inmates are satisfied, the numbers of lawsuits will stay down. If the inmates are not satisfied with the outcomes, once these administrative remedies are completed, then the number of lawsuits will almost surely increase again.

For now, it is more difficult for prisoners to get their cases into federal courts and keep them there. Prisons and jails have more discretion in managing prisoners, and many state corrections departments have established mechanisms—grievance procedures, mediators, and ombudsmen—for resolving complaints about prison conditions short of litigation. Although corrections officials have become accustomed to fighting out prisoners' rights issues in court, they recognize that it is cheaper and easier to resolve complaints internally than to take them into the courtroom.

Prisoners' rights is not a completely dead issue, and no one (except perhaps an extremely conservative Supreme Court justice or two) is suggesting that we return to the hands-off era, but no one outside prison really seems highly interested in expanding inmates' rights as a legal priority for now. We have reached a kind of status quo in this regard.

Some prisoners either have not noticed or do not care. They remain committed to challenging the corrections system through the courts. Some have turned more often to state courts, thinking that state judges may be more sympathetic (more "liberal") than federal judges in the current political environment. Some await political changes at the national level that will result in a different perspective among the federal judges making decisions in prisoners' rights cases (though these political swings can take a very long time and no one really anticipates the activist Warren Court being re-created anytime soon). Some search for new themes and new wrinkles on old themes—anything to keep litigation alive.

Prisoners are captives of their own adversarial mentality. They do not see that their own excesses from the prisoners' rights era, which led them to file not only important suits but also too many trivial suits as **recreational litigation,** when combined with the more conservative turn of the federal courts, have undermined support for any further extension of prisoners' rights. Even the litigation experts who have supported reform have suggested that prisoners need to be more "judicious" in attacking the legal system. Otherwise, they run the risk of further alienating the public, the political officials, and, most important, the judges whose support is essential if they wish to get a fair hearing in court.

COLLATERAL CONSEQUENCES OF A CRIMINAL CONVICTION

One of the traditions left over from civil death is the felon's loss of civil rights, even after discharge from prison or supervision and carrying over beyond the end of his sentence. Diminished civil standing continues even when the criminal punishment is completed. These civil rights, such as voting, holding public office, marital and parental rights, serving on a jury, and possessing firearms, are often lost to the convicted felon until he goes through the formal procedure to get them restored. The **ex-offender,** often labeled an **ex-con** if he or she has been imprisoned, must also comply with administrative and legal restrictions, such as registration or notification of authorities, and employment licensing; he must also deal with the social stigma of being a felon.

These are the **collateral consequences** of a felony conviction. The criminal does his time and comes to the end of his term, as Robert M. A. Johnson, president of the National District Attorneys Association, wrote recently, only to discover that this is not the end:

> Today's offenders learn that they have only begun to suffer the consequences of their convictions after they have satisfied their sentences. State legislators and members of Congress, often motivated by public response to highly publicized cases, have opened the dam on a stream of laws that impose subsequent consequences on those convicted of particular crimes. These collateral consequences are in addition to the sentencing consequences enforced in the courtroom, and unlike the judicial sentence, they do not consider the circumstances of an individual offender or offense and often they are lifetime consequences. The consequences vary from state to state, but they generally relate to voting, occupational licensing, vehicle licensing, firearms restrictions, offender registration, civil forfeitures, and welfare benefits. Federal collateral consequences are much the same as those imposed by state law with the addition of deportation.[50]

Jeremy Travis, former director of the National Institute of Justice, called these consequences **invisible punishments** in that they pose legal barriers harmful to the economic, political, and social well-being of their communities, black communities in particular. National policies, many of them coming out of Congress, significantly affect the life prospects of the 600,000 prisoners of all races released back to the community each year as well as social and economic conditions in the low-income neighborhoods to which most criminals return.[51]

The civil rights lost vary greatly from one state to another. Some states are very restrictive, others much less so. In Mississippi, persons convicted of most felonies (though not drug crimes) lose the right to vote or serve on a jury. All felons post-1992 are disqualified from holding public office. Felons are either barred or subject to discretionary review by licensing authorities for a long list of professional and occupational licenses, including those for architect, nurse, bail agent, insurance agent, physician, social worker, attorney, and schoolteacher.

Persons with drug- or sex-related convicts are barred from working or volunteering with any counseling program in which they would provide services directly to children. Sex offenders are required to register (as indeed they are in every state now). The rights to hold public office and vote are restored by the governor's pardon, as is the right to possess firearms. The court in which the felon was convicted can also grant a "certificate of rehabilitation" restoring firearms privileges if it finds that the criminal has been rehabilitated.[52] (Thus, apparently the Mississippi courts have known all along what others find so difficult to determine—when the criminal has been rehabilitated.)

In Vermont, felons are permitted to vote by absentee ballot even in prison. A felon who has actually served prison time cannot serve on a jury. A felony conviction can also be grounds for denial of some business or professional licenses. Vermont law does not prohibit felons from possessing firearms, though persons on probation may be ordered by the court not to possess firearms. Persons who engage in sexual abuse of children, whether convicted or not, have to register as sex offenders.[53]

Since the specific provisions cited were taken from *Civil Disabilities of Convicted Felons: A State-by-State Survey*, last updated by the Office of the Pardon Attorney in the U.S. Justice Department in October 1996, it is quite possible that changes have occurred recently with regard to the rights of felons in Mississippi, Vermont, and the other forty-eight states. However, we should not assume that the direction of change in general is toward the restoration of lost rights, which some foresaw as a trend in the 1960s and 1970s. When we began to "get tough on crime" in the 1980s and 1990s, however, we also got tough on criminals. Many states reversed directions and imposed collateral consequences on convicted felons (and some misdemeanants) once again. Attention tends to be focused on whatever "crime du jour" happens to hold the political spotlight at the moment—drugs, sex crimes, child abuse, domestic violence, and, most recently, terrorism. All these have been singled out for particular attention at the federal level and in specific states, along with the ordinary murders, rapes, robberies, burglaries, and thefts that make up the bulk of felony crimes.

The list of **civil disabilities** is a long one. Most of us would not quarrel too loudly with the restrictions on firearms possession by convicted felons, the single right that is most likely to be taken away and least likely to be given back. Keeping guns from felons is not such a bad public policy. But voting is almost as widely prohibited. Forty-eight states prohibit voting during imprisonment, thirty-three during parole, and twenty-nine during probation. Seven states permanently bar felons from voting (unless pardoned by the governor or meeting other specific authorizations), while seven others have crime-specific bars or waiting periods. Marc Mauer pointed out that nearly 5 million Americans have currently or permanently lost their voting rights as a result of a felony conviction. This includes 13 percent of black men. The state of Florida, the swing state in the 2000 presidential election, had an estimated 600,000 ex-felons who were unable to vote in that election.[54] If even one-quarter had voted, would this have made a difference?

Other disabilities are less well known, unless you happen to be a felon that runs into the barrier. When Congress passed the welfare reform package in 1996, one of the laws adopted was a lifetime ban on the receipt of welfare and food stamp benefits for anyone convicted of a felony drug offense; states can opt out, but twenty states enforce it in full. Federal laws allow public housing agencies to ban anyone who had engaged in "any drug-related" activity; registered sex offenders are ineligible for housing also. Students with drug convictions face ineligibility periods when they are disqualified from receiving student loans and federal grants for technical and higher education. It is interesting to consider that an armed robber or an arsonist could get governmental assistance, but a single mother convicted of a drug crime could not.

Realistically, many ex-felons probably could not care less about some of the common civil rights they have lost—holding public office, serving on juries, or even voting. But housing, job training, temporary assistance (particularly if they have children), and employment—these are critical to avoiding returning to criminal activities. What they must have, first and foremost, is a job. Ex-felons face employment restrictions, including occupational disability statutes that bar them from licenses in certain trades and professions. When they go in to apply for many jobs, the standard line on the employment application throws them into a quandary: "Have you ever been convicted of a felony?" In some states, the application may ask the broader question about arrests, not just convictions. If ex-offenders answer yes truthfully, their employer may turn them down as criminals (although the official reason would be that they were not right for the job). If they say no, they run the risk of being fired later for falsifying the employment application. Which option would you choose?

The consequences to ex-felons are also consequences to their dependents. More than 10 million American children have a parent who has been in prison. *Every Door Closed: Barriers Facing Parents with Criminal Records*, the 2002 joint report of the Center for Law and Social Policy and Community Legal Services of Philadelphia, explores in detail the impact of criminal records on families. The report looks at six specific aspects of life on which criminal records impose ineligibility or other sanctions:

1. Employment
2. Welfare benefits
3. Subsidized housing
4. Loss of child custody
5. Student loans
6. Immigration

The report's executive summary suggests that these barriers, singly and in combination, tear families apart, create unemployment and homelessness, and guarantee failure, thereby harming parents and children, families, and communities.[55] These barriers (to stable employment needed to earn a living most of all) are intended to reduce crime and enhance community security, yet their effect is just the opposite: they make it more difficult for ex-offenders to take care of their children and avoid criminal activity. In addition, what will happen to the children of the parents to whom "every door is closed"?

CRIMINAL REGISTRATION

The offender's criminal record does not go away by itself at the expiration of the sentence; generally, the offender must pursue legal action at his own initiative to clear his record. The most sweeping—and least available—method of wiping out a record is through what is called **annulment.** The National Council on Crime and Delinquency, in its Model Act for Annulment of Conviction of Crime, states that the effect of an annulment is to restore all lost civil rights and to cancel the record of conviction and disposition. The responsibility for annulment would lie with the court that convicted the offender. The judge would issue the annulment order to assist in rehabilitation when it was consistent with the public welfare.

Little support exists for the practice of annulment at present; the trend seems to be in the other direction, toward maintaining better records on convicted criminals and using the records to impose greater control over ex-offenders. Harry Allen and Clifford Simonsen have described the old local courts' practice of maintaining "vest-pocket" records of criminal offenses, particularly minor offenses, meaning that the records were maintained locally for the information of the local courts but not sent forward into the central repository at the state level.[56] With the computer networks of today, it has become much more difficult to keep records out of the system.

Centralized data banks are often used as sources of information in those states that require **registration of criminals.** Registration of certain classes of criminals, particularly sex offenders, is becoming more common in the United States today. In Europe, where citizens were often required to carry identity papers, former prisoners were once given a **yellow card**—like Jean Valjean in *Les Miserables*—showing that they had been in custody previously. When asked for their identification, they had to show their yellow card to the police, which probably did not do a lot for their credibility as law-abiding citizens. They carried the yellow card for life unless they were pardoned for the crime.[57] The cards were a replacement for branding, which was practiced in early modern Europe as both a form of punishment and criminal identification. Nothing like carrying your criminal history as a permanent mark on your skin.

Although we do not use yellow cards in the United States today, we are marking sex offenders for life by requiring them to register or face criminal penalties for failing to do so. Sex offender registries have existed since California started one in 1947, but they really took off nationally in the 1990s. First, the forcible abduction of Jacob Wetterling, an eleven-year-old Minnesota boy in 1989, prompted Congress to pass the Jacob Wetterling Crimes Against Children and Sexually Violent Offender Registration Act (the Jacob Wetterling Act) in 1994. Criminals who commit sex crimes against children or any violent sex offense against adults must register for a period of ten years from the date of their release from custody or supervision. All fifty states now have sex offender registration laws.[58]

The Jacob Wetterling Act gave states the option of releasing information about registered sex offenders to the public but did not require it. This changed in 1996 when Congress amended the act to require states to disclose information about sex offenders for public safety purposes. This legislation was known as **Megan's Law,** after seven-year-old Megan Kanka, who had been abducted and murdered by a convicted sex offender in New Jersey. States were required to notify citizens of sex offenders in their communities through a variety of methods:

1. Internet postings, including photos (used in thirty-four states by 2003)
2. Media releases or announcements
3. Flyers distributed by offenders or public officials through the mail

4. Door-to-door flyers
5. Public meetings[59]

Virtually all states have adopted some form of **community notification laws** based on some combination of these methods.

The Pam Lychner Sexual Offender Tracking and Identification Act of 1996 amended the Jacob Wetterling Act by establishing a **national sex offender database** maintained by the FBI. This national tracking system gives law enforcement authorities access to sex offender registration data from all participating states.[60] It contained information on about 400,000 registered sex offenders in 2003.

Several objections to the broad scope of sex offender registration have been made:

1. It is permanent, lasting a lifetime, no matter how long it has been since the person last committed a sex crime.
2. Although the intent of the statutes is to protect children and others from sexual predators, all sex offenders who commit listed crimes are required to register. This would include many nonviolent offenders, family offenders, and adults who have had sex with minors.
3. Registration is not based on risk. It feeds a kind of "witch hunt" mentality about sex offenders that is not supported by research. Most sex offenses, especially against children, do not involve strangers, and recidivism rates for sex offenders are no higher (and, in recent detailed Justice Department statistics, are much lower) than for other categories of criminals.
4. Registration further stigmatizes criminals as an additional civil disability added to the other collateral consequences. Convicted sex offenders end up the "lowest of the low" among the criminal caste in American society.

Among the public, political officials, and the legal system, no one seems to find much merit in these objections at present. In March 2003, the Supreme Court announced two major decisions upholding sex offender registries. Offenders in Connecticut and Alaska had claimed that registration violated due process (posting without a hearing to determine dangerousness) and represented an "extra" punishment beyond the criminal sentence. The Supreme Court rejected both arguments. It said registration was based on past acts, not future threats. It also said registration is not a punishment but a regulatory effort to account for the location of sex offenders to ensure public safety, not to humiliate the offender.[61] These decisions clear the way for even more rigorous requirements to register offenders, including tracking down and prosecuting as fugitives the approximately 100,000 offenders who cannot be located in the FBI's database.

CIVIL COMMITMENT

For some sex offenders, the end of the criminal sentence holds an even greater peril than registration—**civil commitment** for treatment as a **sexually violent predator** (SVP). Howard Zonana described the history of civil commitment in a 1997 article:

U.S. society has struggled with the question of what to do with sex offenders. Between 1930 and 1960, a number of states passed "sexual psychopath laws" that offered indefinite hospitalization and treatment in lieu of incarceration for offenders who committed repetitive sexual crimes. When treatment was not sufficiently effective, and when retribution became a more primary goal than rehabilitation, these statutes were repealed or fell into disuse. Sex offenders were then given very long sentences with the opportunity for earlier release if they were deemed safe by parole boards. This era of so-called "indeterminate sentencing" was replaced in the 1980s by the present era of "determinate sentencing." The mandatory sentence now is based on the average time offenders used to spend in prison for a given offense under the old indeterminate sentencing system.

One consequence of this policy change in criminal justice has been that offenders had to be released at the end of relatively brief fixed sentence, and a number of them inevitably repeated some particularly heinous crimes. The legislature of the state of Washington reacted to this by passing the first of the "sexual predator" statutes in 1990. Over the next three years, several states passed similar legislation or revived their old sexual psychopath statutes. These new statutes permitted state officials, under civil law, to commit offenders who were considered dangerous if, at the end of their sentence, they met the criteria of a "sexual predator." In order to do so, offenders had to have a "mental abnormality" that would lead to the commission of further crimes. The definition of "mental abnormality" that is sufficient to meet the legal standard included many disorders that had not been used as a basis for civil commitment for many years. This abnormality can be defined so broadly as to include antisocial personality traits, such as lack of empathy for others or absence of conscience, that could make the offenders likely to repeat their past crimes. If these criteria are met, the person could be confined indefinitely as a "patient" in a psychiatric hospital until it is "safe" to permit that person's return to the community.[62]

Although the practice of civil commitment of the mentally ill had gone out of fashion in America in the 1960s and 1970s, in its focus on SVPs in the 1990s it was welcomed back with enthusiasm. Several states, including Kansas, passed laws modeled on Washington's. Kansas's Sexual Predator Act empowered the state's attorney general to bring civil commitment actions against individuals who are within ninety days of release from criminal confinement and who are deemed, through a review process, to be at high risk to reoffend. Through a civil commitment process, these individuals can be committed to a sexual predator treatment program (SPTP) for treatment until it is determined by treatment staff and the court that they no longer represent a high risk to reoffend. The law cast a broad net, and most sexual behaviors that were illegal could serve as criteria for commitment.[63]

Leroy Hendricks was the first Kansas resident committed to SPTP. When he appealed his commitment, the Kansas Supreme Court ruled the law unconstitutional and threw out his commitment. The attorney general appealed to the U.S. Supreme Court, which in a landmark 1997 decision, *Kansas v. Hendricks,* upheld the law by a five-to-four vote. The majority opinion, written by Justice Clarence Thomas, indicated that constitutional protections apply primarily to criminal, not civil, law. The Court said the Kansas law was not about retribution or deterrence, reasoning that "the confinement's duration is instead linked to the state purposes of the commitment, namely to hold the person until his mental abnormality no longer causes him to be a threat to others." Justice Anthony Kennedy, in his concurring opinion, underlined the importance of treatment and the ability of people to move through the program as central to the position of the court. This ruling seemed to make clear that SVP programs could legitimately hold people in restraint of their freedom only if the programs were willing and able to offer treatment aimed at reducing sex offenders' risk for reoffense and so afford them an opportunity to return to the community.[64]

In a 2002 split decision, the Florida Supreme Court upheld that state's Ryce Act (named after Jimmy Ryce, a nine-year-old boy who was raped and murdered). In the Florida case, *Westerheide v. State of Florida*, the court said the Ryce Act did not violate due process because the state carries the burden, during the civil commitment hearing, of proving by clear and convincing evidence that the person's mental condition requires confinement. In addition, it noted, defendants receive assistance of counsel, trial by jury, appeal, and yearly mental evaluation to determine whether they still require treatment.[65]

Alexander Cockburn, looking at California's SVP law in practice, called the view of sexually violent predators preying on minors of the same sex a "quadruple axel of evil," meaning that such persons are put in a special category apart from other offenders. "There's no quarreling between prosecutor and judge, jury and governor, Supreme Court and shrinks. Lock 'em up and throw away the key."[66]

When the California sex offenders identified as SVPs approach parole, a jury hearing is held to commit them to Atascadero state hospital, the SVP treatment facility. They go to Atascadero for two years, get a hearing to determine suitability for release, and go back for another two years if disapproved.

Marita Mayer, a public defender who represents such men in their hearings, says, "Many of them refuse treatment. They refuse to sign a piece of paper saying they have a mental disease"[67]—which, of course, creates a catch-22 condition: if you will not admit you are sick, then you must be sick, and you cannot be released until you agree to the treatment to cure you of your sickness.

Attorney Mayer concludes,

It's using psychiatry, like religion, to put people away. Why not hire an astrologer or a goat-entrails reader to predict what the person might do? Why not the same for robbers as rapists? What's happening is double jeopardy. People don't care about rapists, but the Constitution is about protections. How do I feel about these guys? When I talk to my clients I don't presume to think what they'll do in the future. I believe in redemption. I don't look at them as sexually violent predators, I see them as sad sacks. They have to register; they could be hounded from county to county; even for a tiny crime they'll be put away. Their lives are in ruin. I pity them.[68]

Criminal defense attorneys are not the only ones who feel this way. Medical professionals have expressed several important concerns:

1. The decision broadly redefines sexual criminal behavior as a mental illness for the purpose of allowing continued preventive detention—an unacceptable **medicalization of deviance.**
2. The legislature's main purpose is preventive detention and not treatment.
3. The criminal conviction assumes voluntary behavior, but the mental disorder assumes that the offender cannot control his behavior, warranting commitment and long-term treatment.
4. If 10 percent of sex offenders are identified as sexual predators, mental health treatment costs—averaging $60,000 to $130,000 per "patient" in maximum-security mental health facilities—will divert funds from other severely mentally ill patients.

5. This is a matter to be addressed by criminal sentencing and not the use or misuse of psychiatry.[69]

RESTORING RIGHTS

The traditional and most available way for an offender to get lost civil rights restored is through the **executive clemency** process under the authority of the governor or president. What the offender needs is a **pardon.** In some states, certain classes of offenders whose terms have expired may be entitled to so-called automatic pardons, where no discretionary board action is needed. In other states, offenders must petition the state pardon board and appear in person to ask for a pardon—either full or conditional—to get those rights restored. The governor remains in charge of clemency, though in some states the pardon board has the authority to make decisions without his approval being necessary. Pardons may be either full, with the restoration of all rights, or conditional, with only certain rights, often excluding firearms.

Even if a pardon is granted to the ex-offender, restoring the lost civil rights, under most state laws the offender still has a criminal record. To get rid of the record, the ex-offender must get an **expungement** order signed by the court in which the offender was sentenced. This order would result in the destruction of the criminal history record related to the instant case. Both manual and computer files at all levels—local, state, and federal—should be purged of all information related to the defendant's involvement in the case. A similar process, called **erasure of record,** is used for juvenile court records, which by law are supposed to be sealed and not mixed with or carried over to the offender's adult criminal records. If the ex-offender follows both tracks—pardon and expungement—legally available in his state, he can get his lost rights back and his record wiped clean. The only limitations may be that he must wait some period of time past the expiration of his sentence to apply for either action, that each disposition on his record must be attacked separately, and that repeat offenders may not be eligible to apply. In truth, many ex-offenders, who are not known for their attention to bureaucratic detail, view these processes as so much mumbo jumbo. They never bother to apply. Ex-offenders are no longer civilly dead, but it still is not easy to make a fresh start.

The public image of the felon released from prison has been shaped not only by legal tradition but also by the media, in particular the crime movies of an earlier era. We think of the tough-talking, amoral ex-con, dedicated to a life of crime, pursuing the company of others living like himself in the criminal underworld, and anxious to resume the criminal activities interrupted by a prison term. In the real world, it is not so simple. Many offenders released from prison want to "go straight" and avoid further run-ins with the law. Half of them may end up back in prison, but this statistic also means that half don't. Ex-offenders have families and friends; they need a place to live, a job, and productive ways to spend their time. It is not easy to leave prison, particularly if you have been away several years, and jump right back into mainstream society—not as an "ex-con."

KEY TERMS

civil death

outlaw

nonperson

Ruffin v. Commonwealth

penal servitude

slave of the state

hands-off doctrine

appeals

torts

criminal charges

writ of mandamus

administrative appeals

habeas corpus petitions

civil rights lawsuits

Eighth Amendment

Bill of Rights

cruel and unusual
punishments

incorporation

Fourteenth Amendment

due process

equal protection

Warren Court

due process revolution

class-action lawsuits

totality of conditions

Holt v. Sarver

Section 1983 lawsuit

under color of state law

court order

injunction

court master

monitor

contempt power

activist

consent decree

access to courts

jailhouse lawyer

law library

Wolff v. McDonnell

liberty interest

DB Court

Estelle v. Gamble

deliberate indifference

right to refuse treatment

informed consent

medicate to execute

personal rights

First Amendment

Black Muslim

Cooper v. Pate

Religious Freedom
    Restoration Act of 1993

legitimate penological
    interests

gender equity

differential treatment

disparate treatment

parity of treatment

parity model

vengeful equity

equal treatment

special needs

grievance procedures

ombudsman

exclusionary rule

Morrissey v. Brewer

frivolous lawsuits

Anti-Terrorism and
    Effective Death
    Penalty Act

Prison Litigation Reform
    Act

rights era

deference era

Bell v. Wolfish

judicial deference

Gregg v. Georgia

Rhodes v. Chapman

Turner v. Safley

Wilson v. Seiter

Lewis v. Casey

reasonable relationship

recreational litigation

ex-offender

ex-con

collateral consequences

invisible punishments

civil disabilities

annulment

registration of criminals

yellow card

Megan's Law

community notification
    laws

national sex offender
    database

civil commitment

sexually violent predator

Kansas v. Hendricks

medicalization of deviance

executive clemency

pardon

expungement

erasure of record

NOTES

1. Donald H. Wallace, "Prisoners' Rights: Historical Views," in James W. Marquart and Jonathan R. Sorensen, *Correctional Contexts: Contemporary and Classical Readings* (Los Angeles: Roxbury Publishing, 1997), p. 249.

2. Ibid.

3. Ibid.

4. Ibid., p. 250.

5. Sheldon Krantz, *Corrections and Prisoners' Rights*, 3rd ed. (St. Paul, Minn.: West Publishing, 1988), p. 125.

6. See Christopher E. Smith, *Law and Contemporary Corrections* (Belmont, Calif.: Wadsworth Publishing, 2000), pp. 30–51.

7. Krantz, *Corrections and Prisoners' Rights*, pp. 254–55.

8. Christopher E. Smith and Steven B. Dow, "Revitalization of the Eighth Amendment," *Corrections Compendium* 27, no. 8 (August 2002): 2.

9. Krantz, *Corrections and Prisoners' Rights*, pp. 199–200.

10. Ibid., p. 200.

11. Ibid., pp. 200–201.

12. Burk Foster, "Angola in the Seventies," in Burk Foster, Wilbert Rideau, and Douglas Dennis, *The Wall Is Strong: Corrections in Louisiana*, 3rd. ed. (Lafayette, La.: Center for Louisiana Studies, 1995), p. 57.

13. Roger A. Hanson and Kenry W. K. Daley, "Challenging the Conditions of Prisons and Jails: A Report on Section 1983 Litigation," U.S. Justice Department, Bureau of Justice Statistics Discussion Paper, December 1994, p. 17.

14. Ibid., pp. 35–36.

15. Ibid., p. 20.

16. *Lewis v. Casey*, 116 S. Ct. 2174 (1996).

17. Rolando V. del Carmen, Susan E. Ritter, and Betsy A. Witt, *Briefs of Leading Cases in Corrections*, 2nd ed. (Cincinnati: Anderson Publishing, 1998), p. 35.

18. Krantz, *Corrections and Prisoners' Rights*, p. 214.

19. Ibid.

20. Laura Failing and Randall Sears, "Medical Treatment and Mentally Incompetent Inmates," *Corrections Today* 63, no. 5 (August 2001): 106.

21. Del Carmen et al., *Briefs of Leading Cases in Corrections*, pp. 84–85.

22. Ibid., p. 95.

23. Smith, *Law and Contemporary Corrections*, p. 110.

24. Ibid., p. 111.

25. Del Carmen et al., *Briefs of Leading Cases in Corrections*, pp. 85–87.

26. Smith, *Law and Contemporary Corrections*, p. 86.

27. Ibid.

28. Del Carmen et al., *Briefs of Leading Cases in Corrections*, p. 73.

29. John McLaren, "Prisoners' Rights: The Pendulum Swings," in Joycelyn Pollock-Byrne, *Prisons: Today and Tomorrow* (Gaithersburg, Md.: Aspen Publishers, 1997), p. 357.

30. Krantz, *Corrections and Prisoners' Rights*, p. 227.

31. Barbara Bloom and Meda Chesney-Lind, "Women in Prison: Vengeful Equity," in Roslyn Muraskin, *It's a Crime: Women and Justice*, 3rd ed. (Upper Saddle River, N.J.: Prentice Hall, 2003), p. 189.

32. Ibid., p. 188.

33. James B. Jacobs, "The Prisoners' Rights Movement and Its Impacts," in James W. Marquart and Jonathan R. Sorensen, *Correctional Contexts: Contemporary and Classical Readings* (Los Angeles: Roxbury Publishing, 1997), p. 233.

34. Ibid., pp. 241–44.

35. Malcom M. Feeley and Roger A. Hanson, "The Impact of Judicial Intervention on Prisons and Jails: A Framework for Analysis and a Review of the Literature," in John J. DiIulio Jr., *Courts, Corrections, and the Constitution: The Impact of Judicial Intervention on Prisons and Jails* (New York: Oxford University Press, 1990), p. 31.

36. James Minton, "Boss Ross Says Federal Court Role Helped Prisons," *Baton Rouge Sunday Advocate*, February 6, 2000, p. 1A.

37. Ibid.

38. Del Carmen et al., *Briefs of Leading Cases in Corrections*, p. 143.

39. Ibid., p. 148.

40. Smith, *Law and Contemporary Corrections*, pp. 198–203.

41. Jack E. Call, "The Supreme Court and Prisoners' Rights," *Federal Probation* 59, no. 1 (March 1995): 36.

42. Ibid., p. 37.

43. These summaries are cited from Del Carmen et al., *Briefs of Leading Cases in Corrections*, pp. xiii–xviii.

44. Ibid., p. 5.

45. Ibid.

46. Fred Cheesman II, Roger A. Hanson, and Brian J. Ostrom, "A Tale of Two Laws: The U.S. Congress Confronts Habeas Corpus Petitions and Section 1983 Lawsuits," *Law and Policy* 22, no. 2 (April 2000): 96–97.

47. "Inmate Lawsuits and Grievances," *Corrections Compendium* 28, no. 6 (June 2003): 12.

48. Ibid., p. 14.

49. Ibid., p. 11.

50. Robert M. A. Johnson, "Collateral Consequences," Message from the President, National District Attorneys Association, May/June 2001, p. 1, *www.ndaa.org/ndaa/about/president_message_may_June.2001.html*.

51. Marc Mauer, "Invisible Punishment," *Focus*, May/June 2003, p. 3.

52. "Mississippi," in "Civil Disabilities of Convicted Felons," U.S. Justice Department, Office of the Pardon Attorney, October 1996, pp. 62–63.

53. "Vermont," in "Civil Disabilities of Convicted Felons," U.S. Justice Department, Office of the Pardon Attorney, October 1996, p. 113.

54. "Felony Disenfranchisement Laws in the United States," The Sentencing Project, January 2004, *www.sentencingproject.org*.

55. Center for Law and Social Policy and Community Legal Services, Inc., *Every Door Closed: Barriers Facing Parents with Criminal Records* (Washington, D.C.: Center for Law and Social Policy, 2000), pp. 1–6.

56. Harry Allen and Clifford Simonsen, *Corrections in America*, 9th ed. (Upper Saddle River, N.J.: Prentice Hall, 2001, p. 560.

57. Ibid.

58. Alan D. Scholle, "Sex Offender Registration Community Notification Laws," *FBI Law Enforcement Bulletin*, July 2000, p. 18.

59. Chad Kinsella, "Court OKs Sex Offender Registries: Recent U.S. Supreme Court Rulings Find State Sex Offender Registries Constitutional, but Implementation Poses Problems," *State Government News* 46, no. 5 (May 2003): 7.

60. Scholle, "Sex Offender Registration Community Notification Laws," p. 18.

61. Kinsella, "Court OKs Sex Offender Registries," pp. 1–2.

62. Howard Zonana, "The Civil Commitment of Sex Offenders," *Science* 278, no. 5341 (November 14, 1997): 1248.

63. Austin T. DesLauriers, "Kansas' Sex Offender Treatment Program," *Corrections Today* 64, no. 6 (October 2002): 118.

64. Ibid., p. 119.

65. Laurie Cunningham, "Justices Uphold Law Allowing Detention of Sexual Offenders," *Miami Daily Business Review*, October 18, 2002, p. A10.

66. Alexander Cockburn, "Evil: The Quadruple Axel," *The Nation* 274, no. 9 (March 11, 2002): 8.

67. Ibid.

68. Ibid.

69. Zonana, "The Civil Commitment of Sex Offenders," p. 1249.

FURTHER READING

DiIulio, John J., Jr. *Courts, Corrections, and the Constitution: The Impact of Judicial Intervention on Prisons and Jails.* New York: Oxford University Press, 1990.

Feeley, Malcolm M., and Edward L. Rubin. *Judicial Policy Making and the Modern State: How Courts Reformed America's Prisons.* New York: Cambridge University Press, 1998.

Martin, Steve J., and Sheldon Ekland-Olson. *Texas Prisons: The Walls Came Tumbling Down.* Austin: Texas Monthly Press, 1987.

Smith, Christopher E. *Law and Contemporary Corrections.* Belmont, Calif.: Wadsworth Publishing, 2000.

WEB AND VIDEO RESOURCES

The *Prison Legal News* Website is *www.prisonlegalnews.org.* This comprehensive site provides links to state and federal prison Websites and to many local jails.

The American Civil Liberties Union maintains a "Prisoner Rights" page at *www.aclu.org/Prison/PrisonsMain.cfm.*

COMMENTARY

17 ## Disenfranchising Felons Hurts Entire Communities

by Marc Mauer

Lumumba Bandele is a teacher and guidance counselor in the Brooklyn neighborhood of Bedford Stuyvesant in New York City. As the father of two, he and his wife struggle to provide a safe and secure environment for their children in a neighborhood with overcrowded public schools, failing small businesses and little affordable housing. Bandele sees political change as the means of improving these conditions, but he's frustrated by declining voter turnout in his community.

Electoral participation is lacking across the country, but in places like Bedford Stuyvesant it takes on a particularly curious slant. With so many of his neighbors unable to vote because they are in prison or on parole, Bandele feels that he, too, has lost political influence. To change that, he is now a plaintiff in a lawsuit challenging New York State's felon disenfranchisement laws, in part because they dilute the vote in communities of color, like his own neighborhood.

"The issue of disenfranchisement is really about power," Bandele says. "As the 'prison industrial complex' grows, one of the results is an increase in the number of people of color who are not allowed to participate in the electoral process. Our communities have been and will continue to struggle for power. The big battle now is to empower our family members who have returned and who are returning home from prison."

The New York litigation is but one aspect of a growing recognition that the vast expansion of the prison apparatus over the last two decades is now hurting not only those incarcerated and their families, but their communities as well. Increasingly, the ability of these communities to gain political representation and influence—and therefore access to public resources—is being thwarted by the American race to incarcerate. The structural racism in the system, an entrenched and often unconscious bias in law enforcement, has weakened Black political power. This affects everything, from elections for township supervisors to the president and all the policies that result.

As we celebrate the 50th anniversary of the historic *Brown v. Board of Education* Supreme Court decision, we can measure the contours of the expansion in incarceration against the background of the intervening five decades. While much attention is being focused on assessing progress in educational opportunity, the contrast with developments in the criminal justice system is quite profound. The figures themselves are shocking even after countless news stories and government reports. On the day of the *Brown* decision in 1954, about 98,000 African Americans were incarcerated. Today, there are nine times that number, an estimated 884,000, which is nearly half of today's total incarcerated population. If current trends continue, one of every three Black males born today will be sentenced to prison at some point in his lifetime. And in recent decades, the combined impact of poverty and the war on drugs has resulted in rapidly escalating figures for Black women as well.

The ripple effects of large-scale incarceration now extend well beyond the time individuals are locked up. We can see this most directly in the way low-income communities have lost political influence as a result of felony disenfranchisement laws. Depending on the state, a felony conviction can result in the loss of the right to vote while serving a sentence or even after completion of sentence. At present, prisoners can vote only in Maine and Vermont. In the other 48 states and the District of Columbia, persons in prison are not permitted to vote; in 33 of these states, persons on probation and/or parole cannot vote either; and in 13 states a felony conviction can result in the loss of voting rights for life. As a combined result of the growth in incarceration and disenfranchisement practices, more than four million Americans will be unable to vote in this year's presidential election. Among African American men, an estimated 13 percent are disenfranchised as a result of a current or previous conviction. And in the states with the most restrictive laws, 30 percent to 40 percent of the next generation of Black males will lose their right to vote if current trends continue.

These dynamics are not just the unfortunate consequences of higher rates of involvement in crime among African Americans. There is documented evidence of racial disparity in criminal justice processing and in the legacy of disenfranchisement being used as a means of restricting Black voting. In the years after Reconstruction in the South, state legislators tailored their disenfranchisement laws with the intent of reducing participation among the new Black electorate. The means by which they accomplished this was to expand disenfranchisement for crimes believed to be committed by Blacks but not for those offenses presumed to be committed by Whites. This led to the bizarre situation in Alabama whereby a man convicted of beating his wife would lose his right to vote but a man convicted of killing his wife would not.

Disenfranchisement laws directly affect the 1.4 million African American men and 245,000 women who cannot vote, but the impact goes well beyond them. The effect on families can be particularly hard when women are incarcerated. "Almost half of all Black families are headed by women. When Black women are disengaged from the political process, the whole family is disfranchised," says Monifa Bandele, field coordinator for the Right to Vote Campaign and wife of Lumumba Bandele.

Communities with high rates of people with felony convictions have fewer votes to cast. All residents of these neighborhoods, not just those with a felony conviction, become less influential than residents of more affluent neighborhoods. Emerging research also suggests that disenfranchisement laws may affect voter turnout in neighborhoods of high incarceration even among people who are legally eligible to vote. Since voting is essentially a communal experience—we talk about elections with our families and often go to the polls together—limitations on some members of the community translate into lower overall participation.

While disenfranchisement policies raise serious questions about democratic inclusion, their practical effect is now of such a magnitude that it may be determining electoral outcomes. On the day of the historic Florida election fiasco in 2000—when 537 votes in the state effectively decided the presidential election—an estimated 600,000 persons who had completed their felony sentences were unable to vote due to the state's restrictive laws. Had these persons been eligible to vote, even a modest rate of participation could easily have altered the national outcome.

Political influence and access to resources are further hindered by the growing tendency to build prisons in rural areas. Prison officials have always sought rural land for prison construction, primarily due to low real estate costs, and these trends have accelerated in recent years. Communities hard hit by the loss of manufacturing jobs and the decline of family farms have come to view prisons—often incorrectly, it turns out—as a recession-proof means of providing jobs. In New York State, for example, all 38 of the prisons built since 1982 have been located in upstate areas, most in rural communities.

Rural prison expansion affects urban communities of color through the mechanism of the census count. The Census Bureau's general rule is to count people in their "usual residence"; for prisoners, this has been interpreted to mean that they should be counted at the prison where they are housed, not in their home communities. The effect of this policy is that sparsely populated rural communities are artificially enlarged through their inmate population consisting mostly of people of color from urban neighborhoods. In Florence, Arizona, for example, two-thirds of the town's 16,000 inhabitants are prisoners, and for every dollar raised by local taxes, the town receives an additional $1.76 from state and federal allocations based on its prison population.

The increased political clout in many areas is now quite significant. In one prison district near Albany, New York, every 93 residents enjoy the political representation that would require 100 residents in other areas of the state, according to Soros Justice Fellow Peter Wagner. Fiscal dynamics created by the census play out in similar ways. Former Soros Senior Justice Fellow Eric Lotke (currently with the Justice Policy Institute) estimates that nationwide each prisoner brings in between $50-$250 a year to the local government in which he or she is housed. Thus, a new 500-bed prison may yield about $50,000 annually in new revenue. If such facilities were located in the urban areas many inmates call home, at least their communities would reap any financial and political benefits. Finally, urban areas suffer from the vicious cycle set in motion by the dramatically high rates of arrest and imprisonment of members of their communities. Eric Cadora of the Open Society Institute, who tracked this geographic concentration in a publication for the Urban Institute, found that New York City taxpayers spend $1 million to incarcerate inmates from some city blocks in Brooklyn. Suppose that this rate of incarceration could be reduced by just 10 percent; that would free up $100,000 in savings that could be invested to provide education, health care, and job training to this distressed area.

In recent years, considerable momentum for change in disenfranchisement laws has developed nationally. Nine states have adopted reforms of their policies since 1996, resulting in a half million persons becoming eligible to vote. The changes represent a growing realization in the states and in Washington that restricting voting rights does not serve a crime control agenda—the goal of racial inclusion or democracy itself. At the federal level, Congressman John Conyers (D-MI) introduced legislation last year that would permit any non-incarcerated person to vote in federal elections, even if prohibited from voting in state elections. He argues that there should be uniformity in electing national leaders. "If we want former felons to become good citizens," he said, "we must give them rights as well as responsibilities, and there is no greater responsibility than voting."

18 "America's Abu Ghraibs"

by Bob Herbert

Most Americans were shocked by the sadistic treatment of Iraqi detainees at the Abu Ghraib prison. But we shouldn't have been. Not only are inmates at prisons in the U.S. frequently subjected to similarly grotesque treatment, but Congress passed a law in 1996 to ensure that in most cases they were barred from receiving any financial compensation for the abuse. We routinely treat prisoners in the United States like animals. We brutalize and degrade them, both men and women. And we have a lousy record when it comes to protecting well-behaved, weak and mentally ill prisoners from the predators surrounding them.

Very few Americans have raised their voices in opposition to our shameful prison policies. And I'm convinced that's primarily because the inmates are viewed as less than human. Stephen Bright, director of the Southern Center for Human Rights, represented several prisoners in Georgia who sought compensation in the late-1990s for treatment that was remarkably similar to the abuses at Abu Ghraib. An undertaker named Wayne Garner was in charge of the prison system at the time, having been appointed in 1995 by the governor, Zell Miller, who is now a U.S. senator. Mr. Garner considered himself a tough guy. In a federal lawsuit brought on behalf of the prisoners by the center, he was quoted as saying that while there were some inmates who "truly want to do better . . . there's another 30 to 35 per cent that ain't fit to kill. And I'm going to be there to accommodate them."

On October 23, 1996, officers from the Tactical Squad of the Georgia Department of Corrections raided the inmates' living quarters at Dooly State Prison, a medium-security facility in Unadilla. This was part of a series of brutal shakedowns at prisons around the state that were designed to show the prisoners that a new and tougher regime was in charge. What followed, according to the lawsuit, was simply sick. Officers opened cell doors and ordered the inmates, all males, to run outside and strip. With female prison staff members looking on, and at times laughing, several inmates were subjected to extensive and wholly unnecessary body cavity searches. The inmates were ordered to lift their genitals, to squat, to bend over and display themselves, and so on.

One inmate who was suspected of being gay was told that if he ever said anything about the way he was being treated, he would be locked up and beaten until he wouldn't "want to be gay any more." An officer who was staring at another naked inmate said, "I bet you can tap dance." The inmate was forced to dance, and then had his body cavities searched. An inmate in a dormitory identified as J-2 was slapped in the face and ordered to bend over and show himself to his cellmate. The raiding party apparently found that to be hilarious.

According to the lawsuit, Mr. Garner himself, the commissioner of the Department of Corrections, was present at the Dooly Prison raid. None of the prisoners named in the lawsuit were accused of any improper behavior during the course of the raid. The suit charged that the inmates' constitutional rights had been violated and sought compensation for the pain, suffering, humiliation and degradation they had been subjected to.

Fat chance. The Prison Litigation Reform Act, designed in part to limit "frivolous" lawsuits by inmates, was passed by Congress and signed into law by Bill Clinton in 1996. It specifically prohibits the awarding of financial compensation to prisoners "for mental or emotional injury while in custody without a prior showing of physical injury." Without any evidence that they had been seriously physically harmed, the inmates in the Georgia case were out of luck. The courts ruled against them.

This is the policy of the United States of America. Said Mr. Bright: "Today we are talking about compensating prisoners in Iraq for degrading treatment, as of course we should. But we do not allow compensation for prisoners in the United States who suffer the same kind of degradation and humiliation."

The message with regard to the treatment of prisoners in the U.S. has been clear for years: Treat them any way you'd like. They're just animals. The treatment of the detainees in Iraq was far from an aberration. They, too, were treated like animals, which was simply a logical extension of the way we treat prisoners here at home.

13 REHABILITATION

Rehabilitated? You know, I don't have any idea what that means. . . . To me, it's just a made-up word. A politician's word. . . . What do you really want to know? Am I sorry for what I did? . . . There's not a day goes by I don't feel regret. . . . I look back on the way I was then—a young, stupid kid who committed that terrible crime. . . . That kid's long gone, and this old man is all that's left. I got to live with that. Rehabilitated? It's just a bullshit word. . . . So you go on and stamp your form, sonny, and stop wasting my time, because to tell you the truth, I don't give a shit.

— CONVICT ELLIS "RED" REDDING, AT HIS PAROLE HEARING AFTER
FORTY YEARS IN PRISON, IN *THE SHAWSHANK REDEMPTION*, 1995.

INTRODUCTION

For the prison generation that fell between "hard labor" and "get tough on crime," rehabilitation was an important concept. Although it did not apply equally to all prisoners in all institutions—and certainly not in jails—it represented a perspective that said one purpose of imprisonment was to promote positive change in the prisoner during confinement. This perspective would be officially abandoned during the 1970s, but it remains part of the prison vocabulary, and it retains adherents among corrections officials, scholars, prisoners, and the public. It is part of the prison landscape even in today's more punitive era. Early signs suggest that rehabilitation in a different form may be making a comeback in American corrections in the early twenty-first century. After reading the material in this chapter, you should be familiar with:

1. The origins of rehabilitation in prison.
2. The post–World War II rehabilitation era.
3. The decline of rehabilitation in the 1970s.
4. Common forms of rehabilitation programs in prison, including education, vocational training, and therapy programs.
5. Issues in the provision of rehabilitation programs in prison.
6. Measuring rehabilitation through recidivism.
7. The rise of rehabilitation in recent years.

THE BIRTH OF REHABILITATION

Rehabilitation is an often-used word in corrections. It is used so often by so many different speakers in so many different contexts that it has ceased to have any real meaning. Saying "rehabilitation" in corrections is much like wishing a friend "good luck"—an expression of optimism that something positive may happen but without any real expectation that it will. Life is about as full of bad experiences as it is good; criminals who leave prison are about as likely to return as not. *C'est la vie*—out of prison and in.

What does "rehabilitation" mean? In the prison setting, a generic definition is "something that makes a prisoner a better person." This is pretty open ended, for it does not describe the change agent, how the change takes place, or the consequences of change—a prisoner can become a "better person" and still be a criminal. A rapist can turn away from violent crimes to committing burglaries instead, or a burglar can go from committing 200 burglaries per year to committing twenty. Is each a better person? Yes, in a manner of speaking, though each remains an active criminal. Is either rehabilitated? Not hardly.

Rehabilitation is often thought of in a more narrow definition today—as specific programs applied within the prison setting (or outside) intended to bring about the end of criminal behavior, called **desistance,** meaning to cease or stop. This can be expressed in a kind of formula: prisoner classification × appropriate programming × positive participation = probability of desistance. The aim of the prison is to get the prisoner into the right program, keep him or her there until the program is successfully completed, and then turn the prisoner out to test the commitment to noncriminal behavior. This is only a general formula, and like many such formulas, it comes with a warning label: "Human behavior cannot be formulized." Two criminals with the same backgrounds could complete the same programs and be turned loose at the same time, one to return immediately to a life of crime and the other to stay straight. What made the difference here?

Speakers at correctional conferences on rehabilitation are fond of referring to the dictionary definition of rehabilitation: "to restore to a previous condition." They then point out what we should know about prisoners by this point: their previous condition was nothing to rejoice in. They are undereducated, badly skilled, substance-abusing, antisocial misfits who would not be making major contributions to society even if they were not behind bars. What these folks need is not to be restored to a previous condition but rather to be raised up to a position they have not previously attained in life. They need transformation, or **habilitation,** before they could hope to qualify for rehabilitation. When you consider what prisons have to work with and where they would like to go, transformation seems an even more daunting task than rehabilitation.

Pessimism—or reality—aside, what do we know about the association of rehabilitation with imprisonment? Rehabilitation is a relatively new concept in imprisonment, born of the increasing influence of social work and the behavioral sciences in corrections during the first half of the twentieth century. Some have suggested that rehabilitation was emphasized first for children being monitored through the juvenile court, then gradually spread through the developing probation and parole alternatives into adult prisons after World War II.

Some people speak of rehabilitation as part of the ideology responsible for the creation of the penitentiary ("The Quakers believed in rehabilitation"), but not much support for this proposition exists historically. The rationalist schol-ars who advocated the replacement of variable punishments—corporal pun-ishment, capital punishment, servitude, and the rest—by imprisonment did so because the old punishments were not working. They wanted punishments that were more certain and more uniformly applied and also generally more appropriate to modern civilized societies than those that had been used throughout history. The penitentiary movement was driven more by deter-rence (the effect of certainty of punishment) and humane concerns (turning away from ugly physical punishments) than by the hope of rehabilitation as we think of it today.

Indeed, rehabilitation is not a word to be found in the arguments about the place of the prison in nineteenth-century American society. What the Quakers believed in was penance, the suffering of punishment inducing the prisoner to express sorrow for his sins and to promise to do good to make up for his evil acts—social change based on the religious transformation that took place within the penitentiary. The penitentiary was a place for penitents to do penance. This was intended to take place in isolation, as one might meditate alone in one's room (or a monk might pray alone in his monastic cell). All the penitentiary did in this design was provide the quiet, ordered, safe environ-ment in which penance was to take place. Change was up to the individual.

As we know, penance and solitary confinement soon yielded to the more practical and economic design of hard labor and congregate confinement—the Auburn model. The regimentation and strict rules of the prisons applying this model, while ignoring the spiritual transformation of the individual, did seek to impose a rigid conformity that might lead to **reformation.** Joycelyn Pollock has suggested that the definition of reformation used in the prison of the latter 1800s was one based on external change rather than internal change. Reform monitors external behavior; success is defined as conformance of behavior to expectations.[1] Thus, what the prison was trying to do through routine, labor, and discipline was teach the orderly habits of good citizens (while paying for the costs of the lessons through the sale of the goods the prisoners produced). In Pollock's view, rehabilitation implies internal change, meaning a permanent change in values, attitudes, morals, or ways of looking at the world.[2]

At the 1870 National Prison Congress in Cincinnati, international penal reformers met to discuss restoring the prison to a positive role in society. They adopted a "Declaration of Principles," the first one of which reads, "Reforma-tion, not vindictive suffering, as the purpose of penal treatment of prisoners."[3] The next year, the National Congress on Prison and Reformatory Discipline, meeting at Albany, New York, made the same point:

> Crime is . . . a moral disease, of which punishment is the remedy. The efficiency of the remedy is a question of social therapeutics, a question of the fitness and the measure of the dose . . . punishment is directed not to the crime but the crimi-nal . . . (in order to reestablish) moral harmony in the soul of the criminal . . . his regeneration—his new birth to have respect for the laws. Hence . . . the supreme aim of prison discipline is the reformation of criminals, not the infliction of vin-dictive suffering.[4]

These principles would be applied not so much in the penitentiary, which remained a mass institution committed to rigid structure and hard labor for another seventy-five years, but in the new institution called the **reformatory.** Zebulon Brockway's Elmira Reformatory, which opened in 1876 in New York, is often cited as the birthplace of prison rehabilitation in America. Brockway combined into one package many of the reforms that had been proposed at the 1870 and 1871 prison meetings:

1. The indeterminate sentence
2. Basic classification of inmates
3. Industrial training
4. Religious and educational instruction
5. Individualization of treatment
6. Parole

These principles would later be incorporated into the rehabilitation model that spread through the American prison in the 1950s. Before this time, however, the ideals that defined rehabilitation (though still not using the term) would continue to be applied not generally but very specifically in reformatory-type institutions. The reformatories for men usually took in younger first offenders who were regarded as more amenable to change through programming. The women's reformatories took in mostly white women who were vice criminals and tried to turn them into "ladies" who would make suitable marriage partners or, failing that, good domestic servants, which might be the same thing without a marriage contract. This new-fangled idea of "rehabilitation," when it began to be called such in the social science literature of the early twentieth century, was applied to the chosen few—juveniles, young adults, whites, English-speaking immigrants, and first-time and lesser criminals (as opposed to habitual and violent criminals). For the mass of prisoners, rehabilitation was like the "Big Rock Candy Mountain," a fantasy place where they could not go. They had too much work to do to be rehabilitated.

THE REHABILITATION ERA

The **rehabilitation era** in American corrections is associated with the two decades from the mid-1950s to the mid-1970s, though in some places the beginnings would be earlier and the ends later, and in other places—particularly in several southern states and in local jails—rehabilitation never took hold as a primary purpose of imprisonment. It is important to remember that even in the states where rehabilitation was emphasized, it was not *the* purpose but rather *a* purpose, right along with whatever else the state might be accomplishing through the operation of its prison system. State corrections departments did not have anything like a mission statement or an outcomes plan to guide them during this time; purposes were described in political statements and often not well defined.

Several circumstances would coalesce to promote widespread interest in rehabilitation by the middle of the twentieth century. First was the growth of **scientific penology** as a movement. James V. Bennett, the director of the Federal Bureau of Prisons from 1937 to 1964, once observed that "penology" was a naive attempt to reduce to a science the unhappy task of punishing people. Yet he became the leading advocate of individualized treatment of criminals based on scientific observations and precepts, leading eventually to the adoption of the medical model in corrections by the last years of his administration.

Scientific penology pre-dated the founding of the Bureau of Prisons by about two decades. John Roberts has reported on the origins of this movement:

> In the early and mid-twentieth century, criminologists, social scientists, social workers, and prison administrators applied theories from the emerging fields of sociology, psychology, and psychiatry to study crime and punishment, and to attempt to create a more beneficial prison environment. Around 1910, university professors and clinical psychologists began establishing research centers connected with courts or prisons to collect and analyze data on offenders.
>
> The Laboratory of Social Hygiene was established at Bedford Hills Women's Reformatory in New York in 1912 to study the psychology of female offenders. In 1916, Dr. Bernard Glueck set up a clinic at New York's Sing Sing Prison to examine each incoming inmate. By the 1920s, Harvard and nearly a dozen other universities and law schools had developed courses on criminal psychology that further fueled the proliferation of clinics and institutes to study criminal behavior and sanctions.[5]

The **Elmira System** of Zebulon Brockway had provided rudimentary classification, programs, and individualized release based on good behavior for its selected clientele. Scientific penology would expand certain aspects of this system while focusing more on studying the individual needs of prisoners and diversifying the types of institutions in which they were confined. Women, juveniles, and young adults already had their own specialized institutions by the 1930s; in the federal system and several states, further specialization for different types of prisoners, such as drug addicts and the physically and mentally ill, began about this time and continued through the 1950s. Prisoners also began to be divided into the basic custody levels we still use today: maximum, medium, and minimum. Prison systems set up classification centers—later known as reception and diagnostic centers—to amplify the needs assessment of incoming prisoners and ensure that the new inmates were sent to the right institutions; or at least that was the ideal theory of classification in the progressive states.

These changes were accompanied by the rapid decline of prison labor, which turned the nature of prison life upside down between 1930 and 1945, except in the federal system and the southern agricultural prisons that escaped the trauma of the industrialized prison states. The states with industrial prisons went from most inmates working in factories in the 1920s to inmates doing internal maintenance chores only by the late 1940s. Increases in inmate populations after the war and general neglect, coupled with the absence of work and other purposeful activities, were blamed for the prolonged period of prison riots and unrest that took place across the country in the early 1950s. Among the reported findings of the McGee Committee appointed by the American Prison Association to identify the causes of the riots were idleness, public (and political) indifference to prison needs and objectives, and lack of funding for treatment.

For the next decade or so, even in many states not known for progressivism, correctional officials were able to steer public policy and public opinion away from traditional notions of punishment and toward treatment. The

American Prison Association changed its name to the American Correctional Association, and there was a burst of energy in corrections lasting through the 1960s that made behavioral science–based rehabilitation programs and the establishment of more humane conditions the primary focus of corrections.[6]

John Conrad has provided a close-up example of the motivation for expanding rehabilitation in the postindustrial prison. In the early 1950s, when Robert A. Heinze was warden of California's Folsom Prison, a disturbance in the prison's Adjustment Center left prison officials wondering what to do to prevent a recurrence. The men had nothing to do except scheme among themselves and wait for an officer to make a mistake to get trouble started. Warden Heinze told his staff at a meeting held after this particular event, "I don't want to run that place without a program any longer." The result was a management program using group counseling, education, daily exercise, and eventually a ticket of leave by which a convict housed in the Adjustment Center could return to regular housing. While it did not accomplish wonders, Conrad pointed out, it *was* a program. Warden Heinze was convinced that it reduced trouble in the Adjustment Center and made it possible to release some people into general population.[7]

Conrad points out that wardens had three choices:

1. Put prisoners to work
2. Offer them opportunities to improve themselves
3. Let idleness prevail

Warden Heinze wanted programs to keep prisoners constructively occupied, and Conrad argues that this principle was justification enough for rehabilitation activities in prison during this era. If prisoners cannot work, and if wardens do not want to let them sit in idleness, then rehabilitation—in whatever form the prison can offer—is the only option.[8]

Many political and correctional officials in other systems would have agreed with this assessment, and rehabilitation enjoyed widespread support for a time. Some systems went much farther than others. The federal system, still under the direction of James Bennett, went farthest of all in its adoption of the **medical model** of rehabilitation:

> In its simplest terms, the Medical Model was a theory of corrections that viewed criminality as analogous to a physical disease. It was the role of prison to diagnose the causes of criminality in individual—social immaturity, psychological maladjustment, alcohol or drug abuse, illiteracy, lack of job skills—and to prescribe a regimen to cure the illness. Treatment programs might involve behavior modification therapy, psychological counseling, addiction therapy, vocational training, or whatever would help induce rehabilitation.[9]

In 1970, the Joint Commission on Correctional Manpower and Training described the medical model in this way:

> The offender is to be perceived as a person with social, intellectual, or emotional deficiencies who should be diagnosed carefully and his deficiencies clinically defined. Programs should be designed to correct these deficiencies to the point that would permit him to assume a productive, law-abiding place in the community. To achieve these goals of correctional treatment, it would be necessary only to maintain the pressure on the inmate for his participation in the treatment programs, to continue to humanize institutional living, to upgrade the educational

level of the line officer, and to expand the complement of professional treatment and training personnel.[10]

For most inmates, the rehabilitation era meant three basic steps: classification on entry into the system, assignment to an institution based on this classification, and participation in an expanded range of programs as a replacement for inmate labor, which was no longer generally available. Achieving "rehabilitation" was also critical to release under the indeterminate sentence; if the warden wanted a program to keep inmates occupied, the inmates said "to get out you have to have a program." Program participation was necessary to prove change. Acquiring program-completion certificates became to the prisoner what résumé-building activities are to college students: documentation to prove your deserts among your competitors.

In the federal system and the few states that chose to devote resources to the medical model, the promise was for even more programs and a customized treatment plan fitted to the individual prisoner. The three parties most concerned with what happens inside prisons—the public, the prisoners, and correctional staff—tuned in to see whether the increased emphasis on rehabilitation was worth the effort: would it truly reduce crime?

THE DEATH OF REHABILITATION

The so-called rehabilitation era, slow in developing and never ripening fully into an integrated, pervasive approach, began its decline about the time people started putting a name to it.[11] The death of rehabilitation is most often tied to one specific historical event—the publication of Robert Martinson's article "What Works—Questions and Answers about Prison Reform" in the journal *The Public Interest* in 1974. In his introduction to the article, Martinson gave this summary: "With few and isolated exceptions, the rehabilitative efforts that have been reported so far have had no appreciable effect on recidivism."[12]

Some people are destined to be remembered primarily—or exclusively—for their pessimistic contribution to history. Colonel George Armstrong Custer is remembered for his ill-advised attack on the Indian village on the Little Big Horn in 1876; his famous line was "Charge!" This may have been followed by "Damn, where did all these Indians come from?" Both remarks have to be attributed since no white man who heard them actually survived the battle. **Robert Martinson** is remembered for his report on rehabilitation: "What works? **Nothing works.**"

Martinson, along with his colleagues Douglas Lipton and Judith Wilks, had been hired to make a comprehensive survey of what was known about rehabilitation. They reviewed 231 acceptable studies from the years 1945 to 1967. While Martinson was left skeptical about rehabilitation, concluding that "it may be . . . that there is a more radical flaw in our present strategies—that education at its best, or that psychotherapy at its best, cannot overcome, or even appreciable reduce, the powerful tendency for offenders to continue in criminal behavior,"[13] his colleagues were guarded in the 1975 final report, published in book form as *The Effectiveness of Correctional Treatment: A Survey of Treatment Evaluation Studies* and bearing all three of their names. They concluded, "The field of corrections has not as yet found satisfactory ways to reduce recidivism by significant amounts,"[14] which is a way of saying we have not found anything that works perfectly well—a **silver bullet** that kills criminal behavior.

Other researchers argued that Martinson's conclusions were too broad, that some particular programs seemed to work well while similar programs in a different locale might not do so well. The National Academy of Sciences Panel on Research on Rehabilitative Techniques reviewed the research by Lipton, Martinson, and Wilks and in a 1979 report found it accurate and fair, agreeing that no known programs or methods of rehabilitation could be guaranteed to reduce the criminal activity of released offenders.[15] Martinson debated the effectiveness of rehabilitation over the years, and then he wrote in a journal article the year before his death in 1980 that, "some treatment programs do have an appreciable effect on recidivism."[16] But the lasting harm to the rehabilitative ideal had already been done: "Nothing works."

In retrospect, it seems about as wrong to put the blame on Martinson for the demise of rehabilitation as it does to put the blame on Custer for the destruction of the Plains Indians. Larger forces were clearly at work in both cases. In the case of rehabilitation, contradictory winds were blowing from all corners against the rehabilitative ideology. As crime rates rose, some "get tough on crime" advocates wanted to do away with any efforts that smacked of being nice to criminals. Conservative scholars argued that retribution and incapacitation were more appropriate objectives of punishment. Norval Morris and other reformers contended that **forced rehabilitation** was an inherently coercive game that could not be played fairly; they objected to sentence length—through release on parole—being tied to participation in rehabilitation. Psychologists in particular objected to the influence of the prison environment on rehabilitation, suggesting that the **crimogenic environment** of the prison caused more new crimes than rehabilitation could prevent. The complete dominance of security over rehabilitation supported this argument.

Prisoners had their own objections to rehabilitation. They faulted the subjectivity of the whole process—who got into the program slots available and who got favorable consideration by the parole board. They claimed that smart sociopaths easily manipulated the system to their advantage, that programs were too few in number, and that the prison seldom made a serious effort to match prisoners and programs. As a convict, you might be interested in learning carpentry skills, but the only class you could get into was auto mechanics. Knowing that you were angry and impulsive, there were no slots in the counseling group, but you could attend Alcoholics Anonymous meetings if you wanted to: "Hello, I'm John, and I'm not an alcoholic, but this was all I could find." Instead of considering individual needs and interests, it was "Here it is; take it or leave it."

The Federal Bureau of Prisons officially gave up its medical model in 1975, announcing its replacement by the **balanced model,** in which retribution, deterrence, incapacitation, and rehabilitation were all considered possible objectives that might apply to different inmates. In the 1980s, a decade dominated by a conservative crime control ideology at the national level, rehabilitation faded in importance. It was easier to write prisoners off as irredeemable or to reduce change to a mystery—akin to a religious experience—that could not be explained.

The death of rehabilitation was most noticeable in regard to sentencing. The indeterminate sentencing structure that had prevailed in most states, allowing generous parole provisions for rehabilitated inmates, was an obvious casualty.

Discretionary release on parole was abolished or cut way back in the federal system and most states from the mid-1980s on. While rehabilitation remained the bedrock of the juvenile courts, longer incapacitative sentences and transfer of more juveniles to the adult system for punishment were popular measures.

Some observers pointed out that it was the *ideal* of rehabilitation—or the emphasis on rehabilitation as a purpose of imprisonment—that had died; rehabilitative *programs* were still alive in most prisons. Some programs were cut back for a while, particularly when money for new prison construction was tight; some programs that were politically dangerous, such as furloughs and educational and work release that took prisoners into the community, were eliminated, as were such politically controversial programs as Pell Grants for prisoner higher education. The relative dearth of programs for substance-abusing inmates and mentally disordered inmates was also noted.

But for the most part, prison officials did not rush to abolish traditional rehabilitative programs—education, vocational training, and counseling—within their institutions. As many researchers have pointed out, prisons were not spending that much money on rehabilitation, generally less than 5 percent of their budget, and officials wanted to keep programs alive for the same reasons Warden Heinze wanted programs at Folsom Prison fifty years ago. Programs give prisoners something to do, something positive in an otherwise stale environment. Programs provide the opportunity to change, and inmates who want to change use programs to help them do so. Prison officials want to facilitate change, and they believe that programs are "part of the package" through which change comes about.

Although late twentieth-century rehabilitation programs were made voluntary rather than mandatory and were usually officially divorced from release consideration, inmates continued to flock to them. Some authorities had predicted that prisoners would stop taking part in programs once it was clear that they would not win early release through their participation, but across the country this did not happen. Even when rehabilitation was dead as an ideology, the percentages of inmates participating in programs remained steady or increased.

RECIDIVISM AND REHABILITATION

One of the troubling aspects of rehabilitation was determining its long-term effects. How does one measure the success or failure of people who have been through rehabilitation? Several measures might be possible: whether they are healthier, happier, "better" people; whether they are more productive in society; whether they avoid various kinds of deviant behavior; or whether they return to criminal behavior but at a less active rate. But we have tended to focus on the repetition of criminal behavior, resulting in arrest, reincarceration, or a new conviction. The term is **recidivism,** which the dictionary defines as "repeated or habitual relapse, as into crime."

Several different levels of recidivism are possible, as Robert Martinson and others found when they were examining rehabilitation studies in the 1970s. Four different measures have often been used to identify **recidivists:**

1. **Rearrest,** being taken into custody for a new offense
2. **Reconviction,** getting a new felony or misdemeanor conviction

3. **Reimprisonment,** returning to prison with a new sentence or as a technical violator of the terms of release under the old sentence
4. **Reimprisonment for a new felony,** the most narrow definition of all because it would involve the fewest number of prisoners

Some ex-convicts—probably most ex-convicts, just like many citizens who are not ex-convicts—commit crimes for which they are never caught. Their "blips" never show up on the radar screen; as far as the system is concerned, they are success cases. If they do get arrested, they are failures even if the charges are minor or were nothing like the original felony conviction (an armed robber picked up for shoplifting) and even if the charges were dropped with no further legal action. It was the arrest of the ex-offender that determined recidivism.

Most men and women released from prison are under some form of supervision—parole or mandatory release. If they violate the terms of release, such as by leaving the jurisdiction without permission or failing to keep in contact with their parole officer, they can be returned to prison. They become recidivists without having actually been charged with a new crime—only technical violations of release conditions. Some will also be charged with new crimes and revoked after probable-cause hearings to determine their guilt; they go back to prison on the old charge even if the new charge is dropped without a new conviction.

Finally, some ex-convicts will pick up new convictions and return to prison as repeat offenders. They are the true recidivists. The public perception is that prison is a "revolving door," that the men and women going out are virtually certain to return convicted of new crimes. On the surface, the numbers appear to support this notion: seventy-five percent of state and federal prisoners have a prior felony conviction that imposed either probation or confinement. But keep in mind that over 10 million adults have at least one felony conviction and that only about 10 to 15 percent of them are in prison at any given time. The other 85 percent—five of every six persons ever convicted of a felony—are loose in society. The ones in prison are the most persistent recidivists, making a life out of crime and incarceration, just like our state legislatures and Congress are full of the most persistent officeholders making a life out of politics. There are many one-term felons, just as there are many one-term politicians.

Minnesota looked closely at recidivism among the 9,000 offenders released from prison or sentenced to probation in 1992:

> The study found that 59 percent of prisoners were *rearrested* in Minnesota for new felonies or gross misdemeanors in the three years following their release, and an additional five percent were rearrested in another state. Forty-five percent of released prisoners were *reconvicted* of felonies or gross misdemeanors within three years. Forty percent of prisoners were *reimprisoned* within three years—28 percent for new crimes and the remainder for "technical violations" of their prison release conditions.[17]

Many studies of recidivism use the first three years after release as the most critical study period, when reoffending rates are highest, but recidivism does not end after three years: it lasts for a lifetime. If you were convicted of a drug charge at nineteen and given probation and then twenty years later, after living a relatively crime-free life, get in a bar fight and pick up an assault charge, you are a recidivist. If you leave the system and return, regardless of the interval involved, you would show up in the recidivism statistics.

When scholars tried to evaluate the effectiveness of various rehabilitation programs, they encountered many obstacles. Different studies used different measures of success, depending on how far into the system the failures went. Some focused on rearrest, some on return to custody (even without new convictions), and some on new convictions. The percentages change significantly depending on the standards used.

In comparing experimental groups and control groups (following ideal experimental protocol), it was difficult to get groups that compared with each other. Bacteria or lab rats can be selected at random and divided into comparable groups. Prisoners cannot. Most rehabilitation programs enroll voluntary participants, so right away you have the problem of motivated versus unmotivated prisoners. Many programs selected the best candidates from a larger field of applicants—a process known as **creaming,** meaning to pick the cream of the crop—which enhances the likelihood of success from the start.

Attrition rates are a problem. Programs that are harder to complete are often more successful than those that have few dropouts along the way, so which is better: the program that more people complete but with a higher failure rate or the program that is more difficult but percentage-wise more effective in reducing criminality?

One of the things researchers were interested in was the concept of a **model program** that could be easily reproduced and exported to other settings. If there was a new program—let's call it "transcendental empathy"—that in ninety days could teach criminals to put themselves in the place of crime victims and thereby cut typical recidivism rates from 50 to 25 percent, this would be a highly effective program. We would want to box it and ship it all over the country. What we might find, however, is that the effectiveness of this program depended on characteristics unique to this program, such as the persona of its leader or the diligence of its staff, rather than its program content—or maybe they were just lucky for a while, or maybe they were lying about the recidivism rate.

In examining similar programs (or programs that claimed to be applying the same type of treatment modality, such as behavior modification), observers noted that few "pure" programs following ideal models could be found. Rather, programs tended to be hybrid models combining different approaches, and these were modified to fix the circumstances of particular settings—meaning they had to be adaptable to the prison routine. This also hampers the idea of **exportabililty,** transplanting a successful model to a different setting.

Robert Martinson found examples of bias in some of the studies he examined. He compared **treatment effects** to **policy effects.**[18] Treatment effects were the *bona fide* results of treatment programs, objectively measured. Policy effects were more subtle. If the people in charge of the program wanted people to succeed—perhaps because they were more humanitarian in their beliefs or because they needed to be successful to get their funding renewed—they could ignore minor violations and call outcomes successful even though a different evaluator might call them failures. Probation officers do the same thing with people violating probation conditions; they become known for giving or not giving people slack, and this influences their revocation rates.

Some programs appeared to achieve such remarkable successes that their results were considered unreliable. A program for juveniles that claimed a

97 percent success rate, for instance, would be highly suspect to anyone used to working with juvenile criminals; we would know that they were jiggling their statistics in one form or another.

The point of all these concerns is that recidivism is not a universal language spoken by all people involved in prison administration and rehabilitation. It is not an absolute. Recidivism is more like a local dialect of a broader language, with considerable variation from place to place. Even as evaluation has become more standardized and systematic in the thirty years since the first rigorous reviews resulted in the death of the rehabilitation ideology, we know that success and failure are not always easy to measure. Rehabilitation is an intervention into people's lives, and its effects have to be viewed from multiple perspectives—those being "intervened," those doing the intervening, and those in whose name the intervention is done.

REHABILITATION IN PRISON

What should be included under the heading of rehabilitation in prison? In theory, any program that makes people better or reduces criminal behavior could be called rehabilitation. In this broad definition, rehabilitation could include several kinds of activities not usually thought of as being part of a program:

1. Religion, including Bible study groups, attending church services, or being a part of a religious congregation in prison. In terms of inmate participation, religion is the biggest program in prison.
2. Recreation, like a sports club or group that meets regularly to enjoy particular activities.
3. Arts and crafts, the use of free time devoted to individual crafts or artistic expression.
4. Service groups that engage in activities beneficial to other inmates or sometimes to people in the free world, such as fund-raising to support juvenile group homes.
5. Self-help groups, including such common groups as Alcoholics Anonymous and Narcotics Anonymous but also Toastmasters, Jaycees, and numerous others.
6. Prison work assignments, the inside jobs inmates are assigned to.
7. Visitation with family and nonfamily outsiders.

The National Research Council's 1979 report *The Rehabilitation of Criminal Offenders: Problems and Prospects* gave a different definition:

> Rehabilitation is the result of any planned intervention that reduces an offender's further criminal activity, whether that reduction is mediated by personality, behavior, abilities, attitudes, values, or other factors. The effects of maturation and the effects associated with "fear" or "intimidation" are excluded, the results of the latter having traditionally been labeled as specific deterrence.[19]

Calling rehabilitation a **planned intervention** narrows the field of activities considerably, excluding the more general aspects of prison life listed previously.

The National Research Council's definition would be more appropriate to the traditional prison-sponsored programs emphasizing education, vocational training, and therapy of different types, but what is it that actually promotes change in criminals? This is a difficult question to answer. Some criminals will tell you they are changed when they know in their hearts they are not, and others will tell you what they believe changed them even if other people who know them might cite completely different reasons.

One thing is for certain: many prisoners will tell stories of change that have little or nothing to do with the formal, planned interventions the National Research Council uses to define rehabilitation. When you talk to prisoners who have been out of prison a long time, you hear stories of what induced change: joining a Bible study group, meeting a woman visitor who eventually became a wife; learning to bake in a prison kitchen; learning to read and joining a book discussion group, attending Alcoholics Anonymous regularly, or getting involved in an antidelinquency program that worked with young visitors to prison. Sometimes it is nothing specific, just growing older, maturing, or deciding not to return to prison again. This is what makes evaluating the effectiveness of rehabilitation so difficult—there is no exact cause-and-effect relationship of the planned interventions to the subsequent behavior of the offender. The results of the interventions take place in the human mind and the human heart, where science cannot peer. We can never be sure whether change took place *because* of the interventions or *despite* the interventions or whether the interventions were merely part of a larger pattern of change that took place over a longer period of time in and out of prison.

Joycelyn Pollock has called this the **black box** of prison:

> Treatment programs are only one part of the prisoner's life. The prison experience is like a "black box" that the researcher cannot look inside. We can measure the outcome of the black box (higher or lower recidivism), but we can never identify which elements of the prison experience contributed to the results. It may be that treatment programs provide positive elements to a course of changing one's life, but the negative aspects of imprisonment—**prisonization** (the socialization to the prisoner subculture), violence, attacks on self-esteem, loss of family support—may override any treatment effects.[20]

Ron Wikberg came to the Louisiana State Penitentiary in 1970 to serve a lifetime for murder. Wikberg shot and killed a grocery store owner who shot at him during an armed robbery. Wikberg went on to become an award-winning staff writer and associate editor of *The Angolite* magazine and was released on parole shortly before he died of cancer in 1994. When asked about rehabilitation in his own case—what had turned his life around—Wikberg said that he became "rehabilitated" as soon as the bullet from the grocer's gun went by his ear. "I knew I wasn't cut out for the career of an armed robber." But it was too late; he shot back, becoming a convicted murderer and being given a life sentence.

Wikberg said he spent the first four or five years in prison trying to survive, including getting involved in petty inmate games and internal prison politics. Then, in his early thirties, he began to think of becoming a better person—"to make up for the harm I've done." He paid for correspondence courses on his own to become a prison paralegal, then began to study sentencing practices and write on legal issues. Wikberg wrote for *The Angolite* for a decade and published two books on corrections. He acknowledged being helped by prison officials who believed in him and put him in positions of responsibility, which gave him a voice and also eventually helped him win parole, but he never participated in any particular prison program intended to rehabilitate him. You could say that he became rehabilitated in prison, but whether prison did it for him or whether he did it for himself was a question he could not answer. He did believe that prisons ought to do much more to enhance rehabilitation than they are presently doing, particularly in regard to education and job training.

We will look next at three main types of conventional prison rehabilitation programs—education, vocational training, and therapy—and then examine new programs that have emerged within the past few years.

PRISON REHABILITATION: EDUCATION

Prison officials have long recognized that prisoners as a group are undereducated. As early as the 1820s, prisons in New York and Kentucky offered brief classes teaching prisoners to read and write. In 1847, New York passed a law requiring the appointment of a full-time teacher in each of its state prisons. Teachers were common staff members in the first reformatories of the late 1800s.

In 1930, **Austin MacCormick,** called the father of modern correctional education, founded the **Correctional Education Association** (now an affiliate of the American Correctional Association). He established the *Journal of Correctional Education* in 1937. MacCormick was an advocate of **individually prescribed instruction** (IPI) in correctional settings, which meant that each prisoner should have his or her own plan of education and that much instruction was intended to be one on one as opposed to group or congregate based. MacCormick was famed for advancing the spread of prison schools and libraries to benefit uneducated prisoners.

As the twenty-first century begins, prisoners remain poorly educated, and prison educational programs are abundant. Caroline Wolf Harlow reported in 2003 that a comprehensive national survey of prisoners completed in 1997 showed that 75 percent of state prisoner inmates, 59 percent of federal prison inmates, and 69 percent of local jail inmates had not completed high school (these figures are slightly higher than the educational attainment percentages reported by institutions). About 11 percent of the state prisoners had some college education. In contrast, among adults in society, only 18 percent were not high school graduates, and almost half of all adults had some college.[21]

To meet these needs, Harlow reported, the great majority of jails and prisons provided educational programs for their inmates. The breakdown of educational programs offered in state, federal, and private prisons in 1995 and 2000 and in local jails in 1999 is displayed in this table.

Prisoners in general take advantage of the educational opportunities available to them while incarcerated. About 52 percent of state prison inmates, 57 percent of federal inmates, and 14 percent of local jail inmates said they had taken educational classes while in custody. By far, the largest category of inmates taking academic classes were those lacking a high school diploma who were preparing to take the GED test.

EDUCATIONAL PROGRAMS

Type	State Prisons		Federal Prisons		Private Prisons		Local Jails
	1995	2000	1995	2000	1995	2000	1999
Any program	88.0%	91.2%	100.0%	100.0%	71.8%	87.6%	60.3%
Basic adult	76.0	80.4	92.0	97.4	40.0	61.6	24.7
Secondary	80.3	83.6	100.0	98.7	51.8	70.7	54.8
College	31.4	26.7	68.8	80.5	18.2	27.3	3.4
Special education	33.4	39.6	34.8	59.7	27.3	21.9	10.8
Study release	12.0	8.8	5.4	6.5	32.7	28.9	9.3[22]

Prisons emphasize attaining the GED in confinement as a measure of success, but research does not indicate that getting a GED has much impact on recidivism. Why not? As one prisoner said, "When you take the elevator from the subbasement to the basement, you're still not on the same level as everyone else." What he meant was that the GED is generally recognized as a substitute diploma for high school dropouts. Thus, getting the GED actually becomes a mark not of attainment but of educational inferiority. The U.S. military no longer accepts enlistees who have the GED but no higher education. Especially when it is concentrated among those younger inmates who have the highest recidivism rates on release, the GED does not appear to have much impact in changing the lives of inmates when they reenter the free world.

At the other end of the scale, prisoners with a college education have fared much better after they get out. Recidivism rates for college-educated inmates are considerably lower than rates for persons with less education. New York state reported in 1991 that prisoners who completed at least two years of higher education had a 26 percent recidivism rate compared to 44 percent overall. The Federal Bureau of Prisons reported that of all inmates released in 1987, those who had earned college degrees recidivated at 5 percent compared to 40 percent overall. Texas reported in 1995 that recidivism rates of those who had earned associate degrees were 13.7 percent; baccalaureate degrees, 5.6 percent; and master's degrees, 0 percent.[23]

So why don't we give all inmates master's degrees and wipe out crime? The fact is that only about 10 percent of prisoners are considered good prospects for doing college-level studies. The other 90 percent are either uninterested, unqualified, or already educated to that level. Many inmates are not motivated to do college-level work, and even if they were, the availability of college courses for prisoners—either inside the walls or through **educational release**—has dropped off over the past decade since Congress killed federal Pell Grants for prisoners with the passage of the Violent Crime Control Act of 1994.

Higher education for inmates had really taken off in the 1970s, following the example of **Project Newgate,** a federally funded program that established college campuses within the walls of several prisons. Many universities and community colleges took their courses into prison or arranged for inmates to come out on furloughs to attend classes on campus. But these programs became politically unpopular during the crime control campaigns of the 1990s, state and federal funding were cut back, and internal support (among wardens and administrators) lagged. Thom Gehring has argued that many institutional staff seem to have an **antieducation bias** against college programs (and a bias in favor of training in manual trades) for inmates. He has also suggested that higher education is not a cure for deviance but rather a tool that "helps people pursue social aspirations." The prisoners who pursue college education, in comparison to those languishing in GED programs, are smarter, sharper, and more motivated, and they have far better career opportunities when they get out; but education does not necessarily turn them into good citizens, no more than completion of an MBA imparts moral virtue to business executives.[24]

PRISON REHABILITATION: VOCATIONAL TRAINING

Vocational training in American prisons was originally reserved for young criminals. Adult prisoners were put to work—doing individual craft work in cells or congregate labor in prison shops—while youthful prisoners were given the job skills necessary to make it in the labor force as an adult. Historians have compared the houses of refuge, training schools, and reformatories that were training youngsters to the apprenticeships they had once served on their way into the skilled trades and crafts.

Adult penitentiaries were factories with walls until the early part of the twentieth century. If you did not know how to work as a new inmate, you were simply assigned to learn a job by doing it (on-the-job training). These prisons did not have highly developed vocational training programs. In the southern prison farm states, mostly black convict populations did agricultural work that required no training.

Not until after World War II, when prison labor was done away with, did progressive prisons begin to offer much in the way of skilled training for inmates. Vocational training was greatly expanded in the 1960s and 1970s during the rehabilitation era in corrections. Prison administrators and staff tend to be more supportive of work training for inmates than they are of college education, so these programs remain more pervasive in American prisons than higher-education programs. In the 1990s, about a third of inmates reported receiving some type of vocational training since entering prison, but this training was not often ongoing. In a given year, fewer than 10 percent of prisoners participate in any kind of vocational training in or out of prison.

Vocational training in prison can be divided into two types: generic and certified. Generic includes job-based work assignments under the direction of staff members who are not certified instructors; they are staff members—correctional officers or civilians—who supervise inmates on the job. The inmates acquire job-related skills, but there is no formal structure to the training, no evaluation, and no certification of expertise at the end of the training period. As an inmate, you may have learned to be a cook, a plumber, or an auto mechanic, but you get nothing to certify your training when you go out into the world.

Certified training, on the other hand, is provided by vocational/technical instructors who could be teaching the same skill to free-world students. The courses are the same as would be offered in a vocational or technical school outside of prison. They have structure, content, and exams, and the prisoners who complete them receive certificates.

Texas has long been recognized as one of the national leaders in providing vocational education to inmates. In 1969, it created the **Windham School District**—the first correctional school district in the nation—to provide educational, vocational, and life skills programs for incarcerated offenders. The Windham School District is a public school district monitored by the Texas Education Agency. In fiscal year 1998, its expenditures totaled $56.9 million. Approximately 39 percent of all prisoners in Texas state prisons and jails participated in at least one Windham-funded program in fiscal year 1998.[25]

Over 20,000 (of Texas's approximately 192,000 inmates, by their count, in 1998) were enrolled in one of three types of certificate programs:

1. *Secondary-level vocational programs—16,293 participants, 7,458 certificates.* Career and technology education (CTE) programs provide occupational training and industrial certification in forty trade areas. Full-length courses offer 600 hours of training focused on industry standards and certification. Short courses are designed to prepare offenders for prison jobs or provide basic skills prior to release. Courses range from 45 to 200 hours of instruction. Over 1,500 certificates were awarded to students meeting industry certification standards in thirty-one trade areas in 1999.

2. *Apprenticeship training programs—1,084 participants, 34 journeyman certificates.* Apprenticeship training programs are offered in thirty-two craft areas, all of which are registered with the U.S. Department of Labor.

3. *Postsecondary vocational programs—3,668 participants, 2,019 certificates.* Postsecondary vocational programs provide training in nineteen course areas. Courses are normally six months in length and result in the awarding of twenty semester hours of college credit on satisfactory completion.[26]

Offenders working in Texas Department of Criminal Justice jobs can also earn on-the-job training credits in over 275 occupations. The district report notes that "these jobs teach marketable skills, help promote good work habits, and reduce TDCJ operational costs."[27]

Vocational training in prison is slanted heavily toward skilled trades, such as carpentry, welding, upholstery, air conditioning, electrical work, auto repair, plumbing, data processing, printing, groundskeeping, and culinary arts. Women's training programs are often more limited than men's (though this has changed in several states as women's prisons have gotten bigger). The most common programs for women include office skills, culinary arts, garment production, the hospitality industry, and cosmetology (or as a woman prisoner said, "secretary, cooking, sewing, cleaning, and beauty shop, you know, pretty much what we've always done.") Programs to train women—and men—prisoners in sales, supervisory, management, health care, and service occupations are pretty slim. The assumption is that these jobs are beyond the skill levels (and outside the interests) of most prisoners.

Elayn Hunt Correctional Center in Louisiana offers five major vocational training programs to the 1,500 men who make up its resident population. These programs and the number of inmates in each include the following:

Air conditioning/heating: twenty

Auto technology: thirteen

Carpentry: twenty-five

Cabling: twelve

Welding: twenty-five

The programs enroll about 7 percent of the institution's population, just below the national average. Another 120 men are taking employability training classes.

PRISON REHABILITATION: THERAPY

When some people think of rehabilitation in prison, they think specifically of **therapy,** a treatment process intended to cure the prisoner of criminal behavior. Such programs do go on in prison, but they are not as plentiful or as important as outsiders might think. If you asked most prisoners what kind of therapy they had been getting since they entered prison, they would either look at you in disbelief or laugh out loud. Therapy is narrow and limited to the most disordered or the lucky few who fall into the slots available. Most prisoners never take part in any type of formal therapy program while they are incarcerated; if they do, it is most likely because they have been identified as falling into one of two groups of special needs offenders: substance abusers or the mentally ill. Sex offenders have also received much more attention as a special treatment category over the past decade or so.

Therapy programs in prison have often been classified as two types:

1. **Psychological therapy,** which deals with the mental state, or **psyche,** of one individual person, especially in regard to motivation
2. **Social therapy,** which concentrates on the relationship between the individual and the people around him

Different therapists, typically with backgrounds in psychology and sociology, have devised **treatment modalities** for the application of their ideas to human subjects in the world at large. Some therapists then take these modalities and apply them to men and women in prison. They recognize the problems with both the "clientele" and the environment, and some therapists refuse to treat criminals as long as they remain in the prison setting. Others have dedicated their life's work to this specific population. We will take a brief look at the most common of these treatment modalities, bearing in mind that they are far more complex than we can get into in this introduction.

Psychotherapy is one option not heavily used in corrections. Most people probably associate Sigmund Freud's **psychoanalysis** (literally the analysis of the psyche) with this form of intervention. It is "talk therapy" and involves one-on-one counseling over an extended period of time. When you look at the hourly rate that private patients pay psychiatrists and psychologists for therapy sessions, you can understand why prisons do not put ordinary inmates into long-term individualized treatment. The MDs and PhDs who work in prison are concerned mostly with diagnosis and treatment plans that will be carried out by others, such as social workers or counselors, and much more often in a group rather than an individual approach.

The perfect psychoanalysis patient has been described by the acronym YAVIS: young, attractive, verbal, intelligent, and successful. Women are also said to make better patients. Other than young, prisoners do not match this stereotype. Prisoners in general are also not known for placing trust—the essence of the patient/therapist relationship in psychotherapy—in "shrinks" who treat "bugs." Some recidivism studies have suggested that prisoners who go through psychotherapy do *worse* than others treated less intensively. This is probably not true. The few prisoners treated with this approach were more disordered to begin with; their high recidivism rates meant simply that they were "less amenable to treatment," as the therapists say.

Another form of therapy that is individual but more humanistic in its approach is **client-centered therapy,** sometimes referred to as Rogerian therapy in applying the principles of Carl Rogers. In this approach, the therapist is a guide as the patient seeks self-understanding. The therapist is supposed to be warm, friendly, understanding, and nonjudgmental. The objective is supposed to be on the positive aspects of the person's life rather than the negative. Some have said this puts the therapist in the position of being the "older brother" or the "cheerleader" for criminals who are often manipulative, violent, or otherwise not very positive folks. They furthermore typically have to live in an environment that is anathema to the positive values the therapist is trying to instill in them.

Behavior modification, in which Edward Thorndike and B. F. Skinner are central figures, emphasizes behavior or conditioning rather than attitudes or self-enlightenment. Its objective is to produce desirable behavior through the strict application of punishments and rewards. One version of this would be **operant conditioning,** which uses highly structured routine, rigorous monitoring, token economies, and earned privileges as rewards. It is often used in prison honor blocks and in juvenile group homes on the outside. Inmates tend to do well within its structure, but problems occur when they are removed from this environment and have to function independently—get up, go to work, go to school, take care of their chores, and perform the routine tasks of daily life without close monitoring and the use of immediate punishments and rewards.

Another version of behavior modification is **aversive conditioning,** which is not favored in Western prisons because of its association, in extreme forms, with **brainwashing.** This approach is illustrated in an article that James V. McConnell, professor of psychology at the University of Michigan, published in *Psychology Today* in April 1970. In the article, titled "Brainwashing the Criminals," Dr. McConnell wrote,

> I believe the day has come when we can combine sensory deprivation with drugs, hypnosis, and astute manipulation of reward and punishment to gain almost absolute control over an individual's behavior. . . . We'd assume that a felony was clear evidence that the criminal had somehow acquired full-blown social neurosis and needed to be cured, not punished. . . . We'd probably have to restructure his entire personality.[28]

Jessica Mitford, in her chapter "Clockwork Orange" (referring to the title of the Anthony Burgess novel and Stanley Kubrick film about "resocializing criminals") in *Kind and Usual Punishment: The Prison Business* (1974), describes the control techniques being applied in some American prisons at the time:

1. **Sensory deprivation:** confinement in sterile "adjustment centers" with no activities for long periods of time
2. **Stress assessment:** complete lack of privacy, often combined with sleep deprivation, to promote conflict and see how much the prisoner can stand without losing his temper
3. **Chemotherapy:** the use of drugs to control behavior
4. **Aversion therapy:** the use of physical pain and fear, through such techniques as electric shock and drug injection, to modify behavior
5. **Neurosurgery:** brain surgery to reduce aggressiveness[29]

One such experimental treatment in California prisons involved injecting violent inmates with the drug Anectine, derived from the curare poison of South America. When injected with the drug, prisoners lost control of all voluntary muscles, which meant they would stop breathing for up to two minutes at a time, creating sensations of suffocation and drowning. While in this "brink of death" state, therapists would warn the prisoner to avoid violence or face more of the same.[30]

Aversive conditioning programs of this type were generally ruled unconstitutional in the courts by around the mid-1970s and went out of fashion with the demise of the rehabilitation model. Some programs of this sort, using drugs and negative stimuli, have been resurrected in recent years for the specific treatment of sex offenders but not for the general treatment of violent or habitual criminals.

Of the various types of social therapies, **group therapy** is the most commonly employed in the most varying forms. It begins with a group—perhaps eight to twelve persons—and a facilitator trained to guide group discussions. The members of the group can be crime specific or diverse—drug abusers, for instance, or residents of a particular dormitory. The group starts together and stays together during regular meetings over a period of time. One of the guiding principles of group therapy is that "what is said in group stays in group." This is an attempt to create solidarity among the members and reduce the likelihood that any revelations in group would be shared with outsiders in the general population.

Groups may be guided by many different approaches or modalities, some much more rigorously applied than others. In general, the idea is to move the group through a series of stages, from introduction (or security) to trust (in each other) to responsibility (for one's actions) to work (on one's problems) to closing, in one example. Groups may be more directive or more open ended by what they allow to go on in their sessions.

Group therapy is recommended in corrections for several reasons. It is more cost effective than individual treatment. The therapist does not have to be trained to the doctoral level. It is very flexible in its content and adaptable to the environment. It also benefits from the peer feedback: "you can't con a con," or so the cons say, meaning that prisoners who lie or pretend to fool therapists cannot as easily pull the same tricks with other prisoners. There is no particular evidence that this is true, but convicts always like to think that they are better judges of the true character of other criminals than noncriminals may be.

Three other forms of social therapy are prevalent:

1. **Transactional analysis.** Eric Berne and his colleagues developed a form of therapy based on communication patterns, particularly our self-images as we think others see us, and life scripts, why people are consistent in their behavior, especially in repeating the same mistakes. In Berne's *Games People Play* and Thomas Harris's *I'm Okay, You're Okay*, transactional analysis concentrated on the barriers that prevent effective communication between adults. These theories were influential in prisons during the 1970s but declined in importance later.

2. **Reality therapy.** Based on the work of William Glasser in California, reality therapy has several features attractive to the prison setting. It focuses on behavior rather than motivation: "What are you doing," not "Why are you doing that?" It teaches that you accept your past but not be controlled by it. "Get over it" would be a useful phrase. It emphasizes three Rs important to good conduct in prison or on the street: reality, responsibility, and right and wrong. This approach has sometimes been called commonsense therapy, in which the therapist is trying to get the prisoner to assess his or her own behavior and figure out how to change it.

3. **Therapeutic communities.** The therapeutic community (TC) is a treatment group sharing a common affliction and living together in a close-knit, family-like environment somewhat insulated from outside influences. Developed originally in British psychiatric hospitals after World War II to be applied to mentally ill veterans, its American prototype was Synanon, a community of former addicts and ex-offenders in California. Under the leadership of Charles Dietrich, Synanon passed from being a therapeutic community to a social movement to a religious group to disintegration in the early 1990s. In a recent article, Douglas Lipton described the model of therapeutic communities that developed in the United States:

> The U.S. model uses the **community of peers** and role models as change agents rather than professional clinicians and trained correctional officers, and it is less democratic in operation and more hierarchical in structure. The U.S. model also is less psychiatric (and less medical) in origin, emerging from a recovered client self-help background. Thus, American therapeutic communities (also called concept-based therapeutic communities) generally subscribe to a self-help, social learning model approach and holistic human change perspective.[31]

After a period of decline, therapeutic communities were reborn in the mid-1990s when treatment alternatives for drug criminals began to be politically popular again. Whether found in special housing units within larger prisons or in community-based residential facilities, TCs have been very effective in using positive peer pressure to control the behavior of their residents. Research has shown that substance-abusing offenders taking part in TCs are less likely to recidivate than offenders pursuing individual therapies. Problems occur, however, when residents have to leave the supportive environment and make it on their own. This has led to the creation of long-term therapeutic communities in some places, such as the Delancey Street Foundation in San Francisco, which operates several private businesses, including a restaurant on the Embarcadero, and houses and employs about a thousand ex-convicts and homeless people for an average stay of two to four years or longer.

QUESTIONS ABOUT REHABILITATION

In asking "What works?" as the preface to his evaluation of rehabilitation, Robert Martinson seemed to be hoping not for the elimination of rehabilitation programs in prison but rather for the abolition—or at least the minimalization—of the use of imprisonment as a sanction. He reasoned that if the purpose of imprisonment was to rehabilitate criminals and it was failing in this mission, then we should reject imprisonment as a change agent and seek something more effective, such as community-based alternatives. Although Martinson's argument was adopted by those who wanted to do less to help prisoners and more to make prisons meaner in spirit, that was not his original argument at all. He wanted to see the prison system vastly reduced in size.

Many of the critics of rehabilitation in the 1970s shared this point of view. They made two main arguments against rehabilitation in prison. First, rehabilitation did not really work appropriately in the high-custody environment of the time, when fortress-style prisoners predominated and most prisoners were still held in higher-custody grades. The nature of the custodial institution—its rules, its oppressiveness, and its brutality and depersonalization—seemed to undercut the positive effects of intervention. Second, the programs that prisons could offer could not really be matched to the individual prisoner. Some prisoners were not suited for rehabilitation, at least not in present time, and others had multiple needs that single-purpose programs did not effectively address.

In the 1970s, these criticisms led to an emphasis on **reintegration** as an alternative to prison-based rehabilitation. Reintegration was community based; it kept offenders out of prison, avoiding the negative effects of imprisonment, and it allowed criminals to take part in a more diverse set of programs (at least in theory) than what they would find in prison. Thus, for a few years, even while the number of convicted criminals under supervision was increasing, the prison population stayed down because more of them were being dealt with through probation, parole, halfway houses, and other community-based programs. Furloughs for education and work release were also common in this era.

But then researchers began to note that the community-based interventions were no more effective and sometimes were even less effective (because they tended to be focused on younger offenders who have higher recidivism rates) than imprisonment. Then, the crime control decade of the 1980s arrived, and the shift from nonsecure alternatives to secure custody began in earnest. Both rehabilitation and reintegration went out of fashion.

Scholars continued to study rehabilitation, however, focusing not so much on broad policy initiatives but on specific features of individual programs that appeared to be successful. The reasoning was that no single form of intervention is going to "cure" criminal behavior. Criminals are far too different (and many of them far too opposed to being cured) for any one measure to have remarkable across-the-board impact. The definition of success has also been defined more realistically. If the three-year recidivism rate for a control group of similar offenders is 48 percent and the rate for the group completing this particular program is 36 percent, is this a successful program? Very much so. The recidivism rate has been reduced by a fourth, resulting in great economic savings when every prisoner costs $20,000 or $25,000 per year to confine, and public safety is increased because (we hope) some of the criminals are much less criminally active on their release from custody.

Paul Gendreau, a Canadian psychology professor, has long been among the adherents of practical rehabilitation programs. Gendreau has emphasized the positive influence of directing intensive services to high-risk offenders, the matching of offenders and intervention, the importance of disrupting criminal networks and providing relapse prevention, and the value of advocacy and brokerage services. He has identified **principles of ineffective intervention,** which include traditional psychodynamic therapies, nondirective relationship-oriented therapies, radical nonintervention (leaving the criminal alone), traditional medical model approaches, the use of intensive services with low-risk offenders, and clinical approaches that encourage externalizing blame to parents and others, venting anger or ignoring the impact of their crimes on the victims.[32]

Gendreau has also been among the critics of the so-called **punishing smarter** strategies, which he says are no more effective long-term than traditional interventions. These new or faddish interventions include boot camps, electronic monitoring, longer periods of incarceration, urinalysis, humiliation, and shock incarceration. Many of these options are politically popular and more likely to receive scarce state or federal funding, but Gendreau's findings, supported by other research, illustrate the frustration of many observers that programs receive political support more for the appearance than the reality of working.[33]

Kaye McLaren, policy and research analyst with the New Zealand Department of Justice, has also studied what works in correctional interventions. She says that successful interventions share certain common components and that together these components form a set of principles of effectiveness that can be applied to many types of intervention in both institutional and community settings. McLaren lists **principles of effectiveness:**

1. A social learning approach that assumes attitudes and behavior can change if noncriminal attitudes and behaviors are introduced and reinforced
2. Clear, consistent rules and sanctions to make legal sanctions certain and understandable
3. Illustration of and support for noncriminal attitudes and behaviors
4. Practical problem-solving skills
5. Positive links between community and program resources
6. Relationships between staff and offenders that are open, emphatic, warm, trusting, and encouraging of noncriminal attitudes and behaviors
7. Advocacy for offenders and brokerage with community resources
8. Use of ex-offenders as positive role models
9. Offenders' involvement with the design of specific interventions
10. Staff focus on strengthening prosocial and noncriminal behavior rather than stopping antisocial and criminal behavior
11. Offender peer groups directed toward reinforcing prosocial and noncriminal behavior
12. Sound theoretical knowledge and adequate resources to apply appropriate principles of effectiveness
13. Multiple methods of intervention rather than reliance on narrowly based interventions

14. Emphasis on relapse prevention and self-efficacy
15. Matching individual offenders with specific interventions[34]

McLaren has noted that none of these principles is set in stone, yet they do provide direction for program design that is based on experience and has passed some evaluative muster. "When it comes to putting offenders in programs," McLaren said, "it's a case of one size doesn't fit all." She recommended three approaches to offender placement: "Put offenders in programs that address problems they actually have, put offenders with more severe problems into more intensive programs, and choose programs that fit what's known about the most effective way to impact a given problem."[35]

In its 2003 report "Programs That Help Inmates Stay Out of Prison," the MTC Institute similarly reviewed principles of effective programming, principles that it maintains can reduce recidivism by 25 to 40 percent. These are divided into two principal categories—educational and substance abuse treatment:

Educational Program Principles

1. *Outcome focus.* Formal education must be focused on specific outcomes, including GEDs and vocational certificates.
2. *Duration and intensity.* Formal education programs must be of appropriate duration and continuity—at a minimum six months or more of daily classes.
3. *Certified curricula and instructors.* Educators and instructors must be certified.
4. *Early assessment.* A formal assessment of the offender on arrival is necessary.

Substance Abuse Treatment Program Principles

1. *Structured and intensive.* Treatment programming is highly structured and intensive.
2. *Cognitive focus.* Treatment has a cognitive focus, meaning an emphasis on thoughts and behaviors associated with drug use and crime.
3. *Assessment guides treatment.* Offender assessment guides programming types and intensity.
4. *Duration and continuity.* Structured substance abuse treatment programs must be of appropriate duration and continuity.
5. *Aftercare.* The program includes an aftercare component that continues after release into the community.[36]

THE "NEW" REHABILITATION

How have prison rehabilitation programs changed over the past generation, from the rejection of the rehabilitation ideology during the 1970s to the resurrection of rehabilitation in the first years of the twenty-first century? We want to briefly touch on five major features of the "new" rehabilitation:

1. Substance abuse treatment
2. Thinking patterns
3. Faith-based programs

4. Work

5. The whole-person concept

We have already looked at the alcohol and drug abuse histories of men and women prisoners and the nature of programs used to treat them in prison in chapters 9 and 11. Many states are taking a close look at expanding substance abuse treatment within prisons, acknowledging that untreated substance abusers have very high failure rates when discharged from prison; generic treatment programs have fared little better.

A program initiated in Delaware in the late 1980s provides a contrasting approach. Delaware's substance abuse rehabilitation program follows three stages. In the first, about a hundred prisoners are pulled together into a separate housing unit away from the rest of the inmate population. Once there, they undergo three kinds of therapy: behavioral, cognitive, and emotional. Treatment continues through stage 2, six months of work release at an outreach center. In phase 3, participants are involved in a six-month aftercare program. They participate in a two-hour group session each week and receive individual counseling and urine testing for drugs. The dropout rate for this program is high—about a third—but the recidivism rate (measured by arrests within eighteen months) was only 27 percent compared to 56 percent among general population releasees.[37] Many other states are considering intensive substance abuse treatment, even if it costs an extra $5,000 to $10,000 per inmate per year, as ultimately being cheaper than the effects of crimes committed by those not receiving treatment.

Therapy in prison has traditionally been **nondirective therapy;** that is, it deals with people's problems and feelings and sense of self-worth. Recent therapy has been more cognitive in nature. It tends to focus more on how people think and how thinking controls behavior or actions. One influential theory is Lawrence Kohlberg's **moral development** theory. Kohlberg believed that people progress in their moral reasoning—in their bases for ethical behavior—through a series of stages. He identified six stages divided into three levels, which can be outlined in this manner:

Level	Stage	Social Orientation
Preconventional	1	Obedience and punishment
	2	Individualism, instrumentalism, and exchange
Conventional	3	"Good boy/good girl"
	4	Law and order
Post-conventional	5	Social contract
	6	Principled conscience[38]

People move through these stages, developing morally through social interaction. Kohlberg believed that most people never reach the higher stages. Prisoners, we would think, start off at a low stage, typically stage 1, and have to be moved along one stage at a time to develop a higher sense of morality. They do this through open discussion of moral dilemmas in a formal classroom setting, like a philosophy class or what Kohlberg called the **moral discussion approach.**[39] In prison you might call it "ethics for convicts": confronting prisoners with complicated moral situations, getting them to discuss their responses, and making them think about how their conduct affects other people.

Another contemporary treatment approach is **cognitive therapy,** which assumes that faulty thought processes and beliefs create problem behaviors and emotions. The most influential cognitive therapists in programs treating criminals are Albert Ellis and Aaron Beck. Ellis's **rational-emotive behavior therapy** follows what he calls an A-B-C approach to defeating negative or irrational beliefs: (A) an activating event, usually a negative stimulus of some kind; (B) the belief system, which is the person's interpretation of the experience; and (C) the emotional consequence, which leads to problem behaviors.[40] Beck's approach is even more geared toward real experiences, as opposed to just talk or self-expression, to help people avoid the behaviors that come from their destructive cognitions.[41] His approach is often called **cognitive-behavior therapy.**

SMART Recovery has attracted recent attention in its application of cognitive therapy to prisoners. This nonprofit program is often cited as an alternative to the religion-based twelve-step approaches of Alcoholics Anonymous and Narcotics Anonymous, both longtime prison self-help staples. SMART (which stands for Self Management and Recovery Training) defines its purpose as supporting individuals abstaining from addictive behavior by teaching how to change self-defeating thinking, emotions, and actions and to work toward long-term satisfactions and quality of life. Its approach does the following:

1. Teaches self-empowerment and self-reliance
2. Works on addictions/compulsions as complex maladaptive behaviors with possible physiological factors
3. Teaches tools and techniques for self-directed change
4. Encourages individuals to recover and live satisfying lives
5. Relies on meetings that are educational and include open discussions
6. Advocates the appropriate use of prescribed medications and psychological treatments
7. Evolves as scientific knowledge evolves[42]

Starting in the community in 1994, SMART began to be applied in prisons in 1997 through a program called InsideOut. Used most extensively in Arizona prisons, SMART is more structured, directive, and technological than Alcoholics Anonymous; it emphasizes **empowerment** and problem solving where Alcoholics Anonymous emphasizes powerlessness and the need to believe in a higher power. For people who do not have religious beliefs and do not plan to get any—and even for believers who seek a more defined educational program—InsideOut is an attractive alternative.[43]

At the opposite pole from SMART's admittedly secular approach are the **faith-based programs** developing in several states, most notably Texas. In 1997, the **InnerChange Freedom Initiative** (IFI) was given about half the beds of the Texas's Carol Vance prison to operate as a Christian prison. Prison ministries are nothing new, and one of the biggest ministries is that of former attorney and Watergate felon Charles Colson, the Prison Fellowship Ministries, sponsor of IFI. Prisoners have to be within eighteen months of release to be sent to the facility. They must be volunteers for IFI placement, as are staff, who must be practicing Christians themselves. The concept is to operate a prison as a Christian community. The warden of the facility, Jack Cowley, who was previously a warden in Oklahoma, says it seemed very strange for him to see—and encourage—inmates and staff to give each other hugs.[44] But that kind of personal contact goes on frequently in a Christian prison.

Not everyone agrees that this is a good concept, especially because public tax dollars are being used to fund the operation. Several groups supporting the separation of church and state argue that prison programs should not be used to indoctrinate prisoners into particular religious beliefs. They also argue that in the multicultural United States, with its mix of many different cultures and religions, it is unfair to non-Christians, such as Muslims, Jews, or others. This opposition, which is countered by support for faith-based initiatives in the George W. Bush White House, has not stopped interest in this approach from spreading to other states. Prison ministries are more active in working inside prisons than they have been since the early days of the penitentiary, and more states are looking at setting up faith-based housing units—looking at them as another type of therapeutic community. IFI is just beginning to get long-term recidivism statistics. The results are mixed, suggesting that the program itself—sixteen months in-house and six months in the community after release—may not be as important as the Christian motivation it takes to get into the program in the first place. But its proponents continue to expect that "something good is going to happen here" (to put it in an evangelical phrase).

So far, we have addressed thinking patterns and religious beliefs, which are obviously two key components of change. But when inmates hit the free world full of the spirit and with their minds right, what is the first thing they need? If they are going to stay out very long, the answer has to be "a job." If the ex-prisoner cannot find lawful work soon after his or her release, the odds of staying out of trouble very long are slim. When money runs out and friends and relatives get tired of footing the bill, ex-convicts find it easier to reenter the underground economy—crime.

How does the need for work in society relate to work in prison? Most prisoners are not doing much to either earn money or improve their employability while they are doing prison time. Some writers have asserted that prison unemployment rates, which are officially said to be in the range of 30 to 40 percent, are more correctly closer to 90 percent since, according to 1990 statistics, only about 7 percent of prisoners worked in manufacturing and another 4 percent in agriculture (most of these in California, Louisiana, Texas, and a few other southern states). The bulk of the prisoners who are working— 41 percent in 1990—are doing in-house chores—food service, laundry, groundskeeping, dorm maintenance, warehouse work, and so on. About 9 percent of prisoners were enrolled in vocational training programs, and fewer than 1 percent were going outside the prison on work release.

As chief justice of the U.S. Supreme Court in the 1980s, Warren Burger proposed that prison be turned into **factories with fences,** providing prisoners with education, vocational training, and work skills necessary to make a living after release. Since then, the percentage of prisoners working has actually declined, overwhelmed by the tremendous increase in prison population.

What is holding back the productive use of prison labor, including both prison industries and private sector employers? Three principal objections have emerged over time:

1. *It takes jobs away from workers outside prison.* This argument has been made by labor unions and their supporters going all the way back to the days of the industrial prison.

2. *It is a form of "slave labor."* Prison activists conjure up images of labor camps in totalitarian countries.

3. *If it involves work release in any form, it is dangerous to public safety.* Victims' rights groups and politicians have often opposed prisoners working among free people, although this is where 95 percent or more of all prisoners will eventually end up seeking employment.

The principal current means for expanding employment opportunities for prisoners is the **Prison Industry Enhancement (PIE) Certification Program.** The PIE Program was created by the Justice System Improvement Act of 1979. It has been expanded twice subsequently. The program is designed to place inmates in a realistic work environment, pay them the prevailing local wage for similar work, and enable them to acquire marketable skills to increase their potential for successful rehabilitation and meaningful employment on release. Corrections departments are allowed to take deductions from prisoners' wages to pay for room and board, taxes, family support, and crime victim compensation. To meet certification requirements, the employer—public or private—must pay prevailing wages, and the program must not displace nonprison workers.

Thirty-eight states were certified to operate PIE programs by the end of 2003. About 200 individual programs were in operation. Most of these were small, employing a total of 4,650 workers, over half of them in just five states: South Carolina (753), Kansas (472), Texas (466), Indiana (397), and Washington (314). Thus, although you may hear noises about increasing employment opportunities for prisoners within prisons, the fact is that less than one-half of 1 percent of inmates are working in PIE-certified programs. California alone has more inmates cleaning toilets than this.

If real work is out (and it is, for the most part), prisons can still teach **workability skills** relating to seeking and finding employment after release. These skills are often taught as part of the **whole-person approach** intended to address multiple needs in a prisoner approaching release. The concept is to make the last six months or so before release a period of intensive programming, aiming for the type of transformation discussed earlier that would bring about habilitation. Prison programs of the past were often criticized for addressing either single needs or the wrong needs, so the whole-person approach attempts to remake the criminal by attacking his or her problems on several fronts simultaneously.

Louisiana's prison boot camp program IMPACT (for Intensive Motivational Program of Alternative Correctional Treatment) is an example of a program taking the whole-person approach. The incarceration phase, which lasts six to nine months, emphasizes discipline, physical conditioning, community service, and, most important, combined therapeutic regimes—substance abuse, values reorientation, self-discipline and responsibility, parenting skills, basic life skills, and education. It is a rigorous program with a high dropout rate, but the successful completers have much lower recidivism rates than the general inmate population.

Louisiana tried a similar approach in another program, **Project Metamorphosis,** from 1997 to 2001. Using a Life Skills Grant from the federal Office of Vocational and Adult Education, three prisons set up intensive prerelease programming for inmates in two men's and one women's prison. The goal was to reduce recidivism by increasing vocational, cognitive, and employability skills and postrelease employment and wage rates.[45] The three-year recidivism rates for inmates completing Project Metamorphosis was about five percentage points lower than that of general population inmates not completing the program. But when federal funding expired in 2001, the program was discontinued.

Missouri has conducted a broad-based whole-person program called **Parallel Universe.** Its premise is that life inside prison would resemble life outside prison, so inmates can acquire the values, habits, and skills needed to function as productive, law-abiding citizens on their release.[46] As a corrections-based reentry program, Parallel Universe has four interactive elements:

1. Offenders participate, during work and nonwork hours, in productive activities that parallel those found in free society. During the workday, offenders attend school and go to work and, if applicable, participate in treatment for sex offenses, chronic mental health problems, and drug and alcohol dependency. During nonworking hours, inmates participate in community service, reparative activities, religious programs, and recreation.
2. Offenders achieve sobriety and adopt relapse prevention strategies to stop the recurrence of antisocial thoughts.
3. Offenders make decisions for which they are accountable.
4. Offenders earn recognition for good conduct and improve their status by adhering to agency rules and regulations.

The reconviction rate of discharged offenders in Missouri fell sharply (from 33 percent in 1994 to 19 percent in 2001) after Parallel Universe was established as a requirement for offenders leaving the prison system.[47]

Although these programs, focused on specific work, cognitive, and substance abuse needs of prisoners, appear to hold promise in changing behavior and reducing recidivism, scholars still have lingering concerns about the effectiveness and fairness of rehabilitation—old and new. In an article in *Criminal Justice Ethics*, Andrew von Hirsch and Lisa Maher discuss several of these concerns:

1. *Amenability.* Rehabilitation works best with selected inmates who want to change; these screened inmates are then placed in specific programs intended to address their needs. Generic programs applied to general populations do not appear to be any more effective than they were in the past.
2. *Resources.* The programs that succeed tend to be well funded, well staffed, and vigorously implemented in an experimental setting.
3. *Humaneness.* Treatment of offenders is really directed toward crime desistance or prevention, not humanitarian concerns. Treatment is not necessarily gentle or "caring" in its approach, and it can be downright oppressive.
4. *Blameworthiness.* How should treatment amenability be balanced with punishment for reprehensible behavior? Should a treatably responsive murderer be released quicker than an uncooperative armed robber whose response to treatment is "Go f——k yourself"?[48]

Von Hirsch and Maher write, "The most dangerous temptation is to treat the treatment ethos as a kind of edifying fiction" in which goodwill justifies any necessary means of treatment. They argue that proportionality, dealing with matters of equity and the diminution of suffering, should remain much more important in criminal sentencing than any inspired hope in the new rehabilitation.[49]

THE LATEST ON RECIDIVISM

With or without rehabilitation, recidivism remains (or should remain) an important component of crime control policy. Do we know more about recidivism than when Martin wrote "nothing works" three decades ago? Is anything—rehabilitation or anything else—effective in reducing reincarceration?

The most recent national survey on recidivism is Patrick Langan and David Levin's "Recidivism of Prisoners Released in 1994," a Bureau of Justice Statistics Special Report published in June 2002. This study tracked 272,000 felony inmates for three years after their release from prison in fifteen states in 1994. This study also compares to a previous bureau study tracking 108,000 prisoners released in eleven states in 1983.

Langan and Levin used the four measures to calculate recidivism rates:

1. *Rearrest.* An estimated 67.5 percent of the released prisoners were rearrested for a new crime (either a felony or serious misdemeanor) within three years.

2. *Reconviction.* A total of 46.9 percent were reconvicted in state or federal court for a new crime (felony or misdemeanor).

3. *Resentence.* Over a quarter—25.4 percent—were back in prison as a result of another prison sentence.

4. *Return to prison with or without a new sentence.* A total of 51.8 percent were back in prison because of a new sentence or because of a violation of conditional release, such as by rearrest, failing a drug test, or absconding on parole. More were returned to prison for release violations—26.4 percent—than for new sentences.[50] This figure is thrown out of balance by California's inclusion in the survey. California has a high rate of returns to prison for failing drug tests and other release violations. Because its number of prisoners released is the largest of any of the survey states, its practices significantly alter these statistics—the return rate would fall to 40.1 percent without California.

For each of the four measures, men had recidivism rates about ten percentage points higher than women, blacks had recidivism rates five to ten points higher than whites, and non-Hispanics had rates about five points higher than Hispanics. Recidivism rates vary sharply with age. Over 80 percent of those under age eighteen were rearrested, compared to 45.3 percent of those forty-five or older.[51] Other studies have shown that this steady decline continues from middle age into old age, making age at release the single best predictor of recidivism. Federal prisoners also appear to have much lower recidivism rates than state prisoners—about 16 percent returning to federal custody in comparison to the 51 percent returning to state custody—but the federal figures do not include ex-federal prisoners who end up in state prisons.

The crime is important also. Released property offenders had the highest recidivism rates. An estimated 73.8 percent of property offenders were rearrested within three years, compared to 66.7 percent of drug offenders, 62.2 percent of public order offenders, and 61.7 percent of violent offenders. By specific crimes, Langan and Levin reported these rearrest rates:

Motor vehicle theft	78.8 percent
Possessing/selling stolen property	77.4 percent
Larceny	74.6 percent
Burglary	74.0 percent
Robbery	70.2 percent
Weapons violations	70.2 percent
Assault	65.1 percent
Drug trafficking	64.2 percent
Arson	57.7 percent
Driving under the influence	51.5 percent
Rape	46.0 percent
Homicide	40.7 percent[52]

The crime-specific observations of Langan and Levin's study are enlightening. For example, within three years, about 2.5 percent of released rapists were rearrested for another rape, and 1.2 percent of released murderers were rearrested for another homicide. But of the released prisoners, those convicted of auto theft were most likely to be arrested for a new murder, and murderers were most likely to be arrested for theft and had a zero likelihood of being arrested for rape. Rapists and other sexual assault prisoners are among the **criminal specialists,** so called because they are more likely to be rearrested for the same offense, but murderers, public order offenders, and drug offenders were much less specialized.[53]

Most felony prisoners are not one-time offenders. The 272,000 released prisoners had accumulated 4,100,000 arrest charges (an average of fifteen each) before their current prison term, and 744,000 charges (2.75 each on average) within three years of release. Prisoners with fifteen or more prior arrests had an 82.1 percent rearrest rate, while those with just one prior arrest (who are very likely to be violent offenders) had a 40.6 rearrest rate. Those who had been in prison two or more times had a rearrest rate about ten points higher (73.5 to 63.8 percent) than those serving their first prison sentence. Langan and Levin reported, "The pattern here is clear: the longer the prior record, the greater the likelihood that the recidivating prisoner will commit another crime soon after release."[54]

In his commentary on the 1983 and 1994 surveys, prison journalist Douglas Dennis points out that recidivism rates increased during the decade of the 1990s, which would seem to undercut notions that new rehabilitation programs are more effective. But much of the higher rate is due to tougher supervision of parolees on the street and higher rates of return after new arrests and technical violations. Most state studies show three-year return-to-prison recidivism rates in the range of 35 to 45 percent, with half or more being new convictions and the rest release violations. Louisiana's five-year recidivism rate averaged about 45 percent in the 1980s and just over 50 percent in the 1990s.[55]

Dennis points out that murderers and sex criminals are the best release risks. He also indicates that failure often comes early. "An ex-con's first year out is the toughest, and most critical to success. Two-thirds of those rearrested were rearrested during the first year, which also produced the highest conviction and reimprisonment rates of the three-year period."[56] During their first year out, 39.1 percent of the 1983 releasees were rearrested compared to 44.1 percent of the 1994 group.

Dennis comments,

> The average released prisoner has little education, lacks job skills or a sound work history, and has no money or possessions beyond a few bucks in his pocket and what he can carry in a paper bag. That, and a stigma riding his back like an 800-pound gorilla. To most people, an ex-con is toxic waste. Nobody wants to hire them, house them, or feed them. A survey of employers in five large cities found that 65 percent would not knowingly hire an ex-convict. Their families are often less than enthusiastic about their return. They seem doomed to fail, a fact that has lately begun to arouse concern.
>
> Prison isn't enough, no matter how many educational, vo-tech or rehabilitative programs might be available. "Reentry" or "after-care" assistance for the 600,000+ prisoners released annually—work-release, job counseling, substance-abuse and anger-management programs, temporary residential care, assistance with job placement, and so forth—is now regarded as essential to public safety.[57]

The state of Florida, one of the fifteen states in Langan and Levin's report, recently completed its own more detailed study of recidivism. This report, "Recidivism Report: Inmates Released from Florida Prison July 1995 to June 2001," tracks almost 100,000 prisoners. It not only tabulates recidivism rates but also evaluates those factors most related to recidivism. Research indicated that in Florida the three-year reimprisonment rate was about 25.7 percent; after five years, it had climbed to 36.9 percent.[58]

In looking at eighteen different factors relating to the prisoner's demographics, criminal history, and record in custody (but not rehabilitation programs completed), the report indicated that for both males and females, the two most influential factors on both reoffending and reimprisonment are prior recidivism and age at release, in that order. Lower tested education levels were also important for males but not so important for females.

Five factors *raise* both reoffending and reimprisonment rates for males and females:

1. Disciplinary reports (more)—especially for female reoffending
2. Prior recidivism (more)—especially for females and for reimprisonment
3. Burglary (worst crime)—especially for females and for reimprisonment
4. Property crimes (more)—especially for males
5. Drug crimes (more)—especially for females

Seven factors *lower* both reoffending and reimprisonment for males and females:

1. Age (older)—especially for female reimprisonment
2. Ethnicity (Hispanic)—especially for female reoffending

3. Custody (low)—especially for males
4. Time in prison (more)—especially for female reoffending
5. Education level (higher)—especially for reimprisonment
6. Homicide (worst crime)—especially for reoffending
7. Sex/lewdness (worst crime)—especially for reoffending and for females

Six factors have *mixed* effects on reoffending and reimprisonment or between males and females:

1. Race (black)—raises recidivism for males but lowers for females
2. Custody (high)—raises recidivism for males but lowers for females
3. Supervision after release—lowers reoffending but raises reimprisonment
4. Robbery (worst crime)—raises reimprisonment but not reoffending
5. Other violent (worst crime)—raises reimprisonment but lowers reoffending
6. Weapons crimes (more)—lowers female reoffending only[59]

It is important to note that these factors apply to prisoners generally and should not be seen as deterministic in their application to individuals. Or as a prisoner once put it, "We can predict with certainty that we are going to die, but we cannot predict when and how, unless we're on death row." Likewise, we can predict that younger property criminals with bad prior records and higher disciplinary violation rates will have higher recidivism rates than older, violent, first offenders with good conduct records, but we cannot be certain which persons in each group will succeed or fail, nor can we tell how prison rehabilitation programs or other factors not evaluated in the Florida study—such as substance abuse history, family support, and postrelease financial assistance—might affect reoffending and reimprisonment.

If recidivism is likened to a science, in which different factors are correlated to produce a predictable result, then rehabilitation is the artistic element (even though it is said to be scientific and behavioral in nature) that throws off these calculations and makes them more difficult to predict. The bad killer with a lifetime criminal history can find God, get an education, get out of prison, become a minister, and spend the rest of his life trying to save the souls of other criminals, while his former cell mate, a burglar, returns to a life of crime and ends up on death row for killing a minister during a botched burglary. How would you predict either outcome? People live their lives, and things happen. For prisoners, rehabilitation is a part of the mix, but it is only one part and too often not the driving force in their lives once they return to the street.

KEY TERMS

rehabilitation	rehabilitation era	nothing works	recidivism
desistance	scientific penology	silver bullet	recidivists
habilitation	Elmira System	forced rehabilitation	rearrest
reformation	medical model	crimogenic environment	reconviction
reformatory	Robert Martinson	balanced model	reimprisonment

reimprisonment for a
   new felony

creaming

model program

exportability

treatment effects

policy effects

planned intervention

black box

prisonization

Austin MacCormick

Correctional Education
   Association

individually prescribed
   instruction

educational release

Project Newgate

antieducation bias

certified training

Windham School District

therapy

psychological therapy

psyche

social therapy

treatment modalities

psychotherapy

psychoanalysis

client-centered therapy

behavior modification

operant conditioning

aversive conditioning

brainwashing

sensory deprivation

stress assessment

chemotherapy

aversion therapy

neurosurgery

group therapy

transactional analysis

reality therapy

therapeutic communities

community of peers

reintegration

principles of ineffective
   intervention

punishing smarter

principles of effectiveness

nondirective therapy

moral development

moral discussion
   approach

cognitive therapy

rational-emotive behavior
   therapy

cognitive-behavior
   therapy

SMART Recovery

empowerment

faith-based programs

InnerChange Freedom
   Initiative

factories with fences

Prison Industry
   Enhancement (PIE)
   Certification Program

workability skills

whole-person approach

Project Metamorphosis

Parallel Universe

criminal specialists

NOTES

1. Joycelyn Pollock, "Rehabilitation Revisited," in Joycelyn M. Pollock, *Prisons: Today and Tomorrow* (Gaithersburg, Md.: Aspen Publishers, 1997), p. 161.

2. Ibid.

3. American Correctional Association, *The American Prison: From the Beginning—A Pictorial History* (Gaithersburg, Md.: American Correctional Association, 1983), p. 71.

4. Ibid., p. 65.

5. John W. Roberts, *Reform and Retribution: An Illustrated History of American Prisons* (Lanham, Md.: American Correctional Association, 1997), p. 120.

6. Ibid., p. 169.

7. John P. Conrad, "What Prospects for Rehabilitation? A Dissent from Academic Wisdom," in Martin D. Schwartz, Todd R. Clear, and Lawrence F. Travis III, *Corrections: An Issues Approach* (Cincinnati: Anderson Publishing, 1980), p. 217.

8. Ibid., pp. 223–24.

9. Roberts, *Reform and Retribution*, p. 170.

10. Ibid.

11. Pollock, "Rehabilitation Revisited," p. 163.

12. Robert Martinson, "What Works? Questions and Answers about Prison Reform," *The Public Interest* 35 (spring 1974): 25.

13. Ibid., p. 49.

14. Douglas Lipton, Robert Martinson, and Judith Wilks, *The Effectiveness of Correctional Treatment: A Survey of Treatment Evaluation Studies* (New York: Praeger Publishers, 1975), p. 627.

15. Lee Sechrest, Susan O. White, and Elizabeth D. Brown, *The Rehabilitation of Criminal Offenders: Problems and Prospects* (Washington, D.C.: National Academy of Sciences Press, 1979), p. 5.

16. Robert Martinson, "New Findings, New Views: A Note of Caution Regarding Sentencing Reform," *Hofstra Law Review* 7 (1979): 244.

17. State of Minnesota, Office of the Legislative Auditor, "Many Adult Felons Commit New Offenses," January 13, 1997, *www.auditor.leg.state.mn.u./pe9701.htm*.

18. Martinson, "What Works?," pp. 44–46.

19. Sechrest et al., *The Rehabilitation of Criminal Offenders*, pp. 4–5.

20. Pollock, "Rehabilitation Revisited," p. 204.

21. Caroline Wolf Harlow, "Education and Correctional Populations," U.S. Department of Justice, Bureau

of Justice Statistics Special Report, January 2003, p. 3.

22. Ibid., p. 4.

23. Douglas Dennis, "Realities of Recidivism," *The Angolite*, September/October 2002, p. 31.

24. Thom Gehring, "Recidivism as a Measure of Correctional Education Program Success," *Journal of Correctional Education* 51, no. 2 (June 2000): 198–201.

25. Criminal Justice Policy Council, State of Texas, "An Overview of the Windham School District," February 2000, p. 4.

26. Ibid., p. 7

27. Ibid.

28. James V. McConnell, "Brainwashing the Criminals," *Psychology Today* 111 (April 1970): 11.

29. Jessica Mitford, *Kind and Usual Punishment: The Prison Business* (New York: Alfred A. Knopf, 1974), pp. 126–27.

30. Ibid., p. 128.

31. Douglas Lipton, "Therapeutic Communities: History, Effectiveness and Prospects," *Corrections Today* 60, no. 6 (October 1998): 107.

32. Russ Immarigeon, "What Works?" *Corrections Today* 57, no. 7 (December 1995): S3.

33. Ibid.

34. Ibid., p. S2.

35. Ibid., pp. S2–S3.

36. MTC Institute, "Programs That Help Inmates Stay Out of Prison: Growing Public Expectations," Management and Training Corporation, Centerville, Utah, November 2003, pp. 8–11.

37. "Program after Prison May Help Addicts," *State Legislatures* 23, no. 7 (July/August 1997): 9.

38. Robert N. Barger, "A Summary of Lawrence Kohlberg's Stages of Moral Development," 2000, *www.nd.edu?˜rbarger/kohlberg.html.*

39. Ibid.

40. Karen Huffman, *Psychology in Action*, 6th ed. (New York: John Wiley & Sons, 2002), pp. 538–39.

41. Ibid, p. 539.

42. See *www.smartrecovery.org.*

43. Jessica B. Konopa, Emil Chiauzzi, David Portnoy, and Thomas M. Litwicki, "Recovery from the Inside Out: A Cognitive Approach to Rehabilitation, *Corrections Today* 64, no. 5 (August 2002): 56–58.

44. Richard Williamson, "Faith-Based Changes Come from Inside a Texas Prison: Programs Reduce Recidivism," *The Non-Profit Times* 16, no. 3 (February 1, 2002): 1.

45. Richard L. Stalder, Secretary, Louisiana Department of Public Safety and Corrections, "Strategies to Reduce the Growth of Incarceration in the State of Louisiana," September 2000, p. 47.

46. Dora Schriro and Tom Clements, "Missouri's Parallel Universe: A Blueprint for Effective Prison Management," *Corrections Today* 63, no. 2 (April 2001): 140.

47. Ibid., p. 152.

48. Andrew von Hirsch and Lisa Maher, "Should Penal Rehabilitation Be Revived?" *Criminal Justice Ethics* 11, no. 1 (winter/spring 1992): 25–28.

49. Ibid, p. 29.

50. Patrick A. Langan and David J. Levin, "Recidivism of Prisoners Released in 1994," U.S. Department of Justice, Bureau of Justice Statistics Special Report, June 2002, p. 7.

51. Ibid.

52. Ibid., p. 8.

53. Ibid., p. 10.

54. Ibid.

55. Dennis, "Realities of Recidivism," p. 28.

56. Ibid., p. 32.

57. Ibid.

58. Glen Holley and David Ensley, "Recidivism Report: Inmates Released from Florida Prisons July 1995 to June 2001," Florida Department of Corrections, July 2003, p. 12.

59. Ibid., p. 25.

FURTHER READING

Bernfeld, Gary A., David P. Farrington, and Alan W. Leschied. *Offender Rehabilitation in Practice: Implementing and Evaluating Effective Programs.* New York: John Wiley & Sons, 2001.

Walters, Glenn D. *Changing Lives of Crime and Drugs: Intervening with Substance-Abusing Offenders.* New York: John Wiley & Sons, 1998.

WEB AND VIDEO RESOURCES

The Center for Alternative Sentencing and Employment Services (*www.cases.org*) in New York provides a range of rehabilitative services to thousands of offenders.

COMMENTARY

19 Reflections on Leaving the Penitentiary: A Psychologist Takes Stock

by Christopher J. Alexander

By training, I am both a child psychologist and a forensic psychologist. Through my work in these specialties, I have conducted evaluations on abuse and neglect, custody determinations, divorce mediation, trauma assessment and play therapy. I also have spent many hours in law offices, judges' chambers and courts of law, always advocating for the best interests of the child. This is the work I devoted the majority of my career to, prior to moving to New Mexico in 1995.

In light of my background, it is curious that I didn't take a job as a private practitioner upon arriving in New Mexico. Rather, I accepted a position as the supervising psychologist at the Penitentiary of New Mexico at Santa Fe. My duties at the North Unit, or maximum security unit, include supervising a staff of five mental health workers, performing personality and neuropsychological evaluations on the male inmate population, and facilitating the training of prison mental health workers throughout the state on understanding the criminal mind. A significant portion of my time also has been spent negotiating my way through the Duran Consent Decree, which was passed after the 1981 riot at the New Mexico Main Unit, giving the federal government oversight of the penitentiary.

As a child psychologist, I dealt primarily with victims. The children I saw were forced to face the brutal realities of divorce, neglect, abuse, violence and overall chaos. Upon arriving at the penitentiary, my role changed. Instead of finding ways to protect our more vulnerable members of society from victimization, I now find myself working with the perpetrators of these crimes. This is particularly so at the North Unit, where the perpetrators I work with often are labeled "mad and bad." Several are neurologically impaired from multiple head traumas and lifelong substance abuse; most have concurrent mood, learning or mental disorders; and all suffer from chronic and severe personality dysfunction.

It took some getting used to, but one aspect of working as a prison psychologist is that you can't create a mental hierarchy based on the crime committed. That is, I find myself treating equally the inmate who raped and killed a child and the one who sold drugs to the undercover officer. When you deal with an inmate population on a daily basis, you see that they really are people, with all the positive and negative attributes common to all of us. With this perspective, it becomes possible to relate to them, not as the horrific beasts that many in society choose to believe they are, but instead as men with families, dreams and feelings of their own.

It often is said that the role of prisons isn't rehabilitation, but rather containment. Thus, I never had any fantasies of transforming the lives of my clients based on my skillful administration and interpretation of psychological tests, careful supervision of the mental health staff or understanding of the criminal mind. But I did hope that I would be able to find some way of affirming my professional integrity and identity, and to feel that I was doing something to help both these individuals and society. This, however, has been difficult to achieve. Guiding someone toward positive mental health often is about encouraging them to explore the different options available to them. When you're incarcerated for life, your options are few.

The world of prison is a harsh and brutal one. The madness that gets played out—by both inmates and staff—is incomprehensible to most people. The sociopathic behavior of offenders doesn't stop once they are imprisoned. On the contrary, prison is the best environment many of these men have ever lived in, and the predictability and relative consistencies of the prison environment permit their antisocial tendencies to grow and thrive. Many of the inmates know which staff members can be bought, how to secure a steady supply of drugs, and how to manipulate and maneuver their way through one of the most controversial and complex systems in our state.

As a learning experience, however, there are few better places than prison. Working in a prison has taught me that standard psychological training simply is incapable of adequately capturing the full extent of the mental functions of the human mind. Since I am accustomed to being cross-examined on the features, causes and treatments for various mental disorders, I know the classification systems well. Yet, when you spend time with pure sociopaths, narcissists and bipolar persons, the failure of our current classification methods to identify the complexity of mental functioning becomes obvious. Prison work, though, really does help one better understand the behaviors of offenders such as Charles Manson, Ted Bundy and Andrew Cunanan, as well as other high-profile criminals.

The extent of head trauma that most male inmates have endured also is notable. Typical causes of these injuries include accidents, gunshot wounds, and beatings. Severe head trauma is directly responsible for everything from personality change to impaired impulse control. When you factor in long-standing patterns of inhalant and other substance abuse, the brain of the typical maximum security inmate is hardly capable of helping these persons negotiate the complexities of a social world.

Perhaps more than anything, working in the prison has reaffirmed for me that it is best that I work, not as a prison psychologist, but as a child psychologist. It is not that prison work exceeds my abilities or interests. Rather, prison work reminds me of a thought I often had when I was working with chronically abused children: "I wish I'd had them sooner." In other words, it really is true that in order to effectively intervene with someone who is on the path toward gang involvement, criminality or other antisocial behaviors, we have to treat or help them while they are young. I'm not yet willing to write off

the incarcerated adults in our nation's prisons. But reversing what for them has become learned and adaptive ways of surviving and functioning in life can often seem an insurmountable challenge.

Working with the incarcerated has made it difficult for me to separate their criminal acts from their broader life picture. For example, when I read of what these inmates did to other humans, it astounds me. The extent of victimization and brutality that many have inflicted on others in society is best left unsaid. But what is equally harsh is the madness many of them had to endure in their own early lives. This certainly doesn't—and shouldn't—excuse what they have done to others, but I do believe we need to maintain some perspective on the issue.

In my work with children, I have had the unfortunate task of reading through medical files and looking at police photos of the worst forms of neglect and abuse. None of this, however, prepared me for hearing what childhood was like for many of the inmates I have evaluated: 4-year-olds being given illicit drugs by their caregivers; 6-year-olds being taken on store robberies with their fathers; mothers engaging their young boys sexually from a very early age; boys being forced to participate in the rape and torture of other children; and boys who were tied to outdoor posts in the winter while being severely physically abused.

It is with these experiences and observations in mind that I return to the private sector. But instead of feeling that I somehow made a wrong turn in my career, I believe that I needed the experience of working in the penitentiary to clarify my understanding of why I do the work that I do. This experience not only has reaffirmed my professional commitment to advocating for the best interests of children, but it has made me realize that each of us has to do whatever it is we can to make life better for all children in our state. As several inmates have told me, "one caring adult in my life would have made all the difference."

20 Why Prisons Don't Work

by Wilbert Rideau

I was among 31 murderers sent to the Louisiana State Penitentiary in 1962 to be executed or imprisoned for life. We weren't much different from those we found

here, or those who had preceded us. We were unskilled, impulsive and uneducated misfits, mostly black, who had done dumb, impulsive things—failures, rejects from the larger society. Now a generation has come of age and gone since I've been here, and everything is much the same as I found it. The faces of the prisoners are different, but behind them are the same impulsive, uneducated, unskilled minds that made dumb, impulsive choices that got them into more trouble than they ever thought existed.

The vast majority of us are consigned to suffer and die here so politicians can sell the illusion that permanently exiling people to prison will make society safe. Getting tough has always been a "silver bullet," a quick fix for the crime and violence that society fears. Each year in Louisiana—where excess is a way of life—law-makers have tried to outdo each other in legislating harsher mandatory penalties and in reducing avenues of release. The only thing to do with criminals, they say, is get tougher.

They have. In the process, the purpose of prison began to change. The state boasts one of the highest lock-up rates in the country, imposes the most severe penalties in the nation and vies to execute more criminals per capita than anywhere else. This state is so tough that last year, when prison authorities here wanted to punish an inmate in solitary confinement for an infraction, the most they could inflict on him was to deprive him of his underwear. It was all he had left.

If getting tough resulted in public safety, Louisiana citizens would be the safest in the nation. They're not. Louisiana has the highest murder rate among states. Prison, like the police and the courts, has a minimal impact on crime because it is a response after the fact, a mop-up operation. It doesn't work. The idea of punishing the few to deter the many is counterfeit because potential criminals either think they're not going to get caught or they're so emotionally desperate or psychologically distressed that they don't care about the consequences of their actions. The threatened punishment, regardless of its severity, is never a factor in the equation. But society, like the incorrigible criminal it abhors, is unable to learn from its mistakes.

Prison has a role in public safety, but it is not a cure-all. Its value is limited, and its use should also be limited to what it does best: isolating young criminals long enough to give them a chance to grow up and get a grip on their impulses. It is a traumatic experience, certainly, but it should be only a temporary one, not a way of life. Prisoners kept too long tend to embrace the criminal culture, its distorted values and beliefs; they have little choice—prison is their life.

There are some prisoners who cannot be returned to society—serial killers, serial rapists, professional hit men and the like—but the monsters who need to die in prison are rare exceptions in the criminal landscape.

Crime is a young man's game. Most of the nation's random violence is committed by young urban terrorists. But because of long, mandatory sentences, most prisoners here are much older, having spent 15, 20, 30 or more years behind bars, long past necessity. Rather than pay for new prisons, society would be well served by releasing some of its older prisoners who pose no threat and using the money to catch young street thugs. Warden John Whitley agrees that many older prisoners here could be freed tomorrow with little or no danger to society. Release, however, is governed by law or politicians, not by penal professionals. Even murderers, those most feared by society, pose little risk. Historically, for example, the domestic staff at Louisiana's governor's mansion has been made up of murderers, hand-picked to work among the chief-of-state and his family. Penologists have long known that murder is almost always a once-in-a-lifetime act. The most dangerous criminal is the one who has not yet killed but has a history of escalating offenses. He's the one to watch.

Rehabilitation can work. Everyone changes in time. The trick is to influence the direction that change takes. The problem with prisons is that they don't do more to rehabilitate those confined in them. The convict who enters prison illiterate will probably leave the same way. Most convicts want to be better than they are, but education is not a priority. This prison houses 4,600 men and offers academic training to 240, vocational training to a like number. Perhaps it doesn't matter. About 90% of the men here may never leave this prison alive.

The only effective way to curb crime is for society to work to prevent the criminal act in the first place, to come between the perpetrator and crime. Our youngsters must be taught to respect the humanity of others and to handle disputes without violence. It is essential to educate and equip them with the skills to pursue their life ambitions in a meaningful way. As a community, we must address the adverse life circumstances that spawn criminality. These things are not quick, and they're not easy, but they're effective. Politicians think that's too hard a sell. They want to be on record for doing something now, something they can point to at re-election time. So the drumbeat goes on for more police, more prisons, more of the same failed policies. Ever see a dog chase its tail?

14   PAROLE AND RELEASE FROM PRISON

"You're an old con. How can we trust you? How do we know what you've been up to? You vanish for months at a time. Then there's this violence in your record."

"That was twenty years ago."

He had the grace to look down. "I know. But that was you out there in Nevada, not someone else."

"It was not me. I am someone else. In the twenty years since that happened I have never stopped trying to change myself."

"How can we know that?"

That was it, wasn't it? They didn't know. How could they know? And since anything I might find to say was selfishly inspired, designed to free me, it had to be discounted. Only the file could be trusted, and here the ink never faded.

When I played this scene over, as I did again and again, the feeling that came over me was the horror of total impotence. There was nothing I could do. No way to demonstrate my sincerity. I had moved beyond the usual pattern and was now abandoned there.

I left the boardroom sure of several things. I was denied. The Adult Authority were probably poorer judges of who would make it and who wouldn't than the average con on the yard. They were taking fifty thousand dollars a year to sit in those big leather chairs and wing it. And, finally and most demeaning, I knew it was somehow more agreeable to Fitzharris to deny me than it would have been to set me free.

— Malcolm Braly, *False Starts: A Memoir of San Quentin and Other Prisons*, 1976

INTRODUCTION

This chapter considers parole and other ways to leave prison and reenter society. Parole was not a part of the original penitentiary, but over time it became a universal practice. Almost all felons were parole eligible, and most—unless they got a pardon or good-time release before they came up for parole—could expect to be released on parole one day. No more. The decline of discretionary parole—and the changed form of the new parole—have had major effects on imprisonment over the past generation. After reading the material in this chapter, you should be familiar with:

1. Parole from the inmate's perspective.
2. Parole and other options to get out of prison.

3. The development of parole as a practice.
4. The "old" parole board and process.
5. The parole officer and parole work.
6. Parole and mandatory release today.
7. Life as a parolee today.
8. The effectiveness of parole.

ON PAROLE

A week after he got out of prison, Jean Sanders shook the hand of the ex-president of the United States. It was February 2001, and Sanders, fresh out of prison for the fourth time—this time after serving seven years for auto theft—went from his homeless shelter in Brooklyn up to Harlem to apply for low-income housing. Former President Bill Clinton (whom some would argue was in need of his own dose of rehabilitation after his controversial second term ended) appeared in the same building to look for office space. Sanders welcomed Clinton to the neighborhood, and he told *Time* magazine writer Amanda Ripley, who kept track of his adventures for a year as part of a cover story on parole she would write in January 2002, "If this is a sign, then I think everything's going to be all right."[1] Meeting the president would be one of the ups in a year of ups and downs.

Jean Sanders was among the more than 600,000 men and women released from prison in 2001, about a quarter of them on discretionary parole, meaning they were released through the authority of a parole board. A greater number were discharged on mandatory parole, or mandatory release, which means they reached a mathematical date based on earned good-time credits—time in prison on good behavior. A smaller number served their full term or were released through other options.

Sanders cashed his $40 release check from the department of corrections and returned home to Brooklyn at age forty-one. He had a three-part plan:

1. Reconcile with his family
2. Find an apartment
3. Get a job

"I want a life," he told Ripley. "I want to be normal again. I want to go to work, come home, see my kids, go on vacation." He has four children, ages eighteen to twenty-one. He has a mother, Ophelia, seventy; two brothers who hold managerial jobs; and an extended family. He also has a twelve-page criminal history as a drug dealer and a car thief and an "epic history of drug addiction." He has spent most of the past fifteen years in prison, and he has lost the trust of his family, but most of the time, Ripley observes, "he is optimistic, almost irrationally so. He envisions a better life for himself, whereas most would see a life half-wasted."

Ophelia Sanders welcomed her son home, visited with him, and fixed dinner for him, but he was not allowed to spend the night. His first night out of prison he spent in a homeless shelter two and a half miles away. The first gigantic brick shelter he stayed in Sanders called "Castle Grayskull." The second he promoted to "Cuckoo-bird Dungeon," saying he was blessed to be there, but as Ripley reports,

Both were trials for Sanders. Inside and out, they alternately reeked of prison or temptation. Within a five-block radius of the second shelter, there were three crack houses. Directly outside the shelter, men worked the corner, smoking and doping. Police made frequent sweeps, stopping whoever wasn't in motion. Sanders was careful not to pause. Even so, over the course of three months, he was searched twice. He was polite and compliant; he joked about how his orange wallet looked nothing like a gun. He was clean both times but so shaken he had to sit and catch his breath.[2]

Sanders was surrounded by homeless people and parolees, the sort of people with whom his parole conditions told him not to associate. He was himself a victim of crime when someone at the shelter broke into his locker and stole his underwear and washcloth. Though he got a closetful of secondhand suits as a gift and applied for hundreds of jobs, he could not get full-time work. The kinds of work he was offered—mostly manual labor and temporary or "off the books" jobs—he could not accept because of an old neck injury or because the jobs were not allowed under parole conditions.

He went to job interviews and he went to meetings: drug treatment, once a week to see his parole officer, welfare meetings, regular job training meetings, appointments to give urine samples, and housing authority. He was busy almost full time without a job. People gave him a hard time as a parolee. A prisoner advocate told Ripley, "The expectations placed on the parolee are disproportionate to what they can assimilate. People are looking over their shoulders waiting for them to fail." Sanders says the prerelease program he completed in prison provided useless or outdated information.

In June, still unemployed, Sanders smoked crack with people near the shelter. Police caught him with a rock in his waistband. He sat in jail thinking he had just sent himself back to prison. But he was charged only with disorderly conduct, not drug possession, and discharged. Knowing his parole officer would learn of the parole violation, he packed his things and prepared to run away. Then he changed his mind, at age forty-one tired of running. He turned himself in to his parole officer, who allowed him another chance. "He wants to do the right thing," she said. "I just don't think he has many friends or many different lifelines."

After his "slip-up," Sanders started attending drug treatment religiously. He did piecemeal work, he visited his family regularly, he found a small room to rent that allowed him to move out of the shelter, and he found a woman to date but quit when he was too poor to buy her dinner. Then came the September 11 terrorist attacks on the World Trade Center. The air was smoky and the sky dark. He was depressed, staying home in bed for two weeks.

In early November, when he was almost out of ambition, he was finally offered a legal job—as a $6-an-hour gas-station attendant. He took it at once. Within a month he had a promotion. Making $13,000 a year, with no benefits, he says he is on cloud nine. "I don't have no issues. I work, I come home tired, I go to sleep, I go back in the morning."

For Christmas he gave his family members cash—fresh, crisp dollar bills— that he had earned himself. He worked on New Year's Eve, then went home to watch the Times Square ball drop on TV with his mother. They said a prayer for the new year, and he went home to his room and went to bed. He had been out of prison for a year, his longest stretch of freedom in fifteen years.[3] Half of all parolees are back in prison within three years after release; Jean Sanders barely made it through the highest-risk period without joining them. What would the next two years hold in store for him? As we will see in the commentary at the end of this chapter, parole is not automatically easier with time—the risks are always there.

LEAVING PRISON

In the 1932 film *I Am a Fugitive from a Chain Gang*, the hard-luck innocent man, Jim Allen, newly arrived on the Georgia chain gang, sees two men leaving the prison camp. Barney walks out, shuffling along in short strides as if the chains are still on his legs. Red goes out in a pine box. Another convict observes, "There's just two ways to get out of here: work out and die out."

Comparatively few prisoners "die out" to get out of prison, although their numbers have grown steadily in recent years, for three primary reasons and one secondary reason. First, the prison population is getting older, the average age of inmates increasing from late twenties to mid-thirties over the past twenty-five years. Second, real, long-term sentences have become much more common. Over 20 percent of all state and federal prisoners are serving sentences of twenty years or longer. A recent report by the Sentencing Project says that almost 10 percent of state and federal prisoners (127,677 in 2002) are serving life sentences; in New York and California, almost 20 percent are serving life.[4] In six states—Illinois, Iowa, Louisiana, Maine, Pennsylvania, and South Dakota—and the federal system, a life sentence now automatically means life without parole, a natural life sentence.[5] Thus, when you hear that an "average" prison term is about five or six years and an "average" inmate serves two and a half or three years before release and you think that sounds about right—or perhaps way too short—keep in mind that a growing percentage of prisoners has a lot more real time to do and that they do not figure in the time-served-at-release averages (which continue to climb) because they are not being released. The third reason relates to the health problems of inmates. Chronic illnesses such as hepatitis C, HIV/AIDS, and tuberculosis have added to the toll imposed by drug abuse and generally deficient health care provided the poor, leaving the life expectancy of prisoners a decade or more shorter than that of the general population outside prison. The fourth reason is the increase in the number of executions in the past decade, rising to a steady level of between sixty and 100 annually.

How many inmates "die out" of prison each year? Camp and Camp report in *The Corrections Yearbook 2001* that in the previous year, 3,203 inmate deaths were reported, about one-fourth of 1 percent of the entire prison population. The leading cause of death (2,509) was natural causes, including hepatitis C–related deaths. Suicide (201) was second, and AIDS (195) was third. Eighty-five inmates were executed.[6]

In *I Am a Fugitive from a Chain Gang*, Jim Allen finds a third way out of prison. He "hangs it on a limb," or escapes. In fact, in the film, as in the real-life adventures of Robert Burns, on whose book the movie is based, he successfully escapes from the chain gang twice. How prevalent are escapes from prison? An average of about 10,000 inmates per year were reported as escapees during the 1990s. But about 90 percent of these were inmates who were in work release or open facilities or who were on furlough at the time; they did not "crash out," they just walked away and did not return when they were supposed to. Fewer than 100 escapes per year are made from medium-

or higher-security prisons.[7] About two-thirds of all escapees/runaways are captured or turn themselves in within seventy-two hours; most of the rest filter back in over time.

For a long time in common law countries, one way out of prison was through a pardon. Parole is often confused with this form of intervention, which is actually one form of **executive clemency.** In earlier times, the king or ruler often intervened—sometimes for cash, which was then okay but is now bribery, a felony—to moderate sentences or prevent them from being imposed, as in a case of capital punishment. Today this traditional executive authority is called clemency. The authority resides in the office of the President of the United States and the governors of the states. Through a legally defined process, often involving preliminary screening done by political appointees serving as a **pardon board,** an executive may intervene in the legal process in several different ways:

1. **Pardon,** which was originally used to set aside wrongful convictions; it is now more often used to restore lost civil disqualifications, such as the right to vote or own firearms. Today we expect the appellate courts rather than the governor's office to overturn wrongful convictions and set innocent people free.

2. **Amnesty,** which is a blanket freedom from criminal prosecution given to a group of offenders, such as those Americans who fled the country to avoid serving in the military during the Vietnam War. Amnesty may be granted before people are charged, or it may be used to set free offenders who are in prison. Amnesty is obviously often set in a political context; someone characterized it as the government's way of saying "I'm sorry."

3. **Reprieve,** which is a stay, usually short term, from the imposition of a sentence. We think of reprieves particularly in regard to executions, as when the offender in the prison movie waits for a last-minute call from the governor's office (that in real life seldom comes).

4. **Commutation,** which is the shortening of a sentence by executive order. Commutations remain very important to sentenced offenders in many states that make abundant use of life sentences and other very long prison terms. If the executive finds the offender deserving, the commutation is an early out (if the sentence is commuted to time served) or an early parole date for the imprisoned offender.

In the present era of "get tough on criminals," many governors are reluctant to use their clemency powers for fear of being called soft on crime. This executive intervention from outside the judicial system, once so common, has become a rare event. No politician wants to be haunted later by his opponent's criticism that he was "too nice to criminals." Clemency options, except for the restoration of lost rights, do not matter nearly as much as they used to. A recent annual count of commutations of terms for prisoners behind bars showed fewer than 1,000 having been granted, and the great majority of these were in two states—Oklahoma and South Dakota—where commutations were used to relieve prison overcrowding. Prisoners are too "hot" to expect a return to the good old days, when a bag of gold or political connections was enough to support a plea for mercy.[8]

A few prisoners do benefit from court intervention to set aside convictions. Sometimes the state or federal court, during the appeal or in postconviction proceedings, will simply overturn the conviction and order the offender discharged. More often, the offender is sent back for a new trial. He may be granted bail while he waits. If the criminal has already done a lot of time or if the retrial case against him is weak, the prosecutor may elect to discharge him without a trial or allow him to plead to a charge for time served, resulting in his release from custody. This outcome is also a rare event, but when it happens, especially with someone who has been in prison a long time, it encourages other prisoners to keep their own numbers in the postconviction lottery. Who knows who might be the next big winner?

When severe prison overcrowding was a commonplace problem in the 1990s, prisoners in several states benefited from so-called **emergency release** provisions adopted by state legislatures. In Texas, for example, when prison occupancy rates climbed above 95 percent, officials had the authority to provide early parole to inmates approaching their release dates. In Florida, a similar "purge" of parole-eligible inmates was used to free up bed space—leading to a side industry of researchers counting arrests and crimes committed by people who should still have been in prison. Many states in the South and elsewhere resorted to such pressure-release mechanisms (like "blowing off steam") to reduce overcrowding at its worst; as prison populations have leveled off the past few years and new prison construction caught up with the need for beds, the use of this measure—which rates about the same popularity as executive clemency—has declined sharply.

Several thousand offenders serving **shock probation** terms will be released from prison to probation, under the authority of a judge rather than a parole board, after serving a short prison term, typically in the range of three to six months. This is one of the practices that has developed within the past three or four decades to make probation tougher, as we will discuss at length in the next chapter. The premise is that the short prison term enhances the deterrent effect of probation since the offenders know what would be facing them if they return to custody. It is unclear whether they consider themselves lucky—to have stayed only a short time—or unlucky to have ever gone to prison at all. The practice has not caught on as some thought it might when it was first proposed in the 1960s. Only about nine states in the Midwest and South, led by Indiana with 3,000-plus inmates, use this practice for more than 1,000 prisoners a year.

Some unlucky prisoners are released at the end of one sentence only to be immediately picked up by authorities from another jurisdiction—state or federal—and transferred to another institution to serve another prison term. Defendants who have been convicted of crimes in more than one jurisdiction are placed under **detainer** if the new jurisdiction wants them when they get done with the present sentence. This prevents them from being discharged from custody; detainers are used in the same way to keep probation and parole violators in jail until a hearing can be held to decide revocation.

Another small group of unlucky prisoners qualify for release each year on what is called **medical parole** or in some states a medical pardon. These are generally terminally ill prisoners—verified as such by medical staff—who are released to go home because they are about to die or because they are suffering from severe, debilitating illnesses that make them a minimal criminal threat. They may also need medical treatment they cannot get in prison. These cases sometimes stir up heated opposition, as when crime victims oppose the release of sick old men, preferring that they "die in prison" as the law provided.

All the release options considered so far amount to no more than about 10 to 15 percent of the total releases in a given year. The three most prevalent forms of release—discretionary parole, mandatory parole, and expiration of sentence—account for the balance, approximately 85 to 90 percent of all discharges from prison annually.

Discretionary parole occurs through the action of a parole board. A prisoner becomes eligible for parole review after serving a specified portion of his or her sentence. If the board grants parole, the prisoner is discharged on **conditional release** to serve the remainder of the sentence in the community under supervision. Into the 1970s, discretionary parole was by far the most common means of leaving prison, with more than 70 percent of all prison releases each year occurring through parole board action. But reaction against the **indeterminate sentence,** which left it up to parole authorities to determine how long the prisoner served, led to the abolition of discretionary parole in sixteen states by 2000 and restrictions on parole eligibility for certain violent and sex offenders in several other states. By 2000, discretionary parole had been abolished for federal felons and convicted felons in these states:

Arizona

California

Delaware

Florida

Illinois

Indiana

Kansas

Maine

Minnesota

Mississippi

North Carolina

Ohio

Oregon

Virginia

Washington

Wisconsin[9]

The decline of the indeterminate sentence has seen the rise of the determinate sentence. The parole board is gone (actually it is not gone because it is still there for the old cons who were sentenced under the old law; it just has no authority over the new inmates sentenced under determinate sentencing statutes). In its place is a technician sitting with a calculator in a records office, tabulating **good-time release** or what has come to be called (probably because prison authorities shy away from the connotation that imprisonment is a "good time") **mandatory parole** or mandatory release. This release date involves a simple mathematical computation: full term less good-time credits earned equals release date. The prisoner is still on conditional release, and he or she can be returned to prison to serve more of the sentence if parole is revoked for failure to comply with parole conditions.

Supervision of mandatory parolees varies widely from state to state—from the same level of supervision as other parolees to lower supervision to no supervision at all. On either discretionary parole or mandatory parole, the former prisoner is still serving the sentence until the sentence expires. Good-time standards vary by crime, by class of offender (which in prison terminology refers to how many prior felonies someone has, not socioeconomics), and by state; by 2000, thirty states and the federal government had adopted the federal **truth-in-sentencing standard** of 85 percent for serious violent felonies. This standard requires the criminal to serve 85 percent of the sentence to reach the mandatory parole date. A criminal serving ten years for robbery who kept all his good-time credits would earn his release after eight and a half years.

The third common release option is **expiration of sentence.** This would apply to prisoners who are ineligible for good time or who lose their good-time credits and serve their full term—every day of it. There used to be very few (fewer than 5 percent, in most states even less) prisoners who would "max out"; they were viewed either with awe (as the toughest or most stubborn of inmates) or with pity and amazement (as the most stupid or lost) by their fellow prisoners. Changing laws have made this exit more common, nationwide almost as common now as discretionary parole.

A criminal whose sentence has expired is not under supervision and has no conditions to abide by, unless he happens to be in the category of federal criminals sentenced to **supervised release.** In the federal courts, a prisoner is given a prison sentence and a good-time release date (all federal prisoners since 1987 have been under the 85 percent good-time rule); he or she is also given a specified length of time, such as twelve or eighteen months, of supervised release after discharge from custody. This is equivalent to the period of mandatory parole supervision in the states. The maximum period of supervised release is five years, except for sex offenders, who can be placed under supervision for life. The federal ex-prisoner who violates parole conditions can be sent right back to prison to serve the rest of the supervised release term behind bars.

Methods of release have evolved over the past two decades, as illustrated in Table 14-1. The use of discretionary parole declined steadily over this period; in 1994, for the first time, more prisoners were released to mandatory parole at their good-time dates than through parole board action. This trend has continued since. Prisoners kept in to full-term expiration of sentence increased, declined in the worst overcrowding years, and then increased again to percentages not seen in the modern parole era.

By 2000, an average felon in a state prison system was serving a sentence of about five to six years in length; he or she could expect to serve about half that time—an average of thirty-four months—in custody before release. The length of time served before release was, as you would expect, higher for violent crimes and lower for property, drug, and public order crimes; violent criminals stayed in on average about twice as long as criminals in the other categories. Interestingly, when violent offenders in the truth-in-sentencing states and the other states without such laws (should we refer to them as the "lying-in-sentencing" states?) are compared, the length of time served before release and the percentage of sentence served before release were not sharply different. In fact, the violent criminals in the non–truth-in-sentencing states actually served more time before release—fifty-five months—than the offenders

TABLE 14-1

Percentage of Releases from State Prison by Method of Release, 1980–2000

Year	Discretionary Parole	Mandatory Parole	Expiration of Sentence
1980	54.76%	18.63%	14.25%
1981	51.44	20.15	13.06
1982	50.28	23.63	13.92
1983	46.32	25.86	15.50
1984	45.23	28.25	16.03
1985	42.55	30.36	16.66
1986	42.65	30.68	14.65
1987	40.07	30.78	16.00
1988	39.82	30.26	16.58
1989	38.36	30.28	15.25
1990	39.40	28.83	12.65
1991	39.72	29.94	10.83
1992	39.54	29.48	11.38
1993	38.82	31.61	11.88
1994	34.99	35.61	12.47
1995	32.33	38.98	14.50
1996	30.35	37.95	16.74
1997	28.19	39.67	16.80
1998	25.98	40.45	18.67
1999	23.71	41.13	18.09
2000	23.87	38.78	19.60[9]

Source: "Reentry Trends in the U.S.," Bureau of Justice Statistics, *www.ojpl.uddoj.gov/bjs*. Page last revised on August 20, 2003.

in the truth-in-sentencing states—fifty-three months—although the truth-in-sentencing offenders served a slightly greater percentage of their term—58 percent—than the non–truth-in-sentencing offenders—54 percent. Both the length of time served to release for all crimes and the percentage of time served before release had increased sharply during the 1990s; time in custody increased by about six months on average, and percentage of sentence served increased by about ten percentage points, to 49 percent.[10]

You could say overall, then, about policies in regard to release from prison in the period from 1990 to 2000, that prisoners were sentenced to about the same amount of time to serve (or a little less) but actually stayed in prison to serve more of it. The greatest number of prisoners were being released on mandatory parole at the good-time dates, and an increasing number of prisoners were being held to expiration of sentence. The big change was the sharp decline in the number of inmates granted discretionary parole; indeed, in the one-third of the states that had eliminated parole by the year 2000, the numbers had been reduced to a veritable dribble in comparison to twenty or thirty years earlier. Where did parole come from? Why did it rise to such a position of prominence as a release mechanism, and what brought its sudden fall from favor? What happened to generate the movement to "do away with parole"?

THE ORIGINS OF PAROLE

In American prisons of the 1970s, parole was an orderly, perfunctory, often arbitrary process in which inmates, after serving some minimum time in prison, came before a parole board that reviewed their files and, usually after a rejection or two for seasoning, turned them loose under the nominal supervision of a professional parole officer to serve the remainder of the sentence in the community. Parole was like a well-oiled machine that, despite criticisms of many kinds, kept performing its mission: approving the conditional release of men and women from prison. Many corrections officials and the great majority of prisoners whose fate depended on its workings probably assumed parole had always been around, working in the past pretty much as it did in the present day.

In fact, parole was only about a century old in the 1970s, having been officially created by a New York statute in 1876. Parole was created as a reaction against the penitentiary and the determinate sentence. Parole and its delivery mechanism, the indeterminate sentence, were first put into practice at Zebulon Brockway's new Elmira Reformatory in July 1876, the culmination of several years of lobbying on behalf of prison reform. Not only had the penitentiary already turned into a brutal and degrading drain on society, Brockway and other reform advocates argued, but it had also failed in its mission of reforming prisoners. Fifty years after it began, the penitentiary was already a sad failure. The reformatory regimen, on the other hand, promised individual management of prisoners and reform based on the reward of release on parole.

Parole had been the talk of progressive penal circles in America since the 1870 National Prison Congress in Cincinnati, an international forum where the principles of parole were discussed at length. The components of parole—classification, the indeterminate sentence, programs and social training, rewards for good conduct, and earned release—were incorporated into the congress's "Declaration of Principles." Parole as such did not exist in an American prison, but it had its antecedents, particularly in the British prison system, in practices both old and very recent.

Indentured servitude was practiced extensively in English courts of the 1600s and 1700s. Convicted felons and debtors were contracted to landowners and businessmen in the American colonies for periods of servitude, typically seven to fourteen years. The criminals were pardoned for their crimes, the crown made money from the sale of the felon's labor, undesirables were removed from the country, and the laborers, if they survived the journey, eventually earned their freedom in the new world. The conditions of indentured servitude have been compared with those of parole as it developed later. One of the conditions of the contract was that the pardon was void if the criminal returned to England, in effect imposing a death sentence on any deported felon who returned (as happened to the transported convict Abel Magwitch in Dickens's *Great Expectations* when he returned from Australia to see how the boy Pip had turned out).

The work of **Alexander Maconochie,** the former British naval officer who became superintendent of the **Norfolk Island** penal colony, was particularly influential in laying the philosophical foundation for parole. Britain had been transporting its convicts to Australia, originally known as Botany Bay, since January 1788. The convicts who committed new crimes after arriving in Australia were shipped east 800 miles to what was called the *ne plus ultra* of convict degradation: Norfolk Island. The men and women sent there, by all accounts, considered it a fate worse than death. It was called the worst place in the English-speaking world or, in Robert Hughes's *The Fatal Shore*, the history of Australia's founding, the "Isle of the Damned."

To this terrible place, more by accident than design, came Alexander Maconochie in 1840. Maconochie was a Scotsman, a lawyer's son who had gone to sea as a teenager. As a young lieutenant in the British navy, he was captured by the French and spent two years as a prisoner of war. As Hughes recounts, "This was Maconochie's one traumatic taste of life in prison, and he never forgot it. Indeed, he was the only major official of the transportation system who had even spent time behind bars."[11]

Maconochie retired from the navy and became a geography professor. He was a geographer, not a prison activist, but when he was sent to visit Australia for the first time in 1837, some friends in the Society for the Improvement of Prison Discipline asked him to write an account of the penal system in Van Diemen's Land (Tasmania). He was horrified at what he saw—brutality, corruption, and exploitation of convict labor—and said so in his report. Initially, he was in big trouble with government authorities and with the local citizens who benefited from the system. They heaped criticism on him. But Maconochie, in his early fifties, like the jail reformer John Howard half a century earlier, had found his mission in life. He wrote in 1839, "The cause has got me complete. I will go the whole hog on it. . . . I will neither acquiesce in the moral destruction of so many of my fellow human beings nor in misrepresentation made of myself, without doing *everything* that may be necessary or possible to assist both."[12]

When the report of the Molesworth Committee recommended an end to transportation of convicts and a shift to free immigration to Australia in 1838, Maconochie suddenly found himself the unexpected hero of the prison reformers. He was sent to Norfolk Island in 1840 to put into practice these new penological ideas that he had been developing the past three years. Maconochie's basic concept was that punishment should be by "task, not time." He developed the **mark system,** based on credits earned for hard work and good behavior, to replace the existing system of punishment by time served. Prisoners would buy their way out of custody (and back to the Australian mainland) with the marks they earned—6,000 to replace a seven-year sentence, 7,000 a ten-year sentence, and 10,000 a life sentence. The moral lesson of the mark system, "nothing for nothing," was applied through a series of stages—from solitary confinement to several levels of individual labor to group labor to discharge from custody through a **ticket of leave.** Some of his ideas were influenced by other thinkers, particularly theologian William Paley, but Maconochie was in a position to actually try out his ideas. As superintendent of a prison colony in a remote corner of the world, he could experiment without interference.[13]

Maconochie put the mark system ideas into practice over the next three years, writing voluminous reports full of reform philosophy and asking for more money and more authority to manage his convicts in accordance with his plan. His reform ideas did appear to be working. The colony was safe, orderly, and productive. Of the more than 900 convicts sent back to Australia during his tenure, by 1845 only twenty were convicted of new felonies—a modern-day recidivism rate of 2 percent.[14] But a high death rate from disease, problems with agriculture, and constant complaints from old-line settlers who advocated a return to harsh treatment of convicts led to Maconochie's recall in 1844. He returned to England and wrote a book in 1846, *Crime and Punishment, The Mark System,* framed to mix Persuasion with Punishment, and Make their Effect Improving, yet their Operation severe. Briefly put in charge of a new prison in Birmingham, he was dismissed after two years of conflict with subordinates who would not put his humane ideas into practice. Bitterly disappointed but too proud for self-pity, he died in 1860, too obscure by then to draw attention at his death.[15] He had no idea he would eventually become known as the "father of parole."

In 1853, the English parliament passed the **English Penal Servitude Act,** which had two important effects on criminal punishment:

1. It substituted imprisonment for transportation, except for sentences of longer than fourteen years.
2. It specified the minimum length of time convicts must serve to be eligible for conditional release on a ticket of leave.

Sentence length was tied to eligibility for release, making this in effect a form of the indeterminate sentence. The monarch, acting through prison officials, was given the authority to grant conditional release to a convict and to revoke the release and have the offender arrested again.[16] When England began to release convicts early, an apparent sharp increase in crime followed. The ticket of leave system took the blame.

The Irish prison system, under the direction of **Sir Walter Crofton,** took a different approach. At his new prison, Mountjoy, he developed a four-stage prison management system:

1. Stage 1 was eight or nine months in solitary confinement.
2. Stage 2 used four grades, with inmates earning marks through labor to move from one grade to the next. It lasted about eighteen to twenty-four months.
3. Stage 3 was the "intermediate stage," a small, open prison. The first was at Lusk near Dublin. It would compare with a prerelease center today.
4. Stage 4 was release on a ticket of leave. Staff members helped prisoners find jobs, and police were given the responsibility of supervising parolees. Police often delegated supervision to volunteer friends who stayed close to the offender after his or her release from custody.[17]

The orderly progression of Crofton's **Irish System** was reported to have a greater crime reduction effect than England's unstructured and unsupervised ticket-of-leave distribution system. It attracted many supporters in Europe and America. His ideas, supplementing Maconochie's concepts of indeterminacy, struck home with the growing number of Americans who did not like what had happened to the penitentiary. Conceived as a reformative, humane alternative to physical punishments, the penitentiary had quickly become a factory with chains—an institution whose operation combined breaking the convict's spirit and cheap management of convict labor.

Americans had been talking about the practice of **parole** since Dr. Samuel Gridley Howe, a prison activist and ardent abolitionist of the day, began using the term in Boston in the 1840s. He based it on a French practice, *parole d'hon-*

neur, or word of honor, a method of release from custody similar to release on recognizance today.

Two other practices in American prisons were also important antecedents of parole. The first, **good time,** was approved by legislative act in New York in 1817. Its purpose was the same as good time today: the criminal's sentence was shortened as a reward for good behavior in custody. Good time was generally adopted as an administrative control device, providing an incentive for good conduct in prison, in other state prisons during the remainder of the 1800s. It started as a minimal adjustment—a few days per month—and then grew more generous to convicts over time.

The second practice was the **conditional pardon,** which was in use in a number of states in the 1800s. In this era, pardons were often used to set convicts free from imprisonment. The conditional pardon was a bit more complicated. It granted freedom but set conditions. The criminal could be returned to custody if he or she violated these conditions, much like what would happen on parole today.

Zebulon Brockway was an experienced prison manager when he came to New York to open the **Elmira Reformatory** in 1876. He was familiar with the progressive practices of Maconochie and Crofton. Elmira was his Norfolk Island and Mountjoy. He believed in classification of inmates according to character, not crime. He wanted to work with young—age sixteen to thirty—first offenders (though he soon found the courts were slipping in recidivists as well). He set up an ambitious program of education, vocational training, military drill, physical training, and religious and moral training—about everything he could think of to try to reform criminals. He wanted the criminals to be absolutely within his control (you may recall that he was eventually removed for excessive paddling of mental defectives). He met with all his criminals individually, and the indeterminate sentence approved by the New York legislature in 1876 gave him authority to release any inmate after a year in custody. He used a grading system, like Crofton, that required inmates to earn credits toward their release. Those who failed to progress could spend up to the full term, five years, in custody. The men who were released, with a place to live and a job, were on parole for at least six months. They had to report on the first day of the month to a volunteer called a "guardian" and provide an account of their situation and conduct. Written reports, signed by the parolee's employer and guardian, had to be sent in to the reformatory each month.[18]

Brockway's experimentation with parole at Elmira proved very influential. Within fifty years, all states except three—Florida, Mississippi, and Virginia—had adopted parole in some form. In 1907, New York became the first state to adopt all the components of a modern parole system: the indeterminate sentence, a system for granting release, postrelease supervision, and specific criteria for parole revocation.[19] Parole was still considered a limited concept, applicable not to all prisoners but just to those on a reform track. Both the indeterminate and the determinate sentence were in widespread use, many times in the same state but applicable to different inmates according to offender class and crime committed. Prisoners were divided into two classes: parolable and not. Parole was all right for the ones who could be reformed; the common view was that most criminals could not, and hard work and the determinate sentence were preferred for them. These inmates would continue to be released from prison at their good-time dates, at sentence expiration, or through pardon or commutation by the governor. Parole was for those "other guys" in the reformatory, not the real men in the penitentiary. Not until the 1930s would the majority of American convicts find that they were parole eligible, making the encounter with the parole board the crucial event in securing release from prison.

"OLD" PAROLE IN TWENTIETH-CENTURY AMERICA

Parole was originally an ill-defined practice. All it meant was that the warden had the authority to turn some prisoners loose early. An 1885 Ohio statute gave authority to the board of managers of the Ohio prison to set up a plan under which any prisoner, except a murderer, who had served his minimum term might be allowed to go on parole outside the buildings and enclosures but to remain while on parole in the legal custody and under the control of the board and subject at any time to be taken back.[20]

In North Dakota, the concept of "parole" was first discussed in an 1888 report from the state penitentiary to the governor of the Dakota Territory. Within a few years, the warden was releasing short-term prisoners to the custody of an employer, typically a farmer. The local sheriff returned to the penitentiary any violators or inmates for whom employers had no further use, such as farmworkers after the harvest was done.

Parole in Texas is traced to a 1905 law that gave the board of prison commissioners and the board of pardons advisers power to make rules and regulations under which certain meritorious prisoners might be paroled. The approval of the governor was required. Within a few years, the position of parole agent was created, though this was an office job not involving supervision; parolees were under no supervision once they left the prison. In the American states adopting parole during this era, supervision was more of an afterthought, in contrast to the Irish System, which emphasized supervision as an important element of the plan. In the United States, someone was usually made responsible for the parolee—such as the local sheriff in Idaho and Louisiana—but no one was directly supervising the parolee in most states in the early years.

Volunteers—as individuals and as a part of charitable organizations—were an important part of early parole. Louis Robinson wrote in 1921,

> In dealing with the problem of releasing men from prison, one should not pass over the work of volunteer societies, which long ago perceived that the sudden thrusting forth into the world of men kept for years behind bars, without friends or without the means of obtaining an honest livelihood, was a poor way of restoring an erring member to society. Homes now exist in many cities to which discharged prisoners are free to go until some provision can be made for their placement. Very often some form of industry is carried on, partly to keep the men employed and partly to help defray the cost of running the establishment. Both the American Volunteers and the Salvation Army have been active in the work, and there are several other smaller agencies or organizations supporting the same cause.
>
> With the growth of parole work there has been some reaction against any arrangement for taking care of discharged prisoners in a group, the thought being that a man should go immediately to a job upon his release from prison and have no further contact with former associates. No doubt this would be best, but until the parole system has been developed to a point where this is possible for every discharged prisoner, the volunteer organizations should be encouraged and supported in their work.[21]

Texas used volunteer local parole boards beginning in 1937, ending the existing system in which no supervision was provided for. Voluntary parole supervisors, who assisted inmates in obtaining jobs and making reports, were appointed in 242 of 254 counties in Texas within a year.

Volunteers were more important in most locales than full-time officers. A 1915 survey of parole found such officers to be scarce, and the number of parolees under supervision ranging from forty per officer to more than 800. In their early years, parole officers were more often housed in prisons and managed files, while the volunteers interacted face to face with the former prisoners in the community.

Old parole emphasized the authority of the prison warden, acting either alone or with the advice of other board members or prison officials, in selecting inmates to be released from prison early. Parole was decided within each prison for its own population, and inmates once paroled were responsible to the prison that released them—and to which they would be returned if revoked.

When federal parole began in 1910, each of the three federal penitentiaries had its own board consisting of the warden, the physician, and the superintendent of prisons of the Justice Department in Washington, D.C. A single three-member board, headquartered in Washington, was created with the founding of the Federal Bureau of Prisons in 1930.

In other states, the same type of movement, from individual institutional control to an independent **parole board** within the department of corrections or another state agency or reporting directly to the governor, took place over time. Parole was seen as being closely linked to executive clemency under the governor's authority. Many states combined the two functions. Texas created a combined board of pardons and paroles in 1929 that still exists today; its dual functions were to recommend prisoners for parole to the governor and to make clemency recommendations as well. Until 1947, paroles in Texas were considered a part of clemency; they were called conditional pardons or executive paroles.

When the National Advisory Commission on Criminal Justice Standards and Goals reviewed the responsibilities of parole boards in the fifty states in 1973, it found these additional responsibilities:

Additional Responsibility	Number of Boards
Holding clemency hearings	28
Commuting sentences	24
Appointing parole supervision staff	24
Administering parole service	20
Paroling from local jails	19
Granting or withholding good time	17
Supervising probation service	14
Granting pardons, restorations, and remissions	1
Fixing maximum sentences	1
Discharging prior to sentence expiration	1
Setting standards for good time	1
Advising on pardons	1
None of these additional responsibilities	5[22]

As the responsibilities of these boards increased, two other expectations changed as well. First, they should be less "political" and more professional in their approach. Although they were then (and still remain in most states today) political appointees, the notion developed over time that parole board members should be more than just political hacks who needed a job; they should have some professional background in the legal system, the behavioral sciences, or some other field connected to law and human behavior. Second, their work should appear to be "scientific," as if they were following a methodology more precise than human intuition. They should be "experts," making expert decisions.

Edwin Sutherland reported in the 1930s that only six states then had full-time salaried parole boards, starting with Illinois in 1927.[23] He commented on the trend toward full-time, professional, independent parole boards composed of experts, adding,

> The trend during the last three decades has been toward centralization of parole authority and toward removal of the parole board from the department of correction. While this has been supported by the prison staff in many cases on the grounds that it relieves them of a troublesome responsibility which interferes with their efficiency in the institutional work, it has been criticized by others on the grounds that the prison staff knows better than any other agency when a prisoner should be released.[24]

It did seem like an odd thing to do, looking back at the original work of Maconochie and Crofton, which emphasized the prison manager's responsibility to keep up with the progress of each prisoner and determine when he was ready for release. To divorce the parole decision from the institution, even to the point in the federal system and many states of not allowing prison administrators or employees to appear at parole board hearings, seemed to move away from the concept that how the criminal behaved in prison—the prisoner as a management problem—was in any way related to his suitability for release. The parole board would have to make its decisions based on two primary criteria: the contents of the inmate's file and the inmate's performance at the parole hearing.

The American Parole Association had adopted a "Declaration of Principles" in 1933, outlining the principles that would be used in determining the time at which a particular offender should be released from prison:

> Has the institution accomplished all that it can for him; is the offender's state of mind and attitude toward his own difficulties and problems such that further residence will be harmful or beneficial; does a suitable environment await him on the outside; can the beneficial effect already accomplished be retained if he is held longer to allow a more suitable environment to be developed?[25]

This put the parole board in the position of predicting the prisoner's behavior based on its interpretation of his state of mind, particularly whether he would be better off in prison or out. Sutherland went on to list numerous arguments against this approach, several of which are highlighted here:

1. The indeterminate sentence takes into account nothing except the reformation of the person, while other things, especially the deterrence of potential criminals, should be considered.

2. No satisfactory method of determining when a prisoner has reformed has been developed; his prison record is generally used, but this is unsatisfactory for the reason that a good prisoner is frequently a poor citizen.

3. It tends to produce sycophancy (which we would call "brownnosing" today) among prisoners, making them work to make friends with the guards rather than work to modify their behavior.

4. Uncertainty regarding the time of release causes much anxiety for prisoners.

5. Prisoners suspect that differences in the length of terms of prisoners convicted of the same offense are due to favoritism or graft.[26]

As a system tying current criminological thought to institutional performance, New Jersey's parole system was much admired in the 1930s. It used a system of classification, reclassification meetings every six months, transfer to the appropriate institution, and training to prepare for release that was very individualized for its day. Parole decisions were made by a full-time board that worked closely with the classification committee (with strong medical and behavioral science representation) at each institution. When approved for release, the parolee was assigned to a full-time, professional parole officer in the community; different levels of supervision and special placements were possible. This system, which incorporated many aspects of the medical model that would be emphasized a generation later, was the most progressive of its day.[27]

Federal parole procedures from the late 1930s, while lacking the classification input, were no less systematic. Prisoners became eligible for parole after serving one-third of their sentence or fifteen years of a life sentence. There followed a sequence of steps:

1. *The application for parole.*

2. *Information about the prisoner.* An institutional parole officer was responsible for preparing the file for review.

3. *The parole hearing.* One member of the parole board came to every federal prison four times per year. The only people present for the hearing were the parole board member, the institutional parole officer, the applicant, and a stenographer; no institutional officers were present, and no one outside the prison was allowed to attend or speak for or against.

4. *The disposition.* A meeting of the full board of parole in Washington, D.C.

5. *Conditions of parole.* The parolee is assigned a volunteer adviser and prepared for release.

6. *Supervision.* Each parolee is assigned to a federal probation officer. He also meets regularly with his volunteer adviser. The parolee must send in reports at least monthly.

7. *Violations of parole.* Any member of the parole board could issue an arrest warrant to return the offender to imprisonment; a hearing was held at the next meeting to revoke or reinstate parole.

8. *Final discharge.* The parolee got a letter notifying him that he had completed his parole successfully.[28]

By the time of World War II, parole had spread across America, and though it ranged in practice from minimalist to fully formed, it had become the most common means of release from prison. Prisoners were learning how to play the parole game because it was the quickest way out of prison, but many of them hated it for many different reasons.

Edwin Sutherland cited this former prisoner's view of parole:

> Parole is the worst thing that can happen in a prison. The prisoner learns that some other prisoner is paroled. The other prisoner committed the same offense and has no more children, no better friends, and the same previous record. This causes suspicion of graft or politics. It makes the prisoner resentful of the entire system. He is willing to pay a regular penalty for a certain crime and regards that as proper and just. When he commits a crime he knows he is likely to get caught and he expects to pay the regular penalty if he does get caught. The underworld has the penalties all figured out, so much for this offense and so much for that, it is a consistent and definite system. They regard the indeterminate sentence and parole as mere camouflage. When a particular prisoner gets out earlier than this system of thought provides, it is graft; when he is held longer, it is a grudge. This disrupts the prison.[29]

Parolees also objected to being supervised after their release from prison, a point made in a 1925 Pennsylvania report arguing in favor of the indeterminate sentence and parole: "Parole is not leniency. On the contrary, parole really increases the state's period of control."[30] If the prisoner was liberated by any other means, he went out of prison a free man. The state had lost its control. Society was no longer safe. Parole, however, kept the convict on a string, even after release.[31]

Parolees recognized that they were the center of attention while on parole—that to the public and law enforcement authorities they were **marked men.** When a sensational crime was committed, the police always went after "the usual suspects," many of them parolees who would be questioned and released, and if a parolee was the one responsible for a terrible crime, the whole parole system was attacked. An inmate-written article, titled "The Parolee's Obligation," in the Iowa State Prison newspaper in 1935 addressed this point:

> From the misstep of any one man a complete case is made against the parole system, and by judicious propaganda the public is led to infer the entire system has broken down and that penal institutions are nothing but factories where prisoners are turned out hardened criminals and that inmates are being mollycoddled to such an extent criminals look forward to a term in prison as a sort of vacation from the rigors of life on the outside. Not one word is ever said of the thousand who have expiated their crimes and gone on to lives of useful endeavor.
>
> It behooves the parole man to watch his step, for if temptation confronts him and he lets go, he then inflicts punishment upon those he has left behind, even though he has no intention of hurting them, because the awaited chance to howl is eagerly grasped by those who enjoy pointing out the faults of those who have once been convicted of wrongdoing.[32]

Some of the prison observers pointed out that what parole had done was replace clemency as the principal method of release. Governors saw parole boards as a way of deflecting away from themselves the political heat that releasing criminals often generated. Thus, even though the governor appointed the parole board members, the board still served as a buffer between an unhappy public and the governor's office.

Convicts knew that the parole board, whether staffed by unpaid amateurs or by professional experts, held the key to their future. Malcolm Braly, the writer and editor, made many appearances before the Adult Authority, California's parole board, in his twenty-year criminal life. He called the annual parole board appearance "in many ways, the worst time of all.":

> The average inmate appears once a year, and you are no sooner denied, flopped over (which in those days meant denial without explanation), knocked down with your rent paid for another year, than you begin to wait for your next appearance. . . .
>
> There was nothing that interested us more and we logged years trying to thrash out a basis on which to predict the Adult Authority. This was our great debate. We knew which programs to try to associate ourselves with and we knew which ploys were now exhausted. We could gauge public pressure and the changing winds of penal philosophy, and we knew which individual members were apt to be liberal and which were conservative. We charted their idiosyncrasies. We hope they were feeling well. . . .
>
> . . . every time I appeared in front of the Adult Authority I found some reason, however wild, to imagine they would free me. These were not dreams of invisibility, this was real hope. No matter how I counseled myself against this irrational optimism it always came to me. It made me crazy to know that these other humans, these walking, talking, shitting and ulcerating humans, could, if the whim took them, order me set free, and no one, not the entire guardline, could change their order. . . .
>
> We had our body of wisdom and our intuitions as to how they must function, but they also had learned something about us. They had been subjected to the most artful and elaborate cons until now they took nothing on faith. They knew we would say anything to get out. Every man who came before them sat there with a single purpose—to somehow leave that room with his freedom restored. Few cared how.[33]

No one paid much attention to what prisoners thought, and parole continued its development—mostly following the track that took it farther away from direct association with prison officials at particular institutions—in the post–World War II rehabilitation era. The basic parole process went like this. States used two types of sentences: determinate and indeterminate. Put yourself in the place of a felon convicted a second time of auto theft. In one state, you might get five years; in another state, you might get one to fifteen. But in both states you were parole eligible. In the determinate sentencing state, eligibility came after some portion of the sentence, most commonly one-third, had been served. A life sentence was calculated in minimum years; lifers were eligible for parole after seven years in Florida, for instance.

In the indeterminate state, you would go to the parole board after your minimum time, but they would just look over your file and deny you; you had not been in long enough. Then you would go back every year until they decided you were ready for release.

The **parole hearing** would typically involve a direct meeting with several members of the board. Boards varied considerably in their makeup, pay, and procedures as well as their responsibilities, as already described. Some states used volunteers who were unpaid amateurs—just public-spirited citizens who were interested. Others had part-time boards, still others full-time, professional boards. Boards started small and got bigger as their responsibilities and the number of cases heard continued to grow. On the bigger boards, smaller panels would go out to hold hearings at the individual prisons; the panel members might rotate their combinations to avoid becoming excessively familiar with the staff of a particular institution, who were known to informally "put in a good word" for inmates coming in for hearing, even if they were not allowed to speak formally on the inmates' behalf.

What was the parole hearing like? One inmate compared it to thirty minutes before God or before St. Peter trying to get to God, another said it was fifteen minutes of sweating blood, and another could not remember anything about it after it was done. One of the parole board members was usually assigned your file. He led the way in discussing the case, asking about the crime and the experience of imprisonment.

Put yourself in the place of the convict again. How would you respond to these questions?

"What were you thinking when you committed this crime?"

"How do you think you've changed in prison?"

"How will you be different if you should be released?"

"Are you a good Christian?"

"What do you think your problem is?"

Let's imagine you answered the questions this way:

"I am an innocent man. I did not commit this crime. The police and district attorney framed me."

"I've become more bitter and frightened—angry at the world."

"I don't plan to do anything different—except not get caught again."

"I am an atheist, though sometimes I'm attracted to Buddhism."

"My problem is that I am in prison, and I want to be somewhere else."

What decision do you think the board would make?

In many states, to avoid emotional confrontations, the inmate was not informed of the board's decision at the end of the hearing. He would return to his cell and wait for the letter of formal notification. If it said "approved," it gave a release date, often contingent on having both a place to live and a job—the **parole plan,** it was called. If it said "denied," that was all it said; sometimes it gave a date to apply again. Inmates called this being **flopped,** as Braly used the term earlier. It meant try again later, though it did not provide guidance about what you should do differently next time. Get a program? Be more respectful? Or just lie more earnestly? You had a year to figure it out.

Most convicts would figure it out, or the board would figure they had done enough time and vote to let them go. Research into parole practices from this era suggests that inmates, whether under determinate or indeterminate sentencing, would end up serving comparable terms in confinement, but some, those who were unruly, uncooperative, quirky, or scary, could end up serving a lot more time in the indeterminate states. They were marked as men not ready for parole.

Parole always operated in a political context. In some states, lots of inmates got parole on their first try; in others, prisoners expected to be denied two or three times on average before they were finally approved. In the 1950s, the U.S. Parole Commission released figures showing that it approved about a third of the federal prisoners coming before it seeking parole while denying the other two-thirds. But the ones denied could come back again and again, and most would eventually get out. As early as the 1920s in New York, about 95 percent of the inmates eligible for parole eventually got it, most of them when they had completed the minimum term.[34] If they did not get parole, there was always good time, which was accepted as a universal prison practice by the early 1900s, years before parole was; or they could seek a commutation or pardon if they had money or political connections.

By the 1960s, the prisoner who served his full term was becoming a rare bird. There were too many options to get out of prison early, and most prisoners found at least one of them, parole most frequently. Parole boards exercised general authority over virtually all inmates, and through the mid-1970s about three-quarters of all inmates discharged from prison each year left on discretionary parole. Then in the 1980s, rehabilitation went south and very nearly took parole with it.

NEW PAROLE AND MANDATORY RELEASE

The movement to abolish old parole began in the 1970s. It came without much warning. One parole official compared it with rolling along, thinking everything was fine, and then discovering that everyone hated you. Everyone—the public, politicians, criminologists, convicts, and prison officials—virtually everyone had terrible things to say about parole. The only people saying much good about parole for a while were the people actually doing parole work, and their remarks often sounded defensive, like they were trying to justify their work and place in the criminal justice system.

Maine was the first state to abolish parole in 1975. It was followed by California in 1976, Indiana in 1977, Illinois in 1978, and New Mexico in 1979. Over the next two decades, they would be joined by a dozen other states and the federal government. The most notable feature of the **new parole** was that it no longer existed in a third of the states by the end of the century; in the remaining states, its form was much changed. The parole tide had flowed in strong at the beginning of the century, and at the end it had ebbed just as strongly.

Joan Petersilia has summarized the criticisms of indeterminate sentencing and parole as falling into three major categories:

1. There was little scientific evidence that parole release and supervision reduced subsequent recidivism.
2. Parole and indeterminate sentencing were challenged on moral grounds as unjust and inhumane, especially when imposed on unwilling participants.
3. Indeterminate sentencing permitted authorities to utilize a great deal of uncontrolled discretion in release decisions, and these decisions were often inconsistent and discriminatory.[35]

As a release option, parole had to confront the crime control politics of this era as well; whatever else it might do, parole let criminals out of prison early. In the context of the most severe approach to crime control, placing emphasis on incapacitation above all else, parole was a bad idea. Any practice that let criminals out early was a bad idea.

Release on parole in America began a major transformation in the late 1970s that continued through the remainder of the century. This transformation, focusing at this point on the role of the parole board, had four major legal and political causes:

1. The outright replacement of discretionary parole by mandatory parole in a third of the states
2. Restrictions on the authority of the parole board to release offenders convicted of certain crimes, particularly violent crimes covered by truth-in-sentencing provisions
3. Raised restrictions on eligibility, based on the proportion of the sentence served required for first review and the portion served by second-time or habitual offenders
4. Political conservatism among appointed parole board members in most states

As Petersilia and others have described, the parole board was abolished in about sixteen states and in the federal system. What used to be the Adult Authority in California is now the **Board of Prison Terms** (BPT). Its powers have changed since the days when Malcolm Braly appeared before it. Its discretionary release authority (subject to the governor's approval) is now restricted to lifers; all other criminals are released on mandatory parole at their good-time dates. The BPT also conducts revocation hearings, handles placements of mentally disordered offenders, holds hearings to label criminals as sexually violent predators, transfers foreign-born criminals to other countries, and makes recommendations to the governor on pardons and commutations. What it does not do is parole the 150,000 parole reentries (many of them the same people going out and coming back and going out again) in California each year.

At the federal level, the Comprehensive Crime Control Act of 1984 created the **U.S. Sentencing Commission,** which sets the sentencing guidelines judges use to fix sentences. The U.S. Parole Commission was abolished, and parole was phased out of the federal system in 1997. Parole has been replaced by supervised release, as discussed earlier, an add-on when the federal prisoner is discharged at his 85 percent good-time discharge date.[36]

Of the states that have not abolished parole, most have adopted truth-in-sentencing provisions applicable to violent crimes. To get parole or good-time release in these states, offenders must serve 85 percent of their sentences, the same standard used in the federal system. State adoption of this standard was tied to receiving federal funds for jail and prison construction and other anti-crime activities.

In the approximately fifteen states that remain outside the "abolish parole" and "truth in sentencing" movements, other legal changes have changed eligibility dates and made some offenders serve more time before getting a hearing. Parole boards have amended their own rules about hearings and rehearings after denial. More than half the states allowing discretionary parole use some type of **risk assessment** instrument to assist in making parole decisions. These instruments, which quantify risk factors in the offender's background and predict the risk of recidivism, have been around since the 1930s, but they have been used more frequently of late—first, because they are more accurate than old "hunch" methods, and, second, because they make the selection process appear to be more objective.

One early device developed by Clark Tibbits in 1931 used twenty-one factors related to predicting parole success; most of these, if supplemented by the seemingly omnipotent factor of drug abuse, would still be considered relevant today. Tibbits's scale gave inmates favorable or unfavorable ratings on these factors. Inmates scoring favorably on fifteen of twenty-one were considered good risks; inmates scoring unfavorably on fifteen of twenty-one were considered bad risks. The instruments used today generally quantify important variables such as prior convictions, drug abuse history, unemployment, and so on; the higher the score, the greater the risk. The current New Jersey parole guidelines provide that each case is to be assessed "in terms of risk and public safety," using four general criteria:

1. Criminal history
2. Prior opportunities on community supervision
3. Institutional behavior
4. The inmate's parole release plan regarding housing, employment, and education

Beyond these legal and administrative restrictions, politics, or the parole board's appreciation of the political environment in which they work, then comes into play. Parole is a political decision, and the people making the decisions today are in general more conservative—or at least more inclined toward a public safety than a rehabilitative perspective—than were members of earlier boards. Discretionary release means that you can say yes, but when you say no, there is not much the prisoner can do about it: there is no right to appeal. Thus, many boards just say no more often. In Louisiana, for instance, the parole board under populist Democratic Governor Edwin Edwards (1992–1996) granted parole in about two-thirds of the cases it heard. Under Edwards's successor, conservative Republican Mike Foster (1996–2004), a different board approved about a third, and this was after some violent criminals had been removed from eligibility, slightly improving the quality of the parole pool. Louisiana's felons are by law entitled to only one parole hearing, so if you are denied in your one appearance, you may never get another chance—you wait for your good-time release.

The composite result of these changes has been to make getting released on parole more difficult. The impact on imprisonment has not been as severe as some people anticipated. The average length of prison term actually served has increased by about five or six months over the past two decades, and the average length of time on parole has increased by about four months, meaning that a typical criminal would be under the control of the corrections system for almost a year longer than he would have been in the 1980s.

We should keep in mind that the profile of imprisoned men and women is different in several respects from that of a generation ago. If violent criminals were apples and nonviolent criminals oranges, then there are more oranges than apples in the prison barrel and lots more than there were twenty or thirty years ago. However, the oranges are now being held in prison as if they were the apples of earlier years, and the apples are being quarantined as if they were poison. Both the apples and the oranges stay longer under the control of the system; when they are released, to be managed under the heightened supervision standards of today, they are more likely to get in trouble, get revoked, and be returned to prison either for a new crime or for a technical violation of parole that involves breaking the rules but no new arrest or conviction. Parole release options have been cut back and made less discretionary during this period of transformation; the same forces have affected the work of the field officers who make up the other part of the parole system.

THE PAROLE OFFICER AND PAROLE WORK

The parole board determines who will be released and when; the **parole officer** supervises the offender once he or she has been released from imprisonment. While discretionary parole release has been sharply curtailed over the past generation, parole supervision has been intensified, particularly in regard to its surveillance component. Just as new parole is very different from old parole, the work of the twenty-first-century parole officer is much different from the work of the officer of a century ago or even twenty years ago.

Parole officers were originally tied to the institutions from which parolees were released. They managed the paperwork and assisted prisoners with getting a job and a place to stay—and they set up the contacts with the **volunteer parole officers** who provided the direct assistance in the community. If the parolee failed, which in the early days meant getting arrested and put back in jail or losing his job and source of income, then the parole officer oversaw his return to prison, which was carried out by law enforcement authorities. The parole officer's job for a long time was more **case management** than provision of direct services.

By the mid-1900s, the parole officer no longer worked for the prison; he worked for the parole board, and his job had become more focused on supervision of parolees. The key measure of workload was the **caseload**—the number of active files the officer was responsible for. The **casework** approach, borrowed from the social services, viewed the parolee as a client whom the parole officer was trying to assist with various social needs. The ideal role of the parole officer combined elements of a mentor, a confidante, an advocate, and a disciplinarian.

By the end of the 1900s, this role had changed again, as Joan Petersilia explained in her book *Reforming Probation and Parole in the 21st Century*:

> Historically, parole agents were viewed as paternalistic figures that mixed authority with help. Officers provided direct services (for example, counseling) and also knew the community and brokered services (for example, job training) to needy offenders. As noted earlier, parole was originally designed to make the transition from prison to community more gradual and, during this time, parole officers were to assist the offender in addressing personal problems and searching for employ-

ment and a place to live. Many parole agencies still do assist in these "service" activities. Increasingly, however, parole supervision has shifted away from providing services to parolees, and more toward providing monitoring and surveillance activities such as drug testing, monitoring curfews, and collecting restitution.[37]

The literature of parole work often makes the contrast between rehabilitation and surveillance, while veteran parole officers used different terminology: they say **law enforcement** has replaced **social work,** and many of them do not approve of the trend. Marc Mauer of The Sentencing Project defines the traditional role as more of a balance—"half cop, half social worker." But the old-timers are on the way out, replaced by a new wave of parole officers who never worked under the old models—when parole officers were more autonomous and less rule oriented.

The parole officer of today is a civil service state employee. Parole is managed as a part of the state corrections bureaucracy in about forty of the fifty states; the older model, in which the parole officer worked directly for the parole board, still holds in about ten states. In about half the states, the same officer or agent is supervising both probationers, released under the authority of a local trial court judge, and parolees, released by the parole board or by the prison on good time. Probation is really a mixed bag, as we will discuss at length in the next chapter, felons and misdemeanants sometimes monitored by the same officer and sometimes by different officers, depending on how governments organize these responsibilities. Probationers outnumber parolees about five to one in 2002 (almost 4,000,000 to 750,000), so if an officer is supervising both probationers and parolees, he or she is likely to have more probationers than parolees and also to have other functions, such as presentence investigation reports, that accompany probation.

During the 1970s, the average caseload of parole officers was said to be in the range of forty-five to fifty, though not all sources are consistent with this figure. The President's Crime Commission, reporting in 1967, found about 112,000 adults and 60,000 juveniles on parole (juvenile parole is correctly titled **aftercare**); 2,100 adult parole officers and 1,400 juvenile parole officers were supervising them. This would mean an average adult caseload of about fifty-five and an average juvenile caseload of about forty-three, making no adjustments for supervisors and managers who might carry reduced caseloads or none at all.[38]

By 2000, the number of parole officers had increased to about 7,000, while the number of combined probation/parole officers stood at over 18,000. Figuring caseloads is more complicated because of the long-term trend to merge probation and parole caseloads in the same officer, but for parole alone, the average for a regular caseload was about seventy-three; for probation and parole combined, it was higher, about ninety-four.[39] Parolees are always assumed to be a higher risk than probationers—because they have been to prison, while many probationers have not—and the traditional expectation was that parolees were in need of more direct supervision—and stricter supervision—than were probationers. Nevertheless, with caseloads in the range of seventy to 100, a parole officer would see the parolees in his caseload perhaps twice per month—maybe once in the office and once on the street. The opportunity to make collateral contacts with family members or employers would also be limited; most such contacts would be by telephone—or now by e-mail.

The movement toward stricter supervision has meant in part tighter enforcement of **parole conditions** the parolee must agree to follow when he leaves prison. Going back to the days of the Irish System, parolees have had such conditions to follow to remain free, but the conditions have tended to get longer and more complicated recently as officials try to come up with more comprehensive "thou shalt not" lists.

New Jersey's current **standard parole conditions** provide an example of a relatively short, focused list:

1. Obey all laws and ordinances
2. Report in person to the parole officer
3. Notify the parole officer immediately after any arrest
4. Obtain approval of the parole officer:
    For any change in resident or employment location
    Before leaving the state
5. Do not own or possess any firearm
6. Do not own or possess any weapon
7. Refrain from the use, possession, or distribution of a controlled dangerous substance
8. Make payment for court imposed penalties
9. Register with the appropriate law enforcement agency subject to the provisions of N.J.S.A. 2C:7-2 (Megan's Law)
10. Refrain from behavior that results in the issuance of a final restraining order
11. Waive extradition to the state of New Jersey from any jurisdiction in which they are apprehended and detained for violation of this parole status[40]

The New Jersey Parole Board can also impose **special parole conditions** specific to the individual. Typical special conditions include abstaining from alcohol, participating in random drug and alcohol monitoring, avoiding contact with their victims or with children, refraining from associations with people involved in criminal activity, attending substance abuse treatment, attending mental health counseling, and abiding by a curfew.[41] The most frequently imposed special condition nationwide is **drug testing,** which, given the drug abuse histories of today's parolees, seems sensible, but it also seems sensible to provide drug treatment to those who want it, which is not being done.

Parolees can be returned to prison in either of two common ways. One is an arrest or a conviction for a new crime; this is called a **law violation.** The other is for violating any of the other conditions of parole; this is called a **technical violation.** Criminal behavior is obviously more important. If you are on parole for armed robbery and are arrested for a string of armed robberies and admit your guilt, you are going back to prison to serve the rest of your term and may well pick up some new time on top of it. If you are late with your monthly report to your parole officer or move to a new address without notifying her, then you could be arrested and held under a **detainer** (a legal order preventing you from being released) until a revocation hearing was held; or the parole officer, when she finds you again, could just read you the riot act and tell you not to do it again. The enforcement of technical violations is up to the **discretion** of the parole officer.

Discretion is not, however, purely a matter of individual belief and choice; it is guided by organizational policy and practice. A generation ago, when parolees were returned to prison, it was likely to be as a result of a criminal law violation. Today more parolees are returned as technical violators than as law violators; the majority of the 200,000-plus parolees sent back to prison each year are returned for not following the rules—particularly those dealing with drug use, maintaining contact with the probation officer, and employment—rather than for criminal behavior.

This shift is indicative of organizational changes in the application of discretion, as Petersilia recently pointed out:

> Newly hired parole officers often embrace the "surveillance" versus "rehabilitation" model of parole, along with the quasipolicing role that parole has taken on in some locales. Twenty years ago, social work was the most common educational path for those pursuing careers in parole. Today, the most common educational path is criminal justice studies.[42]

Richard Seiter studied the changing role of parole officers in St. Louis in research completed in 2002, noting,

> Over the past decade, there has been a transition from the dominant style of casework supervision, which emphasizes assisting the offender with problems, counseling, and working to make sure the offender successfully completes supervision, to a style of surveillance supervision which emphasizes the monitoring of offenders to catch them when they fail to meet all required conditions.[43]

A veteran Illinois parole officer put it this way: "The philosophy of the parole unit has changed. Now they all have cars, guns, bullet-proof vests and badges." Parole officers used to try to help parolees succeed; now they look for ways to put them behind bars.[44] Carl Wicklund, the executive director of the American Probation and Parole Association, calls this orientation "tailing, nailing, and jailing."

In an important 1992 article that has generated considerable debate in parole circles over the past decade, Malcolm Feeley and Jonathan Simon defined what they call the **new penology** as the emerging strategy of corrections, including parole work. Their analysis suggests that corrections is dominated by a systems-analysis approach to the task they call **danger management,** which focuses on the old "dangerous class" of criminals who make up the urban underclass—a segment of the population abandoned to poverty and despair. Whereas the old parole officer focused on individual redemption and rehabilitation, at least making the criminal "normal" enough to lead a productive life, the parole officer of the new penology sees not individuals but a class that cannot be helped. The goal of parole, within the corrections system, becomes that of "herding a specific population that cannot be disaggregated and transformed but only maintained—a kind of waste management function."[45] The dangerous class cannot be helped or transformed, so the mission becomes securing it to minimize harm to society at the lowest possible cost.

Jonathan Simon's social history of parole, *Poor Discipline: Parole and the Social Control of the Underclass, 1890–1990,* carries the concept of **waste management** a step further. The "toxic waste" containment sites would be the underclass communities where those under the control of community corrections would be required to live. Parole officers and others in frontline penal jobs would not try to change people or relate to them as individuals; they would define their mission as managing risk and minimizing damage to the larger society.[46]

Feeley and Simon present the new penology as an ideology, not as a set of procedures formally adopted to carry out public policy. It is clear, however, that parole management has adopted several important features of **risk management** in their application to parole work in recent years. These include the following:

1. Actuarial models based on statistical probabilities
2. Detailed risk/needs assessments of individual offenders based on case histories
3. Emphasizing documentation, records keeping, and data input into computerized databases
4. Caseloads structured by perceived risk, using such designations as regular, intensive, electronic, and special
5. Designation of targeted groups of offenders for concentrated supervision, which in recent years has emphasized sex offenders first and foremost
6. Use of formal monitoring criteria that can be counted and documented—urine tests, meetings attended, appointments kept, and forms submitted on time

The result of this emphasis, tied as it is to computers and paperwork, is actually to reduce the parole officer's fieldwork responsibilities and keep him or her tied more to an office (though in increasing numbers of jurisdictions, laptop computers are being issued right along with .40-caliber automatics and body armor). Mona Lynch's study of the new penology as it applied to a large parole office in California found that the officers resisted the risk management strategy and wanted to spend more time in the field, though their orientation was more toward surveillance and law enforcement rather than counseling and helping, as this quote from an experienced parole officer indicated:

> When you've been in this business so long, you tend to realize that you can't really change these guys. I've been 18 years in law enforcement. I think my goal, basically, is—of course keep the community safe—safety—I think my goals is mainly if any of them are doing anything, to find out what they're doing and stop them from doing that. Prevention. We could do prevention if we had the numbers.[47]

Lynch observed that officers emphasized getting out of the office and using their investigative skills. Prevention was equated with being out in the field, watching parolees, and being ready and able to make arrests at the first sign of trouble.[48]

This is the California approach, which is not necessarily synonymous with parole management in other jurisdictions. Seiter's research in St. Louis asked parole officers to identify the most important aspect of their job in improving a parolee's chance for success (which is not the same thing as "what do you emphasize?" or "what is your most important mission?"). The first choice was the monitoring/supervising/surveillance aspects of the job, cited by 33 percent of the officers; the second and third choices, assessing needs and referral to other agencies and helping maintain employment, were listed as first choices by 28 and 20 percent of the respondents.[49] Thus, even though surveillance was listed as the first choice, offender needs and employment were selected by about half of the officers, suggesting the absence of a uniform perspective on doing supervision.

The **parole revocation** process, like field supervision, has undergone considerable change from the old days. The old parole officer just went to the jail, picked the errant parolee up, and took him back to prison or, in the very old days, just signed for the parolee when the local sheriff returned him to prison custody. Since 1972, parole revocation has been governed by the standards of *Morrissey v. Brewer.* The U.S. Supreme Court ruled in this case that Morrissey, a parolee from the Iowa State Penitentiary, was entitled to a **due process hearing** as part of revocation; the parolee was extended six basic due process rights:

1. Written notice of the claimed violations
2. Disclosure of the evidence against him
3. Opportunity to be heard in person and to present witnesses and documentary evidence
4. The right to confront and cross-examine adverse witnesses (although this can be denied for good reason by the hearing officer)
5. A "neutral and detached" hearing body, which does not necessarily mean a lawyer or a judge
6. A written statement by the fact finders as to the evidence relied on and reasons for revoking parole[50]

Many jurisdictions set up a two-stage revocation proceeding. First, a hearing officer, usually a senior parole officer or supervisor, holds a probable cause hearing to determine if the violation occurred. Many parolees routinely waive this hearing and proceed on to the second phase, the hearing before the parole board. At this **revocation hearing,** the board decides whether to revoke or reinstate parole. The parolee is most commonly held in jail until these hearings are held. The two phases can be rolled into one proceeding, but in many jurisdictions, where offenders are held in county jails first, the preliminary hearing will be held locally before the parolee is transported to a prison for the revocation hearing.

The relationship between the parolee and the parole officer, particularly the parole officer's definition of the supervision role, is a key to determining whether the parolee will succeed or be revoked. Most parolees do "slip up," to use Jean Sanders's term for relapsing into drug use. It is what happens after they slip up—what the parole officer does in response to the violation of parole conditions—that determines the subsequent path. Parole officers, even in California, are not windup robots who mechanically enforce every rule of parole to the letter of the law. While they have less discretion in most jurisdictions than they once did, in regard to both law and technical violations, they still "not revoke" more often than they "revoke" the violators in their caseload. They have to—or ought to—take some action against violators, but it does not have to be putting them back in prison.

Parole officers develop their own styles and management strategies for working with offenders, as numerous research studies indicate. Some are "by the book," some are laid back, some are more detailed manipulators, and others are more remote. One parolee described the relationship between parolees and parole officers as "ranging from the difficult to the impossible." His explanation was that it would be difficult at best because one figure was trying to impose control, and the other was trying to resist it and live his own life without interference; it would be impossible when two personalities were in such conflict that they could not get along at all.

An effective dramatization of the parolee/parole officer relationship can be found in the 1978 film *Straight Time*. Dustin Hoffman portrays Max Dembo, a California parolee who has been in and out of prison since he was a boy. He seems possibly interested in staying out of crime when he gets out of San Quentin this time. When he gets down to Los Angeles, he gets a job and finds a pretty girlfriend. But when Max meets his new parole officer, Earl Frank (portrayed by M. Emmett Walsh), they butt heads from the start. After a series of clashes and a memorable scene in which Dembo turns the tables on Frank in a most embarrassing public way, Dembo returns to criminal life with a fury. But you can almost hear him telling another con (like Edward Bunker, the old California ex-con who wrote the book *No Beast So Fierce*, on which the film was based), "I might have made it, if I'd just had a different PO." See the film and decide for yourself how much difference the parole officer makes.

LIFE AS A PAROLEE

What are parolees like, and what kinds of lives do they live? Their basic situation is defined by two circumstances: they are convicted felons, and they have been in prison. They have to confront all the restrictions, all the disadvantages, and all the stigma of convicts, except they have to do it on the street, among people not in prison. A man who had spent many years in prison and several years on parole put it this way:

> It's easier in prison. You have two classes, the guards and the cons. You know the rules, and the cons are all alike. Being on the street is much more complicated. You are completely responsible for everything you do; it's like living under a magnifying glass. You know everybody is watching you—like you are a threat to them. You are a marked man—you see how people react to you. That's why ex-cons would rather associate with other ex-cons, even though you know that is one of the things that can get you sent back. Even if you want to go straight, it's a hard, uphill climb. You are constantly afraid of making the one mistake that will put you back in prison.

On December 31, 2002, over three-quarters of a million (753,141) adult men and women were on parole, naturally an all-time high. The parole numbers are closely tied to the prison numbers; the ratio of parolees to prisoners has long been in the range of from 0.55 to 0.65 to 1.0—the parole population is a bit less than two-thirds of the prison population at any given time, if we are searching for mathematical formulas. For a few years in the early 1990s, the ratio climbed above 0.7, but a combination of new prison construction and more restrictive laws and policies soon brought it back down within the normal range. In 2002, the ratio stood at 0.55 to 1.0, indicating that parole use has been down slightly the past couple of years.

Five big parole systems dominate the statistics:

California	113,185
Texas	103,068
Pennsylvania	97,712
Federal	82,972 (almost all supervised release, not parole)
New York	55,990

These five systems contain 453,000 parolees, over 60 percent of the national total. On the other end of the scale are states like Maine—which abolished parole and parole supervision almost thirty years ago—with thirty-two parolees in the entire state, Washington with ninety-five, and North Dakota—after a sudden surge—with 149. Maine has the lowest rate of parole at three per 100,000 population; Pennsylvania has the highest by far, 1,037 per 100,000.[51]

Parolees—discretionary and mandatory—look in profile a lot like prisoners, except that the prison population is made up of more violent and long-term criminals who will not be paroled soon—if at all. At least 20 percent of the prison population is serving sentences of twenty years or longer (including life), most of these for violent crimes, which will keep these inmates from being a factor in parole statistics for a long time.

Of the adults on parole in 2002, 40 percent had been imprisoned for drug crimes, 26 percent for property crimes, 24 percent for violent crimes, and 10 percent for public order crimes. Women, as predominantly nonviolent criminals, made up 14 percent of adults on parole, more than twice the percentage of women in the prison population.[52] Whites made up about 39 percent of the parole population, blacks and Hispanics about 60 percent; the parole population is about four percentage points "whiter" than the prison population, mostly because of the greater numbers of minorities serving longer sentences for violent crimes.

Regardless of race, ethnicity, or gender, parolees share the same problems on release. A 1997 California report provided this background of the state's parolees:

85 percent were chronic substance abusers.

10 percent were homeless, but this figure was higher in cities, as high as 30 to 50 percent in San Francisco and Los Angeles.

70 to 90 percent were unemployed.

50 percent were functionally illiterate, reading below a sixth-grade level and unable to complete job forms or compete in the job market.

18 percent had some sort of psychiatric problem.[53]

These background characteristics may be somewhat more extreme than those of parolees in other states but only by a few percentage points. American Radio Works, the documentary unit of Minnesota Public Radio, produced a series titled "Hard Time: Life after Prison" in 2003. In profiling parolees in New Jersey and North Carolina, the documentary points out that 50,000 people leave prison every month. They have been away longer than in the past and are less likely to have gotten any job training or education behind bars—only about a third do so. They typically return home carrying all their old liabilities—addictions, poor education, and bad work habits—and they bring new ones: stigma and damaged relations with families.[54] Eddie, who has done time in New Jersey for having sex with underage girls, cannot find a full-time job:

> Like Eddie, many ex-convicts struggle alone on sporadic, informal work. Researchers have found that a prison term takes a slice out of a person's earning power—a 15 percent slice, on average. Since most people who go to prison have few marketable skills to start with, a 15-percent wage hit often means poverty. Federal and state laws ban many felons from holding jobs in schools, nursing homes, or airport security. Eddie's home state of New Jersey has a long list of jobs off-limits to certain felons—from bartending to firefighting, to working at a racetrack or as a parking attendant. Before his arrest, Eddie held jobs as a postal worker and an optician and he managed a Radio Shack store. Since prison, he says, he's applied for dozens of entry-level jobs.[55]

Every time he filled out an application for permanent employment, his criminal record came up. It took Eddie thirteen months to get two part-time jobs, enough to make ends meet. He is trying to get his own painting business started. On his company's employment applications, he says he would ask, "Have you ever been convicted of a felony?" If they put no, he will tell them he cannot hire them.[56]

Richard Seiter's survey asked parole officers to identify the most important aspect of reentry for improving parolees' chances for success. The top three choices were the following:

1. Steady or continuous employment—34 percent
2. Staying off drugs and alcohol—21 percent
3. A support system (family, friends, church)—20 percent.[57]

For women on parole, these needs are complicated by two important variables: the stigma of being a "woman ex-con," with its connotation of being even lower than a man ex-con, and their children. Patricia O'Brien's 2001 book *Making It in the "Free World": Women in Transition from Prison*, follows eighteen women as they left prison and returned home. Sixteen of the eighteen women were mothers, with a total of forty-four children. Their reintegration into society was greatly complicated by the financial and emotional burdens of caring for their children. As O'Brien indicated, the women described their response to parole supervision as "doing what I have to." Most of them reported that their parole officers were a positive force in promoting their transition despite the intrusion and control that they represented in their everyday lives:

> Women wanted to know the rules and expectations of the parole or supervision process. Some women were frustrated because they felt that parole officers sometimes transgressed their privacy in the name of supervision or the overwhelming nature of the expectations placed on them. Mandi, in particular, represented the extreme example of the expectations that some women have to address: in order to both complete parole and meet demands for regaining custody of her children, she had to manage a number of treatment conditions, report to her parole officer regularly, and work two jobs to generate enough income to rent a house large enough for her and her four children. Initially, she did this without a car.[58]

In her research into the expectations of groups of convicted female felons before and after their release from confinement, DeAnna Talbert found among the in-custody group a sense of optimism one would not expect to find in this population. To a survey questionnaire identifying potential problems after release, these women—who were in profile single mothers living below the poverty line, with relatives and friends who were also criminals, with a background of drug and alcohol abuse, and with a history of physical and sexual abuse—expected to do well and encounter few problems on their release from custody.

A narrative question on Talbert's survey posed this question: "What is your outlook on how your life will be after your release from custody?" The common threads running through the written responses were the following:

1. Accepting responsibility for what they had done
2. Defeating their substance abuse problems
3. Finding religion

They seemed to think that behind bars they had become stronger persons and that this inner strength would carry over to the street after release.[59]

Talbert wrote in her conclusion,

> Behind bars, the women seemed to be content with their situation and living conditions. The researcher believed that they were trying to be patient and wait on their release date. Within the jail, they enjoyed each other's company; they were constantly laughing and talking and joking with each other and the jail staff. Many of these women kept their problems inside; their approach to life behind bars was to get along the best they could day-to-day.
>
> Many of the in-custody group apparently expect this philosophy to carry over into the outside world after their release. Despite the serious problems they have had before, they expect the world to be better this time around. Are these expectations realistic?
>
> The responses of the out-of-custody group seem more in touch with reality. Their concerns are more the concerns of poor single women in American society—housing, employment, earning a living, and transportation. They have been back out on the street long enough to come up against these and other problems that the women behind bars seem to think will not mark their own lives in the future as they surely did the past.
>
> The most immediate need of the staff involved with programs, it appeared to the researcher, was to find a way to keep reminding the female inmates that life on their own on the streets would be much tougher than life in the supportive jail environment. When you had them believing this, then you could try to address the specifics of what they need to survive after their discharge from custody.[60]

Patricia O'Brien asked her eighteen women this question: "What did women identify as necessary for making it in the free world that could be applied to the benefit of others currently in transition from prison?"

The major recommendations that women suggested included the following:

a. Women need to begin the process of identifying sources of support prior to leaving prison.
b. Women need to address issues of abuse and addiction that may prevent them from recognizing their ability to manage the transition.

c. Representatives of the correctional system need to treat women with respect and believe in their potential to transform themselves, and provide training for employment at living wages when released.

d. Association with other ex-inmates can be a source of support—it should not be an automatic risk for violating a woman on parole or supervision.

e. Helping professionals should be educated about the range of needs that women coming out of prison have to face and work with women to define strategies for meeting those needs.

f. The general public, particularly potential employers, should be educated about female offenders and their motivation to succeed, so that they are given an opportunity to (re)establish themselves.[61]

Most of these recommendations are as true for men as they are for women, and one of the issues they touch on is the interaction between the criminal and the parole officer. British criminologist Stephen Farrell has written about this relationship in *Rethinking What Works with Offenders: Probation, Social Context and Desistance from Crime* (2002). Based on hundreds of interviews with probation officers and offenders, Farrell's work—applied to the comparable context of parole—suggests that the road to going straight is hardly straight at all. Offenders and officers disagree about the obstacles to be overcome and how to overcome them. In successful outcomes, they are overcome, but solutions imposed were more ad hoc than focused or sustained, and the important factors were generally outside the control of either party:

> The two factors most favorably reported—by both probationers and offenders—were employment status and family formation. In the end, obstacles were generally, successfully overcome when probationers, rather than officers, initiated actions that led to improved employment and family situations. However, increased probation assistance associated with these particular cases was found to enhance the economic and familial improvements that eventually overcame obstacles.[62]

Farrell concluded,

> If probation work became more desistance-focused rather than offending-related, officers may feel they had a clearer mandate to help probationers tackle family (or economic) problems. This may in turn result in a greater involvement of officers in the attempts to tackle such obstacles and greater success in actually resolving them.[63]

If family connections and economic support are most important to success on parole, we should keep in mind that most criminals released on parole have neither. They are much closer to the position of Malcolm Braly, released from San Quentin for the first time in 1950 at age twenty-five:

> I took the bus to San Francisco, checked my boxes in a locker at the depot, and, on impulse and because I could, I decided to walk down the length of Market Street to the parole office which was housed in the Ferry Building at the edge of the bay. It was a strange walk. I was shocked at how dirty the streets were and the people seemed nondescript. For years my impressions of this world had been formed by

magazine ads and the weekend movies. As the illusion gained substance, if only through repetition, my memories of this ordinary world had faded away. Now I suffered the shock of instant disillusion, and this, too, was the real end of a fairy tale.

My parole officer, a former cop, had no interest in me. I signed papers, received the balance of my release money, and was told, "Good luck."

"Where should I live?"

"Get yourself a room in a cheap hotel. You've got a job waiting. When you get paid you can look for something permanent. Look, you and I aren't going to be any trouble to each other if you remember just one thing, get your report in every month by the fifth."

For years I had been told exactly what to do. I had walked from the most rigid of routines into this strangely empty freedom. I rented a cheap room, recovered my boxes, and went out to walk the streets. I found myself near the top of Nob Hill, where the pavement sparkles outside the Fairmont Hotel. Here was life as I felt I could live it. I repeated my litany: I was young. I was good-looking. I was smart. I could make something happen for me.[64]

Eighteen months later, he was back in San Quentin, arrested after he was caught in a string of burglaries. Malcolm Braly failed on parole three times before he finally enjoyed a "successful outcome"—with a family and a steady income as a writer and editor. When you read of his misadventures in *False Starts*, you cannot help but wonder what, if anything, would have made the difference in his being successful the first time instead of the fourth.

THE EFFECTIVENESS OF PAROLE

"The abolition of parole will save lives and money," begins the article in *Policy Review* by Governor George Allen of Virginia. Allen goes on to explain why and how the State of Virginia abolished parole, established truth in sentencing, and increased as much as fivefold the amount of time that violent offenders will spend in prison in his term of office.

Virginia's new system (in 1995) was attempting, Allen wrote, to unravel thirty years of paper-tiger laws based on the questionable philosophy that people can change, criminals can be rehabilitated, and every violent criminal—even a murderer—deserves a second chance. In his view, "The only foolproof crime-prevention technique is incarceration." He wanted to send violent criminals this message: "We will not tolerate violence, and if you commit a violent crime, you will stay in prison until you're too old to commit another one." Abolishing a "bankrupt" parole system was a major part of Governor Allen's plan to shift the balance of imprisonment in Virginia from 50 percent violent/50 percent nonviolent to 70 percent violent/30 percent nonviolent.[65] (The result of this plan was that, by 2002, the balance had shifted to 53 percent violent/47 percent nonviolent.)

Political officials and corrections officials in many other states and at the federal level shared Governor Allen's views on parole. Joe Lehman, commissioner of the Washington Department of Corrections, said, "We have a broken parole system. Part of the problem is that parole can't do it alone, and we have misled the public in thinking that we can—hence the frustration, and the cries to abolish parole."[66]

The statistics on the effectiveness of parole seem to support these abolition arguments. From the early 1980s to the mid-1990s, the success rate of parole (discharges without revocation) declined from about 70 percent to about 45 percent, where it has remained since. Almost as many parolees are returned to prison as are successfully discharged, and about 10 percent at any given time are **absconders,** meaning they have disappeared and cannot be found.

Parolees are flooding the prison system. About a third of all admissions to prison in recent years are parole violators; more parole violators reenter prison than new admissions for any of the four categories of criminal offenses: violent, property, drug, or public order. Since 1980, the percentage of conditional release violators who had originally left state prisons as parolees, mandatory releases, and other types of releases subject to community supervision has more than doubled, from 16 to 34 percent.[67]

John DiIulio has pointed out that in 1991 nearly half of all state prisoners had committed their latest crimes while out on probation or parole. While formally "under supervision" in the community, their violations included more than 13,000 murders, some 39,000 robberies, and tens of thousands of other crimes. DiIulio calls this system a **revolving door** and says it is even more true for juvenile criminals than adults.[68]

The most recent national recidivism statistics, based on prisoners discharged from prisons in fifteen states in 1994, indicate that within three years of release, 67.5 percent were rearrested, 46.9 percent reconvicted, and 25.4 percent resentenced to prison for a new crime; another 26.4 percent were returned to prison for technical violations of parole. Thus, the general odds on a parolee being back in prison within three years of release are slightly better than fifty-fifty—not exactly stirring fuel for debating the positive role of parole in society.

In some states, the numbers are particularly striking. A recent analysis of California's prisons calls its "take-all-prisoners" approach to ex-convicts a major reason in the state's prison-funding crisis.[69] Over half the inmates in California prisons are parole violators, most of them reincarcerated for technical violations. California has both a huge number of parolees, well over 100,000 at any given time, and the nation's highest violation rate. Forty-two percent of all state parole violations in America were in California.

This is not a recent aberration but rather the result of a policy change going back more than twenty years. In the 1970s, California had an average daily parolee population of about 15,000 and a revocation rate of less than 15 percent, one of the lowest rates in the country. Then California started putting more parolees back in prison. By the late 1980s, California's parole violation rate had climbed to 85 percent (eighty-five of every 100 parolees released were returned to prison each year).[70] It has declined subsequently, remaining at 60 to 70 percent during most of the past decade before falling to 59 percent in 2003, the lowest rate since 1985. This figure does not include absconders who, when added to the total, mean that only about three in ten parolees in California currently complete parole without being revoked.

To get an idea of the impact of parole in California, consider this comparison. In 2001, about 125,000 new prisoners entered California prisons, compared to about 150,000 parole violators, most of them in and out (and often in and out again) within a few months. For many years, the great majority of California parolees were being returned to prison for failing drug tests, more than for all other reasons combined. This was part of the rationale for passage of **Proposition 36,** approved by voter referendum in November 2000; one provision calls for drug treatment for most routine parole violators in lieu of being returned to prison. By diverting drug-using parolees into treatment, this act is said to be partly responsible for the drop in parole revocations, though, with its huge numbers, California continues to overpower the national statistical picture.

PAROLE: ABOLISH OR REINVENT?

The loss of faith in parole in the 1990s brought about two important changes, both of which we have touched on already. First, the use of discretionary parole declined. About a third of the states abolished parole, and its use was curtailed in the other states, resulting in a pronounced shift to mandatory parole as the preferred method of release from imprisonment. Second, the use of parole vis-á-vis imprisonment declined also. Parole usage had increased more than imprisonment in the 1980s, but in the 1990s, when state imprisonment was going up by 75 percent, parole was increasing by only 30 percent (and almost half of that a big one-year jump in 1991). The number of state parolees was virtually flat from 1992 (619,000) to 2000 (652,000).[71]

This was a crisis decade for parole. Governor Allen was among many calling for the abolition of parole, and the trend was in that direction for several years. But after this time of soul-searching, what emerged was a call to **reinvent parole** rather than abolishing it altogether.

Even parole's critics began to notice some good things about it. For one thing, rehabilitation—a more focused form of rehabilitation—is enjoying a comeback. Certain aspects of the new rehabilitation—drug treatment and job training—are highly compatible with parole. For the past two years, California has put many of its parole violators who would have been revoked for using drugs into intensive treatment. This could be done in prison, but most prison systems are in no way prepared to offer more than rudimentary relapse prevention programs that most convicts either disregard or cannot get into.

Texas established **Project RIO** (for Reintegration of Offenders) in 1985 to provide job placement services to parolees. By 1999, Project RIO had grown to sixty-two field offices providing prerelease employment assistance, assessment, job placement after release, and follow-up. Working with about 15,000 parolees per year, Project RIO had reduced recidivism rates at all levels of risk—high, average, and low—well below the rates for ex-offenders not participating in the project. While California was sending two-thirds or more of its parolees back to prison, Project RIO was maintaining reincarceration rates averaging well below 20 percent.[72]

Two aspects of the traditional parole process—parole board discretion and parole officer supervision—also enjoyed revived support. Joan Petersilia wrote in 2001,

> Parole experts have been saying all along that the public is misinformed when it labels parole as lenient. To the contrary, through their exercise of discretion, parole boards can target more violent and dangerous offenders for longer periods of incarceration. When states abolish parole or reduce parole authorities' discretion, they replace a rational, controlled system of "earned" release for selected inmates with "automatic" release for nearly all inmates. Nonparole systems may sound

tough, but they remove an important gate-keeping role that can protect communities and victims.[73]

The role of the parole officer on the street is being reemphasized. Parole supervision is increasingly seen as being effective—whatever its limitations—in both of its primary aspects: helping and surveillance. The parole officer can be an important source of information and referral assistance for parolees; if the parole officer does not perform this role, who would? Likewise, conditional parole release requires someone to monitor compliance with provisions of release—work, residency, treatment, and so on.

If the parole officer's position is abolished, as has happened in a couple of states enthusiastic to "go all the way" in doing away with parole, no one is left to represent the state's interest in monitoring the transition of criminals from prison to community. It is a fine thing to make the abstract argument that individual criminals have "done their time" and deserve to be released free of strings to make their own choices in life, free of state interference. It is another thing in practice to turn loose on society (and left to their own devices) many thousands of young, unattached, unemployed, unskilled, substance-abusing misfits who have been out of society, on average, for somewhere between two and twenty years. Fifty dollars, a bus ticket, and a wish of "good luck" are not going to do the job with most of these men and women.

As states increasingly grapple with the high cost of imprisonment, they look for options to keep more criminals in the community. Discretionary parole, which costs on average about $2,000 annually per offender as opposed to more than $20,000 to keep an offender in prison, is often cited as part of this movement. Many states would like to do what Governor Allen proposed to do but was apparently unable to accomplish in Virginia: release more nonviolent prisoners to discretionary parole earlier in their sentences, thereby gradually shifting the balance of prison beds more toward violent offenders. This trend is already evident nationwide, though in the states many corrections officials seem reluctant to publicize their policies, probably in fear of being criticized for "turning criminals loose."

Parole's supporters argue that parole's declining success rate—or, conversely, its sharply higher failure rate—is not the product of a "crime wave" among parolees. The high failure rate is due not to an increase in law violations by parolees but to an increase in technical violations, which are discretionary with the parole officer. California provides an illustrative example. In the 1970s, most parole violators were returned to prison with a new prison term for a new crime. Two decades later, the number of law violators among parolees had increased slightly (the average was about 10 to 12 percent per year), while the number of technical violators had skyrocketed. After 1996, 80 percent of California's parole violators were being returned for technical violations—failing a drug screen, traffic law violations, and compliance failures that had nothing to do with serious criminal offenses.[74]

The same pattern was evident nationwide. If California is excluded, then about four in ten parolees will be returned to prison within three years after release. About half have new convictions; the other half are revoked for technical violations. There is no real evidence to suggest that today's parolees are any more mean-spirited or criminally active than those of thirty or forty years ago; what is different is that surveillance has been stepped up, and enforcement of noncriminal violations is much more likely to result in revocation now than it was then. In other words, we have created the failure of parole by enforcing the rules as stringently as they could always have been applied.

This creates an interesting statistical anomaly. Outside California, parolees released on discretionary parole under supervision have a successful discharge rate of about 55 percent. Mandatory releasees, on the other hand, who are not supervised to the same extent (or in some places at all) have a successful discharge rate about ten percentage points higher.[75] Thus, the ones parole boards select as good risks and approve for early parole release, the ones who are watched more closely after release, are more likely to fail, which has also been established in research studies emphasizing heightened supervision in small caseloads.

If, on further reflection, parole is a good idea—for public safety, reintegration, and efficiency—after all, then what might we do to "reinvent" it? Joan Petersilia, who has studied probation and parole more thoroughly and written more about them than anyone else over the past two decades, has come up with the most comprehensive plan to reform parole. In her 2003 text *When Prisoners Come Home: Parole and Prisoner Reentry*, she provides a comprehensive list of recommendations to improve the reentry process, emphasizing a revitalized form of parole:

1. Prison administrators should embrace the mission of **prisoner reintegration**.
2. Reentry should be rehabilitated through the implementation of treatment, work, and education tracks in prison.
3. Prisoner responsibility should be encouraged through making prison life as much as possible like life outside prison.
4. Prisoners should participate in their own comprehensive prerelease planning.
5. Risk-based discretionary parole release should be reestablished in all states and at the federal level.
6. Victims should be notified of prisoners' release on parole, including any special parole conditions.
7. Increased monitoring of high-risk violent parolees should be practiced.
8. Treatment and vocational training should be available to any parolees who want it.
9. Parole offices should embrace neighborhood parole supervision strategies.
10. Reentry courts and community partnerships should be developed and evaluated for effectiveness.
11. Parole terms should have definite goals.
12. Prisoners should regain full citizenship rights.[76]

Some of these recommendations are often core elements of other reform proposals as well:

1. More reentry training in prison instead of the "cold turkey" transition
2. Intensive monitoring of high-risk criminals (though this will in all likelihood result in higher revocation rates among targeted groups)
3. Increased availability of drug treatment and job assistance on the street
4. Reentry courts

5. Neighborhood parole
6. Exploring parole options within intermediate sanctions and restorative justice

Reentry courts, charged with overseeing a prisoner's reintegration into society, are already in use in a few places. The judge, already responsible for probation, would monitor parole also. The concept is to keep minor criminal violations and most technical violations at the local level—more support services, graduated sanctions, and local jail time if needed—instead of immediately returning the parolee to prison. Jeremy Travis of the Urban Institute has argued

> for a twist on this approach: making sentencing judges responsible for coming up with a reentry plan for prisoners. Judges would tell men and women they had just sentenced that they must begin preparing in prison for the return home, and would order drug rehabilitation, job training, or whatever other programs were called for.[77]

Martin Horn has suggested that many parolees want to go straight and can make it "if they are literate, civil, and can stay off drugs, remain sober, and get a job." His proposal for reinventing parole is called the **personal responsibility model.** A released prisoner would be given the equivalent of a parole services voucher. For a fixed period of time—say, two years—he can use the voucher to seek education, job training, drug treatment, or other services from state-selected providers. If he wants to help himself, he can. If not, he's on his own.[78]

Joan Petersilia describes **neighborhood parole** as a model of community engagement similar to community policing. Its key components include strengthening parole's linkages with law enforcement and the community, offering a "full-service" model of parole, and attempting to change the offenders' lives through personal, family, and neighborhood interventions. At the core, these models move away from managing parolees on conventional caseloads and toward a more "activist supervision" where agents are responsible for close supervision and procuring jobs, social support, and needed treatment.[79] This may be compared with the proactive community supervision model in probation, to be discussed in the next chapter. It may also be compared with the late 1800s model of volunteers who worked closely with parolees in their communities.

The "offender in community" concept is equally important to Joseph Lehman, the secretary of corrections for the State of Washington, and his colleagues who prepared a Justice Solutions white paper, "The Three 'Rs' of Reentry" in 2002. Taking what they call a "victim-, family-, and harm-centered perspective," they propose an **offender reentry model** built on three considerations:

1. Reparative justice, which focuses on such goals as reducing harm to families and communities, offender accountability, and building competency among offenders and the community
2. Relationships, which centers on getting the offender's family to influence and monitor behavior
3. Responsibility, which is directed to the mutual responsibilities of the offender, the community, and the criminal justice system[80]

This would change parole at its core from "offender centered"—punitive and rehabilitative—to "community centered"—collaborative, reparative, and preventive. In many respects, this approach to offender reentry is the most ambitious because it proposes to do the most *outside* the conventional criminal justice system. Addressing larger issues of harm, victimization, and responsibility in the community context is an ambitious undertaking, particularly in an era still so centered on isolation and punishment of the offender. There are still many critics who wish that Maconochie, Crofton, and Brockway had never invented parole; they would like to return to the days when parole was not an option.

KEY TERMS

executive clemency
pardon board
pardon
amnesty
reprieve
commutation
emergency release
shock probation
medical parole
discretionary parole
conditional release
indeterminate sentence
good-time release
mandatory parole
truth-in-sentencing standard
expiration of sentence
supervised release
indentured servitude
Alexander Maconochie

Norfolk Island
mark system
ticket of leave
English Penal Servitude Act
Sir Walter Crofton
Irish System
parole
good time
conditional pardon
Zebulon Brockway
Elmira Reformatory
parole board
marked men
parole hearing
parole plan
flopped
new parole
Board of Prison Terms

U.S. Sentencing Commission
risk assessment
parole officer
volunteer parole officer
case management
caseload
casework
law enforcement
social work
aftercare
parole conditions
standard parole conditions
special parole conditions
drug testing
law violation
technical violation
detainer
discretion

new penology
danger management
waste management
risk management
parole revocation
Morrissey v. Brewer
due process hearing
revocation hearing
absconders
revolving door
Proposition 36
reinvent parole
Project RIO
prisoner reintegration
reentry courts
personal responsibility model
neighborhood parole
offender reentry model

NOTES

1. Amanda Ripley, "Outside the Gates," *Time* 159, no. 3 (January 21, 2002): 56.

2. Ibid., p. 58.

3. Ibid., p. 60.

4. Fox Butterfield, "Almost 10% of Prisoners Are Serving Life Terms," *New York Times*, May 12, 2004, *www.nytimes.com/2004/05/12/national/12prison.html.*

5. Ibid.

6. Camille Graham Camp and George M. Camp, *The Corrections Yearbook 2001* (Middletown, Conn.: Criminal Justice Institute, 2002), p. 44.

7. Ibid., p. 33.

8. A comprehensive national review of executive clemency can be found in Clifford Dorne and

Kenneth Gewerth, "Mercy in a Climate of Retributive Justice: Implications from a National Survey of Executive Clemency Procedures," *New England Journal on Criminal and Civil Confinement* 25, no. 2 (summer 1999): 413.

9. Timothy Hughes and Doris James Wilson, "Reentry Trends in the United States," U.S. Department of Justice, Bureau of Justice Statistics, updated April 14, 2004, *www.ojp.usdoj.gov/bjs*.

10. See table 6.37, "Mean Maximum Sentence, Mean Time Served, and Percent of Sentence Served for Violent Offenders," and table 6.38, "Mean Sentence Length and Mean Time Served for First Releases from State Prison," in *Sourcebook of Criminal Justice Statistics, 2002, www.albany.edu/sourcebook/1995*.

11. Robert Hughes, *The Fatal Shore* (New York: Vintage Books, 1986), p. 489.

12. Ibid., pp. 492–93.

13. Vergil L. Williams, William A. Formby, and John C. Watkins, "Development of Parole," in *Introduction to Criminal Justice* (Albany, N.Y.: Delmar Publishers, 1982), p. 369.

14. Hughes, *The Fatal Shore*, p. 519.

15. Ibid., p. 521.

16. Williams, et al., "Development of Parole," p. 370.

17. Ibid., pp. 371–72.

18. Joan Petersilia, "Parole and Prison Reentry in the United States, Part I," *Perspectives,* summer 2000, p. 36.

19. Ibid.

20. Lawrence M. Friedman, *Crime and Punishment in American History* (New York: Basic Books, 1993), p. 162.

21. Louis N. Robinson, *Penology in the United States* (Philadelphia: John C. Winston Company, 1921), p. 238.

22. National Advisory Common on Criminal Justice Standards and Goals, *Corrections* (Washington, D.C.: U.S. Government Printing Office, 1973), p. 396.

23. Edwin H. Sutherland, *Principles of Criminology*, 4th ed. (Chicago: J. B. Lippincott Company, 1947), p. 530.

24. Ibid.

25. Ibid., p. 520.

26. Ibid., pp. 526–28.

27. Fred E. Haynes, *The American Prison System* (New York: McGraw-Hill, 1939), pp. 348–49.

28. Peter B. Hoffman, "History of the Federal Parole System: Part 1 (1910–1972)," *Federal Probation* 61, no. 3 (September 1997): 28.

29. Sutherland, *Principles of Criminology*, p. 528.

30. Friedman, *Crime and Punishment in American History*, p. 305.

31. Ibid.

32. Haynes, *The American Prison System*, pp. 344–45.

33. Malcolm Braly, *False Starts: A Memoir of San Quentin and Other Prisons* (Boston: Little, Brown, 1976), pp. 252–53.

34. Sutherland, *Principles of Criminology*, p. 520.

35. Petersilia, "Parole and Prison Reentry in the United States, Part I," p. 38.

36. Ibid., p. 40.

37. Joan Petersilia, *Reforming Probation and Parole in the 21st Century* (Lanham, Md.: American Correctional Association, 2001), p. 159.

38. President's Commission on Law Enforcement and Administration of Justice, *Task Force Report: Corrections* (Washington, D.C.: U.S. Government Printing Office, 1967), p. 70.

39. Camp and Camp, *The Corrections Yearbook 2001*, pp. 195, 222–23.

40. New Jersey State Parole Board, "Myths of Parole," *www.state.nj.us/parole/myths.htm*.

41. Ibid.

42. Petersilia, *Reforming Probation and Parole in the 21st Century*, p. 161.

43. Richard P. Seiter, "Prisoner Reentry and the Role of Parole Officers," *Federal Probation* 66, no. 3 (December 2002): 54.

44. Douglas Dennis, "Realities of Recidivism," *The Angolite,* September/October 2002, p. 30.

45. Malcolm M. Feeley and Jonathan Simon, "The New Penology: Notes on the Emerging Strategy of Corrections and Its Implications," *Criminology* 30, no. 4 (November 1992): 470.

46. Mona Lynch, "Waste Managers? The New Penology, Crime Fighting, and Parole Agent Identity," *Law and Society Review* 32, no. 4 (1998): 840.

47. Ibid., p. 851.

48. Ibid.

49. Seiter, "Prisoner Reentry and the Role of Parole Officers," p. 52.

50. *Morrissey v. Brewer*, 408 U.S. 471 (1972).

51. Lauren Glaze, "Probation and Parole in the United States, 2002," U.S. Department of Justice, Bureau of Justice Statistics Bulletin, August 2003, p. 5.

52. Ibid., p. 6.

53. Petersilia, "Parole and Prison Reentry, Part I," p. 42.

54. "Collateral Damage: East Durham," in "Hard Time: Life after Prison," American Radio Works, 2003, *www.americanradioworks.org/features/hardtime/durham1.html*.

55. "Hard Time—Scraping By," in "Hard Time: Life after Prison," American Radio Works, 2003, *www.americanradioworks.org/features/hardtime/full.html*.

56. Ibid.

57. Seiter, "Prisoner Reentry and the Role of Parole Officers," p. 52.

58. Patricia O'Brien, *Making It in the "Free World": Women in Transition from Prison* (Albany: State University of New York Press, 2001), p. 123.

59. DeAnna Talbert, "What Did They Expect? What Did They Find? A Study of Women Prisoners Released from Custody in Louisiana," unpublished paper, November 2000, p. 10.

60. Ibid., p. 11.

61. O'Brien, *Making It in the "Free World,"* p. 124.

62. As cited in Russ Immarigeon, "Parole, Probation and Prisoner Reentry," *Federal Probation* 67, no. 3 (December 2003): 74.

63. Ibid.

64. Malcolm Braly, *False Starts*, pp. 201–2.

65. George Allen, "The Courage of Our Convictions," *Policy Review,* spring 1995, pp. 4–7.

66. Petersilia, "Parole and Reentry in the United States, Part II," *Perspectives* fall 2000, p. 43.

67. Ibid., p. 42.

68. John J. DiIulio Jr., "Reinventing Parole and Probation," *Brookings Review*, spring 1997, p. 41.

69. "Parolees Filling California Prisons," *Baton Rouge Advocate*, March 8, 2004, p. 2.

70. "Total Felon Parolees Returned to California Prisons," in "Rate of Felon Parolees Returned to California Prisons," California Department of Corrections, May 2004, p. 1.

71. Timothy A. Hughes, Doris James Wilson, and Allen J. Beck, "Trends in State Parole, 1990–2000," U.S. Department of Justice, Bureau of Justice Statistics Special Report, October 2001, p. 2.

72. Peter Finn, "Job Placement for Offenders: A Promising Approach to Reducing Recidivism and Correctional Costs," *Journal* (National Institute of Justice), July 1999, pp. 6–7.

73. Joan Petersilia, "Prisoner Reentry: Public Safety and Reintegration Challenges," *Prison Journal* 81, no. 3 (September 2001): 312.

74. "Total Felon Parolees Returned to California Prisons," p. 1.

75. Hughes et al., "Trends in State Parole, 1990–2000," p. 12.

76. Immarigeon, "Parole, Probation, and Prisoner Reentry," p. 73.

77. Margaret Talbot, "Catch and Release," *Atlantic Monthly*, January/February 2003, p. 100.

78. DiIulio, "Reinventing Parole and Probation," p. 42.

79. Petersilia, *Reforming Probation and Parole in the 21st Century*, pp. 185–86.

80. Joseph Lehman, Trudy Gregorie Beatty, Dennis Maloney, Susan Russell, Anne Seymour, and Carol Shapiro, "The Three 'Rs' of Reentry," Justice Solutions, Washington, D.C., December 6, 2002, pp. 1–18.

FURTHER READING

Maruna, Shadd. *Making Good: How Ex-Convicts Reform and Rebuild Their Lives*. Washington, D.C.: American Psychological Association, 2001.

Petersilia, Joan. *When Prisoners Come Home: Parole and Prisoner Reentry*. New York: Oxford University Press, 2003.

Simon, Jonathan. *Poor Discipline: Parole and the Social Control of the Underclass*. Chicago: University of Chicago Press, 1993.

Travis, Jeremy, and Sarah Lawrence. "Beyond the Prison Gates: The State of Parole in America." Research Report, Justice Police Center, Urban Institute, November 2002.

WEB AND VIDEO RESOURCES

The Fortune Society (*www.fortunesociety.org*) has been active in helping ex-prisoners and at-risk youth since 1967. It publishes the journal *Fortune News*.

21 The Struggle to Stay Outside the Gates

by Amanda Ripley

Lying in bed late one night last spring (2002), a few months after appearing in a *Time* In Depth story about the challenges facing ex-convicts, Jean Sanders evaluated his options. Compared with most men just out of prison, he had it all. After a year of scraping and pleading, he had moved out of a homeless shelter and into a rented room in Brooklyn, N.Y. He had apologized to his mother and grown daughters for his years of drug dealing and addiction, and despite a sense of foreboding, they had taken him back. He had finally found a job, as a gas-station attendant. And the *Time* article about his return to society had inspired people to send letters of support and checks totaling close to $2,000. At 42, he was clean and free for the first time in 15 years. "I am on cloud nine. I am going places," he told *Time*.

Sanders was one of some 600,000 people to leave prison in 2001, more than ever before. The record was broken again last year. The crowds that filled the prisons in the 1990s are streaming back out. Their return to civilian life is the biggest problem facing the U.S. criminal-justice system. Within three years, most ex-inmates are rearrested. That night last spring, Sanders got out of bed and walked outside, telling himself he was going to buy cigarettes but knowing he wasn't. Instead, he went to the corner and bought himself a beer. Next came weed and then crack. "I was thinking, Damn, I did it. Then I was like, Give me more," he remembers. Most ex-inmates trying to stay off drugs slip repeatedly, even the ones who eventually succeed. "It's like having a disease, like cancer," Sanders says now. "You can put it in remission, but it can come back, like a demon."

After Sanders began using crack again, the fissures in the rest of his life widened. In April he was fired by the gas station for being too friendly with female customers. Then he did something he never would have done 10 years ago. "One Sunday morning I found myself on the corner looking for drugs when I should have been in church," he says. "I just knew it was not my destiny." Two days later, he took the subway to see his parole officer and turned himself in. In some states, Sanders would have been sent back to prison.

But he was taken to an inpatient treatment program in Queens. It had a tough, institutionalized atmosphere, and was filled with ex-inmates. Sanders sank into depression. He did not call his family to tell them what had happened or where he was. He spent his days contemplating his failures, which disgusted him. When doctors told him his prostate-specific antigen levels were high, which can be a harbinger of prostate cancer, he refused to get a biopsy.

In October, exasperated by the program's rigidity—which made it hard to contact family or go to church regularly—Sanders walked out and spent the weekend at his mother's home in the Bushwick section of Brooklyn. He went to his parole officer that Tuesday and was put in handcuffs. Parolees cannot change their address without permission. Finally, his parole officer agreed to let him try another program.

Phoenix House is probably Sanders' last chance. Since Thanksgiving, he has shown signs of progress at the drug program's Bronx center, where he now lives. He has earned permission to look for a job. He has handed out flyers for a cell-phone store. He returned to the gas station to see whether he could get his old position back. Brad Goodman, the owner, told him maybe. "I might be stupid," says Goodman, "but he's a likable guy." Sanders has been allowed to leave the center on recent Saturdays, going to church and then to his mother's house. His family is quiet around him. "It's like they're holding their breath," he says. His mother has reluctantly agreed to let him move in with her, temporarily, after his scheduled release from Phoenix House on February 24.

Like most who leave prison, he will be returning to the scene of his crimes. When he walks down the street, he is greeted by those he did drugs with over the past two decades. "How you doing?" they ask. "Ain't seen you in a while. You looking good. You need something?"

Today when Sanders talks about the future, his optimism is muted. He once spoke of earning enough to put his 19-year-old daughter through college and take a vacation. Now he just talks about staying off drugs. He has been clean for nine months—and counting.

Postscript: After three years on parole, Jean Sanders was discharged on March 25, 2004. This was the first time he had ever successfully completed parole. "Successfully" is a complicated word in the language of parole. He had violated his parole conditions by using drugs more than once. In other states he would likely be back in prison, but his parole officer gave him second and third chances to complete treatment programs.

Sanders remains somewhat estranged from his daughters, to his dismay. He lives with his mother. He has never found a "good job." But for the last year of his parole, he worked steadily as a "flyer guy" in Brooklyn. He hands out flyers for a cell phone store to passers by on the sidewalk. This means he is outside on his feet all the time, gets low pay, and, of course, no benefits. But he likes playing "mayor" to all the people on the street, saying hello to the babies, flirting with the ladies, and generally feeling acknowledged.

As the end of parole approached, Sanders was equal parts ecstatic and anxious. He had problems sleeping. As much as he wanted to be free of all the oversight and hassle, he said, he was nervous about the independence. "I can't even explain to you all the things I'm feeling. Nerves in my heart, in my stomach. It's great!" he said, calling from a payphone after his last parole visit.

To celebrate, *Time* took Sanders and his fiancée, Pat, out to eat at Junior's, the famous Brooklyn diner. The very next day, his first day off parole, he had to go to the courthouse to appear on a charge of "aggressive solicitation." He had been picked up in a police sweep of flyer guys, evidently after complaints that their salesmanship constituted a nuisance. He wanted to fight the charge on principle, insisting he had done nothing illegal. But on the advice of his court-appointed lawyer, he decided to take a plea instead. His sentence? Community service.

COMMENTARY

22 Parole's Positive Threat

by James Q. Wilson

"For a drug treatment program to work for a person on parole, the state must have some way of forcing parolees to stay in one: the threat of incarceration."

Most criminologists never give up their hostility to prisons. When the crime rate was starting to increase in the 1960s, they argued for rehabilitation instead. Now that the crime rate is dropping, in part because more people were imprisoned, they say we incarcerated too many people. And from first to last they often claim that we incarcerate too many ethnic minorities.

The newest argument is that we are returning too many parolees to prison. Fox Butterfield, in a recent *New York Times* story, showed that two-thirds of the people sent to prison last year were on parole, and most of these went back inside because of "technical violations of the terms of their parole," such as failing a drug test. The result of this, Butterfield argues, is the creation of a "self-perpetuating prison class" that is an unexpected, and presumably undesirable, consequence of our get-tough-on-crime philosophy.

I have a different view. Prison has not made these people bad; they were bad before they went to prison. Prison may rehabilitate a few inmates, and the prospect of going back to prison may frighten others into becoming law-abiding, but there is very little evidence that prison alone makes most offenders either better or worse. Butterfield's data make the point. Inmates today are overwhelmingly drawn from the ranks of drug users; many are illiterate or mentally ill, and few have much chance of holding a decent job. In California many come from the ranks of street gangs and return to those gangs once they are free. They were sucked into crime on the streets, and when returned to the streets they will be sucked back in again.

When we realize that some people are drawn into crime before they ever see a prison, we will stop expecting so much from either prison or parole and will worry more about preventing crime when would-be offenders are still young. Taking this view calls into question the opinion of many criminologists that prison was better when its inmates served flexible sentences and were released only when a parole board thought they were rehabilitated.

There was no evidence then that parole boards knew who, if anyone, had been rehabilitated. Though rehabilitation does occur on occasion, parole boards, like criminologists, can't predict who the beneficiaries will be. The flexible sentences that were once the rule did not mean rehabilitation, they meant discrimination. Two people with the same record who had committed identical crimes served different prison terms based on a parole board's guess as to who had changed.

There is one thing that prisons and parole can do, however: They can supply drug treatment programs in prison, and parole officers can insist that parolees stay in those treatment programs when they are back on the streets. Butterfield notes the gains made by Phoenix House in one of its programs for released offenders in California and rightly suggests that more such efforts be made. But he omits a crucial point. Treatment programs tend to help people the longer they remain in them. For a drug treatment program to work for a person on parole, the state must have some way of forcing parolees to stay in one. The only means the government has to do this is to threaten inmates with more incarceration. Experience in California and elsewhere has shown that for most drug users, coercion has to be used to keep them in treatment. Those who experience this pressure do at least as well as, if not better than, those who stay in them voluntarily.

Perhaps a return to prison is an excessive sanction. Maybe we could send inmates who drop out of treatment programs back to local jails. But there must be a credible threat that they will be sent somewhere unpleasant, and the threat must be enforceable by administrative, not judicial, action. Judges take too long to decide, and their court dockets are congested. And so parole officers must do exactly what some criminologists think they shouldn't. Where criminologists are right is that society must be prepared to pay the bill for these treatment programs.

15

PROBATION AND COMMUNITY CORRECTIONS

The extension of probation for felonies still encounters strenuous antagonism and distrust. Most of this antagonism flows from the fear that probation will undermine the efficiency of punishment as a deterrent of crime. Formerly, severity of punishment was believed to be the great deterrent. Severity of punishment has not deterred crime to any great extent.

— FRANK WADE, CONGRESS OF THE AMERICAN PRISON ASSOCIATION, 1923

INTRODUCTION

This chapter considers those forms of correctional supervision that take place outside secure confinement in jails and prisons. These alternatives, founded on probation and the suspended sentence, supervise more than twice as many offenders as are held in secure confinement. Probation is the principal option to imprisonment, but increasingly other intermediate sanctions are being used to fill the gap between prison and probation, which has led to the vast expansion of formal community corrections alternatives over the past thirty years. After reading the material in this chapter, you should be familiar with:

1. The history of the suspended sentence and probation in America.
2. Probation work and administration.
3. Probation as a sentence and a process.
4. The profile of probation clients.
5. Questions about the effectiveness of probation.
6. The range of controls provided by intermediate sanctions.
7. The options available under community corrections.
8. The pros and cons of intermediate sanctions and community corrections.
9. The future of probation and community corrections.

CORRECTIONS OUTSIDE INSTITUTIONS

When Americans think of punishment for serious criminality, we are predisposed to imagine removing the criminal from society and putting him or her in a secure box—jail or prison—to spend a block of time. Punishment is time in isolation, replacing the "normal" community of somewhat law-abiding citizens with a different community—a community of antisocial lawbreakers controlled by authoritarian keepers. The ideology of imprisonment is so strong that when you suggest decreased use of secure custody and working with more criminals under community supervision, people look at you as if you have suddenly begun speaking an alien language. "Leave criminals in the community? Not on your life."

To which you can make two sensible explanatory (and defensive) responses. First, only in the past 200 years have large numbers of criminals been locked up in jails and prisons. Before the 1800s, whatever punishment was applied to criminals, it was done *in* the community, not out of it. Unless they were banished, criminals were beaten, executed, humiliated, fined, or otherwise punished while they remained in the community—indeed, often with the community observing the punishment. The criminal did not go anywhere; punishment was close to home. As scholars have pointed out, one of the attributes of retribution is that once the punishment is over, things are all square. There are no collateral consequences, no stigma, and no disqualifications following the criminal around—except whatever sense of shame the criminal might feel in a close-knit community. Even after prisons began to be used to punish serious criminals, the rates of imprisonment were low, well below 100 per 100,000 throughout the 1800s, in contrast to combined jail and prison rates averaging five to seven times that at the beginning of the twenty-first century. Thus, it is imprisonment or, more specifically, the extensive use of imprisonment that is the new idea, not community corrections.

Second, the criminals are already in the community. That's where they were before they ran afoul of the legal system. That's where ninety-eight out of every 100 will eventually return as they leave prison. They are all around you. An estimated 10 million adults have at least one felony conviction. With only 1,300,000 of them in prison at present, that means the other 87 percent are out there in society, roaming around loose. Look around you. One in every twenty adults is a convicted felon. Granted, it is a lot higher in some neighborhoods than others, so depending on where you live, it may be a lot higher or a lot lower than this. In 2002, when there were more than 2 million adults in jail and prison, over 4.7 million adults were under correctional supervision—some form of probation or parole—outside secure institutions. For every one criminal behind bars, just over 2.3 criminals are supervised *outside* confinement. The point is clear: criminals remain a part of society no matter where they are.

The question about community corrections—nonsecure supervision—becomes one of degree: how much of the criminal population should be managed in the community, and how much of it should be kept behind bars? When we look at how the federal government and the states answer this question, we see vast differences from one place to another, as you can see in Table 15-1. Nationwide, about 30 percent of our correctional population is incarcerated, but there is quite a range from high to low. The high-end states include Mississippi (58.7 percent), West Virginia (54.1 percent), Virginia (53.7 percent), and Nevada (50.3 percent); the federal government, operating under strict sentencing guidelines, is high also (58.1 percent). On the low end of incarceration are Minnesota (8.9 percent), Vermont (11.4 percent), Rhode Island (12.5 percent), and Washington (14.4 percent).

The state-to-state contrasts can be interesting. Minnesota and Louisiana have similar populations, 5 million and about 4.5 million people. Louisiana's

TABLE 15-1

Adults under Correctional Supervision and Number Supervised per 100,000 Adult Residents, by Jurisdiction, Year-End 2002

Region/ Jurisdiction	Under Supervision	On Probation or Parole	In Jail or Prison	Supervision Rate per 100,000 Adults	Percentage Incarcerated
U.S. total	6,732,400	4,698,000	2,034,300	3,125	30.2
Federal	272,500	114,300	158,200	126	58.1
State	6,459,900	4,583,700	1,876,100	2,999	29.0
Northeast	1,051,200	778,700	272,500	2,545	25.9
Connecticut	72,000	53,200	18,700	2,747	26.0
Maine	12,600	9,500	3,100	1,275	24.7
Massachusetts	70,900	47,700	23,200	1,434	32.7
New Hampshire	9,200	4,700	4,500	960	49.2
New Jersey	190,400	146,200	44,200	2,923	23.2
New York	357,000	254,000	102,900	2,448	28.8
Pennsylvania	299,500	228,500	71,000	3,179	23.7
Rhode Island	27,700	24,300	3,500	3,390	12.5
Vermont	11,900	10,600	1,400	2,554	11.4
Midwest	1,392,100	1,040,300	351,900	2,866	25.3
Illinois	238,900	177,000	61,900	2,542	25.9
Indiana	147,300	112,500	34,800	3,213	23.6
Iowa	37,900	26,300	11,600	1,711	30.6
Kansas	34,000	19,200	14,800	1,692	43.5
Michigan	257,000	189,900	67,100	3,443	26.1
Minnesota	136,200	124,000	12,200	3,654	8.9
Missouri	106,500	68,100	38,400	2,515	36.0
Nebraska	26,300	19,700	6,600	2,050	25.0
North Dakota	5,000	3,300	1,700	1,055	33.6
Ohio	291,900	227,400	64,500	3,412	22.1
South Dakota	10,700	6,600	4,100	1,919	38.3
Wisconsin	100,400	66,100	34,300	2,469	34.2
South	2,642,800	1,812,100	830,700	3,422	31.4
Alabama	80,800	43,500	37,300	2,405	46.2
Arkansas	56,300	39,700	16,600	2,783	29.5
Delaware	27,700	20,800	6,900	4,557	25.0
District of Columbia	17,400	14,400	3,000	—	—
Florida	427,100	295,100	132,000	3,314	30.9
Georgia	470,100	387,800	82,300	—	—
Kentucky	55,100	30,400	24,700	1,783	44.8
Louisiana	103,600	56,600	47,100	3,166	45.4
Maryland	121,200	85,200	36,100	2,973	29.8
Mississippi	42,700	17,600	25,100	2,038	58.7
North Carolina	164,100	115,700	48,300	2,601	29.5
Oklahoma	62,100	32,800	29,200	2,389	47.1
South Carolina	78,000	45,200	32,800	2,536	42.1

(continued)

Region/ Jurisdiction	Under Supervision	On Probation or Parole	In Jail or Prison	Supervision Rate per 100,000 Adults	Percentage Incarcerated
Tennessee	88,600	49,800	38,900	2,024	43.9
Texas	737,400	526,600	210,900	4,682	28.6
Virginia	96,900	44,900	52,000	1,753	53.7
West Virginia	13,700	6,300	7,400	980	54.1
West	1,373,700	952,700	421,100	2,842	30.7
Alaska	9,900	5,500	4,400	2,186	44.8
Arizona	116,100	74,200	41,900	2,896	36.1
California	711,200	471,300	239,900	2,756	33.7
Colorado	89,300	60,400	28,800	2,646	32.3
Hawaii	24,400	19,300	5,100	2,587	20.8
Idaho	42,200	33,300	8,900	4,396	21.1
Montana	12,100	7,500	4,500	1,777	37.5
Nevada	32,700	16,300	16,500	2,030	50.3
New Mexico	25,600	13,600	12,000	1,904	46.9
Oregon	83,100	65,000	18,000	3,129	21.7
Utah	22,200	12,300	9,900	1,394	44.6
Washington	197,200	168,900	28,300	4,348	14.4
Wyoming	7,900	5,200	2,700	2,142	34.6

Source: Lauren E. Glaze, "Probation and Parole in the United States, 2002," U.S. Department of Justice, Bureau of Justice Statistics Bulletin, August 2003, p. 7.

overall crime rate is higher, but Minnesota has more convicted criminals under supervision (136,000) than Louisiana (103,000). Minnesota has about 12,000 people in jail and prison, while Louisiana has almost four times that number (47,000). Why would states differ so much in their use of confinement as part of a crime control policy (if indeed they actually *have* a crime control policy, as opposed to a collection of laws imposing punishments without an overall sense of direction)?

This question is being asked more frequently as state policymakers face issues related to the social and economic costs of imprisonment. Since the 1980s, the United States has pursued a **bricks-and-mortar solution** to increasing correctional supervision. We have built new prisons and jails to increase the number of jail and prison beds from fewer than 500,000 to more than 2 million in twenty years, in an era when the crime rate has remained flat (except for a spike in the late 1980s to early 1990s) or in decline. We have also increased the numbers of persons under community supervision by pursuing the policy of net widening, which means pulling lesser offenders into the system under more formal controls than would have been the case previously. Thus, both populations—the incarcerated and the nonincarcerated—have increased dramatically in a relatively short period of time.

The question now being asked in many states is, "Are prisons at a turning point?" Although our prison population has been climbing steadily for thirty years, has the time come to narrow the role of the prison and provide for community supervision of an even greater percentage of criminal offenders? Some criminologists and corrections experts argue that the proper role of the prison is **selective incapacitation**—protecting the public not equally from all criminals but from those high-rate and violent criminals who pose the greatest threat to public safety. These **chronic offenders** will be confined in prison. Other offenders will be supervised under less severe (and less expensive) sanctions in nonsecure settings. If prison populations are to be brought under control, to level off, or even go into decline, as some advocates have argued should happen, the system of dealing with criminals outside jail and prison must be more coordinated and highly developed. If the pendulum should swing back from increased incarceration, what will it swing toward? What are the **front-end solutions** to America's punishment dilemma?

THE HISTORY OF THE SUSPENDED SENTENCE AND PROBATION

Probation is the chief means of supervising criminals outside confinement. As an alternative to imprisonment, probation is considered a modern sentence, but it has its roots in earlier forms of withholding punishment—what we often refer to as the **suspended sentence.** The **right of sanctuary,** under Hebrew law, set aside holy places for offenders to seek protection from secular laws; this practice continued under the Catholic Church. **Benefit of clergy** similarly allowed religious officials to avoid punishment in the criminal courts, also allowing them to avoid the stigma of a criminal conviction and retain their church duties after a period of penance. English courts also recognized the practice of **judicial reprieve,** a delay in sentencing after conviction. Sometimes this delay became permanent, and the criminal never had a sentence imposed. American courts used a similar practice called **filing of cases** or recognizance.

Predecessors of probation in use in English and early American courts allowed judges to informally withhold punishment for deserving offenders. In practice, this suspended sentence had a more narrow meaning than contemporary probation; it did not require supervision or impose conditions on the offender, as probation does. The traditional European model of **surcease** withholds punishment if the offender commits no new crime during the period of suspension.

Part of the Enlightenment argument in favor of imprisonment was that these methods of withholding or minimizing punishment had to stop. Judges had grown too "soft" to impose the physical punishments that prevailed in Europe through the end of the 1700s. Too many criminals were "getting off." A more certain punishment with greater deterrent effects was needed, scholars argued, and imprisonment emerged over time as this punishment. All serious criminals—both misdemeanants and felons—were supposed to do time. Time was to take the place of pain, and it could be measured in units just like the individual strokes of a flogging. When someone was sentenced to thirty lashes, he got thirty lashes; when he was sentenced to thirty months, he was supposed to do every day of the thirty months. No provisions existed for a suspended sentence (to keep him from going to prison) or good time or parole (to let him out early). To achieve deterrence, discretionary imposition of penalties had to be done away with. Cesare Beccaria, the Italian legal reformer of the late 1700s, insisted that the law, to be effective, must be applied with certainty and uniformity. Punishment must be seen as the inevitable consequence of crime.

Thus, in the American courts of the early 1800s, the intent was that a serious or repeat criminal would spend some time in custody. But almost at once, court officials began to look for ways *not* to punish certain offenders they believed did not deserve imprisonment.

The origins of modern probation in America are often traced to the work of **John Augustus,** a Boston shoe manufacturer and civic reformer of the 1840s and 1850s. Augustus had a shoe shop on Franklin Avenue in Boston near the police court. One day in August 1841, he was in court observing as a member of the Washingtonian Total Abstinence Society, a group devoted to the idea of abstaining from alcohol and helping alcoholics. Augustus spoke to a man convicted of drunkenness and decided he could be reformed. The judge let Augustus bail him, and Augustus guaranteed the court that the alcoholic would appear for sentencing three weeks later. That man became the first "official" probationer.[1] He stopped drinking. When Augustus took him back to court, he looked neat and healthy. The judge was pleased. The usual sentence would have been a jail term in the House of Correction. Instead, the judge fined the man 1 cent and court costs for a total of $3.76.[2]

This started Augustus's unplanned career as the father of American probation. His work provided the model for probation as we know it today. Virtually every basic practice of modern probation was originally conceived by him. He was the first person to use the term **probation**—which derives from the Latin term *probatio,* meaning "a period of proving or trial." He developed the ideas of the presentence investigation, supervision conditions, social casework, reports to the courts, and revocation of probation.[3]

Until he died eighteen years later, Augustus bailed out almost 2,000 men, women, and children from Boston's city courts, keeping records that showed a very high success rate in reducing recidivism. He was not indiscriminate in his interventions, and he developed one of the first risk/needs assessments procedures. He believed in careful screening of potential probationers, as he wrote later:

> Great care was observed, of course, to ascertain whether the prisoners were promising subjects for probation, and to this end it was necessary to take into consideration the previous character of the person, his age, and the influences by which he would in the future be likely to be surrounded.[4]

Augustus would clean up his probationers and help them find a job and a place to live. He could not personally supervise more than a hundred criminals a year, so he recruited other volunteers as **probation officers.** These volunteers, whom Augustus specified should have a "good heart," were often drawn from Catholic, Protestant, and Jewish church groups.[5] Augustus would ask them to work one on one with offenders for short periods of time.

Augustus was a modest and selfless person who spent his life helping criminals. He had many critics in his day. Some have accused him of exploiting criminals by recruiting "slave laborers" for his business and those of his friends, but in fact he apparently became so committed to his volunteer work that he neglected his successful business and lost money. When critics said he was helping criminals escape punishment, he replied that society benefits when the offender is kept out of prison. He felt it is the harshness of prison life that makes people commit more crimes, not the mercy of probation. The records he kept showed probation to be more effective than imprisonment in preventing future crimes. For those who would not accept the effectiveness argument, Augustus told them it was cheaper to use probation than to use imprisonment.

Boston's judges supported Augustus's work. An early supporter was Judge Peter Oxenbridge Thacher, city court judge from 1823 to 1843. Judge Thacher was a practitioner of **recognizance,** a form of release from custody—with or without the posting of money bail—used with petty offenders. Long before Augustus appeared in court, Judge Thacher would sometimes permanently release offenders on recognizance, meaning that they would never return to court to have a sentence imposed. He did this informally at first and then in 1836 Massachusetts passed a law formally recognizing recognizance.[6] The law allowed petty offenders to be released at any stage of the legal process if sureties—financial guarantees—could be provided. Augustus took this a step further, in effect serving as a friend of the court in monitoring those persons released in his custody.

Massachusetts, encouraged by Augustus's successful example, passed the first probation statute—for juveniles—in 1878. Several other states followed, and the rise of the juvenile court in the early twentieth century promoted the continued expansion of formal probation services (see Table 15-2).

Juvenile probation spread more quickly than adult probation, but in both courts the concept of probation as the principal alternative to imprisonment gradually gained widespread legal acceptance. Probation began informally in many jurisdictions, often making use of volunteers who reported directly to local judges. The volunteers were often successful civic figures or religious activists who saw their role more as helping or serving as a **mentor** or father figure than a paid supervisor with a checklist in hand. When probation became a formal governmental function, police were often asked to supervise probationers. It was also common, when the courts began to request presentence investigation reports and other formal documentation, to hire retired law enforcement officers to work directly for the judges who imposed probation.

PROBATION ADMINISTRATION AND THE WORK OF THE PROBATION OFFICER

As probation developed, it meant a status or a sentence under the general authority of the trial judge, but in practice the means for carrying out probation varied widely. No standard model of probation administration developed, with the result that today probation administration differs from city to city and state to state. To understand the nature of probation in a particular locale, you need to answer five basic questions:

1. Is probation a function of state or local government?
2. Is it placed in the executive or judicial branch of government?
3. Are felons and misdemeanants supervised from the same office?
4. Are adults and juveniles supervised from the same office?
5. Is probation work combined with parole work?

Probation was originally very decentralized under the control of local courts, but over time the trend has been toward centralization of adult and juvenile probation at the state level—most often as a division of the state department of corrections.[7] California places both adult and juvenile probation

Table 15-2

Significant Events in the Development of U.S. Probation

Year	Event
1841	John Augustus introduces probation in the United States in Boston.
1878	Massachusetts is the first state to adopt probation for juveniles.
1878–1938	Thirty-seven states, the District of Columbia, and the federal government pass juvenile and adult probation laws.
1901	New York is the first state to adopt probation as a legal sentence for adult criminals.
1927	All states but Wyoming have juvenile probation laws.
1954	All states have juvenile probation laws.
1956	All states have adult probation laws (Mississippi becomes the last state to pass authorizing legislation).
1973	The National Advisory Commission on Criminal Justice Standards and Goals endorses more extensive use of probation. Minnesota is the first state to adopt a Community Corrections Act; eighteen states follow by 1995.
1974	Robert Martinson's widely publicized research purportedly proves that probation does not work.
1975	U.S. Department of Justice conducts the first census of U.S. probationers.
1976	U.S. comptroller general's study of U.S. probation claims to reduce recidivism and costs.
1982	Georgia's intensive supervision probation program claims to reduce recidivism and costs.
1983	Electronic monitoring of offenders begins in New Mexico, followed by larger program in Florida.
1985	The Rand Corporation releases study of felony probationers showing high failure rates; replications follow, showing that probation services and effectiveness vary widely across nation.
1989	General Accounting Office shows all fifty states have adopted intensive probation and other intermediate sanction programs.
1991	U.S. Department of Justice funds nationwide intensive supervision demonstration and evaluation.
1993	Program evaluations show probation without adequate surveillance and treatment is ineffective, but well-managed and adequately funded programs reduce recidivism.
1999	"Broken windows" model of probation, emphasizing that supervision is not effective when conducted solely in officers' offices, is endorsed by the American Probation and Parole Association.

Source: Adapted from Joan Petersilia, *Reforming Probation and Parole in the 21st Century* (Lanham, Md.: American Correctional Association, 2001).

under the control of judges at the county level. Colorado and several other states place both adult and juvenile probation under the control of the state judiciary. Texas has a structure that splits adult and juvenile probation into separate offices at the county level. Juvenile probation is directed by a board of judges and funded mostly through the county commissioners. Adult probation (now called "community supervision") is under the direct control of judges in each judicial district. Texas's parolees are supervised by state parole officers who work for the Texas Department of Criminal Justice.

In Louisiana, both adult and juvenile probation officers work for the state-level department of corrections (although the legislature has acted to move juvenile probation into a separate new juvenile justice department not yet completed), but adult probation officers supervise only felons, while juvenile probation officers supervise all delinquents put on probation, whether felons or misdemeanants. Probationers and parolees—adults and juveniles in separate offices—are supervised by the same agents. An adult probation and parole officer might have a caseload of 120—100 probationers and twenty parolees—assigned at random. Misdemeanor probation in Louisiana is optional. Some state courts and some city courts have it; it may be provided as a part of the court budget, or it may be under the control of some other government office, such as the district attorney's office or the central city or parish government.

It would be easy to spend the rest of the day arguing about the advantages and disadvantages of various types of probation organization. Probation administered by a local government unit is said to be smaller, more flexible, and better able to respond to the unique problems of the local community; it can also work more closely with local government and make better use of existing resources.[8] But local probation offices often suffer from the same types of problems as local police organizations, including inconsistent standards, inadequate funding, lack of training, and inconsistent policies and procedures. Juvenile probation is generally perceived as working better under decentralized control; thus, it is more likely to be operated at the local level than is adult probation, which in most states is provided by agents who work directly for the state (though operating out of offices at regional and local levels).

For the probation officer in a typical state, county, or city probation office, the key term is **caseload,** referring to the number of clients supervised by the probation officer. Think of a caseload as number of files to be managed. For those states in which probation officers are supervising only probationers (including all felons and misdemanants), the official average caseload per officer in the year 2000 was 133; where probation officers were also supervising parolees, official caseloads were lower, averaging ninety-eight per officer.[9]

What do these numbers mean in terms of supervision or services provided clients? Think of it this way. If a probation officer works full time, he or she puts in about 180 hours of work each month, making no deductions for holidays, vacation time, sick leave, training, or other time out of the office. If your caseload is 100 or over, this means that if the client came to you, you might be able to spend an hour or so each month visiting with him and then making a few notes in the file. You would see each case once a month for an hour—not a very high level of supervision. If you left the office to see the client in the field, with travel time and missed connections, you would be lucky to see him once a month for a fifteen- to thirty-minute visit—hardly enough time to really keep up with his business.

This scenario is based on the premise that supervision is all parole officers do, which in fact is not the case for most officers. The probation officer's job today is diverse and demanding, far beyond balancing the schizophrenic supervision role of surveillance and helping. Supervising a caseload is only a part—in many offices a small part—of a much larger function. The officer does **presentence investigation reports** for the court; the information in these reports often makes up the basis of the offender's permanent file, used in later cases and in parole- and clemency-related matters. The officer spends time in jail, in court, in sentencing hearings, and in probation revocation proceedings.

Probation officers complete paperwork to transfer offenders from one jurisdiction to another, and they must complete reams of forms to bureaucratically
manage the clients of today.

Camille Camp and George Camp, in *The Corrections Yearbook 2001*, estimate
that about 72,000 people were working for county, state, and federal probation and parole agencies on January 1, 2001. This figure is admittedly incom-
plete because about half a dozen states did not submit information, and many
city and county probation offices are not counted as well. When Cunniff and
Bergsmann profiled probation administration in 1990, they found that only
slightly more than half the staff were **line probation officers** providing direct supervision of criminals. The rest were management and supervisory staff,
clerical workers (necessary to process the high volume of paperwork), and
support staff, such as technicians, treatment specialists, trainers, custodians,
and others.[10] Camp and Camp found similar numbers in 2001. About 57 percent of probation staff were line officers, while the remaining staff were performing supervisory, support, and other functions.[11] The number of officers
actually carrying a caseload is further reduced when you remove from the to-
tals those officers supervising juveniles and performing pretrial and investigative duties not involving direct supervision. In ballpark or unofficial figures,
we probably had about 2 million felons being supervised by something fewer
than 20,000 officers. This would average out to more than 100 felons per probation officer, not far removed from official numbers.

The issue of reducing caseload size to an ideal number has been argued for
a long time. In 1917, a group of probation administrators suggested an ideal
caseload of fifty. This recommendation, later modified to include investigations,
was never validated.[12] The President's Crime Commission made the following
recommendation in 1967 in its report *The Challenge of Crime in a Free Society*: "All
jurisdictions should examine their need for probation and parole officers on the
basis of an average ratio of 35 offenders per officer, and make an immediate start
toward recruiting additional officers on the basis of that examination."[13] The
Commission estimated that this would require doubling the number of juvenile
probation officers, tripling the number of adult felony probation officers, and
increasing more than sevenfold the number of misdemeanor probation officers.

In its *Task Force Report: Corrections*, the Commission discussed the caseload
concept:

> The concept of an "average caseload" is administratively convenient when calculat-
> ing broad estimates of the resources necessary to effect some improvement in
> staffing ratios. However, this useful idea usually becomes translated into the "stan-
> dard caseload" that each officer should carry. Differences in individual probationers'
> needs require different amounts of time and energy from a probation officer. The
> typical probation caseload is usually a random mixture of cases requiring varying
> amounts of service and surveillance but usually treated as if all the cases were much
> the same. Clearly, the value of differential treatment requires that probation man-
> power ratios vary directly with the kind and amount of services to be performed.[14]

The Commission noted that experimental studies had been carried out
using reduced caseloads at different levels—seventy-five, thirty, or even as
low as fifteen. What would you expect to happen when caseload size was reduced, ostensibly to allow probation officers more time to assist their clients?
Do you think the officers would throw themselves into more prolonged

interaction with their clients, getting to know them better and counseling them at greater length about their problems? Not exactly or, really, not at all. When caseload size was reduced, the two most notable results were, first, that the officers spent a lot more time getting their paperwork right (because this was seen as the key to professional advancement), and, second, that revocation rates went up because when the officers supervised their clients more closely, they caught them doing wrong more often. Thus, reducing caseload size, by itself and without changing other aspects of the work, either was unrelated to the quality of supervision or resulted in more unsuccessful terminations as the level of supervision increased. Thus, put it back the way it was because it was cheaper to have fewer officers supervising more criminals.

Few states have made a long-term commitment to holding down caseload size. Joan Petersilia has noted that Arizona probably has the most ideal system in this regard. In 1987, the Arizona legislature wrote into statute that felony probation caseloads could not exceed sixty offenders to one probation officer, and they allocated state funding to maintain that level of service. As a result, probation departments in Arizona are nationally recognized to be among the best, providing their offender with both strict surveillance and needed treatment services.[15] In 2000, Arizona was still maintaining its sixty-felon standard, the lowest of any state in the country.

If caseload is important as a measure of workload, a related term, **casework,** also has a history in probation work. Casework applies to an approach or methodology, typically a treatment-oriented model associated with the medical model in corrections. A 1942 manual published by the National Probation and Parole Association, *Probation and Parole in Theory and Practice*, discussed the development of social work skills in interviewing, creating therapeutic relationships with clients, counseling, providing insight, and modifying behavior. When practitioners began to view themselves as "therapists," one consequence was the practice of having offenders come to the office rather than the workers going out into their homes and communities.[16]

The casework approach was probably much more influential in juvenile probation than it ever was in adult probation, and juvenile probation officers were much more inclined to see themselves as social workers with a rehabilitative mission. Adult probation officers, many of whom had a background in law enforcement, typically lacked the training, time, and inclination to "treat" offenders. They managed their files, they referred clients to other community programs where such options existed, they took clients to court when necessary, and they put them behind bars when they failed, but for the most part probation officers did not comprehensively engage in providing treatment services. Probation has tended to move away from the casework model in recent years as the emphasis on surveillance and crime control has increased.

In recent years, caseload management has been affected by two important trends: structure and specialization. Probation work is caught up in the effort to provide greater accountability based on outcomes. Many probation agencies use some type of **risk/needs assessment** instrument in determining how to manage their clients most effectively. Risk/needs assessment is based on those variables in a criminal's background that are known to be related to recidivism—such elements as age, criminal history, substance abuse, employment history and income, family life, education, and so on. Points are assessed for each variable, and the criminal is assigned a total score, like an exam grade, except here the higher the score, the greater level of risk—a 93 is high risk, a 60 is a moderate risk, and a 27 is a low risk. The needs part of the assessment is supposed to be individualized; that is, given the risks that have been calculated, what are the needs of the criminal that must be addressed to increase the likelihood of successful completion of probation?

Caseloads are structured by level of supervision, based on frequency of contact, from minimal to intensive. Here is an example from Langan and Cunniff's 1992 study of felony probation:

Supervision Level	Prescribed Number of Contacts	Percentage of Caseload
Intensive	Nine per month	10
Maximum	Three per month	32
Medium	One per month	37
Minimum	One per 3 months	12
Administrative	None required	9[17]

The concept here is that criminals would be placed at a level appropriate to their risk assessment. They would be moved up or down the scale over time as they adapt or fail to adapt to supervision. This implies some degree of management as opposed to the prevailing practice of a generation ago in which all probationers were supervised in general caseloads with the same general level of supervision. It was then left up to the officer, using his or her discretion in an approach often described as **crisis management,** to decide how many times a month clients would be seen. The operative principle was that you would not see most people more than once a month, or some not at all, as long as they appeared to be doing okay and kept sending in their monthly reports. However, when you got calls from mothers, girlfriends, or employers that so-and-so was drinking again, had quit his job, or had simply disappeared, you tried to deal with that person's crisis as an immediate concern. Structuring caseload supervision formalizes what was once an informal practice.

In Langan and Cunniff's classification scheme, about 20 percent of felons on probation were being seen in person less than once a month or not at all, while about 10 percent were on the opposite end in intensive caseloads requiring two or three contacts a week. The practice of **intensive supervised probation** (ISP or IPS) developed in Georgia in the early 1970s. Faced with severe overcrowding in its prison system, Georgia developed a model in which felons who would ordinarily have gone to prison were placed under ISP.

Billie S. Erwin, who helped implement this model, described its operation several years later:

> Georgia's IPS is characterized by caseloads limited to 25 probationers supervised by two officers (or caseloads of 40, with three officers) who work staggered hours. One officer specializes in rehabilitative programming and court liaison, and the other specializes in surveillance. Supervision standards include five contacts per week during initial stages, curfews enforced by frequent home visits, employment verification, unscheduled drug screening, and alcohol breath tests. Standard

equipment for IPS officers consists of walkie-talkies to provide back-up capability in field situations; breathalyzers; in some cases, portable EMIT urine testing machines; and, more recently, Roche urinalysis kits. About half the officers carry guns. State-of-the-art crime information systems provide the capability for quick response to any violations.[18]

When Georgia evaluated the effectiveness of this model in 1985, the most impressive finding was the achievement of effective control of subsequent crime by those supervised under IPS, while simultaneously demonstrating a significant cost savings—about $6,000 per offender. Although the close supervision gave officers more information than usual regarding technical violations and may have led to more probation revocations, there was a notable absence of violent crime and personal injury among the IPS group and a pattern of less serious subsequent crimes than was found in the comparison cohorts (prison releasees and high-risk probationers).[19]

Coming as it did in a time when crime control policies were being emphasized, this model was extremely influential in three respects:

1. The emphasis on **surveillance**—through daily contacts—tightened supervision and confronted one of the persistent criticisms of probation, namely, that offenders were not monitored closely enough.
2. IPS established that it was an effective alternative for controlling habitual but nonviolent offenders, who make up about half the American prison population.
3. It broke down the generalist model of probation into a specialized model based on function and type of caseload or level of supervision.

Probation at the federal level and in many state and local jurisdictions has subsequently employed a **team approach**—a model in which probation officers specialize in performing one part of the process or in supervising one particular type of client. One officer might only do presentence investigations, for instance, or handle revocation hearings. Another might only supervise intensive probationers or DWI (driving while intoxicated) offenders. These officers are often referred to as **specialists** as opposed to traditional **generalists** who would supervise a mixed cased of randomly assigned probationers without regard to crime or treatment needs.

The Dallas County, Texas, Community Supervision Corrections Department (the name has been changed from Probation Department) provides an example of specialization within a generalist approach. Probation officers might be assigned to a regular caseload of felons, misdemeanants, or DWI offenders, but they could also be assigned to several specialized caseloads:

1. *Pretrial services.* These officers recommend to the court and then monitor defendants released from jail on recognizance.
2. *Sex offenders.* With an average caseload of sixty-five cases, these officers supervise only sex offenders.
3. *Special supervision unit.* A maximum supervision caseload requiring at least weekly contact with offenders.
4. *Day reporting center.* A unit that monitors younger, unemployed probationers who report in for programs on a daily basis.

5. *Restitution center.* A fifty-bed coed residential facility used as an intermediate sanction.

6. *Neighborhood services unit.* A storefront office in a high-crime area; it emphasizes community contacts and supervision of community service hours.

7. *Mental illness/mental retardation.* Officers assigned specifically to work with small caseloads of mentally ill or mentally retarded offenders.

8. *Substance Abuse Felony Punishment Facility.* SAFPF officers work with caseloads of no more than forty-five offenders each; these offenders have been released from a prison therapeutic community known as SAFPF. The officers assigned have received special training in this therapy.

9. *DIVERT court.* A small unit that works with selected offenders before trial. If the offenders complete prescribed rehabilitation successfully, their criminal charges are dismissed.

Some of these assignments in Dallas also provide examples of how the team approach is used in probation today. The team approach develops team members' expertise in regard to specific client needs, such as mental health services or substance abuse counseling. The "War on Drugs" has further increased the number of probation clients with substance abuse problems, often with other mental health, physical health, and interpersonal issues. Probation officers have had to learn a whole new lingo, the language of drug treatment, if not to treat then to understand the treatment their clients are undergoing. The officers are dealing with many clients who suffer from comorbidity, or drug abuse in combination with other intrapersonal problems. They must also be familiar with many different treatment modalities, including some, such as family counseling, that involve not only the client but other family members as well. As if life were not complex enough.

Federal probation is often used as a model of what probation might become at the state level if it had more resources and an expanded role. The Federal Probation Act of 1925 established a probation system in the U.S. courts and gave courts the power to appoint probation officers and to place defendants on probation. Today this system is known as the U.S. Probation and Pretrial Services System, a part of the federal judiciary. Federal probation officers have three core responsibilities:

1. *Investigation.* Officers investigate defendants and offenders for the court by gathering and verifying information about them. Pretrial services officers investigate defendants who are charged with federal crimes and awaiting a court hearing. Probation officers investigate offenders who are convicted of crimes and awaiting sentencing as well as those who are serving a term of supervision after release from prison.

2. *Report preparation.* Officers prepare reports that the court relies on in making decisions. These are pretrial services reports that help the court decide whether to release or detain defendants while they are waiting for trial and presentence investigation reports that help the court impose fair sentences for offenders in accordance with federal sentencing guidelines and applicable federal law. Officers also prepare other reports for the court, including reports that address individuals' adjustment to supervision and their compliance with conditions of release.

3. *Supervision.* Officers supervise defendants and offenders in the community and in doing so reduce the risk these persons pose to the public. Pretrial services officers supervise defendants released pending trial. Probation officers supervise offenders conditionally released on probation by the court and on parole or supervised release after they are released from prison.[20]

Each of the ninety-four federal district courts has a probation office, ranging in size from about ten to more than 200 pretrial services and probation officers. In 2002, the 4,300 officers (not including supervisors and support staff) supervised about 186,000 defendants and conducted more than 156,000 investigations. To house an offender in a federal prison costs almost $61 per day as compared with less than $9 per day to supervise that person in the community.[21] Nevertheless, the increased emphasis on imprisonment in the federal system means that more federal offenders are behind bars than under supervision in the community at any given time.

Federal probation differs from typical state or local probation in several respects. First, the pretrial services officers pick up defendants at the point of arrest rather than on conviction or after sentencing, as is more often true in state and local systems. This provides for more information and greater continuity of supervision. Second, the supervision caseloads are small, averaging about forty to fifty per officer throughout the system; this is lower than any state system. In the larger districts, caseloads are specialized by crimes and treatment needs. Third, the relative permanence of court staff—judges, probation officers, clerks, and other officials—promotes a very close working relationship and a team-oriented perspective of probation work.

Federal probation work is highly bureaucratic in that the work is prescribed in detail in guidelines, manuals, policies, and procedures. Monograph 109, *The Supervision of Federal Offenders*, provides, for instance:

> the federal supervision model is founded on the conditions of release and comprised of both controlling and correctional strategies consistent with those conditions that are sufficient, but no greater than necessary, to facilitate achievement of the desired outcomes.
>
> The officer's responsibility within this model is to assess and manage risk by engaging in an ongoing process of investigation, assessment, planning, implementation, and evaluation that will begin at or—for offenders coming from prison—before the beginning of the term of supervision, and continue throughout the course of supervision.[22]

This manual defines the major **principles of good supervision** to be directed toward achieving desired outcomes with offenders:

Individualized: tailored to the individual offender

Proportional: not overly intrusive but what is necessary to address relevant sentencing purposes

Purposeful: applying specific goal-directed objectives

Multidimensional: using multiple intervention strategies from a variety of disciplines

Proactive in implementation: based on fieldwork and collateral contacts rather than supervision from an office

Responsive to changes: adjusting supervision as required based on compliance or noncompliance with conditions of release.[23]

PROBATION AS A SENTENCE AND A PROCESS

In the early years of the penitentiary, probation for convicted felons was the exception. Now **felony probation** is an accepted practice. In most jurisdictions, more felons get probation, either directly or after a short jail term, than go straight to prison. But is probation a real sentence, a serious punishment, or did the criminal "get away with it"? There is no doubt that both the conditions of probation and probation supervision in practice have gotten tougher in recent years. Probation is more restrictive and more costly to the probationer, and probation violation rates are up in most jurisdictions as probationers are monitored more closely.

More than twice as many offenders are on probation as are confined in state and federal prisons. In most jurisdictions, first-time nonviolent offenders—and some repeaters and less serious violent criminals—are routinely put on probation as a second chance. In many jurisdictions, probation is combined with a short jail term in what is called a split sentence. As a practice, probation has come to mean the following:

1. A disposition, with different provisions for controlling the offender's behavior
2. A status, which allows the offender to remain in the community under supervision
3. A subsystem of criminal justice
4. A process, involving such elements as investigating, reporting, and supervising

Not all offenders are eligible for probation. Many states use **statutory restrictions** to deny probation to certain violent criminals and to repeat offenders. Offenders placed on probation are subject to required conditions that fall into one of three realms:

1. **Standard conditions** imposed on all probationers, including such requirements as reporting to the probation office, notifying the agency of any change of address, remaining gainfully employed, and not leaving the jurisdiction without permission.
2. **Punitive conditions** established to reflect the seriousness of the offense and increase the painfulness of probation. Examples are fines, community service, victim restitution, house arrest, and drug testing.
3. **Treatment conditions** imposed to force probationers to deal with a significant problems or need, such as substance abuse, family counseling, or vocational training.[24]

If you were a criminal sentenced to felony probation in Lafayette Parish, Louisiana, you would be provided with the following legal notice (in abridged form) for your signature:

Conditions of Probation

It is the Order of the Court that you comply with the following required conditions of probation:

> Refrain from criminal conduct and pay a supervision fee to defray the costs of probation supervision.
>
> The Court has ordered you to pay a supervision fee of $_____ per month and it is to begin on _____.

The following specific conditions have also been imposed:

1. Make a full and truthful report at the end of each month.
2. Meet your specified family responsibilities, including any obligations imposed in a court order or child support.
3. Report to the probation officer as directed.
4. Permit the probation officer to visit you at home or elsewhere.
5. Devote yourself to an approved employment or occupation.
6. Refrain from owning or possessing firearms or other dangerous weapons.
7. Make reasonable reparation or restitution to the aggrieved party for damage or loss caused by your offense in an amount to be determined by the court.
8. Refrain from frequenting unlawful or disreputable places or consorting with disreputable persons.
9. Remain within the jurisdiction of the Court and get the permission of the probation officer before making any change in your address or employment.
10. Devote yourself to an approved reading program at your cost if you are unable to read the English Language.
11. Perform community service work.
12. Submit yourself to available medical, psychiatric, mental health, or substance abuse examination or treatment or both when deemed appropriate and ordered to do so by the Probation and Parole Officer.

Failure to comply with the foregoing conditions may cause your probation to be revoked. During the period of probation, you shall be subject to arrest at any time by the Probation and Parole Officer, either with or without a warrant, for the purpose of returning you to the Court for further disposition.

If you were a probationer in Dallas County, Texas, you would be obliged to review and sign a similar form—a three-page form for ordinary probationers or a four-page, more detailed form for sex offenders. The first ten conditions are the same on both forms:

a. Commit no offense against the laws of this or any other state or the United States, and do not possess a firearm during the term of probation.

b. Avoid injurious or vicious habits.

c. Do not use marijuana, narcotics, dangerous drugs, inhalants, or prescription medication without first obtaining a prescription for said substances from a licensed physician.

d. Avoid persons or places of disreputable or harmful character and do not associate with individuals who commit offenses against the laws of this or any other state or the United States.

e. Obey all the rules and regulations of the probation department, and report to the probation officer as directed by the judge or probation officer, to-wit: weekly, monthly, twice monthly.

f. Permit the probation officer to visit you at home or elsewhere, and notify the probation officer not less than twenty-four (24) hours prior to any changes in your home or employment address.

g. Obtain and maintain employment that is approved by this court and actively seek a job during any unemployment periods that may occur during the term of community supervision.

h. Remain within a specified place, to-wit: Dallas County, Texas, and do not travel outside Dallas County, Texas, without first having obtained written permission from the court.

i. Within 14 days of date below or release from custody report to the Dallas County District Clerk Collections Department, Frank Crowley Building, 5th floor, Room C-2, 2–4–653–5784, to arrange payment of court costs, fine, and court-appointed attorney fees.

j. Support your dependents.

For a regular probationer, the remaining conditions deal with payment of fees, restitution, community service, education, drug testing, avoiding contact with certain persons, jail confinement, special restrictions for persons convicted of drunk driving, and participation in other required treatment programs or special housing. Sex offenders may have to meet these special conditions and several of their own, such as registration, a polygraph exam, avoiding contact with children, avoiding schools or other places frequented by children, no possession of pornography in any form, no surfing the Internet for porn, and submitting a DNA sample for inclusion in a criminal database.

Violation of any general or special conditions can lead to **probation revocation.** This generally occurs in a two-step proceeding. The probation violator is held in jail under a **detainer** that prevents him or her from bonding out until a hearing is held. A hearing officer will first hold a probable cause hearing to determine that the violation—a new crime or technical violation—occurred. Then the sentencing judge to whom the probationer is responsible is required by the U.S. Supreme Court decision of *Gagnon v. Scarpelli* to hold a due process hearing before revoking probationary status. Being rearrested for a new felony offense is highly likely to result in revocation in most jurisdictions. Misdemeanor arrests and technical violations allow the court more wiggle room. Judges often admonish defendants and impose more restrictive conditions, but they are less certain to revoke probation for misdemeanors and other noncriminal behavior. Judges often practice tourniquet sentencing, which we will look at later in this chapter, tightening the rules, such as through curfews and drug testing, to control unlawful behavior. It is apparent that many probationers do not take probation at all seriously; they make little effort to change their lifestyles and avoid wrongdoing. Judges and probation officers today have more tools to use to get the attention of these offenders, who, if they are convicted felons, could just as easily be serving time in prison.

THE PROBATIONER: A PROFILE

What are probationers like, or, more specifically, how are people on probation different from people in prison? The most notable difference to keep in mind is that virtually all men and women serving prison terms are convicted felons, while about half of all probationers are misdemeanants under supervision for drunk driving, drugs, and assaults, among other misdemeanor crimes (though keep in mind also that many persons with misdemeanor convictions were originally charged with felonies and have pleaded them down). Probationers also tend to be younger and have less of a criminal history, especially for violence, than felons. Joan Petersilia and Susan Turner examined the criminal records and case files of more than 16,000 felons in California in 1986, trying to identify the specific factors that distinguished who was granted probation and who was sentenced to prison. They found that a person was more likely to receive a prison sentence if the following applied to him or her:

Had two or more conviction counts (in other words, was convicted of multiple charges)

Had two or more prior criminal convictions

Was on probation or parole at the time of the arrest

Was a drug addict

Used a weapon during the commission of the offense or seriously injured the victims[25]

Thomas Bonczar's report "Characteristics of Adults on Probation, 1995" is the most comprehensive national overview of men and women on probation. Probationers do look somewhat different in profile than prisoners is some key aspects:

Women make up about 21 percent of probationers, more than twice as high as their jail and prison percentages.

Whites make up about 62 percent of probationers, with blacks, Hispanics, and others making up the balance. This is almost exactly the reverse of jail and prison figures.

Probationers are more likely to be married and to have completed high school.

Probationers are also younger than prisoners (which is probably directly related to the criminal histories they are building up to deserve imprisonment in the future).[26]

The majority of probationers surveyed in this report were on probation for one of five offenses:

Driving while intoxicated—17 percent

Larceny/theft—10 percent

Drug possession—10 percent

Drug trafficking—10 percent

Assault—9 percent[27]

In an updated report on probation and parole completed in 2003, the numbers were about the same, except that the number of people on probation for drugs had increased sharply, as had the number of theft offenders. These increases are likely reflective of policies reducing the use of imprisonment for nonviolent criminals.

By year-end 2002, almost 4 million people were on probation, equally divided between felons and misdemeanants. Texas had the most people on probation, 434,000, although Georgia, California, and Florida were not far behind. If you took the probationers from these four states and added them together, their combined population of almost 1.5 million would make them the thirty-ninth largest state in America, just ahead of Idaho. If you took everyone on probation across the nation, the entire "State of Probation," they would make up the twenty-seventh most populous state, just ahead of Oregon and Oklahoma.

The majority (60 percent) of adults on probation in 2002 were sentenced directly to that status. The rest were given either a suspended sentence (31 percent) or a **split sentence** (9 percent) involving jail or prison time followed by probation. The split sentence is most common for people held in jail until they plead guilty; they get **credit for time served** and are then discharged to probation.

For most people on probation, the status comes with strings attached—additional conditions tacked on to probation supervision. Bonczar found these conditions commonly imposed in 1995:

Supervision fees—61.0 percent

Fines—55.8 percent

Court costs—54.5 percent

Mandatory drug testing—32.5 percent

Restitution to victim—30.3 percent

Alcohol treatment—29.2 percent

Community service—25.7 percent

Drug treatment—23.0 percent

Other treatment/counseling—17.9 percent

Education/training—15.0 percent

Virtually all offenders, 98.6 percent, had at least one additional condition imposed on them beyond obeying the law and complying with supervision procedures.[28]

The average length of time spent on probation at the time of the 1995 survey was about eighteen months, though this would naturally vary sharply according to whether one was convicted of a misdemeanor or a felony. How successful is probation in terms of outcomes? It is hard to give a general answer to this question: it depends on how you define "success," and it depends on the severity of the sanctions applied to those who fail, which is really a local practice and not something for which national standards apply. Bonczar's 1995 survey found that about 18 percent of probationers had faced a disciplinary hearing after entering probation. The five most prominent reasons given for these hearings included the following:

Absconded/failed to maintain contact—41.1 percent

Arrested or convicted of a new offense—38.4 percent

Failure to pay fines or restitution—37.9 percent

Failure to attend/complete treatment program—22.5 percent

Positive drug test—11.2 percent[29]

Some people qualified with more than one reason—a few probably with all five and more reasons not listed.

At any given time, about one in nine probationers has simply disappeared or **absconded,** which means the parole officer does not know how to find him or her. When this person gets caught, particularly if it involves an arrest for a new crime, you would imagine they are in big trouble. They probably go straight to prison, right? The answer is not necessarily. The largest category are returned to supervision, more often with a higher level of supervision and new conditions added. About a third are directly incarcerated; felons are much more likely to be incarcerated for disciplinary violations than misdemeanants are.

Let's look at the bottom line: does probation work? How do people leave probation: successful terminations, incarceration, or absconding? Over the past decade, the success rate has been very consistent in the range of 60 to 62 percent described as "successful completions," which means they were discharged from probation on time or early. The percentage returned to incarceration has declined from about 21 to 14 percent in 2002, indicating either that people are doing better or that we are giving them more slack when they do wrong (or that definitions of wrongdoing that would serve as the basis of revocation, such as failing drug tests, have been modified). The absconded and other unsuccessful category remains at about the same level, 16 percent. The leftovers make up a category known as "others." What this means is that at present, about three of every five people put on probation complete it without being revoked or otherwise failing to comply with supervision.

Researchers offer contradictory observations that confuse the public and political officials. Todd Clear and Anthony Braga wrote about probation in 1995, "Studies show that up to 80 percent of all probationers complete their terms without a new arrest." But Patrick Langan and Mark Cunniff draw a different conclusion:

> Within three years of sentencing, while still on probation, 43 percent of these felons were rearrested for a crime within the state. Half of the arrests were for a violent crime (murder, rape, robbery, or aggravated assault) or a drug offense (drug trafficking or drug possession). The estimates (of recidivism) would have been higher had out of state arrests been included.[30]

Joan Petersilia uses these examples to point out how definitions of target groups and standards of success and failure may vary. Clear and Braga are talking about the entire probation population—felons, misdemeanants, and DWIs—and only about arrests, not about other compliance violations. Langan and Cunniff are discussing persistent criminal behavior resulting in the arrest of felons on probation, whether the arrest results in revocation or not. Petersilia comments,

> In reality, then, there are two stories to be told in terms of recidivism rate of probationers. . . . On the one hand, recidivism rates are low for the half of the population that is placed on probation for a misdemeanor—data suggest that three-quarters of them successfully complete their supervision. Of course, previous

data has shown us that misdemeanants typically receive few services and little supervision, so in essence, they were "rehabilitated" either as a result of their own efforts, or simply being placed on probation served some deterrent function and encouraged them to refrain from further crime. . . .

The other story is that for *felons* placed on probation, recidivism rates are high, particularly in jurisdictions that use probation extensively, where offenders are serious to begin with, and supervision is minimal. In 1985, RAND researchers tracked, for a three-year period, a sample of 1,672 felony probationers sentenced in Los Angeles and Alameda Counties in 1980. Over that time period, the researchers found that 65 percent of the probationers were rearrested, 51 percent were reconvicted, and 34 percent were reincarcerated.[31]

Research in other jurisdictions has found considerable variation in arrest and revocation rates, but it is clear that many probationers, misdemeanants as well felons, do not view probation as a sign from God that they should turn their lives around. Many probation officials suggest that the lower recidivism rates for misdemeanants are not in fact due to lower rates of criminal conduct (or more effective rehabilitation) among misdemeanants. They offer two alternate explanations. First, misdemeanants are not supervised as closely as felons; thus, much of their bad behavior is never discovered unless they are arrested. Second, even if their misbehavior becomes known, they are at the bottom of the priority list for incarceration. In crowded times, felons get put behind bars, and misdemeanants are sent forth with instructions to "sin no more."

THE EFFECTIVENESS OF PROBATION

Probation has had its ups and downs over the past three decades. The rehabilitation and reintegration era of the 1960s and 1970s emphasized probation as the preferred option to imprisonment. Even after the American crime rate began a period of steep increase, the increasing use of probation for convicted felons, especially drug and property criminals, kept prison populations low. During the 1970s, straight probation was the most common sentence for convicted felons—more common than either imprisonment or a jail term followed by probation. This momentum carried probation through the end of the decade.

But by the middle of the crime control decade of the 1980s, this began to change. Probation fell out of favor for reasons we will explore momentarily, and by the end of the decade imprisonment had become the sentence of choice. The relative use of probation and imprisonment can be tracked over this period by comparing the ratio of persons on probation to persons in prison.

Year	Probation	Prison	Ratio
1980	1,118,097	319,598	3.50
1983	1,582,947	423,898	3.73
1986	2,114,621	526,436	4.02
1990	2,670,234	743,382	3.59
1993	2,903,061	909,381	3.19
1997	3,261,888	1,185,800	2.75
2000	3,826,209	1,316,333	2.90
2002	3,995,165	1,367,856	2.92[32]

It is easy to track the ebb and flow of probation over time. The change in the ratios from the peak use of probation in 1986 to its lowest point a decade later is indicative of a remarkably rapid change of public policy. Two further observations should be made. First, by 1997, America had more people *in prison* than it had on probation in 1980. Second, although the ratio of probationers has been increasing in the early years of the twenty-first century, the head count suggests that most of this increase is due to more use of formal probation for misdemeanants, that is, more people being brought under probation supervision who would not have been there before. Thus, while figures may show that probation is growing faster than imprisonment again, leading some analysts to declare the rebirth of reintegration (with its attached rehabilitative components), the recent increase is due more to net widening than to any ideological shift in favor of nonsecure management of felons.

If we view sentencing as three basic options—prison, jail (often credit for time served pretrial) followed by probation, and straight probation—then here is the plain truth: for all violent felonies, for all property felonies, for all drug felonies, and for all weapons felonies and other felonies, prison is used more often than straight probation; for most of these felony crimes, it is used more often than jail and probation added together. Thus, when some "policy wonks" (a term John DiIulio applies to himself and others) argue that most felony defendants are sentenced not to prison but to probation, they are lumping together the vast numbers of felons convicted of larceny, fraud, and drug possession, who get jail and probation or straight probation with greater frequency, with the smaller numbers of felons in other categories. In fact, if you are convicted of homicide, rape, robbery, aggravated assault, sexual assault, burglary, or drug trafficking, you are more likely to go to prison than to jail or directly to probation.

The most dramatic example of the change in probation vis-á-vis imprisonment is in the federal system. In 1975, the federal system had 64,000 probationers and parolees and 21,000 Bureau of Prisons prisoners, a ratio of slightly more than three to one. By 1997, the number of probationers and parolees had increased to 91,000, while the number of prisoners was also at 91,000. In two decades, the ratio had gone from three to one to one to one. By 2002, the number of federal prisoners stood at about 161,000, while the number of persons supervised in the community—probationers, parolees, and mandatory releasees—was at 109,000. Only 31,000 federal felons were on probation, less than one-fifth the number serving prison terms. In the federal system, probation has moved all the way back to the days of John Augustus.

What caused probation to lose favor and yield so much ground to imprisonment so quickly? Three main criticisms were directed at probation:

1. Probation was not controlling enough. Supervision was too lax.
2. Probation was ineffective in changing behavior. Probationers kept on practicing deviant behavior and eventually matured into habitual criminals who ended up in prison.
3. Probation was not punitive enough. It was not perceived as a **real punishment** either by criminals or by the public.

The position of probation officials and of scholars studying probation practices moved through a series of responses to these criticisms. The first wave of responses often followed the traditional **more resources** argument: "If we had more people, better people, and paid them more, if we had smaller caseloads and could provide more services, we could do a better job with criminals." As a correctional function, one of probation's advantages is its cost. Joan Petersilia wrote at one time, when average spending for supervision was about $200 per year per offender, "It is no wonder that recidivism rates are so high." Think of it this way. To keep 100 criminals in prison would require the services of twenty to thirty staff, costing from $15,000 to $25,000 per year, depending on the state. To keep those same 100 criminals under probation supervision would require one probation officer and another clerical person to help manage the reports; the average cost per criminal is in the range of $2 to $3 per day, or about $700 to $1,100 per year. Thus, imprisonment costs about twenty to twenty-five times as much as probation, which makes investing more in probation a reasonable argument.

The second wave of responses fell into the **greater accountability** group. This reflected an effort to make probation more "scientific." By using behavioral models, technology, and statistics, probation managers could require probation officers to manage their caseloads more diligently. Caseloads were structured according to levels of supervision required, offenders were assigned to levels on the basis of some sort of risk/needs instrument, specialization was emphasized, and officers were issued laptop computers plugged into information databases and told to keep up with their criminals better.

When neither of these approaches (not to imply that they swept uniformly across the country, bringing more resources and better management in their wake) seemed to make probation generally better or more popular with the public and the political officials who define its mission and approve its budget, a third wave began to build in the latter part of the 1990s; this wave, which seeks not only to change probation management but also to redefine its philosophy, is most often called **reinventing probation.**

The leading advocate of reinventing probation is John J. DiIulio Jr. He has argued that probation and parole fail to protect the public by failing to adequately supervise offenders and apply sanctions to violators. Probation thus becomes a kind of do-nothing status, playing no real part in society's efforts to control crime. To reinvent probation, DiIulio argues, we will need to reinvest in it. More money, more agents, and closer supervision are just the first phase. Equally important is what he sees as "creative and critical thinking."[33]

DiIulio is a member of the **Reinventing Probation Council,** most of whose members are probation managers who are associated with the National Association of Probation Executives of the **American Probation and Parole Association,** an organization that traces its origins to 1907. The council's August 1999 report "'Broken Windows' Probation: The Next Step in Fighting Crime" acknowledges that "widespread political and public dissatisfaction with community corrections has often been totally justified."[34] The report highlights a number of reasons "why probation isn't working":

Inadequate funding and understaffing.

The **fortress probation** approach, which brings offenders to the probation office for brief contacts rather than taking the probation officer out into the community

Ineffective drug testing and follow-up enforcement[35]

In a speech accompanying the report's release, one of the council members, Mario Paparozzi, added several other important failures of substance:

Emphasis on referrals but failure to engage offenders in change

Officers being content with contacts rather than involvement

Satisfaction with monitoring (or counting) instead of meaningful intervention[36]

In a section of the report titled "How Probation Can Work," the council identified seven key strategies of **broken windows probation:**

1. Placing public safety first
2. Working in the community
3. Developing partners in the community
4. Rationally allocating scarce resources
5. Enforcing conditions and penalizing violations
6. Emphasizing performance-based initiatives
7. Encouraging strong and steady leadership[37]

Broken windows probation is derived from the broken windows model of policing suggested in a 1982 essay by James Q. Wilson and George Kelling. This model focused on physical deterioration and public disorder as key features of high-crime neighborhoods. It suggested that police work with people in communities to address these problems.

In probation, broken windows is seen as combining elements of community policing and private business management to take probation officers out of the office and into the community, where they will work with police and community organizations to supervise offenders more closely. In its partnership with policing, broken windows probation clearly emphasizes the enforcement authority of its officers—and their accountability for the criminal behavior of the offenders in their caseload. It incorporates the first two waves of probation change—more resources and greater accountability—into a third giant wave (sort of a "probation tsunami") designed to wash away the old bureaucracy and replace it with a new, decentralized, but tightly managed strike force of probation monitors.

Well, that's an idea that is sure to be politically popular, broken windows' critics reply, but what about offenders? How does this "tight-ship" probation officer, running around the city in body armor and carrying a .40-caliber Glock—to be better prepared to take enforcement action—how does this surveillance-minded operative deal with the problems and needs of the criminals in his caseload?

A sharp rejoinder to broken windows is contained in "The Truth about 'Broken Windows' Probation: Moving Towards a Proactive Community Supervision Model," a paper (and article) written in 2001 by Faye Taxman and James Byrne, longtime advocates of expanded community corrections alternatives. Taxman and Byrne offer a treatment-based strategy they call **proactive community supervision** probation; their approach is sometimes also referred to as the **what works model,** referring to Robert Martinson's 1974 rehabilitation essay. The emphasis of the proactive supervision model is on offender change, not merely surveillance and control. Taxman and Byrne call the broken windows model a "step in the wrong direction for all the wrong reasons" and offer this explanation:

> Our rejection of the "broken windows" probation model is based on a belief that despite its "social ecological" rhetoric, this proposal is a throwback to the "get tough" surveillance-oriented community sanctions championed during the late eighties and early 90s. The fact that the Council has attempted to "reinvent" probation by turning it into community policing suggests to us that there may actually be a link between financial (need) and intellectual bankruptcy. Probation certainly needs additional resources, particularly if we expect probation officers to provide adequate supervision and treatment (resources) to offenders. But a "broken windows" probation strategy is not the *only* option available to administrators attempting to increase public support (and resources) for their agencies. One only has to look at recent reform efforts in California and Arizona for evidence that the public currently supports *treatment* and is willing to pay for it.[38]

A December 2002 editorial by James Gondles, the executive director of the American Correctional Association, made the same point about treatment:

> Today, tough on crime rhetoric persists, but it is losing its popular foothold as the public embraces a myriad of alternatives to incarceration. Programs emphasizing alternatives to sentencing—including prevention, treatment, and rehabilitation—are gaining support among the general population and, thus, lawmakers. New polls find that the public believes that laws should be changed to reduce the incarceration of nonviolent offenders and that rehabilitation should be the No. 1 purpose of the justice system.[39]

In an article titled "Much Ado about Nothing: 'Broken Windows' versus 'What Works,'" Mario Paparozzi has called for reconciliation between the two paradigms, which he sees as being caught up in ideological conflicts about conservatism and liberalism. This is how he defines the contrasting models:

> When applied in a community corrections context, broken windows refers to community-centered strategies that call for the amelioration of social problems related to crime and disorder. Additionally, broken windows protocols expand professional responsibilities for increased services to individuals and communities victimized by crime. On the other hand, what works strategies are offender-centered, and focus the professional work of community corrections agencies solely on the individual rehabilitation of the offender under supervision. Moreover, what works principles eschew making families, neighborhoods, and communities the centerpieces of community-based offender supervision practices.[40]

While what works focuses on reducing individual offender recidivism, broken windows, in its broader focus on public safety and community wellness, "presents an opportunity for what works principles to become compelling rather than optional," according to Paparozzi. He offers the following "brief and somewhat simplistic summary" of the most important broken windows theories:

> The profession's customers (the public) are those who foot the bill for goods and services provided.
>
> Professionals are part of the customer base, and they get an equal but not greater voice in determining the values of goods and services provided.
>
> Professionals are burdened with the primary responsibility of providing leadership in the public discourse, determining what results can be achieved and

which strategies produce the desired results (and why), implementing strategies that produce the results and documenting results in simple terms (e.g., success/failure).

If there is at least sound theoretical relevance and, at best, strong empirical evidence regarding the positive correlation between strategies and results, the strategy should be implemented and evaluated, and the results should be articulated.

Professionals should broaden their views about their work responsibilities to include individuals under supervision as well as families (significant primary groups), neighborhoods, and communities.

Professionals should acknowledge that crime is an individual and a social problem that is optimally addressed through coalescence, not fragmentation, across the spectrum of professionals, community members, and education, economic, health, social service, and law enforcement agencies.

Professionals should find the will and methods to incrementally expand into the practice grounded in broken windows and not maintain the status quo in the name of impoverished resource allocations, outdated and ineffective bureaucratic constraints, and a disinterested (or mean-spirited) political environment.[41]

These arguments about new perspectives come at an important time. As the emphasis on intermediate sanctions grows and many states look for ways to reduce their prison populations by supervising more criminals in the community, probation officials will have to determine what principles are most important in managing those to whom these sanctions will be applied, the criminals living in the "state of probation." What should be the emphasis in developing the intermediate sanctions that we will look at next—surveillance and control or treatment and rehabilitation? Papparozzi suggests,

If being a what works proponent includes a desire for civility when it comes to punishment, humanitarianism and altruism for all (including victims), and being a broken windows proponent includes paying attention to the will of the majority, providing leadership on the quest to a better place while respecting the customer base, then community corrections professionals can feel comfortable with a reconciliatory approach to these two very important models for corrections.[42]

INTERMEDIATE SANCTIONS

For many years, the courts faced a simple "either/or" choice in sentencing convicted felons—either nonsecure probation, allowing offenders to roam free under minimal supervision, or secure imprisonment, which isolated offenders from society. Since the **reintegration era** began in the 1970s, we have seen the development of a wide range of **intermediate sanctions** that impose more controls and restrictions over offenders. Most intermediate sanctions are considered a part of **community corrections,** keeping offenders at home or in a community-based residential facility. But some involve placement in jail or prison settings for short periods in combination with other periods of supervision in the community. Intermediate sanctions can be seen as providing more individualized controls matched to the offender's behavior; these sanctions also make the probation function more punitive by imposing greater costs on the offender's liberty. They are sometimes referred to as **enhancement programs** because they enhance both the treatment options for the offender and the control options for the state. Their objective is to achieve the goal we have previously discussed, **desistance,** which is defined as the system's effort to get the offender to cease criminal behavior.

Michael Tonry and Richard Will provided many of the philosophical justifications for intermediate sanctions in the introduction to their early report *Intermediate Sanctions,* written in 1988. Among their justifications are the following:

1. *The need for alternatives.* "The prison or nothing psychology of American sentencing is unimaginative and underdeveloped and has impeded efforts to develop constructive non-incarcerative correctional programs."

2. *The need for just deserts.* "There has been little meaningful proportionality in punishment for those who are not bound for prison. . . . Intermediate sanctions may provide the successive steps for a meaningful ladder of scaled punishments outside prison."

3. *The need for fairness and equity.* "The creation of meaningful intermediate sanctions removes the arbitrariness and unfairness that occur when prison and probation are the only choices available to the judge."

4. *The need for intermediate punishments.* While the possible net-widening effect of intermediate sanctions should be examined closely, "not all intermediate sanctions . . . need to be designed as alternatives to incarceration. Some may be designed as punishments for people whose crimes and criminal records make it inappropriate to do nothing to sanction their criminality and yet unduly harsh . . . to incarcerate them."

5. *The need to distinguish general and specific sentencing aims.* "Individualized efforts to fit the punishment to the offender and the applicable purposes of sentencing are, however, possible only when a range of punishment options is available, and that is part of what intermediate sanctions provide."[43]

James Byrne has represented common sentencing options on a continuum or scale of controls, from least to most punitive. These are shown in Figure 15-1. The idea of a scale of options fits the scheme of **tourniquet sentencing,** or tightening controls over the offender until desistance occurs. The corrections system is put in the business of **risk management,** which has to do with assessing risk and providing structured controls appropriate to the degree of risk the offender is believed to represent.

Restitution is at the low end of this scale. Restitution, which is akin to the old practice of *wergeld,* is accomplished through **restitution orders** that require the offender to repay the victim for economic losses; it is used more often in property crimes but can be used in violent crimes where injury also results.

Next on the scale is the **day fine,** which has been in use in European countries for many years. Instead of a flat fine, such as $500 for DWI that all offenders pay, the fine is expressed as a part of the offender's income. Each crime is worth so many **punishment units.** The judge sets a number of units for this specific offense, and these units are multiplied by a standard percentage of the offender's income (such as one one-thousandth of his annual income) to come up with a specific financial obligation. If both a business executive who earned $100,000 per year and a college student who worked

```
Prison                          ████████████████████████████████████
Jail                            ██████████████████████████████████
Split Sentence                  ███████████████████████████████
Residential Community Corrections  ████████████████████████
House Arrest                    ███████████████████████
Intensive Probation             ████████████████████
Active Probation                ███████████████████
Community Service               ████████████████
Day Fine (Plus Restitution)     ██████████
Restitution                     █████████
```

FIGURE 15-1 Sentencing options on a scale of punishment.
Source: James Byrne, "The Future of Intensive Probation Supervision," *Crime and Delinquency* 36, no. 1 (January 1990): 29.

part time and earned $10,000 per year were convicted of second-offense drunk driving, they both might be fined forty units of income. This would cost the businessman a fine of $4,000, while the student would pay $400. The premise, difficult to apply in practice, is that of equal impact. A number of American jurisdictions have experimented with the day fine, but it has not proven as popular here as it has in some of the more self-consciously egalitarian European countries, such as Germany, where it is the most common criminal punishment.

Community service or **community work orders** are next up on Byrne's scale. Offenders are ordered to put in so many hours of time devoted to some public service or charitable work. Sometimes the work is skill related, as a doctor who might provide free medical care; more often it involves social services, such as visiting a nursing home, or manual labor, such as picking up trash in a park. The idea is that the community work is more productive and more morally effective than being locked up or being let off with a fine or a suspended sentence.

Standard probation remains an option, though with typical caseloads of greater than 100, it provides minimal supervision. As we have already noted, many jurisdictions now structure probation supervision from administrative to low to regular to intermediate to high, with the highest level being ISP, which has spread nationwide since Georgia's experiment in the 1980s. Intensive probation has several standard features: small caseloads; frequent, sometimes daily, contacts between probationers and probation officers; drug testing; supervision fees; curfews; and participation in treatment programs. In some states, those offenders assigned to intensive supervision would otherwise have been sent to prison. They are usually repeat property or drug offenders. In other states, intensive supervision is part of an enhancement program; that is, it provides stepped-up supervision for regular probationers or parolees who have failed to comply with the conditions of less intensive caseloads. Their supervision is enhanced as an alternative to imprisonment.

Other intermediate sanctions center on confinement at home. This practice is related to the **furloughs** many states once used to allow inmates short visits home, often during the holidays, for family emergencies, or prior to release from custody. Furloughs have been less popular in recent years, primarily because political officials cannot take the heat when a criminal on furlough commits a new crime. Violent crimes committed by Willie Horton, a Massachusetts prisoner who absconded while on work furlough, became an important issue in the 1988 presidential election, with George Bush using the issue to claim that Michael Dukakis, then governor of Massachusetts, was "soft on crime." Furloughs are still legally available in about half the states and the federal system, but only three states—Indiana, Maine, and New York—have made much use of them recently.

House arrest, or **home detention,** is an intermediate sanction now used in many states and local jurisdictions. It may be a part of probation or a sentence in itself, as it is in Florida's Community Control Program. Home detention can be very restrictive, particularly when it is combined with **electronic monitoring** to impose even stricter controls over the offender's movements and whereabouts. The use of technological devices to monitor offenders was proposed in 1964 as **electronic parole,** but it has come into general usage only within the past decade. About one-third of offenders on house arrest nationwide are monitored through various types of electronic systems—some of which now have video and breath-testing capabilities. Global Positioning Satellite (GPS) technology is already in use in several jurisdictions to monitor high-risk or high-profile criminals such as sex offenders. It is technologically conceivable that within a few years, *every* probationer or parolee could be required to wear a bracelet or have an electronic chip implanted to facilitate GPS tracking.

Although such programs are often criticized as net widening, in many jurisdictions the offenders sentenced to house arrest and electronic monitoring are people who would otherwise be sent to prison under existing sentencing standards. Thus, house arrest and electronic monitoring have thus far probably kept as many people out of prison, at substantially reduced cost, than they have brought into the system under higher degrees of supervision. Success rates for electronic monitoring tend to be in the same range as routine probation, around 75 percent or higher. The probation officer's work seems likely to be increasingly tied to new monitoring strategies and technologies.

If offenders cannot live at home, the next step up the scale is to place them in a nonsecure residential facility. These facilities were typically called **halfway houses** at one time. They became popular in the mental health field and spread to community corrections in the 1960s and 1970s, when the reintegration era was in vogue. Their name came from their place—halfway between freedom and confinement. They were used both for offenders exiting the system—on prerelease, parole, or discharge—and for probationers who required stricter supervision. **Community residential treatment centers** today are almost always tied to employment, education, or treatment programs of some sort. Their emphasis is on making offenders productive and on providing intensive services that offenders cannot get as easily at home.

In some jurisdictions, the latest twist on the halfway house is the **day reporting center** (called the **day attendance center** in Australia and in some other models). Offenders live at home, but they report to another site each day to report in and take part in specific programs, usually treatment, education, or vocation focused. They then go home at night under curfew; with telephone checks or electronic monitoring added on, day reporting centers can be made nearly as restrictive as community residential centers.

Intermediate sanctions are usually tied to the community, as in recent **drug court** programs now proliferating in many urban areas, but there are variations that involve confinement in secure jails or prisons. Intermittent or "weekend" jail sentences and split sentences involving prison and probation are common in many jurisdictions. Accelerated or "shock" programs are another recent sanction combining time in secure custody with time under supervision—often intensive supervision—in the community. **Shock probation** was established in Ohio in 1965. The Ohio model uses a three- to four-month prison term followed by the offender's return to probation in the community. The judge is the official with authority to recall the inmate from prison and set the conditions for probation.

Georgia (1983) and Oklahoma (1984) were the first states to establish a different kind of shock program: **shock incarceration** or **boot camp.** These programs spread across the country within a decade. People liked the *idea* of boot camp. It reminded them of the old-fashioned idea of sending a troubled young person off to the military so that they could come back in a couple of years, all short-haired, clean-cut, well disciplined, and grown-up—having been "made a man of" or, in some cases, "made a woman of." The people who were actually in the military know that this premise often did not work. The military has plenty of criminals of its own and no longer allows confirmed criminals to enlist on active duty. Wonderful old movies like *The Dirty Dozen* aside, criminals tend to make bad soldiers. The people who came to military life as a refuge from a messed-up civilian life often replicated the mess they were trying to leave behind, finding that "it's the character, silly, not the locale." Thus, they ended up being problem children in the military, too, and getting an early discharge to go home.

Dale Parent, who has studied boot camps for more than a decade, described the boot camp approach in a 2003 report:

> As the name implies, correctional boot camps are in-prison programs that resemble military basic training. They emphasize vigorous physical activity, drill and ceremony, manual labor, and other activities that ensure that participants have little, if any, free time. Strict rules govern all aspects of conduct and appearance. Correctional officers act as drill instructors, initially using intense verbal tactics designed to break down inmates' resistance and lead to constructive changes.[44]

This idea really caught on, and by 1995 state correctional agencies were operating seventy-five boot camps for adults. Another thirty juvenile boot camps were operated by state and local government, and several large county jails had established similar programs, such as the "About Face" program in New Orleans, Louisiana. Boot camps had three main goals: reducing recidivism, reducing prison populations, and reducing costs (through shorter stays in prison). When the early results showed that recidivism rates of boot camp graduates were comparable to those of ordinary convicts, many boot camps retooled their programs, as Parent describes:

> Although first-generation camps stressed military discipline, physical training, and hard work second-generation camps emphasized rehabilitation by adding such components as alcohol and drug treatment and prosocial skills training. Some also added intensive postrelease supervision that may include electronic monitoring, home confinement, and random urine tests. . . . Recently, some boot camps, particularly those for juveniles, have substituted an emphasis on education and vocational skills for the military components to provide comparable structure and discipline.[45]

The long-term results have been mixed, according to Parent's summary:

1. Participants reported positive short-term changes in attitudes and behaviors; they also had better problem-solving and coping skills.
2. With few exceptions, these positive changes did not lead to reduced recidivism. The boot camps that did produce lower recidivism rates offered more treatment services, had longer sessions, and included more intensive postrelease supervision. However, not all programs with these features had successful results.
3. Under a narrow set of conditions, boot camps can lead to small relative reductions in prison populations and correctional costs.[46]

The use of boot camps declined in the latter part of the 1990s as the faddishness wore off and results fell short of early expectations. About a third of them had closed by 2000, and the average daily population of participants had dropped by about 30 percent also. One of the programs that has lasted a long time and shown positive results recently is Louisiana's IMPACT program (for Intensive Motivational Program of Alternative Correctional Treatment) at Elayn Hunt Correctional Center in St. Gabriel. After about a decade, in which the program's recidivism rates almost exactly paralleled the rates of ordinary prison releases, IMPACT was redesigned. It became, in Warden C. M. Lensing's description, "a treatment program within a military framework." The program was made longer—at least six months—and components of substance abuse education, social and work skills, and classroom education were added. More intensive aftercare is provided on release. The program is still tough, and dropout rates remain high (about 40 percent), but the three-year recidivism rates of recent graduates have averaged about 28 percent, just over half that of general population inmates.

There are two major limitations to the boot camp approach. First, they are focused on younger offenders, who are often the least interested in changing. Their motivation is to get the program quicker and get right back to the life they were leading before (even if they politely tell you something else when they are standing at attention in the boot camp dormitory). Second, although they do satisfactorily in the artificial boot camp environment, it is too short to change their basic values, to which they revert as soon as they are released back into society. They benefit from the structure; it just does not last long enough to make a permanent change in their behavior.

Shock incarceration is said to be a new approach, yet its regimen is very similar to the first American reformatories of a century ago. Reformatories did not achieve remarkable success rates, and so far boot camps have not done so either. But at least boot camp is quicker and cheaper, so corrections officials keep modifying its content in hope that its effectiveness can be substantiated. On James Byrne's scale, boot camp is the most severe of the intermediate sanctions and the closest to imprisonment. Fail here, and you're already in prison. All you have to do is take off your fatigues and put on the uniform of an ordinary convict.

DIVERSION: KEEPING THE OFFENDER OUT OF THE SYSTEM

Boot camps are at the high end of the scale of intermediate sanctions, closest to ordinary confinement. At the opposite end, before the offender acquires a record of criminal conviction, is another option called **diversion.** Diversion programs are said to be of three types: community based, police based, and court based. **Community-based diversion,** which is more likely to be used with at-risk juveniles than with adults, sends the offender into an alternative treatment program prior to arrest and filing of charges. There may be some question of just what legal compulsion the offender is under in this arrangement since diversion is based on the assumption that the offender can be returned to court for conventional processing if he or she fails to live up to the terms of the diversion contract.

Police-based diversion gives police officers the authority to send certain types of offenders, such as those involved in incidents of domestic violence, into counseling or treatment programs. A prime example of the impact of this type of diversion is the practice of taking common drunks to hospital **detoxification centers.** The prevalence of "detox" has resulted in a sharp decline in the number of drunks put in jail and processed as criminals. Police sometimes do not want this formal authority, to not put people in jail, which is based on the informal discretion that is already so much a part of routine police work.

Court-based diversion programs have become the most common. They are based on the concept that the judge has the authority to dismiss criminal charges if the offender completes a specified program of rehabilitation or self-improvement within a mandated time period. The offender signs a contract with the court to complete the program; if he or she fails to do so, the original charges are reinstated. Many jurisdictions operate **pretrial intervention programs,** under public or private authority, to get the offender to "take charge" of his or her life before the case comes to trial instead of waiting until after conviction to start corrective action. The big incentive to the offender is avoiding the stigma of a criminal conviction. Some diversion programs feature treatment in substance abuse rehab facilities or other hospital environments. This is considered medical treatment, which requires the informed consent of the offender before participation, just as consent was required in the earlier period—from the 1930s into the 1970s—when prisoners took part in the preapproval testing of new drugs. The "hottest" form of court-based diversion going in the United States today is the drug court movement. These treatment and monitoring–oriented courts, operating under the direction of judges who want to work with drug offenders as a special purpose clientele, have been established in hundreds of local and state trial courts across the country.

COMMUNITY CORRECTIONS: OPTIONS

One of the most direct applications of community corrections alternatives is to aid offenders in making the transition from prison to the community as they approach the end of their sentence. The **Federal Prisoner Rehabilitation Act,** passed by Congress in 1965, provided several options—work release, furloughs, and community treatment centers—to assist in reintegration. Many state laws today do the same, though many of the statutes may exclude more offenders than they include.

Work release was first authorized at the state level in a 1913 Wisconsin statute allowing misdemeanor offenders to work at outside jobs while they spent their nights in jail. Practically all states have some felons on work release today. Work release is not only good for the offender, by helping him or her get back in touch with society and make some money; it also benefits society through taxes, welfare savings, and offenders bearing the costs of their incarceration while living in work release facilities. Many authorities do not like to mix work release and non–work release inmates in the same secure facilities because of the problems of contraband being brought back in and conflict among inmates, but most correctional officials have no problem with work release inmates living in separate wings of secure prisons or living in the community in nonsecure residential facilities.

The halfway house, which is now often called a **community residential center,** is probably used more today as a work release facility than for any other purpose. When halfway houses first gained popularity in the 1960s, they more often housed parolees and other discharged, homeless ex-offenders. Over time, their purpose has changed to include more offenders still in custody— some in prerelease programming, some in educational release or taking vocational training, but mostly offenders in work release status. They live in the halfway house under varying degrees of restriction and work at full-time jobs they have been placed in.

Halfway houses today may be publicly operated or privately operated either for profit or, more commonly, by **nonprofit organizations**—religious, charitable, civic, or purely correctional in nature. Most offer residential facilities housing anywhere from a dozen to several dozen residents, often in an old residence in an urban neighborhood, though some halfway houses may use old apartment buildings or even former motels. Programs and services vary widely, but work is a constant, as are limited resources with the private facilities. Most of the private centers operate in a "break-even" mode. Most contract with local, state, or federal correctional institutions to provide housing and certain specified services for a particular type of offender, usually the inmate who qualifies for work release at the end of his or her sentence. The small size of their operation is great for flexibility and making changes, but it makes the operation vulnerable to catastrophic events. The loss of one contract, for instance, can kill an otherwise viable halfway house. Likewise, because these small facilities must either carry expensive liability insurance as protection against lawsuits or go the self-insured route with their own usually meager cash reserves, one important legal action can virtually wipe out the operation financially or make it impossible for the organization to continue to get insurance coverage.

Many states and the federal government operate a different type of facility called a **prerelease guidance center,** or prerelease center, for inmates at the very end of their sentence. It is usually located in larger metropolitan areas, and inmates from those areas are sent home a few weeks early to get counseling, find a job, and establish contact with their family again. If the state uses the furlough at all, as a form of **partial incarceration** reestablishing family and community ties, it can be attached to these centers.

INTERMEDIATE SANCTIONS AND COMMUNITY CORRECTIONS: PROS AND CONS

When community corrections alternatives first began to be emphasized during the early days of the reintegration era of the 1970s, the emphasis was on the "community" benefits. As James Byrne and other scholars have pointed out, the more recent popularity of intermediate sanctions seems more related to the "sanctions" part—to the stepped-up controls and penalties applied to those criminals who are not locked up. How did the kinder, gentler community corrections scheme of thirty years ago morph into the hard-nosed sanctions of today? What are the pluses and minuses of these two strategies, both of which rely on nonsecure alternatives but are very different in practice?

In 1898, the Irish author Oscar Wilde published a long poem, "The Ballad of Reading Gaol," after spending two years in prison for homosexuality. Stanza 5 of part V of this poem reads,

> The vilest deeds like poison weeds
>
> Bloom well in prison air:
>
> It is only what is good in man
>
> That wastes and withers there:
>
> Pale Anguish keeps the heavy gate
>
> And the Warder is Despair.

This verse could have served as the credo of the early community corrections movement, especially in sharing Wilde's aversion to prison air. Its members believed that "prison air"—the entire prison environment and experience—was naturally unwholesome and unhealthy to those forced to breathe it; the air of prison experience made people worse. The converse, then, was that the free air of the community was naturally healthy and healing. Therefore, corrections should have two primary goals:

1. Keep as many criminals in the community as possible, sending only those from whom society needed to be protected to prison
2. Among those people in prison, get as many of them back into programs in the community—rather than in prison—when they were ready for such programs

This was what Robert Martinson actually meant when he argued against rehabilitation—that if it was the purpose of imprisonment and it obviously did not work, then criminals should be dealt with through a different approach that did not involve isolation behind bars.

Supporters of community corrections marshaled several important arguments in favor of diminishing the use of imprisonment (or abolishing altogether its use as a punishment, except for the relative handful of truly dangerous criminals, although we really do not know how many there are or who they are, except judging by their past behavior). These arguments would include the following:

1. Community corrections offered a normal, humane environment, as opposed to prison's artificial environment. This was the environment the offender would have to deal with if he or she were to be successful and avoid a life of crime. People adapt to prison life—prisonization—but it only makes them better prisoners, not better free people.
2. Responsibility was placed on the criminal. Prison takes responsibility away and treats criminals like very bad children who are required to follow detailed, strict rules of daily living. Prisoners make almost no decisions on their own. When they get out, they have to get up in the morning, go to work, pay their bills, avoid bad-news friends who want to get them into trouble,

and fill up their idle time. These actions require responsible decision making, which prisoners are not very good at.

3. It was cheaper than imprisonment. Mainly because of the high levels of staffing necessary for security, prison is far more costly than community corrections.

4. For most criminals, community corrections was the appropriate alternative— the **least restrictive alternative**—it was less trouble.

5. A much broader range of referrals was available, and the programs were real-world programs, not those operating piecemeal under constraints of prison routine.

Thus, when we began to move more criminals—not everyone but larger numbers of felons—into probation and the community options, were these claims proven out? The critics of community corrections came back with their own set of responses:

1. The public was often apathetic or openly hostile to community-based programs, especially when residential programs put criminals into neighborhoods. The phrase **NIMBY** (not in my backyard) often came up when any type of residential facility was discussed. People might express favorable ideas about treatment programs but only as long as the facilities providing such programs were located away from neighborhoods, schools, and any place that had to do with children. In other words, it was all right to treat criminals like normal people as long as they did not actually come in contact with normal people. For prisoners, seedy downtown areas full of commercial properties and other social service programs were the natural environment—basically areas where there were no neighbors to complain.

2. Many programs were meagerly funded, hand-to-mouth operations that provided only minimal services. Many of the residential facilities were essentially just places to stay, like overcrowded rooming houses (or "flophouses," as residents sometimes put it), with any programs offered off-site. The staff were often low paid and transitory, not much different from the residents, and far from any notion of dedicated professionals with the background and calling to do this kind of work with criminals.

3. Because of whom they were operated by (often small nonprofits) and their meager resources, many community-based programs suffered from the same failing as prison programs: they were single-purpose programs that could not meet the multiple needs of offenders. A facility with an alcohol-based treatment program, for instance, would find that its residents also lack vocational skills, education, and social skills. What could it do for these other needs? "Sorry, we only do substance abuse." This limited approach often yielded recidivism rates that were as high or higher than conventional prison programs.

4. Persistently high recidivism rates were a serious problem of community-based programs. If community corrections were inherently superior to the prison, why did it have such high failure rates? Much of this likely had to do with two basic failings underlying assigning people to programs. First, as we just noted, assignments to programs were often random in nature or addressed only one problem, and, second, community alternatives tended to be

offered most readily to younger offenders who were most likely to disregard their positive aspects and continue with criminal behavior. Many people also expected unrealistic performances from these programs; if a normal recidivism rate was 50 percent and this program's rate was 40 percent, was it a failure? No, it was 20 percent *more* successful than the conventional prison approach. But it was hard to live with such a high failure rate in a program based on belief in making a difference.

5. Some community alternatives were not much cheaper than incarceration, and some, especially for juveniles, were much more expensive than incarceration. The more staff a program employed, especially the more counseling and treatment staff, the more it cost. Therapeutic programs using social workers, psychologists, and other specialists (prisoners sometimes refer to them as "letter people," like PhD, MSW, CSAC, and so on, not to mention MD), could be prohibitively expensive.

6. The lack of security was a problem, especially in regard to public concerns about the program. Each year, the great majority of prison "escapes" are runaways or walkaways from open facilities of this type, many of them work release, prerelease, or treatment facilities. For people who live around these facilities, the notion that criminals are coming and going at will is hard to take. If the facility has a problem with runaways or persistent misconduct, leading to a perception of lax supervision, its credibility will suffer, and God forbid that one of the residents should commit a violent crime in the neighborhood—like robbing and raping a little old lady. Entire facilities serving dozens of offenders have been shut down in the aftermath of such crimes, leading to public uproar and political intervention. A work-training facility in New Orleans, the only prison in Louisiana located in an urban area, was shut down after an escapee raped and murdered a woman living nearby.

Many of these problems rolled together to create serious operational and perceptional problems for community corrections programs in the 1970s and early 1980s. Many of these programs began with a dual approach—"good intentions" and "hope and a prayer" combined, often with federal funding or other grant funding of limited duration. When the money ran out, programs were cut back or eliminated altogether. Because many of them were privately operated outside the public criminal justice system, they lacked any real basis of continuing support from within the system. They were helpful for a time in relieving overcrowding pressures when institutional populations began to rise, but they were not founded on any philosophy of long-term commitment from politicians or correctional officials. Thus, when politics took a hard right turn in the direction of crime control, it was easy to abandon community-based programs as haphazard and ineffective. "They just don't work," officials said as they turned away from community corrections in favor of secure custody.

The emergence of intermediate sanctions in the 1990s has led to a resurgence of interest in community-based corrections, though this time the emphasis is placed more on public safety and victims' rights than on reintegration into the community and rehabilitation of the individual offender. Several scholars, including most notably James Byrne and Andrew von Hirsch, have pointed out the dangers of the new, hard-edged community corrections.

The philosophical foundation of the new community corrections rests on what von Hirsch call the **anything-but-prison theory:**

> Intervention in the community is tolerable irrespective of its intrusiveness, this theory asserts, as long as the resulting sanction is less onerous than imprisonment. This is tantamount to a carte blanc: Because imprisonment (at least for protracted periods) is harsher than almost any other community punishment, one could virtually never object.[47]

This view, that anyone who gets off with less than a jail or prison sentence (or more commonly a suspended jail or prison sentence assuming satisfactory completion of the community corrections alternative) is "getting a break," has several important consequences. First is **net widening,** which, as we have mentioned before, involves pulling minor offenders farther into the system and threatening them with confinement if they fail to comply with any intermediate sanctions that may be applied to them. More and more minor offenders, who in most other countries and until recently in the United States would have simply been discharged with a fine and a suspended sentence, are subject to more rigorous penalties, with the possibility of incarceration hanging over their heads if they fail to comply. It has led us to formalize controls over relatively minor offenders, which is why the number of misdemeanor probationers is growing more rapidly than the number of felony probationers.

Another consequence is the disregard of proportionality, a concept important to both Byrne and von Hirsch. **Proportionality** applies as much to a noncustodial as to a custodial sentence:

> A sanction levied in the community, like any other punishment, visits deprivation on the offender under circumstances that convey disapproval or censure of his or her conduct. Like any other blaming sanction, its degree of severity should reflect the degree of blameworthiness of the criminal conduct. In other words, the punishment should comport with the seriousness of the crime.[48]

When the offender is not locked up but is subject to other intermediate sanctions, such as intensive supervision, electronic monitoring, community service, restitution, and supervision fees, we often tend to overlook proportionality; after all, he could have gone to prison as allowed by law. It is a bit like looking at someone lying in traction in a hospital after a bad traffic accident; the injured party has both arms and both legs broken, a broken jaw, and various internal injuries that will take months to heal. "Well," you say, cheerfully, "it could be worse." Perhaps it can always be worse, up to the point of a horrible, lingering death by torture, but it can also be completely out of proportion with the harm done by the act.

Byrne comments on the legal system's tendency to engage in **sanction stacking.**[49] To make a point with criminals and perhaps to appear "tough" on criminals, the courts often stack intermediate punishments on top of each other. You get restitution, a day fine, community service, day reporting, a curfew, and a weekend in jail to start it out. He points out that each of these is actually a stand-alone option, and he argues that we need to treat each of the sanctions on his scale as unique rather than as elements of single, comprehensive intermediate sanction—which again is an "easy" penalty because it does not involve prison time. The courts have often failed to make this distinction, with the result that someone can leave court after a relatively minor property or drug crime under a relatively heavy financial and liberty burden.

Todd Clear, Joan Petersilia, and other researchers have described what happens when intermediate sanctions are seen by offenders as being too punitive and too difficult to comply with: they choose to do the time and get it over with. As Byrne comments, "It appears that some offenders would rather *interrupt* their lifestyle (via incarceration) than deal with attempts to *change* it (via compliance with probation conditions)."[50] This is particularly true in those neighborhoods where little stigma (or even positive value) is attached to having done prison time. There are lots of people who would rather do more time than have the system "keep messing with" them.

Von Hirsch suggests that the application of sanctions should be guided by the idea of **acceptable penal content:**

> The penal content of a sanction consists of those deprivations imposed in order to achieve its punitive and preventive ends. Acceptable penal content, then, is the idea that a sanction should be devised so that its intended penal deprivations are those that can be administered in a manner that is clearly consistent with the offender's dignity.[51]

He would reject, for instance, those punishments "purposely designed to make the offender appear humbled or ridiculous," such as wearing Hester Prynne's scarlet letter "A" (or a striped prison uniform) around, displaying a drunk driver sticker on your vehicle, or posting a sex offender warning sign in your front yard. Many people take a contrasting point of view, by the way, arguing that **shame** ought to be a common part of intermediate sanctions, but von Hirsch suggests that we steer clear of punishments intended to make the person see himself or herself as a "moral pariah."[52]

James Byrne asks another question that persists as we imagine tightening controls (tourniquet sentencing) of offenders: how do we convince policymakers that it is useless to focus only on techniques for the formal social control of offenders? He contends that the dual strategies of increased surveillance and/or increased control over offender noncompliance with technical conditions are self-defeating because they ignore the underlying problems of offenders and communities.[53] Just making the rules tougher does not solve the problems of employment, family life, substance abuse, peer relationships, emotional health, and social standing that plague criminal offenders and generate much of their criminal behavior. To change behavior, he says, you must address offenders' problems, and you must do so in the broader contexts of lifestyles and communities.[54]

Byrne also argues that recent efforts to increase the rule-enforcing authority of probation officers undercut the ideal of a close relationship developing between the probationer and the probation officer. When the probation officer becomes little more than a mechanical "bean counter," he loses the moral authority of the mentor figure that was seen as being the essence of the role in the past. This role is still emphasized in certain other cultures, such as Japan, where middle-age and older adults continue to play a key role as volunteer probation officers.

Andrew von Hirsch urges more considered thought as we move toward the development of a more comprehensive system for applying intermediate sanctions. He leaves us with a cautionary warning:

> With adequate ethical limits, community-based sanctions may become a means of creating a less inhumane and unjust penal system. Without adequate limits, however, they could become just another menace and extend the network of state intrusion into citizens' lives. We should not, to paraphrase David Rothman, decarcerate the prisons to make a prison of our society.[55]

COMMUNITY CORRECTIONS IN THE FUTURE

At the center of the movement toward community-based corrections is the **community correctional center.** This facility is an expanded or enhanced version of the current halfway house or community residential center, serving as the location for a wider variety of residential and nonresidential programs for pretrial and sentenced offenders. You can almost envision it as a hotel with multiple floors: first floor, pretrial release; second floor, diversion; third floor, drug court; fourth floor, work release; fifth floor, day reporting; sixth floor, **halfway-out** prerelease inmates; seventh floor, **halfway-in** probationers in trouble; eighth floor, **reintegration centers** for closer monitoring of parolees in trouble for technical violations; and ninth floor, electronic monitoring and house arrest.

Any number of programs and combinations of supervision—both residential and nonresidential—are possible within this unified structure. In this combined facility different options can be interwoven to be applied to individual offenders and offenders can be moved from one option to another as their behavior and needs change. The possibilities of the enhanced community correctional center seem exciting; the most obvious problem is that it does not yet exist in this comprehensive form.

Who would operate such a facility? The ideal candidate seems to be the local sheriff, who through the community correctional center would provide outreach options to the jail while working closely with the local and state probation officers who would be the official monitors of behavior and treatment.

Richard Seiter has proposed a model of offender management that would fit the community correctional center very nicely. Seiter's model is called the **integrated contract model.**[56] This model could work through local jails as intake facilities, or it could also work out of purely state-operated facilities— the present classification units—dispersed around the state. It would require the convicted felon to choose either punishment or reintegration. Some offenders would not get a choice. First-degree murderers, rapists, major drug dealers, third-time convicted felons, and firearms violators would go to prison to serve incapacitative sentences.

If an eligible offender chose reintegration, he or she would be placed in a comprehensive reintegration plan that described the services to be provided, victim restitution, the least restrictive environment, and the treatment and management of the offender. A binding contract between the legal system and the offender, providing for a range of options, levels, and controls, would be drawn up and signed by all parties. The offender would be obligated to work toward defined goals within the contractual time period. Fail to live up to the contract, and you would go to prison after all.

The integrated contract model would keep out of prison a large number—certainly more than half—of all persons currently being admitted to prison each year. Like the enhanced community correctional center, it remains more a dream than reality. But as the costs of imprisonment continue to rise and concern over the impact of imprisonment on large numbers of marginal offenders grows, the integrated contract and the community correctional center have a better chance to be put into practice. The **social justice model,** which Harry Allen and Clifford Simonsen see as a possible long-term end of corrections, suggests that community corrections is more just and fair to most offenders than imprisonment—and it is better for society in the long run.[57]

As expenditures for corrections continue to increase, drawing money away from other governmental services, the key word becomes **accountability.** If community corrections can control offenders more cheaply, with better results, with less trouble, and without compromising public safety, it can probably draw increased popular and political support in the future. Allen and Simonsen have suggested that no more than 15 to 20 percent of convicted felons require imprisonment; the rest could be served by an expanded community corrections network.[58] Several of the more progressive states are already moving in this direction.

As more states pass **community corrections acts** to provide for a better-organized network of intermediate sanctions and alternatives at the local level, more of a burden is placed on state and local probation and parole officers to monitor the performance of the local programs. Probation and parole are the longest-established representatives of the corrections system in the community. Community corrections legislation, intended as an enabling mechanism to bring together offenders, private alternative programs, victims' groups, employers, activist citizens, juvenile advocates, and public agencies, often gives probation and parole the task of coordinating this ambitious (and very undefined) undertaking.

Most of us prefer simplicity; trying to put the many unconnected and sometimes seemingly contradictory people and programs together in a network of intermediate sanctions and community-based corrections is just the opposite—it is more complex than most of us would care to attempt. It makes the probation and parole officer's job much more complicated. Instead of just doing investigations, writing reports, conducting field supervision, and going to court, the probation and parole officer becomes the **change agent** responsible for managing the offender's movement among a range of control levels. Instead of a simple yes/no determination, the community corrections program of the future might have a scale of ten different major options with lesser adjustments attached to each. Using his or her **risk-control tools**—residence, day reporting, curfew, community service, drug testing, electronic monitoring, and so on—the probation and parole officer would manage the offender individually, tightening or loosening controls over time in response to the offender's behavior. This is a much more sophisticated approach than the current practice of probation and parole, and not all probation and parole staff can be expected to move cheerfully into this problematic future. We can imagine this prospect, but it is easier to have the vision than to follow through and make it real. The prison is a much simpler reality.

KEY TERMS

bricks-and-mortar
  solution

selective incapacitation

chronic offenders

front-end solutions

suspended sentence

right of sanctuary

benefit of clergy

judicial reprieve

filing of cases

surcease

John Augustus

probation

probation officers

recognizance

juvenile probation

mentor

caseload

presentence investigation
  reports

line probation officers

casework

risk/needs assessment

crisis management

intensive supervised
  probation

surveillance

team approach

specialists

generalists

federal probation

principles of good
  supervision

felony probation

statutory restrictions

standard conditions

punitive conditions

treatment conditions

probation revocation

detainer

Gagnon v. Scarpelli

split sentence

credit for time served

absconded

real punishment

more resources

greater accountability

reinventing probation

Reinventing Probation
  Council

American Probation and
  Parole Association

fortress probation

broken windows
  probation

proactive community
  supervision

what works model

reintegration era

intermediate sanctions

community corrections

enhancement programs

desistance

tourniquet sentencing

risk management

restitution

restitution orders

day fine

punishment units

community service

community work orders

furloughs

house arrest

home detention

electronic monitoring

electronic parole

halfway houses

community residential
  treatment centers

day reporting center

day attendance center

drug court

shock probation

shock incarceration

boot camp

diversion

community-based
  diversion

police-based diversion

detoxification centers

court-based diversion

pretrial intervention
  programs

Federal Prisoner
  Rehabilitation Act

work release

community residential
  center

nonprofit organizations

prerelease guidance center

partial incarceration

least restrictive alternative

NIMBY

anything-but-prison
  theory

net widening

proportionality

sanction stacking

acceptable penal content

shame

community correctional
  center

halfway-out

halfway-in

reintegration centers

integrated contract model

social justice model

accountability

community corrections
  acts

change agent

risk-control tools

NOTES

1. Virgil L. Williams, William A. Formby, and John C. Watkins, "Probation in America," in *Introduction to Criminal Justice* (Albany, N.Y.: Delmar Publishers, 1982), p. 378.

2. Ibid.

3. Joan Petersilia, "Probation in the United States, Part I," *Perspectives,* spring 1998, p. 33.

4. Donald G. Evans, "Probation: Strength through Association," *Corrections Today* 57, no. 5 (August 1995): 100.

5. Petersilia, "Probation in the United States, Part I," p. 33.

6. Williams et al., "Early English Practices," p. 377.

7. Petersilia, "Probation in the United States, Part I," p. 38.

8. Ibid.

9. Camille Graham Camp and George M. Camp, *The Corrections Yearbook 2001: Adult Systems* (Middletown, Conn.: Criminal Justice Institute, 2002), p. 195.

10. Cited in Joan Petersilia, *Reforming Probation and Parole in the 21st Century* (Lanham, Md.: American Correctional Association, 2001), p. 33.

11. Camp and Camp, *Corrections Yearbook 2001*, p. 223.

12. National Advisory Commission on Criminal Justice Standards and Goals, *Corrections* (Washington, D.C.: U.S. Government Printing Office, 1973), p. 318.

13. President's Commission on Law Enforcement and Administration of Justice, *The Challenge of Crime in a Free Society* (Washington, D.C.: U.S. Government Printing Office, 1967), p. 167.

14. President's Commission on Law Enforcement and Administration of Justice, *Task Force Report: Corrections* (Washington, D.C.: U.S. Government Printing Office, 1967), p. 29.

15. Petersilia, "Probation in the United States, Part I," p. 38.

16. National Advisory Commission, *Corrections*, p. 317.

17. Petersilia, *Probation and Parole in the 21st Century*, p. 35.

18. Billie S. Erwin, "Old and New Tools for the Modern Probation Officer," *Crime and Delinquency* 36, no. 1 (January 1990): 62.

19. Ibid., p. 63.

20. Administrative Office of the U.S. Courts, "The U.S. Probation and Pretrial Service System," *Court and Community*, January 2003, n.p.

21. Administrative Office of the U.S. Courts, "Benefits of Supervision," *Court and Community*, January 2003, n.p.

22. Administrative Office of the U.S. Courts, *The Supervision of Federal Offenders*, Monograph 109, revised March 2003, p. I–2.

23. Ibid., p. I–7.

24. Petersilia, "Probation in the United States, Part I," p. 35.

25. Petersilia, *Reforming Probation and Parole in the 21st Century*, p. 27.

26. Thomas P. Bonczar, "Characteristics of Adults on Probation, 1995," U.S. Department of Justice, Bureau of Justice Statistics Special Report, December 1997, p. 2.

27. Ibid.

28. Ibid., p. 7.

29. Ibid., p. 10.

30. Petersilia, *Reforming Probation and Parole in the 21st Century*, pp. 55–56.

31. Ibid., pp. 56–57.

32. Kathleen Maguire and Ann L. Pastore, eds., "Adults on Probation, in Jail, and on Parole," table 6.1, *Sourcebook of Criminal Justice Statistics 1997*, U.S. Department of Justice, Bureau of Justice Statistics (Washington, D.C.: U.S. Government Printing Office, 1998), p. 464.

33. John J. DiIulio Jr., "Reinventing Parole and Probation," *Brookings Review* 15 no. 2 (spring 1997): 41.

34. Center for Civic Innovation at the Manhattan Institute, "Broken Windows Probation: The Next Step in Fighting Crime," Civic Report No. 7, August 1999, p. 1.

35. Ibid., p. 5.

36. Donald G. Evans, "Broken Windows: Fixing Probation," *Corrections Today* 61, no. 7 (December 1999): 30.

37. Center for Civic Innovation, "Broken Windows Probation," pp. 5–9.

38. Faye S. Taxman and James M. Byrne, "The Truth about 'Broken Windows' Probation: Moving towards a Proactive Community Supervision Model," *Perspectives*, spring 2001, p. 16.

39. James A. Gondles Jr., "Alternatives to Incarceration Mentality Is Emerging," *Corrections Today* 64, no. 11 (December 2002): 6.

40. Mario Paparozzi, "Much Ado about Nothing: 'Broken Windows' versus 'What Works,'" *Corrections Today* 65, no. 1 (February 2003): 30.

41. Ibid., pp. 32–33.

42. Ibid., p. 33.

43. Cited in James M. Byrne, "The Future of Intensive Probation Supervision and the New Intermediate Sanctions," *Crime and Delinquency* 36, no. 1 (January 1990): 15.

44. Dale G. Parent, "Correctional Boot Camps: Lessons from a Decade of Research," U.S. Department of Justice, National Institute of Justice, June 2003, p. 2.

45. Ibid.

46. Ibid., p. ii.

47. Andrew von Hirsch, "The Ethics of Community-Based Sanctions," *Crime and Delinquency* 36, no. 1 (January 1990): 165.

48. Ibid., p. 163.

49. Byrne, "The Future of Intensive Probation Supervision," p. 29.

50. Ibid., p. 23.

51. Von Hirsch, "The Ethics of Community-Based Sanctions," p. 167.

52. Ibid., p. 168.

53. Byrne, "The Future of Intensive Probation Supervision," p. 31.

54. Ibid., p. 33.

55. Von Hirsch, "The Ethics of Community-Based Sanctions," p. 172.

56. Cited in Harry E. Allen and Clifford E. Simonsen, *Corrections in America*, 9th ed. (Upper Saddle River, N.J.: Prentice Hall, 2001), pp. 652–53.

57. Ibid., pp. 654–55.

58. Ibid., p. 655.

FURTHER READING

Byrne, James M., Arthur J. Lurigio, and Joan Petersilia. *Smart Sentencing: The Emergence of Intermediate Sanctions.* Newbury Park, Calif.: Sage Publications, 1992.

Clear, Todd R., and Harry R. Dammer. *The Offender in the Community.* 2nd ed. Belmont, Calif.: Thomson/Wadsworth, 2003.

Dressler, David. *Probation and Parole.* New York: Columbia University Press, 1951.

Morris, Norval, and Michael Tonry. *Between Prison and Probation: Intermediate Punishments in a Rational Sentencing System.* Oxford: Oxford University Press, 1990.

Petersilia, Joan. *Reforming Probation and Parole in the 21st Century.* Lanham, Md.: American Correctional Association, 2001.

WEB AND VIDEO RESOURCES

The American Probation and Parole Association Website is *www.appa-net.org.*

A good site for information related to alternative dispute resolution is *www.adrr.com.*

COMMENTARY

23 Restorative Justice and Community Corrections

by Clifford Dorne

Less punitive than incarceration in jails and prisons, community correctional programs have been generally designed to reform or rehabilitate offenders as a primary goal. As of the early 1980s, however, community correctional policies became more concerned with monitoring and controlling offenders in the interest of public safety and with the intention of keeping them drug free while under supervision—a law enforcement approach as opposed to the previous rehabilitation-oriented social work approach. Currently, it is arguable that more of a balance prevails between the two approaches.

A variety of intermediate sanctions were also developed that were either closely related to community corrections or actually part of such programs: day fines, forfeitures, restitution, community service, intensive probation supervision, house arrest and electronic monitoring, day reporting centers, shock incarceration (correctional boot camps), and residential centers (halfway houses). These sanctions are said to exist "in between" community corrections and regular incarceration.

Regular community correctional programs—and the intermediate sanctions that have become so integrally related to them—have fallen short of some important justice-related attributes. The needs of crime victims have often not been addressed. Even in restitution programs, only the monetary needs are covered while the psychological needs of the victim may be neglected (e.g., to gain an understanding from the offender as to why they were chosen as victims).

Moreover, most community correctional programs do not involve direct input from volunteer community members (though volunteers serve in some support roles), and as such, may reinforce the view in some or many communities that the justice system is remote, out-of-touch, and generally far less responsive to community needs than it could be.

Finally, most community correctional programs set offender rehabilitation as their main goal, perhaps second only to community safety. Traditional notions of rehabilitation were based on the medical model of human behavior or determinism. That is, offenders were not viewed as being responsible for how they are (personality) or for what they do (conduct). Among correctional treatment staff, psychological or environmental variables supposedly existing outside of the offender's control or volition were often considered criminogenic. In a word, historically, traditional rehabilitation failed to hold offenders directly and personally accountable for their criminal behavior.

These observations, in part, resulted in the founding of the restorative justice movement. In the mid-1970s, probation officers in Kitchener, Ontario (Canada) were assigned to some young probationers who were under supervision for vandalism. These officers required the youths to meet with each victim (there were many) and offer restitution and apologies. The interactions between the offenders and the victims were said to have been not only rehabilitative in effect but also reintegrative. The remorseful youths were then permitted to reintegrate back into the community with full forgiveness resulting in satisfaction for the victims, offenders, and for the community.

The Mennonite Central Committee in northern Indiana soon embarked on the development of the first U.S. victim–offender mediation (VOM) program initiative. This idea was emulated throughout the 1980s as many states developed programs that were placed within diversion and probation programs, respectively, and training curricula were implemented to prepare cadres of volunteer mediators to work in court-based and non-profit mediation centers or community justice centers. Restorative justice introduced a new paradigm of justice emphasizing that crime is a breach of relationship within the community and that mercy, forgiveness, community involvement, mixed with offender personal accountability should, when taken together, result in the peaceful reintegration of the offender back in to the community's fold. Currently, about half of the states have restorative justice-related statutes on the books.

The restorative justice movement is based on a variety of theoretical roots that include the victims' rights movement, some justice-related practices derived from various indigenous cultures with community involvement at the center of their justice processes, and faith-based initiatives, especially (but not limited to) Mennonite theology and peacemaking initiatives. Indeed, pacifism is related to restorative justice to the extent that the traditional criminal and juvenile justice systems may be considered to overuse incarceration—analogous to the official overuse of methods based on violence. From this perspective, the "get tough" approach to crime represents overkill and restorative justice advocates prefer a selective incarceration approach—only imprison those who pose a direct threat to society. They would prefer more widespread use of community corrections with restorative justice programs at their core.

In addition to VOM, restorative justice programs include school–peer mediation, school truancy mediation, family-group conferences, and circle sentencing (and the spin-off referred to as reparative probation). The goal is to restore or repair harm or breach of relationship caused by crime to victims, offenders, and communities. Also, restorative justice programs attempt to involve community members and crime victims in key decision-making capacities, both at policy levels and within individual cases.

There is a close relationship between restorative justice programs and traditional community correctional agencies. Restorative justice programs have been placed within them or alongside them (offender referrals), and some advocates would like restorative justice programs to replace traditional community corrections altogether. Thus, there is an ongoing debate about whether restorative justice should supplement traditional community correctional programs (or be placed within them), or actually supplant them altogether. Some advocates arguing for the latter would actually like to see restorative justice completely and holistically replace the traditional juvenile and criminal justice systems. This is a radical position and is unlikely in the foreseeable future.

Restorative justice advocates have not adequately addressed the problems of attempting to use these programs for offenders who have committed very serious or heinous crimes, for offenders who show no remorse or lack a conscience (e.g., anti-social personality), or for offenders that are members of criminal gangs or organized crime groups. Moreover, restorative justice programs tend to work best when there is a clear, innocent victim involved in the case. What about cases of consensual or "victimless" crimes in which the "victim" is also an offender? For instance, if one drug dealer assaults another drug dealer, this case would not be a very good candidate for victim-offender mediation.

Restorative justice programs seem best suited for cases in which the offender committed a non-serious offense and came from the same local community as the victim. Furthermore, the victim should be innocent in the case and should not be involved in a life of crime; after all, why would we want to socially reunite one violent, high-level drug dealer to another in the interest of improving the community? Finally, the presumption is that the community is socially integrated and stable.

Advocates of restorative justice tend to play down the use of coercion in getting offenders to participate in these programs. Restorative justice advocates are often relatively optimistic—and some would say overly optimistic—with respect to the motivation and willingness of offenders to be successfully reintegrated into the community with full forgiveness. Only research will determine if this view reflects reality. Currently, there are substantial survey data indicating that participants in restorative justice programs (victims, offenders, mediators, etc.) are satisfied with their experiences and subjectively deem the programs to be successful. However, there is not enough hard data indicating that restorative justice programs reduce recidivism when compared to more traditional programs, though additional research in this area is ongoing. Also, some rehabilitation programs have actually met their goals reducing recidivism, but, as Sharon Levrant et al. noted in a 1999 *Crime and Delinquency* article, "Reconsidering Restorative Justice: The Corruption of Benevolence Reconsidered," restorative justice has not yet been systematically linked to these successful programs.

Overall, restorative justice programs seem to have much to offer communities in certain types of delinquency and criminal cases. They have the potential to facilitate and improve upon the services offered by diversion and probation programs at the juvenile and adult levels. Restorative justice can pull communities together in crime prevention initiatives and get more volunteers centrally involved in both juvenile justice and criminal justice community correctional programs.

16 CONTRASTING PHILOSOPHIES: AMERICAN AND INTERNATIONAL CORRECTIONS TODAY

I don't care about making prisons "more this" or "less that" because I do not think that prisons represent an even vaguely sensible approach to dealing with many of those who have been found guilty . . . . Without wishing to sound like a 1970s punk anarchist screaming "smash the state," I no longer wish to see prisons improved, if these "improvements" mean that they are further legitimated and as a result their usage increased. This is not to say that I wish to see prisons return to some sort of Dickensian hell-hole. Rather, what I would like to see is first a serious, considered debate about disposals which take as many people out of prison as is possible, and then a programme designed to achieve just that.

— STEPHEN FARRELL, 2000

We believe in making people pay for their crimes, in protecting the weak from the vicious. We believe in justice. And we believe in simple truths. So much so that we might find it hard to accept this complex possibility: that our strivings to protect society may have weakened it. At the very least, our policies have arguably hurt certain communities. But they may also be doing deeper damage, for they fuel the notion that we can afford to throw human beings away. And they discourage us from asking whether it is morally or economically justifiable to invest so much in locking lost souls down and so little in salvaging them. In fact, a strategy of human reclamation may be the only thing that makes sense in the long run, not only for those fated to spend time locked down, but for the communities to which they seem destined to return— communities that now are doubly damned: to suffer when wrongdoers are taken away and yet again when they come back.

— ELLIS COSE, "THE PRISON PARADOX," *TIME*, 2000

INTRODUCTION

This chapter compares contemporary American corrections with the rest of the world. Comparative criminal justice scholars talk about the "global village" and convergence—the tendency of nations to become more alike over time— but it is apparent that in regard to imprisonment, the United States has gone its own way, following a path others may or may not choose to follow. Not only does it have the highest imprisonment rates in the world, but it is making no real effort to change its standing—viewing the high level of imprisonment not as a problem to be addressed but rather as a necessary, even desirable feature of modern society. In this chapter, we will look at the rest of the world and then return to focus on the United States, discussing the influences on correctional philosophy and practice that make us different. We will end with some thoughts on the recent past and the near future of American corrections. After reading the material in this chapter, you should be familiar with:

1. The crime problem as a worldwide concern.
2. An overview of the corrections systems of seven major foreign nations: Canada, England, Germany, Russia, Saudi Arabia, China, and Japan.
3. How other nations view the use of imprisonment.
4. What the experience of imprisonment is like in other countries.
5. How and why America differs from other nations in its approach to corrections.
6. The ideology of American punishment.
7. How recent history has widened the gap between the United States and other nations.
8. The possibilities of the near future in American corrections.

CRIME: A WORLDWIDE PROBLEM

For German prison warden Volker Bieschke, his November 1999 tour of six California prisons was "eye opening." His most striking impression: the size of the institutions. "It was my first time to see such large prisons," he said, pointing out that, among the handful of big prisons in Germany, the largest holds about 1,500 inmates—about a third the size of the average California prison.

Bierschke is a criminologist by training. His prison houses 120 inmates who leave the facility each day for jobs in the community and return each evening to sleep. Their access is not restricted by officers or fences, but Bierschke said escapes rarely occur. After spending their first year in a conventional secure facility, many German inmates qualify to transfer to these small, community-based institutions. But they know that any abuse of the freedoms they enjoy will land them back in a secure prison.

Bierschke had several reservations about what he saw. He wondered whether the large prisons actually help individual inmates. He was disquieted by the physical environment of the Security Housing Unit at Pelican Bay, California's supermax prison. The small size of the cells and the general absence of windows for both staff and inmates drew his attention. But he acknowledged the greater risks presented by the more violence-prone American inmates and the difficulties American wardens have in managing such inmates. German prisons have almost no violence, and no prison riots have been reported in the past forty years. "My problems are not their problems," he said.[1]

Many international visitors to American prisons make similar observations. Depending on their own prison cultures, they comment on the size of the institutions, the emphasis on security, the many prison programs but the general lack of meaningful work, the predominatly minority inmate populations, the isolation of inmates from society, and the philosophical differences in corrections policies. When they find out how many people are in prison— California, with 40 percent of Germany's population, has three times as many criminals in jail and prison, 240,000 to 80,000—their own worries seemed minor in comparison. They ask, "Is crime really that bad to justify keeping that many people locked up?"

Good question. With less than 5 percent of the world's population, the United States has 25 percent of the world's prisoners—2.25 million adults and juveniles behind bars at the end of 2003, out of a worldwide imprisoned population of just under 9 million. One of every four prisoners in the world is behind bars in America. We knew that we were ahead in obesity and Nobel prizes; how did we come to lead the world in this other category? Do we have 25 percent of the world's crime, or is our imprisonment rate clearly out of line with our crime problem?

In shaping their views of the use of imprisonment, many Americans would probably agree with these three basic assumptions about crime:

1. It began in the Garden of Eden with the theft of an apple.
2. It has been on an unbroken upward climb ever since.
3. It has somehow climbed far higher in the United States than anywhere else in the history of the world.

Criminologists offer three responses in return:

1. Crime is related most directly to modern industrial society, particularly the growth of the city.
2. Crime goes up and down over time, according to conditions in society.
3. Crime in America, except for some crimes of violence, is no higher than in the other industrialized nations with which we most closely compare.

Comparative criminologists who study international crime suggest that crime has been an important domestic political issue not only in America but also in other industrialized and developing nations since the late 1960s to early 1970s. The **crime problem** internationally is often broken down into several component parts:

1. Increased rates of traditional crimes, especially property crimes
2. Increased juvenile violence and public misconduct (behavior so commonplace in Europe that a term, "hooliganism," developed to describe it)
3. Increasing criminalization of political corruption and economic misconduct
4. Increasing criminality of women, though more for nonviolent than violent crimes
5. Increased role of alcohol and drug abuse in criminality
6. Increased public awareness—"fear of crime"—generating political attention
7. Increased incidence and visibility of political terrorism in cities

But the American public tends to be ignorant of or to disregard the concerns of other nations as they reflect on our own problems. Where crime is concerned, we tend to think and act as if we are in a class by ourselves, with the result that our extreme devotion to the use of imprisonment has made that tendency a real public policy. Most other nations pursue different policies in which imprisonment is not used as much, though most have taken a turn in our direction of late.

TABLE 16-1

Reported Crime Rates (crimes per 100,000 in 1994)

Country	Homicide	Rape	Robbery	Burglary
United States	8.9	39.2	237.7	1,041.8
Canada	2.0	108.4	98.8	1,326.2
England/Wales	1.4	9.9	116.2	2,445.4
Germany	1.7	7.5	71.0	1,927.1
Russia	20.2	9.4	126.0	262.3
Saudi Arabia	0.9	0.6	0.04	—
China	0.2	3.4	—	45.2
Japan	0.9	1.3	2.2	198.1

Source: INTERPOL crime data reported in Frank Hagan, *Introduction to Criminology,* 4th ed. (Chicago: Nelson-Hall, 1998).

TABLE 16-2

Criminal Victimization (percentage of survey population reporting victimization with a five-year survey period)

Country	Burglary	Theft	Contact Crimes[1]	Assaults (Women)	Assaults (Men)	Any Crime
United States	23.4	28.5	19.8	5.7	7.0	64.1
Canada	19.7	28.9	18.5	7.7	6.0	64.3
England/Wales	22.5	21.1	16.7	4.5	6.6	63.4
Germany	11.7	30.2	18.0	3.6	3.7	62.4
Russia	17.1	32.6	22.2	8.4	8.2	62.8
Saudi Arabia	—	—	—	—	—	—
China	9.1	44.2	12.9	3.7	2.7	52.2
Japan	—	—	—	—	—	—

[1]Robberies, sexual offenses, threats, and assaults.
Source: United Nations Office for Drug Control and Crime Prevention, *The Global Report of Crime and Justice, 1999,* pp. 283–84.

In the next section of this chapter, we will look briefly at the corrections systems of seven major foreign countries: Canada, England, Germany, Russia, Saudi Arabia, China, and Japan. They represent different legal systems, different cultures, and different parts of the world. But look at Tables 16-1 and 16-2 first. They provide a recent overview of reported crime and victimization in the United States and each of these nations; the figures are those of INTERPOL and the United Nations.

In interpreting these numbers, we should first heed the cautionary advice of Erika Fairchild and Harry Dammer, who warn us of the dangers of direct comparisons of **international crime statistics**—underreporting, nonstandard definitions, varying collection practices, and political manipulation of data.[2] It was difficult to accept the reliability of either crime or imprisonment data from the old Communist bloc countries of Eastern Europe, for example. Crime was supposed to have "withered away" under Communism, so it was always underreported and manipulated by governments that wanted Communist society to look better than its capitalist competitor. The full scale of crime and social problems in these countries was revealed after the collapse of Communism in the 1990s.

But looking cautiously at those data on crime incidence and victimization, we can get a sense that being a victim of crime is a pretty commonplace experience around the world today. In most countries, about two people in three could expect to be crime victims over a five-year period. Looking at all the data beyond those given in these small tables, researchers suggest that victimization is generally lower in Asia and higher in Africa and Latin America, with Europe and the English-speaking New World countries somewhere in between. Most of the European countries have property crime rates higher than or comparable to our own (though some suggest that our reporting rates are lower than theirs).

The overall rates of violent crime are higher in the United States than in other Western countries, but we are not alone in our problem with criminal violence. Several of the former Soviet bloc countries, including Russia, had murder rates higher than ours in the 1990s, and numerous Latin American countries, led by Colombia and the Bahamas with their drug-related violence, had murder rates far higher than ours. Likewise, several Latin American countries have higher robbery rates than we do, and Canada, several Latin American nations, and several African nations have higher reported rates of rape than we do. When you look at the whole picture, the United States is far from the most crime-prone nation on earth. But many Americans would never accept this, or they would argue that the only reason it is so is because we have used such rigorous punishments recently; thus, to control crime even more effectively, punishments should be made even more severe.

WORLD IMPRISONMENT: AN OVERVIEW

In modern society, crime is what happens; prison is one way of responding to it. Table 16-3 shows the imprisonment response of the eight countries featured in this chapter.

In comparing rates of imprisonment, as British researcher Roy Walmsley has pointed out, countries with the highest prison populations may not necessarily be the most punitive. They may have the most serious crime to contend with, they may be more effective in bringing to justice those who commit serious crime, or they may be more punitive in regard to certain crimes and less punitive in regard to others.[3] Research in individual countries has established that these kinds of detailed differences underlie the mathematical computation of the **punishment scale** based on numbers behind bars versus national populations. Nevertheless, for international comparisons, this computation is the only standard we have at present, and even it lacks consistency. Some nations do not keep records on or report their pretrial populations held in what are commonly called remand institutions; we call them jails, and in

TABLE 16-3

Imprisonment in Selected Countries

Country	Year	National Population (in millions)	Prison/Jail Population	Imprisonment Rate (per 100,000)	Number of Institutions	Occupancy Level (%)	Ten-Year Rate Trend (per 100,000)
United States	2002	290.0	2,033,331	701	5,059	106.4	Up 196
Canada	2001	31.1	36,024	116	221	94.3	Down 2
England/Wales	2004	52.8	75,324	143	138	112.7	Up 37
Germany	2003	82.6	79,153	96	222	100.5	Up 25
Russia	2003	145.0	846,967	584	1,013	90.7	Up 97
Saudi Arabia	2002	21.6	23,720	110	30	—	Down 8[1]
China	2003	1,304.2	1,549,000[1]	119[1]	689	—	Up 10[1]
Japan	2002	127.6	69,502	54	189	106.5	Up 11

[1]Sentenced prisoners only.
Source: International Centre for Prison Studies, 2004.

the United States, they generally hold about a third of the population in confinement. But in many civil law (or civil-law influenced) countries that combine lengthy pretrial investigations with no right to bail, more people are confined *awaiting trial* than are held *serving sentences*. When we think of the American prison population, we think of convicted felons in state and federal prisons; other countries think of everyone behind bars and in some countries people living in community-based facilities as well. It has become standard practice in the United States in recent years to combine jail and prison figures in calculating our national imprisonment rate, as is done in Table 16-3.

Major contrasts are apparent in this table, and we will look at each of these countries in turn, returning to make a general assessment of the role of prisons and the nature of contemporary prison life around the world before making some final points about American corrections. But first let us take a brief overview of world imprisonment, relying primarily on information presented by Roy Walmsley at a United Nations workshop in Vienna, Austria, in 2001. In his presentation titled "An Overview of World Imprisonment: Global Prison Populations, Trends and Solutions," Walmsley made these points about world imprisonment:

1. The world prison population rate is approximately 140 per 100,000 citizens.
2. About two-thirds of the nations of the world have rates of 150 per 100,000 or below.
3. Ten countries have rates of at least 460 per 100,000, led by the United States and Russia. After these two countries come a group including Belarus, Kazakhstan, Kyrgyzstan, the Pacific island of Guam, and four small states in the Caribbean—the Cayman Islands, the Bahamas, the U.S. Virgin Islands, and Belize.
4. In the decade of the 1990s, prison populations increased steadily worldwide, with a median growth of about 40 percent over the decade. Prison growth was most notable in the Western Hemisphere, where in the five most popu-

lous countries—the United States, Mexico, Argentina, Brazil, and Colombia—increases were between 60 and 85 percent.

5. In the 118 countries (more than half the world's nations) for which consistent statistics for the entire decade were available, prison populations increased in 73 percent. This included ten of thirteen African countries, twenty-five of thirty-three countries in the Americas, eighteen of twenty-one Asian countries, twenty-seven of forty-two European countries, and six of nine countries in Oceania.

6. Where declines occurred, they were generally smaller and marked by ups and downs in the rate from year to year. In only one country, Finland, which decided to pursue a national policy of decarceration, was there a consistent downward trend throughout the entire decade.[4]

Canada

Although Canada has faced considerable internal political pressure to modify its imprisonment policies more in line with its southern neighbor, it has managed to maintain a stable prison population over the past decade. In a series he wrote for the *Ottawa Citizen* in 2002, journalist Dan Gardner described Canada's corrections system as

> suspended somewhere in the mid-Atlantic, halfway between the American model and the Western European. We imprison more offenders than western European countries, but far fewer than the United States. Some of the sentences we hand out are similar to western European norms, but some, especially for the worst crimes, are in line with American norms. Some of our prisons look and operate like Western Europe's while other are in the American mould.[5]

Canada has a **dual correctional system** comparable to the federal/state split in the United States. Canada's provincial governments are responsible for probation and the confinement of short-term prisoners given sentences of less than two years. The federal government confines offenders given sentences longer than two years and manages parole.

The split works out to about 60 percent (19,000) provincial and 40 percent (13,000) federal. In 2001, there were also an estimated 100,000 probationers and 8,500 inmates on parole and supervised release. The federal corrections organization is the **Correctional Service of Canada** (CSC), operating under the control of the solicitor general, a position comparable to the American attorney general.

For the past decade and more, the direction of Canadian federal corrections has been guided by the **Corrections and Conditional Release Act** of 1992. This act emphasizes public safety—"protection of the public"—but does so, as the current mission statement of CSC provides, "by actively encouraging and assisting offenders to become law-abiding citizens, while exercising reasonable, safe, secure and humane control."

The mission is guided by five **core values**:

Core Value 1. We respect the dignity of individuals, the rights of all members of society, and the potential for human growth and development.

Core Value 2. We recognize that the offender has the potential to live as a law-abiding citizen.

Core Value 3. We believe that our strength and our major resource is achieving our objectives is our staff and that human relationships are the cornerstone of our endeavor.

Core Value 4. We believe that the sharing of ideas, knowledge, values and experience, nationally and internationally, is essential to the achievement of our Mission.

Core Value 5. We believe in managing CSC with openness and integrity and we are accountable to the Solicitor General.[6]

Sometimes it is hard to tell, from idealistic statements, whether governments mean what they say. The high-minded, democratic values of the Soviet Constitution of 1936, proclaimed when Stalin was conducting political purges of his enemies and vastly expanding the network of prison camps that came to be known as the Gulag, would be a good example. But in the case of Canada's CSC, they apparently have tried to put these values in practice as policies, which has caused them considerable controversy with conservative politicians and victims' advocates who would prefer more of an American-style corrections system.

In the 1990s, Canadian corrections was dominated by the philosophy of Ole Ingstrup, who twice served as commissioner of CSC. Ingstrup, a Danish-born Canadian who expressed his philosophy as "evidence-based corrections," was accused by his critics of importing liberal western European ideals into Canada, an infestation that inevitably leads to "coddling criminals." (Beware of foreign imports: next thing you know, we will be electing an Austrian body-builder governor of a large American state.)

Ingstrup's overall plan consisted of three main parts:

1. Holding down the prison population
2. Preparing offenders for reintegration and then reintegrating them under supervision
3. As a philosophical approach, adopting restorative justice using three core models: victim–offender mediation, family group conferencing, and circles (derived from aboriginal practices)

CSC called the means to accomplish this plan **effective corrections.** One of its guiding principles was this statement: "Prison is the right place—the only place—for some offenders, but it is also the wrong place for others." Andy Scott, the Canadian solicitor general, made this point in a speech to the American Correctional Association in 1998:

> Effective corrections is built on the premise that we must do what we can to assist offenders in reintegration into the community. One of the ways we help offenders to rejoin society is by giving them the treatment and skills they need through correctional programming. CSC is known for its pioneering work in this area. Educational upgrading, literacy training, violence prevention, living and cognitive skills training, substance abuse and sex offender treatment, and vocational training are some of the core treatment programs offered in our institutions. Almost all federal offenders—100 percent of those who are able to participate—engage in correctional programming.[7]

Canadian corrections emphasizes a gradual, supervised transition to release after programming. About 65 percent of Canadian federal prisoners are serving sentences of ten years or less—although 20 percent are serving life or indeterminate sentences, mostly for murder. Canadian corrections is much more focused on violent criminals; about 75 percent of federal prisoners in 1999 were convicted of crimes against persons. Although Canada is the world's second-leading nation in per capita drug arrests, it puts very few drug criminals in prison—fewer than 1,100 in 1999, or about 8 percent of the prison population, in comparison to 250,000, or 21 percent, in the United States.[8]

From the time the sentence begins, the plan is to return the offender to the community through a series of steps:

1. Eligibility for unescorted temporary absence after one-sixth of the sentence or three years, whichever is shorter
2. Eligibility for day parole, under accelerated review, for low-risk offenders after one-sixth of the sentence
3. Eligibility for day parole six months prior to one-third of the sentence
4. Eligibility for full parole after one-third to one-half of the sentence
5. Statutory release after two-thirds of the sentence
6. End of sentence at expiration of conditional release

This regimen of treatment, programming, services, and graduated supervision makes, as you might expect, for an expensive system, which is one of the common criticisms directed at CSC. The average cost to keep an inmate in a federal prison is over $50,000 (American) per year, more than twice the average cost of imprisonment in the United States. For the 353 women inmates (who would not even fill up a wing of a big-city jail in the United States), the average cost is over $80,000 per year and for young offenders over $100,000 annually. Parole even costs $12,000 a year, more than six times what it costs on average in the United States—and more than the per capita costs of some of our cheapest prison systems, such as South Dakota and Louisiana.

CSC has to contend with other problems in its operations. One major concern is that prisoners find it relatively easy to get illegal drugs. Generous visitation practices, including conjugal visits, and the daily flow of inmates in and out of prison make drug smuggling common. Large numbers of **aboriginals,** mostly First Nations (Indians) and Inuits, find their way into the prison system; making up about 2 percent of the Canadian population, they make up 15 percent of federal prisoners.[9]

But as Canadian corrections pursued it "effectiveness" agenda in the 1990s, its persistent problem was defending its costly, reintegration-centered corrections policies against those who want to see an "Americanized" approach. Journalist Michael Harris published a best-selling book, *Con Game: The Truth about Canada's Prisons* (2002), condemning the CSC and offering the provincial Ontario model, based on American practices, as an alternative and the conservative Canadian Alliance (in 2003 joined with the Progressive Conservatives to reform the Conservative Party) as the party to accomplish correctional change.

Dan Gardner wrote in the *Ottawa Citizen* in May 2002,

American cultural exports consist of more than just Hollywood and Coca-Cola. Public policies are also sold internationally, and few fields of American public policy have been exported more successfully than criminal justice.

Across the western world, politicians have heard that the United States has found the solution to crime. They have also learned from American experience that crime can be the perfect political tool. Motivated by both principle and self-interest, many have begun pushing their nations to adopt American justice policies. In no country is this truer than Canada.

The government of Ontario's approach to crime is a virtual duplicate of the American model. So is the crime platform of the Canadian Alliance. Even the language many Canadian politicians use when they talk about crime—"zero tolerance," "truth in sentencing," "adult time for adult crime,"—was invented by American politicians to sell American reforms.

We should be concerned. While it's true that Americans overwhelmingly credit the get-tough approach with reducing crime, the few who disagree include the experts who actually study crime: Most criminologists believe tougher laws did little to make the streets safer. Punishment is simply not an effective way to cut crime. Even something as draconian as, say, sentencing a man to life in San Quentin for possession of crack won't stop crack dealers from popping up on street corners.[10]

Canadian political officials responsible for corrections policies have argued that they are charting an independent course balancing the interests of the public and offenders. Solicitor General Scott has said,

Canada's incarceration rate, at 133 per 100,000 citizens (in 1998), although much less than that of the United States, is quite high compared to most Western democracies. This is all the more disturbing given that our crime rate is falling and research shows that locking up more people does not contribute to a safer society.

There are no cold, hard facts to indicate that keeping offenders in jail longer reduces the possibility of them committing more crimes. . . . That is why our government is placing so much emphasis on making our corrections system more effective.[11]

Canadian officials have pointed out that twenty years ago, the Canadian imprisonment rate was about half the U.S. rate. It is now about one-sixth the U.S. rate. While crime has been on a steady decline in the United States as prison populations have increased sharply (lending support to arguments about the incapacitative effects of imprisonment), it has also declined in Canada as prison populations have declined (lending support to the reintegration arguments, or to arguments that crime levels and levels of imprisonment are not strongly related).

Two Canadian police associations have recently gotten involved in corrections politics, focusing on violent criminals. They are saying what police worldwide tend to say, that criminals are getting out of prison too quickly—"faster than we can put them in," the phrase usually goes. Among their issues: first-degree murderers should do at least twenty-five years in prison, removing early release as a possibility for other violent offenders, tighter laws and prison policies, and more victim input into sentencing and release decisions.[12]

So far, the CSC is holding the line. Ole Ingstrup is gone to serve as the first president of the new **International Corrections and Prisons Association**—through 2004—funded primarily by CSC and intended to promote global correctional reform and exchange of "best practices," an idea developed by the American Correctional Association. But the policies established during his era remain in effect, and incarceration rates have declined steadily as CSC and most provincial governments have moved more offenders out of prisons and into community supervision. The key to being able to do this politically has been to convince the Canadian public that this approach is working. They call it "citizen engagement," which includes several approaches to soliciting feedback, seeking public input, and public information. The CSC also maintains a very productive research division whose task is to generate the information that political officials need to convince the Canadian public that "effective corrections equals public safety."

England

The view from the continent is that England's prison system is the "most troubled" in western Europe—most troubled is like "the worst" but said politely and with no malice toward those practitioners who manage the corrections system and work in it. Its continental critics view English prisons as captives of the old (architecture and tradition) and the new (conservative politics). Fairchild and Dammer wrote in 2001,

> England's current correctional system appears to be in a state of crisis, and there seem to be few solutions in sight. The familiar continuum of increased crime, hardening of attitude, crowding of prisons, deterioration of conditions and relationships within prison, and desperate temporary measures to decrease the prison population characterize the English system today.[13]

The **National Prison Service** oversees the operation of all prisons in England and Wales—137 public and nine private prisons holding just over 75,000 male and female inmates in April 2004. The official capacity of these prisons is 66,722, so the occupancy level is 113 percent. Its imprisonment rate of 143 per 100,000 is second only to Portugal in western Europe. Scotland and Northern Ireland, though properly a part of the United Kingdom of Great Britain and Northern Ireland, each have their own separate correctional systems; the independent Scottish Prison Service is among the more highly regarded in Europe for its efforts to provide rehabilitative services to prisoners.

England classifies prisons into five types:

Remand centers, also called local prisons, but comparable to larger American jails, that hold pretrial and short-term inmates

Medium-term institutions holding inmates sentenced to terms of eighteen months to four years

Long-term prisons housing inmates serving longer than four years

Dispersal prisons, housing high-security and dangerous inmates, including members of the Irish Republican Army and others considered terrorists

Young prisoner centers, secure prisons for young adults, comparable to American reformatories[14]

In the early 1900s, England developed an early model for youthful offender housing, the **borstal,** which became well known around the world. The borstal was a small, campus-like facility, like a boarding school for criminals between the ages of sixteen and twenty. The residents lived in houses under the direction of a headmaster. While they took part in education and work training, they also set a lot of their own rules and managed behavior within their "houses." The use of peer pressure in this form was an early example of the therapeutic community concept. Borstals have lost favor today, becoming institutionalized and replaced by boot camps in the popular and political vernaculars.

English prisons are regulated through mechanisms both internal and external. Her Majesty's **Chief Inspector of Prisons** is independent of the Prison Service and reports directly to the home secretary on the treatment of prisoners and prison conditions. The **Prisons and Probation Ombudsman** is an independent point of appeal for prisoners and those supervised by the Probation Service. As an independent government official with authority to investigate complaints and recommend corrective action, the ombudsman has long been used by Scandinavian governments; lately, it has spread throughout English government as well. The prison ombudsman was given responsibility in 2004 for investigating all deaths that occur among prisoners in custody. The **Independent Monitoring Board** (IMB) is a group of local political officials and private citizens who monitor each prison in England and Wales. Each board has about fifteen members. The IMBs were formerly known as boards of visitors, but the name was recently changed to avoid confusion with the **Prison Visitors,** a program set up to match private persons with prisoners who had no visitors. The IMBs are appointed by the home secretary to monitor the welfare of staff and prisoners and the state of the premises. They have access to all parts of the prison at any time.

England also has a strong tradition of private activist organizations supporting prisoners and prison reform, perhaps more so than any other country. Established organizations include the Prison Reform Trust, the Howard League, NACRO (National Association for the Care and Resettlement of Offenders), UNLOCK, and the Penal Affairs Consortium. Newer organizations include Action for Prisoners Families, the National AIDS and Prisons Forum, and Partners of Prisoners.

Many English prisons are old, going all the way back to the 1700s and 1800s, though the high-security prisons (especially the supermax dispersal prisons) built in the 1960s and 1970s also get a large measure of criticism. The physical limitations of the prison system were aggravated by the steady increase in prison population that began in the 1980s and the lack of capital for new prison construction. From the early 1980s through the first years of the twenty-first century, England's prison philosophy was viewed as being remarkably similar to America's (which is probably another reason for skepticism on the part of the other western European nations). The primary difference would obviously be that England has a national system under the direction of the **Home Office,** an important cabinet-level office generally responsible for all public safety functions, thus making prison policies a matter of national political import. As Ronald Reagan is often cited for the "War on Drugs" that fueled American prison expansion in the 1980s, British Prime Minister Margaret Thatcher, whose Conservative government ran England from 1979 to 1993, set the tone for a similar hard-nosed approach to crime in England. Julie Sudbury wrote in 2000,

> Britain's love affair with incarceration can be traced to the legacy of the Thatcher years and the special relationship developed between the Iron Lady and Ronald Reagan. During 14 years of Thatcherism, a blend of nationalistic populism, free-

marketeering, and trenchant attacks on organized Labour and Left activism, "law and order" became a key weapon in the right-wing arsenal.[15]

According to Sudbury's analysis, three features marked Thatcher's correctional politics: harsher punishments of street criminals, emphasizing **racial politics** targeting recent immigrants and dark-skinned minorities; a **common sense** connection between crime and punishment that overlooked the social context; and **privatization.** As inmate numbers increased steadily, prisons were overwhelmed. British politicians and prison administrators were won over to the American private prison model, which offered the advantages of cost cutting, modernization, and prison expansion without public capital investment in prison construction. Privatization was presented as a panacea to the problems facing the Prison Service: overcrowding, old buildings, high annual costs, resistance to reform, and a rigid prison guard culture reinforced by the powerful Prison Officers Association.[16]

As the American prison population increased by 75 percent during the 1990s, the English prison population increased sharply as well, by over 60 percent. When the National Prison Service tried to reduce the use of imprisonment in favor of more community-based sanctions, politicians attacked the bureaucracy's "soft on crime" approach. Home Secretary Michael Howard's famous **"Prison Works"** speech of 1993 articulated incapacitation and deterrence as the goals of increased use of imprisonment. He argued for an austere prison environment to protect society and "make many who are tempted to commit crimes think twice."[17]

Even after the Labour Party under Prime Minister Tony Blair took office in 1997, correctional policies did not change substantially for several years. Prison populations continued to increase steadily, and the old problems with overcrowding persisted. In 2001, the **National Probation Service** was created to provide more centralized management of what had previously been a function directed by local probation boards. In 2003, Parliament passed the **Criminal Justice Act,** containing provisions for sentencing reforms that would back away from the punitive ideology established in the 1980s.

The view of increasingly vocal prison critics was that twenty years of punishment had made prisons "the most shameful of all Britain's awful public services," as a review of a 2003 prison exposé by former Chief Prison Inspector Sir David Ramsbotham summed up his observations:

> Over and over again, Sir David lays the blame for the miserable performance of the Prison Service not so much on those at the bottom of the hierarchy as on those at the top—the area managers, their superiors, the top civil servants, and, not least, the ministers. These are the people who have read, or should have read, report after report, study after study, all showing that you cannot cut reoffending rates, let alone suicides, if you cram more and more prisoners into understaffed jails designed (often 100 years or more ago) to hold a fraction of their present number and, more fundamentally, if you refuse to treat prisoners as human beings. The upshot is hugely overcrowded prisons which allow fewer and fewer opportunities for education, exercise, or any other purposeful activity—the absolute prerequisite for any kind of rehabilitation and thus for the claim that "prison works."[18]

The Home Office's response to such criticism was to order yet another study, this one a comprehensive review of sentencing and corrections in England and

Wales, culminating in Patrick Carter's December 11, 2003, report "Managing Offenders, Reducing Crime." This report compares with the internal management reviews often done with federal or state government offices in the United States, reports that are read, discussed, and then abandoned in file drawers as "politics as usual" reestablishes the status quo. But in this case, the recommendations of Carter, a wealthy private businessman, and his study team have been adopted by the Home Office and are being put into effect as 2004 progresses.

The Carter Report observed that the use of both prison and probation had increased steadily over the past decade, while the numbers of people arrested and sentenced has remained constant. Sentencing had grown more severe over this time; sentences had grown longer by an average of two to five months, the percentage of felons getting a custodial sentence had increased from 15 to 25 percent, and the number of first offenders given imprisonment had jumped as well. Crime had fallen steadily, by about 30 percent since 1997, but the increased use of imprisonment was credited (by econometric analysis) with only about a sixth of the drop.[19]

The Carter Report recommended that sentencing be much more targeted on certain offenders. Under the 2003 Criminal Justice Act, for instance, murderers will serve minimum sentences of fifteen years, thirty years, or natural life based on their age and the circumstances of their crime. England in 2001 had 3,387 murderers in custody, which is fewer than the number of homicide offenders imprisoned in the state of Louisiana alone. The report also suggested that "the system needs to improve its grip on persistent offenders," those with multiple previous convictions who are said to be responsible for the bulk of criminal offenses (similar to high-risk offenders once targeted through selective incapacitation in the United States). The Criminal Justice Act had introduced the **persistence principle,** whereby persistent offenders would be treated more severely.[20] In regard to sentencing, the Carter Report had several recommendations:

> A renewed focus on paying back to the community, emphasizing diversion, reparation, and community work for low-risk offenders
>
> Fines rebuilt as a credible punishment, including the importation of day fines heavily used in Germany and Scandinavia
>
> More demanding community sentences, with three different levels of programming and supervision
>
> More extensive use of electronic monitoring
>
> Greater sanctions and help for persistent offenders
>
> More effective use of custody, including doing away with very short-term sentences—from a few days to a few months—for low-risk offenders, a general reduction in the length of prison terms for ordinary criminals, and longer sentences for persistent offenders and violent criminals.[21]

At the national level in corrections, the Carter Report recommended that the Prison Service and the Probation Service be combined into a single **National Offender Management Service** (NOMS) within the Home Office. The concept is to establish a consolidated system focused on the "end-to-end management" of offenders throughout their sentence, with a clear responsibility for reducing reoffending two years after the end of the sentence.

The perception is that the separate Prison Service and Probation Service have not worked very well together within their respective "silos"—their national bureaucracies. The NOMS executive would be responsible for management of all offenders, whether given custodial or community sentences.

The Home Office moved to implement these recommendations in early 2004, appointing the first NOMS chief executive and announcing plans to set up ten NOMS regions in England and Wales. Opposition to the NOMS proposal then began in earnest. Because the Carter Report called for downsizing both prisons and probation through more use of fines, employee organizations had reservations about job security. They also decried the complete lack of consultation with political officials before the plan was announced. Probation groups had concerns about the report's emphasis on **contestability,** the contracting of public services to private and volunteer providers as competitive alternatives to public providers. Contestability is viewed as further evidence of the trend toward privatization in corrections, which is generally opposed by employee unions. The Probation Service, only nationalized three years earlier and already reeling from budget cuts and increased workload, was reportedly in "chaos" after this next major reorganization was announced, and the speed with which the report was prepared and the brevity of its contents left many in doubt about the depth of thinking that had gone into it.

The NOMS proposal, which quickly became the NOMS reality in June 2004, does have two positive features that make many prison reformers in England and elsewhere happy. First, it provides centralized management over offenders with the specific goal of reducing reoffending; the combination of custodial and community corrections under one manager is a bold idea—English officials repeatedly used the word "radical." Second, the target is to reverse the long-term trend and make significant reductions in the size of the prison population. Over 100,000 offenders were sentenced to some time in prison in England in 2003, an all-time record that many policymakers and researchers call scary.

Criminologist and prison critic Stephen Farrell, of Keele University, whose quotation opened this chapter, has gotten the two things he asked for: a debate with the Labour government about taking people out of prison and a program designed to do so. Without this program, England was projected to have 100,000 people behind bars by 2010—or even sooner. Even with the reduction hoped for under NOMS, it will still have the second highest rate of imprisonment in western Europe, its prisons will still be old and overcrowded, and its concentration of poor people and dark-skinned minorities in prison will still trouble penal reformers.

Germany

Among the major European countries, Germany has been considered the trendsetter in recent years. Its prison population climbed steadily during the 1990s—attributed mostly to the assimilation of former East Germans into the united Germany after October 1990—but reached a stasis level of ninety-six per 100,000 in 1998 and has remained at that level since.

Germany is a federal republic similar in structure to the United States. It has a national government that makes laws to be carried out in the sixteen *Läender,* or states. No national prisons exist; each state operates an independent prison system but under the control of the Ministry of Justice in the national government.

The 222 German prisons held almost 80,000 men, women, and juveniles in custody at the end of 2003. This averages about 360 prisoners per institution; most prisons are smaller than this, but a few larger institutions pull the mean upward. About 21 percent of German prisoners are in remand status awaiting trial. Thirty percent are foreign nationals, mostly young male **guest workers** from foreign countries: Turkey, eastern and southern Europe, and Spain. The European nations in general incarcerate foreigners in high numbers, similar to what the United States does with minorities and the other English-speaking countries do with aboriginals and immigrants. German prisons, though commonly said to be "nice," are full—at 100.5 percent of capacity at year-end 2003.[22]

Germany was said to have a typically European correctional system in the latter 1800s. When the German states were unified in 1871, the penal code provided severe punishments centering on confinement in big maximum-security prisons and, by the 1920s, the **progressive system** based on English and Irish models that emphasized movement through different levels culminating in reintegration into society.[23] The prison system was nationalized under Hitler's National Socialist government from 1933 to 1945. It became a huge system holding several million prisoners by late in World War II: Jews, foreign nationals, military prisoners of war, political dissidents, and even a few ordinary criminals.

At the end of World War II, the traditional state prison system was reestablished. It provided retributive, liberty-depriving punishments comparable to other European countries. In 1969, Germany adopted the First Penal Reform Law, which set up the system of **day fines** already in use in Scandinavian countries. Over the next thirty years, the day fine would become the principal criminal punishment in Germany. It is used to resolve over 80 percent of all criminal and traffic cases in German courts, typically as a replacement for a short sentence to confinement.

German day fines are collected in daily rates, which depend on the defendant's daily net income. The number of days may range from a minimum of five to a maximum of 720. The minimum day fine is 2 German marks (worth about 90 cents in 2001), and the maximum is 10,000 marks (or $4,500). This would presumably be used in a situation when someone like Donald Trump was arrested for drunk driving; poor college students would fall on the other end of the scale. Fines can be paid in installments. Failure to pay fines results in jail time—one day of jail for every day of fine unpaid. The percentage of days fines resulting in jail terms is usually between 5 and 10 percent, depending, as you might expect, on employment and economic conditions.[24]

In 1968, the year before day fines were adopted, 184,000 sentences to prison were handed down; twenty years later, the number had shrunk to just 48,000. During the same period, the number of criminal convictions rose from 573,000 to 609,000. Imprisonment, which through the 1950s was being used as the disposition of choice in about 40 percent of criminal cases, was being used in fewer than 10 percent a generation later.[25] So it has remained into the early years of the twenty-first century.

Sentencing practices are obviously more complicated than merely changing a law to allow a monetary fine in place of incarceration. Germany's penal policies changed over time from pure punishment toward practices inherent in the state's responsibilities for its citizens. Humanity is employed as the basis of criminal politics, and the social state's obligation is to treat rather than punish the criminal.

Officials in the legal and correctional systems are skeptical of the value of imprisonment. They see incarceration as counterproductive in society. Research indicated that youthful offenders sent to prison had higher rates of recidivism than those given alternative sanctions. Removing youths from society—even when incarceration included job training—appeared to negatively affect their ability to find employment when released. To German officials, these findings suggested that when youths were imprisoned for offenses, they were more likely to later embrace criminality than young people given alternative sentences. Judges, therefore, began to avoid giving prison sentences to the extent possible.[26]

The German **Prison Act of 1976** set out a model of imprisonment that is still in effect today. This legislation stresses rehabilitation and reintegration as the primary purposes of imprisonment. It also defines the legal rights of prisoners as citizens, including visiting rights, home leave, medical care, and productive paid labor. Many of these provisions were already in effect before they were written into law. When Robert Goldman of the Ford Foundation visited German prisons during a prolonged 1973 European tour, he found these prisons focused in large part on **normalization** of the prisoner's life—getting the prisoner back into society and better equipped than he was before. He was most impressed with a small prison in Frankfurt, the Gustav Radbruch Haus, which held 250 inmates of all types in the last few months of their sentences. Prisoners worked at regular jobs in private industries. They paid for their room and board, and they put the balance of their income into bank accounts to prepare for their release.[27]

Ira Schwartz of the Chicago John Howard Association visited West German prisons in 1976. He found that 40 percent of German prisoners were working in private industry, making everything from auto parts to luggage to skis. He agreed that German prisons were far more humane than American prisons in this era:

> Each West German prisoner, even in institutions built at the turn of the century, has his or her own individual room. There are no cells with bars. Inmates are allowed to decorate their rooms as they please. Medical facilities and staff are excellent, and, miracle of miracles, the prison kitchens are clean and the food quite good. In addition to being more humane and bringing a greater sense of dignity to prisoners, West German penal institutions are also less expensive to build than their U.S. counterparts. In short, the West Germans have created a sane environment in which to house their criminal offenders.[28]

This environment persists nearly three decades later. German prisons are small and located in or near cities, making work, visiting, and home leave more accessible. Prisons in Germany look less like secure correctional institutions and more like factories or hospitals. The belief is that keeping the physical appearance more like that of a factory and creating more "normal" living conditions will promulgate rehabilitation.[29]

Community contacts are an important part of the prison experience. Low-custody prisoners get **home leave**—an average of two or three visits home each year. Married inmates get family visits in prison with their spouses and children. In the *Freiganger,* or **half-open release** program, inmates who have served half their sentences go out to work or to school during the day and return to the prison at night. Inmates would be paroled after two-thirds of their sentences unless they were classified as a risk or unless they declined parole.[30] All German prisoners are parole eligible. Most lifers would expect to be paroled after about eight to twelve years in prisons, and mandatory release for lifers occurs at fifteen years.

When you look at Germany's approach to corrections, specifically at how it manages to keep the incarceration rate below 100 per 100,000, several key features emerge: first, the use of diversionary practices involving day fines; second, the expanded use of probation for most other convicted criminals, in combination with avoiding very short sentences to confinement; and third, short prison terms focused on reintegration. Only about 10 percent of prisoners have sentences longer than five years; the "average" prisoner is in custody less than a year.

Germany has managed to avoid the influence of the American tough-on-crime model and maintain both the size and the philosophy of its correctional system over a long period of time. There is no public pressure or political advocacy to boost incarceration rates. German criminologists and prison officials, if they are seeking direction for new ideas and new programs, are far more likely to look to the north, especially to their neighbor across the Baltic Sea, Finland, than across the Atlantic to America. Finland, which through the 1950s had a Soviet-style prison system and an incarceration rate of 200 per 100,000, has over the past forty years lowered its rate to fifty-two per 100,000, the lowest of the major European countries. This is the model that interests the Germans.

Russia

Anne Applebaum's masterful 2003 book *Gulag: A History* tells the history of the network of labor camps, the *Glavnoe Upravlenie Lagerei,* or Main Camp Administration, that existed in the Soviet Union from 1918 until 1986—almost the entire life of Communist Russia. At its apex in the early 1950s, about the time Josef Stalin died, the **Gulag** consisted of almost 500 camp complexes—thousands of individual camps—holding more than 2.5 million people. Some of these people were ordinary criminals, but most of them were "political" criminals, which at the time meant only that they had run afoul of the secret police for political reasons. Alexander Solzhenitsyn, the Russian writer who compiled his own work on the camps, the three-volume *Gulag Archipelago,* was a decorated army officer when he was arrested near the end of World War II for making "political" remarks about Stalin in a letter. He was a prisoner for eight years and in internal exile for three more until he was granted amnesty.

The worst camps were in the Siberian wasteland, where weather extremes aggravated the effects of disease, chronic malnutrition, and forced labor. About a quarter of the Gulag prisoners, an estimated 4.5 million of the 18 million who passed through the camps, died or disappeared. Mikhail Gorbachev finally began the dissolution of the political camps in 1987, shortly before the Soviet Union itself was dissolved.

For the Russian prisoner of today, the end of the Gulag has created one of those good news/bad news scenarios. The good news is that you will not freeze to death in some godforsaken Siberian labor camp. The bad news is that you will die of tuberculosis in some godforsaken Siberian prison. One horror replaces another.

For most of the twentieth century, the prison system of Russia and the Soviet Union was the largest in the world. The tradition of operating such a system, making use of both conventional prisons and internal exile, and holding not only ordinary criminals but also political criminals and unproductive or marginal citizens ("parasites" in later Soviet nomenclature) was handed down from czarist Russia of the 1800s. What the czar began, Stalin perfected with his expansion of labor camps in the 1930s and 1940s.

When Communism finally collapsed and the half-size Russia replaced the previous Soviet Union in 1990, the Russian prison system was placed under tremendous strain for several years. In the chaos that marked Russian society throughout the nineties, crime flourished. Organized crime, attributed to the old network of gangsters—including the **thieves in law** and the **Chechens** from the rebel state of Chechnya—and now known as the **Russian-Mafia** dominated the economy, sucking money from legitimate businesses and corrupting police and government officials.

Violent crime—murders, rapes, robberies, and assaults—shot sky high; the murder rate was at least twice as high as in the United States. A Russian businessman said it was easier to kill off your competition than buy them out; the futility of the justice system was openly mocked. Alcoholism and drug abuse increased sharply. The removal of restrictions on internal travel made it easy for poor people from remote locales to flock to the city looking for jobs; many fell into lives of vice and crime in the new Russia, where "everything was for sale."

Yuri Ivanovich Kalinin, who headed the Russian Prison Administration in the early 1990s and later became Russian deputy minister of justice when the prison system was moved from the Ministry of the Interior to Ministry of Justice, gave a lecture at King's College in London in 2002 reviewing the recent history of the Russian penal system. In it he described several reasons for the collapse of the penal system after the end of Communism: the conservative mind-set of the Ministry of the Interior, lack of financial resources, no history of concern with prisoners' legal rights, the remote location of many of the labor colonies, and the underlying political turmoil that marked the transfer of power.[31]

Legal reforms took several years, culminating in the transfer of all institutions and agencies administering the punishment of criminals from the Ministry of the Interior to the Ministry of Justice on August 31, 1998. It might seem to outsiders like a trivial bureaucratic move, but to Russians it meant a break with the past—with the law-and-order mentality and the camps—and a move toward legalism and decarceration. By the time the transfer was made, the entire penal system, containing more than a million men, women, and juveniles, was in critical condition.

Roy King, who made an extended visit to Russian's prisons in 1992, gave this overview of the system. The majority of male sentenced prisoners were held in **corrective labor colonies** of several types:

1. General regime colonies, confining those serving sentences of up to three years
2. Reinforced regime colonies for those serving longer than three years
3. Strict regime colonies for recidivists and more serious offenders
4. Special regime colonies for dangerous recidivists and those formerly sentenced to death
5. Colony settlements, like open prisons without fences, for minor offenders and those transferred in on good behavior from stricter regimes

There were also separate hospital colonies, protection colonies, two different levels of women's colonies, education labor colonies for minors ages fourteen to eighteen, and reinforced colonies for juvenile recidivists.[32] Normal correctional colonies were isolated institutions enclosed by barbed wire, fenced with alarm systems, and patrolled by armed guards and dogs. Fences divided the colonies into zones: work, housing, punishment, hospital, school, administrative. Men and women were kept separate. Different levels of internal treatment—light, general, and strict—were used within the camp, like trusty grades, according to behavior and length of stay.[33] An average colony might hold 1,500 to 2,000 prisoners, though some were as small as 500 and others as large as 3,000. Inmates typically slept in open dormitories holding twenty to fifty inmates or in large locked cells of comparable capacity.

Two other types of facilities—cellular prisons and remand prisons—round out this system. Cellular prisons, holding only about 1 percent of the convicted criminals, are used to isolate particularly dangerous recidivists or long-term offenders. Prisoners are kept in small, multiperson cells that they leave only for work, exercise, or visitation. This is the strictest possible regimen in Russian prisons.

Remand prisons, known as "SIZOs," are jails, usually in urban areas, holding inmates up to time of sentencing. This can be pretrial; during the trial, which in a civil law country like Russia is often interrupted with long breaks; or after trial awaiting imposition of sentencing. Inmates are not supposed to spend more than a year in remand, but this rule is often violated.

The worst conditions in Russian prisons in the 1990s were in the remand prisons. On his visit in 1992, Roy King toured four remand prisons, including the well-known Butyrskaya Prison in Moscow. This prison was built in 1771, restored in 1878, and left pretty much as is since. It has 434 cells—a hundred large cells intended to house about twenty to twenty-five prisoners each, the rest smaller cells holding no more than four prisoners. The capacity was intended to be about 3,500 with about twenty square feet of space for each prisoner. But in November 1992, the prison held 5,100 inmates, causing severe overcrowding. Inmates in some cells had less than ten square feet of space to live in; they had to share beds and sleep in shifts.[34]

Critics might say that English prisons were the worst in western Europe at the end of the twentieth century, but the magnitude of Russia's prison problems made its system the worst on earth. Sentences were long, very similar to America—sixty-six months officially on average, thirty-seven months to release. Facilities, especially the remand prisons, were badly overcrowded. Inmates shared their domiciles with infestations of lice and cockroaches. Money was tight, so prisons had little to spend on inmates—less than a dollar per day per inmate for food, no money for medicine or medical treatment, and no programs whatsoever. Just guarding and, in the colonies, work—to earn money to buy necessities. Sickness was rampant. A third of the inmate population had a psychiatric disorder. About 11 percent of inmates, more than 100,000 men and women, were infected with the **prisoners' plague,** or tuberculosis (TB), about a third of these with the drug-resistant strains that derive from interrupted treatment. Four percent of prisoners were HIV positive, much higher than in the United States. Three percent had syphilis. Drug addicts were growing in number. Gangsters ran the inside of many prisons, exploiting other inmates, and violence was a daily occurrence. A Russian politician who had done time in a labor camp in the 1970s compared old prisons to new prisons. "Stalin was a splendid torturer," he said, "but prison life in Russia today may be even worse than it was under him."[35]

Though many feared a violent uprising that would destroy the prison system, it did not happen, and gradually reforms began to take hold after prisons were transferred to the Ministry of Justice. Medical treatment improved. Aggressive programs to separate and treat TB-infected inmates lowered the rate of infection by a third within five years. As the social order was restored, the crime rate began to fall. Fewer arrests were being made, which eased the pressure on the severely overcrowded remand prisons. The laws on pretrial release were changed also, making it possible to turn more defendants loose, and by the end of 2003 the remand prisons held about half the number of inmates from five years earlier. The number of sentenced prisoners was in decline also, dropping by about 30,000 in 2003, and more prisoners were being moved into open colony settlements from secure colonies. In five years, Russian's overall incarceration rate had dropped from 688 per 100,000 to 584. The prison system was said to be "stable," and Russian officials were happy to acknowledge they had lost a major battle: the United States, with its incarceration rate of over 700 and still climbing, had officially won the world war of imprisonment.

Saudi Arabia

Imagine that you are arrested and locked up, but you are not told why. You are not allowed to make a telephone call or contact anyone outside the prison. This would be terrifying enough by itself. Now imagine that your jailers begin torturing you. The only way to stop them is to sign a confession, which you eventually do. Then you are convicted on the basis of that "confession" after a summary trial that is held in secret. You have no access to a lawyer and you are not offered the opportunity to defend yourself. Finally, imagine you are living in a country where the punishment you might face after such summary justice could be death, amputation of a limb, or flogging.

Welcome to Saudi Arabia, according to Amnesty International.[36]

Saudi Arabia, as the oldest of the modern Islamic states, is often used as an example of Muslim penal philosophy. The most obvious feature of the Saudi prison system is its small size, which is a consequence of the very limited use of imprisonment under Shari'a law as practiced in Saudi Arabia. Saudi Arabia's incarceration rate in the year 2000 was 110 per 100,000. With an estimated national population of 21.6 million, just 23,720 were behind bars in thirty prisons. Only a third of these, 8,100, were sentenced prisoners. The balance, almost 16,000, were pretrial detainees.

The official explanation for the low rate of imprisonment is twofold. First, because of the strict morality in Islamic society, the crime rate is low. Second, among the penalties provided under Shari'a law, imprisonment is considered a last resort; it is used primarily for recidivists after other measures—the corporal punishments prescribed in the Qur'an—have failed. There are elements of truth in both explanations, but also elements of evasiveness.

The Saudi crime rate is among the lowest in the world, but criminologists suggest that this is due not only to high moral standards but also to the lack of reporting of many criminal offenses, especially those occurring within the family and among friends. Society is so structured under the domination of the male head of household that many internal crimes are never reported to authorities; it would be like trying to compare crime rates in the religious settlements of early colonial America with crime rates in the same geographic areas today.

The possibility of severe penalties—flogging, amputation of hands and feet, and death by stoning or beheading—for criminal offenses is a further inhibitor of crime reporting, as are the high standards of proof required under Islamic law. Adultery by a married person is a death penalty offense, for instance, but conviction requires the testimony of four male witnesses or a confession—and one principle of Islamic law is that confessions may be revoked by the confessor up to the point of conviction in court. There are not many executions for adultery, though we always seem to be hearing about the possibility of an execution for adultery in some Islamic country somewhere, whether it actually takes place or not (and usually it does not). We also hear about possible amputations of the hands and feet of thieves. This happens occasionally but in actuality no more than a handful of times (no pun intended) each year. Understanding the application of the criminal law in Saudi Arabia is a bit like watching an earthquake—the driving force may be far away and hidden far beneath the surface.

Saudi law, which makes noises of strict impartiality under the Qur'an, is in fact one of the most arbitrary and political on earth, though it must always be expressed against a backdrop of religious beliefs—of what is allowed or required by Islam. Saudi Arabia is a hereditary monarchy in which virtually every government official is a member of the royal family. Decisions about criminal punishments are political decisions that consider the criminal's nationality, importance, and affiliations—his or her place in society. Americans or English or Canadians might *commit* a death penalty offense, but in fact the ones who get *executed* are low-life drug smugglers, armed robbers, thieves, murderers, and rapists, many of them foreigners from other Arab or Islamic countries. Lately, terrorists and bombers opposed to the royal family or to the kingdom's Sunni Islam official religion have been added to the list of likely death penalty candidates.

A third of the people living in Saudi Arabia are foreigners, most of them there to work. Over half the prison population is foreign, and in most years a majority of the eighty or 100 people beheaded in public squares for capital crimes are also foreigners. This is, of course, a polite warning to foreigners to watch out. The U.S. embassy in Riyadh, the capital, warns American visitors on its Website about possession of alcoholic beverages, controlled drugs, and pornography, reporting that Americans have received seventy-five or more lashes for failing a blood alcohol test or a year in prison for alcohol-related offenses. The same or more serious penalties apply to other contraband items. The embassy also describes the role of **Mutawa,** the morals police, who might arrest American men or women for appearing in public inappropriately dressed—or for being found in possession of a Valentine card, which is also contraband.[37]

Once taken into custody, arrested persons, whether Saudis or foreigners, exist in a legal world very different from the West. The United Nations Committee against Torture, responding to a Saudi report in May 2002, noted the following problems with Saudi custodial practices: corporal punishment, including flogging and amputation of limbs; prolonged incommunicado detention, including lack of access to legal and medical assistance; minimal judicial supervision of pretrial detention; lack of criminal sanctions for the crime of torture by officials; and prolonged pretrial detention and denial of consular access to detained foreigners for extended periods. The committee also questioned the role of the religious police and the lack of procedures to investigate possible cases of torture—often torture during pretrial confinement carried out by the **Mubahith,** or political police.[38]

The approach of Saudi investigators is very old-fashioned, according to the reports of such watchdog organizations as Amnesty International and Human Rights Watch. Police focus on getting a confession and will hold a suspect in isolation under the most extreme coercive conditions until they get one. When the confession is signed and verified in court, the confessed criminal is then sentenced. "When was my trial?" you might ask. "That was your trial"— in secret, with no lawyer present or witnesses to confront, and documents written in Arabic.

English-speaking citizens of common law countries are confounded at the complete absence of procedural controls. A new code of criminal procedure was adopted on May 1, 2003, according to Human Rights Watch, placing limits on the powers of officials and providing for elements of due process, but it appears these provisions were not put into effect immediately. For the 100 to 200 political detainees estimated held in Saudi jails, at least, it was reported that old practices were still in use. The five Britons and one Canadian citizen imprisoned for car bombings in 2001 had described these interrogation techniques:

> Continuous sleep deprivation for up to ten days; abrupt slapping on the face and punches to the body; forcing them to stand while their hands were shackled to the top of a door; hanging them upside down, with their hands and feet shackled; and threats to harm their relatives if they did not agree to sign dictated confessions.[39]

Once they confessed and received their prison sentences, the Saudi government proved its generous and forgiving nature by beginning to deport them almost at once. To cries of fraud and shame, the government responded, "What? They all confessed."

Criminals, especially political suspects, are held in pretrial confinement for years. If they survive detention, questioning, and sentencing, they may enter the Saudi prison system, which is under the authority of the directorate-general of prisons with the Ministry of the Interior. The Prison and Detention Regulations of May 28, 1978, indicate that the directorate-general supervises prisons for men eighteen and over and prisons for women thirty and over. The Ministry of Labor and Social Affairs operates social surveillance centers for men under eighteen and welfare institutions for young women under thirty.

The adult prisons are said to be subject to the supervision of the judiciary, who are trained in Shari'a law, and the Public Investigation and Prosecution Department, comparable to the procurator's postsentencing role in some legal systems. The Saudi position is that criminal penalties

> are based on an important principle, namely the need for the social rehabilitation of convicted persons, which is one of their basic rights since a criminal who has suffered from social circumstances that led him into crime has a right to be freed, by the State, from those circumstances and to be reintegrated one day in society as an upright citizen.

Prisons are described as

> model institutions that meet all the requisite criteria for the implementation of re-form and rehabilitation programs based on religious instruction, social reorientation, education, cultivation of the mind, training, and work. The Kingdom's regulations ensure that convicted persons are treated in a proper dignified manner.[40]

Prisoners are subject to psychological examination on entry into the prison system, followed by classification according to gender, age, type of offense, duration of sentence and criminal record, state of health, and social circumstances and cultural circumstances (such as religious beliefs). In addition to secure custody, the regulations allow for other individualized sentences, including suspended sentences, pardon, release on probation, release on health grounds, and semiliberty (work release). On the whole, the Saudi prison administration finds that its Prison and Detention Regulations "transcend" the United Nations Standard Minimum Rules for the Treatment of Prisoners, first adopted in 1955. In its view, Saudi prisons are highly focused, carefully monitored, and effectively performing their limited mission in the modern Islamic state.

China

In prison circles, Chinese prisons are often referred to a **bamboo gulag,** a reference to the labor camps of the Soviet Union. The dual basis for this reference is, first, the political nature of imprisonment, and, second, the emphasis on full-time work as the pathway to reform in prison.

The details of imprisonment in China remain somewhat foggy to outsiders. The People's Republic of China is a totalitarian Communist country, and even as its leaders encourage capitalist policies to develop China's vast economic potential, they resist efforts to make government and social policies more transparent and open to debate. For every claim, there is a counterclaim that refutes it. China still speaks with one voice—following a script written by the Communist Party.

At the end of 2003, China counted 689 prisons holding 1,549,000 sentenced prisoners. This is more sentenced prisoners than the United States, but remember that China has more four times as many people as the United States—1.3 billion to 295 million. The official imprisonment rate is 119 per 100,000, which is comparable to many Western nations.[41]

Many outside observers and Chinese political exiles argue that the official number is a lie in two respects. First, it is a deliberate distortion, underreporting the number of persons imprisoned in labor camps for political and social reasons. Second, it does not count prisoners held in pretrial detention and administrative detention. China is said to keep two sets of books on prisons: the one it shows to the world and the true record known only to party officials.

In China, sentenced prisoners are held in institutions under the authority of the Ministry of Justice, while pretrial detainees are under the control of the Ministry of Public Security, which is also responsible for policing. Five types of secure-custody institutions exist:

1. Detention houses (the *kanshou* houses or detention centers), which hold pretrial and short-term sentenced inmates.
2. Juvenile reformatories (or reform houses), which house fourteen- to eighteen-year-olds who are considered more serious criminals.

3. Criminal detention houses (or reeducation through labor—*laojiao*—facilities), which hold those in the status of **administrative detention.** The status of *juyi,* or criminal detention, is an administrative determination without a trial; the offender is fined and placed in custody for an indeterminate period, commonly up to three or four years. His status is considered noncriminal, or administrative, even though he is locked up. Many political offenders are held in this status. It was widely used in the aftermath of the Tiananmen Square Massacre of June 1989 (which officially never occurred) to punish and separate participants in China's incipient democracy movement.

4. **Reform through labor camps** (commonly called *laogai*), which house criminals serving sentences of from one to ten years.

5. Prisons, holding those serving sentences longer than ten year, a life sentence, or a death sentence.

Noncustodial sanctions are also used. The principal one, similar to probation, is called *guanzhi,* also known as control or **public surveillance.** The offender continues to work and earn regular wages while reporting to the local public security office regularly. The normal period of surveillance is two years, but it can be extended. Other options include suspended sentences and fines. Minor criminals may also have some of their civil and property rights suspended, and they may be subject to censure or requirements that, under the direction of local committees—referred to as reconciliation and mediation committees—they renounce their crimes before gatherings of their neighbors or coworkers. This reflects the emphasis on group harmony that is generally important in Asian corrections.

Harry Wu, who served nineteen years in Chinese prisons before emigrating to the United States and becoming the foremost critic of human rights abuses in China, has called attention to the *laogai* prisons as the most obvious means of Communist Party repression. He calls the *laogai* "a repressive mechanism to control and, in effect, eliminate anyone whose political, religious, or societal views differ from those of the Communist Party." He adds, "The laogai is not simply a prison system; it is a political tool for maintaining the Communist Party's totalitarian rule. A fundamental policy of the laogai states that 'forced labor is a means toward the goal of thought reform.'"[42] Wu estimates that the 1,100 *laogai* he and his associates have identified, plus the *laojiao* facilities, the detention centers, the juvenile camps, and other centers for "forced job placement," hold 6.8 million people.[43] Others provide estimates of up to 10 million or even 20 million total prisoners, which would put China's incarceration rate up with that of Russia and the United States or way beyond it.

These high estimates include those persons under administrative sanctions or in involuntary labor status though not convicted of a crime. From the 1960s through the 1990s, China used a practice called **shelter and investigation** to pick up, detain, and relocate unattached citizens—unapproved migrants, transients, the unemployed, and in some cases political activists. They were managed under administrative policies and were subject to detention and relocation at the discretion of the police. This practice had reportedly been abandoned by the end of the century.

The government's response to Harry Wu's criticisms is to label him a thief, a liar, and an agitator. Criminals are treated humanely and their rights respected:

In reforming criminals in China, the emphasis is on education. In addition to legal, moral, cultural and technical education, physical labor is of great importance.

> Criminals are encouraged to realize gradually the harm they have done to other people and to the society, to give up the idea of obtaining personal gain through criminal means, to form the habit of respecting other people and society in general.
>
> Through physical labor, moreover, criminals learn they can transform themselves from society's liabilities into society's assets. Physical labor also makes them aware they can obtain the skills needed for later employment so that after their release they may become law-abiding and useful citizens.[44]

Chinese prisons draw their operating philosophy from old traditions filtered through Communist Party ideology. Erika Fairchild and Harry Dammer cite the influences of the ancient traditions of Confucianism and legalism. Confucianism, which flourished around 500 B.C., emphasized social harmony as best secured by moral education to bring out the good nature of all; this was achieved through informal social pressure from family and community. Legalism, which followed later in China, emphasized formal laws and strict punishments. Later these traditions merged. Under the Communist doctrine of Mao Zedong (Chairman Mao), who led Communist China from 1949 to 1976, moral education and law were joined under the direction of the party.[45] The basis of social control was through the committees in the neighborhoods and workplaces; prison was simply a more strict environment for control and education. Mao's maxim was "Our prison is no longer a prison of the old society; it should be run like a school, a factory, or a farm."

Chinese citizens are obligated to work, and so are prisoners. The 1994 **Prison Law,** Article 69, states, "Any criminal with the labour capacity must participate in labour." It adds, "The prison should, according to the criminal's individual circumstance, organize the criminals to work rationally in order to redress their bad habits, to cultivate working habits, to learn production techniques and to create employment conditions after their release from prison."[46] About 85 percent of prisoners are working, some of them in manual labor jobs such as farming, clearing land, and building roads in rural areas, but many now working in industrial jobs in factories near cities.

Western visitors to Chinese prisons are struck by the fact that virtually all prisoners are productively occupied. If they are not working, inmates are in class, in group recreation, or in counseling sessions called "political study," which is really about why their selfish criminal attitudes do not fit the social harmony of Communism. Chinese prisons are big, many of them averaging 2,000 to 3,000 inmates living in separate units. Inmates live in congregate cells typically housing ten to twenty prisoners each.

Eugene Miller, visiting several institutions in 1982, well before the latest round of reforms, found that Chinese prisoners had few creature comforts (nor did people out of prison in China at the time) but that institutions were clean, well run, and completely free of violence and escape attempts. Discipline was maintained by the **five rewards and five punishments.** The rewards were praise, bonuses, recording merits in the official file, reduction of the sentence, and parole. The punishments were group criticism, an official warning, recording demerits, solitary confinement, and increasing the sentence.

In a work-study school for girls in Shanghai, an administrator told Miller, "The students are flowers and the teachers are gardeners. The girls here are contaminated blossoms."[47] It is difficult to imagine an American juvenile facility administrator expressing a similar view.

When Robert Elegant toured China in 1988 to write about its legal system, he was struck by the diligence with which prison officials worked to change prisoners. One prison official told Elegant, "Everyone can be reformed."[48] Even lifers and death-sentenced inmates, many of whom were granted two-year reprieves to prove that they wanted to reform, were allowed to renounce their old ways and eventually rejoin society when prison authorities believed they had changed. This process often took many years.

Using work, peer pressure, and indoctrination techniques, prisons worked to accomplish **thought reform,** which at one time was said by outsiders to be like brainwashing but is now viewed as being more akin to the cognitive training—addressing thinking patterns—that has become more prevalent in Western prisons. Prisons are full of inspiring slogans and propaganda, like a high school before the big game. "Become a new man." "Study Marxism and Maoist thought." "Plead guilty. Obey the rules." "Support the government and reveal improper conditions in the prison." "Support the dictatorship of the proletariat."

Americans who espoused such slogans would, of course, be locked down as revolutionaries (or killed by the other inmates as rats), but you get the idea of how these simple messages, repeated endlessly over time, fit into the campaign to remold behavior. Does it work? Prison officials in the 1980s claimed very low recidivism rates of 4 or 5 percent, and even today, when authorities acknowledge that crime and the prison population are increasing as China's economy grows, the official recidivism rate remains under 10 percent.

Although Chinese prisons are said to "work" in terms of the role they play in society and have undergone substantial reforms in the past decade since the enactment of the Prison Law, they continue to draw criticisms on several fronts. Forced labor by nonsentenced prisoners is one. The international sale of unmarked prison-made goods is another. The U.S. government has laws in effect to prevent items manufactured by prison labor from entering this country, but these laws have not been applied to exclude Chinese products.

China is the most prolific applier of the death penalty as a criminal punishment (as opposed to simply executing one's political enemies) in the world. In most years, it may execute more criminals than the entire rest of the world added together. In one of its periodic anticrime campaigns (often called *yanda,* or "strike hard"), China executed more than 5,000 people in three months in 1983, according to Amnesty International. In 1995, more than 2,100 were executed.

A *yanda* campaign in April 1996 resulted in more than 1,000 executions for a variety of crimes—murder and rape but also graft, bribery, organized crime, drug trafficking, prostitution, pornography, theft, and other crimes. On June 26, 1996, Anti-Drugs Day, 1,725 people were convicted of drug crimes, 769 sentenced to death, and at least 230 publicly executed at mass antidrug rallies. Forty-four crimes that "seriously endanger public security" are capital offenses, although many criminals given death sentences are not executed if they repent during their two-year reprieve period.

Government officials and businessmen guilty of corruption and abuse of their privileged positions (and obviously out of favor with the party) are often subject to execution. Executives of such American businesses as Enron, Tyco, MCI, and others involved in recent scandals would already be dead in China—executed with a single bullet to the brain fired at contact range. Favored executives are simply removed from office and placed on house arrest for the rest of their lives, so perhaps we are not so different after all.

What happens after the execution is also a matter of controversy. Many criminals are asked—or required—to sign consent forms allowing their organs to be donated after death. When the criminal is shot to death, medical staff are "standing by" not to save a life but to harvest the organs for transplantation. Kidneys, corneas, livers, hearts, and lungs—the corpse is stripped of all usable parts, which are then distributed to recipients around the country, most notably in Beijing, Shanghai, and Hong Kong. Sometimes the organs are donated, and sometimes they are sold, with a kidney reportedly worth in the range of $30,000 to $40,000 on the organ market.

The prisoner whose labor is no longer available makes a last donation to the government responsible for his death. Presumably, this could be considered a conflict of interest among party officials, who might order a *yanda* when revenues are low, but thus far it has not been prohibited as a practice. With waiting lists for organ donors all over the world, the Chinese view organs harvested from the dead as another valuable item in international trade.

Japan

Visitors to Japanese prisons often make comments similar to those who visit China. If you were to take out Confucianism and replace it with Shinto and Buddhism and replace the single-party Communist Party rule with the single-party Liberal Democratic Party (which is actually a conservative, business-oriented party) that has dominated Japan for the past half century, the prison cultures are nearly mirror images.

At year-end 2002, the seventy-two Japanese prisons and 117 detention houses—all under the direction of the Correction Bureau in the Ministry of Justice—held 69,502 prisoners. With an estimated national population of 127.6 million, the incarceration rate is calculated at fifty-four per 100,000. Texas, in contrast, with a population of 22 million, held three times as many prisoners in custody, over 210,000, in 2002. While Japanese imprisonment rates remain among the lowest of the industrialized nations, they are a cause for concern. In 1990, the rate was only thirty-two per 100,000, so a sharp increase took place over the next decade as Japan struggled with economic malaise and increasing crime. The increased number of prisoners overwhelmed prison capacity, set officially at 65,264; the occupancy level figures out to 106.5 percent in a system that was never too generous with space to begin with.[49]

Western prison visitors are often taken to Japan's largest prison, Fuchu, in a Tokyo suburb. Fuchu is an old prison built on the American maximum-security model and surrounded by high stone walls. Prisoners sleep in either small individual cells or large, multiman cells. Designed for 2,600 prisoners, Fuchu held over 3,000 in 2003. In an unheated cell that would measure about fifteen by fifteen square feet, seven inmates slept head to toe, sharing a single sink and toilet.

When American writer James Webb visited this prison in 1983, he cited the experiences of James Arnett, an American who spent two years there after he was convicted of possessing two kilos of marijuana. Arnett spent most of his time in solitary. He got frostbite in his unheated cell in winter. He was held under very strict supervision—no writing materials; no personal possessions; censored mail; a diet of mostly seaweed, fish, and rice; and no communication with other inmates. In his cell, he was not allowed to touch his bunk or lie down on it during the daytime. He had to work eight hours per day making paper bags in his cell, and his diabetes went mostly untreated, causing him to lose fifty-five pounds in prison.

Sound like grounds for a lawsuit in America? Yet Arnett expressed a preference for Japanese imprisonment:

> They never tried to trick me, even in the interrogation. They were always trustworthy. I could have got five years and they gave me two. The Americans who were helping them wanted me to get 20. The guards at Fuchu were hard, but they never messed with you unless there was a reason. You didn't have to worry about the other prisoners coming after you, either. And the laws of Japan are for everybody. That's the main thing. The laws in this country depend on how much you can pay. I'd rather live under a hard system that's fair.[50]

The **Prison Law** of Japan, enacted in 1908, is still in effect today. It is long on granting authority to prison officials and short on the rights of prisoners. The prison approach is militaristic. Prisoners are subject to searches several times a day, beginning each day with a naked strip search in the cell. Prisoners call it the "cancan"—like the dance because they have to raise their arms overhead and stand on one foot and raise the other leg for the guard's inspection. The rules are very detailed. Many prisons require prisoners to march in military unison from place to place. Talking in the workplace is forbidden—looking directly at another prisoner is forbidden.

Prisoners work forty to forty-four hours per week; about two-thirds of all inmates worked in industrial production in 1994, mostly through contracts with private employers outside. Most of the remaining convicts work at the internal chores—cooking, cleaning, and maintenance—necessary to maintain the prison. Prisoners receive no wages, but a small gratuity—about a dollar per day in 1994—that is put into an account they may draw out on release. In some prisons, prisoners in the workplace begin the work day shouting out the **five principles** in unison:

1. Always be honest
2. Sincerely repent
3. Always be polite
4. Keep a helpful attitude
5. Be thankful

Elmer Johnson, writing on Japanese prisons in 1994, commented,

> A new Japanese inmate is greeted by an ongoing system of ritualized regimentation that constrains his deportment by enveloping him in routines, patterns of surveillance, body searches, shakedowns of living quarters, and control of movement around the prison. . . .
>
> Official policy stresses that the most trivial rule violations should be reported. The uniform administration of penalties is essential to convincing inmates that all incidents receive similar treatment and that treatment safeguards the weak from the strong inmates.[51]

This all appears more than a little authoritarian, more like the American penitentiaries of the early 1800s or something we would expect in totalitarian China. But in democratic Japan? How do they get by with treating prisoners in this manner?

The answer to this question is that prisoners, once they have proven themselves deserving of imprisonment, are dealt with harshly until they reform themselves and conform to the interests of society. Longtime observer of Japanese law and society John Haley has written, "From the initial police interrogation to the final judicial hearing on sentencing, the vast majority of those accused of criminal offenses confess, display repentance, negotiate for their victims' pardon, and submit to the mercy of the authorities. In return they are treated with extraordinary leniency."[52]

Extraordinary leniency is the dominant principle of the Japanese legal system. Criminals who prove themselves deserving of leniency, by expressing sincere contrition and making amends for wrongs done, avoid imprisonment or get very short sentences. The Japanese legal system provides six main penalties:

1. Minor fines (less than 10,000 yen)
2. Penal detention (less than thirty days)
3. Fines (more than 10,000 yen)
4. Imprisonment without labor (rarely used)
5. Imprisonment with labor
6. Death

The death penalty is applied sparingly in Japan. A majority of the public approves of its use, and Japan continues to sentence a handful—perhaps five to ten—criminals to death for murder and maintain them in prison awaiting execution, but executions have become rare events. Some years, no one is executed. When the death penalty is carried out, it is done by hanging.

Fines predominate, and suspended sentences without supervision are more common than probation. Imprisonment, mostly with labor but sometimes without, is reserved for those criminals not deserving leniency. Who would these unfortunate souls be, one might wonder? Several types of criminals float to the top of the "we are not worthy" pot—gangsters of the *yakuza* organized crime families, who are estimated to make up one-fourth of the prison population; gun and drug smugglers; foreigners, especially other Asians such as Koreans and Chinese, and Japanese *burakumin* (the native untouchable caste); habitual offenders; and those who defy leniency by fighting the system (such as Americans who keep screaming, "I know my rights," forgetting they are in someone else's country).

Violent criminals may also be in this bunch, but they may not be in prison long if they are considered one-time offenders and have expressed real contrition. In most years, 80 to 90 percent of Japanese criminals sentenced to imprisonment receive sentences of fewer than three years in prison, including some violent offenders who would expect much longer sentences in the United States. It is not uncommon for criminals to get probation for robbery, rape, attempted murder, or even murder.

Japan has an expansive system of probation and parole under the Rehabilitation Bureau of the Ministry of Justice. The great majority of juvenile offenders (criminals under age twenty) receive probation, as do many adults. The probation network in Japan emphasizes the work of **volunteer probation officers,** now numbering more than 50,000. Most of the volunteers are middle-age and older private citizens who wish to work one on one with one or two younger offenders at a time. Their role has been compared to that of the older brother or sister or sometimes the wise elderly grandparent, who is traditionally revered in Japanese culture. The volunteers have been part of the probation system since 1922, and, though critics often complain that they have outlived their usefulness, they show no sign of going away. The professional probation officers work with the more difficult cases and handle the paperwork on the routine cases where the volunteers provide the direct contact.

Japan has no real tradition of citizen activism in prison affairs or public support for prisoners in custody. Fairchild and Dammer have offered a good reason why:

> Because of the strong emphasis on conformity in Japanese life, prisons are a symptom of failure, and being a prisoner is a particular disgrace for both the inmates and their families. The Japanese believe that the tough methods used in prisons are necessary costs for a safer society. Thus, there is little public involvement in prison conditions, and the correctional process remains an operation that receives little public scrutiny.[53]

Absent outside intervention and without the resources devoted to rehabilitation found in some Western prison systems, the Japanese system emphasizes the role of the prison officer as a combined moral educator, lay counselor, security monitor, and "reformer." Elmer Johnson wrote,

> The roles are in fundamental conflict and led to the policy of American prisons that prohibits "fraternization" with prisoners, because possible manipulation by inmates would weaken security measures . . . .
>
> Contrary to American policy, Japanese correctional policy does not oppose personal contacts between officers and prisoners. . . .
>
> The Japanese culture and official requirements instruct officers to act as surrogate fathers or brothers toward inmates. Their own socialization impels most of the inmates toward cooperative relationships with officers who act as moral instructors and lay counselors. The sternness of the prison environment is eased, and the emphasis on security is counterbalanced. The officers are given access to the personal satisfactions of being helpers, not only security monitors.[54]

Most Japanese prisons for adults do not offer anywhere near the range of educational, vocational, or recreational programs that would be found in Western prison systems that devote more resources to rehabilitation. The most pervasive therapeutic approach in Japanese institutions is **Naikan,** a form of therapy with philosophical roots in Buddhist spiritual practices. It has been used in Japanese prisons since the 1950s:

> The essence of Naikan is revealed in the meaning from the Japanese words "nai," meaning inner, and "kan," meaning observation or introspection. Personal problems and dissatisfactions are often the result of the discrepancy between the actual self and the ideal self, or what is and what should be. Buddhism teaches that experience of living is far more valuable than metaphysical speculations. To philosophize

too much about existence is a waste of energy, just as preoccupation with one's condition. Even to focus too much on a problem can lead to attachment. Yet Buddha taught that life should not be seen as a mystery to be figured out. No, life should be lived, simply and practically, accepting events and circumstances as they occur.[55]

As practiced in prison, Naikan uses a week of intense (up to sixteen hours per day) guided meditation in isolation. This immersion phase is focused on getting the prisoner to ask and answer a series of questions focusing on the important relationships in his life, especially the troubles the prisoner has caused these other people. Counseling continues on a weekly or less frequent basis as the prisoner continues to meditate and develop insight into living a constructive life in harmony with others.

The authoritative approach of Japanese prisons is a concern to many human rights organizations that point out that "big brothers" are often abusive to "little brothers." This is happening with greater frequency, they maintain, as Japan's prisons have to cope with persistent overcrowding. The plain, dilapidated prisons; the five-and-a-half day workweeks; the meticulous enforcement of the rules; and the absolute monotony of the prison routine have reportedly led to more resistance by prisoners and more coercive responses by prison officers in recent years.

Prison officials focus on maintaining order. Japanese prisons have no history of escapes, riots, or inmate violence. Prison officials like to tell the story of the 1923 earthquake that knocked down the wall of a major prison. "No one escaped," they say, pointing out the difference between Japanese and American inmates.[54] Japanese prisoners, even if they are viewed as weak and not evil, are expected to obey and conform. Disobedient prisoners can expect to be isolated and placed under even greater restrictions until they comply.

This tight disciplinary regime invites abuses—long periods in solitary confinement kneeling or sitting in a fixed position, leather handcuffs and body belts that are kept on for days at a time, kicking and beating of unruly prisoners, and denial of medical treatment. Prisons are as secretive and autocratic as they were in the early part of the twentieth century in America, before "prisoners' rights" had any widespread meaning.

Kevin Mara, an American who had spent four years in Fuchu Prison on drug charges before his release in 1997, sued the prison for physical abuse and was awarded $5,000 in damages by Japanese courts—an unusual instance of a prison being held accountable for wrongdoing. Prison officials had maintained that they were only trying to keep order and protect inmates from each other. Mara said fellow inmates were never his greatest fear. "A child molester can be fairly safe from the wrath of other prisoners in Japanese prisons," he said, "but no prisoner is safe from the guards."[56] Not only in spirit but also in regard to human rights, Japan's prisons are increasingly compared with China's. The main thing missing is the propaganda.

THE USE AND PURPOSE OF IMPRISONMENT

The prison is universal in modern society, but its use within a given country is highly individualized. Within each nation, the prison meets a certain purpose, but the purpose is defined within a social, political, and cultural context.

Country to country, certain patterns emerge. Wealthy countries can devote more resources to maintaining nice jails and prisons if they choose to.

These countries often have nationalized corrections bureaucracies that oversee a network of specialized institutions. Less developed countries with lower standards of living often have low rates of imprisonment. Their justice systems are often localized so that punishments are informal and occur outside the national system. They also cannot afford to maintain expensive prison systems applying rigorous international standards of confinement. Conditions in their jails and prisons are comparable to what one would find in American institutions fifty or 100 years ago.

What about a nation's legal family—common law, civil law, socialist law, or Islamic law? Do these influence or determine imprisonment rates? Philip Reichel has suggested that in regard to rank order of countries on the world list of imprisonment rates,

> there appears to be no pattern based on the legal tradition to which the country belongs. Statistics are mostly unavailable in the socialist and Islamic families, but civil and common law countries are well dispersed throughout the list. It would be difficult to argue that use of imprisonment is a function of a country's legal family.[57]

Two observations can be made about this point. First, although civil and common law countries are intermingled in the rankings, civil law countries often hold a greater percentage of their prisoners in remand status, awaiting trial. This results from the civil law practice of holding accused persons in detention until trial while the thorough pretrial investigation is conducted. France is an example of such a nation. Until recently, a majority of its prisoners were pretrial detainees; the figure was down to about 38 percent in 2004, which is still about double the average rate of 20 percent or less that prevails in common law countries. The disproportionate number of pretrial detainees also appears in numerous other non-European countries whose legal systems are based on civil law, including most nations in Africa and Latin America. In these regions, the majority of all prisoners are awaiting trial. This is also true, however, in common law India, where 70 percent of prisoners are detainees. Part of this is attributable to holding arrestees without bail and part to very slow-moving, overburdened justice systems, particularly in those countries that have experienced social and political instability and significant "crime waves."

Second, Islamic countries often do have lower imprisonment rates. Islamic law deemphasizes locking people up as punishment. It is also most prevalent in Asian countries where imprisonment rates are lower regardless of the legal system. Pretrial incarceration rates are often high in Islamic systems, but the relative informality of the legal system and the use of economic and corporal punishments tend to hold down the numbers of sentenced prisoners. The use of confinement to stifle political and religious dissidents in many Islamic countries also inflates their detention rates; these countries hold suspects in isolation for long periods of time with no real plans to ever bring them to trial (as the United States has done with many Arabs and Islamic terror suspects in the wake of the September 11, 2001, terrorist attacks).

Countries experiencing prolonged periods of internal instability often see their imprisonment rates climb. This was surely noticeable in Russia; in many of its former components in northern Europe, central Asia, and central Europe that were reborn from the former Soviet Union; and in many of the eastern European nations that had been under Soviet dominance for a good part of the twentieth century. Fifteen years after the collapse of the Soviet Union, the rates of imprisonment in the former Communist states remain on average two or three times as high as the rates in western Europe. Russia seems to have a handle on controlling imprisonment at present, but its rates are five times the western European average.

The high rates of imprisonment in the former Communist countries are related to the combination of Communist politics and tradition in establishing a philosophy of imprisonment and then experiencing social chaos when the old structures break down. In such conditions, there is always an impetus to respond punitively, and most nations do. It takes a real effort to establish a different philosophy—and work toward an alternative social and political order in which imprisonment is used less often. Imprisonment is the convenient response to increasing crime and social disorder, but it is not the only response.

Finland is a prime example. In the 1960s, its penal system was "in the Russian tradition," according to Norwegian criminologist Nils Christie.[58] When the Finns discovered that their imprisonment rate—in the range of 200 per 100,000, considerably higher than that of the United States at the time—was totally unlike those of their Scandinavian neighbors, they debated their practices and decided their position "was a kind of disgrace." Over the next two decades, a long series of policy changes were implemented, all united by one goal: to reduce imprisonment either by diverting offenders to other forms of punishment or by reducing the time served in prison.

By pursuing this policy consistently from the 1970s through the 1990s, Finland was able to reduce its imprisonment rate to fifty-two per 100,000 in 2002. In a given year, over 90 percent of its convicted felons receive noncustodial sentences—day fines, probation, or community service. Fewer than 10 percent receive prison sentences. After thirty years, Finland's imprisonment rate is slightly lower than its Scandinavian neighbors. Its crime rate, which went up steadily during the reform period, as did the rates in its neighboring countries, leveled off in the early 1990s and has declined steadily since then. Ultimately, Finland's choices about how to punish crime had little or no effect on the crime rate.[59]

Dan Gardner has made a similar observation about the relationship between imprisonment and the crime rate, only his attention was focused on the United States:

> Can a jurisdiction curb crime by putting more offenders in prison longer? Most criminologists think not. State-by-state comparison suggest they are right.
>
> Take New York State. The spectacular decline in crime in New York City between 1992 and 1997 is justly famous. Less well known is the fact that over the same period, the number of state prisoners (the vast majority of whom are from New York City) grew slowly compared to that in other states. In fact, over those five years, New York State prison expansion was the second-slowest in the U.S.
>
> Over the same period, California's prison population grew nine times as fast as New York's. But the incident of crime in California did not drop by the same proportion. On the contrary, violent crime fell far more sharply in New York State, with the drop in California only reaching 40 percent of the decline in New York State.
>
> Or consider the two Virginias. West Virginia boosted its prison population by 131 percent over the last decade and saw a four-percent drop in crime. Across the border, Virginia's prisons grew by 28 percent, while the state enjoyed a 21-percent drop in crime.[60]

Marc Mauer of The Sentencing Project has consistently made the point that the use of imprisonment in America is not directly tied to the crime rate or, conversely, that changes in crime have not been the driving force in expanding the prison population over the past thirty years. Citing the analysis of Alfred Blumstein and Allen Beck (in "Population Growth in U.S. Prisons, 1980–1996," appearing in Michael Tonry and Joan Petersilia, *Prisons: Crime and Justice-A Review of Research*, 1999), Mauer indicates that changes in crime accounted for only 12 percent of the prison rise, while changes in sentencing policy—more direct sentences to prison, mandatory sentencing, truth in sentencing, "three strikes and you're out" laws, natural life sentences, and other changes leading to longer prison terms—accounted for the rest. The prison is used more because the justice system is far more punitive than in years past.[61]

This is not to suggest that if we were to abolish prisons altogether, crime would go away (though some criminologists have suggested that if we did completely abolish prisons, the effect on crime would be minimal). It does suggest that the use of prisons in a given country is determined by many conditions of which the crime problem is only one. Baroness Vivien Stern, senior research fellow at the International Centre for Prison Studies, Kings College, London (which generates the most comprehensive international prison statistics; see *www.prisonstudies.org*), made this point in a 2003 speech:

> It is not obvious that one country's model is better than another. There is no model of the right prison. Prison is an intensely cultural institution. The models of imprisonment in Western Europe and North America are imbued with Christian ideas of guilt, punishment and atonement. They are modelled on the monastery with individual rooms that are called cells. The Russian concept is of banishment and work. In the East, in China and Japan, the aim is to remould the person into conformity. In other parts of the world the whole idea of the prison as the main punishment for crime is an imposition, a colonial legacy, and still sits uneasily in the thinking of Africa or India. What is deemed right to take away from prisoners is cultural. What prisoners will see as legitimate deprivations and what they will not accept is also rooted in their ideas of right and wrong.[62]

WHO GOES TO PRISON?

If we were to line up all the people behind bars in almost 200 nations worldwide, what would we notice about them? The first thing we would notice is that overwhelming numbers of men were elbowing the women out of line or trying to take advantage of them while they waited. The individual country statistics available from the International Centre for Prison Studies indicate that around the world only about 6 percent of prisoners are women.[63] In countries where the percentage is higher—in the United States it was 8.5 percent of all jail and prison inmates in 2003—this is attributed mostly to the involvement of females in drug and vice crimes. Females make up more than 10 percent of the imprisoned population in several major countries, led by Thailand, Bolivia, Paraguay, and Costa Rica. In most countries, females make up a small portion of the prison population—a portion that is often ignored and treated as an afterthought in comparison to the country's male prisoners.

The next thing we would likely notice is that a great number of the imprisoned are not "like us," if "us" is defined as native-born members of the dominant racial group. Around the world, minorities and foreigners always show up in disproportionate numbers behind bars. In the United States, blacks make up 12 percent of the general population but more than 40 percent of the population behind bars. Hispanics are also overrepresented, though not to this degree. Thirty percent of the federal prison population is made up of noncitizens, primarily from Mexico and other Latin American countries.

In England, the minorities are blacks—from the Caribbean and Africa—and dark-skinned Asians. In western Europe, it is the young male guest workers from southern Europe, the Middle East, and North Africa and the transient foreigners who stand out. In some European countries, such as the ethnically homogeneous Switzerland and Luxembourg, two-thirds or more of all prisoners are foreigners. In Hungary, 40 percent of the prison population is made up of Gypsies—this nation's "usual suspects." In Australia, the Aboriginal natives make up less than 2 percent of the population but 19 percent of prisoners. Canada has a similar experience with its First Nations peoples (as we do with our own Native Americans, though not to the same degree). Cultural and socioeconomic differences persisting over long periods have intensified social problems in these groups, and their resulting abundance behind bars is a national embarrassment. It is disparity and disadvantage, for certain, if not discrimination, and the problem is pervasive, as Michael Tonry has pointed out: "Members of minority groups are overrepresented among crime victims, arrestees, pretrial detainees, convicted offenders, and prisoners in every Western nation."[64]

Partly connected to both the numbers of women and the numbers of foreigners in jails and prisons is one other group: drug offenders. Contrary to what it might seem, the United States is not the toughest nation on earth for locking up people for drug use and distribution. Although we have the most in custody in absolute numbers, more than 400,000, Human Rights Watch reports that Ecuador (50 percent) and several Asian countries—Malaysia (40 percent), Singapore (47 percent), and Taiwan (over 50 percent)—have a larger portion of prisoners in custody directly for drug use or trafficking than we do. Many of these prisoners are women, and a large percentage are foreigners also.

We have already noted that pretrial detainees, including people in custody for political, religious, and other noncriminal reasons, are more common than sentenced prisoners in many countries—they make up about half of all prisoners worldwide. Among sentenced prisoners in the Western nations, prisoners convicted of crimes against persons predominate. In part, this is because they get longer sentences. The property criminals, public order criminals, and drug criminals are more numerous among the admissions to prison each year, but the personal offenders stay longer and build up in population. Canada is a good example of this; 75 percent of its federal inmate population have been convicted of crimes against persons; in the United States, it is not quite 50 percent, though the rate has been increasing steadily for a decade because of longer sentences and less use of prison for drug criminals. Thus, if you are in a Western prison, the odds are even or better that the person you are looking at is serving a sentence for a violent crime. In prisons elsewhere, the person might be in for a drug offense or other nonviolent crime. In many countries, the person is more likely to be a pretrial detainee, facing years in custody before his case is disposed of.

Finally, we would notice, among those behind bars, a very small number of juveniles. This gets very complicated to calculate mathematically because of different definitions of juvenile status and different correctional measures, but the United States, with about 100,000 juveniles in secure custody outside its adult prisons and jails, is likely the largest confiner of juveniles not only in numbers but also in percentages (about five juveniles for every 100 adults).

The **Beijing Rules** (formally the United Nations Standard Minimum Rules for the Administration of Juvenile Justice, adopted in 1985) define juvenile status not by age, which varies widely from system to system, but by a legal process different from that applicable to an adult. These rules encourage dealing with juvenile criminal behavior outside of court except in the most serious of cases. They encourage noncustodial sanctions, and they forbid the application of the death penalty to persons under the age of eighteen, which in 2004 was still allowed by law in eighteen American states (though only seven have executed juveniles in recent years). Texas is actually the leading executioner of juveniles in the entire world.

Philip Reichel discusses four models of juvenile justice used in different countries:

1. The **welfare model** prevails in many Western countries. It centers on treatment and the delivery of social services outside the formal legal system. Some nations, especially Australia and New Zealand, have moved on to a restorative justice model that is more reconciliatory and community oriented rather than treatment oriented.

2. The **legalistic model,** which deals with the juvenile more formally under the strict control of the court.

3. The **corporatist model,** of which England is a good example at present, which merges government officials and other public and private professionals into Youth Offender Teams to manage juvenile justice at the local level.

4. The **participatory model,** of which China is a good example, which tries to work with juveniles through local neighborhood committees outside the formal system. The emphasis is on reeducation and surveillance within the neighborhood.

Reichel also gives an example of the **benign-neglect approach** (adopted from James Hackler), which suggests that many underdeveloped countries (the example used is Fiji) are dealt with very informally, not locked up, and "corrected" by school and vocational training. The important difference is there is no juvenile justice bureaucracy to monitor them and intervene in their lives.[65]

The application of any of these models will result in fewer juveniles being dealt with through secure custodial measures. Although international studies suggest that juvenile crime rates peak out in the mid- to lateteen years, the preferred response is to practice leniency and await the maturing that often comes with adulthood. The United States does this, too, but we practice rehabilitation within a secure institutional setting more than other nations do.

THE PRISON EXPERIENCE

One of the truisms of imprisonment, as applicable to other countries as it is to the United States, is that once you get past the condition of being locked up, the quality of your life in prison depends on the prison in which you are confined. The United Nations has adopted about two dozen standards pertinent to human rights and the administration of justice. These are available through the Office of the High Commissioner for Human Rights (available at *www.unhchr.ch*). They are divided into two types—conventions, covenants, and protocols are binding on all members, while rules and principles are nonbinding. The most important of these agreements to prisoners are the following:

1. The Standard Minimum Rules for the Treatment of Prisoners, first adopted in Geneva in 1955
2. The International Covenant on Civil and Political Rights, adopted in 1966 and effective March 23, 1976
3. The Second Optional Protocol to the International Covenant on Civil and Political Rights, aiming at the abolition of the death penalty, adopted in 1989
4. The Convention against Torture and Other Cruel, Inhuman or Degrading Treatment or Punishment, adopted 1984, effective June 26, 1987
5. The Optional Protocol to the Convention against Torture and Other Cruel, Inhuman or Degrading Treatment or Punishment, adopted in 2002
6. The Basic Principles for the Treatment of Prisoners, adopted December 14, 1990

The standards of the Basic Principles for the Treatment of Prisoners, for instance, deal with such issues as avoiding discrimination, respect for human dignity, avoiding solitary confinement, paid work, access to health services, and reintegration into society. Needless to say, all nations regularly fall short of meeting the custodial standards set by these agreements. Both **Amnesty International** and **Human Rights Watch** prepare annual reports highlighting specific problems with treatment of prisoners around the world.

Some nations—and their prisoners—have a lot more problems than others. The most pervasive problem worldwide is overcrowding. Prisons are expensive to build and operate, and most countries want to expand the size of their systems only *after* populations have grown. They are always behind the power curve, and their prisoners suffer the effects while political officials debate policies and financing.

Only about one in five countries on which the International Centre for Prison Studies maintains population statistics is below 90 percent of its maximum prison capacity—a level considered desirable for flexibility in housing prisoners safely. The majority of the world's prison system are above 100 percent capacity, several way above. Among the major countries—mostly in Africa and Asia—whose prison occupancy levels are more than 200 percent over capacity are Cameroon, Bangladesh, Zambia, Iran, Thailand, Kenya, Pakistan, and Rwanda; Honduras in Central America is also on this list. What are conditions like in these countries? Roy Walmsley has pointed out that overcrowding brings

a host of other major problems. Not only restricted living space, but also poorer conditions of hygiene and poorer sanitation arrangements and less time for outdoor exercise. In many countries there is insufficient bedding and clothing for prisoners when there is significant prison population growth, and the food is less satisfactory in terms of quality and quantity. Health care is more difficult to administer effectively in such conditions and diseases spread more rapidly and spread into the community when prisoners are released. There is more tension, with more violence between prisoners, more violence against staff. Risks of self-injury and suicide also increase.

When there is growth in prison numbers the staff-prisoner ratio invariably falls. Staff are rarely recruited speedily enough to maintain that ratio at a satisfactory level. Reduced staff-prisoner ratios are likely to mean less effective supervision by staff and less time for them to organize activities to ensure that the institution is run in a positive way which maximises the chances of successful reintegration into the community on release. Treatment programmes, including pre-release courses, are likely to be negatively affected. Further, the reduced staff-prisoner ratio and increased tension and violence by prisoners are likely to have a harmful effect on staff in terms of increased stress and sickness levels. There are also likely to be harmful effects on families and friends outside the prisons, in so far as they are of the increased levels of tension and stress affecting both prisoners and staff.[66]

The consequences of these problems are commonplace in international news. The prisons of Russia and central Asia have high rates of MDR-TB. Many African prisons have very high rates of HIV and AIDS. British prisons suffered through riots attributed to overcrowding in the 1990s.

Prison violence has been endemic in several overcrowded Latin American prison systems—Bolivia, Brazil, Peru, and Venezuela—for more than a decade. In 1994, Venezuela, with a prison population of about 23,000, counted 274 inmates killed by other inmates. To compare, if the United States experienced a similar level of homicidal violence, over 15,000 prisoners would have been murdered last year (as opposed to about fifty). Venezuela also has one of the world's worst recent histories of prison riots, with hundreds of inmates killed by other prisoners, burning to death in fires, and shot to death by police and troops during the course of riots. The Venezuelan prison murder rate is estimated to be more than forty times the national average.

Much of the level of violence in Latin American prisons goes beyond overcrowding into related issues of drugs and internal corruption. A May 2004 riot at the new Benfica Prison in Rio de Janeiro, Brazil, was attributed to conflict among three rival drug gangs. The three-day riot left one guard and thirty-three inmates dead; in a scene reminiscent of the Santa Fe, New Mexico, prison riot of 1980, most of the inmates were decapitated and their corpses burned. "It was a truly horrific scene," a legislator said. "There were bodies dumped in garbage containers, heads, body parts." A Rio university researcher said that gangs completely controlled all aspects of prison life—stronger in prison than out. "Inmates do not receive such basic things as toilet paper and soap, so many end up completely dominated by gang leaders just to get toilet paper," she said.[67]

In such systems, of which the drug-money-rich Latin American countries are just the extreme example, prisoners are at the complete mercy of guards and officials for basic necessities of life. Corruption is a way of life in these systems. Congregate housing, easy access to weapons (including firearms), and low levels of staffing complicate prison life for ordinary inmates. Influential prisoners with money live well in these prisons, with private rooms, cell phones, family visits, and special meals. Other prisoners barely get by day to day, enduring a climate of fear, violence, sexual exploitation, and extreme deprivation that is completely contrary to the rights and dignities set forth in UN agreements.

The only redeeming factor in many of these countries is that their overall rates of imprisonment, even with overcrowding, are low. Venezuela's current rate of imprisonment is only about seventy-six per 100,000, Bolivia's 102 per 100,000. Thus, when outsiders say anything about terrible prison conditions or levels of prison violence, officials respond with "It's just prisoners" or "It's just prisoners killing prisoners." That puts everything in context.

EXPLAINING DIFFERENCES

American jails and prisons rank moderately low on the international scale of human rights abuses of prisoners. Our prisoners are relatively safe and adequately cared for in comparison to those of many other countries, and most American prisoners are no longer held in badly overcrowded facilities. They have access to legal assistance and the courts, and they are not for the most part "lost in the system," as prisoners in other countries are often said to be. But our correctional institutions do draw critical attention in regard to several human rights issues:

1. Overuse of solitary confinement, especially the conditions of prolonged isolation in supermax prisons.
2. Isolation of state and federal prisoners in rural institutions far from visitors, work, and treatment programs.
3. Imprisonment of drug addicts who are perceived elsewhere as a public health concern.
4. The traditional use of extralegal physical punishments of inmates by staff in several jail and prison systems.
5. Overcrowding and lack of activities and services in many local jails.
6. Overuse of secure custody for juveniles.
7. Continued use of the death penalty, which remains on the books in thirty-eight states and at the federal level.
8. Overrepresentation of blacks and Hispanics behind bars.
9. Finally—and most noticeably—the extreme overuse of incarceration, making our custodial rates the highest in the world at more than 700 prisoners per 100,000 citizens. Once you take Russia and South Africa out of the mix, the United States locks up its citizens at a rate about five to eight times higher than other industrialized nations.

Why does America have such a high rate of imprisonment, especially in comparison to the other Western nations with which we are culturally most similar and usually compare ourselves? There are two tracks to take in answering this question—a statistical track and a cultural track. The statistical track asks the "how" question: how did we get here? The cultural track asks the more profound "why" question: why is America so punitive?

The how question has been answered most often and most ably by Marc Mauer and his colleagues at The Sentencing Project. In "Comparative International Rates of Incarceration: An Examination of Causes and Trends," a report presented to the U.S. Commission on Civil Rights in 2003, Mauer reviews the causal factors responsible for high imprisonment rates. Although our rates of property crimes are only average in comparison to those of our Western neighbors, our rates of violent crime, especially gun crime, are much higher.[68] The use of firearms to commit murders, robberies, attempted murders, and assaults generates much greater numbers of criminals warranting imprisonment.

Violent criminality is however, only a minor part of the overall picture. In the 1980s and 1990s, the greater part of the increase in the jail and prison population was not violent criminals but drug criminals, as the number increased from 40,000 to more than 400,000. This occurred not as a result of a dramatic increase in drug usage but as a result of a policy change written into law: "Put more drug criminals in prison."

Sentencing of all criminals got tougher during this era as well. Prison was viewed as the more appropriate destination for more nonviolent criminals. The likelihood of imprisonment increased, and the length of prison terms imposed and terms actually served before release increased also. Really long sentences—natural life, "three strikes," and habitual felon—were used more often. Release mechanisms were altered to keep people in prison longer. So that is the easy answer to the "how" question: "Sentencing changed. We got tougher on crime."

The response to the "why" question is more complex. At its heart is the concept of **punitiveness,** defined as support for inflicting punishment. International research suggests that punitiveness is a cultural trait, an aspect of one society that can be compared to a corresponding society. How do you think Americans would rank on the international punitiveness scale? Not as badly as you might think, actually. Confronted with this scenario—"how would you punish a twenty-one-year-old repeat burglar?"—about 40 percent of 130,000 respondents in sixty countries chose imprisonment. Respondents in Asia and Africa were most punitive; three-quarters favored imprisonment. In North America and Latin America, it was about half; in western Europe, it was about one-quarter. There was a general connection between punitiveness and the crime rate, except in Asia, which has generally lower crime rates, and less support for noncustodial sanctions in those countries where they are not already well developed and available (in other words, where such alternatives are only imagined and not observed). Finally, there was little connection between imprisonment preferences and personal victimization; punitiveness was not based on personal experience or contact with crime.[69]

A later study posed this same situation—a twenty-one-year-old recidivist burglar—to citizens in a smaller group of seventeen industrialized countries. Given a wide range of sentences, the most punitive, in their combined preference for imprisonment and a longer term behind bars, were people from the United States and Japan. Citizens of western European countries preferred community service and alternative sentences to imprisonment, and the average length of prison sentences they imposed was shorter by about half on average (except for the hard-liners in Poland) than the preferred sentence of thirty-one months in America.[70]

If you put these studies together, some basis of understanding punitiveness as an influence on national policy begins to emerge from the fog of name-calling: "Americans are meaner than the rest of the world!" Not exactly. There are lots of people who think like we do, all over the world. (Research suggests, for instance, that even in nations that do not have the death penalty and have not had it for a long time, a strong minority or sometimes a majority of its citizens believe that some criminals who commit the most heinous murders deserve death; their political officials just do not think this is a good idea in practice, and thus they do not make it available as an option.)

But most of these people are not in countries that have combined rates of crime—personal, property, drug, and public order—anywhere near the level that we do. Asians might be as punitive as Americans, but they have much lower crime rates to contend with. Africans might be as punitive, but their criminal justice systems are small, underfunded, and overworked; they ignore a lot of crime or punish less severely because their systems cannot afford to punish more harshly—and also because justice is still seen as more of a local concern based on old tribal or kinship networks than of a matter for national determination.

The western Europeans and English-speaking industrialized nations who do face crime rates comparable to ours are not as punitive. They are more supportive of alternatives and short sentences. They do not have to live with the same perceived levels of violent crime that Americans do. In most of these nations, people are also more constrained by the practice of criminal justice within a national framework—and perhaps by views on how fiscal resources ought to be used (e.g., in prevention as opposed to punishment). That is, although there might be geographical hotbeds of punitiveness (such as Alberta and Ontario of late in Canada), a more moderate overall policy predominates. In Germany, some states are known to be more punitive that others, but all follow federal laws.

The variables are beginning to add up. The United States has citizens who not only think more punitively but also have more **real crime**—especially violent crime (though most of this happens to lower-class people in cities)—than our neighbor nations. We are an affluent nation that can afford to maintain a more expensive criminal justice system. In 2004, the United States spent more money in support of its mission to impose democracy on Iraq than it will on all its entire correctional system; imprisonment is just one more drop in a huge national bucket.

Our system is an odd hybrid—a nonsystem, it is often called—of local, state, and federal organizations. In the past, punishment was driven mostly by local officials, but over the past generation, politicians at all levels seem to have agreed on a high-pitched, high-priced crime control policy that emphasizes imprisonment within an expanded framework of social control. We are more aware of the increase in the population behind bars, but the noncustodial population—those on probation, parole, or other forms of community supervision—has increased right along with the custodial. We have gone from fewer than a million people under correctional supervision in 1970 to almost 7 million in 2004. Is all this just the product of fear of crime in combination with political opportunism—crime victims and crime fighters in a fortuitous encounter in late twentieth-century America?

Those who study social class in American history suggest there is more to it. The big boost in imprisonment in the past twenty years of the twentieth century is the most recent incarnation of society's ongoing effort to control the dangerous classes. Scott Christianson's *With Liberty for Some: 500 Years of Imprisonment in America* traces the history of imprisonment from Columbus to the end of the twentieth century. He documents the concentration of immigrants and nonwhites in jails and prisons throughout this period, suggesting that the class-based focus of confinement has found a permanent target in America's poor urban minorities. The prison has become the most forceful mechanism for maintaining the status quo.

It is black and Hispanic males (and more recently black females as well) in American cities who have born the brunt of the vast increase in correctional intervention over the past generation. This is particularly noticeable in the sixteen southern states, twelve of which have majority black prison populations, as do ten other states outside the South. Other nations tend to do the same thing with the poor, immigrants, and people of color, as we have seen; they just do not have as many of them to contend with as we do, nor are they generally perceived to be as physically threatening to the social order—**social dynamite,** in Steven Spitzer's definition of dangerous deviance.

One of the key elements in determining "punitiveness in practice," as opposed to "punitiveness in theory," is the contrast between homogeneity and heterogeneity. Nations made up of people who are very much alike—same ethnicity, religion, and values—tend to be much less punitive than nations made up of people who are very different from each other. It was no big surprise, in the 1990s, that the three leading countries in world imprisonment rates were the United States, Russia, and South Africa. Not only were Russia and South Africa going through major periods of social upheaval after changing governmental regimes, but both nations were also multicultural societies in which vastly different peoples were mixed together under extreme pressures. The criminal law and criminal punishments were used increasingly to impose formal order on these disorderly, conflict-ridden societies.

The perfect analogy is the **war on crime,** which makes law-abiding people "the good guys" and criminals "the bad guys" in an ongoing civil war. Or, to carry the analogy forward into confinement, as Baroness Vivien Stern suggested in a 2003 lecture, the prisoner is seen not as a citizen but as the **enemy of the state.** Her position is straightforward:

> Prisons are not places to hold people deemed to be enemies of the state. Prisons have nothing to do with the military or defence, or enemies. In a democratic society prison is a public service. Prisons are places like schools and hospitals. They should be run by the civil power. They should have the objective of contributing to the public good. Therefore prison authorities should have some accountability to the elected parliament. The public should be regularly informed about the state and aspirations of the prisons. Government ministers and senior officials should make clear that they hold prison staff in high regard for the work they do. The public should frequently be reminded that prison work is an important public service. So first of all, the State's responsibility is to run prisons as part of civilian society, as a public service accountable to Parliament.[71]

But many Americans would not agree with this position: the whole direction of American thought and public policy for a generation has been to see prisoners as the enemy. The political hyperbole and exaggerated punitiveness only make it more difficult for us to see them as fellow citizens in need of assistance rather than evil adversaries to be feared, loathed, isolated, and controlled in perpetuity.

In 1956, Reed Cozart, an attorney and former prison official who was then an official of the U.S. Justice Department, told the story of a Finnish prison official who had completed a six-month tour of state and federal prisons in the United States. This was at a time when Finland had a higher per capita rate of confinement than the United States did, but the official pointed out that there was a basic difference of perspective between Finnish and American prisons. Cozart reported his colleague's observation:

> He said that whereas in Finland the offender is regard as a fallen brother and it is the obligation of the state or society to restore him to the brotherhood, he found that in the United States an offender is normally regarded as an enemy of society and an outlaw.[72]

Perhaps the official was ill informed or exaggerating, but a few years later his nation set out to reduce its prison population, while the United States declared war on its criminal enemies. Almost forty years later, which nation is better off?

AMERICAN CORRECTIONS: THE RECENT PAST AND THE NEAR FUTURE

In 1930, the prison incarceration rate in America was 104 per 100,000. Forty years later, after a period of remarkable stability in the use of imprisonment, the rate was ninety-six per 100,000. It stayed below 100 through 1973, and in 1974 it climbed to 102, then to 111 in 1975. In corrections, everyone was still talking about rehabilitation and its ideological successor, reintegration, not yet fully aware that one was a failure and the other unwanted. By the turn of the twenty-first century, the combined jail and imprisonment rates were five times higher than they had been thirty years earlier, and people were talking about—what, rehabilitation and reintegration again?

Where is American corrections headed in the near future? It is hard to predict with much hope of accuracy: psychics should avoid corrections, just as they avoid picking lottery tickets. The people who work in corrections are fond of pointing out that they have very little control over what they do—their work is delivered to them at the end of a very long process. It starts with conditions in society, crime, and law and then the police and courts, and finally it comes to corrections, which does its best to sanitize the residue before returning it to society. This attitude allows corrections to function with a kind of "hey, what can we do about it?" attitude.

There is much truth in this position, particularly in the United States, as opposed to other countries. The American position on imprisonment, in the extreme form practiced today, has developed since the 1960s, and it is almost entirely politics driven. Politics driven is used in contrast to other possibilities, such as research driven or knowledge driven (much less humanity driven). American corrections is driven by the actions of local political officials—district attorneys, sheriffs, and judges—and local legislators who make state laws, making criminal justice policy an amalgam of fifty state systems and one federal system.

Correctional policies are formed and implemented primarily within the states—over 90 percent of prisoners are held in local and state institutions—with the federal role being primarily to provide funding in support of particular policy initiatives, such as jail and prison building funds for states that adopted truth in sentencing in the 1990s. But both state and federal politicians have been speaking the same language in recent years. Their criminal justice politics has been the language of sound bites—beginning with "law and order" in the 1960s and 1970s and continuing forward to "tough on crime," "just say no," "three strikes and you're out," "truth in sentencing," and "victims' rights."

Most correctional policy, whether at the state or the federal level, is based far more on ideology or belief than on fact or plan. This is the politics of **expressive justice,** as David Anderson has referred to policies based on how you feel rather than knowledge and reasoned thought. They have developed into a national model in response to what is often seen—incorrectly—as a constantly rising flood tide of crime in America since the 1960s. People have repeated the slogans so long that they have become part of our way of thinking—a personal and often wrongheaded view of crime and criminals.

In foreign countries, where corrections policies are made at the national level, research divisions conduct major national research projects and prepare important reports to inform policy decisions. There is a sense that researchers and academic criminologists are contributing to the shaping of public policy, that experts are part of the team. In the United States, where corrections is a hodgepodge of local, state, and federal officials responding to the immediate needs of an agitated electorate (or perhaps drawing power by creating the agitation itself), researchers at the national level gather statistics that are "interesting" but go nowhere, and the most important policy research is done by private organizations—The Sentencing Project, the Death Penalty Information Center, the National Council on Crime and Delinquency, the Center on Juvenile and Criminal Justice, the Urban Institute, and many others. What do criminologists do? Well, they teach criminology, not shape or greatly influence public policy. In the United States, politicians, led by or leading the public, decide on the policy first, then seek the research (or useful statistics) to support their position and establish policies. Criminologists, systems experts, and often practitioners are out of this loop.

Not all states have followed the politics-driven approach. The few that have swum against the flood tide of imprisonment—such northern states as Maine, Minnesota, New Hampshire, North Dakota, and Rhode Island, all with imprisonment rates of less than 200 per 100,000—have managed to maintain their state policies over long periods of time, mostly because—like the European countries—they have not had to contend with a punitive electorate. Just coincidentally, or perhaps not, eleven of the twelve states without a death penalty also rank below the national average imprisonment rates. In the South, where the death penalty is strongest, all states except Kentucky, North Carolina, and West Virginia rank above, most of them far above, the national average imprisonment rates.

The punitiveness concept applies not only to nations but also to areas within each nation; it is striking, within the United States, how much imprisonment rates vary from state to state, the numbers a composite formed by policies based on various internal conflicts–urban/rural, class, racial, religious, and cultural. The differences have always been there, but when imprisonment rates were much lower across the board, they were not as noticeable. Since the early 1970s, the polarization of American politics has accentuated differences in imprisonment policies. Of the twenty states with imprisonment rates above the national average (373 per 100,000) at year-end 2000, seventeen gave their electoral votes to George W. Bush. Only three—California, Connecticut, and Michigan—went for Al Gore. Gore won in twenty states, seventeen with below-average imprisonment rates and three with above-average rates. Imprisonment is more closely associated with ideology than crime.

Imprisonment is said to be the reverse of prevention, and this is most noticeable in regard to children. Each year, the Annie E. Casey Foundation publishes the Kids Count Survey ranking the fifty states according to ten variables related to child well-being:

Percentage of low-birth-weight babies

Infant mortality rate

Child death rate

Rate of teen deaths by accident, homicide, and suicide

Teen birthrate

Percentage of teens who are high school dropouts

Percentage of teens not attending school and not working

Percentage of children living in families where no parent is permanently employed

Percentage of children living in poverty

Percentage of families with children headed by a single parent

Year after year, the states at the top of the list, in terms of being good places for children to live, are states with low rates of imprisonment; states with high imprisonment rates are worse places for children. A table comparing child well-being and imprisonment is reproduced here.

Recent research by LuWanna Brown[73] and separately by the Oklahoma Department of Corrections[74] has verified the clear-cut inverse relationship between child well-being and imprisonment. Part of this might be socioeconomic ("poor or bad-off children grow up to become criminals"), but a good part of it is strictly financial. Brown's research established that the states ranking high on the Kids Count Survey spent larger percentages of the state budget on services to children than states ranking lower, while the lower-ranking states spent more on imprisonment. Her findings were like the Midas commercial: "You can pay me now, or you can pay me later." Either you use the resources to prevent crime now, or you wait until the criminals grow up and put them in prison. This approach gives rise to a kind of "reverse welfare system" in America—spend nothing now, then spend $20,000 to $25,000 per year keeping criminals safe and secure in prison as adults.

KIDS COUNT AND IMPRISONMENT RANKINGS, 2001

State	Kids Count Ranking	Imprisonment Ranking/Rate (per 100,000)	
Minnesota	1	49	132
New Hampshire	2	46	188
New Jersey	3	32	331
Iowa	4	39	272
Utah	5	43	230
Vermont	6	45	213
Connecticut	7	22	387
North Dakota	8	48	161
Massachusetts	9	41	243
Nebraska	10	44	225
Wisconsin	11	23	383
Maine	12	50	127
Pennsylvania	13	35	310
Virginia	14	17	431
California	15	13	453
Washington	16	40	249

State	Kids Count Ranking	Imprisonment Ranking/Rate (per 100,000)	
Indiana	17	29	341
South Dakota	18	25	370
Rhode Island	19	47	181
Hawaii	20	37	298
Oregon	21	38	295
Kansas	22	34	318
Ohio	23	20	398
Wyoming	24	30	340
New York	25	27	355
Michigan	26	11	488
Maryland	27	18	422
Colorado	28	21	391
Idaho	29	14	451
Montana	30	26	368
Illinois	31	27	355
Nevada	32	12	474
Missouri	33	8	509
Florida	34	16	437
Delaware	35	9	504
Texas	36	3	711
Kentucky	37	24	371
Oklahoma	38	4	658
Alaska	39	36	300
Georgia	40	6	542
North Carolina	41	31	335
West Virginia	42	42	231
Tennessee	43	19	411
Arkansas	44	15	447
Arizona	45	10	492
South Carolina	46	7	529
Alabama	47	5	584
New Mexico	48	38	295
Louisiana	49	1	800
Mississippi	50	2	715

Sources: Annie E. Casey Foundation, "Kids Count Data Book Online," *www.aecf.org/kidscount/databook.summary.htm,* and U.S. Department of Justice, Bureau of Justice Statistics; *Sourcebook of Criminal Justice Statistics 2002, www.albany.edu/sourcebook/1995.*

Lately, there have been indications that several states would like to move in the direction of downsizing their prison systems. There is more talk of **smart justice,** a term that has come to mean more efficient use of resources, as in fewer prison beds and more community-based alternatives. The main motivation for this move appears to be the cost of imprisonment. As its share of state budgets increases, corrections has been consuming resources government would prefer to spend on other services—education, health, transportation, and the environment. Much of smart justice is directed toward increasing controls over criminals under community supervision (which ultimately has the potential to put more people in prison). Although public support for rehabilitation of drug and nonviolent criminals is reportedly increasing, it does not appear to be politically appropriate to speak of community corrections as "helping criminals" or to point out how unproductive to society prisons are—that prison is two groups of people: one group doing nothing, the other group being paid to see that they do it securely.

Although several northern states have already been mentioned as having been successful in keeping their imprisonment rates low, the state that has held down the growth of its prison population most effectively over the past twenty-five years is North Carolina. In 1980, North Carolina had the highest imprisonment rate in the country, 248 per 100,000. By 2001, this rate had increased by only about 35 percent, to 335, the second lowest in the South and well below the national average. Most of the other southern states had doubled or tripled (or, in the case of Louisiana, quadrupled) their imprisonment rates in the same period. Even some of the low-end states, like Maine and Minnesota, had more than doubled their rates over this period. How did North Carolina control its prison population, even reducing its use of imprisonment after 1995, when it was obliged to temporarily store its excess prison population in private prisons out of state?

According to an analysis by Judith Greene and Vincent Schiraldi, North Carolina has managed to depoliticize crime policy over the past decade since sentencing reforms were enacted:

> Sentencing guidelines have brought a great deal of stability to the system. The impact of proposed sentencing reforms can be projected with confidence; sentencing debates are generally focused on the fiscal impact of any proposed changes; proposals to 'get tough' have largely faded while the dollars saving in correctional costs are shifted to the education budget.[75]

The numbers of drug offenders sentenced to prison time has been reduced by more than half, and the length of drug sentences has been sharply reduced also as the state emphasizes treatment over incarceration. Prison beds are use primarily for violent offenders, who are more likely to get prison time than they were previously. No crime wave has resulted. Both violent and property crimes have declined over the past decade, and the prison system is holding steady at about 95 percent capacity.

It is amazing, to some critics with a sense of history, that we now accept as the norm rates of imprisonment that were unimaginable a generation ago. If you suggest cutting the prison population in half, the reaction is "No way. We could never do that." To which the answer is "Oh, yes, we can. That's where imprisonment rates were in 1987, right before the last period of violent crime increase." Violent crime went down later, but imprisonment has yet to follow in decline.

It is not hard to find lists of what we could be doing differently. The American Bar Association's "Blueprint for Cost-Effective Pretrial Detention, Sentencing, and Corrections" (2002) is included as a commentary at the end of this chapter. On the international scene, Roy Walmsley outlined seven critical measures to reduce jail and prison populations in a recent paper:

1. Less use of pretrial detention
2. Quicker movement of cases to disposition, reducing the period of pretrial detention
3. Increasing the availability of alternatives to prison sentences
4. Encouraging all courts to make use of alternatives
5. Making prison sentences as short as possible
6. Increasing the use of early release
7. Using amnesties, which in this country would mean going back and clearing out a lot of drug criminals and long-term inmates sentenced under recent punitive laws[76]

The International Penal Reform Conference, held in London in 1999, came up with its own list of seven measures to reduce the prison population. Its report reads as follows:

International instruments on the treatment of offenders require minimum use of imprisonment. . . . In addition, further steps, which accord with human rights instruments, need to be taken to reduce inappropriate use of imprisonment:

A planned reduction of the prison population is preferable to ad hoc amnesties.

There has to be a programme of public education to increase awareness of the limitations of imprisonment as a way of protecting society.

Methods of evaluating the effectiveness of the police and the courts must be devised which do not rely on numbers of persons arrested and incarcerated.

There should be a strict limit on the length of pre-trial detention.

The use of effective pre-release methods should be promoted.

Drug abusers should be diverted from the criminal justice system into the health care system.[77]

It is hard to say how much influence such international proposals have in the United States. We should keep in mind that not everyone—and certainly not all or many political officials—at home and abroad think that putting a lot of people in prison is a bad idea. It may be that we do choose to change our policies as reformers suggest, or the opposite may occur: at least in the more affluent or troubled nations, the American model of imprisonment may prevail. As they say in a political campaign—which is essentially what the making of corrections policy in the United States is—this one is too close to call.

KEY TERMS

crime problem

international crime statistics

punishment scale

dual correctional system

Correctional Service of Canada

Corrections and Conditional Release Act

core values

effective corrections

aboriginals

International Corrections and Prisons Association

National Prison Service

remand centers

dispersal prisons

young prisoner centers

borstal

Chief Inspector of Prisons

Prisons and Probation Ombudsman

Independent Monitoring Board

Prison Visitors

Home Office

racial politics

common sense connection

privatization

"Prison Works"

National Probation Service

Criminal Justice Act

persistence principle

National Offender Management Service

contestability

guest workers	Mutawa	*yanda*	Amnesty International
progressive system	Mubahith	Prison Law (Japan)	Human Rights Watch
day fines	bamboo gulag	five principles	punitiveness
Prison Act of 1976	administrative detention	extraordinary leniency	real crime
normalization	reform through labor	volunteer probation	social dynamite
home leave	camps	officers	war on crime
half-open release	*laogai*	Naikan	enemy of the state
Gulag	public surveillance	Beijing Rules	expressive justice
thieves in law	shelter and investigation	welfare model	smart justice
Chechens	Prison Law (China)	legalistic model	
Russian Mafia	five rewards and five	corporatist model	
corrective labor colonies	punishments	participatory model	
prisoners' plague	thought reform	benign-neglect approach	

NOTES

1. "German Warden Tours California Facilities," *Corrections Forum* 9, no. 4 (July/August 2000): 21.

2. Erika Fairchild and Harry R. Dammer, *Comparative Criminal Justice Systems,* 2nd ed. (Belmont, Calif.: Wadsworth/Thomson Learning, 2001), pp. 25–29.

3. Roy Walmsley, "An Overview of World Imprisonment: Global Prison Populations, Trends and Solutions," paper presented to the United Nations Programme Network Institutes Technical Assistance Workshop, Vienna, Austria, May 10, 2001, p. 1.

4. Ibid., pp. 2–3.

5. Dan Gardner, "Behind Bars," *Ottawa Citizen,* March 16, 2002, p. 1.

6. Correctional Service Canada, "Mandate, Mission and Core Values," *Report on Plans and Priorities 2003–04, www.tbs-sct.gc.ca/est-pre/20032004/csc-scc/csc-sccr34_e.asp.*

7. Andy Scott, "Canada's Vision of Effective Corrections," *Corrections Today* 60, no. 7 (December 1998): 147.

8. Correctional Service Canada, "Offenders: The Facts," *Inside Out,* May 2002, p. 2.

9. Correctional Service Canada, *Report on Plans and Priorities* 2003–04.

10. Gardner, "Behind Bars," p. 1.

11. Scott, "Canada's Vision of Effective Corrections," p. 146.

12. "Canadian Police Want Corrections Reforms," *Corrections Digest* 33, no. 7 (February 15, 2002): 4.

13. Fairchild and Dammer, *Comparative Criminal Justice Systems,* p. 253.

14. Ibid., p. 254.

15. Julie Sudbury, "Transatlantic Visions: Resisting the Globalization of Mass Incarceration," *Social Justice* 27, no. 3 (fall 2000): 134.

16. Ibid.

17. Michael Howard, "Prison Works," speech to the Conservative Party Conference, October 1993.

18. "Rambo's Lament; British Prisons," *The Economist* 369, no. 8350 (November 15, 2003): 78.

19. Patrick Carter, "Managing Offenders, Reducing Crime," *Correctional Services Review,* December 11, 2003, pp. 10–16.

20. Ibid., p. 18.

21. Ibid., pp. 26–30.

22. "Prison Brief for Germany," International Centre for Prison Studies, *www.kcl.ac.uk/depsta/rel/icps/worldbrief/europe_records.php?code=139.*

23. Rajko Jelen, "German and U.S. Penal Systems," unpublished paper, November 1, 2001, p. 4.

24. Ibid., p. 7.

25. Ibid., p. 6.

26. "Alternative Sanctions in Germany: An Overview of Germany's Sentencing Practices, " U.S. Department of Justice, National Institute of Justice Research Preview, February 1996, p. 2.

27. Robert B. Goldman, "Impressions of Correctional Trends in Europe," *American Bar Association Journal* 60 (August 1974): 948.

28. Ira Schwartz, "West German Prisons: Humane and Sane," *Prison Journal,* autumn–winter 1976, p. 29.

29. Fairchild and Dammer, *Comparative Criminal Justice Systems*, p. 258.

30. Ibid.

31. Yuri Ivanovich Kalinin, "The Russian Penal System: Past, Present and Future," lecture delivered at King's College, University of London, November 2002, pp. 4–10.

32. Roy D. King, "Russian Prisons after Perestroika: End of the Gulag?" *British Journal of Criminology* 34 (annual 1994): 72.

33. Gary Hill, "Russia's Correctional System," *Corrections Compendium* 28, no. 12 (December 2003): 7.

34. King, "Russian Prisons after Perestroika," p. 73.

35. "One Day in the Life of . . . ," *Time International* 150, no. 39 (May 25, 1998): 38.

36. Amnesty International Saudi Arabia Campaign, "Secrecy and Suffering," *www.amnesty.org/ailib/intcam/saudi/briefing/1.html*.

37. Embassy of the United States of America, Riyadh, Saudi Arabia, "Travel Tips on Saudi Arabia," *usembassy.state.gov/riyadh/wwwhcn29.html*.

38. "Saudi Arabia," Human Rights Watch World Report 2003: Middle East and Northern Africa, *www.hrw.org/wr2k3/mideast6.html*.

39. Ibid.

40. "The Post-Trial Stage: Penalties," Saudi Arabia, Human Rights: Judicial System 2000; *www.saudiembassy.net/Issues/HRights/hr-judicial-7-penalties.html*.

41. International Centre for Prison Studies, "Prison Brief for China," *www.kcl.ac.uk/depsta/rel/icps/worldbrief/continental_asia_records.php*.

42. Harry Wu, "Labor Camps Reinforce China's Totalitarian Rule," Visions of China, CNN.com, *www.cnn.com/Specials/1999/china.50/red.giant/prisons/wu.essay*.

43. Harry Wu, "The Abuse of Prison Labour," Public Hearing on the Social Clause: Human Rights Promotion or Protectionism, June 17 and 18, 1997, Brussels, Belgium, *www.europarl.eu.int/hearings/sc1b/soclause/doc6_en.htm*.

44. Liu Zhengrong, "Lies Will Collapse on Themselves," Visions of China, CNN.com, *www.cnn.com/Specials/1999/china.50/red.giant/prisons/liu.essay*.

45. Fairchild and Dammer, *Comparative Criminal Justice Systems*, p. 259.

46. Yanling Dai, "The Labour of Criminals in Chinese Prisons," Institute for Crime Prevention, Ministry of Justice, China, March 2002, p. 1.

47. E. Eugene Miller, "The People's Republic of China: Successful Reintegration," *Corrections Today* (December 1982): 58–59.

48. Robert Elegant, "Everyone Can Be Reformed," *Parade*, October 30, 1988, pp. 4–7.

49. International Centre for Prison Studies, "Prison Brief for Japan," *www.kcl.uk/depsta/rel/icps/worldbrief/continental_asia_records.php*.

50. James Webb, "What We Can Learn from Japanese Prisons," *Parade*, January 15, 1984, *www.jameswebb.com/articles/parade/japanprison.htm*.

51. Elmer H. Johnson, "Orderliness of Japanese Prisons: The Roles of Prison Officers," *CJ International* 10, no. 4 (July–August 1994): 13–14.

52. Ibid., p. 11.

53. Fairchild and Dammer, *Comparative Criminal Justice Systems*, pp. 263–66.

54. Johnson, "Orderliness of Japanese Prisons," pp. 14–15.

55. M. Honore France, "Naikan: A Buddhist Approach to Psychotherapy," 2000, *www.educ.uvic.ca/faculty/hfrance/naikan.htm*.

56. "Japan Prisons Struggle with Abuse," Reuters, February 9, 2003, *www.fccj.or.jp/modules/wfsection/article.php?articleid=97&category=22*.

57. Philip Reichel, *Comparative Criminal Justice Systems*, 4th ed. (Upper Saddle River, N.J.: Prentice Hall, 2005), p. 317.

58. Dan Gardner, "Why Finland Is Soft on Crime," *Ottawa Citizen*, March 18, 2002.

59. Ibid.

60. Dan Gardner, "Law and Disorder," *Ottawa Citizen*, March 16, 2002.

61. Marc Mauer, "Comparative International Rates of Incarceration: An Examination of Causes and Trends," paper presented to the U.S. Commission on Civil Rights, June 20, 2003, p. 6.

62. Vivien Stern, "Prisoners as Enemies or Prisoners as Citizens? The Responsibility of the State," speech to the International Commission of the Catholic Pastoral Care Congress, August 19, 2003, p. 6.

63. Cited in Reichel, *Comparative Criminal Justice Systems*, p. 322.

64. Michael Tonry, "Ethnicity, Crime, and Immigration: Comparative and Cross-National Perspectives," in *Crime and Justice: A Review of Research* (Chicago: University of Chicago Press, 1997), p. vii.

65. Reichel, *Comparative Criminal Justice Systems*, pp. 336–56.

66. Walmsley, "Prison Population Size," p. 6.

67. Andrei Khalip, "Rioting Kills 34 at New Brazilian Prison," Reuters, June 1, 2004, *www.alertnet.org/thenews/newsdesk/N01362518.htm.*

68. Mauer, "Comparative International Rates of Incarceration," pp. 4–5.

69. Fairchild and Dammer, *Comparative Criminal Justice Systems*, pp. 246–47.

70. Reichel, *Comparative Criminal Justice Systems,* pp. 285–86.

71. Stern, "Prisoners as Enemies of Prisoners as Citizens?" p. 3.

72. Reed Cozart, "Rehabilitation of Criminal Offenders: The Protection of Society," *Vital Speeches of the Day* 22, no. 14 (May 1, 1956): 445.

73. LuWanna Brown, "Counting Kids, Counting Cons," unpublished paper, 2002.

74. "Comparing Rankings of the U.S. States for Child Raising Quality and Incarceration Rate," Data Analysis Unit, Oklahoma Department of Corrections, *www.doc.state.ok.us/docs/childrearing.htm.*

75. Judith Greene and Vincent Schiraldi, "Cutting Correctly: New Prison Policies for Times of Fiscal Crisis," Policy Report, Center for Juvenile and Criminal Justice, February 12, 2002, p. 19.

76. Walmsley, "Prison Population Size," pp. 6–7.

77. "A New Agenda for Penal Reform," Report of the International Penal Reform Conference, London, April 13–17, 1999, pp. 8–9.

FURTHER READING

Applebaum, Anne. *Gulag: A History.* New York: Doubleday, 2003.

Austin, James, and John Irwin. *It's about Time.* Belmont, Calif.: Wadsworth/Thomson Learning, 2001.

Elsner, Alan. *Gates of Injustice: The Crisis in America's Prisons.* Upper Saddle River, N.J.: Pearson/Prentice Hall, 2004.

Fairchild, Erika, and Harry Dammer. *Comparative Criminal Justice Systems.* 2nd ed. Belmont, Calif.: Wadsworth/Thomson Learning, 2001.

Punishment and Society: The International Journal of Penology (Sage Publications,).

Reichel, Philip L. *Comparative Criminal Justice Systems.* 4th ed. Upper Saddle River, N.J.: Pearson/Prentice Hall, 2005.

Stern, Vivien. *A Sin against the Future: Imprisonment in the World.* Boston: Northeastern University Press, 1998.

WEB AND VIDEO RESOURCES

For international prison information, reports, and statistics, look to the International Center for Prison Studies at *www.prisonstudies.org.*

The *World Factbook of Criminal Justice* is available at *www.ojp.usdoj.gov/bjs/abstract/wfcj.htm.*

Human Rights Watch is available at *www.hrw.org.*

Amnesty International is available at *www.amnesty.org.*

The Office of the High Commissioner for Human Rights of the United Nations is available at *www.unhchr.ch.*

The International Corrections and Prisons Association Website is *www.inpa.ca/home.html.*

The United Nations Office on Drugs and Crime Website is *www.unodc.org/unodc/index.html.*

The United Nations Crime and Justice Information Network is available at *www.uncjin.org.*

These Websites provide information for these countries:

Canada: *www.csc-scc.gc.ca/text/home_e.shtml; www.stat.can.ca; www.canada.gc.ca*

England: *www.homeoffice.gov.uk/justice/prisons; www.britainusa.com*

Germany: *www.germany-info.org*

Russia: *www.russianembassy.org*

Saudi Arabia: *www.saudiembassy.net*

Japan: *www.moj.go.up/English/CB/bc-01.html; www.us.emb-japan.go.jp; www.jnto.go.jp*

China: *www.qis.net/chinalaw; www.china.org.cn/english/index.htm*

24 The Globalization of Punishment

by John Pratt

It is well-known throughout the corrections industry that the United States leads the rest of the modern world in levels of incarceration. The U.S. rate has increased from about 230 per 100,000 of the population in 1979 to 709 per 100,000 in 2000, according to Nils Christie's *Crime Control as an Industry.* However, if such a rate and pace of expansion dwarf those in other English-speaking countries, it should not obscure the fact that in such countries, prison levels also have grown—dramatically, in some cases—to levels that were not anticipated nor planned for as recently as 15 years ago.

In New Zealand, for example, the incarceration rate increased from 75 per 100,000 in 1986 to 160 per 100,000 in 2000, per Department of Corrections records. In England and Wales, the incarceration rate increased from 93 in 1986 to 125 in 1997, according to a 1998 Home Office report. In Australia as a whole, the rate increased from 65 per 100,000 in 1996 to 106 per 100,000 in 1998. As in the United States, there are differing levels of incarceration across the Australian states. According to research by Carlos Carcach and Anna Grant, in New South Wales, the incarceration rate increased from 70 per 100,000 in 1986 to 125 in 1998; in Queensland, from 68 to 124. In contrast, the incarceration rate in Victoria only increased from 50 per 100,000 to 61 during the same period.

In other words, there are similarities as well as differences between prison developments in the United States and other modern societies—similarities in terms of the expansion of prison populations and differences in relation to the pace and extent of this development. How might we begin to explain these seemingly ambiguous trends?

It has become clear that many of the expectations associated with penal development in modern societies for much of the 19th and 20th centuries have been put into reverse or taken off on new tangents. During most of that period, governments generally were intent on restricting the use of incarceration, sanitizing penal conditions and developing community-based sanctions to act as alternatives to prison. As such, legislative barriers were placed in front of the prison for an ever-expanding group of offenders—juveniles, the mentally ill, the elderly, alcohol-dependent offenders, women, first-time offenders and in some of these countries, even property offenders. By the 1970s, these trends had reached their apex as prison came to be seen as an expensive and inhumane folly.

Thereafter, all these expectations began to change. Instead of high levels of incarceration being seen as a sign of shame, they now are more likely to be regarded as an indicator of political virility, something to be proclaimed rather than embarrassed about. Again, there is a new belief in what prison might now be able to achieve: it works not in the sense of rehabilitating offenders but in terms of at least being able to keep them off the streets for long periods of time. In these respects, punishment, like other aspects of modern life, has been "globalized," i.e., trends that can be found in the United States are likely to be replicated in other countries.

A new language of punishment has developed in these English-speaking societies, including terms such as "zero tolerance" and "three strikes" (or, in some cases just two or even one strike). There also are new tactics of punishment—exemplified by the three-strikes laws themselves—indicative of a growing intolerance of offenders and a determination to place responsibility for their actions on them and to meet this with longer prison terms. For example, offenders may face long, mandatory sentences (even life) in three-strikes provisions or derivatives, or with additional indefinite detention under the U.S. sexual predator laws and their equivalents elsewhere. Further, in England, there are two-strikes provisions for property offenders and a commitment to ensure longer prison terms for repeat offenders. In New Zealand, there are new proposals to extend the minimum term of life sentences for murderers from 10 to 17 years. This "will be just a starting point," said New Zealand's minister of justice, the Hon. Phil Goff, in a March 15, 2001, media statement. "Judges will be able to impose much longer minimum periods before parole eligibility."

Other proposals include abandoning automatic release after two-thirds of a prison sentence has been served and an extension of the availability of preventive (indefinite) detention and restriction on parole opportunities for this group. In Northern Territory, Australia, and in Western Australia, one-strike mandatory incarceration terms for young, first-time property offenders and car thieves have been on the legislatures' statute books for several years. In New South Wales, Australia, commitment to truth in sentencing since 1989 has significantly extended long-term prison sentences and restricted opportunities for parole.

In these respects, the trend toward increased incarceration in the Anglophone countries mentioned is evident. Although it may not necessarily be in terms of exact replicas of U.S. measures that have become icons of this "new punitiveness" (indeed, it has been claimed that their importance in escalating the use of incarceration has been rather overstated, as noted by James Austin, John Clark, Patricia Hardyman and D. Alan Henry of the George Washington University), but perhaps instead, and more mundanely, by governments being prepared to increase already existing prison terms. The courts in the current climate then may be prepared to make use of them, and community corrections agencies may be more prepared to revoke parole or probation licenses for prisons that contribute to this.

Why is it, though, that this new punitiveness is being expressed and articulated across these societies now? There seems to be no doubt that this is connected to the social, political and economic changes that have taken place across Western society since the mid-1970s. This was centered on a retreat from the ideals characteristic of so much postwar social reconstruction. This was predicated on an increased role for the state and its organizations in managing everyday life, to a much more restricted role, with its place as a guarantor of security and well-being increasingly curtailed, as individuals have been given the freedom to, as it were, "take care of themselves." As a result, security itself becomes a commodity to be purchased like any other, rather than a duty of the state to provide, according to David Garland of New York University. In these respects, there is a growing acceptability of social and economic forces that lead to increased social division—a growing tolerance of inequality coupled with an increased sense of anxiety at the presence of those who might threaten the newfound freedoms that these broader changes have brought with them. Such risks in their own turn then are globalized as a result of the growing power and intrusion on everyday life of the mass media and information technology. In such ways, danger is made to seem more omnipresent and incalculable. We become consumed with worry with what can happen to us today, rather than what is likely to happen, and we conjure monsters that seem to be lying in wait for us in the shadows of everyday existence.

This facilitates an abandonment of liberal penal provisions and a general questioning by the public and politicians about the seemingly excessive leniency of the criminal justice system, and demands that judges impose, instead, sentences that are more in keeping with contemporary fears and anxieties. For example, 80 percent of the New Zealand electorate voted in November 1999 in a citizen-generated referendum in support of still longer prison sentences for violent offenders and "hard labor" prison regimes, the proportion of the vote being 92 percent in favor and 8 percent against. Again, the New Zealand government now has acted on this expression of public will with its revised sentencing proposals detailed above, estimating that this would necessitate another 300 prisons at a cost of $90 million New Zealand dollars ($40 million U.S. dollars). Similarly, the collapse of faith in government organizations and in their ability to provide security, lead to a new alliance between governments and the general public. Increasingly, this alliance becomes the new driving force of penal development, with discredited bureaucratic expertise bypassed, as Franklin Zimring effectively illustrated in his 1996 *Pacific Law Journal* article with reference to the passage of California's three-strikes laws.

However, it is not just penal values that have changed during this period, but the economics of punishment as well. The cost of incarceration no longer seems prohibitive. There are a number of factors behind this:

- New-generation prison architecture, which makes prisons less costly and easier to build;
- Use of the private sector to cut losses;
- Emasculation of prison unions and the curtailment of the perks and privileges that they had previously won for their members; and
- A readiness of governments to spend revenue on prison development while cutting back expenditures in other areas of social responsibility.

In such ways, the economic urgency to restrict the growth of incarceration that was so central to penal thinking during the 1970s seems to have been significantly reduced, making it possible for governments to lock up more people without the previous financial pressures that might have obstructed it. Again, it is as if with all the extra investment poured into prison building during the last two decades, the business of crime control becomes one of the most significant 21st century industries, replacing those that have become redundant, such as mining and steelworks, providing secure jobs and a boost to local economies. According to Christie, there is little wonder that traditional resistance to prison building is crumbling away in some places.

These, then, are trends that occur across most modern, democratic societies, creating the demands for new levels of incarceration. Why is it, though, that these trends in the United States are so dramatically ahead of those in any other corresponding society? Could it be that in the United States, the anxieties and concerns of everyday life are more pronounced and profound—with correspondingly less by way of some residual level of state support that might provide security against them and solutions to them?

In the United States, the extremes of wealth and poverty, often adjacent to each other, urban excitement and conflict, cosmopolitan excitement and angst, accelerate the sense of fear and distrust that seems endemic in late modem society. And it is in the United States where the central state seems to have the most reduced role, placing the emphasis on local individuals and communities to take responsibility for their own security—through insurance, private policing, surveillance systems, etc. It is in the United States, perhaps, that the emphasis on "taking care of oneself" (because there is unlikely to be anybody else who will), has helped instill a sense of anxiety, threat and distrust of others. This emphasis has become so pronounced as a global phenomenon and seems to have had a tremendous impact. In addition, the necessity to win public approval by judges, prosecutors and the like in the United States through elections, in contrast to their appointments as part of a bureaucratic process that exists in all the other societies that have been considered in this article, inevitably allows current public sentiments on crime and punishment to have considerably more direct political purchase there. Not only are public officials likely to have to take a strong stand on law and order to facilitate their reelection, but the availability of plebiscites in some state jurisdictions allows for public-sponsored proposals to be given legislative authority, as Zimring illustrated in a 1996 *Pacific Law Journal* article. Overall, we can see that the new axis of penal power—the alliance between government and the general public—has been cemented more firmly in the United States than in any other country.

In England, for example, demands for community notification procedures similar to the United States' Megan's Law were rejected by the government, which insisted that it would keep to existing arrangements whereby only police and penal professionals would be notified. In these other societies, there still is a hold on the incarceration accelerator. In the United States, the hold has been released. This helps to explain not only the differential levels and rates of incarcration between the United States and other countries, but also the differing conditions of containment within the prisons.

The use of supermax prisons in the United States is not being followed elsewhere: In most of these other societies, the new, more hygienic conditions of private prisons seem to have become the way forward and the benchmark for the public sector to match. In America, it is as if the very creation of a massive prison population, many of whom will never be released and thereby have nothing to lose from disorder or disobedience, in itself only generates these additional problems of security, to which the supermax prison, rightly or wrongly, is seen as the solution. In these other societies, where the penal bureaucracies have not been pushed so far out of the way, there still are significant voices that worry about the rise in the prison population and conditions within the prisons. And, thus, in New Zealand, while the government has been prepared to act on public demands for longer prison sentences, it has not been prepared to act on demands for tougher prison sentences.

Clearly, the growth of incarceration in the United States and other similar societies during the last two decades represents a significant change in the framework of punishment in the modern world. Its boundaries of acceptability have been pushed further and further, thereby incorporating previously unthinkable, impossible levels of incarceration. At the same time, we should not just be aware of the "American difference" in these features, but also of the social and political arrangements that account for this, and which show how far along this new penal path it is possible to go.

COMMENTARY

25 Blueprint for Cost-Effective Pretrial Detention, Sentencing, and Corrections Systems

by the American Bar Association

Fiscal Accountability

1. Each state and the federal government should require the preparation of correctional/fiscal impact statements and their consideration by legislators and the governor or President before legislation is enacted that would increase the number of persons subject to a particular

criminal sanction, or increase the potential sentence length for any criminal offense.

2. Each state and the federal government should make laws increasing the number of persons who will be incarcerated or the length of their incarceration subject to a sunset provision when the money to fund the projected increase in the prison or jail population is not appropriated.

Sentencing and Community Corrections

3. Each state and the federal government should adopt and implement a comprehensive community corrections act that provides the structure and funding for the sanctioning of nonviolent offenders within their communities.

4. Community corrections systems should be structured to avoid unnecessary supervision and incarceration, in part through the expanded use of means-based fines.

5. Each state and the federal government should review their sentencing laws, and sentencing or parole guidelines, to accomplish the following objectives: (a) to provide that a community-based sanction is the presumptively appropriate penalty for persons who do not present a substantial danger to the community; and (b) to ensure that the populations subject to the jurisdiction's prison, jail, or community-sanctioning systems do not exceed each system's rated capacity.

6. Each state and the federal government should review the length of sentences prescribed by law, and sentencing and parole guidelines, to ensure that they accurately reflect current funding priorities, as well as research findings that question the utility of long sentences, whether incarcerative or community-based, for certain kinds of crimes.

7. Each state and the federal government should repeal mandatory sentencing laws that unduly limit a judge's discretion to individualize sentences so that the sentence in each case fairly reflects the gravity of the offense and the degree of culpability of the offender.

8. Each state and the federal government should review and revise sentencing laws and court procedures to provide for appropriate com-munity-based responses to drug offenses, including treatment, in lieu of incarceration.

9. State and federal prosecutors should regularly examine their policies concerning charging, plea-bargaining, and sentence recommendations, in order to avoid overcharging, and to make greater use of community-based sanctions.

Sentence Modifications

10. Each state and the federal government should structure its sentencing system to permit a graduated response, when appropriate, to violations of the conditions of parole or other community release. The sentencing system should provide that a community-based sanction is the presumptively appropriate penalty for persons who do not present a substantial danger to the community.

11. Each state and the federal government should establish a mechanism to apply the above-described sentencing reforms retroactively, where appropriate, to currently incarcerated inmates.

12. Each state and the federal government should adopt and fully implement mechanisms for the expeditious consideration of early release for prisoners who are terminally ill or physically incapacitated, and each jurisdiction should assess the desirability of applying such mechanisms to elderly or other prisoners in specified circumstances.

Reentry and the Reduction of Recidivism

13. Each state and the federal government should adopt a comprehensive plan to reduce return rates to prison and jail, that includes the development of reentry plans, procedures, and services to facilitate released inmates' reintegration into the community, and relief from legal obstacles that impede reintegration.

14. Local, state, and federal governments should implement and fully fund programs within prisons and jails, and within community-based sanctioning programs, to provide educational opportunities, vocational and job

training, mental health and substance abuse treatment, counseling, and other programs designed to reduce recidivism.

Pretrial Detention

15. Local governments, working in partnership with the state government, should adopt, expand, and refine pretrial services programs to reduce unnecessary detention, to save jail space for persons who need to be incarcerated.

Correctional Operations and Facilities

16. Local, state, and federal governments should adopt performance standards for prisons, jails, and community-sanctioning programs, to ensure that the effectiveness of correctional practices and programs can be assessed and improved.

17. Local, state, and federal governments should utilize information, management, and evaluation systems that regularly identify and rectify inefficiencies in judicial case management systems and correctional processes that unduly prolong incarceration in correctional facilities, that result in the inappropriate designation of offenders to high-security institutions, or otherwise increase costs.

18. Correctional officials in each local, state, and federal government should be granted and exercise the authority to designate a halfway house or other community residential facility as the site of an inmate's incarceration when such a placement comports with public safety.

19. Local, state, and federal correctional officials should establish linkages with universities, colleges, and community colleges through which research and service learning can be better utilized to reduce correctional costs.

20. The decision to close correctional facilities for budgetary reasons should be subject to the following requirements: (a) the selection of the facilities to be closed should be informed by and based on input from correctional officials regarding which facility (or facilities) it would be most advisable to close from a fiscal and correctional-management perspective; (b) the closing of a correctional facility should not result in the transfer of inmates to any facility already operating at or above its rated capacity; and (c) the selection of the facilities to be closed should take into account the desirability of permitting appropriate visitation by family members, in order to facilitate inmates' eventual reintegration into the community.

INDEX